I0754839

# Fetish
## and the Art of the Teese

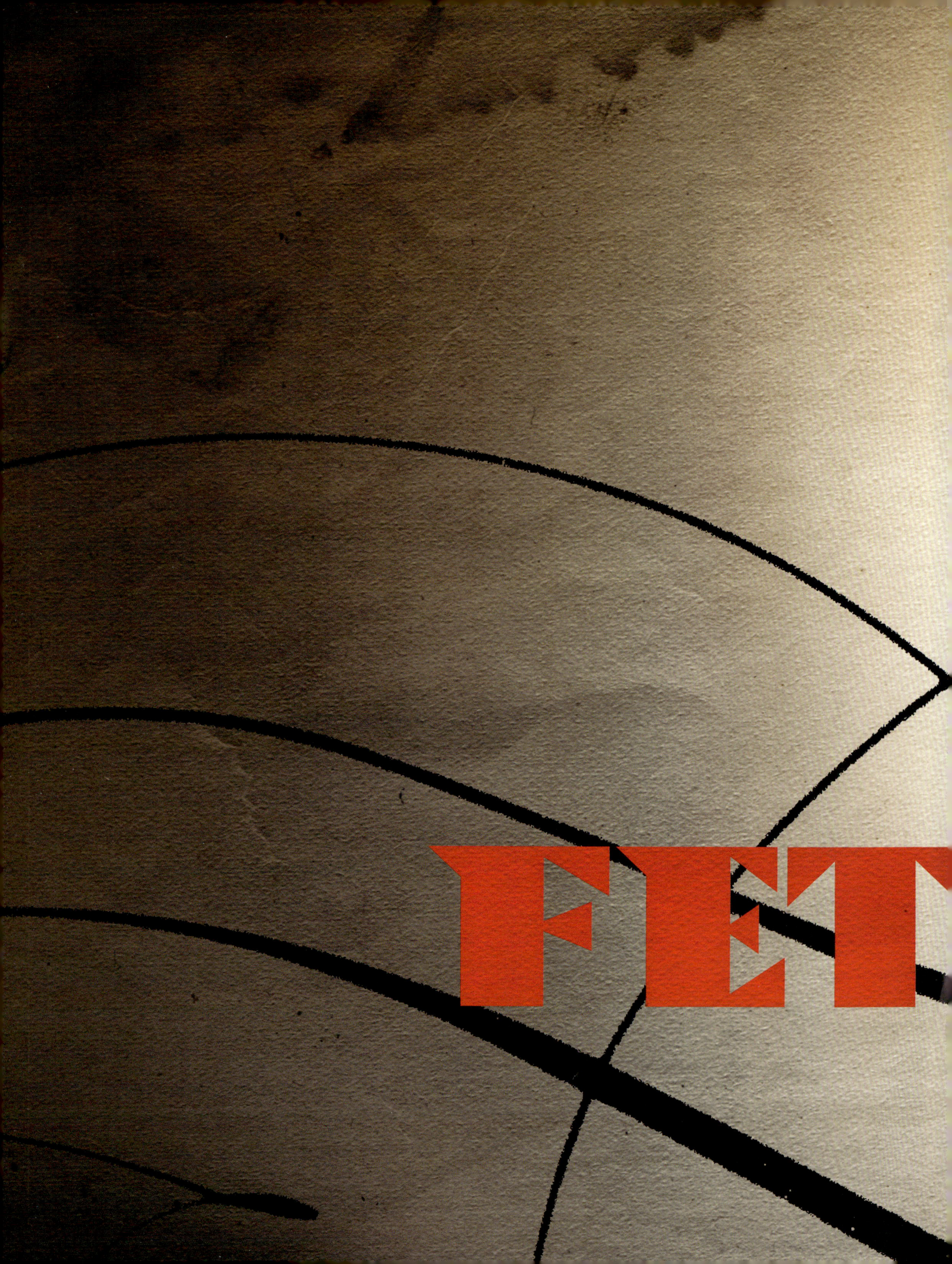
FET

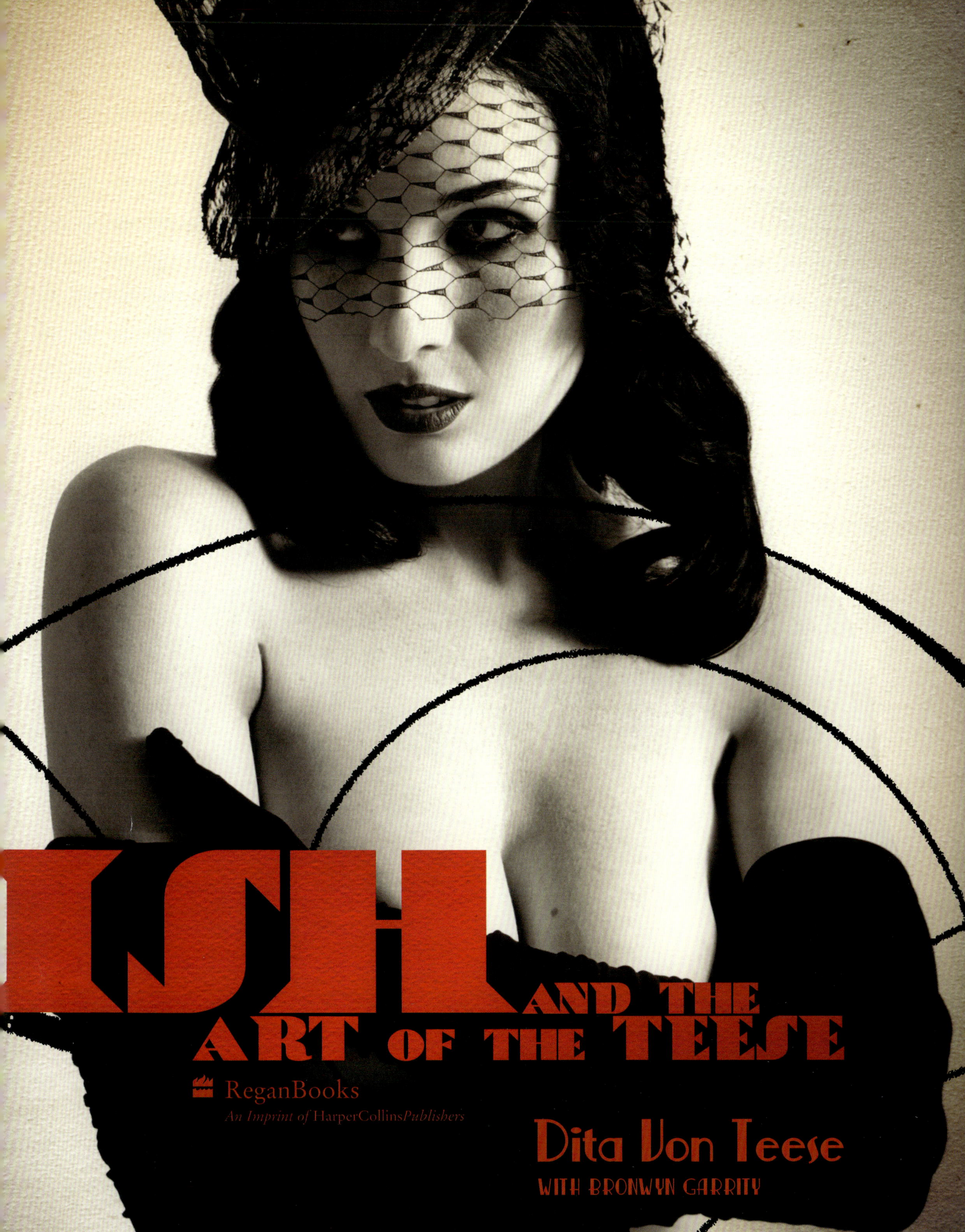

# ISH AND THE ART OF THE TEESE

ReganBooks
*An Imprint of* HarperCollins*Publishers*

Dita Von Teese
WITH BRONWYN GARRITY

www.Dita.net

See pages 130–31 in *Burlesque and the Art of the Teese* for Acknowledgments and Sources.



HarperCollins books may be purchased for educational, business, or sales promotional use. For information please write: Special Markets Department, HarperCollins Publishers Inc., 10 East 53rd Street, New York, NY 10022.

FIRST EDITION

*Designed by P.R. Brown @ Bau-da Design Lab*

Printed on acid-free paper

Library of Congress Cataloging-in-Publication Data

Von Teese, Dita, 1972–
Burlesque and the art of the Teese ; Fetish and the art of the Teese / Dita von Teese.— 1st ed.
p. cm.
No collective t.p.; titles transcribed from individual title pages.
ISBN 0-06-059167-6
1. Von Teese, Dita, 1972– 2. Stripteasers—United States—Biography. 3. Striptease—United States. 4. Burlesque (Theater)—United States. 5. Fetishism. I. Title: Fetish and the art of the Teese. II. Title.

PN1949.S7V66 2006
792.7—dc22

2004050914

25 RTLO 20

In memory of

Cory Thompson

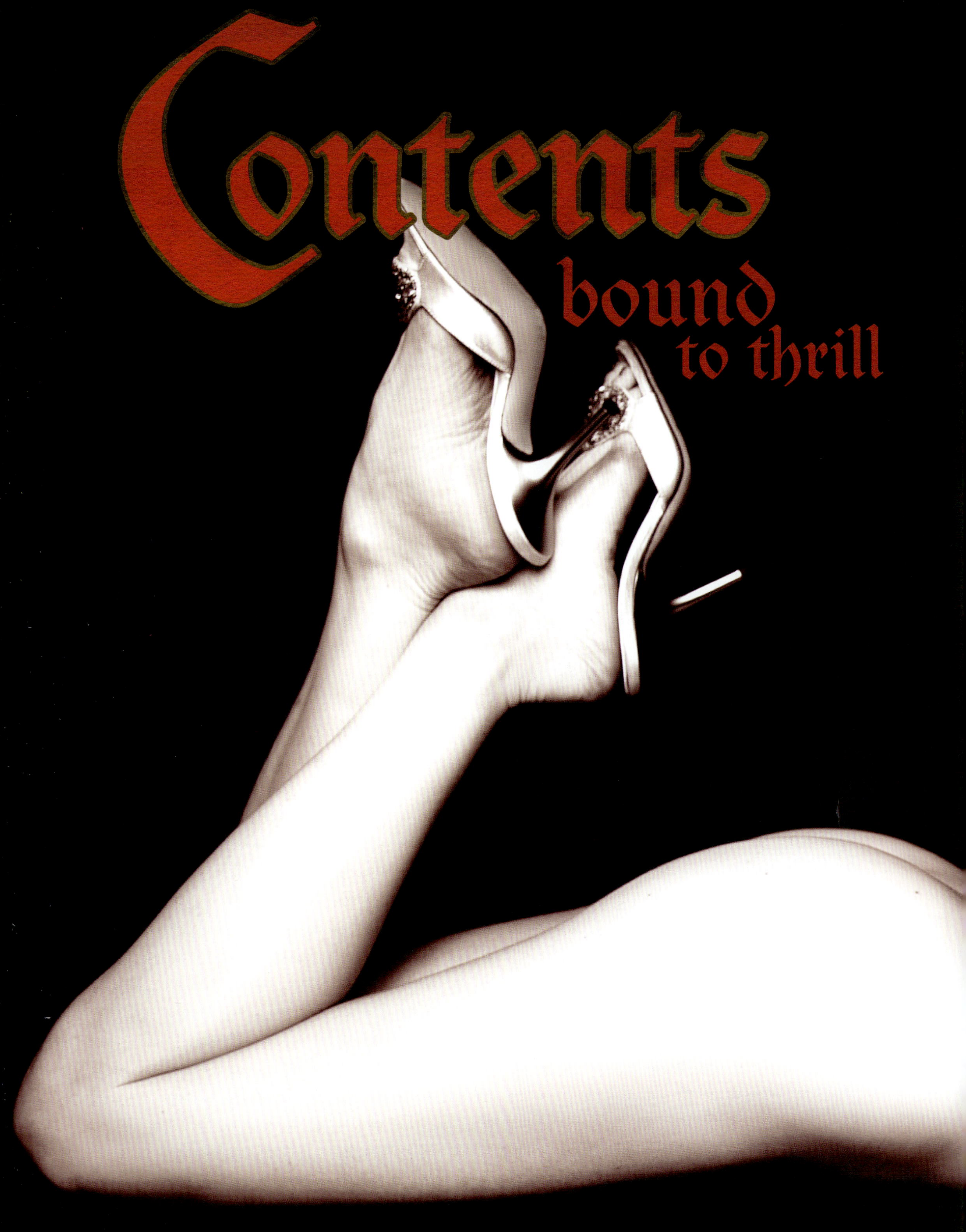
Contents
bound
to thrill

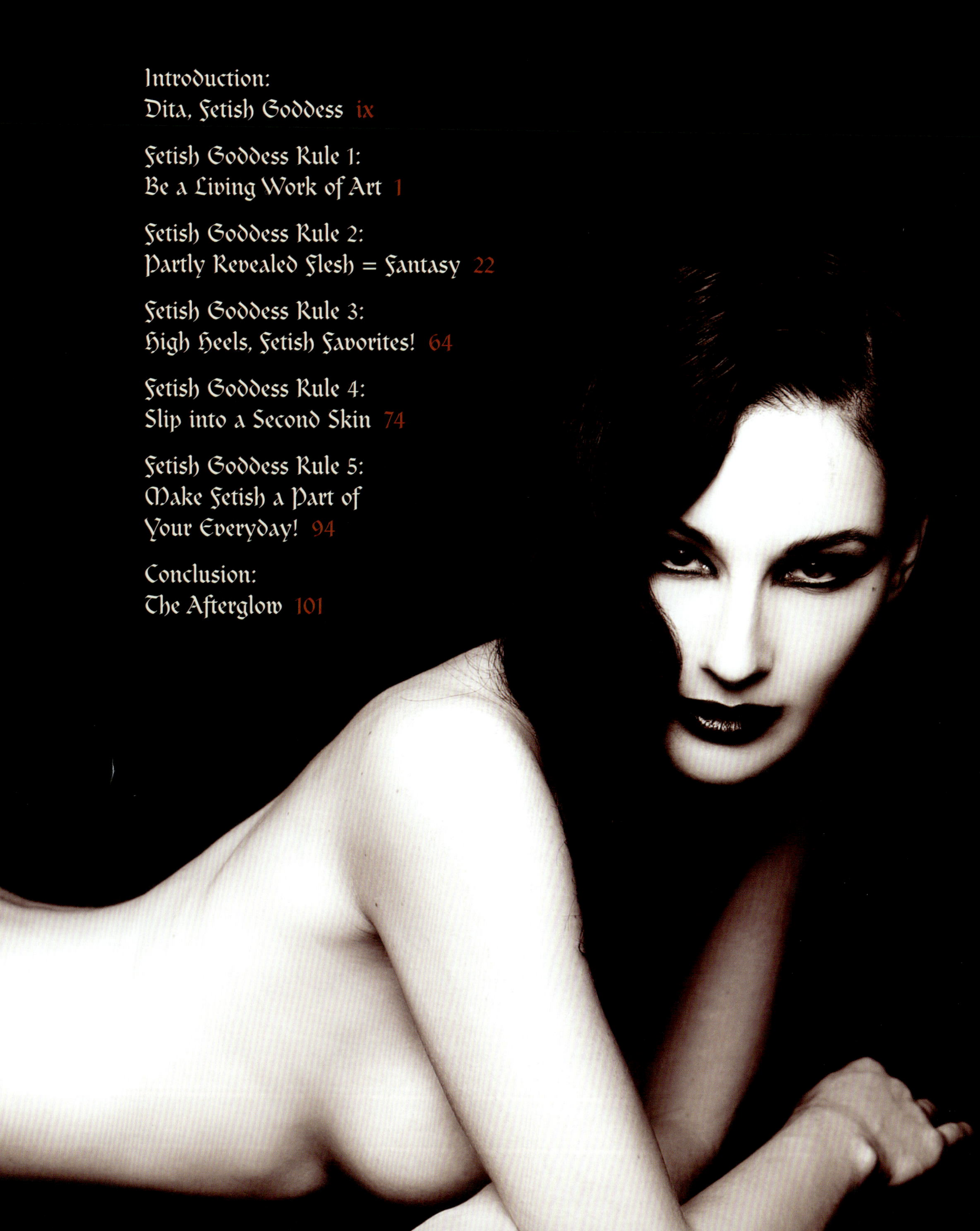


Introduction:
Dita, Fetish Goddess ix

Fetish Goddess Rule 1:
Be a Living Work of Art 1

Fetish Goddess Rule 2:
Partly Revealed Flesh = Fantasy 22

Fetish Goddess Rule 3:
High Heels, Fetish Favorites! 64

Fetish Goddess Rule 4:
Slip into a Second Skin 74

Fetish Goddess Rule 5:
Make Fetish a Part of
Your Everyday! 94

Conclusion:
The Afterglow 101

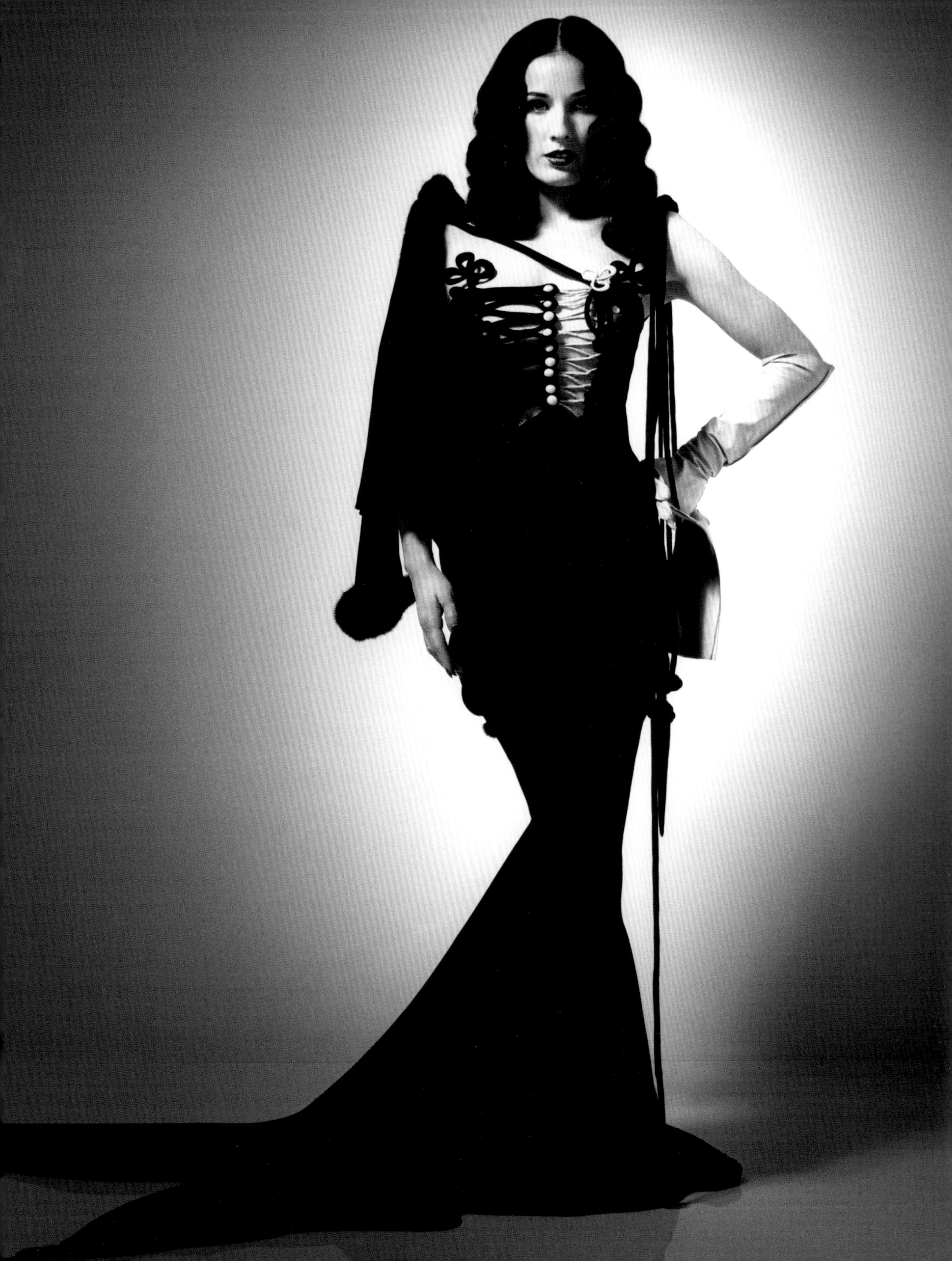

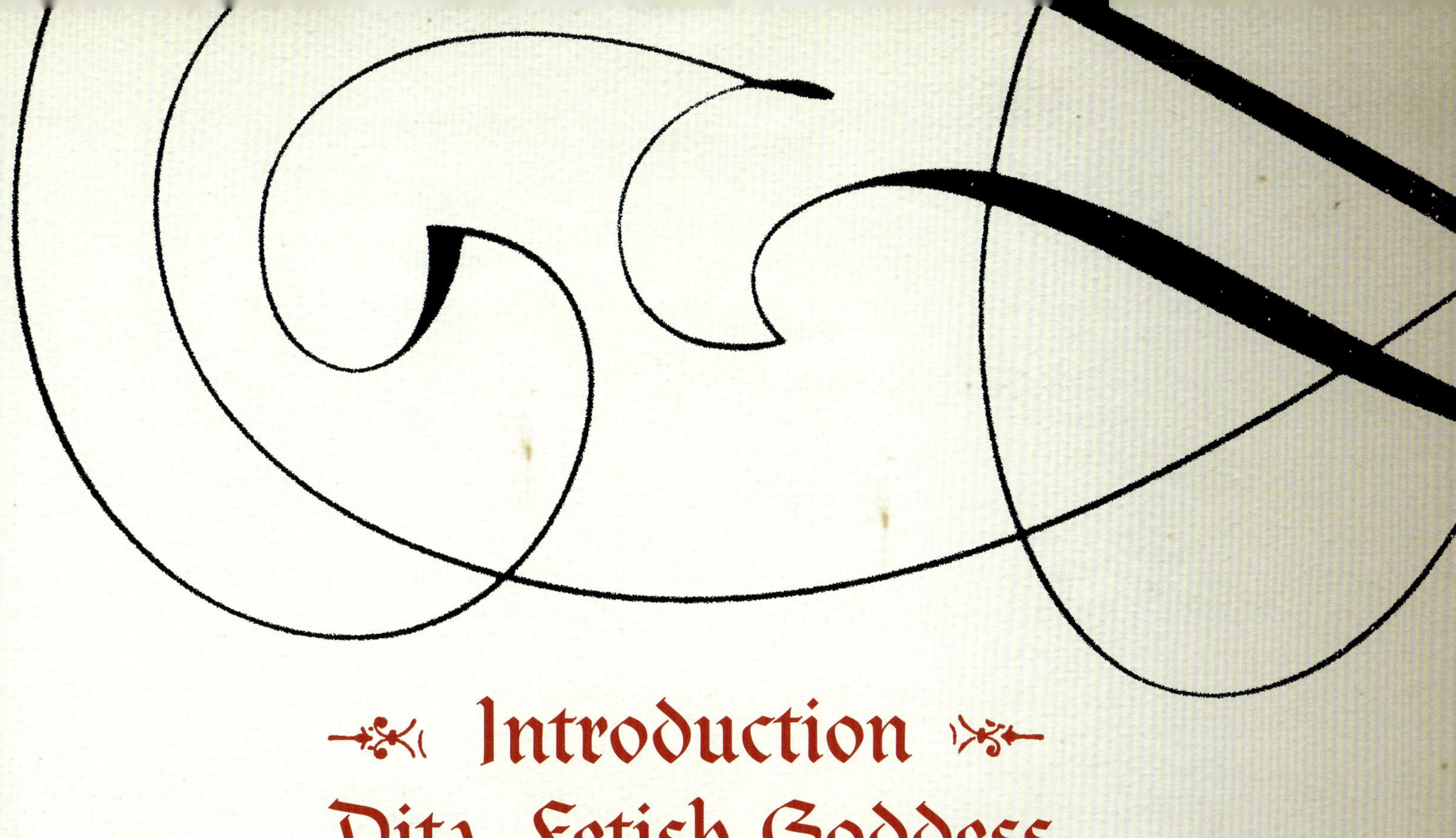

# Introduction
# Dita, Fetish Goddess

You may be one of two people.

You may be a person whose primary interest is in the starry, big band days of burlesque. You may have come for the cotton candy, the feel-good fluff, the star peelers, the cheesecake. Maybe you are seeking a few lessons on the art of the striptease or tales of Minsky hurly burly. Whatever your motivations, I will wager that you did not come for the kink, that you are merely sneaking a peek at this mysterious and peculiar *other side.*

Or perhaps you are the person whose total concentration is on dangerously high heels and the scent of polished latex. You may be a girl who revels in wearing black satin corsets laced tight, or a boy who loves a girl bound to thrill. Maybe you desire a look into the dungeons I have seen. Maybe *you* have come for the fetish.

Whoever you are, I imagine you are holding this book's two sides between your fingers, wondering what could burlesque and fetish possibly have in common? Would you believe me if I told you *everything?*

At least the way I view them, burlesque and fetish are peas of a pod, two snaps of a garter, the committed disciples of the art of the tease. Old burleycue may be stage performance, but fetish is theater just the same. You see, while the burlesquer *emerges* as the vixen by stripping away layers of clothing to reveal more and more flesh, the fetish goddess transforms into a similarly captivating seductress with the objects she keeps *on*—high heels and fully-fashioned seamed stockings, corsets, gloves, furs, to name a few of my own favorite fetish classics. In simply tweaking costume, burlesque and fetish draw their "audience's" minds closer and closer to sex and then—as good temptresses must—snatch it away.

Recently, I performed one of my burlesque shows at a party during fashion week for a fine jewelry company. The audience was wildly enthusiastic—I was draped in priceless jewels as I bathed in my cocktail glass! After drying off, I made my way through the party, chatting with old friends and making new ones. This audience had heard about burlesque's revival and was no doubt curious about its history. But, what else, wondered one group of women, was involved in the execution of my show? Why—since I didn't take off *all* my clothes—were these modern men carrying on so? Certainly they'd seen nearly naked women before—there were some scantily clad ladies in this very room!

My answer was simple and powerfully disagreeable: "Fetish."

For the sake of style, for my own indulgence, and because certain objects have always triggered male hysteria, I incorporate elements of fetish into my burlesque performances. Corsets, high heels, long red fingernails, seamed stockings—to name a few standards—have unfailingly aroused men for centuries. Why should my audience be any different?

Well, the women suddenly looked very uncomfortable. All of them, except one young girl in patent leather stilettos. "What do you mean?" she whispered. "Like torture and whips and stuff?"

Her question was puzzling, since I hadn't employed torture or whipping in my act. But, you must understand, this word *fetish* is powerful—and powerfully encumbered by shock, sex, and the hard core. It smacks of wickedness and perversion. For one thing, our publicity is terrible. Just the other day I read in the newspapers about a German man who killed and ate another man—all in the name of fetish! Must it really be said that cannibalism is not a prerequisite?

There are simple things. Glamorous things. Things for girls like us to love. I pointed at this lovely lady's feet. "Fetish, like the stilettos *you're* wearing."

Well, she was taken aback, of course. *Was I calling her a fetishist?* Certainly not—though stilettos *were* filched from the fetishist's closet. "Women are the fetish goddesses," I said. This girl peeked at her shoes, pleased as Dorothy to discover their power. "Magical charms," I winked.

If you have ever slipped into a pair of high heels you'll know what I mean when I say these shoes are physically *transformative*. Walk across the room and feel the muscles up and down your legs flex and tense, your bum bump into the air, your hips swerve with each step. Your foot, too, looks lovely and tiny, but it's more than that. You are sex on heels. And yet, dressed this way, you are also formal, perfect, unattainable (and therefore more desirable). High heels' double powers of transformation and innuendo have made them centuries-old staples for the fetishist *and* are the reason modern designers produce them for their runways. You didn't think these things were invented for comfort's sake, did you? They were created so that *we* could perform magic.

My friend from the party shook her head and giggled coyly, knowingly—I mean no oxymoron. She was nibbling on the fruit of the fetish pie, sweet with contradictions, juicy with secrets and preserved with the salty timelessness of human desire. Fantasy, of course, is nearly always about what we cannot, or currently do not, have. The allure of denial is as provocative

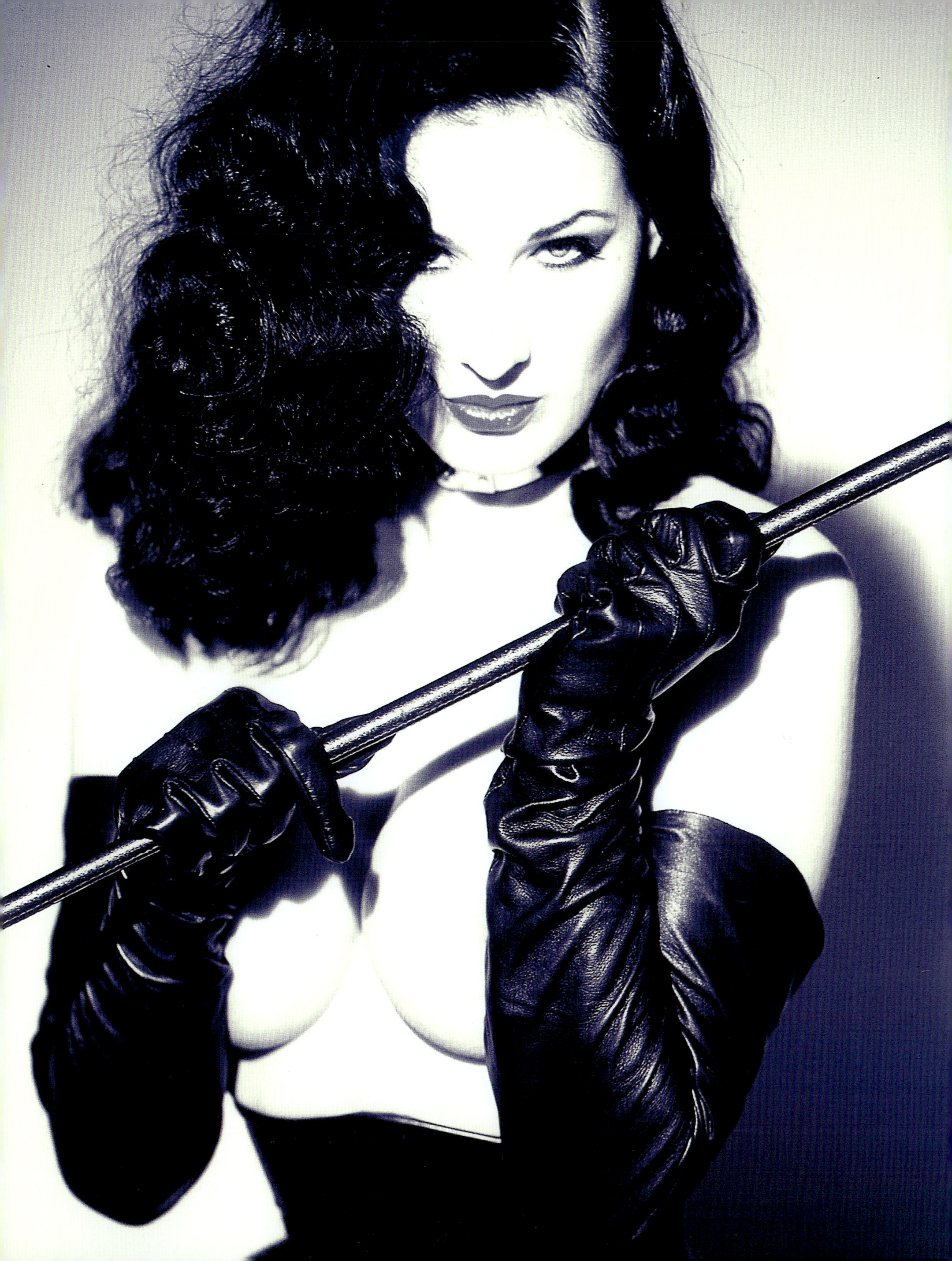

as any embrace—I learned this from the fetishists. It is precisely for this reason that something like a corset is a bona fide fetish icon. This garment (which I wear in *all* my shows) turns nearly any body into Marilyn Monroe's, accentuating the breasts and hips and narrowing the waist—drawing the observer's attention to the wearer's loci of sex appeal. Yet, in an enchanting twist, these very same elements that enhance sensuality also restrict access to it—those straight lines of steel or (in the golden days) whalebone pull tight against the body as a sort of armor. The corset is a real historical artifact and a bracing, teasing paradox. And the boys, they love it.

If you look around, you'll find fetish everywhere. You can right now see it represented in advertisements, movies, fairy tales, cartoons, fashion runways, your own closet. Major designers find inspiration in fetish's sexy standards—and they call it avant garde when it hits runways. Remember, for example, Madonna's pink, lace-up satin corset with the projectile breasts by Jean Paul Gaultier. Gaultier is one of our most revered fashion designers, and he never denied his fetish foundations. "The first fetish I did was a corset," he once said. "That was because of my grandmother." He first found her pink, lace-up corset in her closet as a very little boy, and was captivated—and inspired by—what he saw as "one of the secrets." Gaultier isn't the only designer to sample the fruit de fetish. Vivienne Westwood often works in fetish fabrics and styles. Remember those skyscraper shoes Naomi Campbell was wearing when she fell down on the runway? Fetishists (and their models) have been taking tumbles for fetish for years. John Galliano, Thierry Mugler, and Louis Vuitton (to name just a few) are similarly inspired. In fact, one season Louis Vuitton introduced a series of rubber trench coats.

As couturier John Galliano said after one of his shows: "There has to be a sexual chemistry for the clothes to work." Or, the way I think about it—if the clothes work, there will be sexual chemistry. I should remind you that by *sexy* I do not necessarily mean scandalous or obvious or scanty. A tailored suit can have chemistry if it colludes with the right accouterments. The official definition of fetish covers a vivid spectrum of possibility: "something, such as a material object or an often nonsexual part of the body that arouses or gratifies sexual desire." *Gratifies* is, of course, one thing—we're talking unusual excitement, reserved for a select set of people. But, *arousal*? What man doesn't thrill to see a beautiful pair of legs stroll the runway in a figure-enhancing dress and a strappy pair of heels?

Am I saying all men are fetishists? More or less, yes. Nothing to be embarrassed about, fetish enthusiasm may be a kinky vestige of our days in the jungle when men relied upon visual clues for quick mating. This is Darwinian Natural Selection—heady, I know, but bear with me—where the imagery of voluptuous breasts, slender waists, and creamy complexions alerted passing males to fertile young females. Of course, since men were free back then from child rearing, they coupled and moved along, cuddling as many honeys as possible, spreading genes (among, perhaps, other things). They relied upon quick visuals, in other words. Fetishes, Darwin would say, are simply secondary sexual characteristics, visual clues drawing the viewer's eyes to the prize.

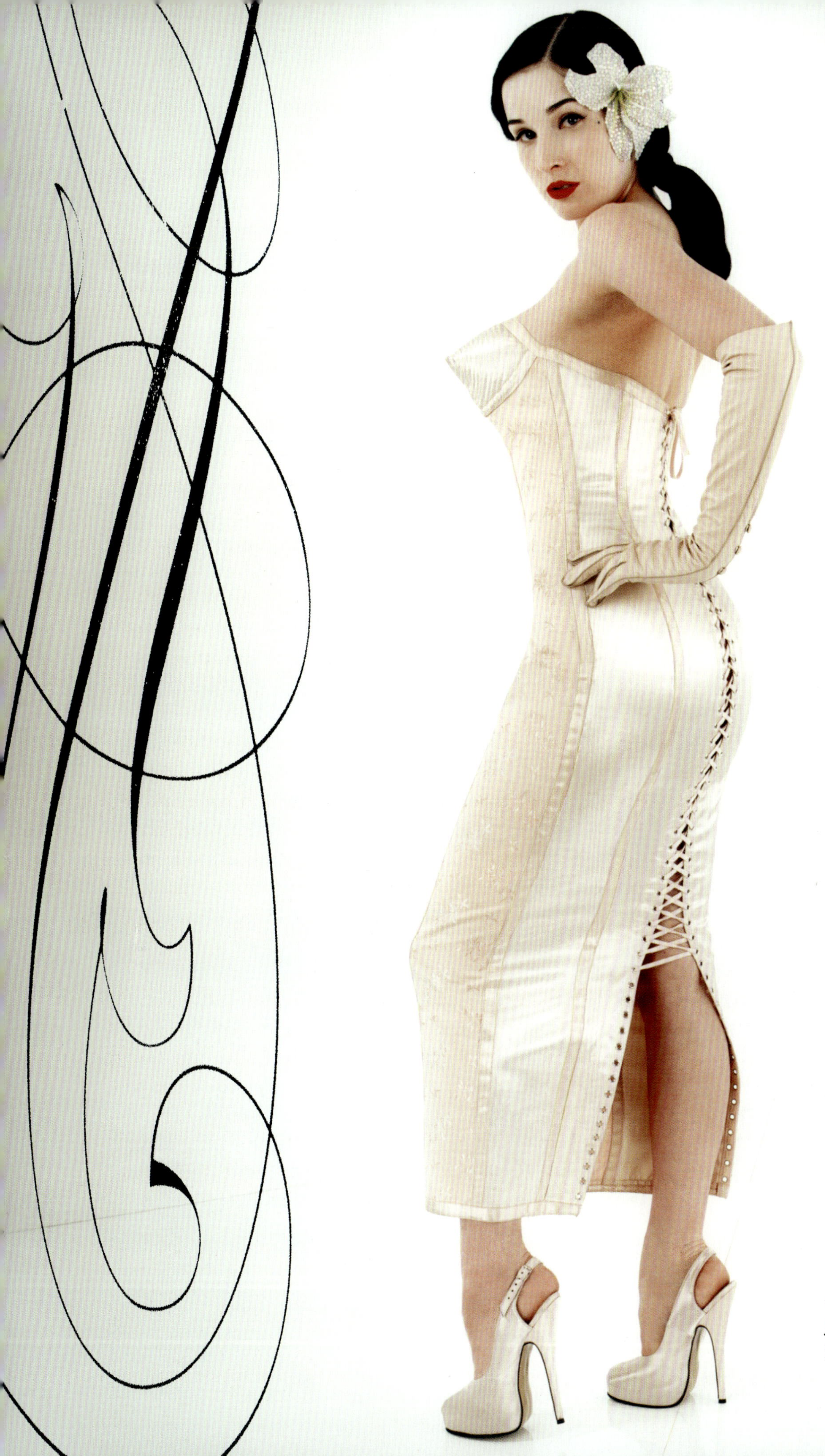

*Cinched into one of Jean Paul Gaultier's famous corset dresses*

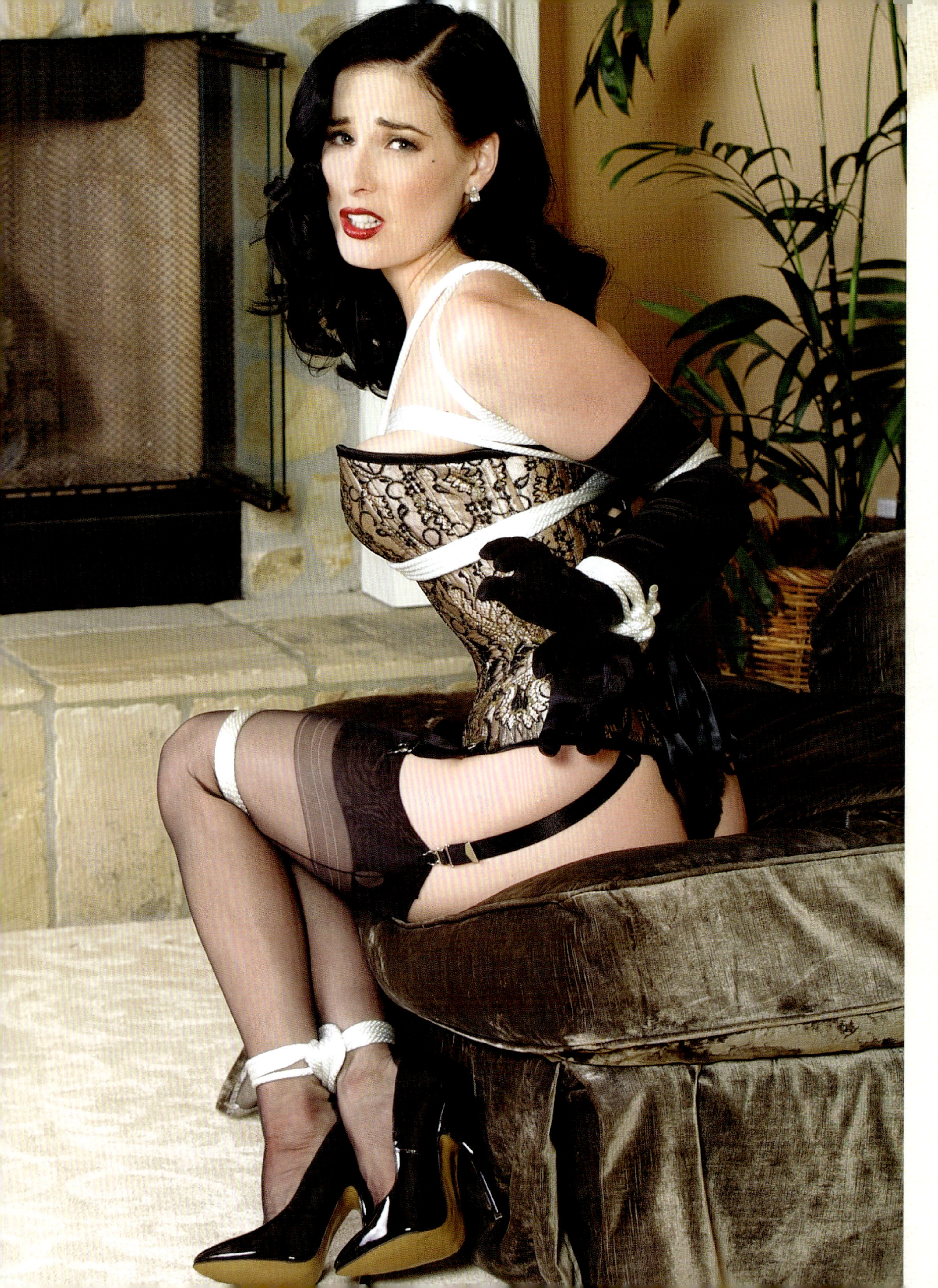

Some fetishists, of course, may experience only mild titillation at seeing long, gorgeous legs in sheer black stockings and heels. Others may spend the entire evening with the stockings themselves. I would however suggest that the prevailing belief in fetish enthusiasts as perverts who grow sexually excited by objects *rather* than by bodies is generally false. Most fetishists I know require a body with their corset or shoe or rubber mask, the arousal having something to do with the flesh that is confined or accentuated or protected by it. I've heard it said that the nearness of the skin soaks into the garment, charging it with the sensuality of the body part itself. I would say this is true and then some—a bit of clothing leaves the imagination necessarily running.

Magic.

Indeed, before the word *fetish* bloated with "obsessive" and "perverse" sexual connotations, the word meant, quite simply, "magical charm." Isn't that lovely? In ancient times, human beings worshipped these idols and amulets, hoping for rain or fertility or food. Over time, evidently, people hoped predominantly for sex because the definition grows increasingly carnal as it nears the modern age. For me, fetish is a sensual magical charm.

I love fetish for its powers of transformation and also for its beauty. To me, there's no lovelier image than that of a sobbing, exquisitely attired lady tied to the railroad tracks as a train roars near, her hero racing to save her. John Willie, Bettie Page, Irving and Paula Klaw—these are my heroes. I have always been inspired by the gorgeous girls they depict in their work, the hourglass figures, the classic fashions, the lingerie (corsets, stockings, girdles), and second skins (furs, satins, silks, latex), the high-heeled shoes. I love those images because they are—above all—beautiful.

Sigmund Freud claimed that fetishizing has something to do with a young boy's fear of being castrated like his mother. This boy, Freud postulated, worships the fetish—whether it is silk stockings or high-heeled shoes—as the mother's penis substitute. Naughty Freud. I offer his analysis as evidence that the famous shrinky was possessed by his own devious fantasies. I don't mean to cast Freud as *the* pervert here—even though his ideas are awfully wicked. No, no, I mean to say *human beings* are perverts. And as for this case study, I would suggest that this boy is celebrating his mother's sensuality, perhaps even her unattainable *difference*.

At the end of the day, though, I have no idea. I cannot explain why fetishists like what they do. The fetishists themselves cannot seem to explain it, and I've asked them, believe me. The only thing we can do, my friends, is enjoy it.

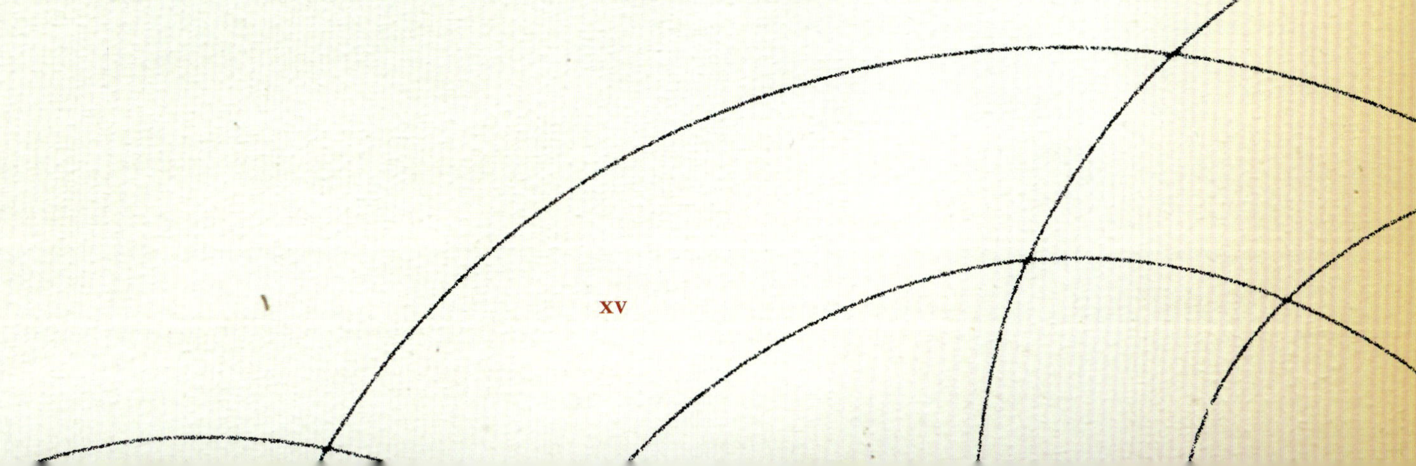

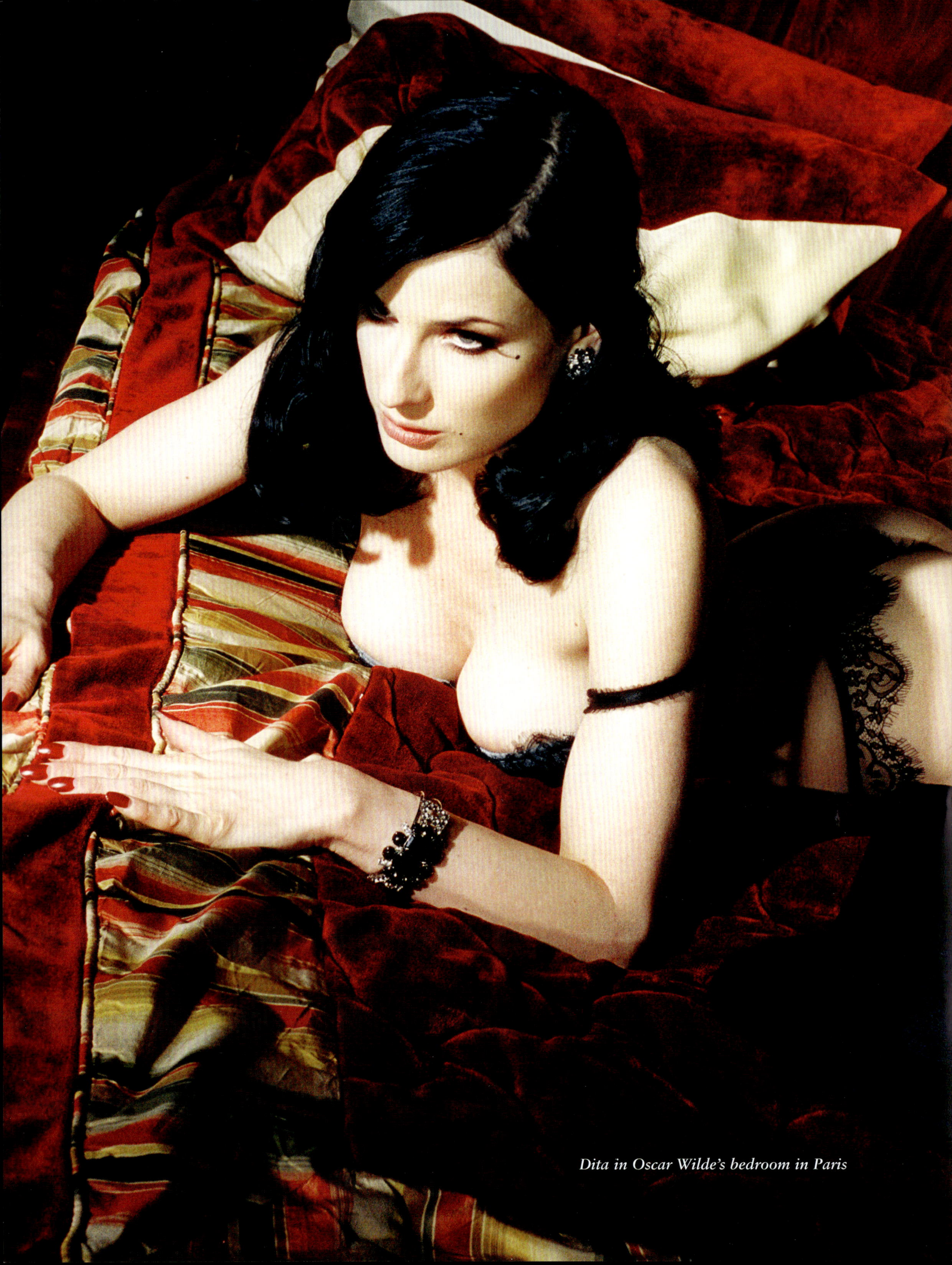

*Dita in Oscar Wilde's bedroom in Paris*

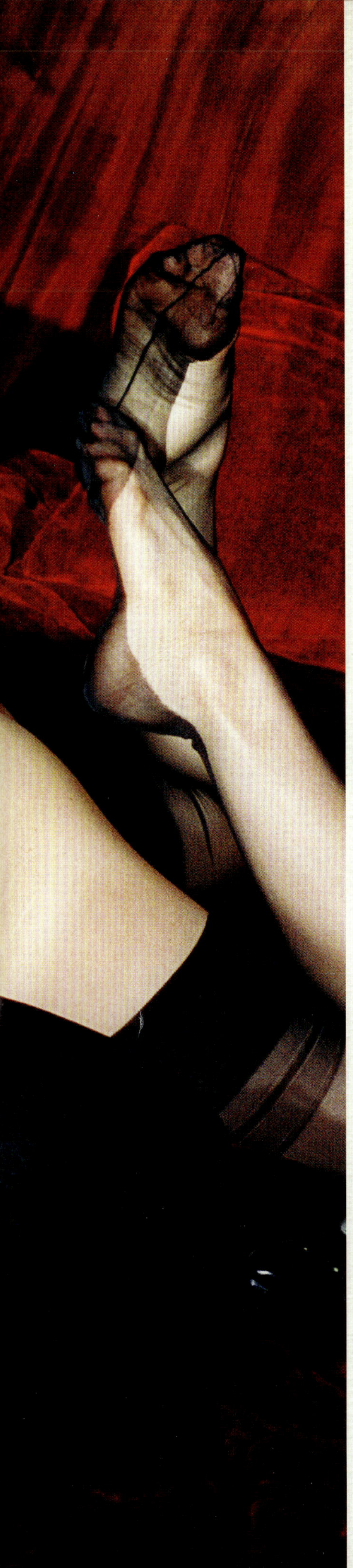

# Dita's Favorite Perverts!

- Seamed Stocking Fetishists
- Corset Aficionados
- Foot Fetishists
- Heavy Rubberists
- Bondage Fans (those that love the classic damsel in distress!)
- High-Heel Worshippers

# FETISH GODDESS

## *Be a Living Work of Art*

*"In art, only the bizarre is beautiful."*
—CHARLES BAUDELAIRE

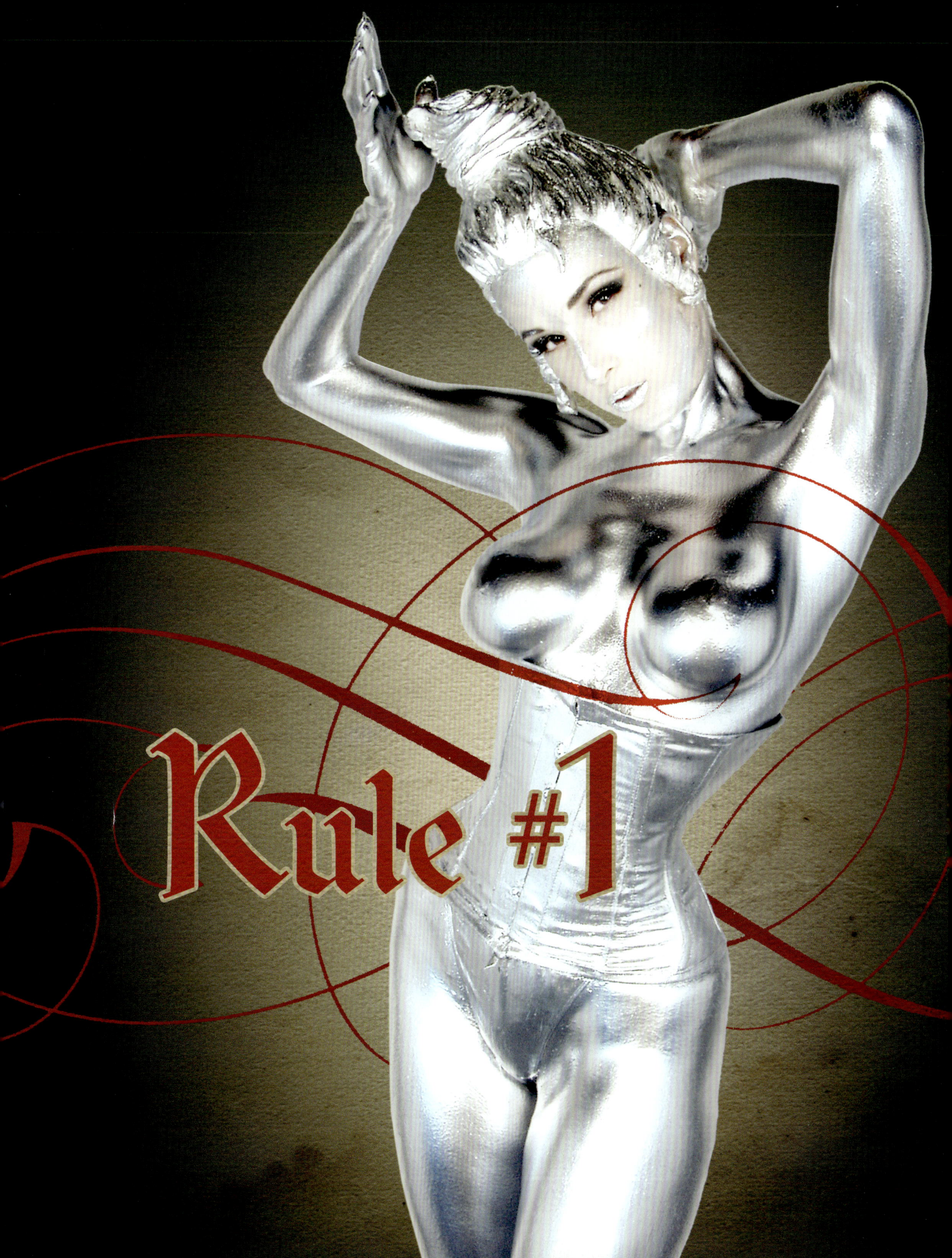
Rule #1

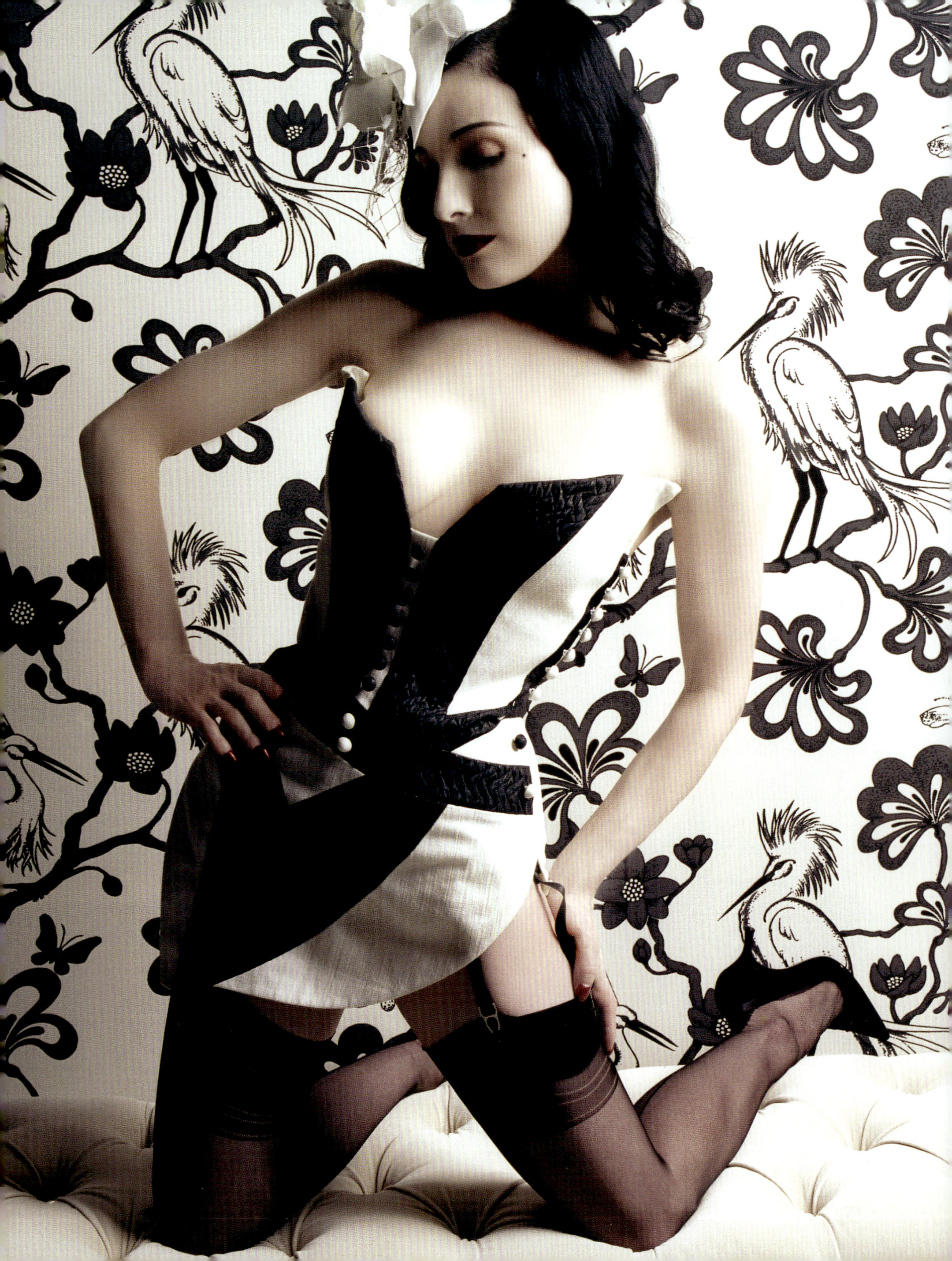

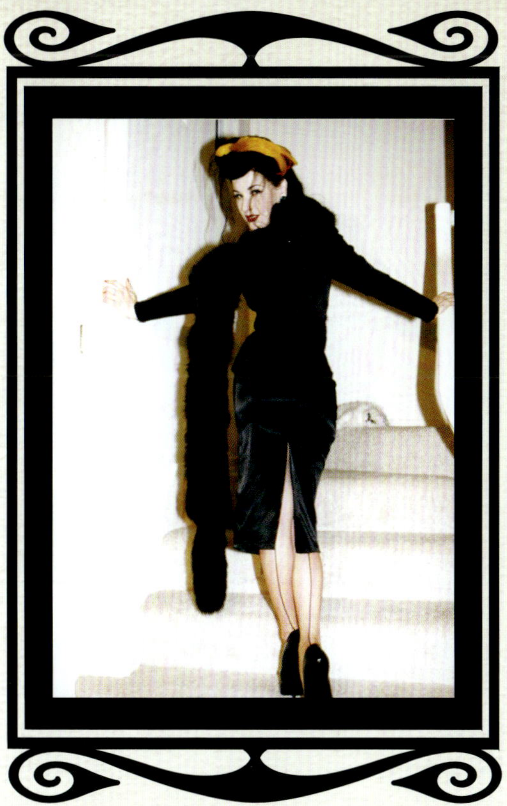

# Pervert Without Precedent

It may seem weird—even dangerous—to acknowledge the power of clothing. After all, doing so would seem to limit a woman's freedom to dress any way she pleases. One might ask, "If I wear this short skirt, this cleavage-inducing/enhancing bustier, and these high stilettos, will men really think I want sex?"

Yes. I can't be sure, but the outfit just described sounds awfully *obvious* in its use of fetish triggers. Of course, this may be the way you want it. Clothing is what we show the world of our bodies and, in a culture of crowds, our personalities. It is through clothing that we define ourselves as femme fatales, businesswomen, bikers, ladies of leisure, or intellectuals. Doesn't each of these personalities have its own distinctive costume?

When I have finished one of my burlesque performances, I purposely finish in nothing but a G-string and pasties. This moment is the culmination of my striptease, the payoff. I want the punters to be thinking about sex—and I want them to think I'm thinking about it too. This is the fantasy. That's the point.

Outside in the world, if I'm going to wear fetish accoutrements, I prefer to disguise them. I might wear a fitted suit with the sheerest dernier black seamed stockings and perilously high heels. Or maybe I'll wear a corset as an undergarment with a dress tailored to show off my silhouette. (Walk around town in a nothing more than a corset, seamed stockings, high heels, black rubber gloves and you'll have a million guys following you around!) Of course, this doesn't mean that I dress *normally*. No, no. A fetish goddess is always dramatic.

I am well aware that most people do not walk around modern America looking the way I do, that some people may find my appearance shocking or inappropriate. Then again, some consider it a nice change. Just the other day, in fact, I was off to a party, and I was dressed in a black satin suit tailored to fit my corseted waist, pale beige stockings with black seams running up the backs of my legs, and five-inch heeled Christian Louboutin pumps. My hair was upswept, pinup style, topped off with a classic veiled tilt hat from the '30s. My makeup? Tasteful but complete, with my signature scarlet lips, of course. I cannot recall whether I was wearing gloves. Anyway, I realized en route that I had forgotten a bottle of champagne for my hostess and so I pulled over to a local grocery store to pick up a bottle. Waiting in line at the checkout, I noticed a little boy, about five years old, holding his father's hand, staring at me, enamored, his mouth half open. The child whispered, "Daddy, look at that pretty lady!" The father did look, in fact he glowered. "I don't think so," he said, pulling the small boy away from the wicked city woman, effectively reprimanding him, teaching him that his reaction to me was wrong—and therefore even more potent. You see, there's a good chance this father's reproof implanted a secret desire into that little boy's brain—one he could carry with him all his life. Believe me. I've talked to enough fetishists to know that in twenty years this little man might just be the guy offering someone big money to dress like the "pretty lady" from the grocery store. It's quite natural to want what you *shouldn't* have.

You may as well know that the chief disadvantage of being a fetish goddess is that people's reactions may be rather mean-spirited. (But, in order to have memorable personal style, one must not be afraid to take risks!) Still, what surprises me is not that some people grow uncomfortable by my appearance, but that they so often identify the source of my "weirdness" as pop-culture America, MTV, and lax Internet laws. These people see me as a pervert without precedent.

Not so.

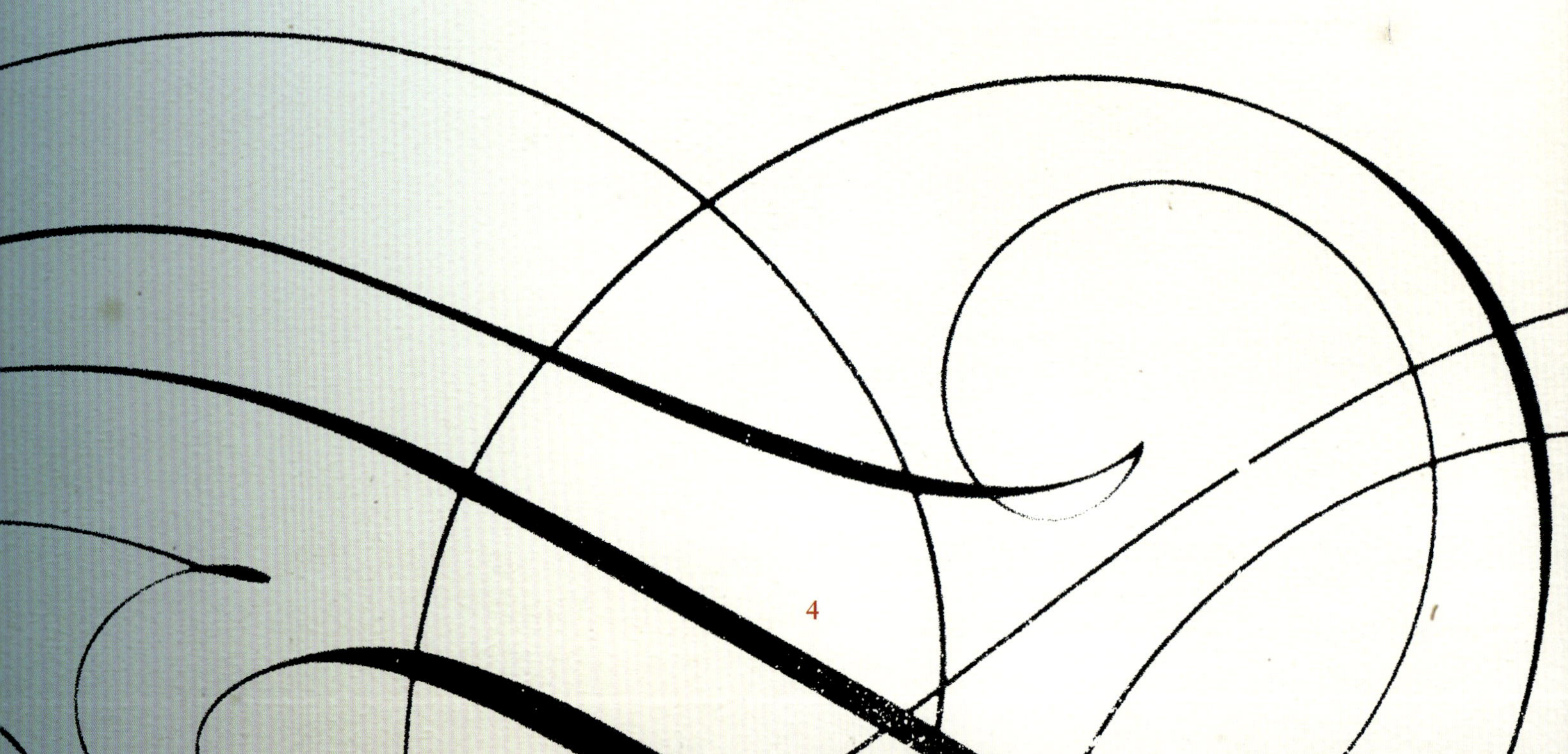

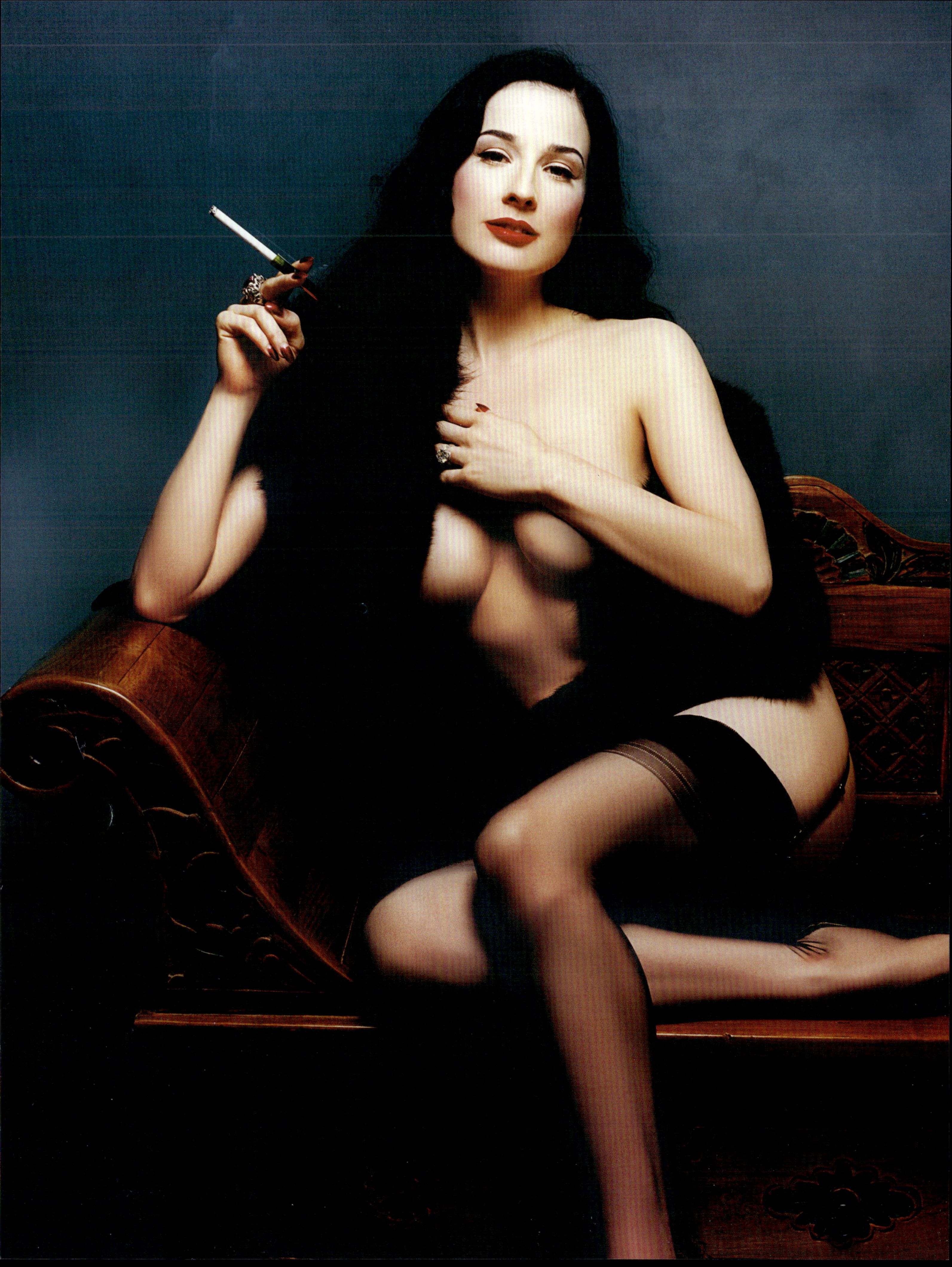

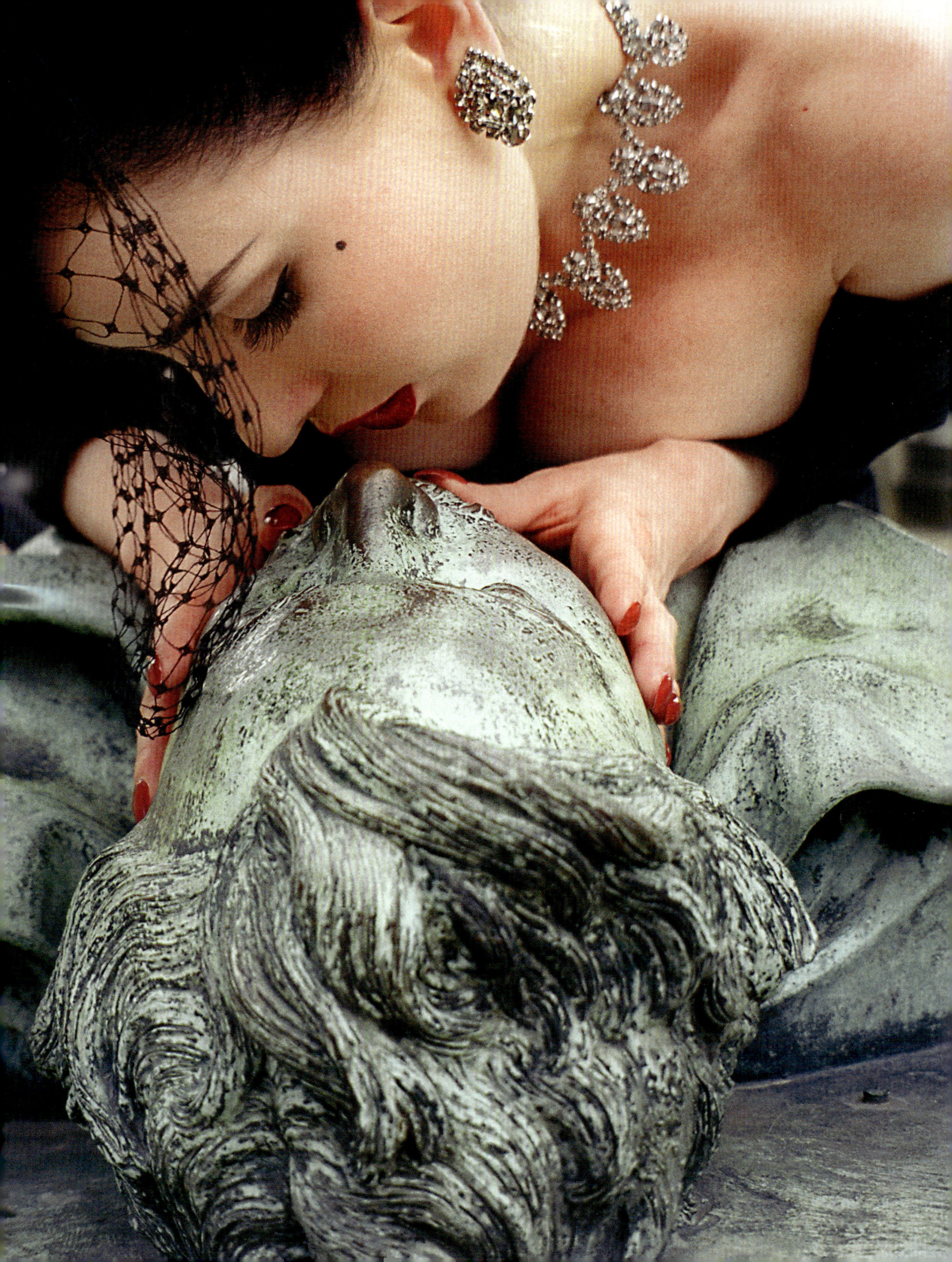

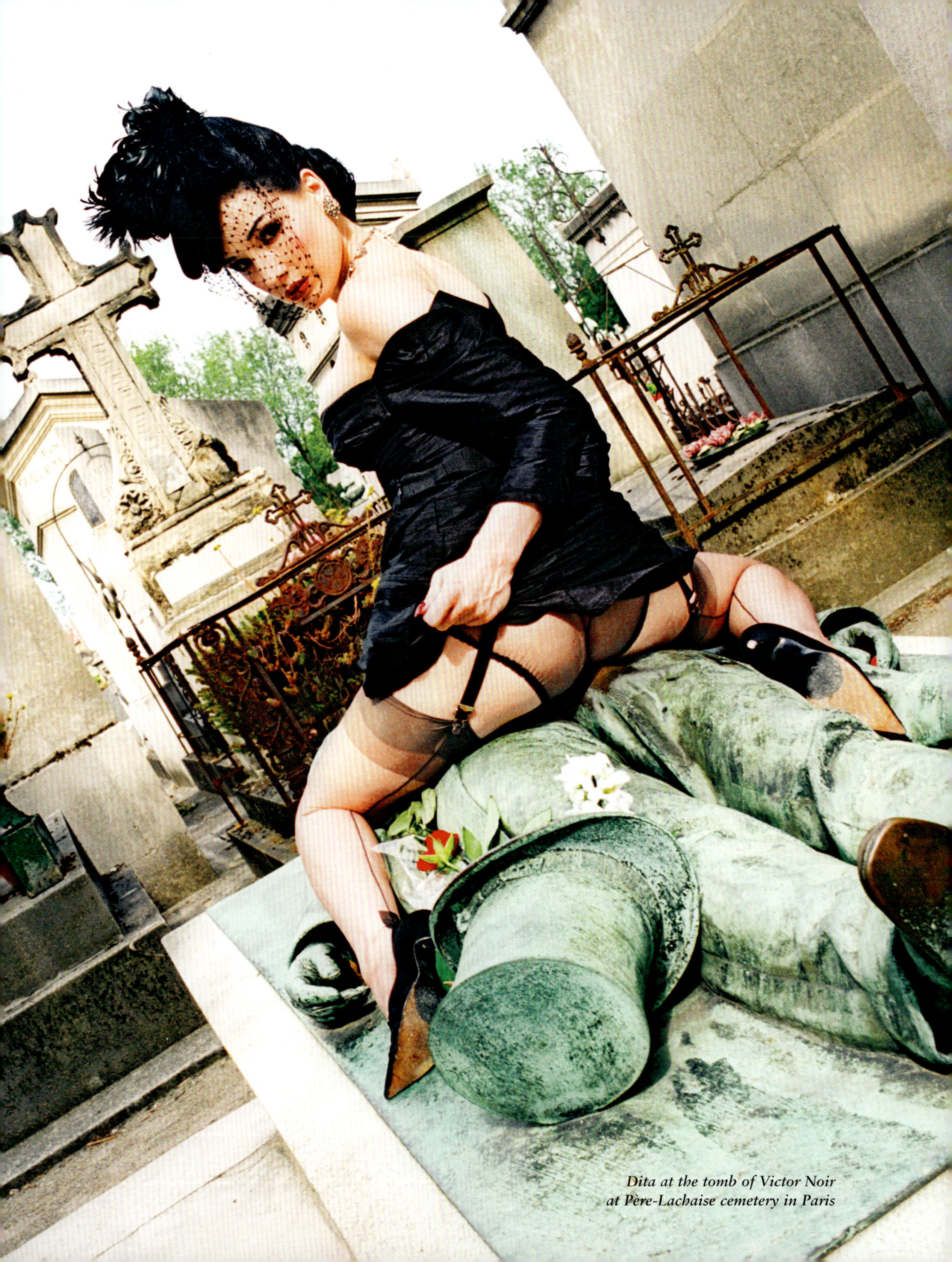

*Dita at the tomb of Victor Noir*
*at Père-Lachaise cemetery in Paris*

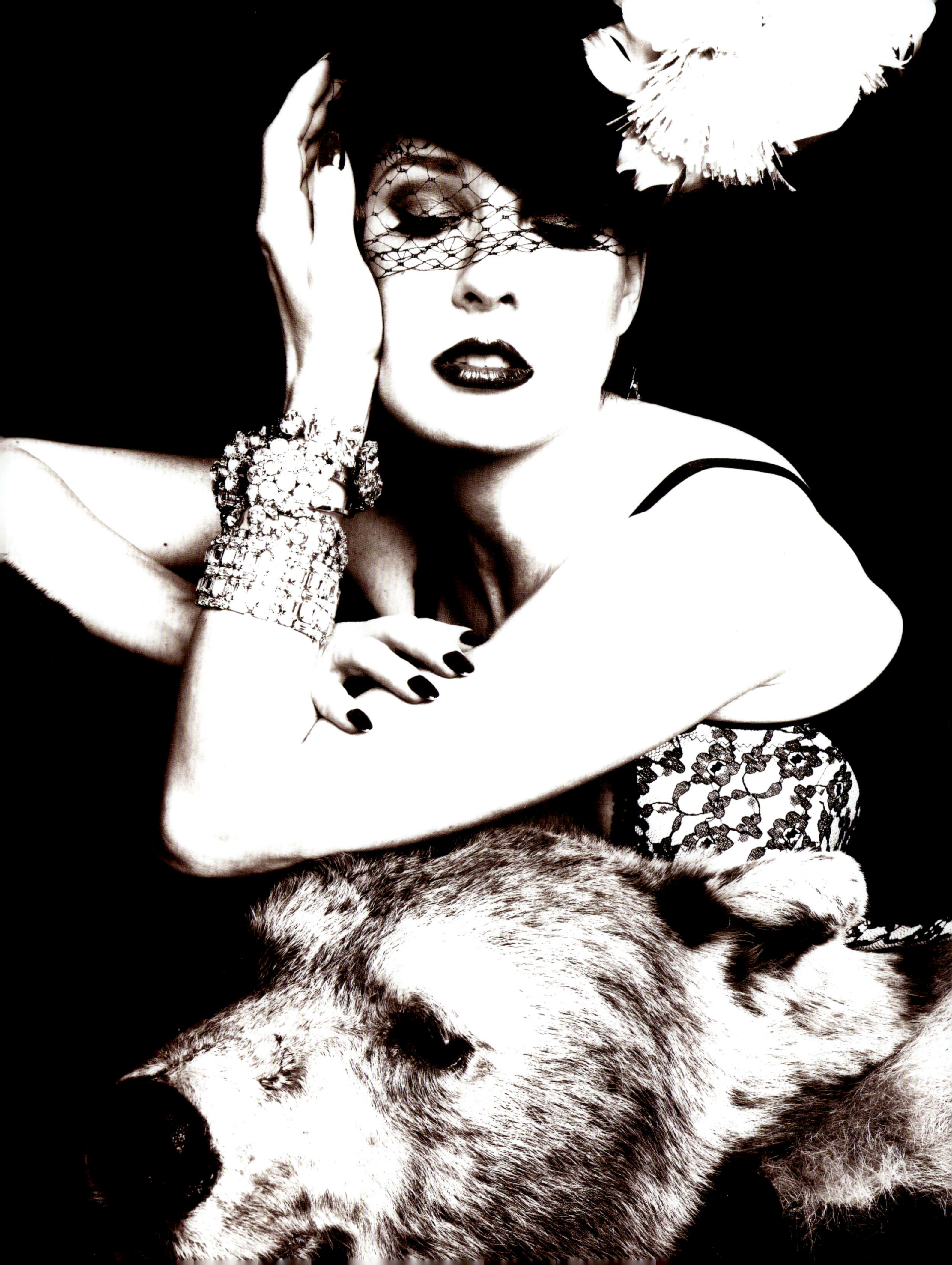

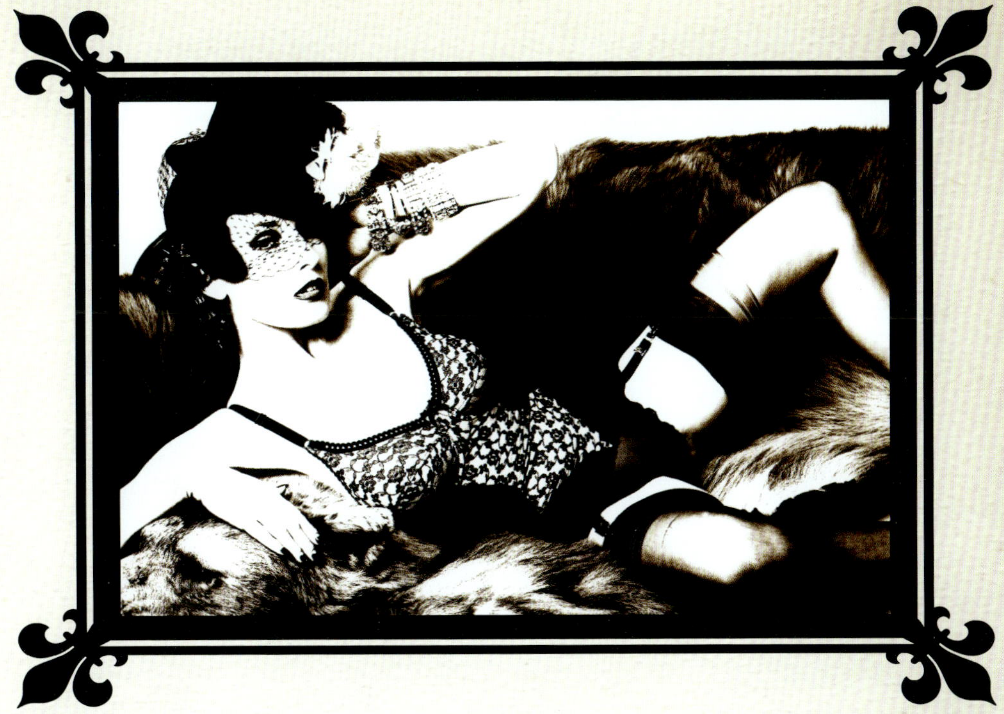

# The Divine Marquise

Follow me to Paris, 1920, to glimpse my fetish forebear in all her shocking glory. Climb the crumbling steps of her Palais Rosé, the pink marble mansion, set like a giant dusty gem on the Grand Canal. Quick! Duck your head! Her pet albino blackbirds—perhaps dyed blue or red to suit the evening's decor—swoop from the sky. The Divine Marquise herself stands at the top of the stairs greeting her revelers, her large green eyes twinkling under glued black velvet strips. Her name is Marchesa Luisa Casati. Wraithlike, her skin cadaverously pale, her pupils vast with belladonna, her hair a vermilion flame, this woman—if you can call her that—wears live snakes around her neck and a crown of white peacock feathers dripping in blood. (You learn over dinner that her chauffeur slaughtered chickens for the added touch of color and that her fur coat was fashioned from a beloved household pet who had passed on of natural causes.)

You enter the grand hall, decorated with floral arrangements made of precious gems, mechanical birds flapping jeweled wings in exquisite gilded cages, and exotic pets, including cheetahs, boa constrictors, and monkeys. A nude, gilt-encrusted manservant takes your coat, holding a torch to illuminate the rooms of endless, enchanting madness.

Eighty years ago, this woman was more shocking than anyone has been since. She designed her costumes to be bizarre and striking. Yet, her transformations were so marvelous, so enchanting that the Marchesa Casati should be remembered as a quintessential fetish fashion goddess.

"I want to be a living work of art!" she shrieked at the world. As luck would have it, fetish means "something that shocks the sensibilities," in the art world. Indeed, if the volume of art inspired by her (paint, film, and writing) is any indication, Casati was a masterpiece. She was captured on film by Man Ray, Cecil Beaton, and Baron Adolph de Meyer. She was the art muse of Giovanni Boldini, Augustus John, Kees van Dongen, sketched by Drian, and sculpted by Jacob Epstein. She inspired the famous "Panther" design for Cartier. In fact, this very fetish goddess is the most artistically represented woman after Cleopatra and the Virgin Mary. True, she commissioned many of these portraits herself—for display in her own gallery—but even after her time, Casati continued to inspire, especially out on the runway. Designers like John Galliano and Tom Ford have invoked Casati's legend.

True, she was a bit more eccentric than I (and anyone for that matter!), but I like to think of Casati as a kindred spirit. Like me, she entered the world as a shy plain Jane and rediscovered herself through costume. In fact, though she is admired by fetishists, Casati was regarded even in her own time as a "fascinatrix." I like the idea. Less dominatrix, more fascinatrix—now those are words to live by!

More to the point, Casati defined showmanship for the everyday woman. She wasn't a dancer at the Moulin Rouge. She didn't wear these costumes just to the opera. She dressed like a maniac *every single day*. She was utterly captivating. A writer of her time, Philippe Jullian, recalled her costumed transformation from human being to something quite different this way: "On this skeleton tawdry fineries had acquired an elegance beyond the canons of any fashion. This figure could arouse panic . . . but pity, never." Casati was a one-woman fetish theater.

In the end, of course, they say she had no interior. Who cares? It was her stated goal to be a work of art, a painting, a thrilling show for the masses. That she descended into poverty as a result of her excesses is a sad but good example of her devotion. By 1930, you see, Casati had amassed a debt of twenty-five million American dollars, escaping to London when her Palais Rosé and all of her possessions were auctioned off. (Coco Chanel was among the bidders and Peggy Guggenheim eventually bought the palace.) Though destitute in London, Casati again became the muse of writers and artists who recorded her movements—even her rummaging through trashcans in search of shreds of lace and velvet for her costumes—with devotion fit for the fetish legend she was.

How can I admire so frivolous a life, you wonder? How can I *not*? Casati's entire identity lay in the creation of fantasy. She made Europe more colorful. She sought immortality and she got it. What more can a fetish goddess ask for?

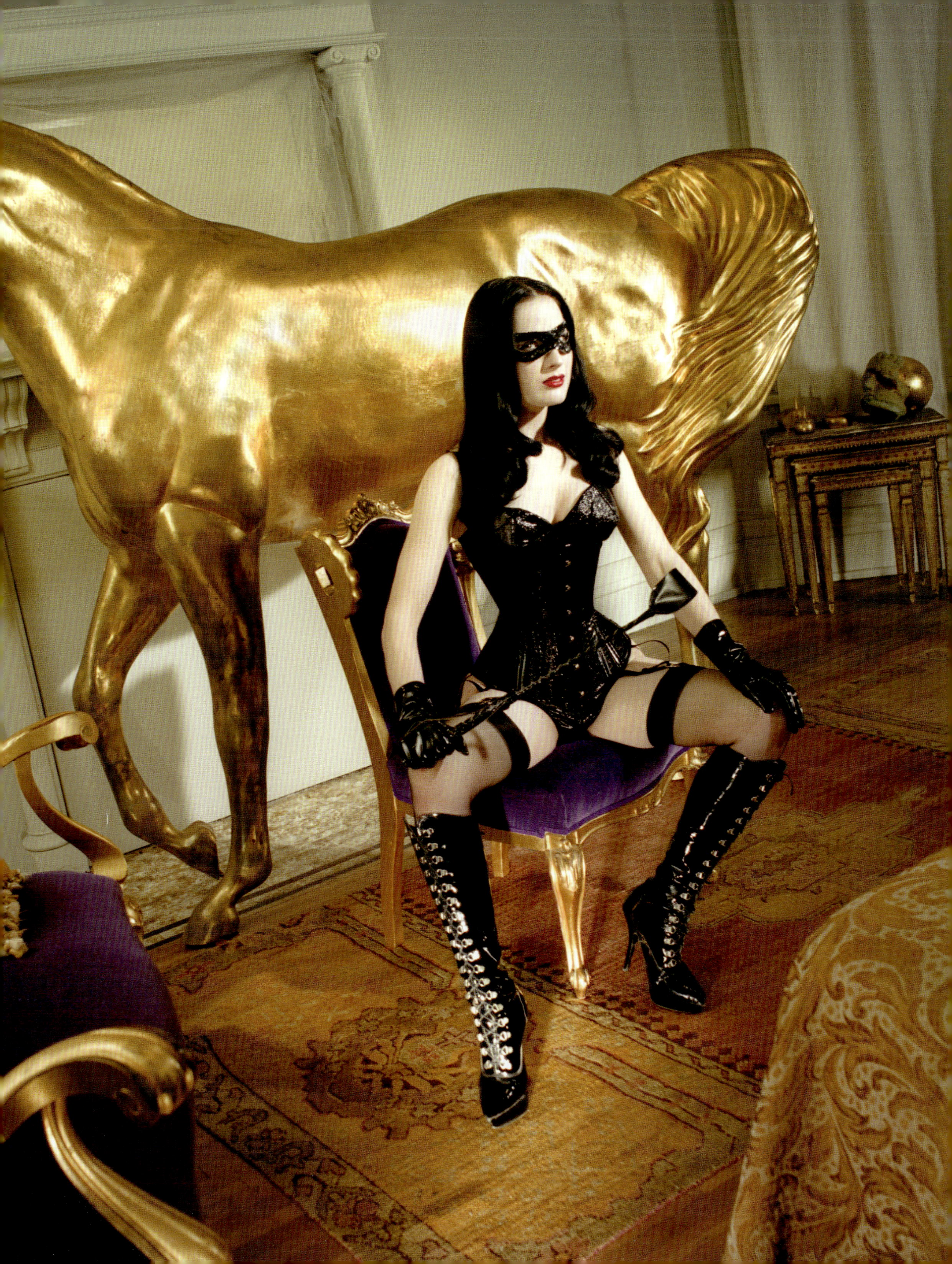

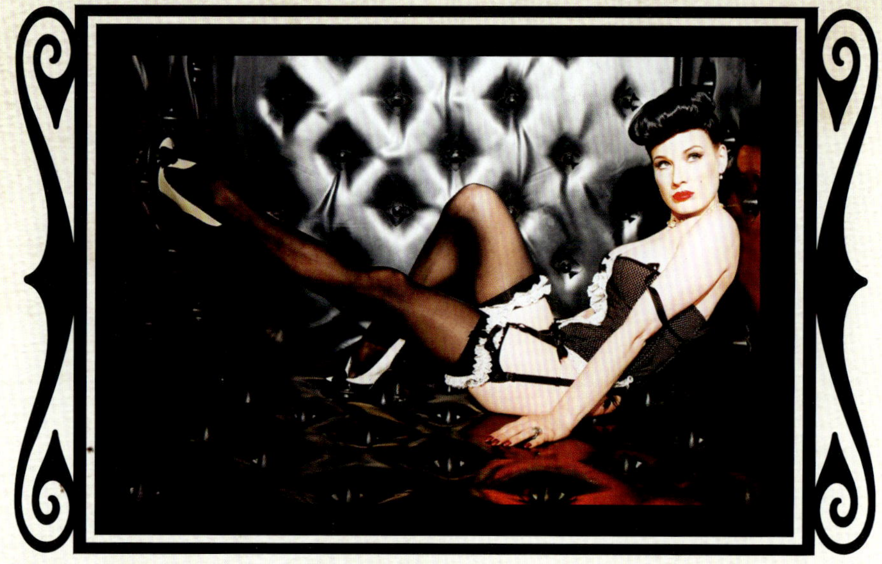

# Modern Fetish Deities

The first fetish goddess I knew was Mistress Antoinette, the owner of Versatile Fashions, where I bought my first corset at the age of eighteen. I kept in touch with the clerk who laced me up that day, and eventually I met and befriended Antoinette, an icon in the fetish world. Now, she was extravagant! One of those ladies who gets her hair done once a week, when she flounced out of the salon, her 'do was big and flaming red, her nails were shiny crimson talons, and her makeup was thickly severe. No matter what her agenda, Mistress Antoinette *always* donned a corset, a miniskirt, and a pair of stiletto boots. And oh yes, she was in her sixties—something that made her all the more shocking to most passersby. On one occasion, I recall traveling with her, and I was washing my hands in an airport bathroom when I heard a group of women waxing impolite about how bizarre my friend looked. I gently explained that Mistress Antoinette was a fetish idol, her style revered the world over, and that men quite literally fell and worshipped at her feet. When I politely asked the women whether they had experienced any such reactions to their own style, they held oddly silent.

I have had boyfriends say to me, "Dita, why do you have to dress like this and have people stare at you? Why don't you take it down about three notches?" Three notches? I wouldn't be myself! I dress in a way that makes me feel glamorous. One may consider my look extravagant, but I simply wouldn't be comfortable in sweatpants or jeans. Artificial and theatrical as I may appear to some people, my style is "natural" for me. And these days, I would never accept anything less in a lover than total appreciation and encouragement to dress as I please.

Of course, there is a difference between the sort of fetish fashion I wear every day and what I wear to transform myself for photos or performances. I cannot very well walk around town in one of my jewel-encrusted burlesque costumes or a French lace, corseted Victorian ball gown. Nor can I show up to the post office rope-tied in just stockings and brassiere, as you might find me in a fetish photograph. This is why I adore the fantasy of my photos. But I can wear stockings and garters and heels every day. . . .

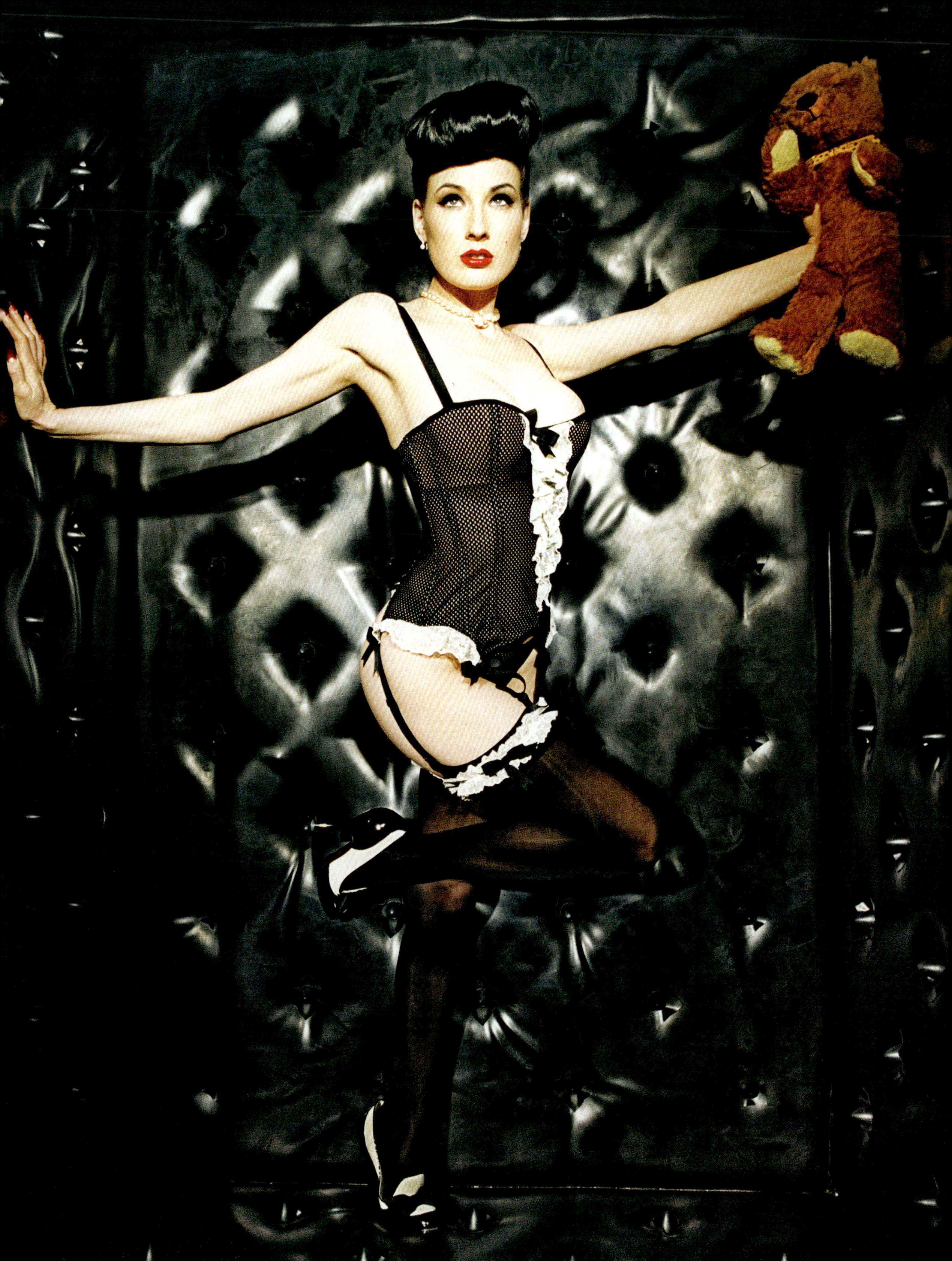

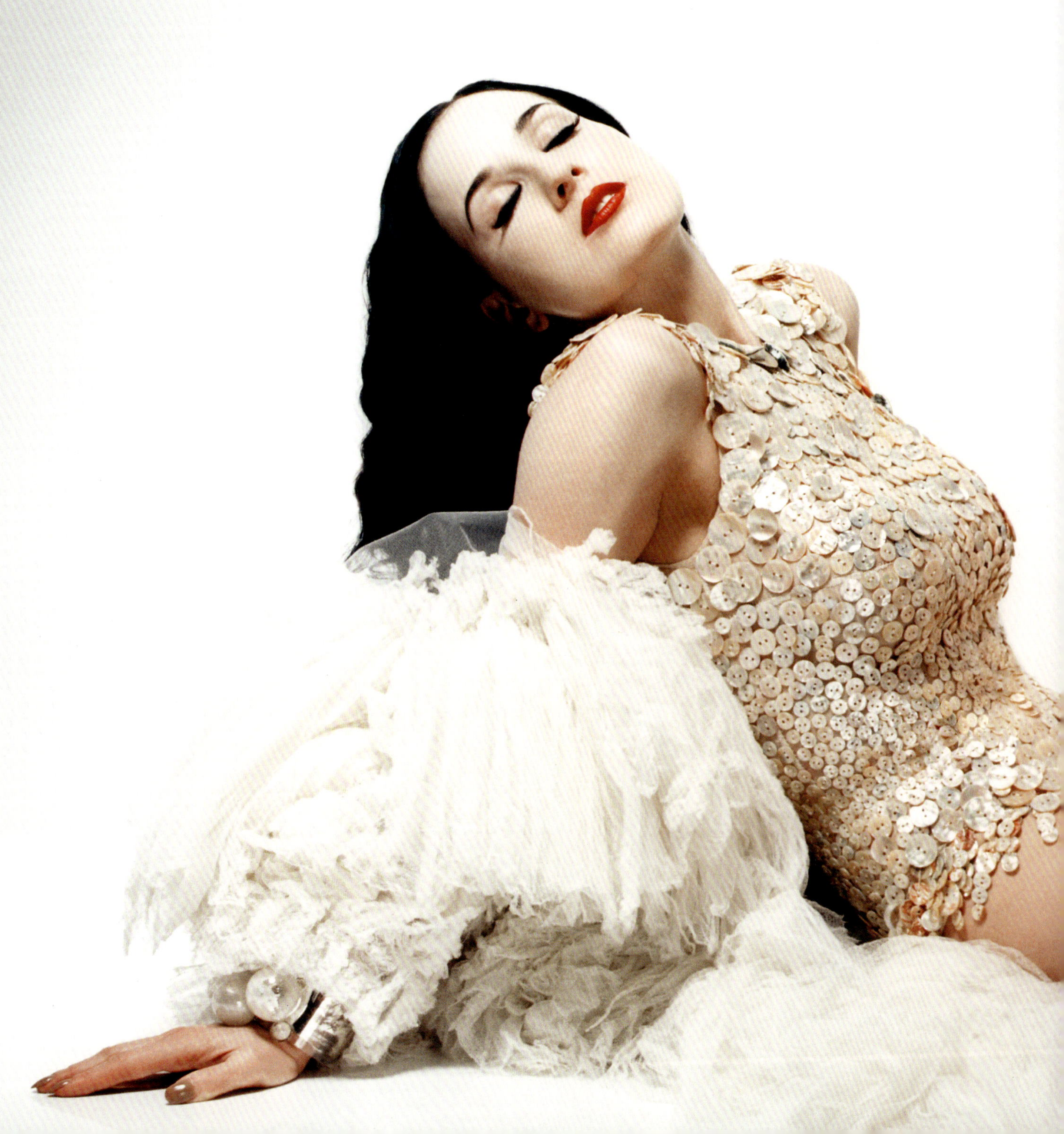

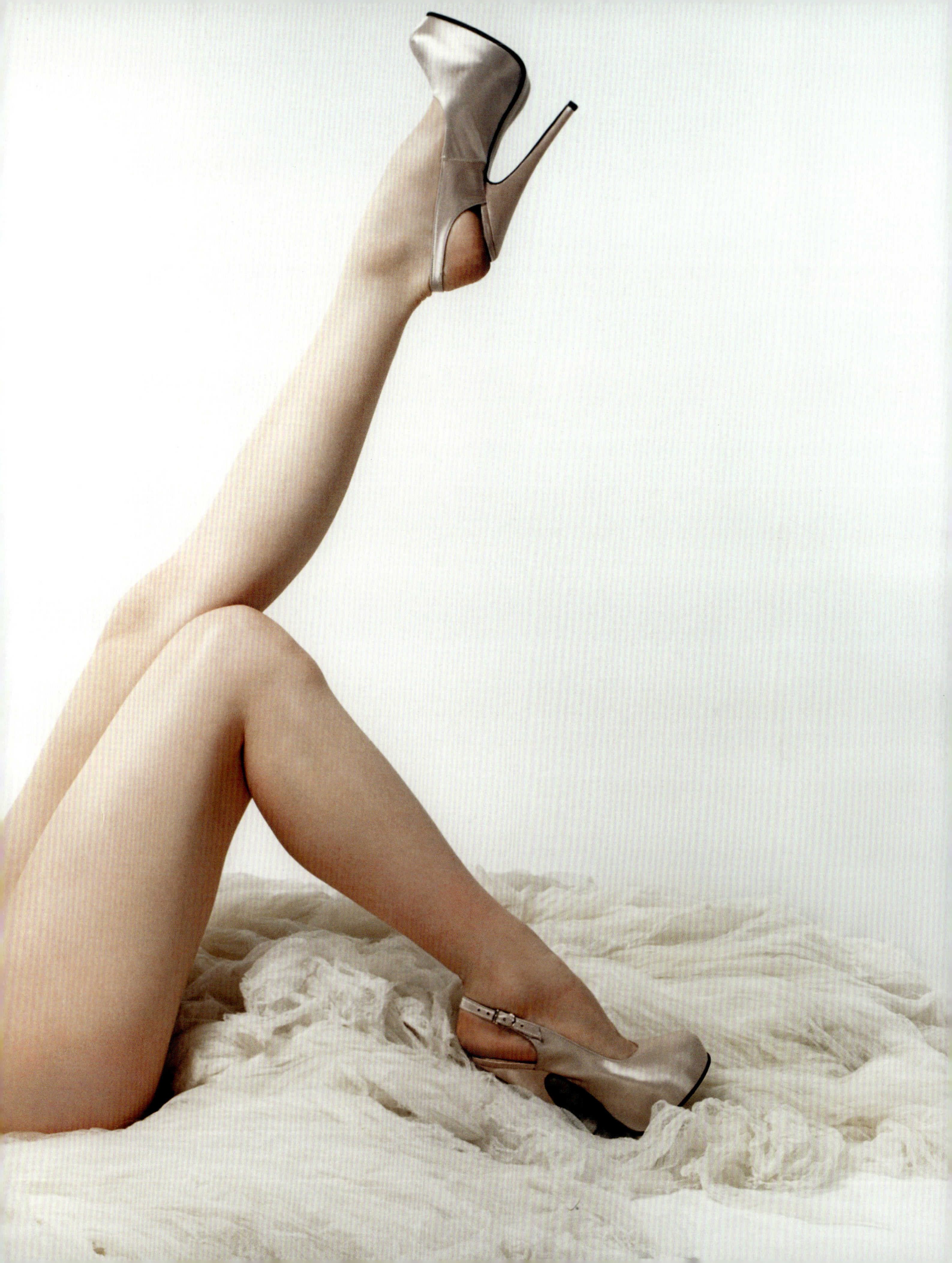

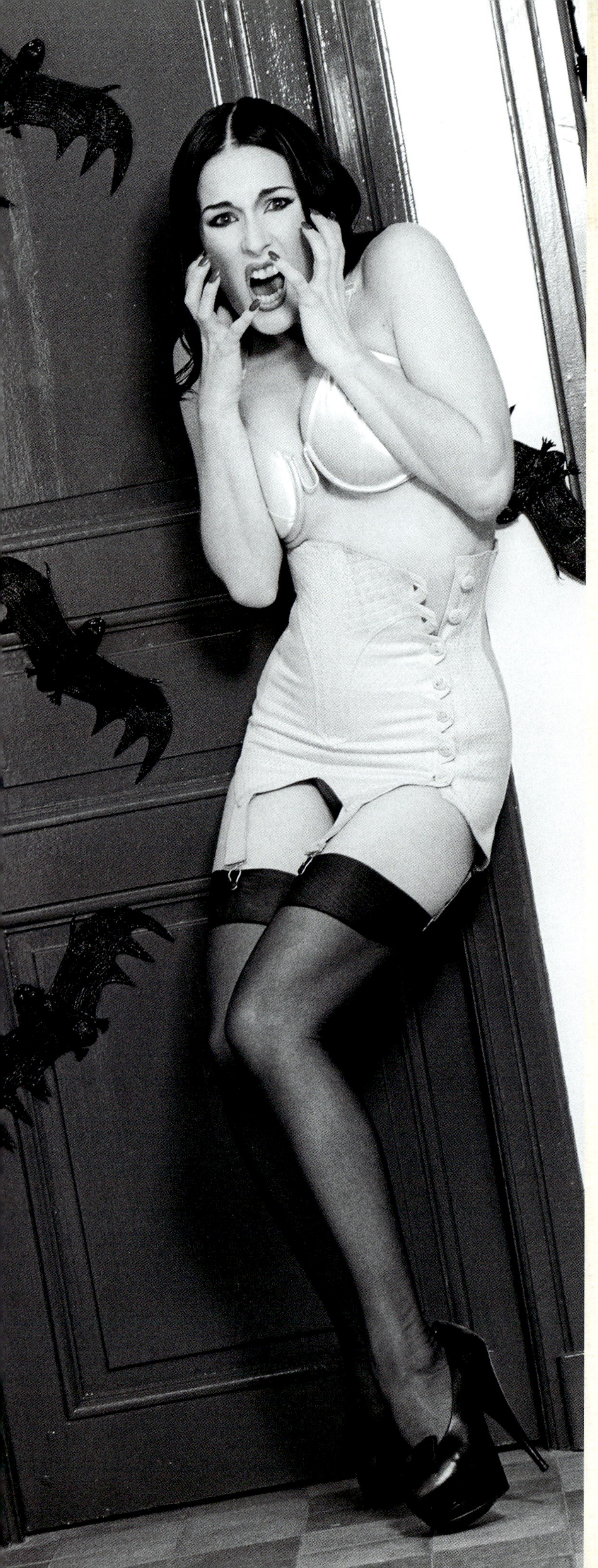

# Damsel in Distress

For me, fetish's allure is in its classics. No matter how many times I portray the damsel in distress, I never tire of her. Hers is the fetish scenario with which I most identify because she is timeless and feminine, beautiful, and typically from the fetish era I love most (the 1940s and '50s). Her clothes—usually she's wearing a slinky but feminine dress, garters, and seamed stockings—are right up my alley. Besides, the damsel is never harsh, never masculine. She's beautiful, vulnerable, and waiting for a big strong man to save her. She's all-American. I've read about her in books and seen her in films—even cartoons! Would you believe I remember watching *Bugs Bunny* as a little girl and seeing my first damsel tied to the tracks? *Bugs Bunny* introduced me to fetish!

When I'm on camera—whether I'm tied up in the jungle or bound to railroad tracks—I imagine that I'm really that girl, in the 1940s or '50s, waiting for my hero to arrive on the scene and save me. What girl doesn't occasionally dream about this?

People are sometimes shocked to learn that I prefer the damsel to the domina. Though I admire her outfits and her strength, the dominatrix must be aggressive and cruel—expressions that don't come naturally to me. Indeed, I have a hard time drumming up enthusiasm for humiliating someone, for giving orders like, "Lick my boots, scum." In fact, I finally had to admit to myself that I just don't take pleasure in

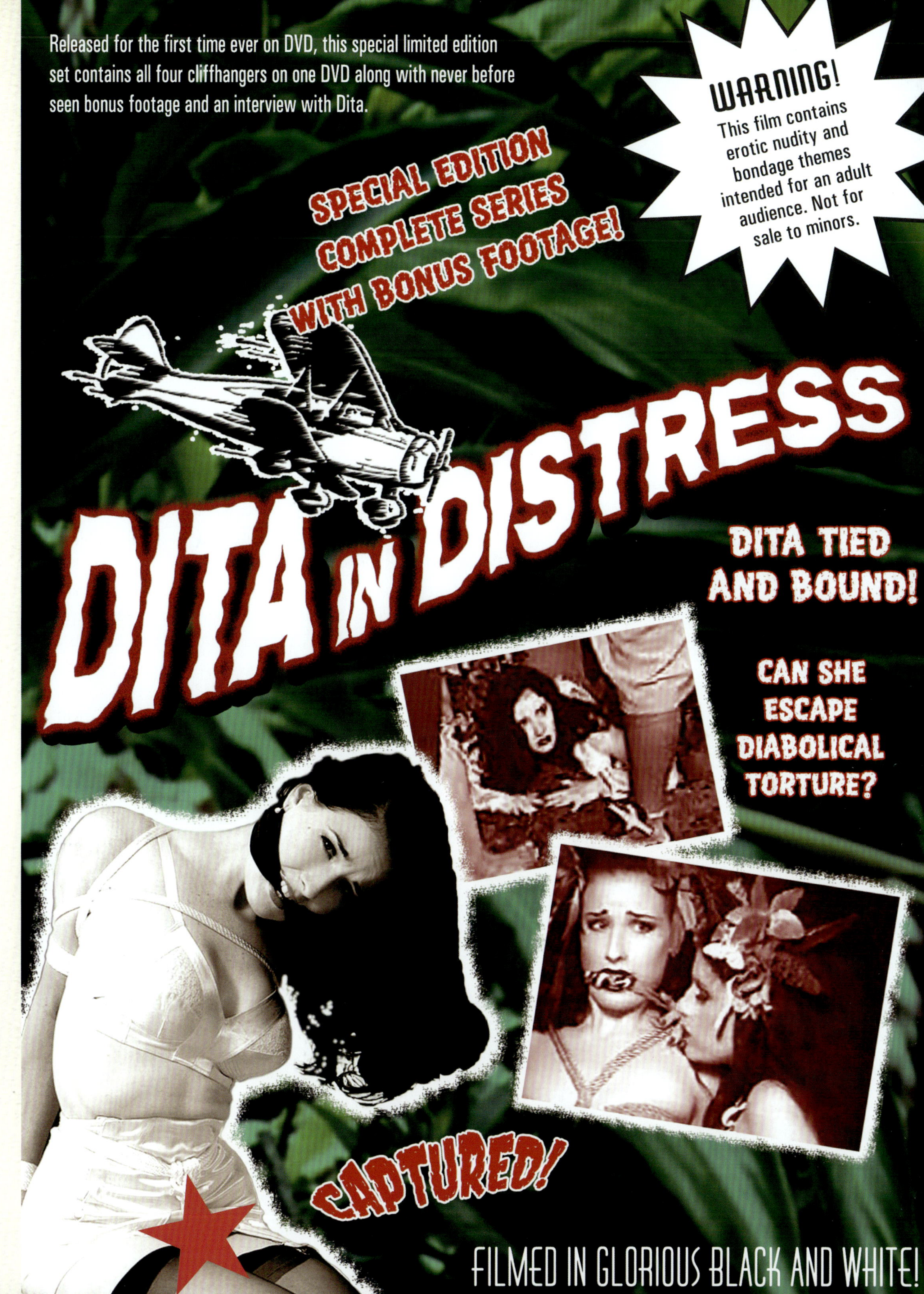

Released for the first time ever on DVD, this special limited edition set contains all four cliffhangers on one DVD along with never before seen bonus footage and an interview with Dita.
WARNING!
This film contains erotic nudity and bondage themes intended for an adult audience. Not for sale to minors.
SPECIAL EDITION
COMPLETE SERIES
WITH BONUS FOOTAGE!
DITA IN DISTRESS
DITA TIED AND BOUND!
CAN SHE ESCAPE DIABOLICAL TORTURE?
CAPTURED!
FILMED IN GLORIOUS BLACK AND WHITE!

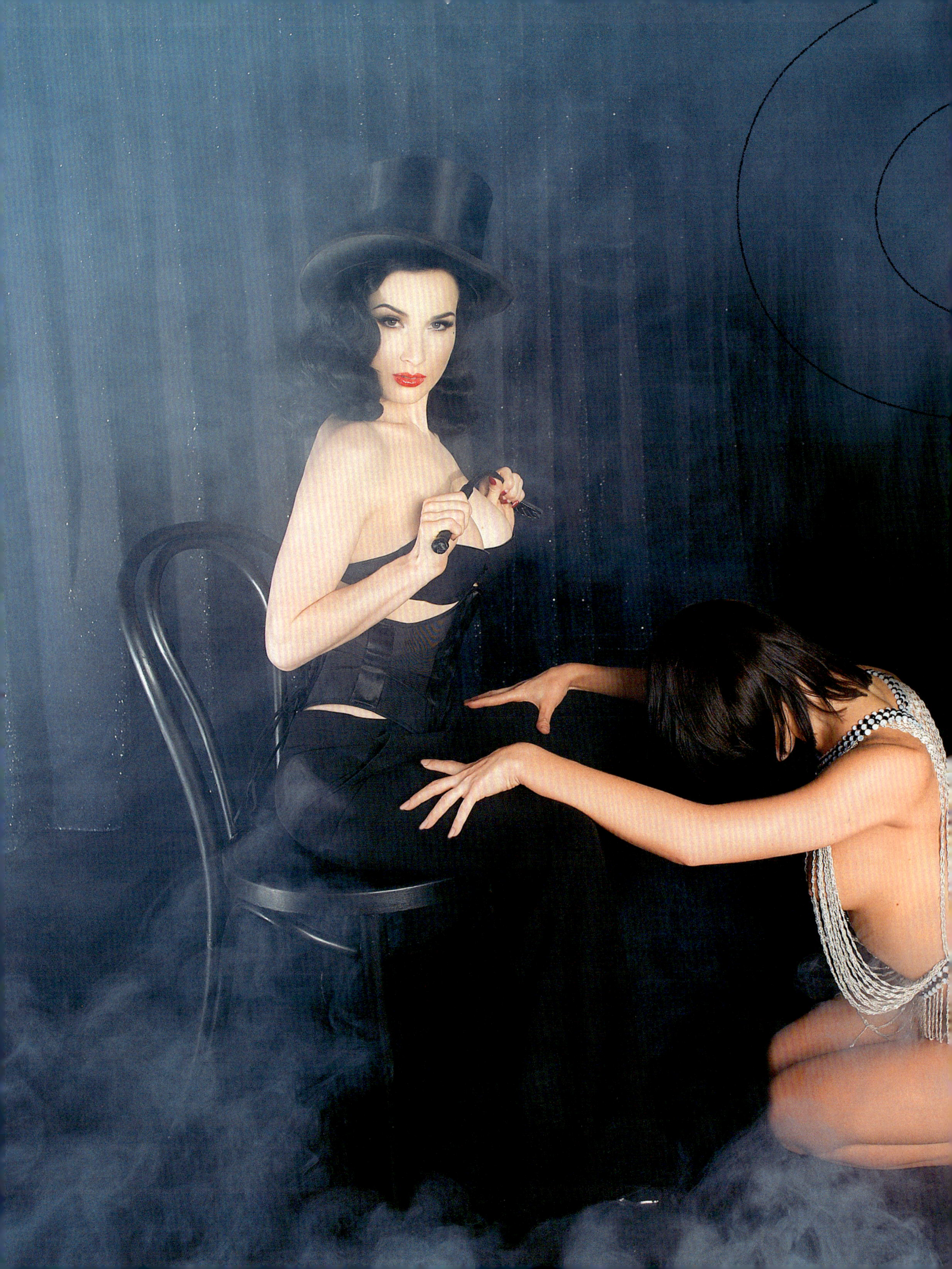

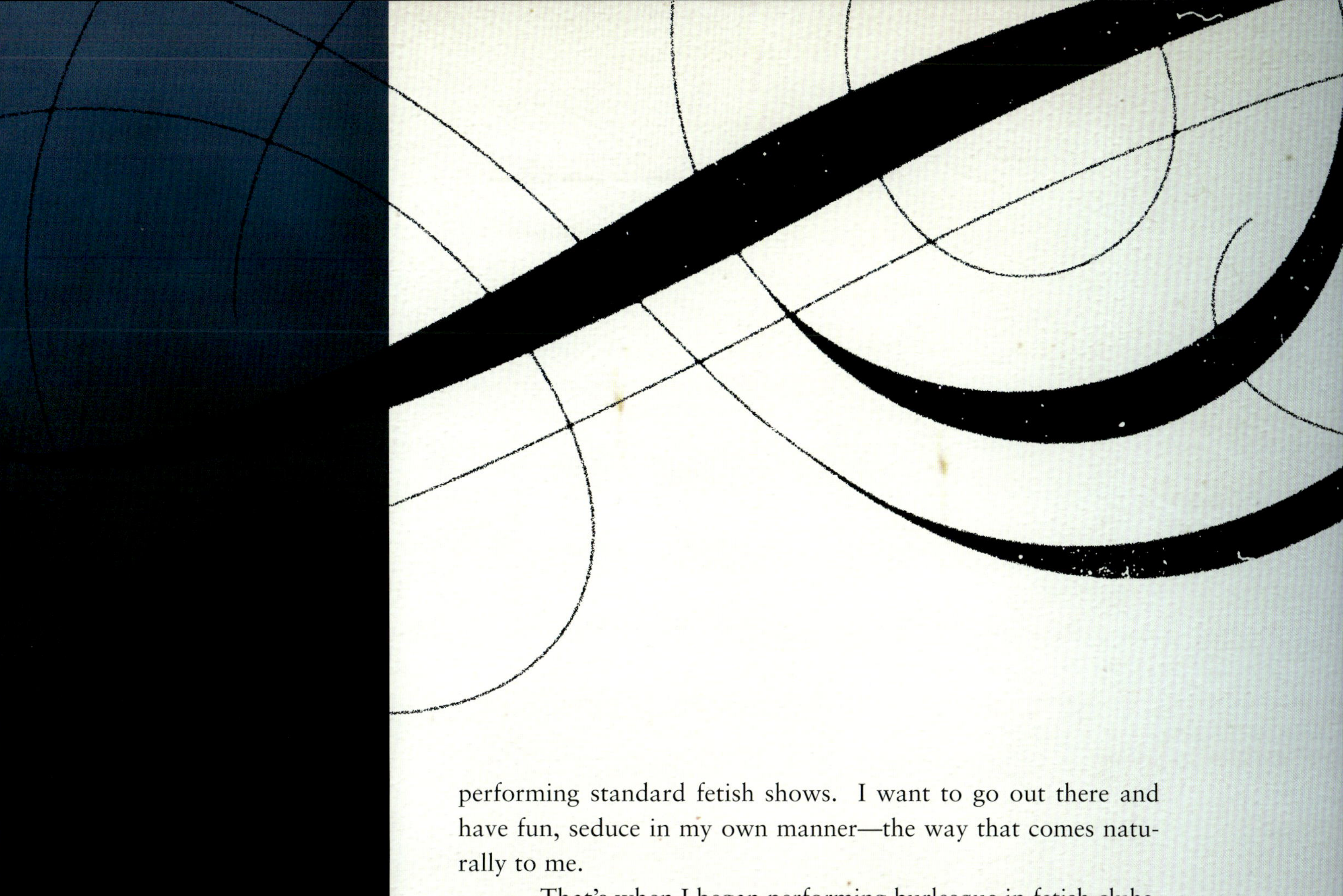

performing standard fetish shows. I want to go out there and have fun, seduce in my own manner—the way that comes naturally to me.

That's when I began performing burlesque in fetish clubs. With burlesque, I involve fetish elements in a fun and unique way. I don't wear a corset because I am a dominatrix on this stage. No, no. I wear it because it is an exaggeration of the feminine form, aside from being pretty and fun to unlace and remove.

When I first began performing my burlesque shows in the fetish scene, some people criticized my act by claiming that there was nothing "fetish" about what I was doing. Listen, if somebody's not seeing the fetish in what I'm doing, then she is not looking closely enough. She's not looking at the tightly laced corset. She's not looking at the silky seamed stockings. She's not looking at the way I navigate the stage in five-inch heels, or at my French maids catering to their mistress' whims. I enjoy adding in as many elements as I can—disguising them for fun and intrigue. For example, a foot fetishist might watch my show and delight in the removal of my stockings and baring my feet. On the other hand, if you have just come for the burlesque, you will watch this same movement and say, "She's stripteasing and it's elegant." The intersection is so complementary that you don't really notice it unless you wish to.

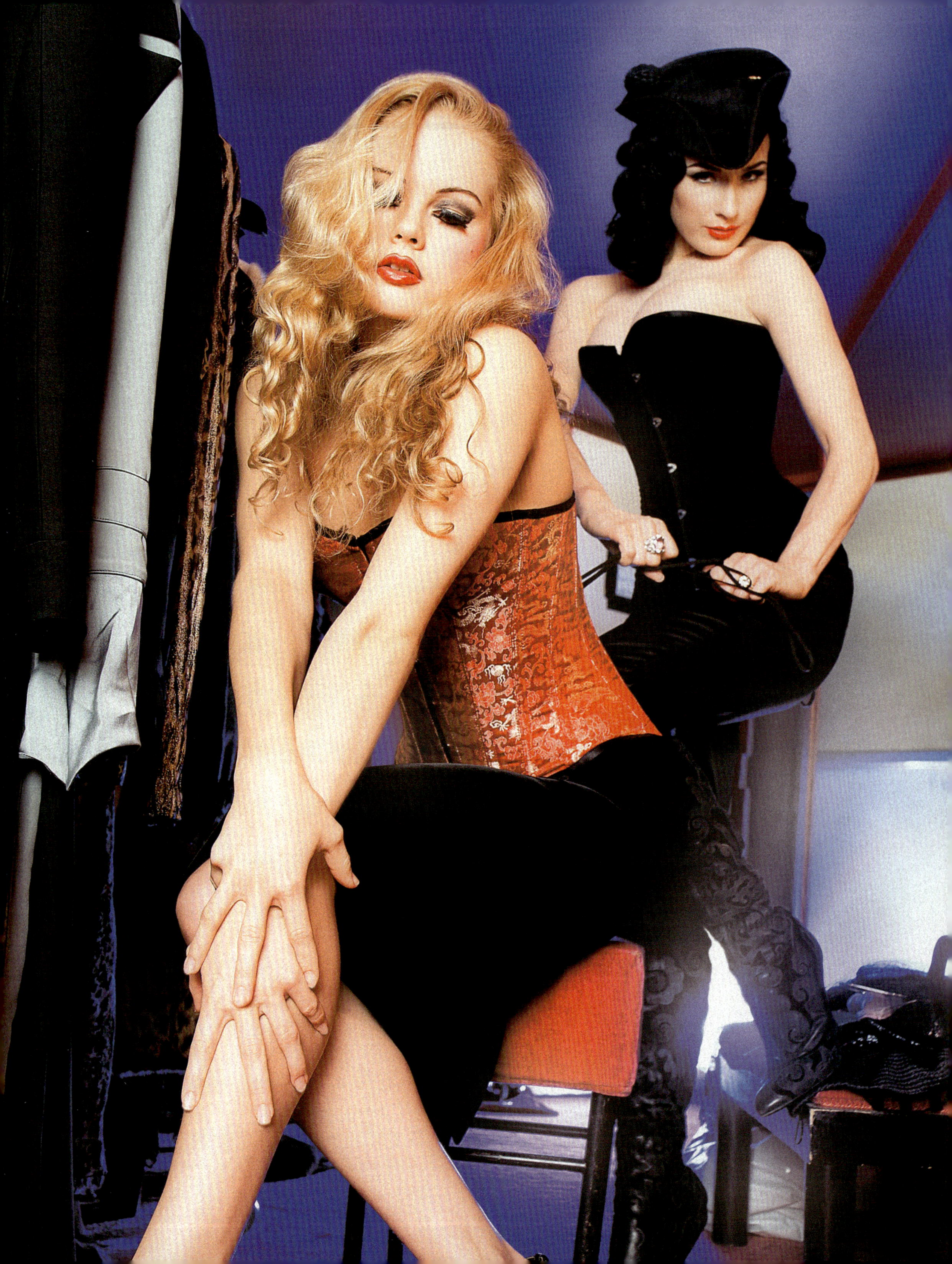

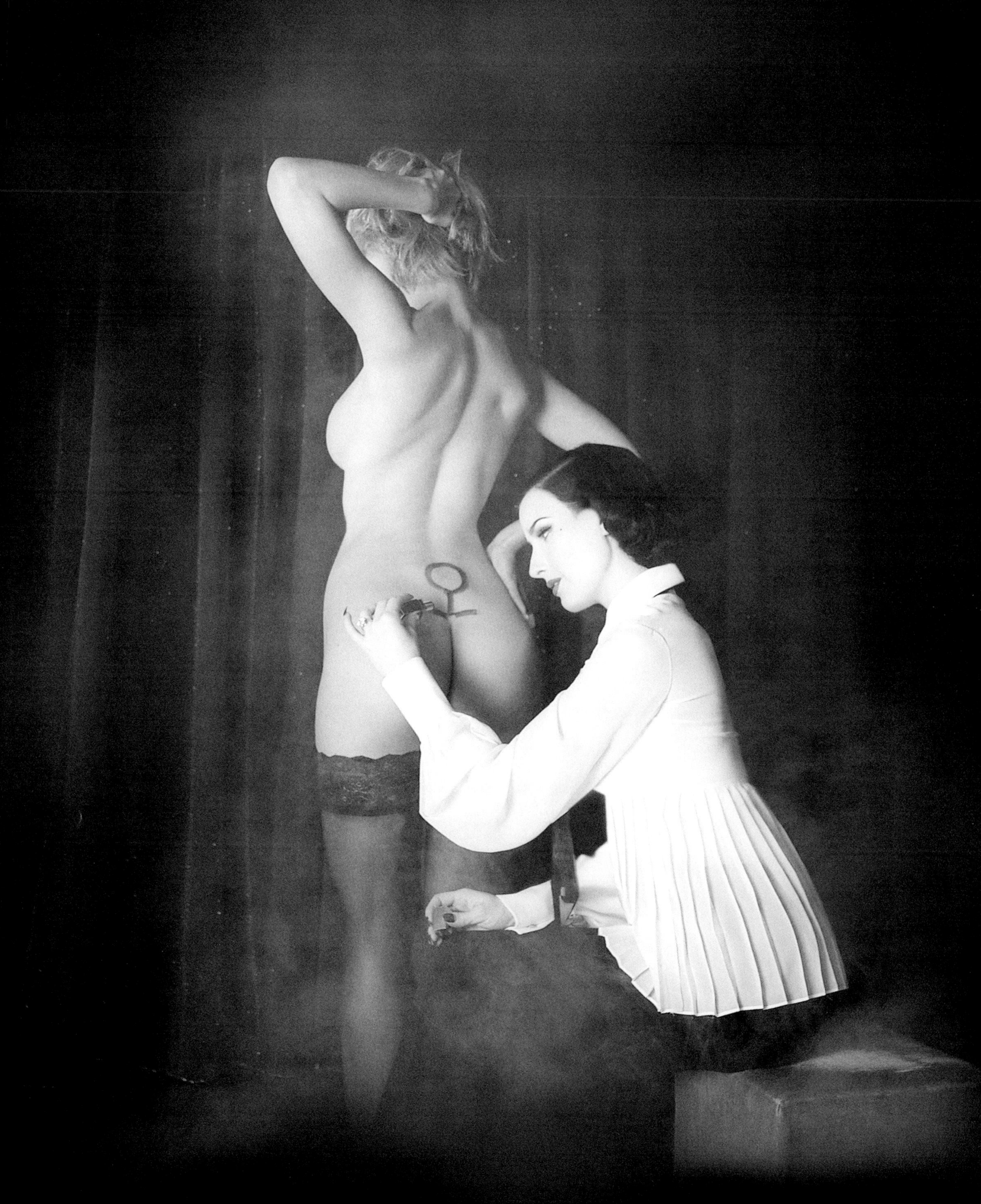

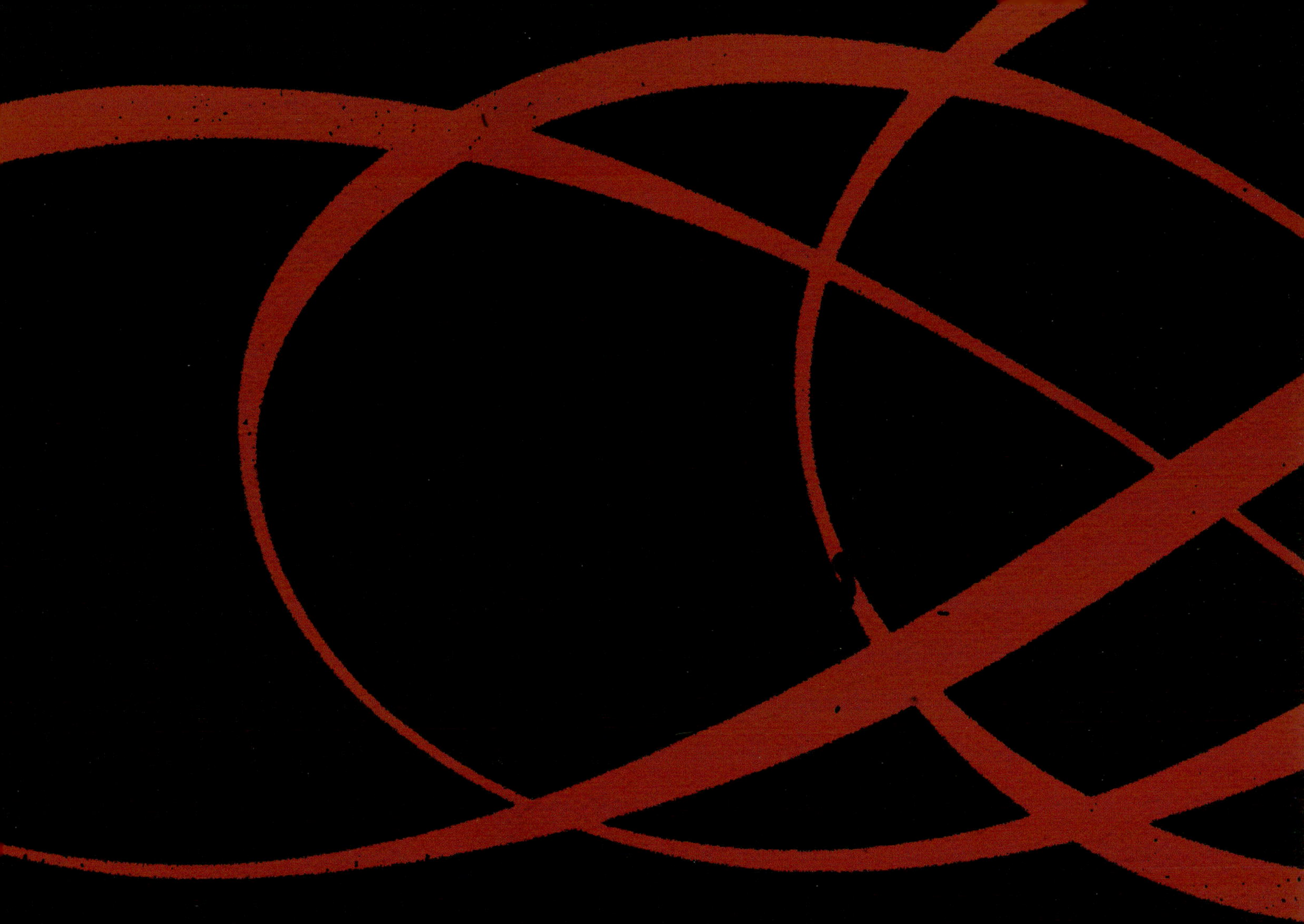

# FETISH GODDESS

## *Partly Revealed Flesh = Fantasy*

*"At the sight of her lying on the red velvet cushions,
her precious body peeping out between the folds of sable,
I realized how powerfully sensuality and lust are aroused
by flesh that is only partly revealed."*

–FROM VENUS IN FURS

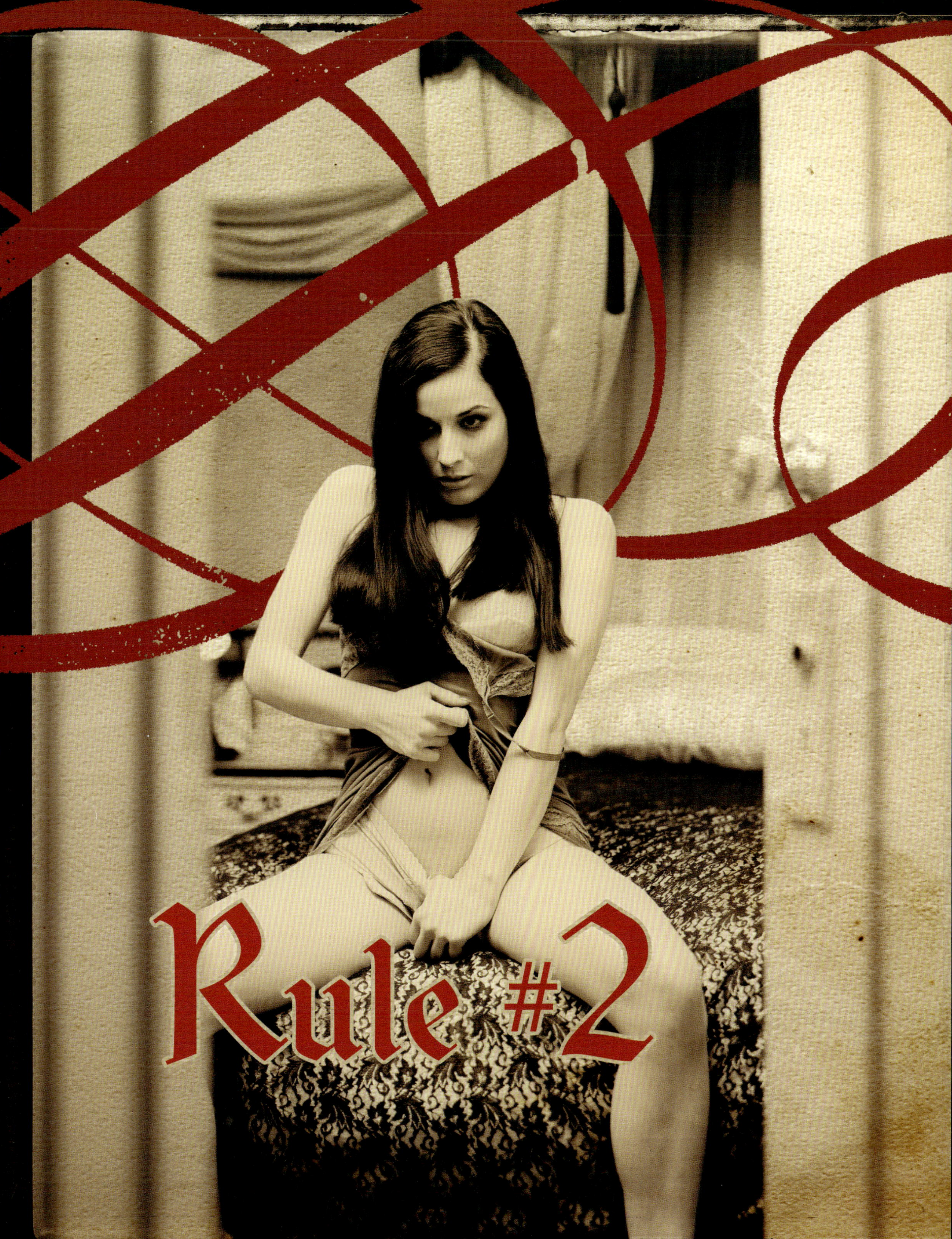

# Rule #2

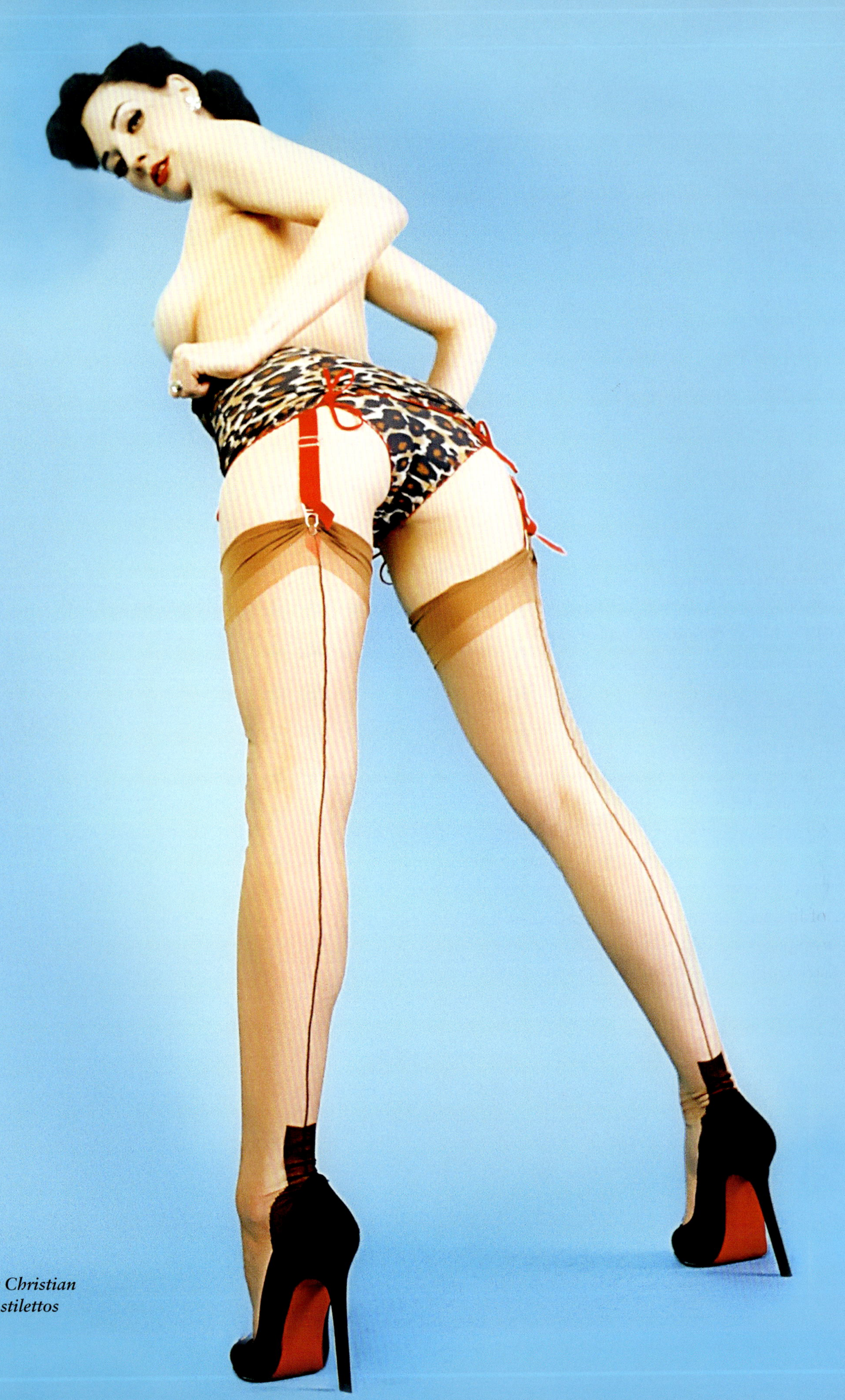

*Dita in her Christian Louboutin stilettos*

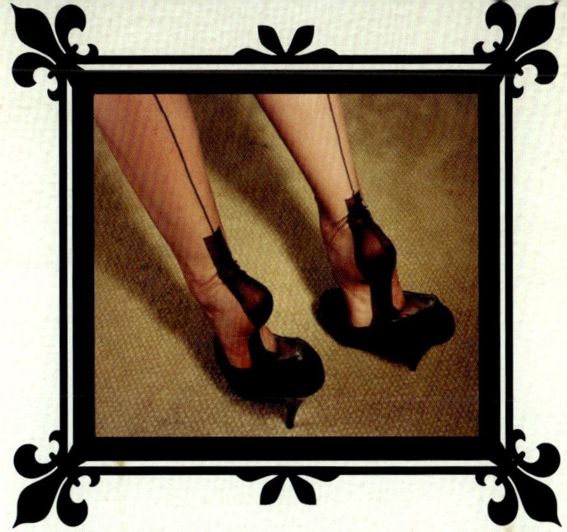

# Seamed Stocking Paradox

You know, I cannot remember the last time I wore a stocking without a seam up the back. What a world it must have been when no lady left her house without pulling on a pair! I think I would feel naked walking out into the world without the tight run of stitching clasping my calves, pulling at my heels, my gams. I believe I would miss the rasp the nylon makes when I cross my legs, the way the garters pull them taught, gently restraining me. What's more, they're something for a lover to grab hold of on certain occasions or to caress under the table at dinner. Oh, they are delicious! A delicate union of modesty and naughtiness stitched into one. What fetish goddess wouldn't want that? I, for one, go through about four pairs a week—and have since I was eighteen. I'm no mathematician, but it seems to me that's a lot of stockings!

I have a friend in Paris named Yves. I have known him for more than a decade, and he has always been the perfect French gentleman. By this I mean he is dedicated to making the world a better place by keeping the women he knows in the finest couture stockings. Indeed, seeing what the world has lost with the advent of pantyhose, he had a hand in resurrecting the mills that make fully fashioned seamed stockings in Europe. I believe that Yves is somewhere in his sixties or seventies—I can never tell age in a man, can you? Anyway, he contacted me through a favorite photographer in Paris during my first trip there and he presented me with the most sumptuous gifts of lingerie. Authentic pale peach 1930s girdles and brassieres (some of them quite racy, with the top part of the breast cut out). He even presented me with the first perfect pair of fully fashioned stockings from the newly running Dior Mills! Anyway, I recall holding these luxurious treats in my arms, and being simply overcome, whispering, "Yves, I should be your girlfriend." Now, naturally, I wasn't being serious, I was flirting. But Yves is a serious man.

"Dita," he said, tenderly, "you are too young, and therefore you are not yet interesting enough for me." Well, I laughed of course. He's candid, this perfect French gentleman.

Since our first meeting, Yves has gone on to become my very own lingerie benefactor. With each visit to Paris, I receive a stunning new prize. But I cannot help wondering, are his gifts simply contributions toward my efforts in fetish goddessness? Is it, perhaps, just generosity? Or maybe, like a classic fetishist, Yves enjoys knowing I will not only appreciate but wear these things beneath my clothes and of course, in photo shoots. That's what the fetishists did in the good ol' days, you know. In the 1940s and 1950s, these boys customized their own fetish photo fantasies.

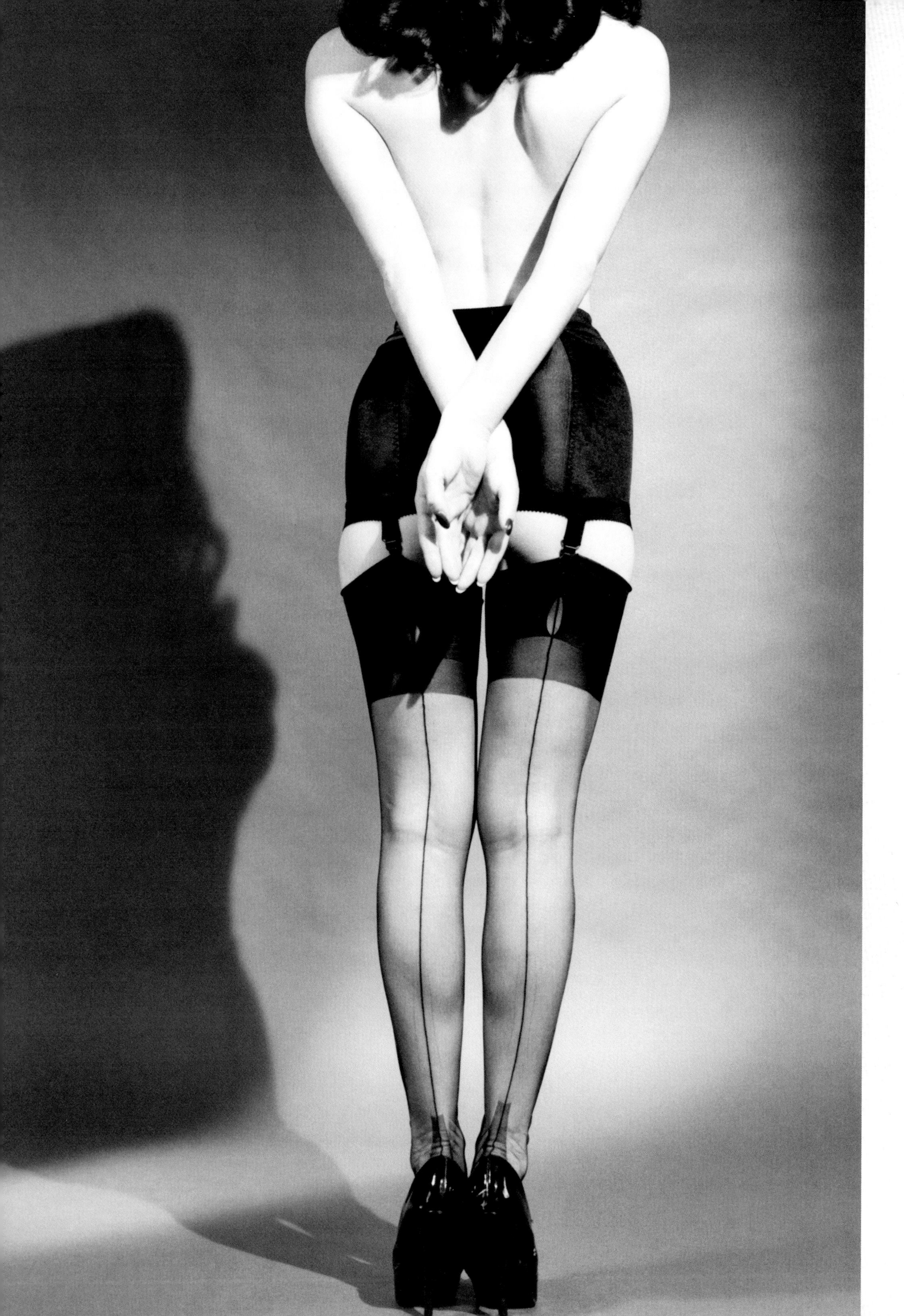

# Anatomy of a Seamed Stocking!

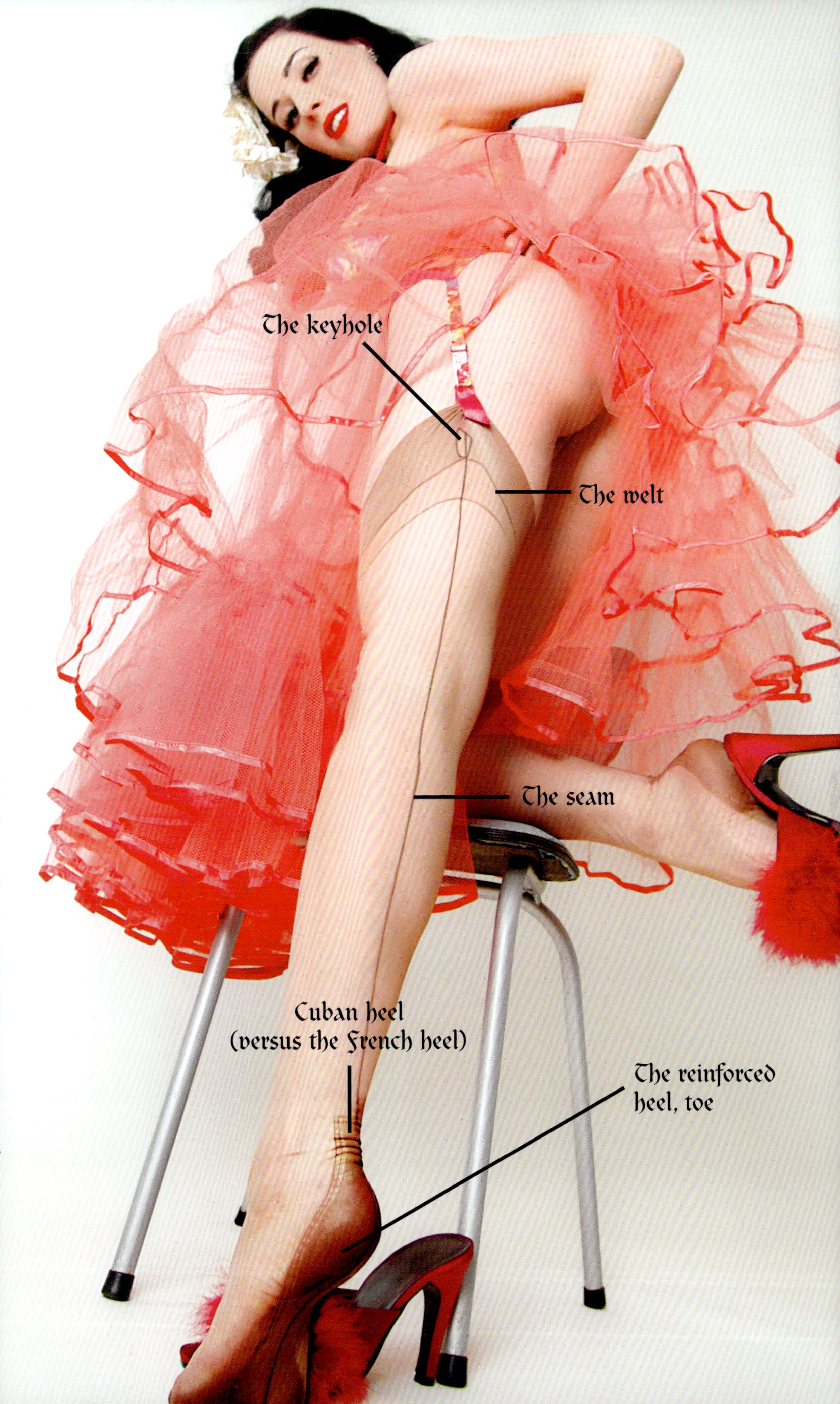

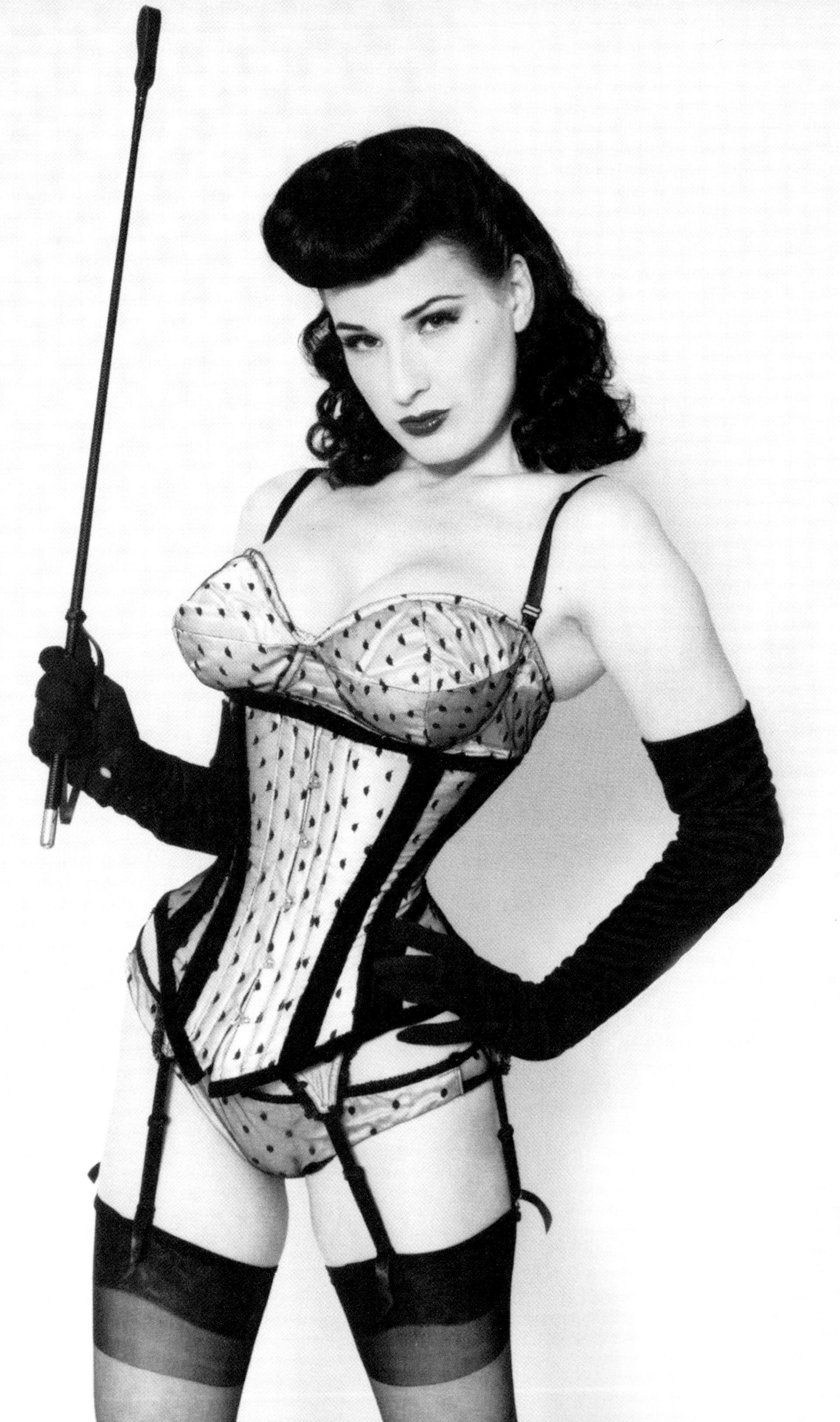

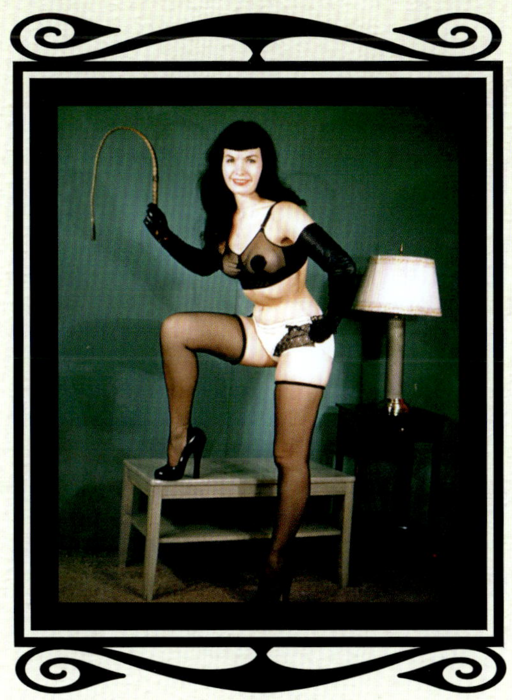

# Bettie Page: Not the Girl Next Door

Bettie Page was Irving and Paula Klaw's greatest fetish model. If you don't know of the Klaws, they were a fabulous brother and sister team running what was, initially anyway, a business selling publicity photos of movie stars out of their 14th Street storefront in New York City. It was the 1950s, and at the outset, business was simple: they bought publicity photos from the Hollywood studios and sold them to customers in their shop or through mail-order catalogs. Everything changed for the better one day when a petite gentleman who liked to be called Little John walked into the store with a single question. The Klaws did some of their own photography—very minimal at that point—and Little John wondered if they would produce a few for him, shot to reflect his personal fantasies.

A brief aside: I have always enjoyed the fetishist who doubles as an ordinary chap during the day, a *normal* man with a sexy secret. Some might see it as a proof of deviousness. I see it as evidence that fetish can be worked into any life. In other words, there are all kinds of fetishists. Fetishists who live in their dungeons and fetishists who go there only on weekends. I've met some truly interesting black and whiters: big company chiefs, doctors, and all sorts of prominent citizens who visit dungeons. Lawyers who wear diapers and like to be babied. The list is endless and always fascinating.

Once, in fact, I was doing a photo shoot in a lovely garden owned by the CEO of one of America's biggest companies (a lady never gives names!). The shoot was arranged by a fashion magazine to take advantage of this beautiful Beverly Hills estate, and once I stepped onto the grounds, I understood why. Rolling hills of jade and winding blue lakes, I felt as if I had happened upon a magical forest. This CEO evidently knew something more about me than I understood when we first shook hands upon my arrival. When I retired to the house for a bit of water, he whispered, "Would you like to see my dungeon?"

Heavens, yes, I wanted to see his dungeon!

The tall, groomed gentleman in the tailored heather suit led me to a secret door and down a dim, winding staircase to a sprawling stone room with every gadget—ropes and chains, pulleys, levers, and wardrobe racks filled with every fantasy one could ask for. I can only imagine the activities and parties for which this room was outfitted. However, as I've said, while I am fascinated by dungeons and what happens in them, I prefer to play in the privacy of my own bedroom with select company.

What I really enjoy is learning people's secrets.

Anyway, back to the Klaws and their unusual customer. So, Paula Klaw alleged that this man Little John was a high-profile federal agent. If you find this astonishing, I ask you, who more than a federal employee needs richness in his fantasy life? Well, Little John offered to pay the models for their time, provide the costumes and ropes and gear, and buy the photos. In exchange, the Klaws would own the negatives and sell them to whomever might buy them. It seemed worth trying. They were adventurous siblings. Little John brought in a series of damsel in distress images he wished to emulate. The subject matter may have seemed slightly suspicious to the Klaws, but John showed them the ropes, if you will, teaching Paula proper tying technique. (Good rope bondage should hold you firmly in place, hurt so good, if you know what I mean, but *never* harm you.)

Well, the pictures were good and more importantly, they were unusually titillating for those times. What's more, Little John was the best kind of customer: he leaked word to other fetishists about the Klaws. Pretty soon, enthusiasts of all sorts were coming in for customized fantasy shots. As Paula remembers it: "A leather enthusiast would bring in leather outfits, and someone who liked chains would bring in a chain outfit. Then the rubber people would bring in something custom-made in Italy. Then there were guys who brought me the shoes with the extremely high heels they had made by an Italian boot maker. We had the spanking fanatics, and those who liked to see girls fighting. We had the garter belt customers, the bare-feet customers—all the fetishists." As you can imagine, it took no time at all for the Klaws to themselves become fetish experts. Pretty soon, business was so good they began shooting their own bondage scenes on the second floor of their 14th Street building, selling the photos downstairs in the store and through mail-order catalogs.

And then, it happened again. With the new business up and running, another man walked into the Klaws' shop, changing their lives forever. And as far as I'm concerned, changing the world. He was an amateur photographer, this one, whose name no one seems to remember. He entered the store and showed the Klaws photos of a beautiful, black-banged young model named Bettie Page. Bettie was popular with the controversial New York camera clubs of the time, and this man was a member. Camera clubs were viewed with suspicion by the public because, unlike published photography—controlled by censorship laws—camera club photos were free to explore all kinds of forbidden terrain. For this reason, the images that survive are rather daring for the 1950s, and rather nude. It all reminds me of Flo Ziegfeld's use of naked women in his "artistic" tableaus. I really believe that if people would just admit that everyone enjoys seeing a naked woman, the world would be a much happier place.

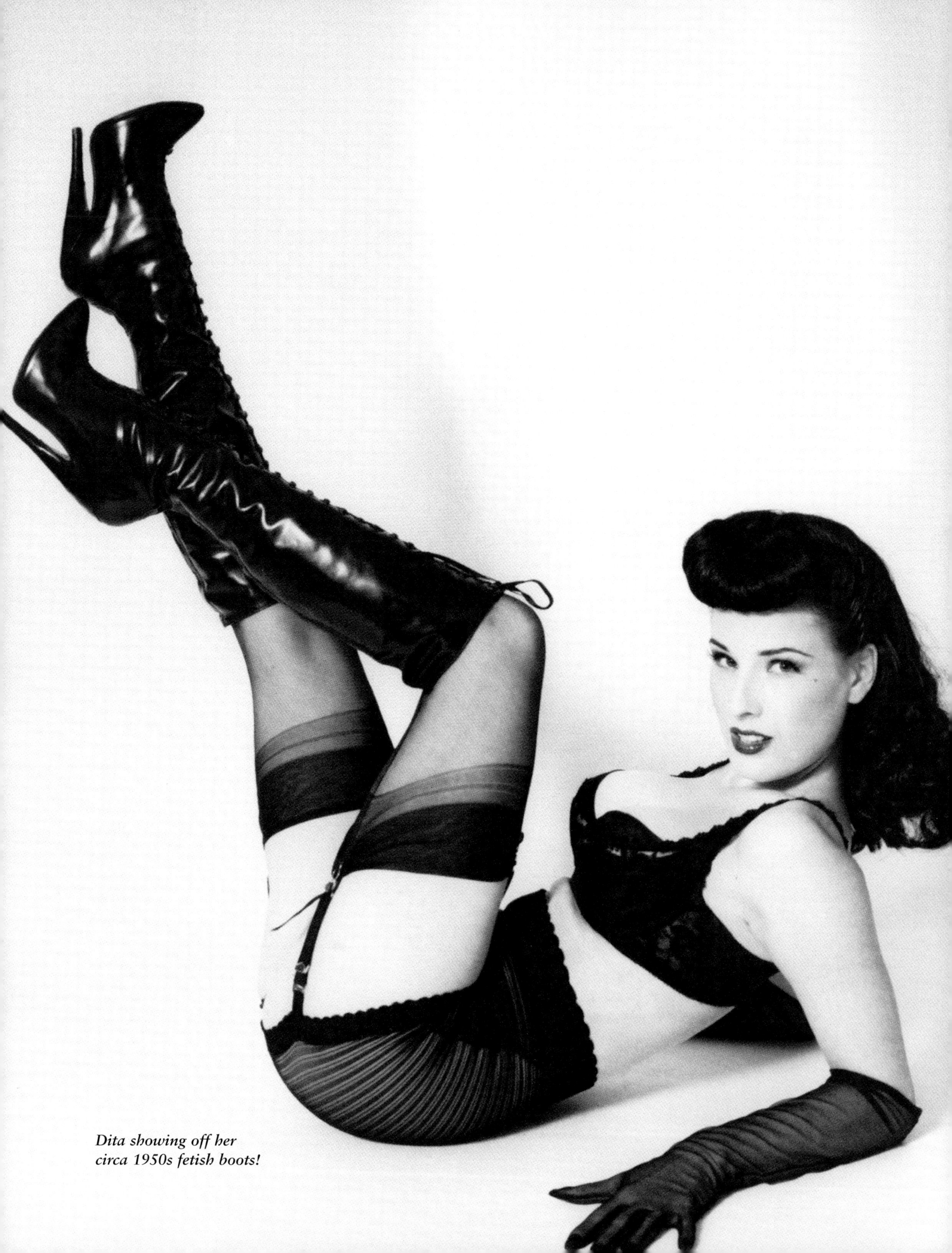

*Dita showing off her circa 1950s fetish boots!*

Anyway, the camera clubs developed sordid reputations as voyeurs who just wanted to be near pretty, *naked* girls. There were even those who claimed that the photographers didn't put film in their cameras. Yet, some of Bettie's best pinups come from this period in her life—by amateur photographer Art Amsie. You know those wholesome pinup shots of Bettie on the beach? Those are Art's.

Of course, she wasn't always wearing a bathing suit. Sometimes she was wearing just stockings and heels, sometimes nothing at all. Yet, Bettie never thought of her nudity as embarrassing or wrong—a pretty perverse perspective for the 1950s! "It just seemed natural to me," she said later. "I was always very happy walking around the house in the nude. When the camera clubs would shoot outdoors in New Jersey, I would go traipsing around in the woods in the buff. I was never self-conscious about it."

People always ask me the same question. Like Bettie, I too am comfortable with nudity. I think, perhaps, it has something to do with the *Playboy* magazines I sneaked from my dad's hidden trove. As far as I was concerned, those were the prettiest girls in the world, and I wanted to grow up and be just like them. I never looked at nudity as pornography. In fact, when I did my very first photo shoot in the buff—save for my new cotton-candy-pink satin and black velvet corset—I was fully at ease. I admit, I was surprised to feel this way—I did worry that I might get nervous and dash out of the studio at the last second. But I was working with someone who made me feel safe—a friend who had earlier photographed my sister. Besides, I've always been comfortable with my body. (And now I work my butt off to keep feeling that way!)

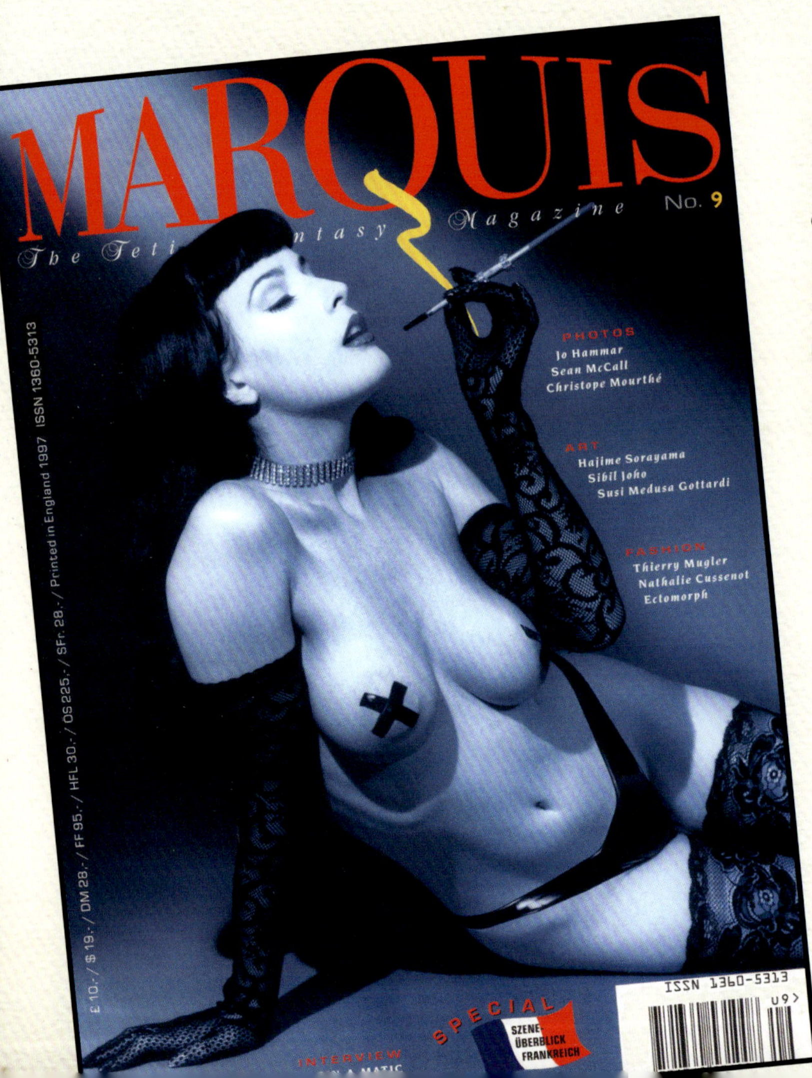


## Best Fetish Magazines

- Marquis
- Skin Two
- Taboo
- Secret

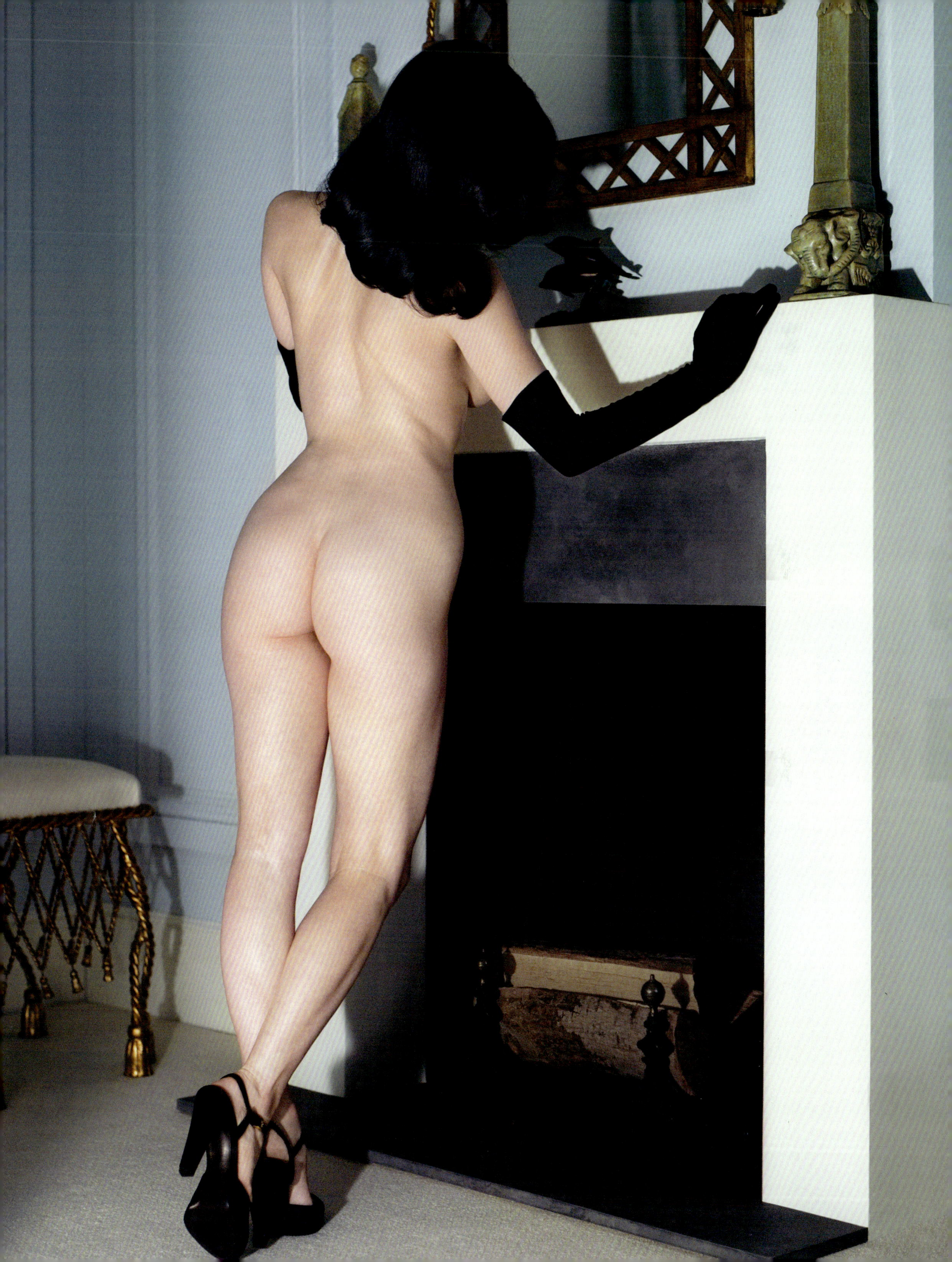

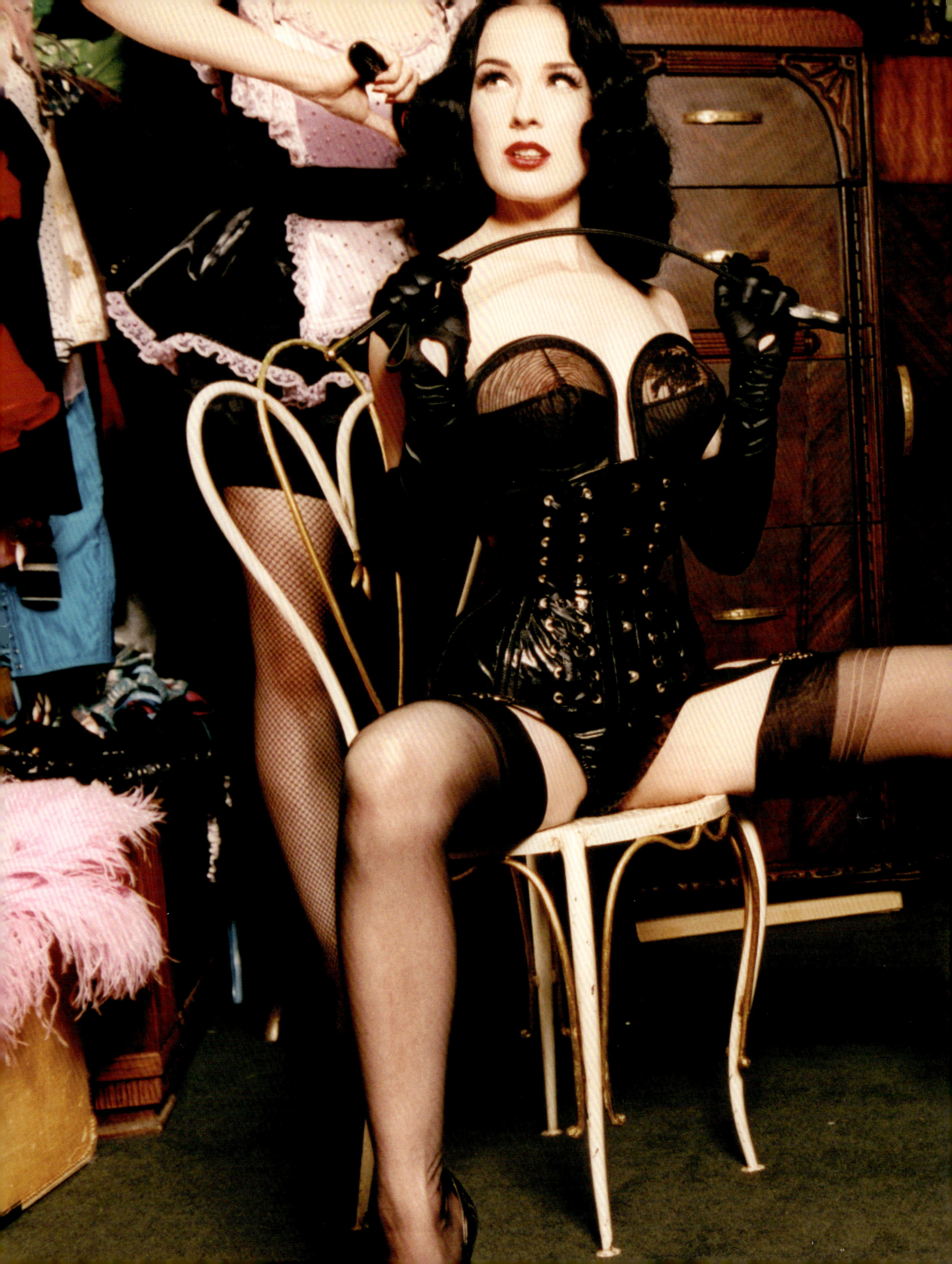

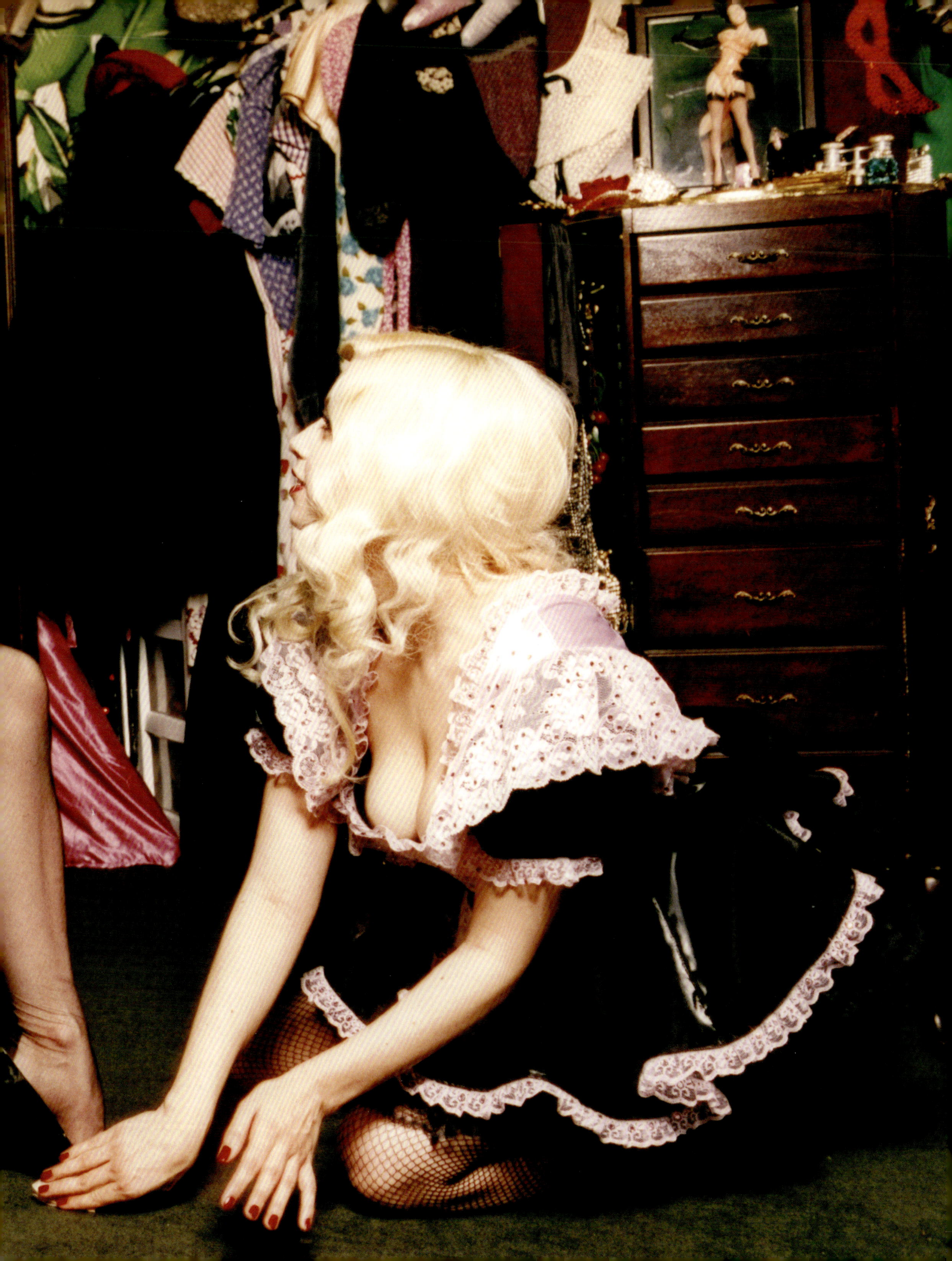

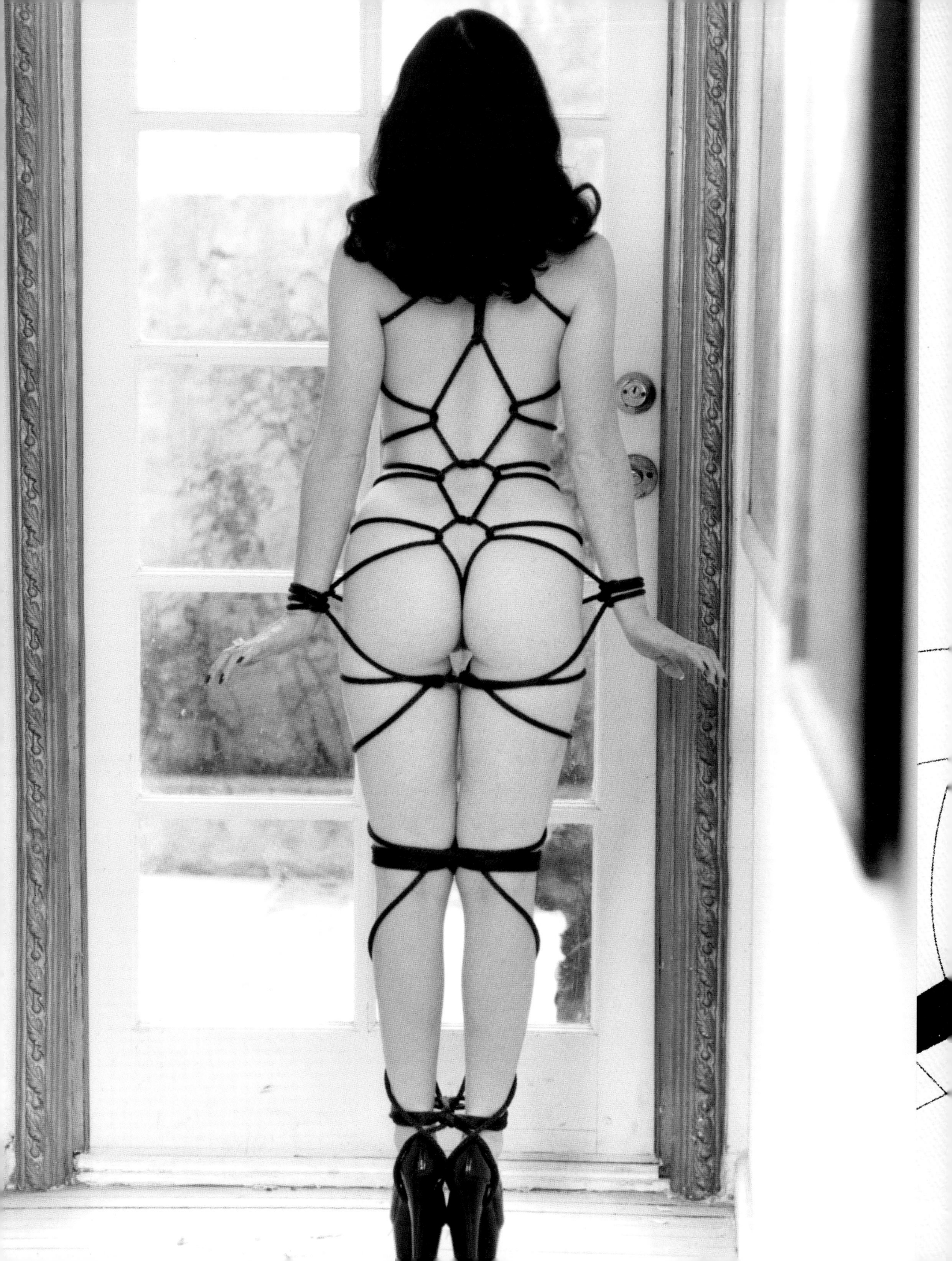

At any rate, it wasn't long before Bettie was the most popular camera club model in New York. Of course, outside such groups, she remained unknown. Then, one club member—whose name again seems to have been lost to history—approached Robert Harrison, the publisher of some of the leading men's magazines of the time, with pinup shots of Bettie. Harrison promptly hired the beautiful brunette for *all* of his publications: *Wink, Titter, Beauty Parade, Eyeful.* These were post-war magazines, and pinups were in. But sometimes, Bettie got to have more fun with the camera, acting out spoof scenarios in comic-strip style spreads (running around town with a man in a gorilla suit is one of my favorites). These assignments were right up Bettie's alley. By the mid-fifties, national men's magazines were full of Bettie shots, but none were explicit. That's not to say they were unavailable—Miss Bettie Page was leading a double life.

I still remember the day in the early 1990s when I saw old bondage glossies of Bettie in the cluttered little fetish shop where I bought my first corset (see *Burlesque,* page 103). I mentioned to the clerk that I wished to see pictures of women wearing corsets, and he happened to have some on hand, showing me a bouquet of different shots. Mind you, most of them didn't catch my eye—but then I saw the vibrant vintage photos of Bettie Page. They were classic and intriguing. She was gorgeous, and more importantly, she looked like she was having a good time. Her expression captured the exhilaration I felt wearing my own corset. The clerk explained that this Bettie Page had a huge following—forty years later. *Are there any fetish models trying to*

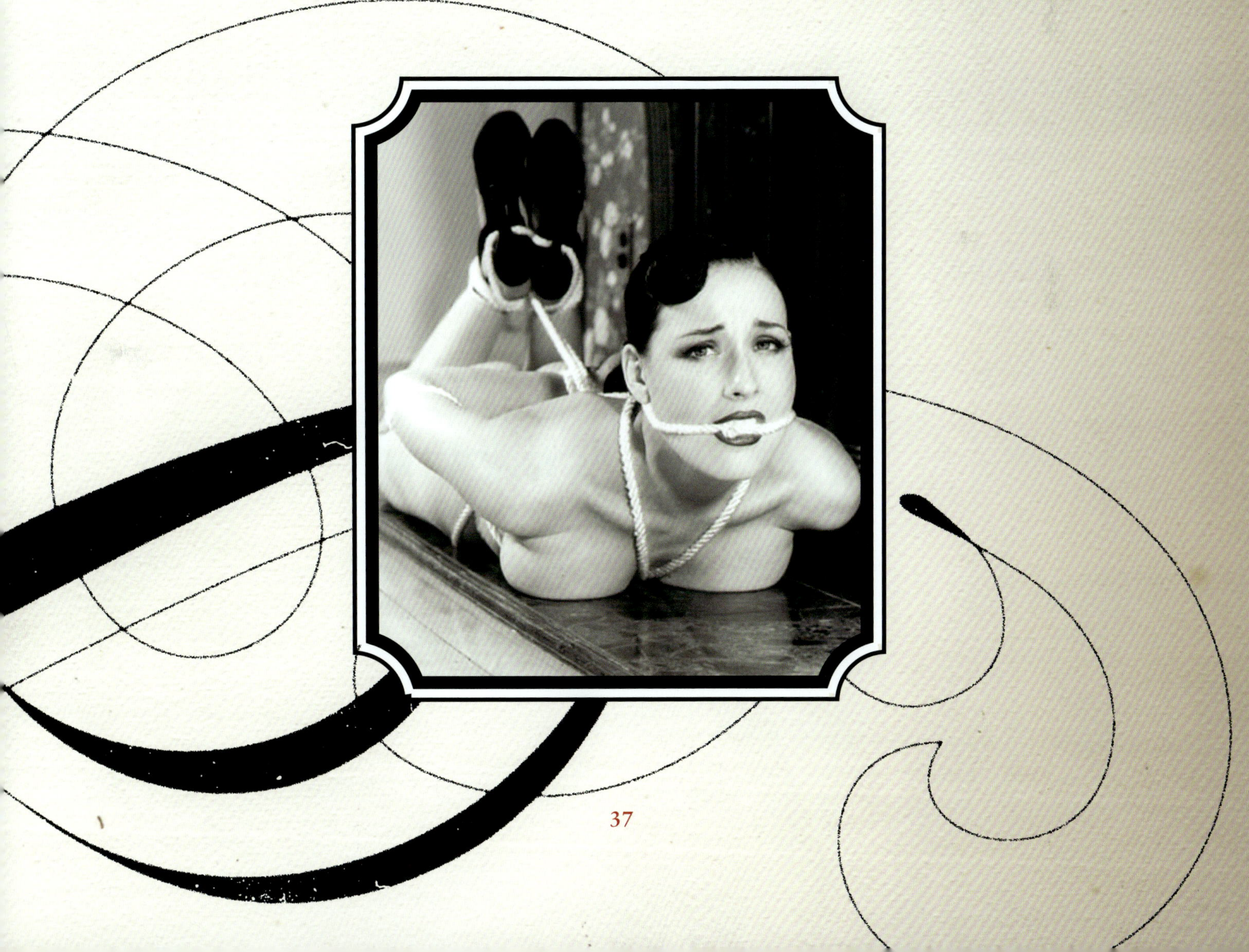

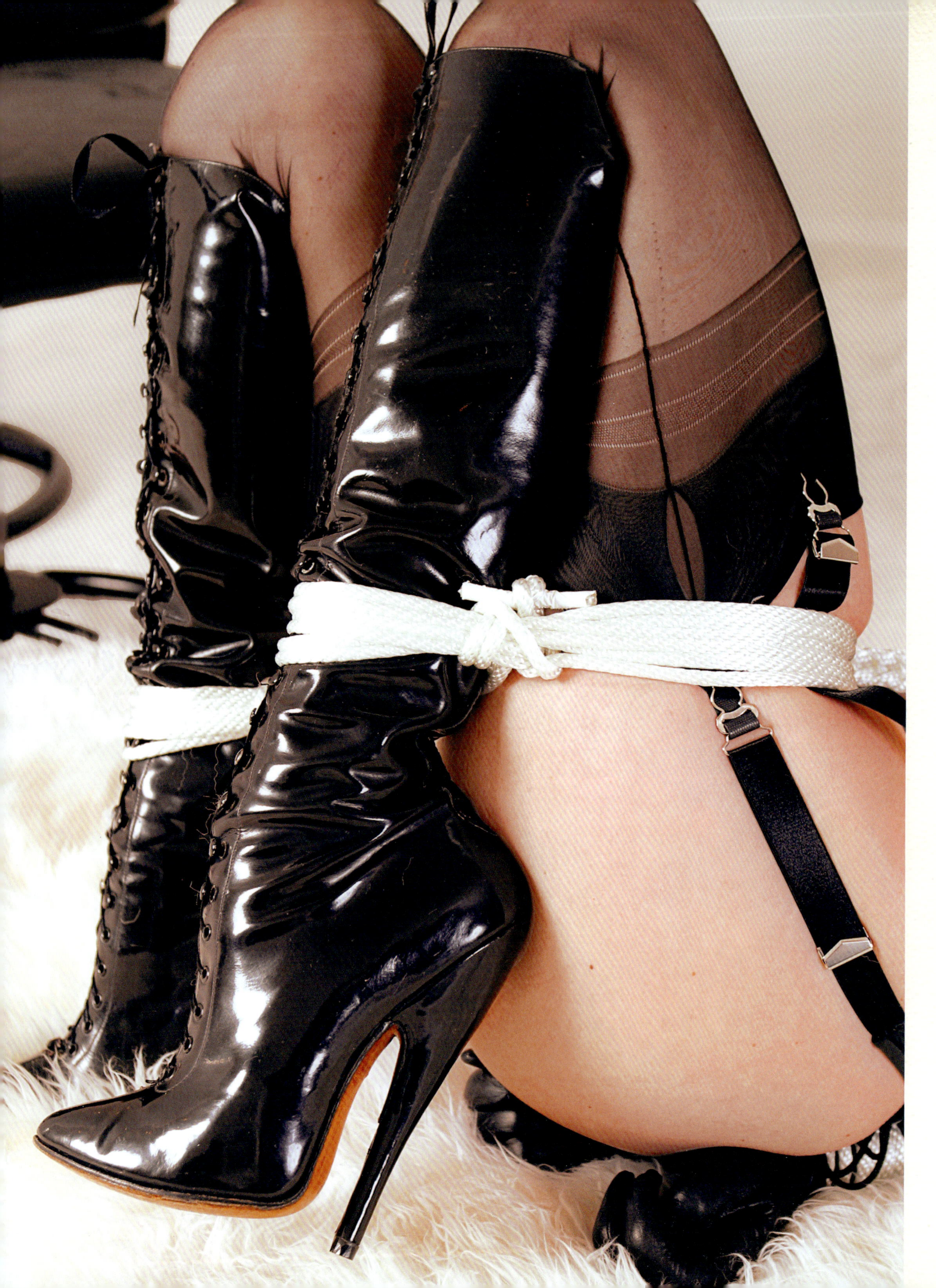

*bring this look now?* I asked. "Not really, not like this," he said, shaking his head sadly, "and, it's a real shame."

Well, I determined that this woman would be my muse, my inspiration. I would emulate her look. I would be a fetish model if that's what Bettie had been. Why not? The ropes (some of the shots were bondage photos) didn't scare me—in fact, they kind of turned me on. And Bettie made it all look like play. Besides, I loved the vintage lingerie she wore: bullet bras and girdles, vintage stockings. Of course, I loved these underpinnings because they were pretty and feminine—I was only now realizing that people wore these things for kinky reasons. But, that intrigued me, too—this other sexy world. That is how at the same moment, I discovered fetish and Bettie Page.

Bettie Page, though she was little known in her heyday outside fetish circles, holds a title for more magazine appearances than Marilyn Monroe and Cindy Crawford combined. The hundreds and hundreds of photos of Bettie—few of which she owns—range from a pure good girl on the beach to a somber if still cherubic fetish goddess in black kid leather gloves and high black heels. Sometimes she is bound and gagged; sometimes she is suspended in midair. But, no matter how serious the scenario, Bettie appears to be at play. "I would often think of the camera as a man," she said.

*She was smart and pretty, that Bettie Page!*

Though bondage photography has been around since nearly as long as the camera itself, Bettie helped glamorize it, her sweet smile and all-American looks breaking down some of the taboo. She was the quintessential pinup, inviting the viewer into her scenarios, smiling brightly enough to make it all okay. Remember that the '50s were a time of rather prudish morals in America. Sex was itself considered perverse. And fetishism? Well, it was a deviance of a very dark kind. But with Bettie as a mascot, I like to think that fetishists started to feel a little more welcome in the world.

At least they were welcome at the Klaw's 14th Street studio, where Bettie was very quickly becoming a star. Paula remembers that, "Once she started working for us, we could tell right away by the sales that our customers liked her, so we used her at every shoot. Besides, she was great to work with." Everyone loved Bettie. She gave her best to each photographer no matter if he was a college student or *Vogue's* favorite contributor (of course, Bettie never did make it into the fashion magazines. In those days, overt sexuality and sensuality were distinctly *not* in vogue).

In October 1953, Bettie was hired to appear in a burlesque film called *Striporama*, produced by burlesque theater owner Martin Lewis. The film, which starred another one of my personal heroes, Lili St. Cyr, was such a hit that the Klaws decided to get in on the action. A year later, Irving Klaw produced *Varietease*, also starring St. Cyr, using Bettie as a dancer. In fact, it was this particular Klaw film with Bettie performing that introduced me to burlesque (see *Burlesque*, page 104). It's funny—Bettie was never actually a burlesque dancer, but her connection to this film brought me to burlesque's glittering theater forty years later!

Of course, not everyone saw bondage imagery as such a positive thing.

In 1955, a United States senator and presidential hopeful named Estes Kefauver initiated a crackdown on pornography which, he argued, influenced juvenile delinquency. His Senate subcommittee maintained that Irving Klaw was "one of the largest distributors of obscene, lewd,

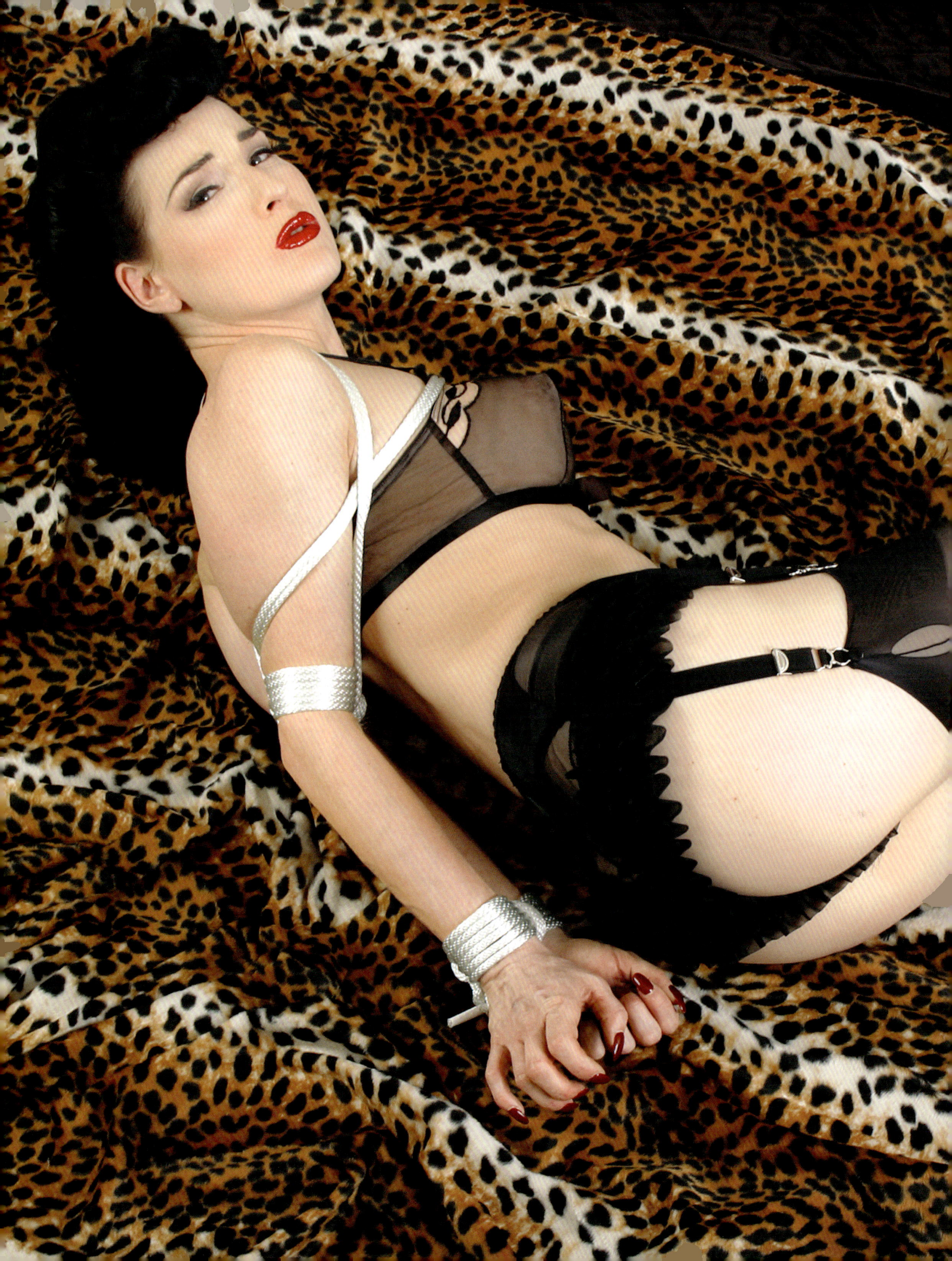

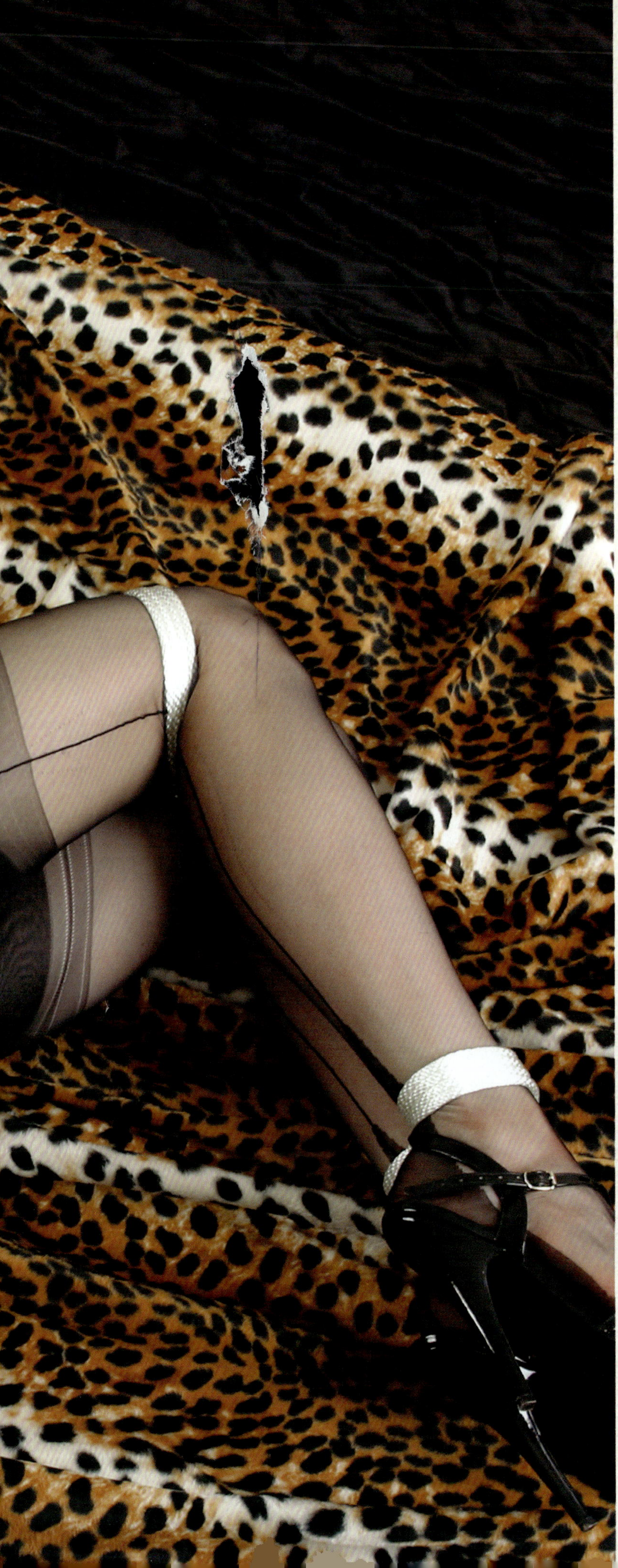

and fetish photographs throughout the country by mail." Unfortunately, Irving and Paula had continued selling publicity shots, even after setting to work on fetish photos and movies—and 65 percent of his buyers were juvenile girls. To Kefauver, this was proof that the Klaws were out to corrupt the minds of children. In a hearing, the senator called on Dr. George W. Henry, a psychiatrist from Cornell University Medical College, to analyze the data. Henry diagnosed the purpose of the one Klaw publication, *Cartoon and Model Parade* as meant to "stimulate people erotically in an abnormal way." I do not know what this means.

Then one day, two representatives from the Senate subcommittee showed up at Bettie's door, requesting testimony that the Klaws sold porn. "I told them very frankly that Irving Klaw never did any pornography at all, not even nudes, and that I would say that if they put me on the stand," Bettie recalled later. When they finally did haul her in, it was only to sit her down alone in a room for sixteen hours. Still, Irving Klaw was shaken up—by 1957 he halted production of pinup and bondage photography. Then, in 1963, after being charged with "conspiracy to send obscene materials through the mail," Klaw cut a deal to be released on $10,000 bail, providing that he shred the offending negatives. Though he tried, his sister Paula saved many of those depicting Bettie Page.

In a strange twist, one men's magazine embracing female nudity and sexuality was simultaneously *thriving*. It was *Playboy*, of course. Naturally, the young editor, Hugh Hefner, called on men's magazine cutie Bettie Page to pose for his new rag. Who could refuse Hef? For the 1955 holiday issue, Bettie holds a Christmas ornament and wears nothing but a Santa Claus cap.

# PLAYBOY

ENTERTAINMENT FOR · www.playboy.com • DECEMBER 2002

*Gala* CHRISTMAS *Issue*

BLOODY NEW FICTION FROM SCOTT TUROW

SEX STARS 2002

PLUS: 20Q WITH GREG KINNEAR TOM ARNOLD HOLLYWOOD'S UNSOLVED MURDERS DMX STYLE SATURDAY NIGHT LIVE PLAYBOY MUSIC POLL PINK AND MORE

DITA VON TEESE THE RETURN OF FETISH

DENZEL WASHINGTON PLAYBOY INTERVIEW

WOMEN OF WORLDCOM NUDE

COLLEGE BASKETBALL PREVIEW

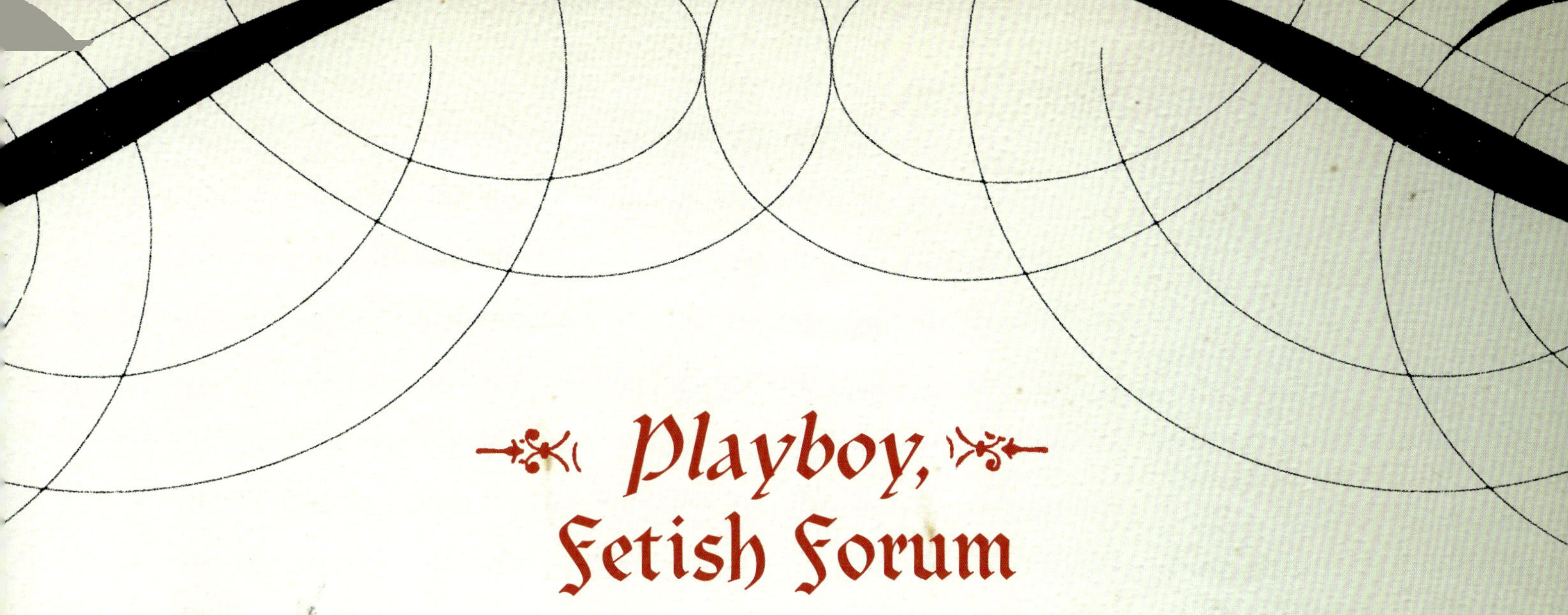

# Playboy, Fetish Forum

I wonder what it was like for Bettie, modeling for this rebellious new magazine just hitting its stride. For me, forty years later, modeling for *Playboy* was the pinnacle, the event that launched all other events, opening doors all over the world to me. But, my goodness, I got turned down so many times!

My first appearance was in *The Book of Lingerie* in 1996. *Lingerie* is one of their special editions. Nonetheless, I went on three or four casting calls, and each time, they said, "No, no, no, you just aren't what *Playboy* stands for. You're not the girl next door."

Not the girl next door? Good!

As luck would have it, the editors shopped for costumes at a store in Hollywood called Trashy Lingerie—a place I also happened to frequent. The gentleman who owns the landmark store was at hand one night after another of my unsuccessful casting calls. One day, the editors happened into the store, undoubtedly seeking lingerie for their models. Well, my good friend at the counter called them over and said something along the lines of: "You know, if you don't use Dita, you're making a big mistake. You should really capitalize on her image. That girl is different and that's good. She has a lot of fans out there." (Aren't my fans the best?)

A day or two later, the editors called for a final, successful casting meeting. Of course, they asked their makeup artist to make me look more "normal" (I promptly un-normalized myself!). It was for this particular issue, actually, that I flipped through the phone book and found my name: Von Treese. (*Playboy* insisted that I use a last name.) The magazine printed it up as Von Teese, and here I am! (Smart typo, don't you think?)

After that issue of *Lingerie*, I received a lot of fan letters, and the editors began featuring me in issue after issue. It was great, but now I wanted to test for a layout of my own in *Playboy* magazine. *No, no,* they said. Playboy *won't feature you once you've been seen naked in* Lingerie. *They want fresh, unseen talent, girls no one has ever seen nude.* So I received a few rejection letters, and I never ever in a million years thought that I would one day be on the cover.

Then one day in February 2002, I was performing a burlesque show and my fans—it seems I had quite a fan base inside *Playboy*'s offices—once again went to bat for me, making sure Mr. Hefner knew about the event. I couldn't believe my eyes when I saw him seated at the best table in the house in front of the stage of the El Rey Theater in the Miracle Mile area of Los Angeles. I performed my ballerina and martini glass shows, and afterward, he walked right up to me and introduced himself! Now, there's a charming man.

Well, it wasn't more than three days later that I was in bed with a touch of a hangover. It wasn't much of a morning until *Playboy* magazine called, and I quite literally began jumping up and down on the bed. This time, the editors agreed to allow me to style the entire pictoral the way I wanted—makeup, clothes, props. I got to dream up the whole thing myself. I even chose the photographers. I wanted the photos to represent who I really am and what my shows really look like. To that end, the wardrobe and props were all my own. The best part: Hef himself edited the layout and oversaw the entire pictorial. It was an amazing time.

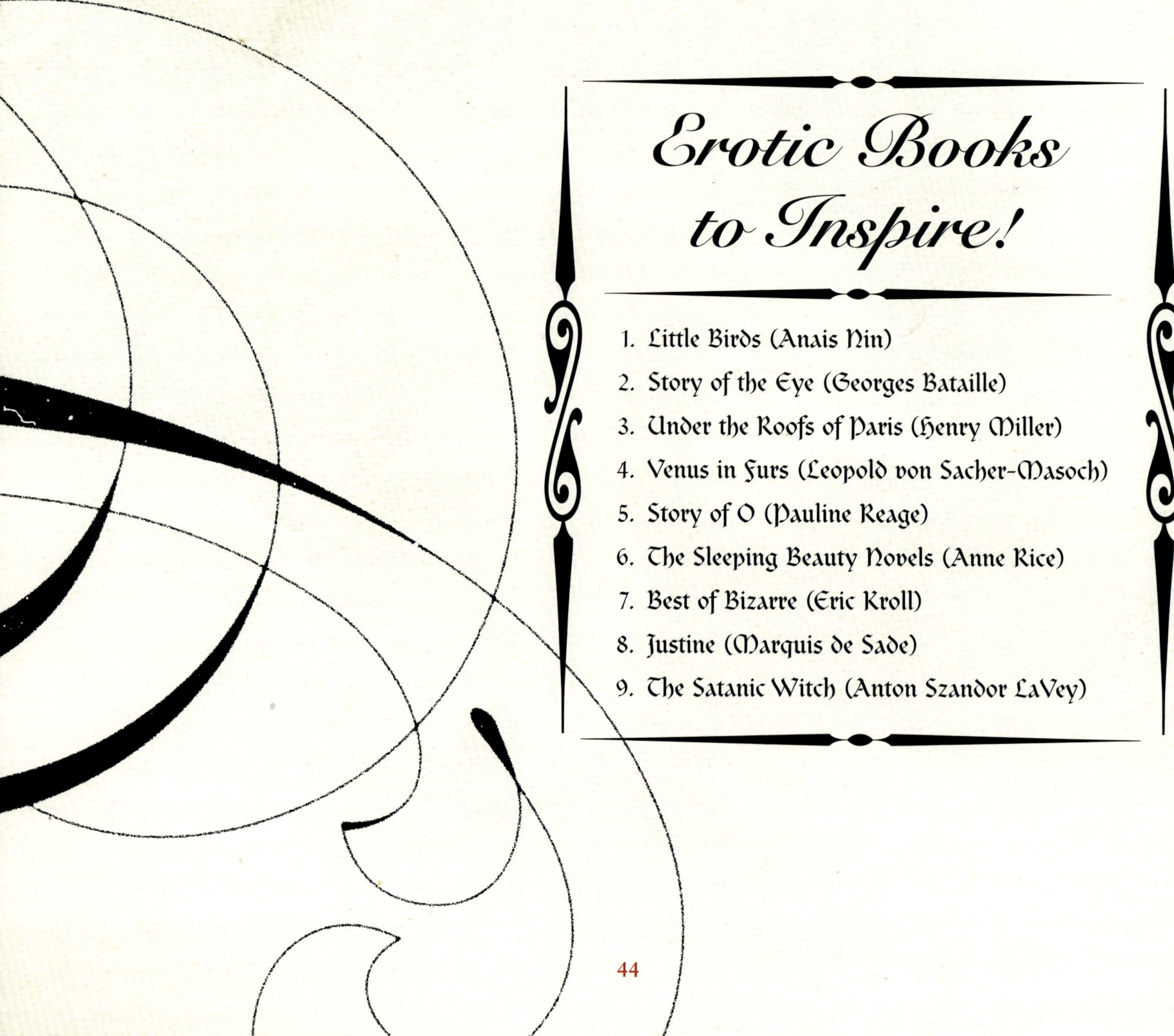

## Erotic Books to Inspire!

1. Little Birds (Anais Nin)
2. Story of the Eye (Georges Bataille)
3. Under the Roofs of Paris (Henry Miller)
4. Venus in Furs (Leopold von Sacher-Masoch)
5. Story of O (Pauline Reage)
6. The Sleeping Beauty Novels (Anne Rice)
7. Best of Bizarre (Eric Kroll)
8. Justine (Marquis de Sade)
9. The Satanic Witch (Anton Szandor LaVey)

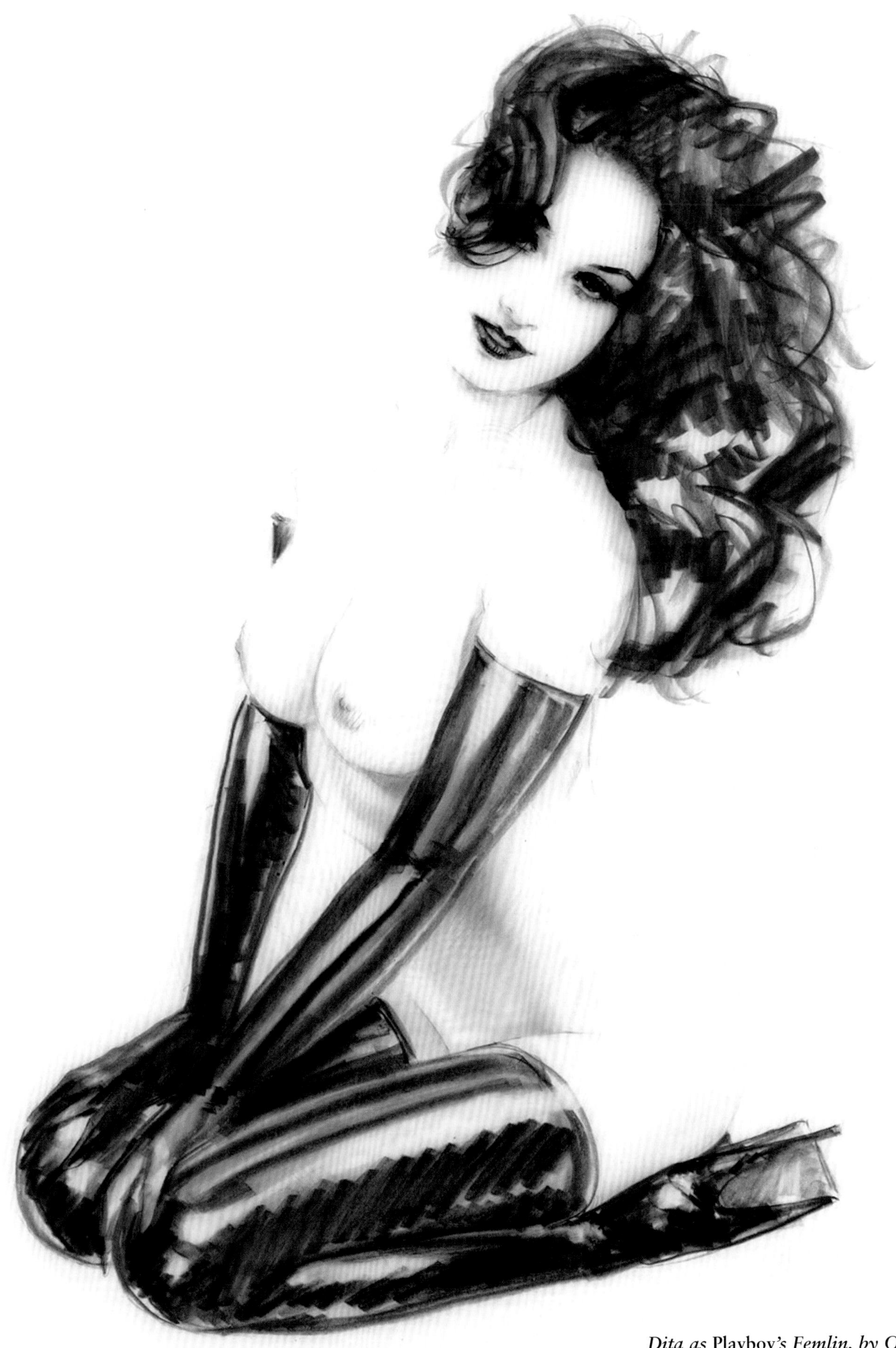

*Dita as* Playboy's *Femlin, by Olivia*

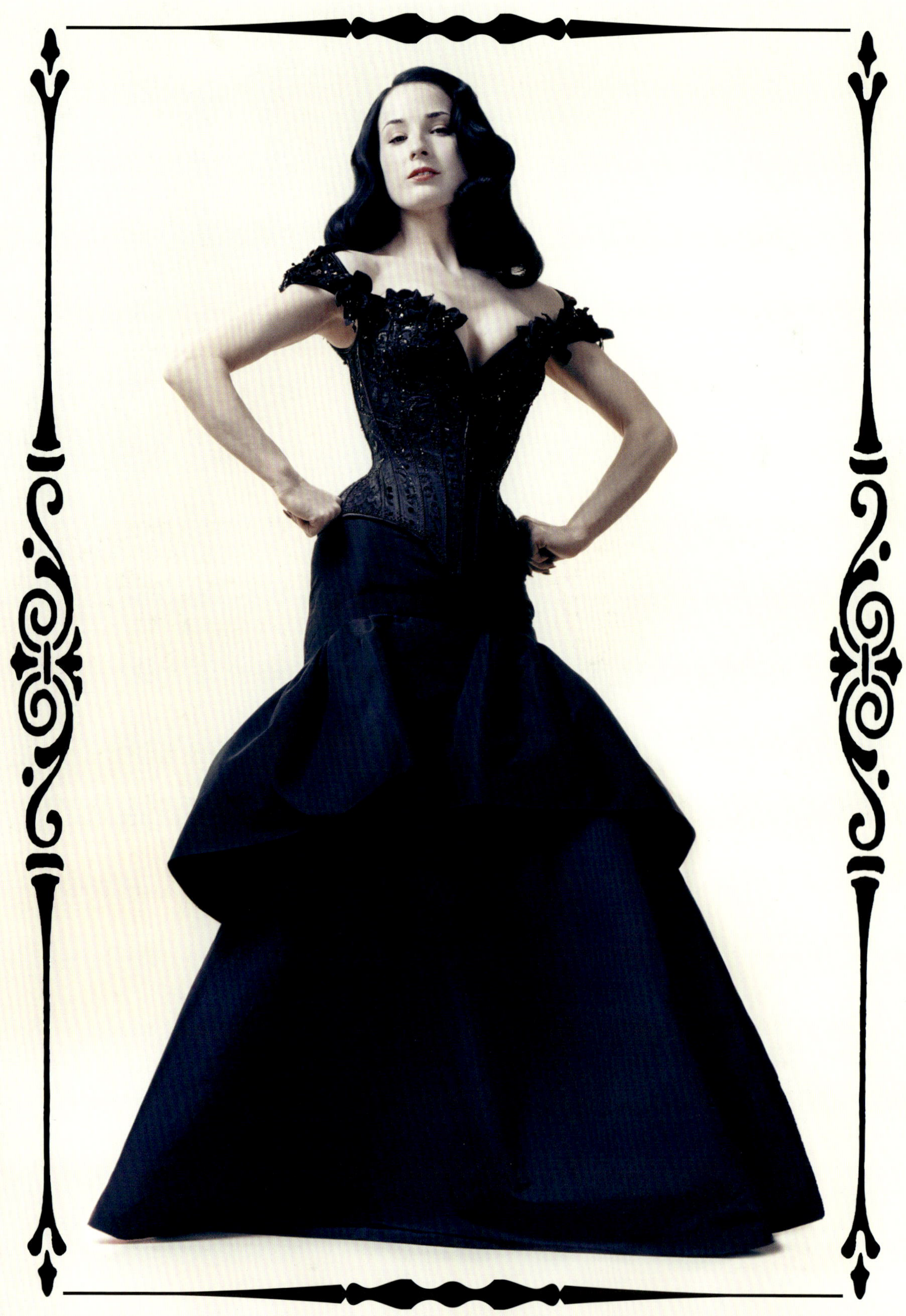

*Corset by Mr. Pearl*

# Swishing Petticoats, Foaming Frills

I would wager that even people who do not consider themselves fetishists can understand (and experience) the thrill of a beautiful body dressed in lingerie. The experience is of seeing someone at once dressed and undressed, accessible and untouchable. Besides this, lingerie is constructed of materials that are themselves fetishes—smooth silks, satins, laces.

Have you ever stopped to consider the function of your underwear? Do you wear it for comfort, for support, for hygiene, to give your body an added lift of sexiness? Would you believe there was a time *before* underwear, when it was not considered healthy or ladylike to wear panties? When women and men were naked beneath their clothes?

The earliest bras, however, can be traced back at least as far as ancient Greece where Minoan vases depict female athletes fastening their breasts before sporting events. Later, in ancient Rome, women evidently experimented with another early prototype of the bra, called the *strophium,* also depicted in murals and other artwork. Historians argue that these renderings confirm that early lingerie was used in a purely functional way. While this is possible, I read the evidence as proof to the contrary. Let's be honest. This art was not made for the sole purpose of serving as records of daily habits for future generations. No, no: vases and murals were *artwork*, one might even say *entertainment*—set out in the home to be admired and enjoyed. At the very least, the female body was considered beautiful. Though we may never know what the images of women strapping up their breasts inspired in the brains of ancient men, I think we can assume that some degree of voyeurism was present in Ancient Greece. This was, after all, the era of great theater!

For a long time after, there seemed to be something of an underpinning of the Dark Ages. Then, during the nonbathing Middle Ages, underclothes were developed to protect expensive fabrics from dirty bodies. (Little did they know these very same garments would attract them, so to speak!) Of course, such garments were not exactly the lacy G-strings and push-up brassieres we own today. These garments were billowing, foamy clouds of fabric piled high underneath heavy outer materials. Still, say historians, underwear was merely functional. I will wager once again that *someone* out there found his heart beating a little more quickly at the sight or sound of a swishing petticoat.

By the eighteenth century, underwear was becoming increasingly eroticized, reaching a sort of frenzied pinnacle in the minds of the public between 1890 and 1910. In fact, in England, for example, fashion writers admonished women to wear erotic underwear to sustain "mystery and coquetry" in their marriages. In France, writers further fetishized the garments, with Comtesse de Tramar calling lingerie "the veiled, secret part, the desired indiscretion conjured up" in 1903.

The lingerie fetish had arrived.

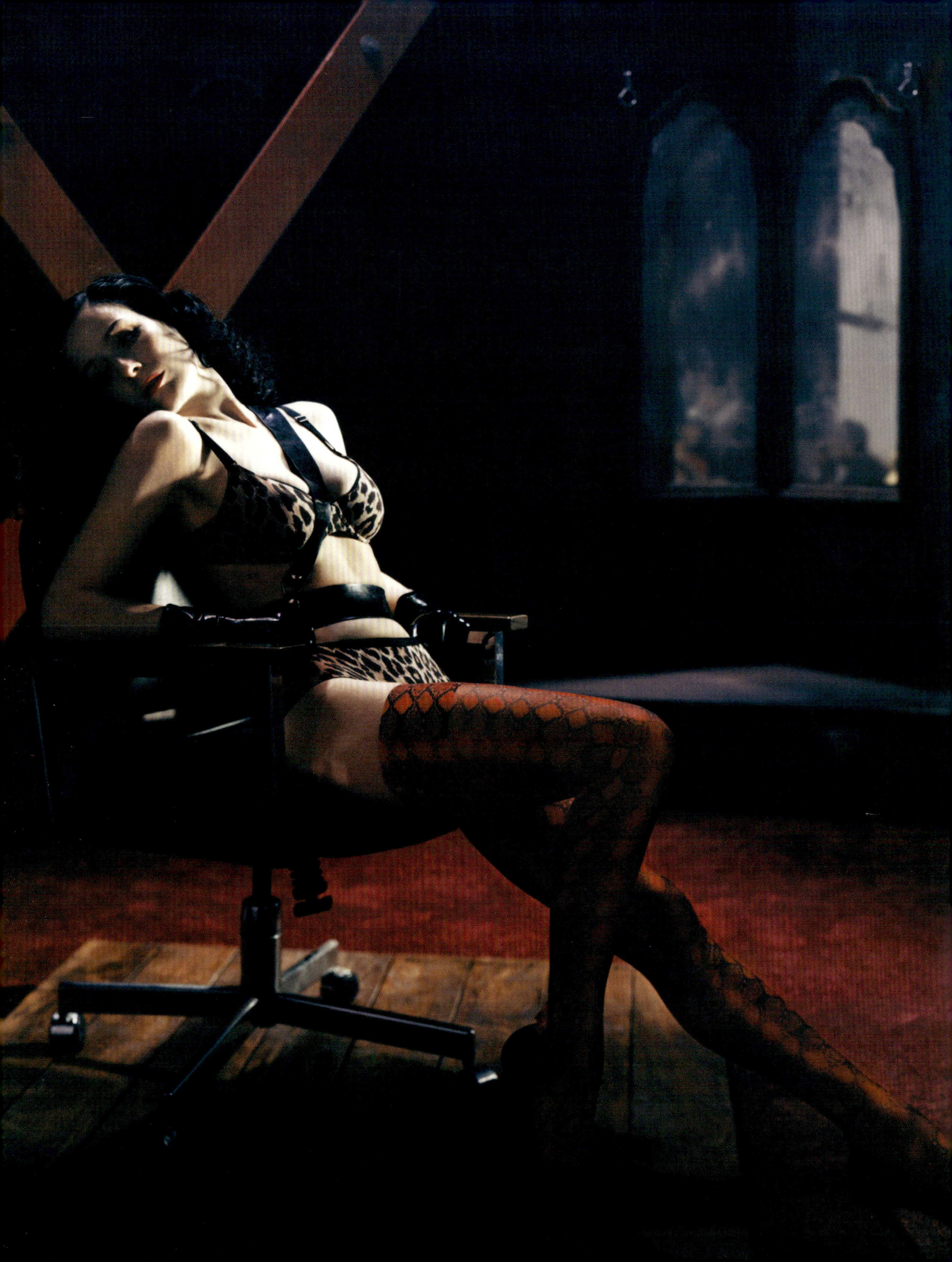

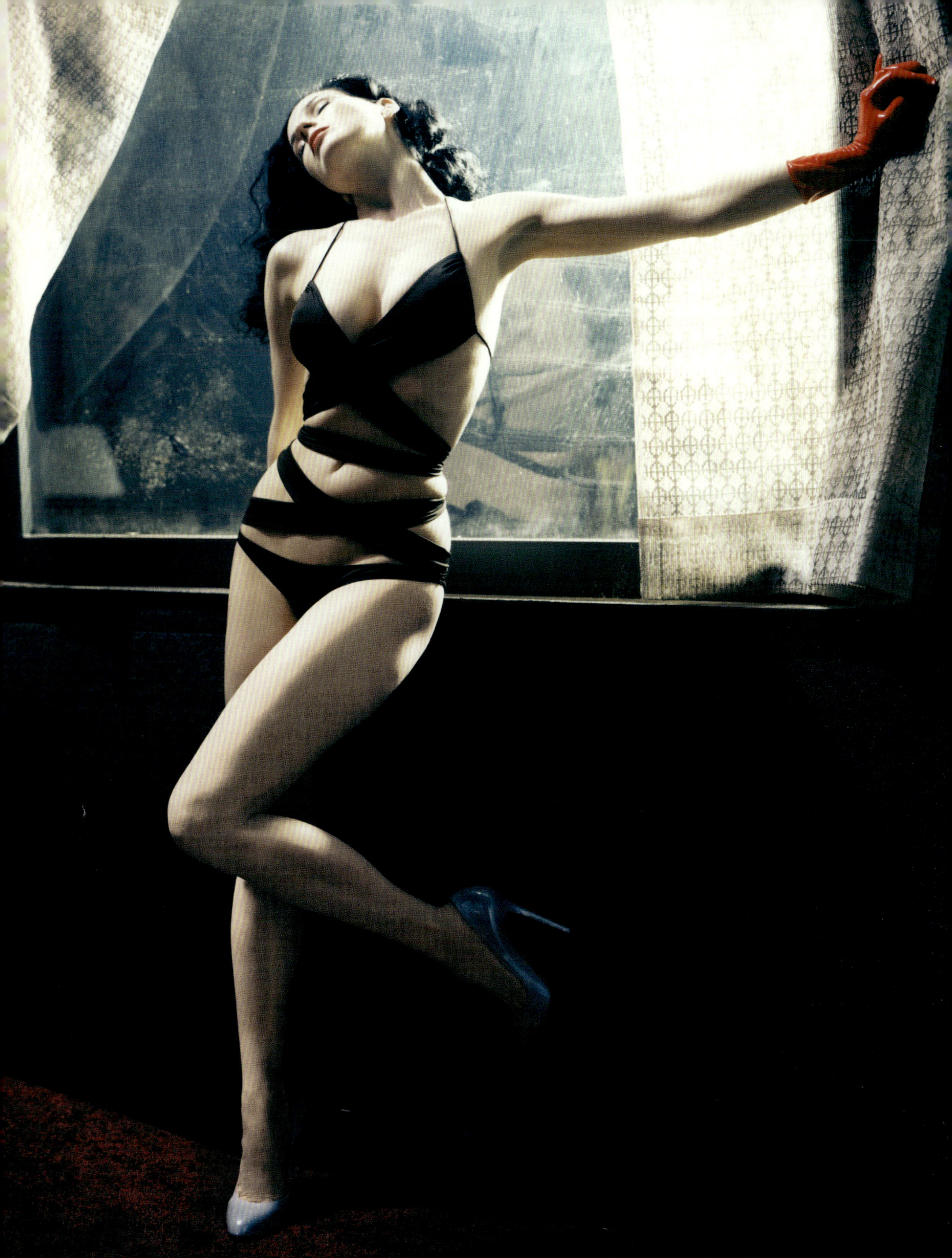

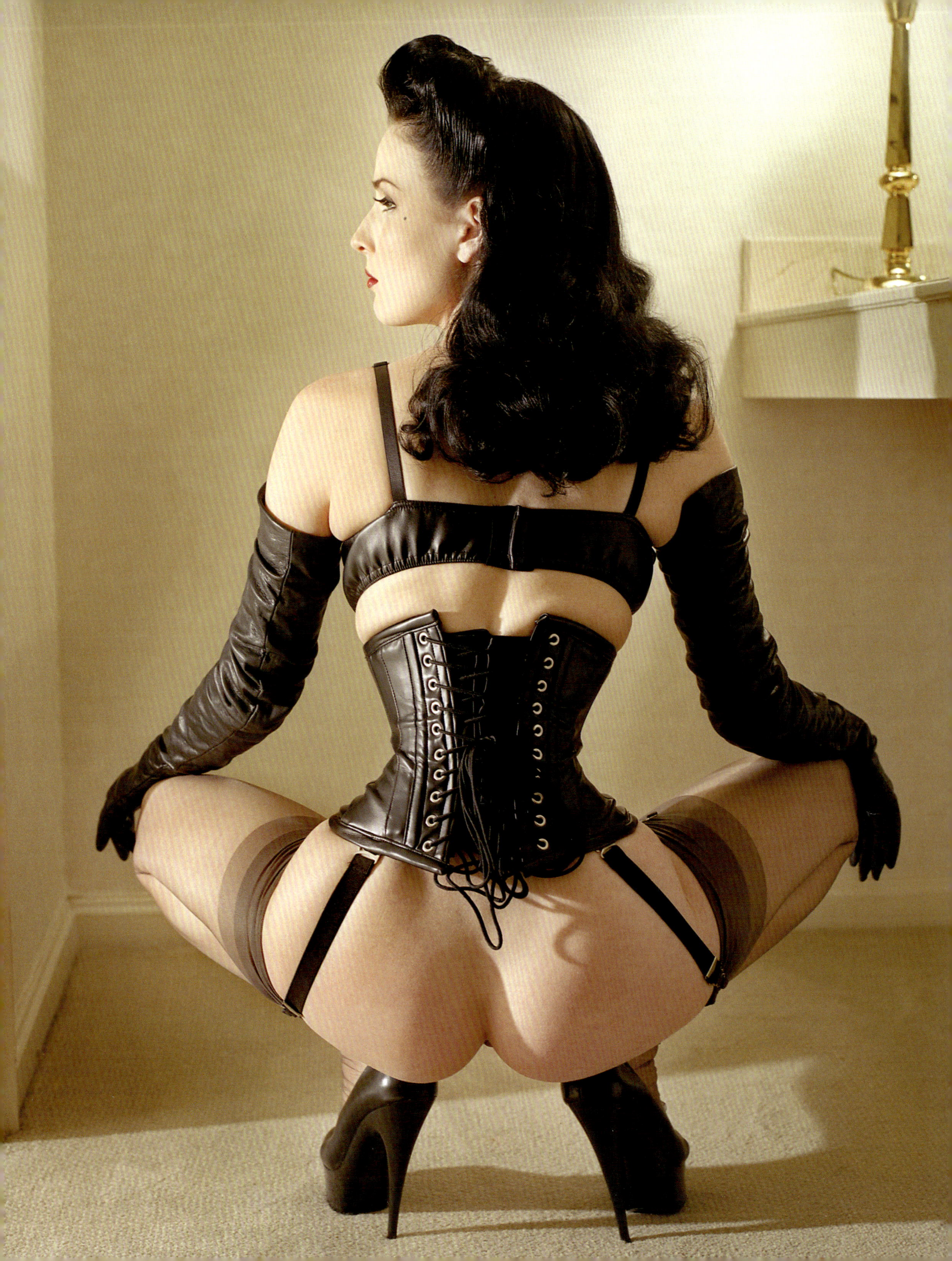

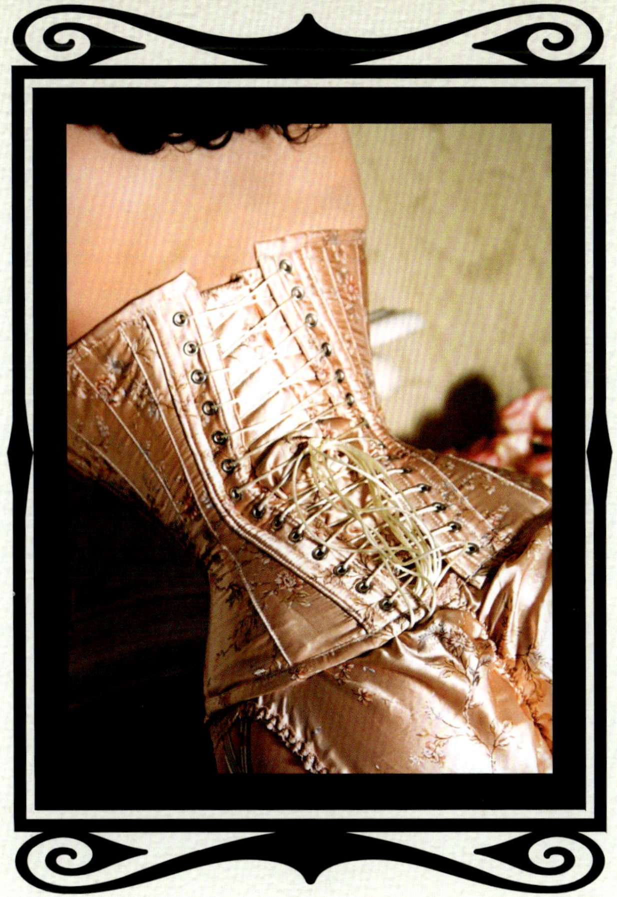

# A Corset in History

Now, while any piece of lingerie can be fetishized, by far the most potent in my experience is the one thing many of us have ceased to consider underwear: the corset. For me, the corset has always been the ultimate piece of lingerie. For one thing, it is a classic—and not in the sense of silk stockings and garters. No, no. I mean classical, ancient Greece. A Cretan statue of a snake goddess dating from about 2000 BC, dons something that cinches her waist and pushes up her breasts. Historians dispute this garment's likeness to a corset, but having worn them for the last fifteen years, I can tell you that it looks a good deal like something I might lace up myself.

For me, there's something subtly erotic about wearing a piece that has been with humanity so long, that women have historically endured for beauty. When I was little, I watched a lot of westerns and a lot of movies set in the Victorian era, in which beautiful girls wore tightly laced corsets. I loved these movies, and I think it is to them that I owe my abiding interest in the corset. Yet, according to fashion historian Valerie Steele, who performed extensive research on women in the Victorian era, these depictions of tightlacing are inaccurate. Steele reported that: "though most Victorian women wore corsets, they were not usually Tightlacers with 16-inch waists any more than most women today wear fetish shoes with 7-inch heels." In fact, though our movies and legends suggest otherwise, average Victorian women's waists were *not* waspy. The majority of women seemed to have waists measuring between 18 and 36 inches.

This makes me wonder if those films I loved as a little girl were really just fetish flicks. Where did this legend come from that everyone tightlaced? Why would modern humanity—with its penchant for accuracy and research—believe that *all* women living in the Victorian era tightlaced? Because the idea is sexy. Because people see history as they *desire* to see it.

Oh, there are so many interesting myths about corsets. Another prevailing tall tale—and one I've seen presented as fact in many books—is that the first widely worn corset was "a tortuous device of steel" made mandatory by a European queen named Catherine de Medici. The 1868 book, *The Corset and the Crinoline,* seems to have influenced a great many researchers, none of whom realized they were reading the work of a fetishist's imagination. I read the following in a book just the other day: "Catherine de Medici, often considered to be on the cutting edge of fashion, actually dictated a rigid construction of the female shape with an ideal waist measurement of thirteen inches!" The author goes on to describe iron cages worn by women of the era. This statement is a fantasy (and a delicious one!). Though iron corsets did exist, records indicate they were used to correct back problems. Again, as far as I'm concerned, this myth is a sort of universal fetish fantasy. You can see how it makes wonderful erotica: the torturous queen with her servile subjects, bound to please. My goodness, it reads like a classic erotic fairy tale. (I recommend Anne Rice's *Sleeping Beauty* books for an uncanny comparison!)

## The Best Places to Buy Corsets

- Mr. Pearl (Paris)
- Dark Garden Corsetry (San Francisco)
- Versatile Fashions (Anaheim, California)

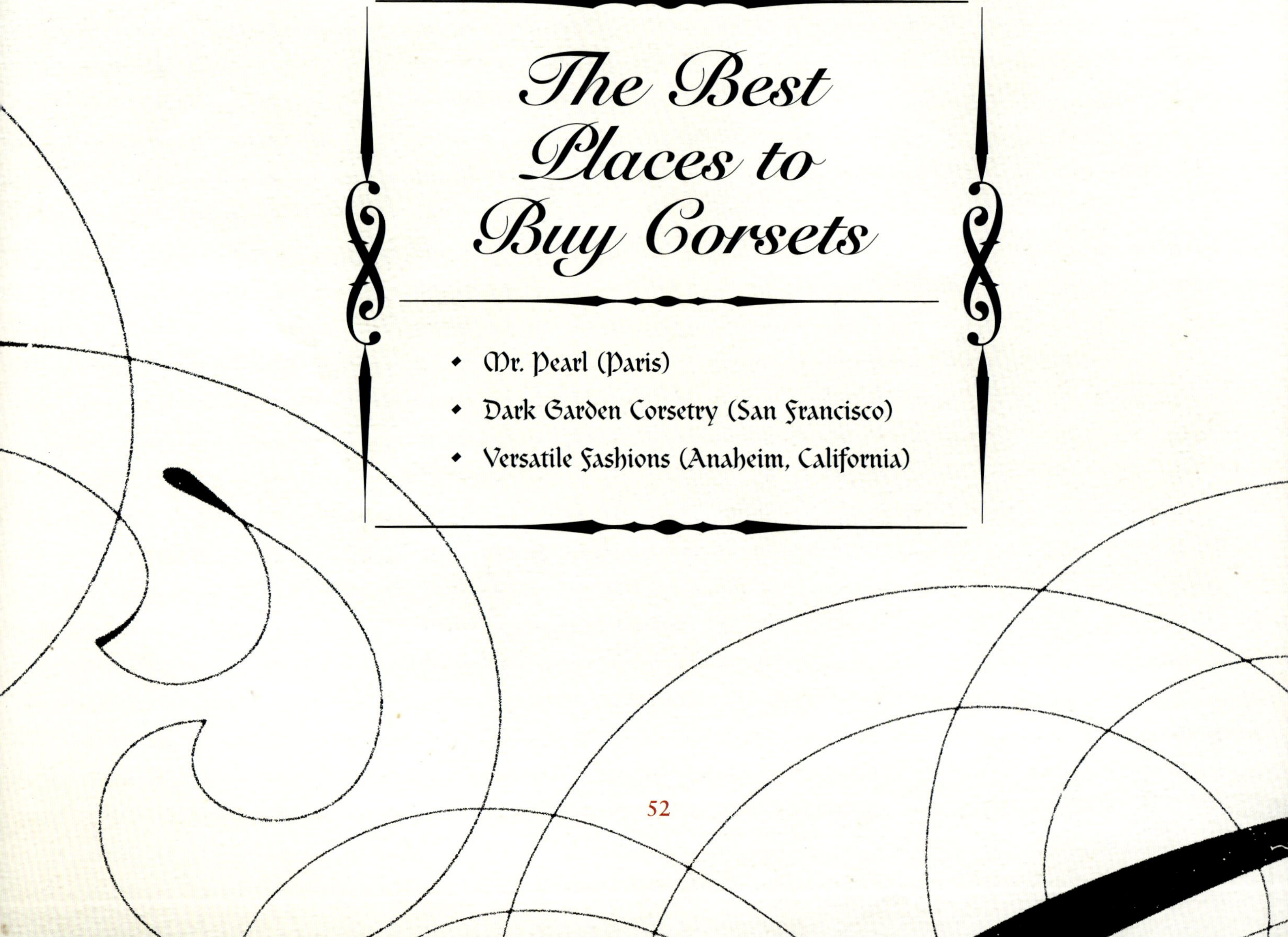

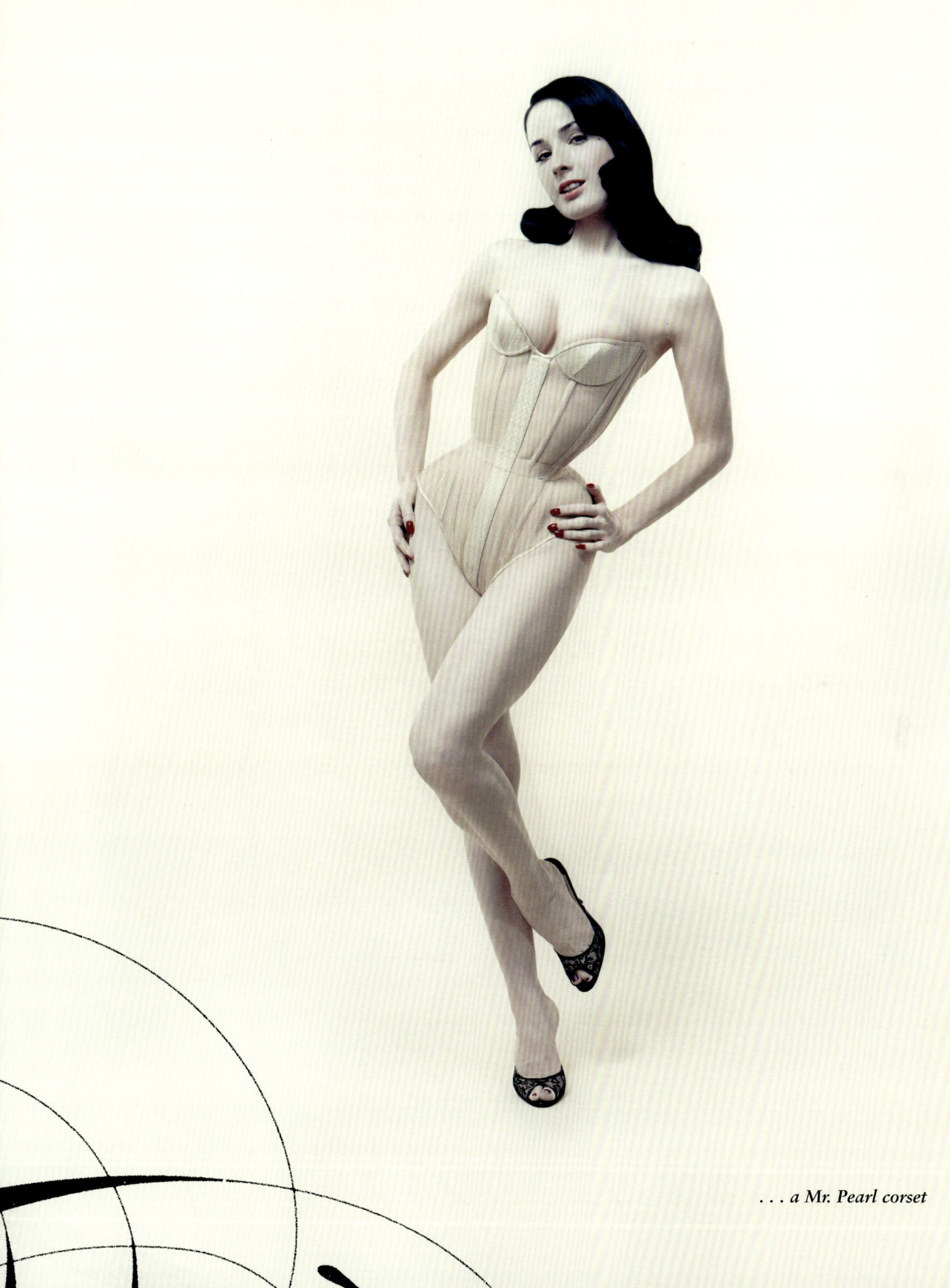

*. . . a Mr. Pearl corset*

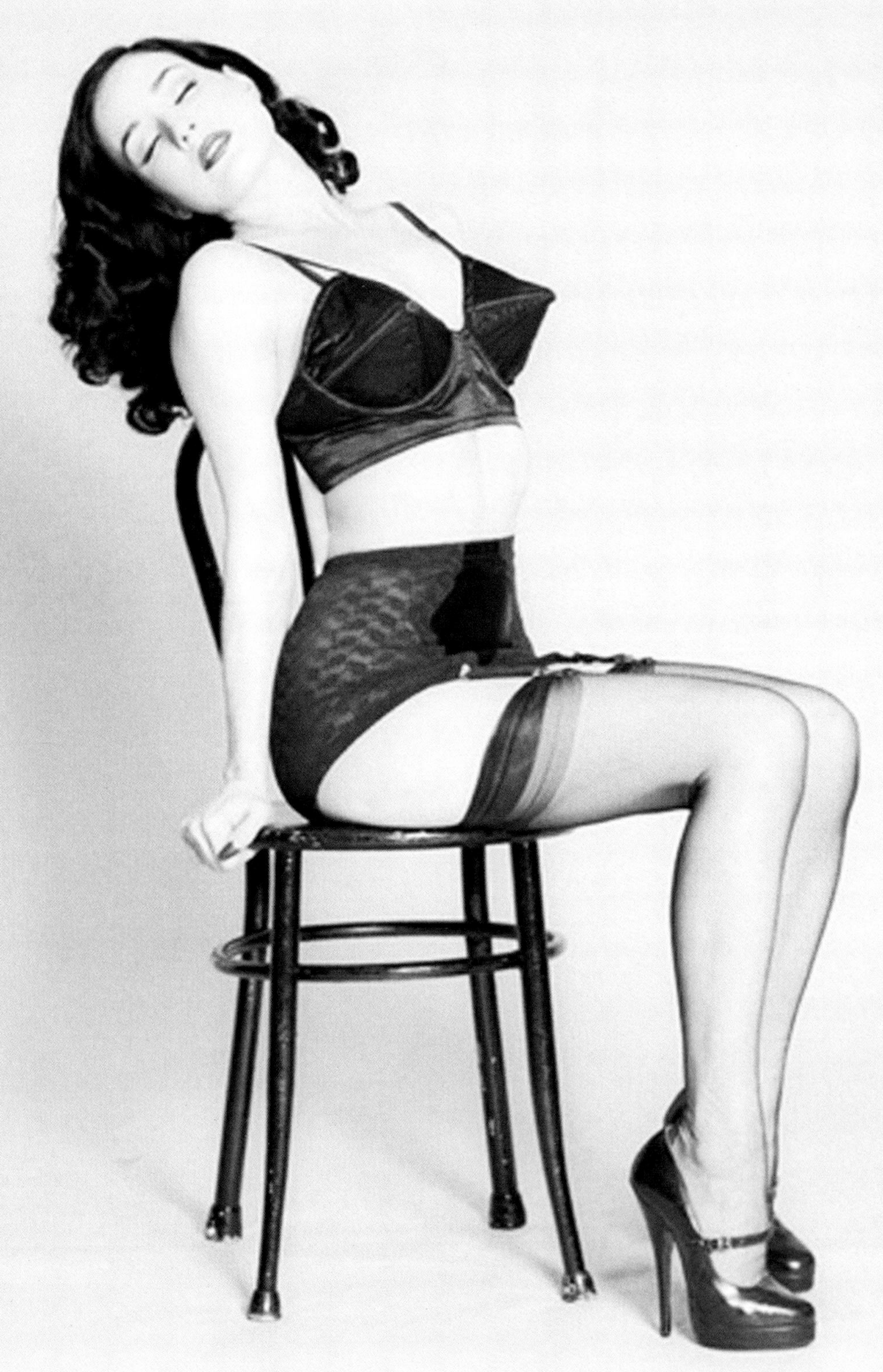

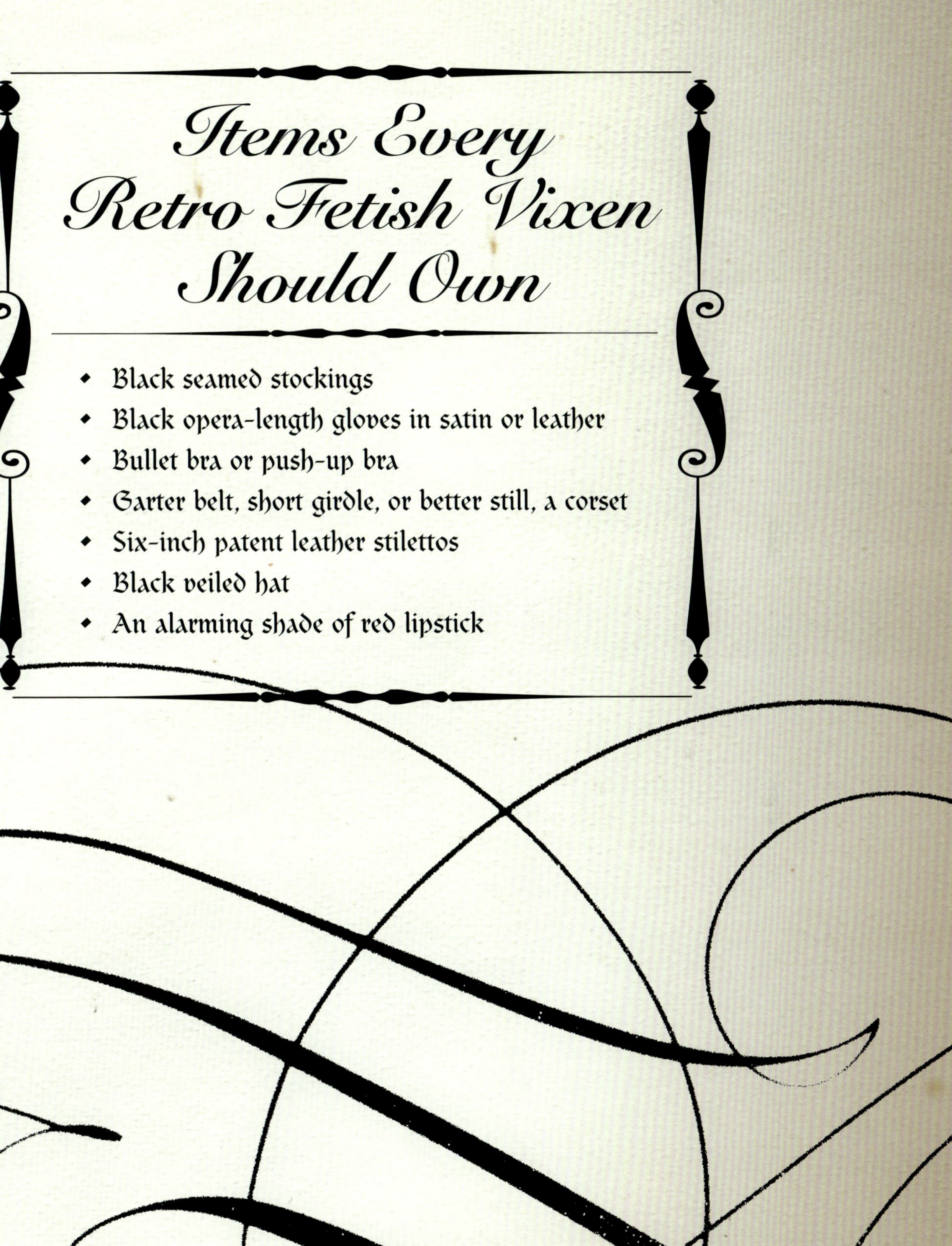

# Items Every Retro Fetish Vixen Should Own

- Black seamed stockings
- Black opera-length gloves in satin or leather
- Bullet bra or push-up bra
- Garter belt, short girdle, or better still, a corset
- Six-inch patent leather stilettos
- Black veiled hat
- An alarming shade of red lipstick

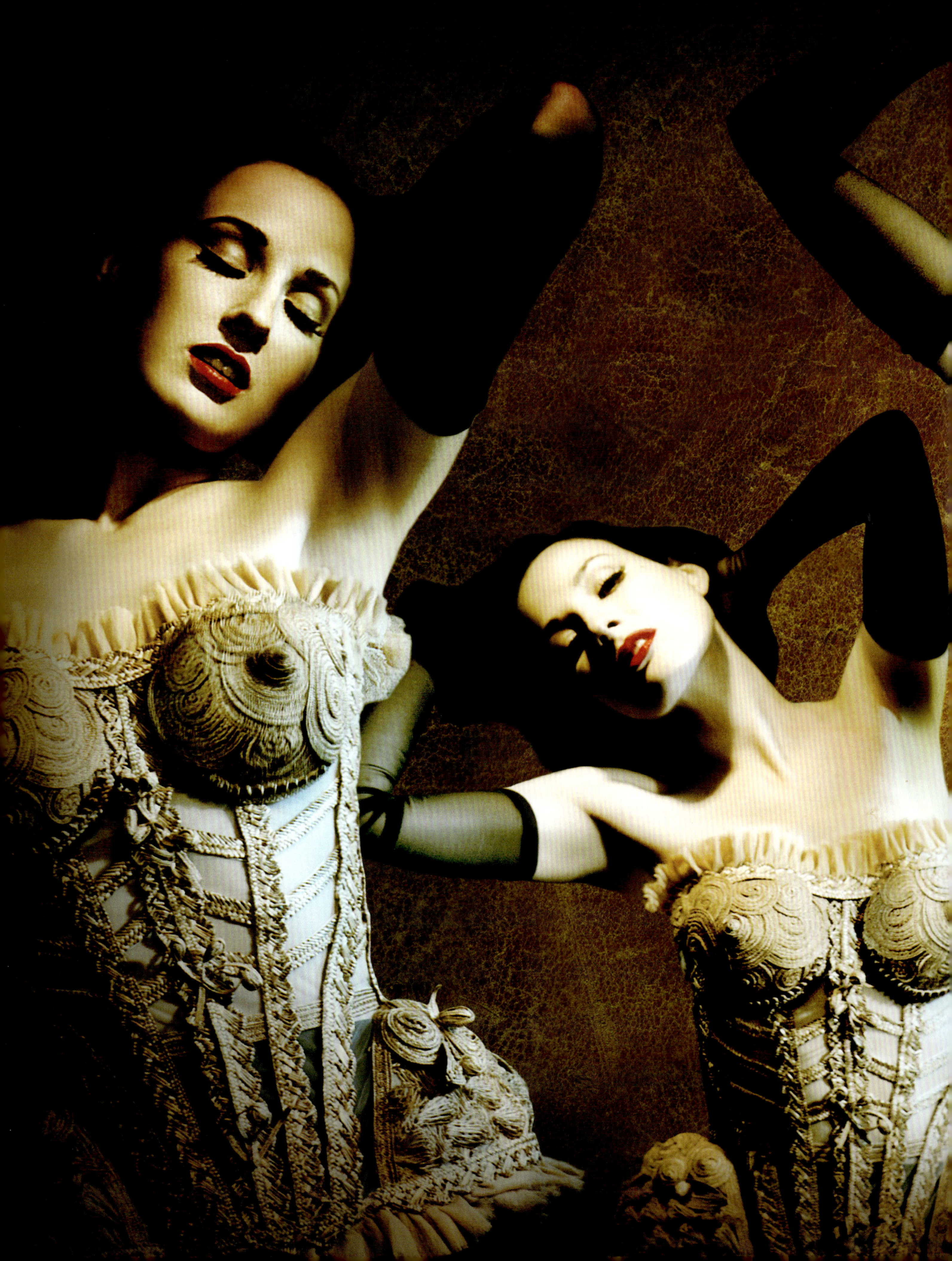

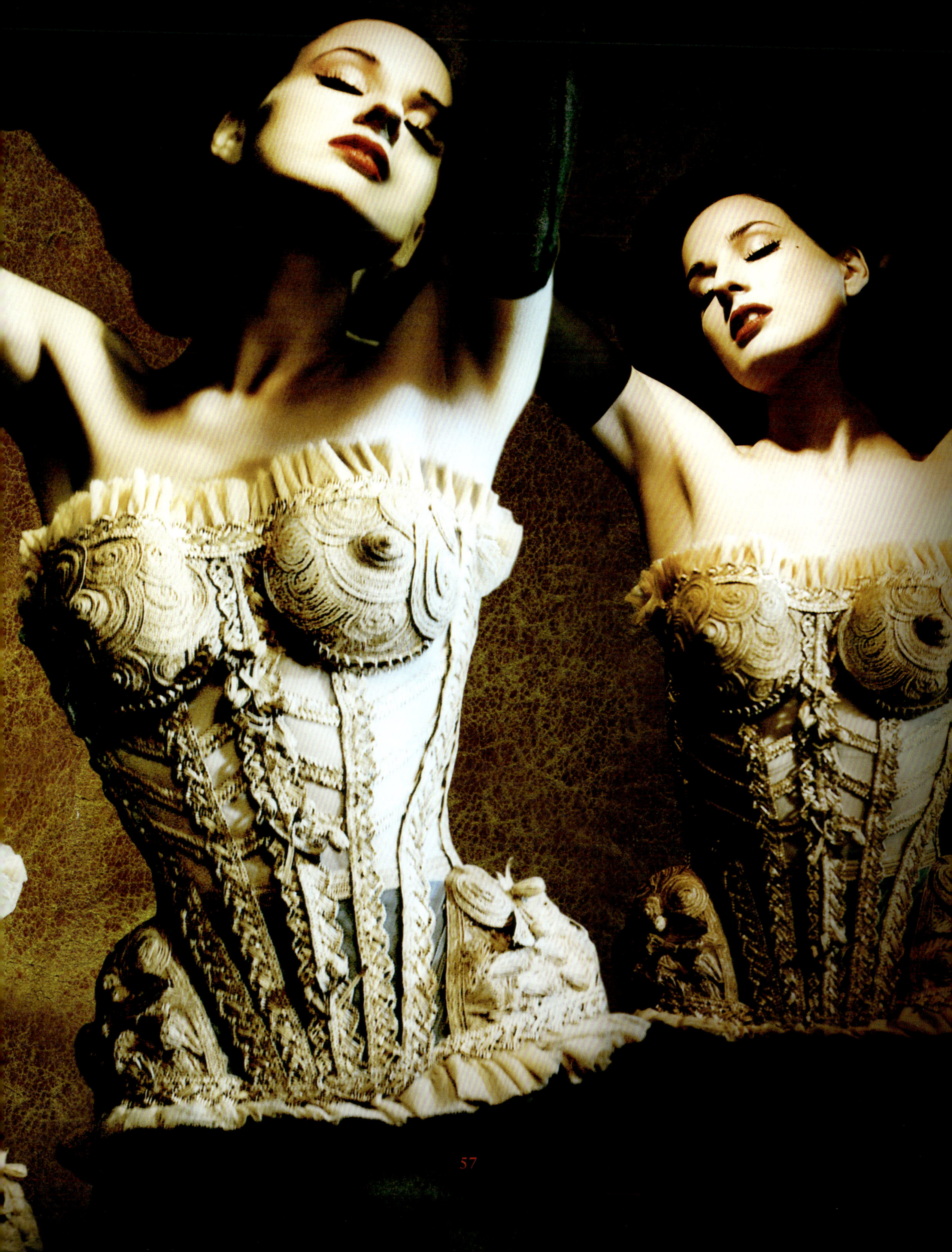

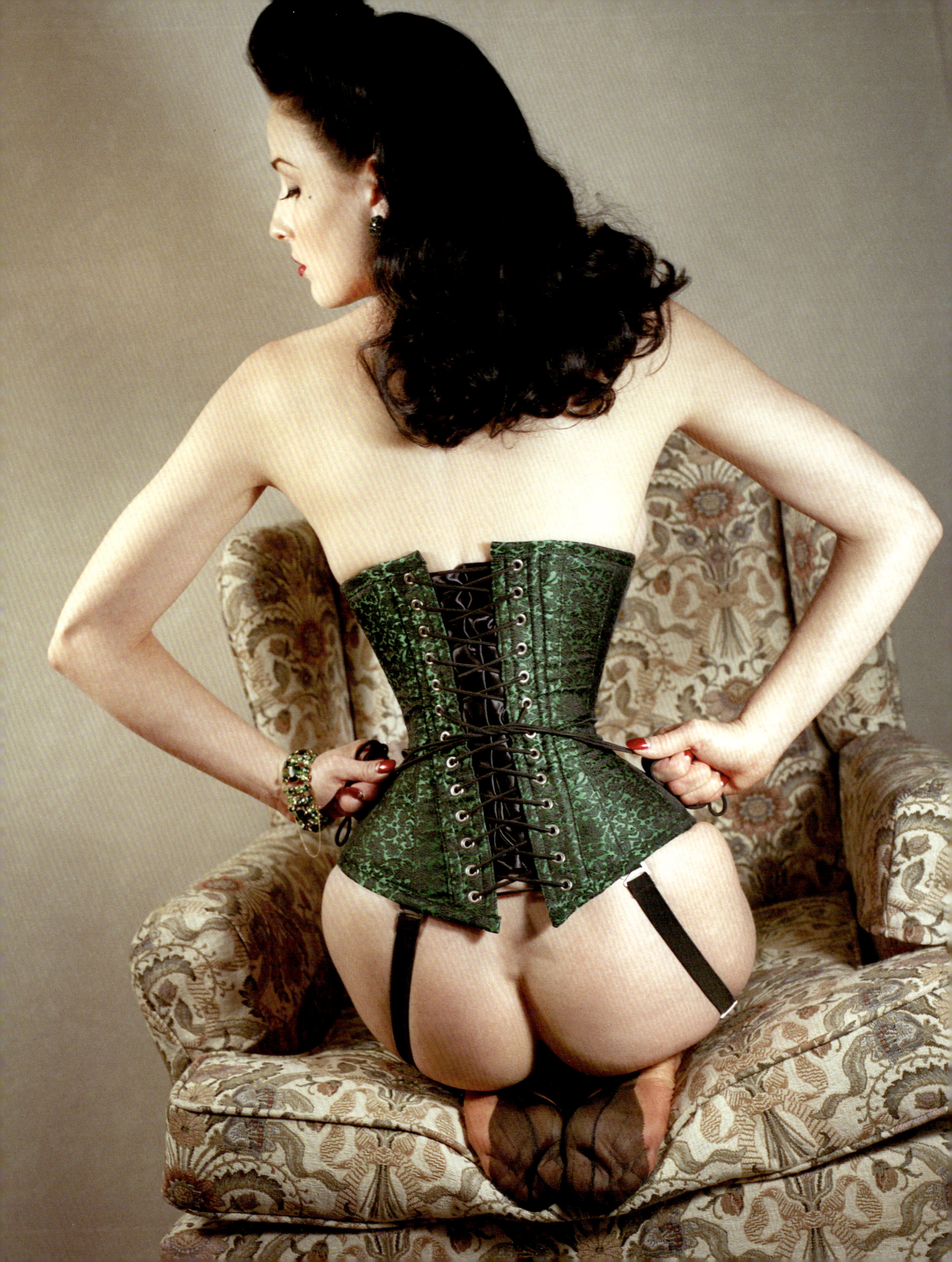

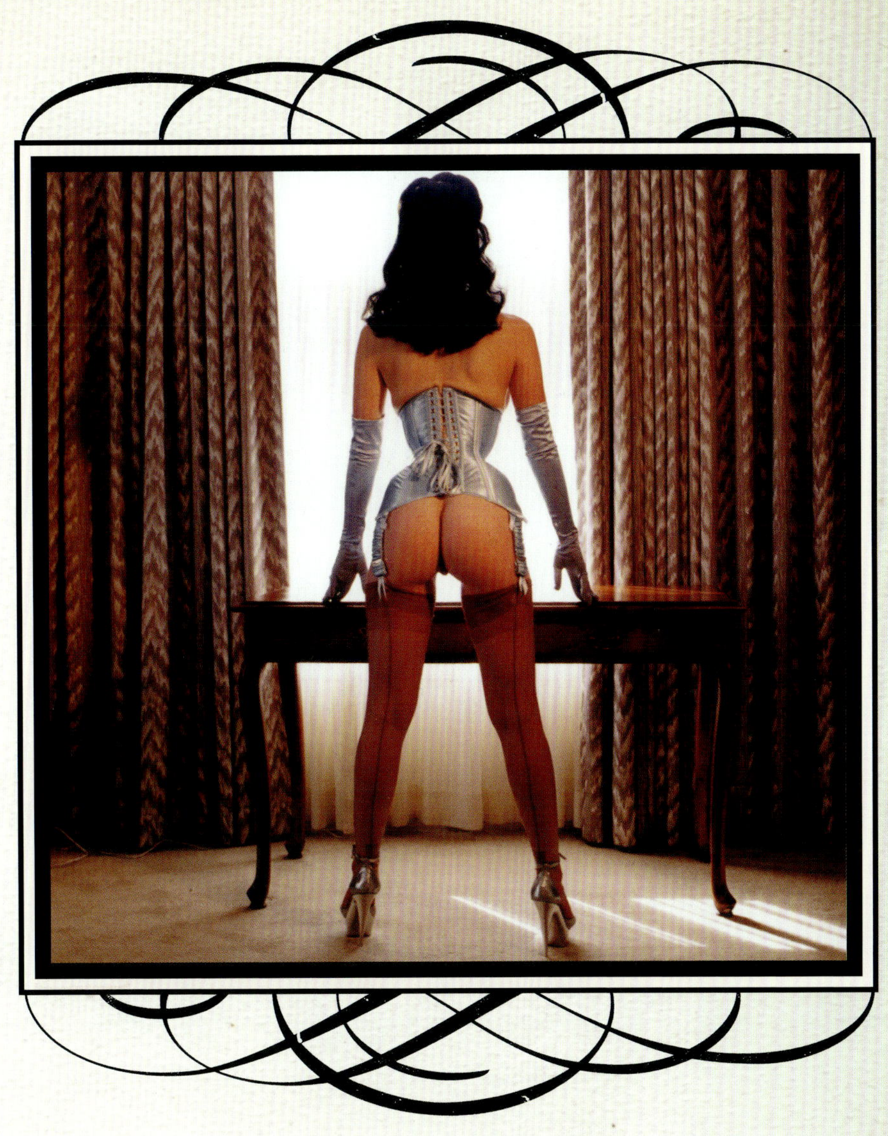

## Dita Von Tightlace

As for tightlacing, I enjoy it more knowing about its imagined history. Though it's never been my goal to have the smallest waist, I love the challenge of tightlacing. I love the extreme feminine curves that result, the sense of discipline I have in wearing it. Best of all, I like taking it off. Sometimes I'll get bruising from my corsets—I even have little tiny scars on my back from the laces—but it's worth it. Like any good bondage, a tightlaced corset is *not* comfortable in the average person's sense of the word, but it is exhilarating.

I'm a small girl; I have a small waist. If I can pull my midsection down from twenty-one to sixteen, that's nice, but it is not as impressive as someone with a larger frame—someone like Mr. Pearl—training his waist size down from a thirty to an eighteen. For Mr. Pearl, "The waist-size magic number is eighteen. Any number below eighteen becomes extremely potent—yes, I would say magical." For me, well, I'm a *performer*. If my waist *looks* small, I

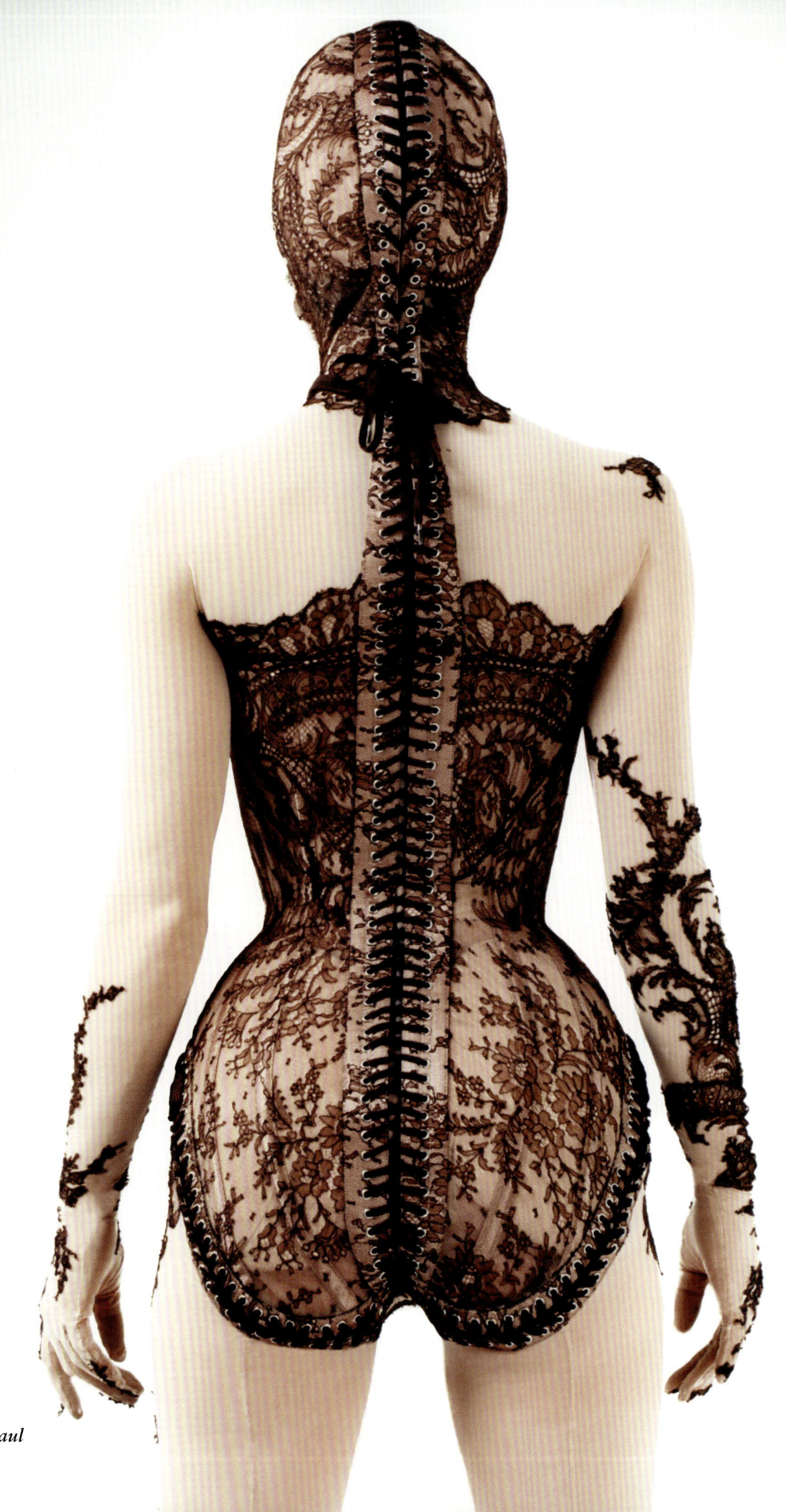

*Laced into Jean Paul Gaultier couture*

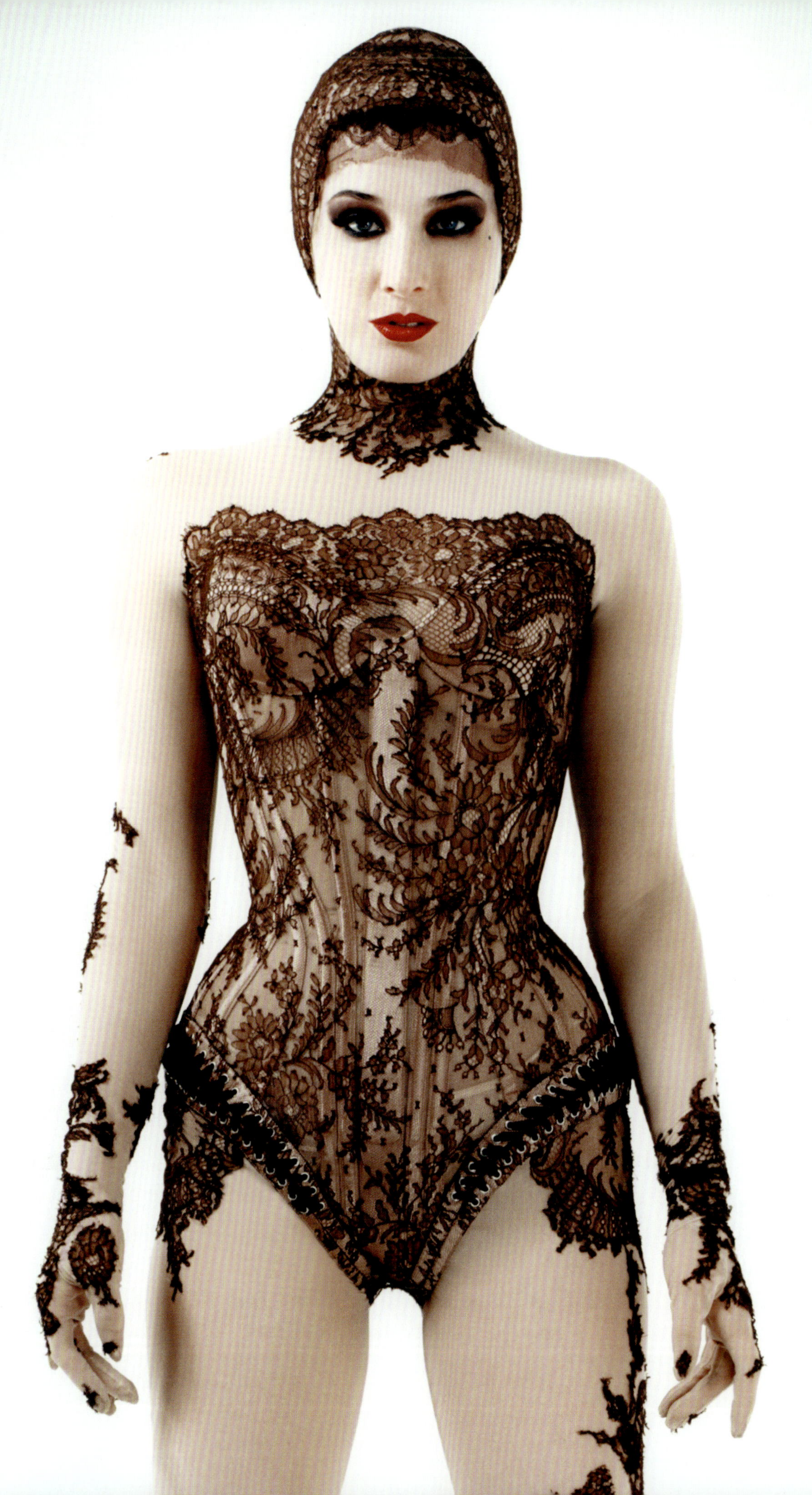

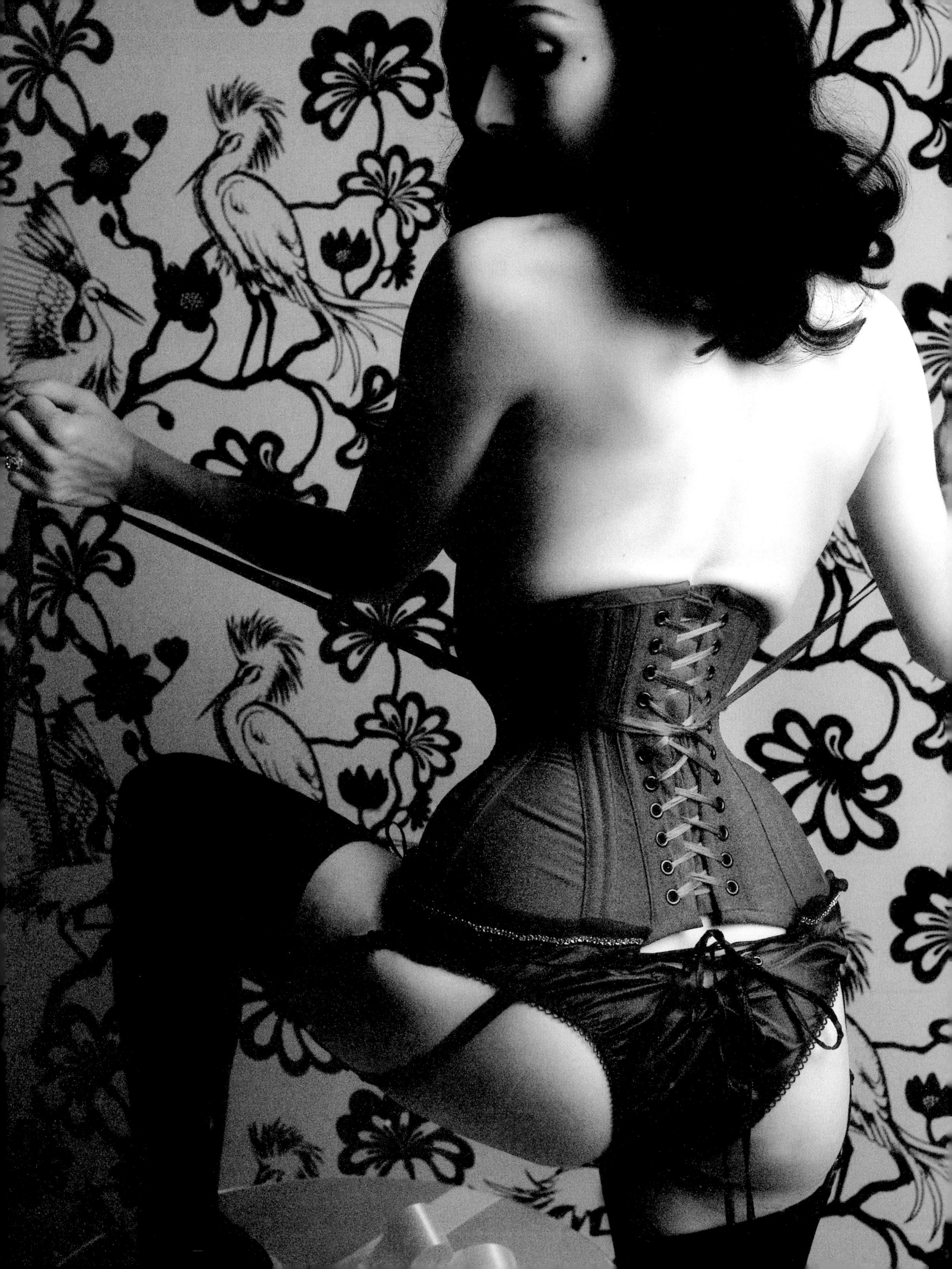

have achieved my goal. Besides, nobody but Mr. Pearl can eyeball my waist and tell if it's twenty inches or sixteen.

Oh, that Mr. Pearl is a marvel. Would you believe he wears his corset twenty-four hours a day, taking it off only to bathe? He loves the corset because it is a "disciplinary" garment. "You can't slouch," he explains. Or eat too much, or run wildly through the streets. Every step you take in the world must be graceful and careful, utterly civilized. Did you know that men once wore corsets? That's right—along with women in the Victorian era, male dandies laced up.

I possess well over four hundred corsets. When I became a model, you see, I often worked in exchange for these gorgeous garments. People knew my weakness: "Let's do a photo shoot, Dita," they would say, "and we'll give you ten corsets made to order in exchange for posing." Well, I could never resist. Still, my very favorites—besides the sumptuous Pearl corsets for which I've flown to and from Paris several times for fittings—are the authentic beauties I found myself at Parisian flea markets. They appear to be from the 1800s, and made of the most beautiful lace and satin, with embroidery and lovely little bows. It's such a shame designers don't make them this way anymore—except for Mr. Pearl, of course. The detail on his corsets is spectacular, everything is exquisitely made by hand. My own Pearl corset is constructed of black Chantilly lace over peach netting with fancy silk embroidery, tulle trimming, and jet glass beaded details.

The day Mr. Pearl fitted me for my corset—a gift from my sweetheart—we drank violet-infused Champagne from crystal glasses and talked about his special brand of corsetry. Mr. Pearl told me he lived with his grandmother when he was a little boy, and she wore a corset to correct a spinal injury. He used to help her lace it up, and in seeing her discipline, he discovered his own need for it. Today he lives and works from an apartment just steps away from the Notre Dame Cathedral in Paris. You know, I would rather have a corset like that than a diamond necklace any day.

## Noted Tightlacers

- Ethel Granger: holds the record for the smallest waist at 13 inches!
- Empress Elizabeth of Austria (1837-1898): 16 inches
- Polaire, French actress (1879-1939): 16.5 inches
- Mr. Pearl: 18 inches
- Cathie Jung: 15 inches
- Dita Von Teese: 16.5 inches

# FETISH GODDESS

## *High Heels, Fetish Favorites!*

*"Black leather, vinyl, nothing's more classic than that."*
—THIERRY MUGLER

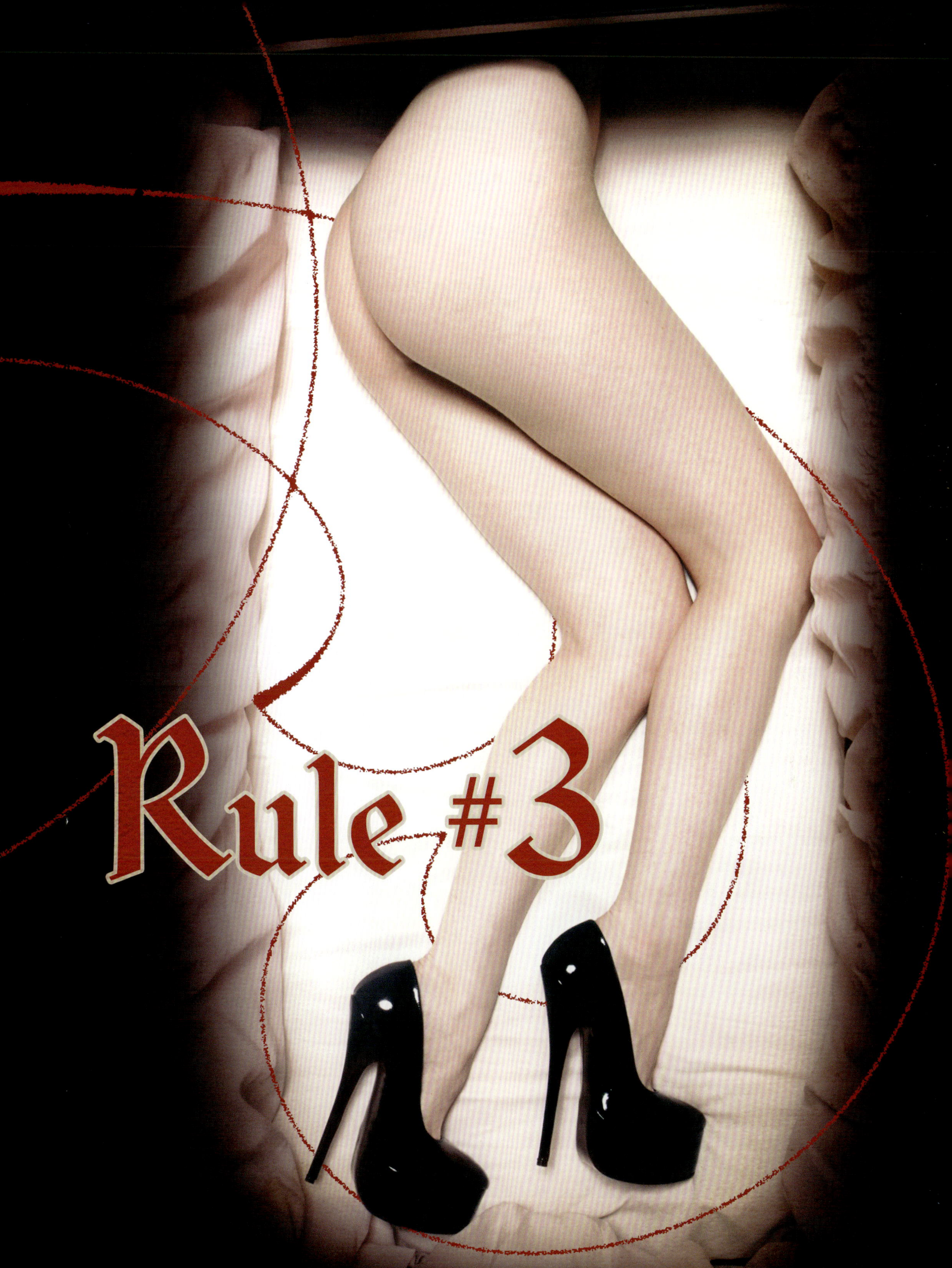
Rule #3

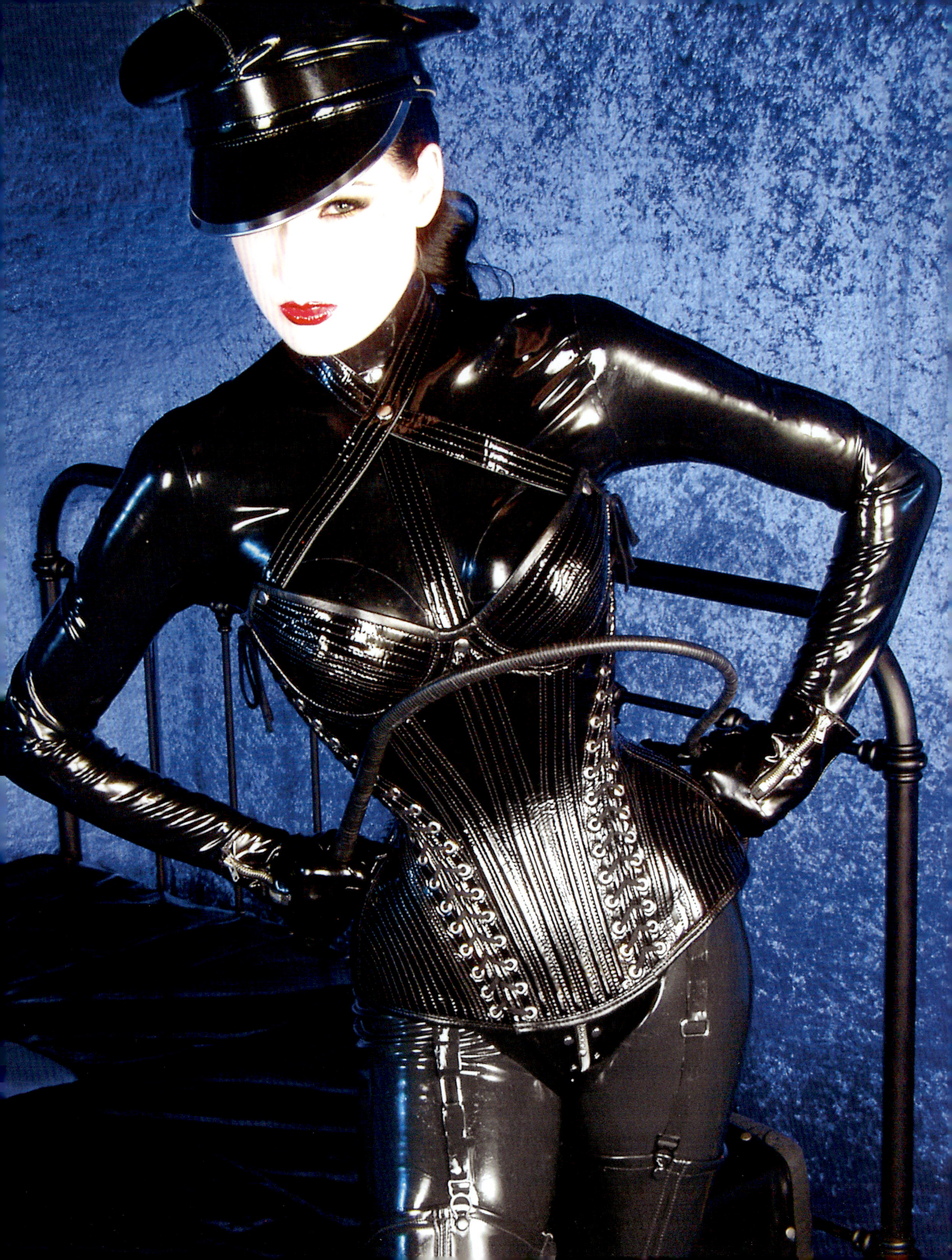

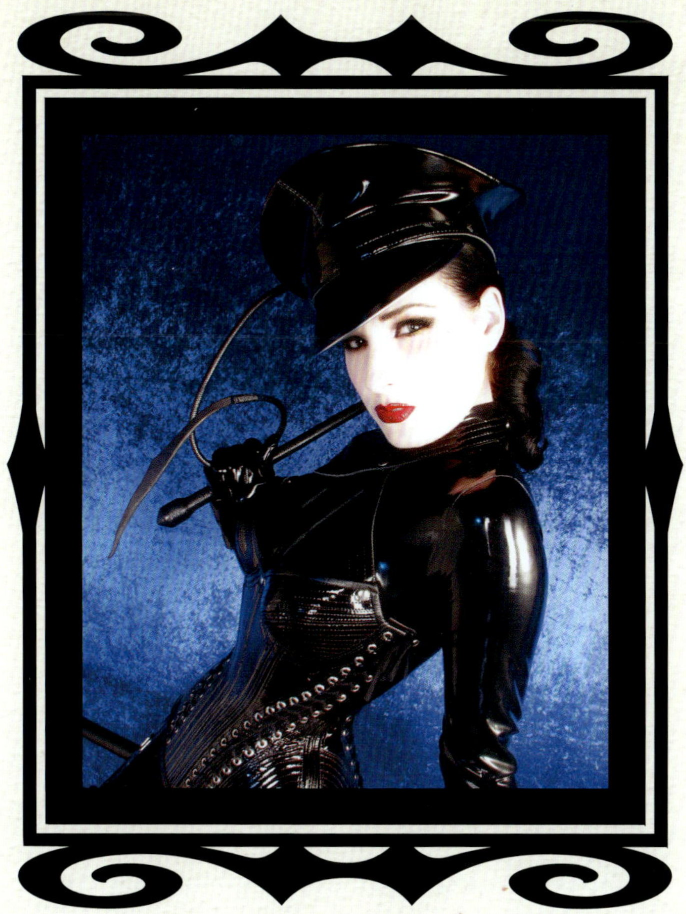

# Bow Down

I was nineteen or so and I was dancing for a customer in a gentleman's club. I had just begun to peel away my layers when I noticed that my audience—a quiet man in a fine suit—wasn't watching. Let me rephrase that. He was watching, he just wasn't watching the usual. This gentleman was watching *my shoes*.

I could see his point—they *were* fabulous. Six-inch crystal-encrusted heels with a little platform and an ankle strap. I felt exactly the same way, I thought, when I saw them on the shelf at Bergdorf's.

"Dita?" he asked, holding up one hand. "Would you mind not dancing, just sitting here next to me, so that I can see your feet?" He seemed slightly embarrassed, but I was more than happy to oblige. It was a simple request, and I'd been dancing all night.

I pulled up a chair and held up a foot. He expressed his gratitude, and asked if he could hold it. I laughed. Why not? As luck would have it, I, too, think I have very nice feet, and I was touched someone else would notice. I lifted the left foot right up into his hands. He had them cupped, like pillows awaiting a precious gem. And when it was in his hands, he just held it. At one point he raised it up, closer to his eyes.

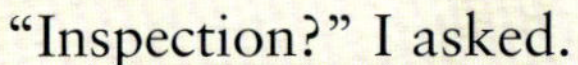

"Inspection?" I asked.

"Appreciation," said he.

It was the sweetest thing I'd seen for ages. Remember, this was a strip club. The man now looked at me again, with big nervous eyes. I shushed him gently.

"Whatever you want," I told him, "as long as they stay in your hands." He knew what I meant. He unbuckled the ankle strap first, sliding the shoe slowly from my foot. Now, I am not a foot fetishist, but this was sensual. Plain and simple. That is not to say I was attracted to this man. No, no. But, maybe my feet enjoyed it.

And then, he gave me a delightful foot rub. At the end of the hour, he paid me for the privilege of having massaged my feet. Ladies, I ask you, who doesn't want this?

When he stood up to go, he told me that if his wife knew what he had done she would be angrier than if he had had sex with me. It was then that the power of fetish really dawned on me.

"Do you think I'm weird?" he asked me.

"Absolutely not," I replied. "Men have been worshipping women's feet since antiquity."

"The Golden Lotus," he nodded.

## Famous Foot Fetishists You Should Know

Charles Baudelaire

Giacomo Casanova

F. Scott Fitzgerald

Von Goethe

King Ludwig I of Bavaria

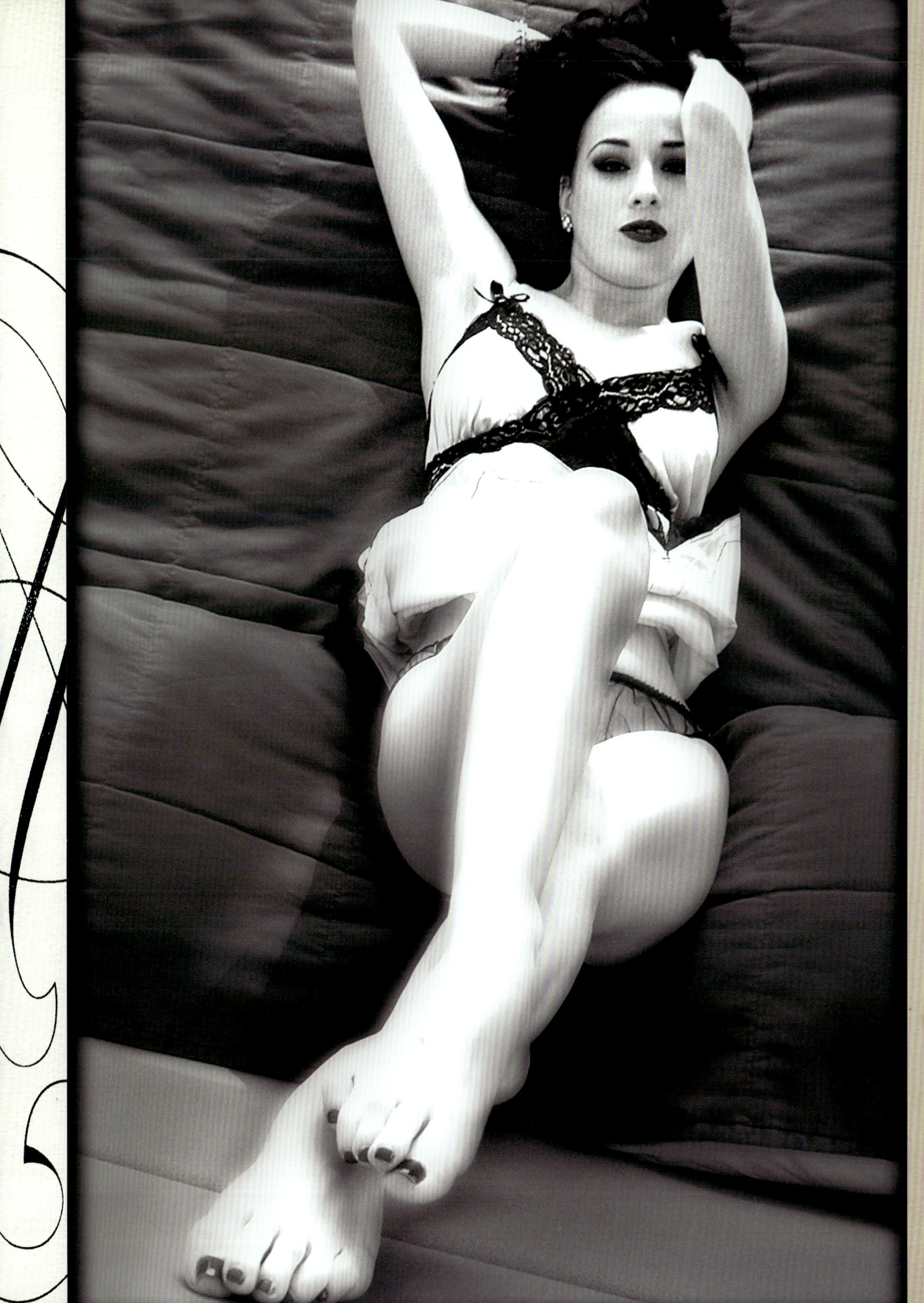

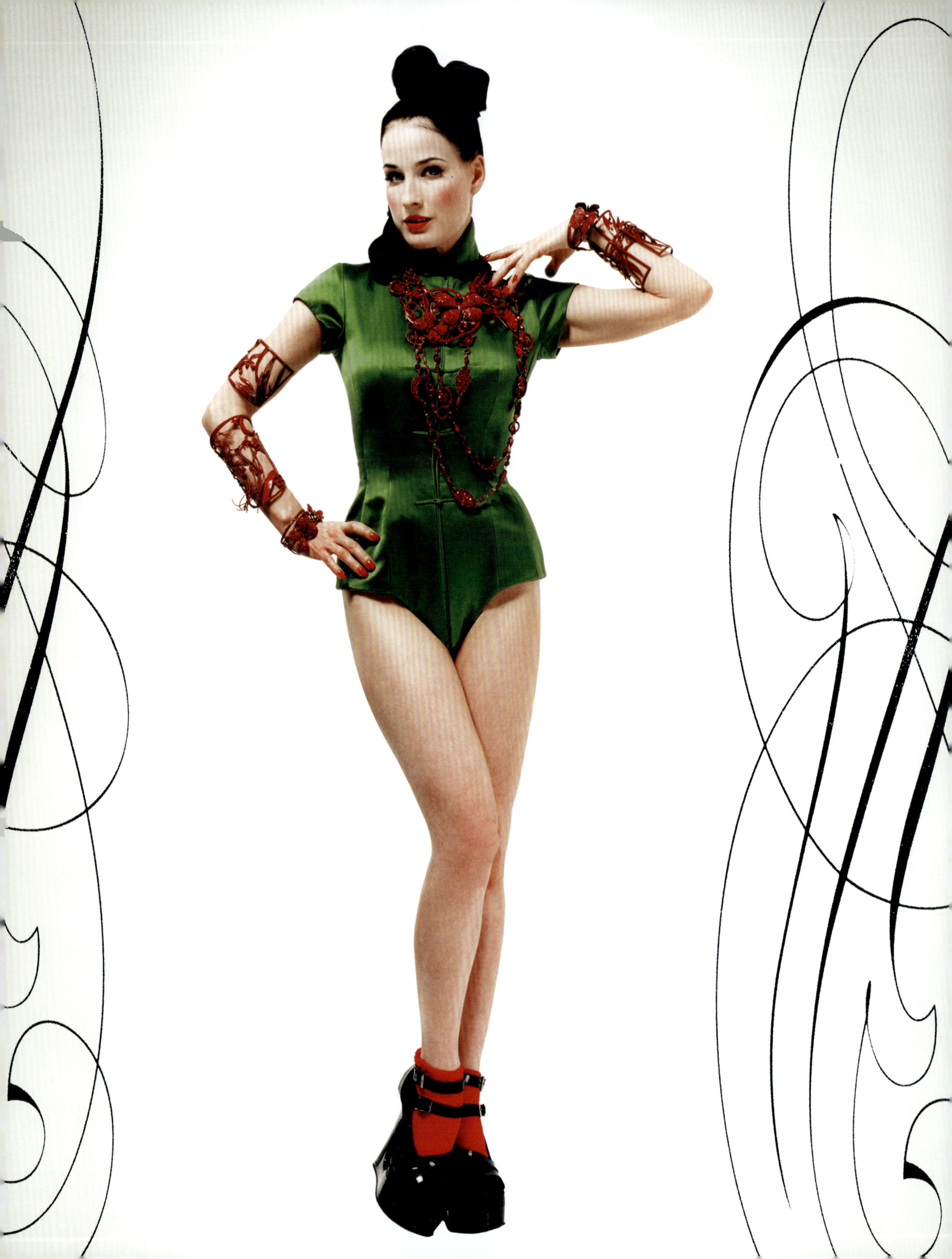

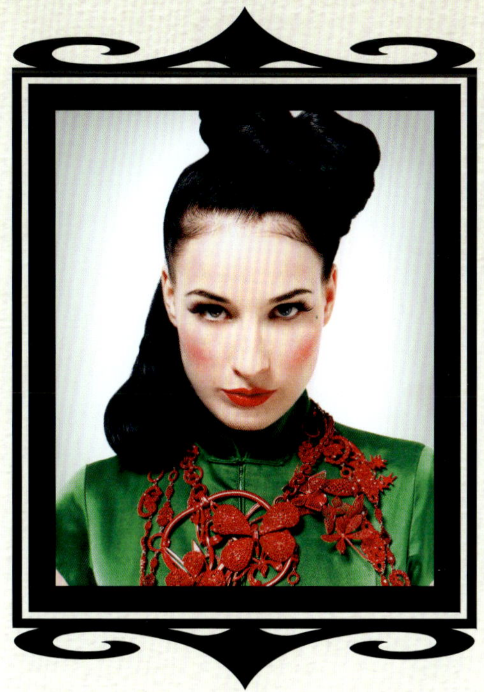

# The Golden Lotus

He was a foot fetishist—of course he'd heard of the Golden Lotus, the mythological three-inch Chinese foot, the holy grail of feet. My own were, by comparison, hulking at size six-and-a-half.

Foot binding, as most people know, was once customary in ancient China. Emerging in the Chinese Imperial Court during the tenth century, it was initially associated with dancers who wrapped their feet with cloth. Later, during the Sung Dynasty, the custom proliferated as a mark of status and grew physically deforming. By the fourteenth century, foot binding was ritualized even in the peasant population.

The process was intended to be debilitating—the more hobbled the woman, the more help she needed, the higher her status. To this end, starting when girls were aged four to eight, the four little toes were pushed under the ball of the foot—with only the big toe left jutting out. The forefoot and heel were then pushed together, breaking bones and forming a high cleft in the sole of the foot. Erotic literature of the era—one of our main sources of information about the practice—suggests that the protruding toe was used as a phallic substitute during sex, while the cleft may have been used as a surrogate vagina. The shoe was also eroticized; I find this is generally true of foot fetishists today, too. Made of vividly colored silks, and even perfumed, the shoe was said to play a prominent role in male rituals such as drinking games.

Some historians contend that foot binding was not a form of fetish because, well, everyone did it. The major source of our knowledge about bound feet is from Chinese erotic literature and Western missionary accounts. I repeat: the erotic literature was *written about feet.* If this is not fetishistic, I don't know what is. What's more, according to these accounts, Chinese men typically cradled the tiny feet in the palms of their hands (much like my friend from the club), kissing them, fondling them, and licking them (unlike my friend in the club).

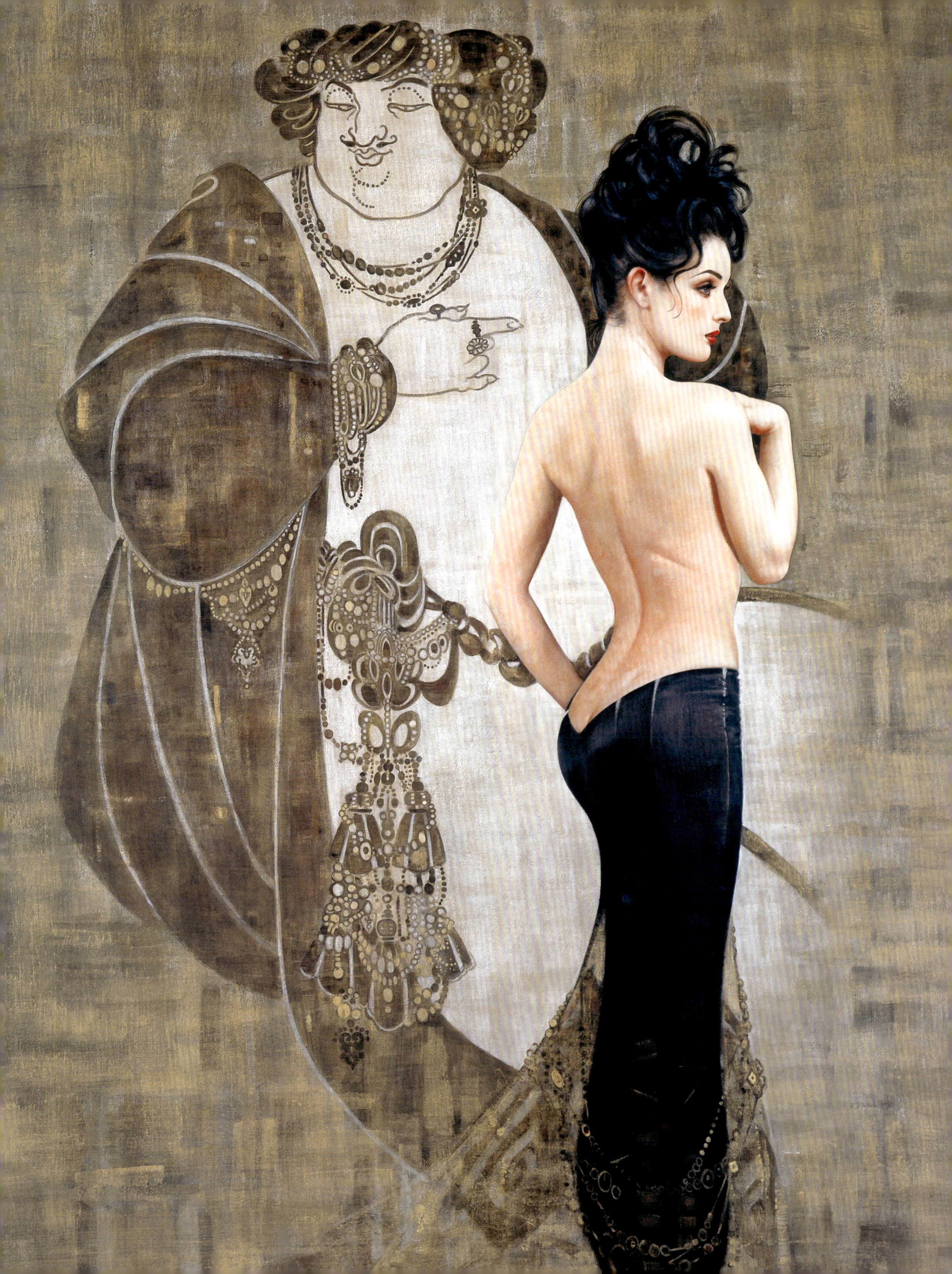

I'm not here to condone foot binding, but I imagine there are plenty of things we do today in America that our global progeny will look at as uncivilized. I will say that it sounds awfully painful, and besides, there was no getting out of it, no return to normalcy when the women tired of being erotic subjects. Still, I also have to admit that one of my own greatest vanity fears is having big feet. I love having small feet. I love them fresh with a fresh coat of red polish. I especially love them in high heels or pointe shoes—people have called high heels the foot binding of the West. While the permanence is obviously a difference, the similarities are striking.

In profile, with that high cleft, a bound foot looks something like a high-heeled shoe. Where the bound foot *is* smaller, the high heel makes the foot *look* smaller. Costuming. Both (especially really high heels) encumber the walker, something fetishists enjoy because it implies the endurance of pain, the transformation toward weakness, bondage.

But, where bound feet seem to have been predominantly about submissiveness and servitude (perhaps because they could not be "removed" like high heels), high heels are sometimes worn for empowerment—in dominatrix scenarios, say, and in the boardroom. In the fetish world and on the street, the higher the heel, the more sexual the connotations—a six-inch heel in the boardroom will result in the men's thinking about only one thing, and it won't be the PowerPoint presentation.

Foot and shoe fetishists are not only my favorite guys, but they may be the most prevalent group of fetishists out there. Some men seem to love the dainty, manicured foot while others enjoy feet for the "crush fantasy," in which the fetishist imagines himself being trampled underfoot by a dominatrix wearing, for example, high-heeled, open-toed shoes with dagger-like red toenails. Whatever floats your boat, as they say. I have no problem with the man who looks at them and fantasizes about this.

Regardless of the fantasy, most foot fetishists—and other body part fetishists—enjoy the attendant costuming. The foot fetishist, in my experience, tends to crave not just a bare foot, but one beautifully *presented*. Perhaps he desires to see and touch a foot dressed in a sheer pair of stockings—the foot at once visible and inaccessible. He may also like to see the objects of his attention in high heels; perhaps he is even interested in garters and girdles. For him, this foot is the star of the show, but the theater (the leg and the clothing) is crucial to the drama. In fact, generally the action peaks with the clothes' removal—the slipping off of the shoe and the unrolling of the stockings. The climax, so to speak!

As a fetish goddess, I wear garters and stockings under my clothes whenever I go out. It doesn't take so much longer to put them on, and they transform you, trust me. Besides, you can wear seamed stockings with just about anything. They are titillating and elegant and have the added allure of being adored by fetishists.

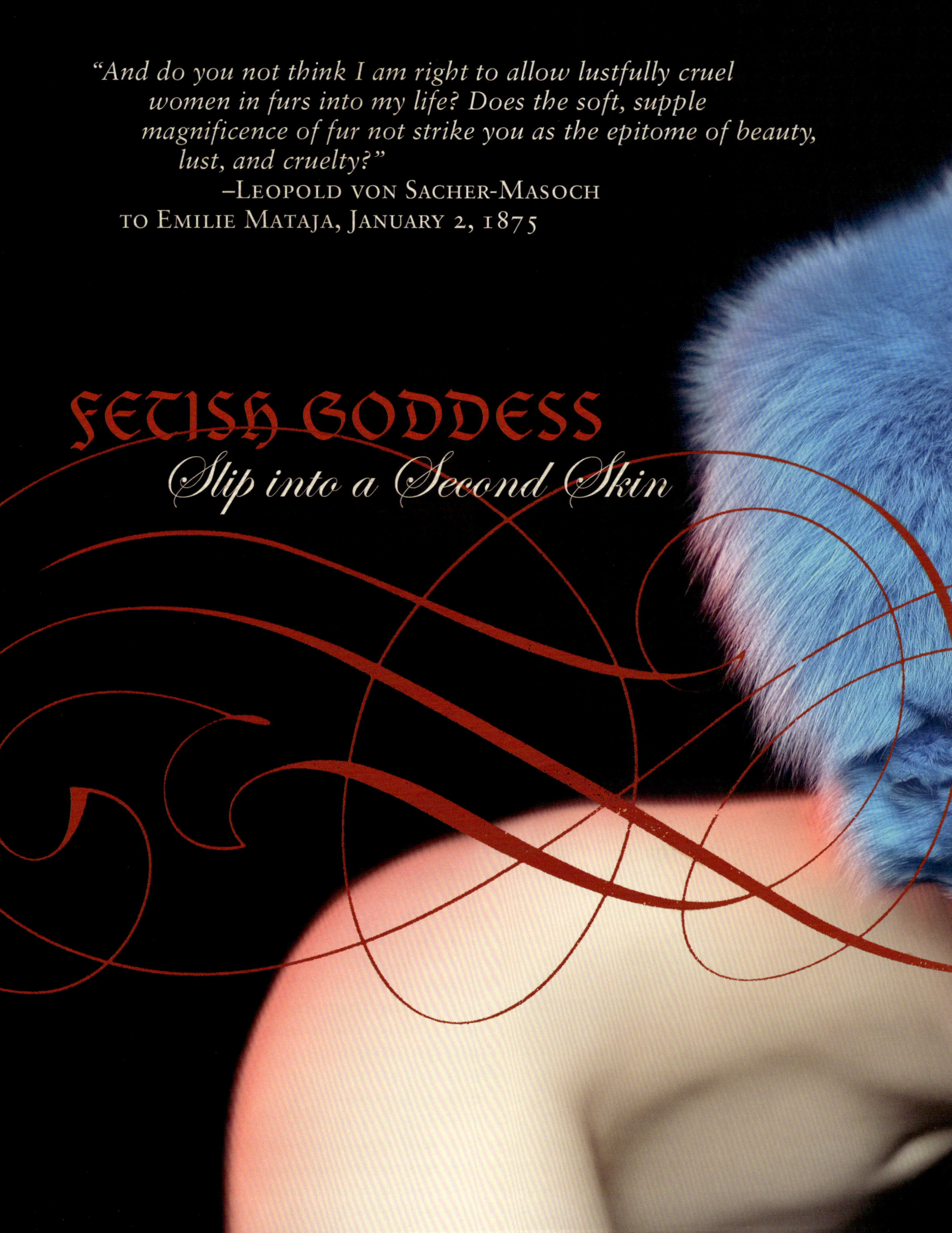
"And do you not think I am right to allow lustfully cruel women in furs into my life? Does the soft, supple magnificence of fur not strike you as the epitome of beauty, lust, and cruelty?"
–Leopold von Sacher-Masoch to Emilie Mataja, January 2, 1875
Fetish Goddess
Slip into a Second Skin

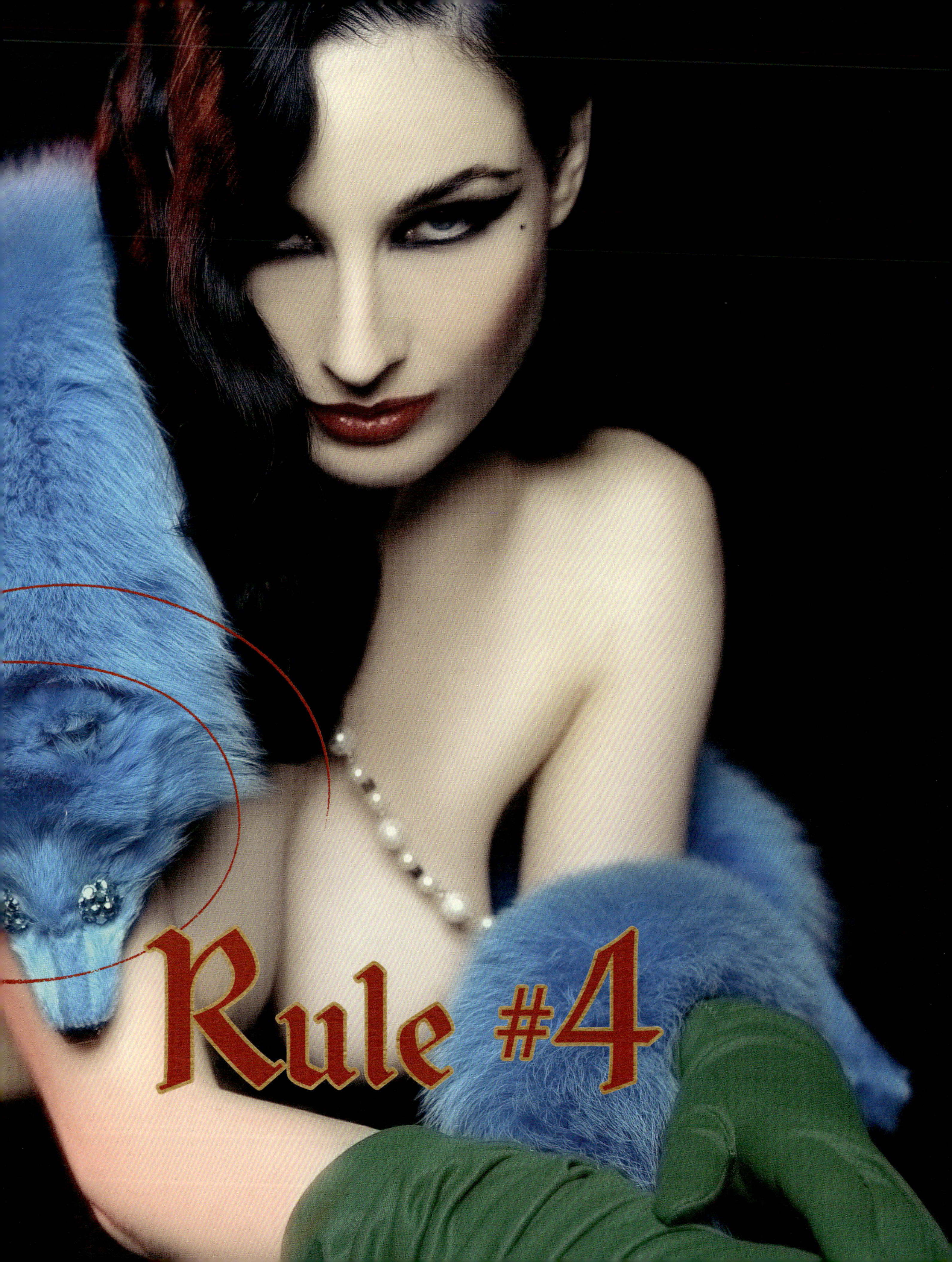

# Rule #4

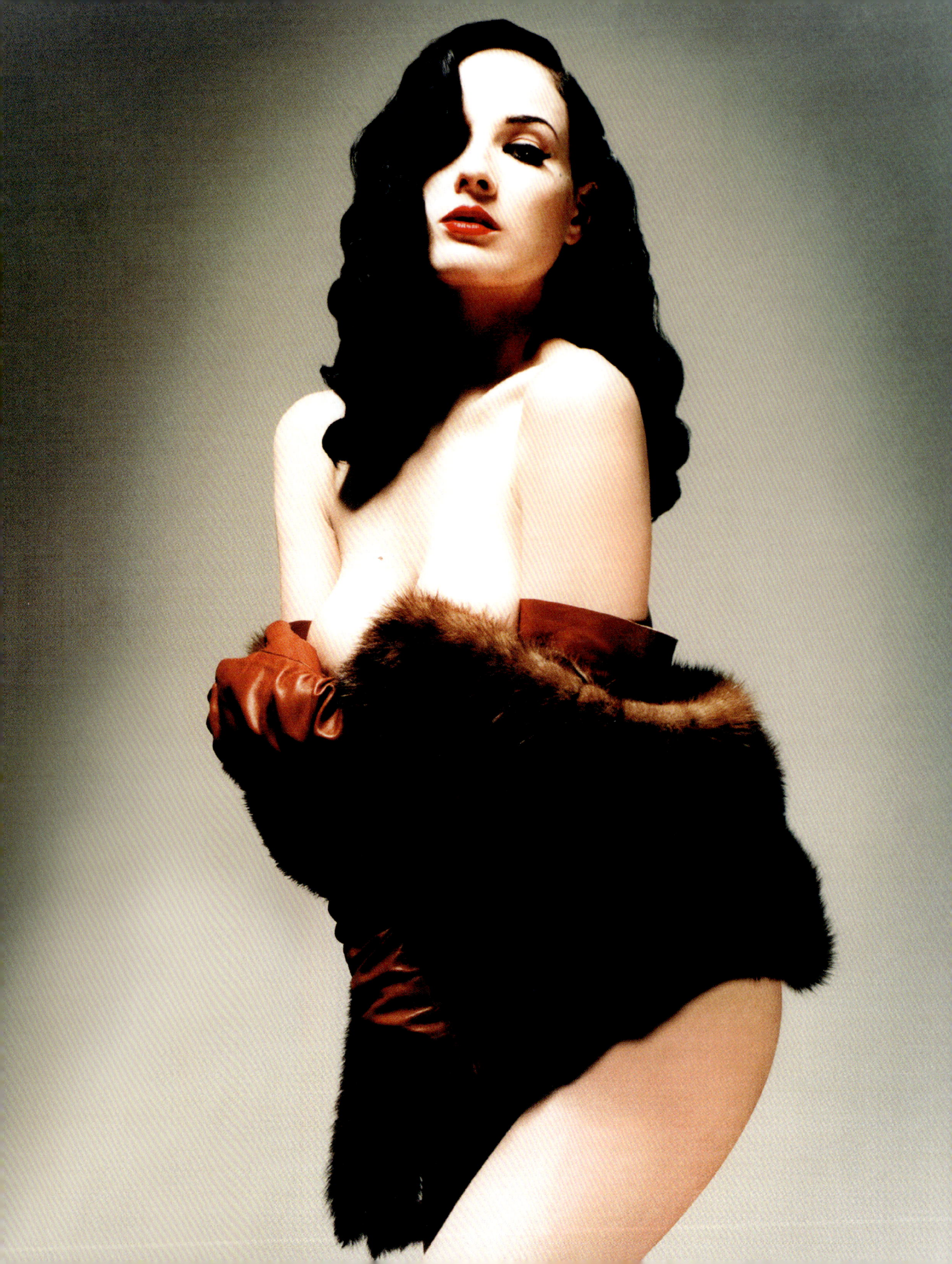

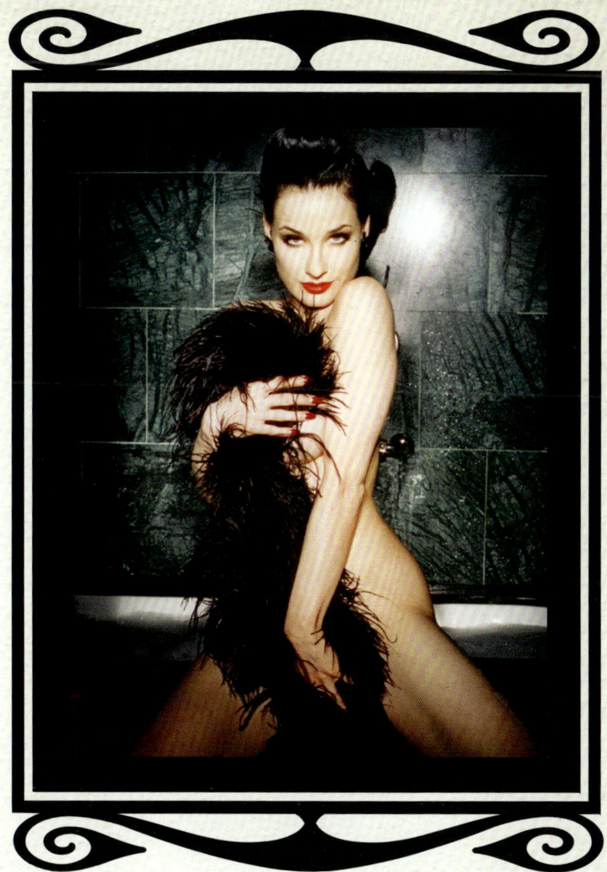

# Lustful, Supple Classics

To Leopold von Sacher-Masoch, the legendary author of the fabulous fetish novel *Venus in Furs,* fine furs or velvet were enough to transform a woman of plainness into one of majesty and cruelty. (Our word *masochist* comes from this man.) Of course, not all second-skin fetishists seek cruelty in the person wearing their favored material. Some simply delight to the sight (or touch) of lush silk against skin, of the light-reflecting qualities of velvet, the prickly sensation of fur against bare skin, or the way smooth satin hugs the flesh.

Second skins wrap our bodies close (like, yes, skin), falling against our curves, caressing us, accentuating us, making us shine. For hundreds of years, my favorite fetish objects—corsets, shoes, and gloves—have been made from these materials.

Who wouldn't love an opportunity to don a cuff of mink given them as a gift, or to wrap a luscious stole of fox around her shoulders on a chilly day? (I guess there are some people out there that wouldn't want to, but I am definitely not one of them!) Silks, satins, furs—I have crowded rooms of such sumptuous materials—are decadent. I've always loved these materials for their softness, their beauty, and the added luster of femininity they bestow upon me when I wear them.

These ultrafeminine materials have long been fetishized because they are as luxurious to the touch as the skin they cover. They caress and they stimulate. Take fur. Soft but sometimes prickly, fur is also thick and voluptuous. Silks and satins are slippery, smooth, and sensual.

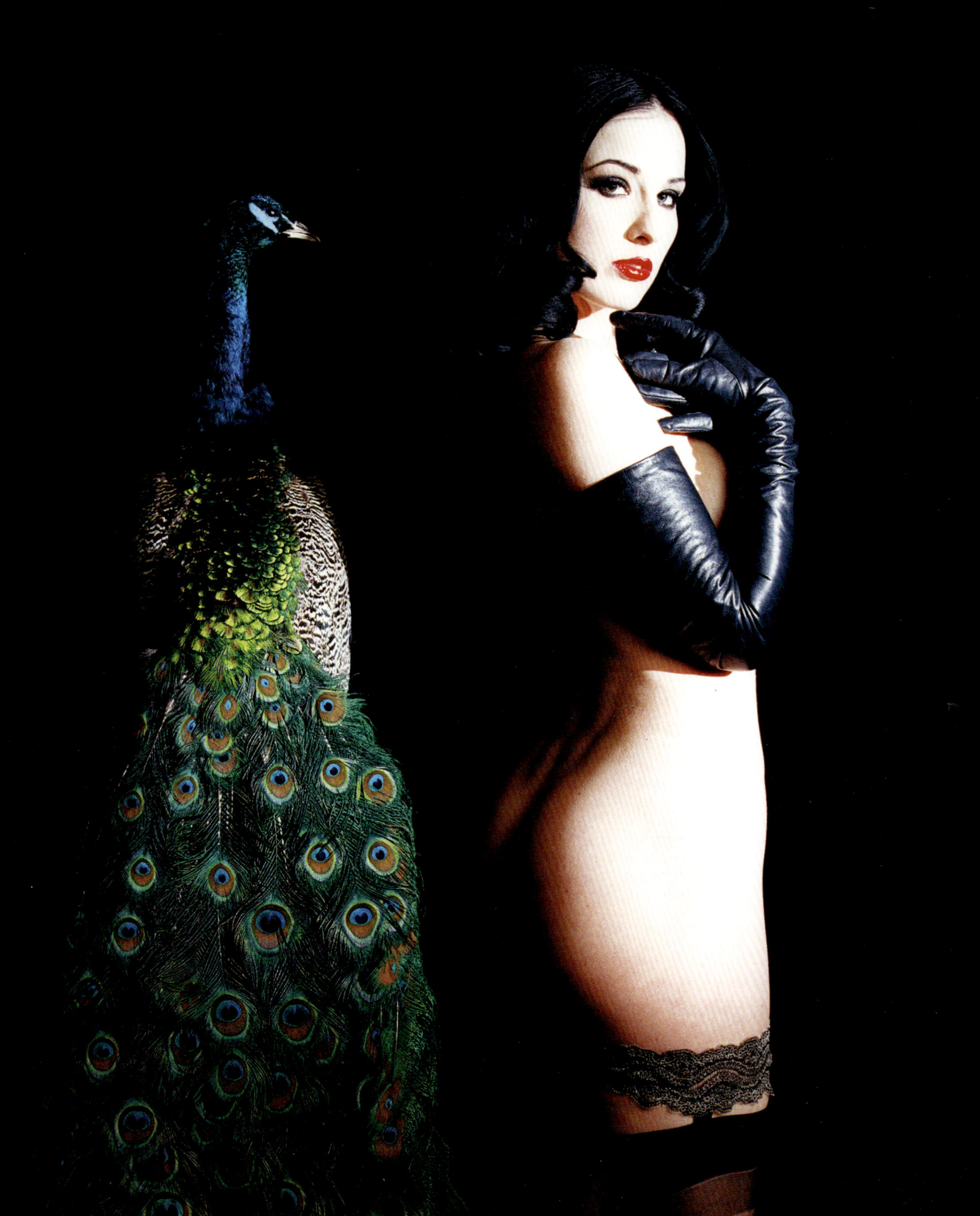

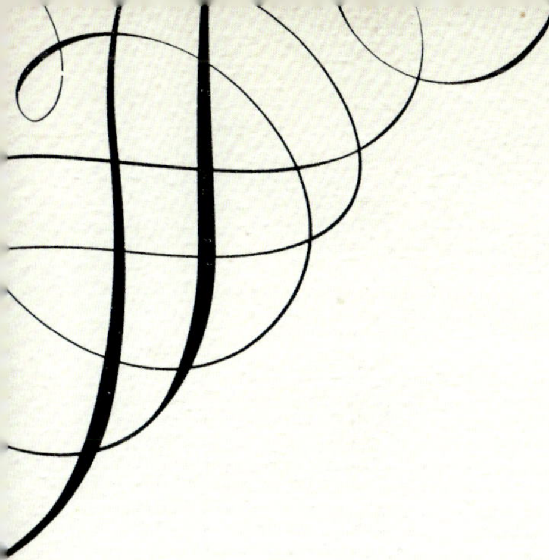

# Fetish Wardrobe Must-Haves

- Black corset
- Latex opera gloves
- Riding crop
- Fishnet hose or better still, fully fashioned black stockings
- A collar and leash
- Something, anything in leather
- Patent leather stilettos with five- to six-inch heels . . . or even higher if you don't mind crawling or being carried!
- Vintage-inspired lingerie in black (bullet bra, girdle)

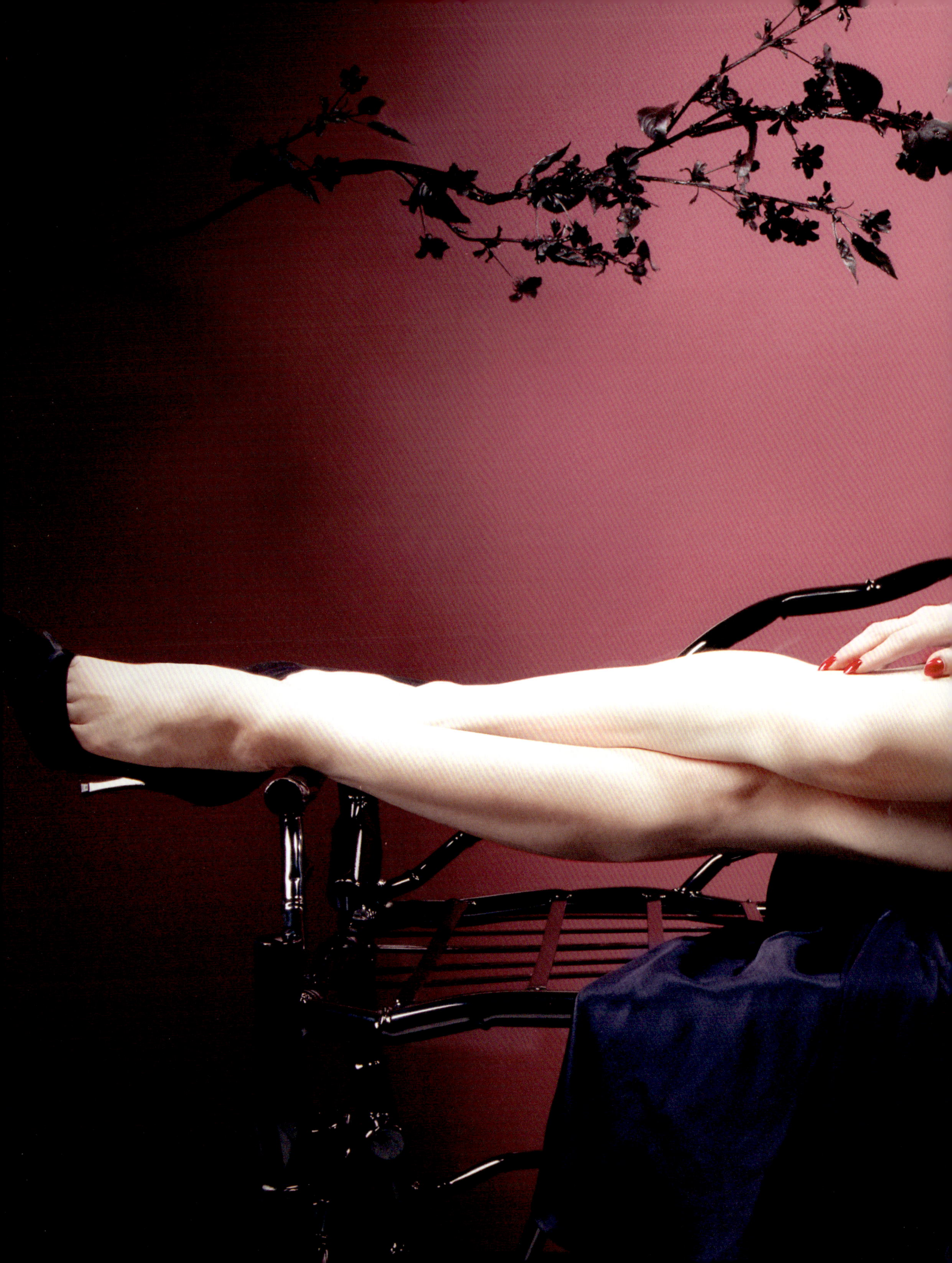

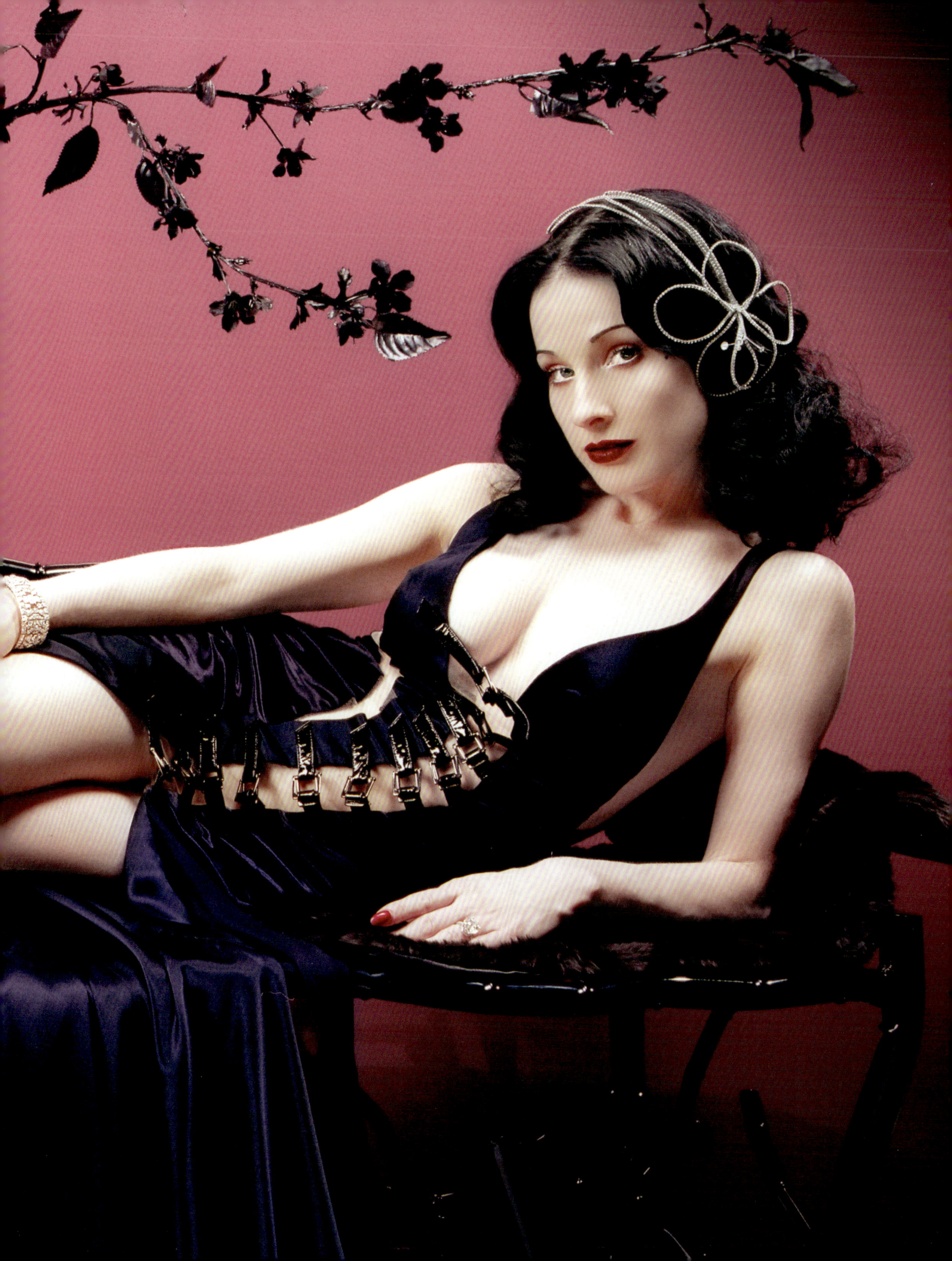

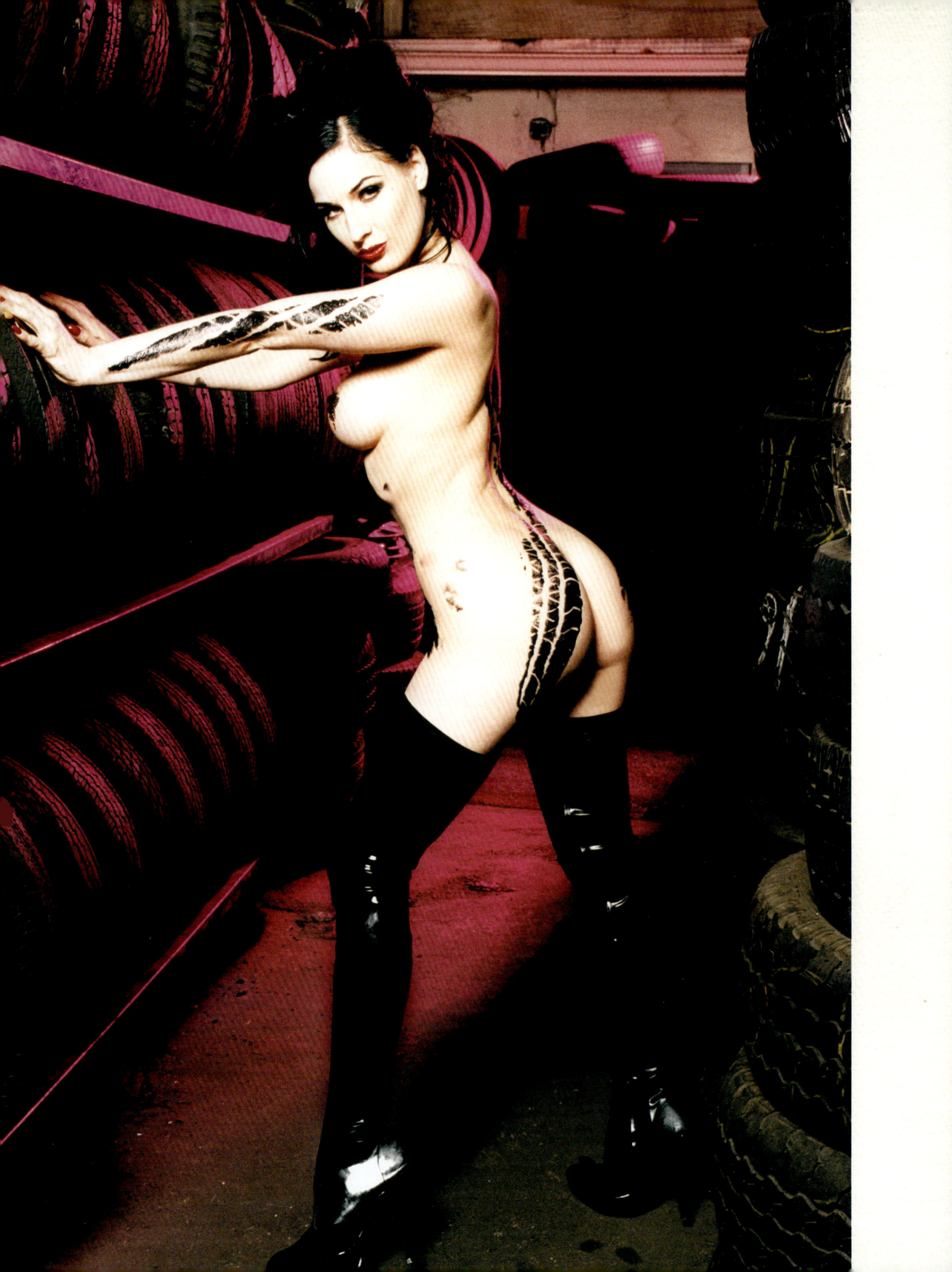

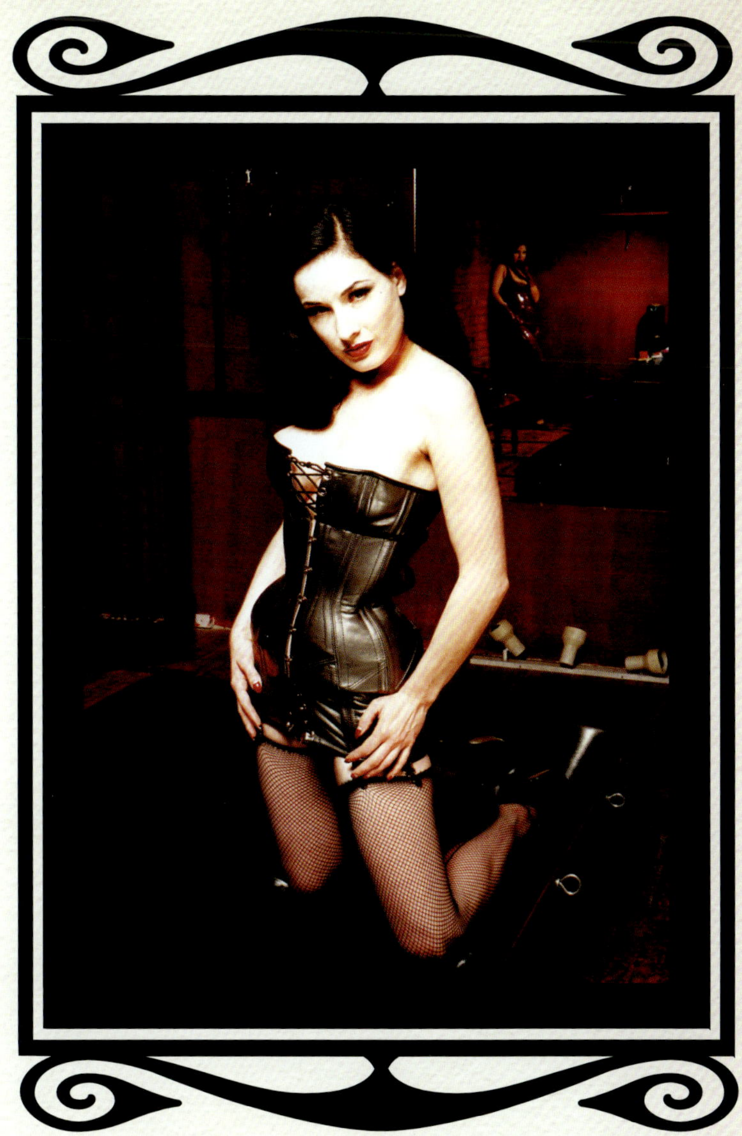

## A Run on Rubber

Of course, with the arrival of better, shinier, tighter fabric-making technology at the end of the twentieth century, the fetish world began to take the idea of second skin more literally, worshipping the new materials that enveloped the skin as skin itself wraps the body. Thanks to mass-production, these new materials—leather and then rubber and plastic—were plentiful, and fetishists embraced them readily.

Rubber, for example, was invented in the nineteenth century as "health clothing" to encourage perspiration, but fetishists quickly adopted it for their own pleasure. By the 1920s, a variety of rubber clothes was available in Germany, England, and the United States, including raincoats, referred to as mackintoshes. For a long time, raincoat adoration reigned as the preeminent rubber fetish.

Now, the standard rubber fetish fashions don't particularly appeal to me—the red and black cat suits, or heavy black dresses. As a committed fetish goddess, however, I find ways to incorporate the material into my wardrobe in classic, cleverly glamorous ways. To this end, I have rubber clothes constructed according to the same designs of say, a 1930s gown, or a Marilyn Monroe-style wiggle dress. I enjoy wearing rubber in pastel pinks and blues and yellow instead of the predictable reds and blacks. My favorite latex garment, in fact, is a pink rubber dress with red cherries—a custom-made piece inspired by classic 1950s style.

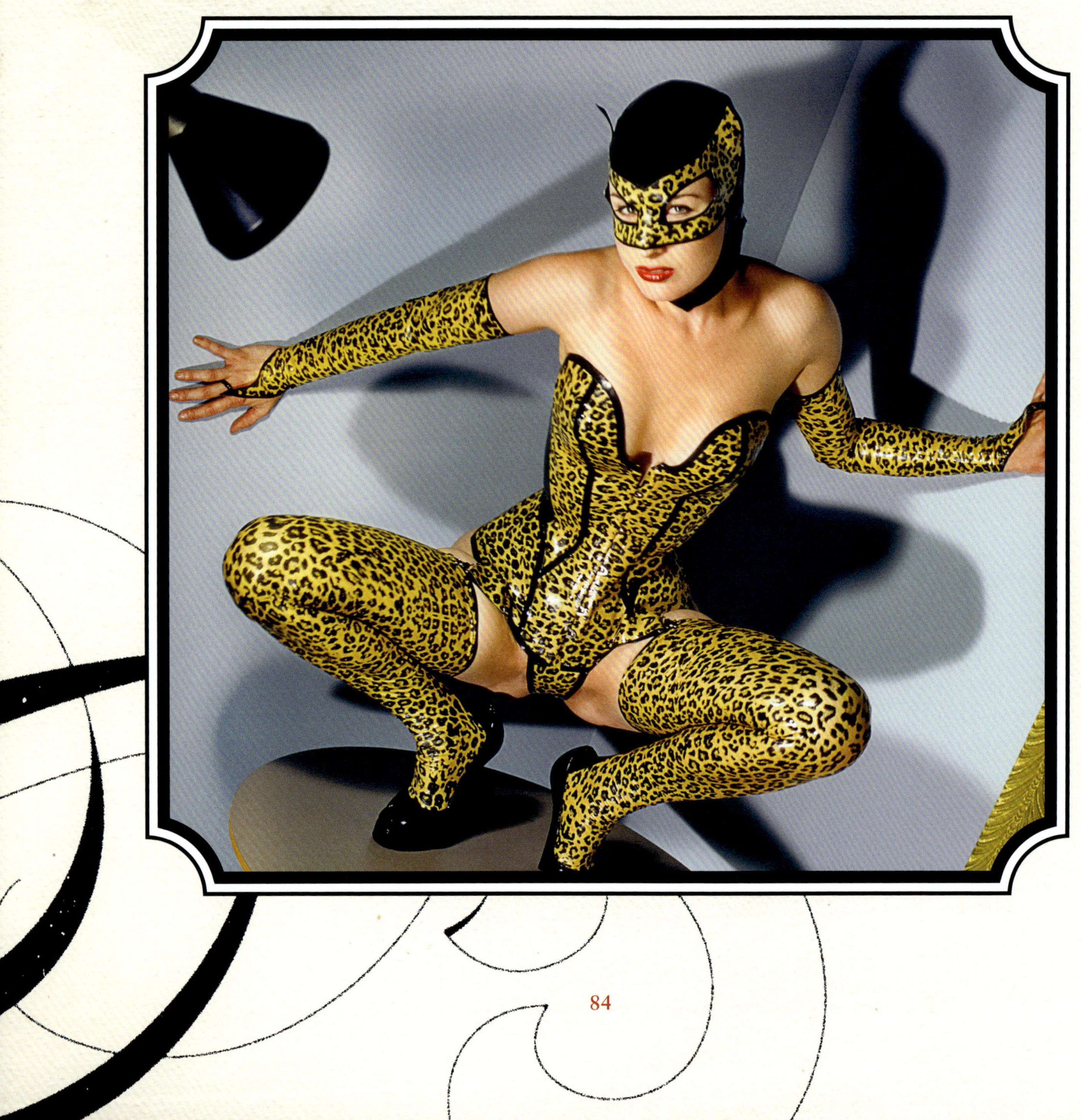

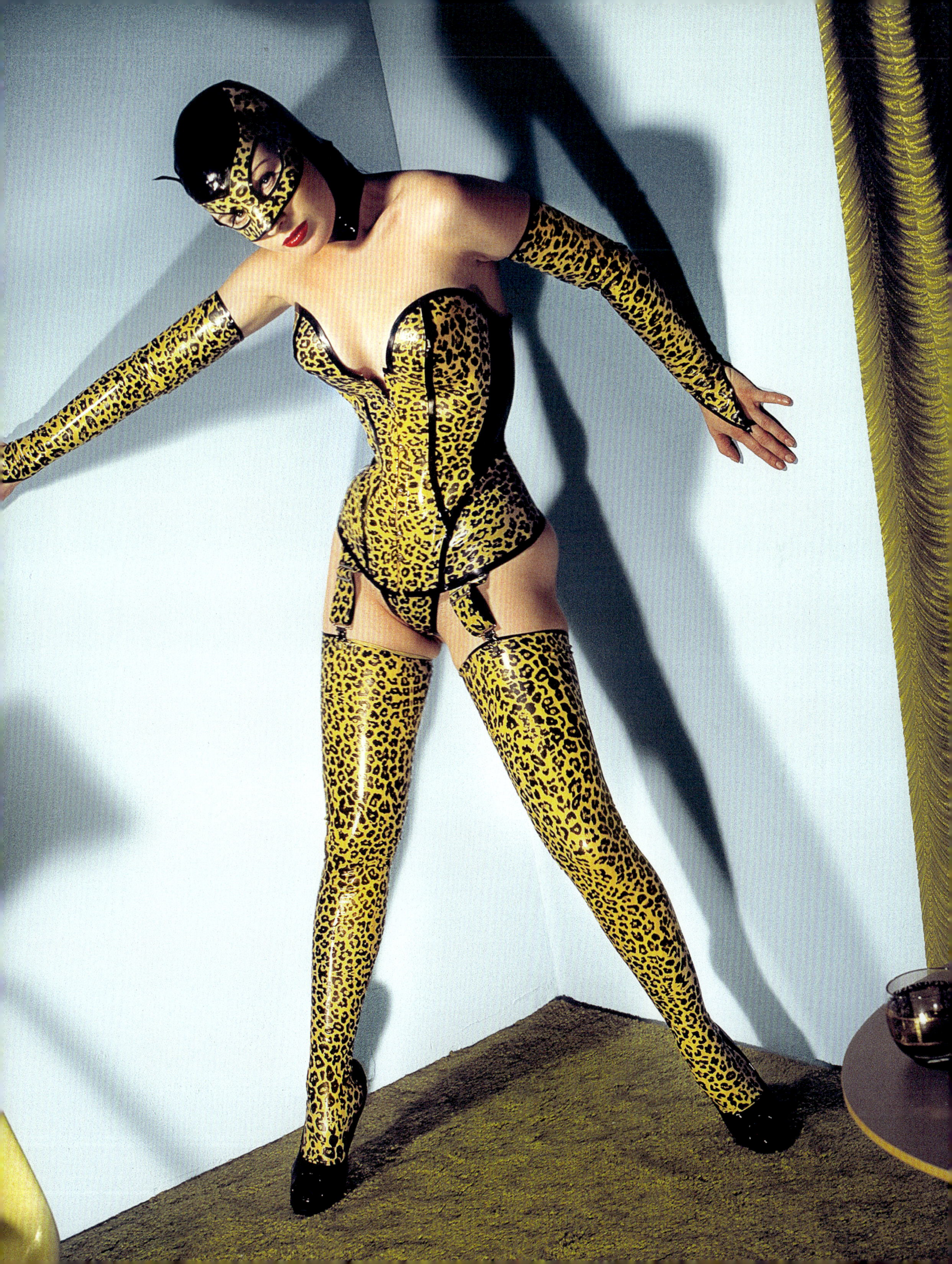

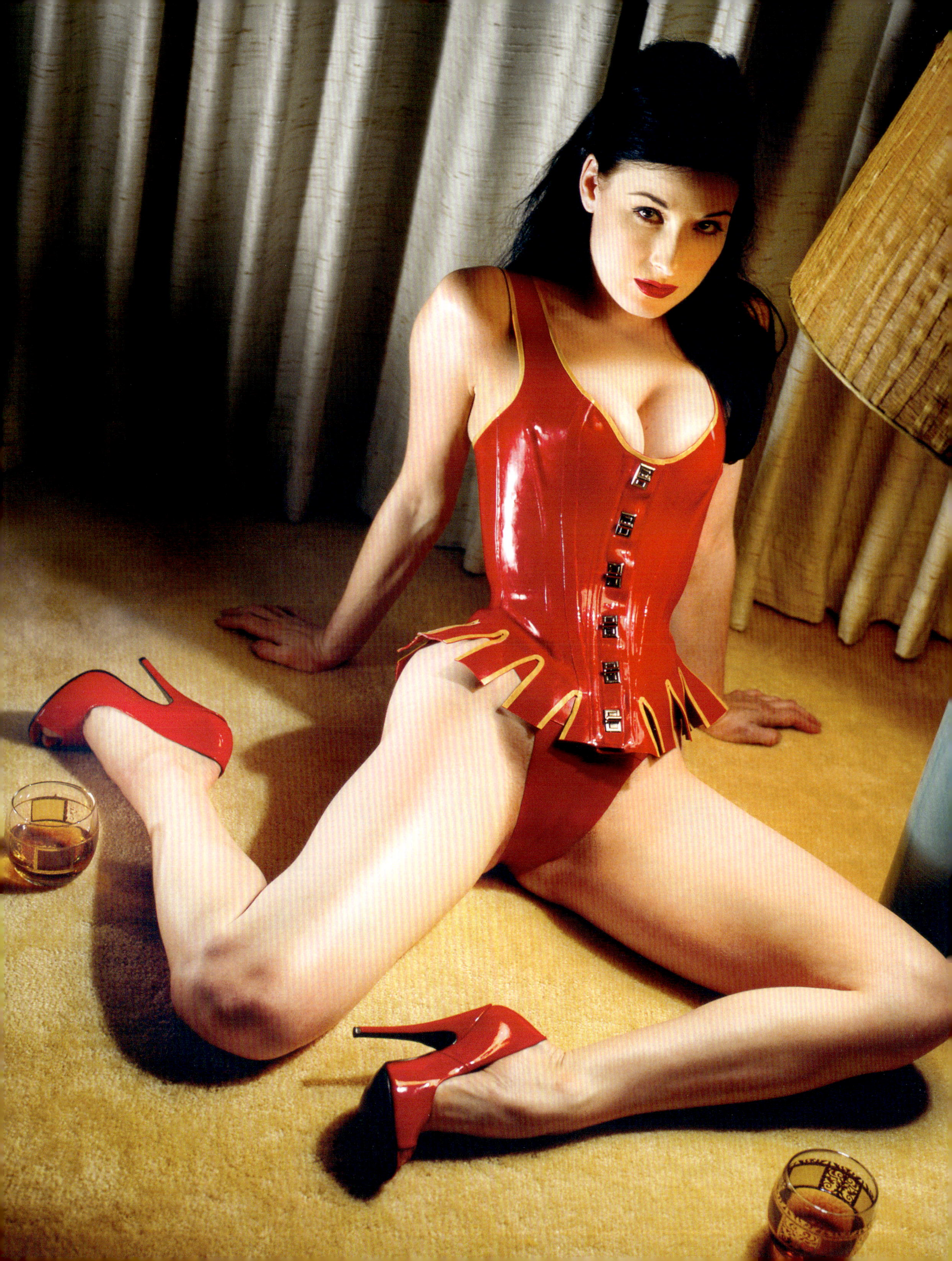

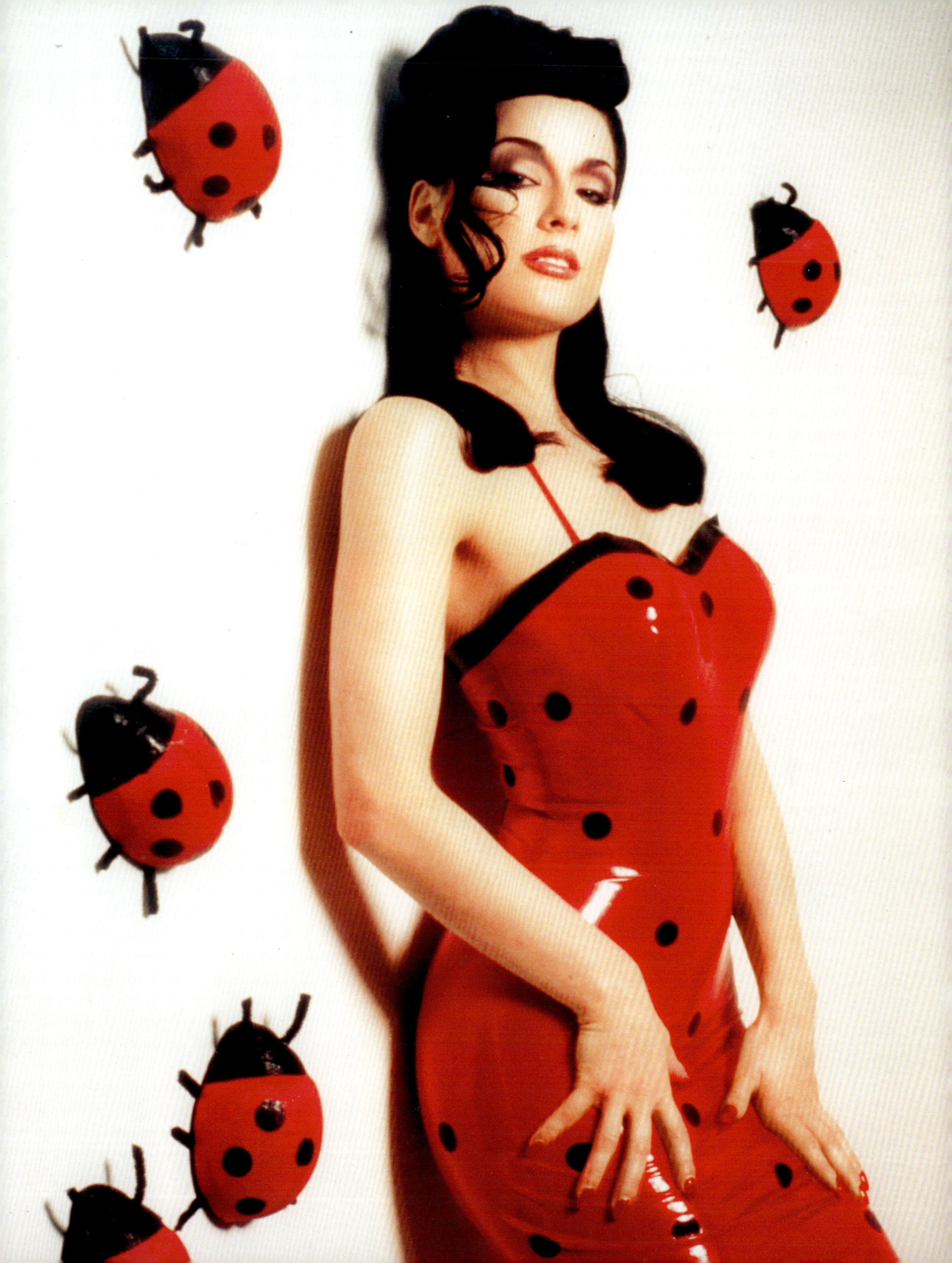

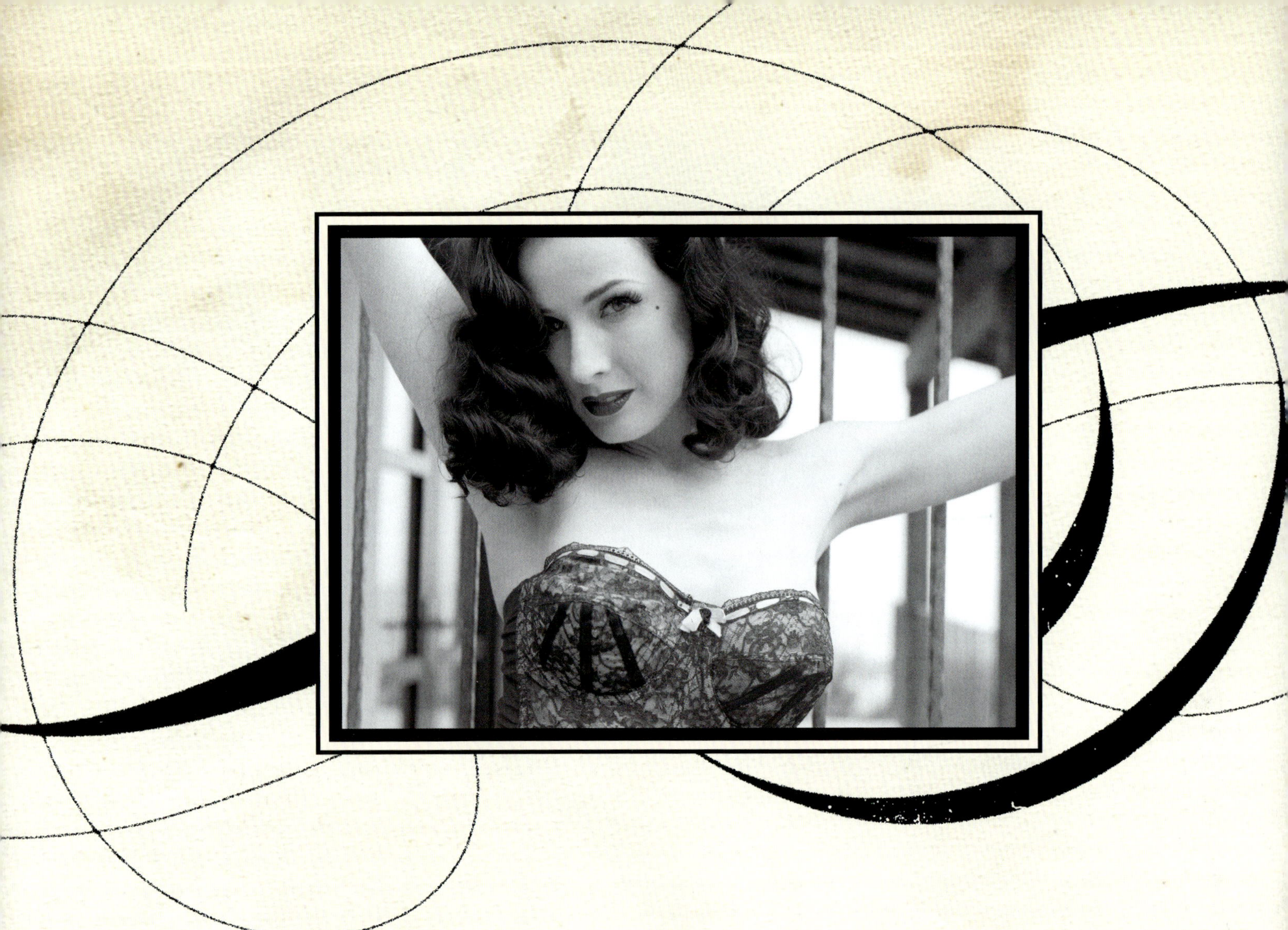

# Find Your Personal Fetish Style

Should you, as a budding fetish goddess, wear the new second skins or the old? Combine! The classics—the corset, seamed stockings, high heels—aren't going anywhere. Take fully fashioned seamed stockings, for example. Though they can appear in the theater of foot fetishism, they are also second skins because they are thin, transparent, pulling, and clinging to feminine limbs, accentuating, tightening the flesh. You get it. Well, for a little twist on occasion, I will wear rubber stockings with rubber seams up the back. The fetishists—who are aware of both fashions—love such combos! It is true that generally I prefer a more classic, elegant fetish style, but rubber is so malleable and so fun (and quite stimulating to your skin) that I can have it made into any of my silhouettes.

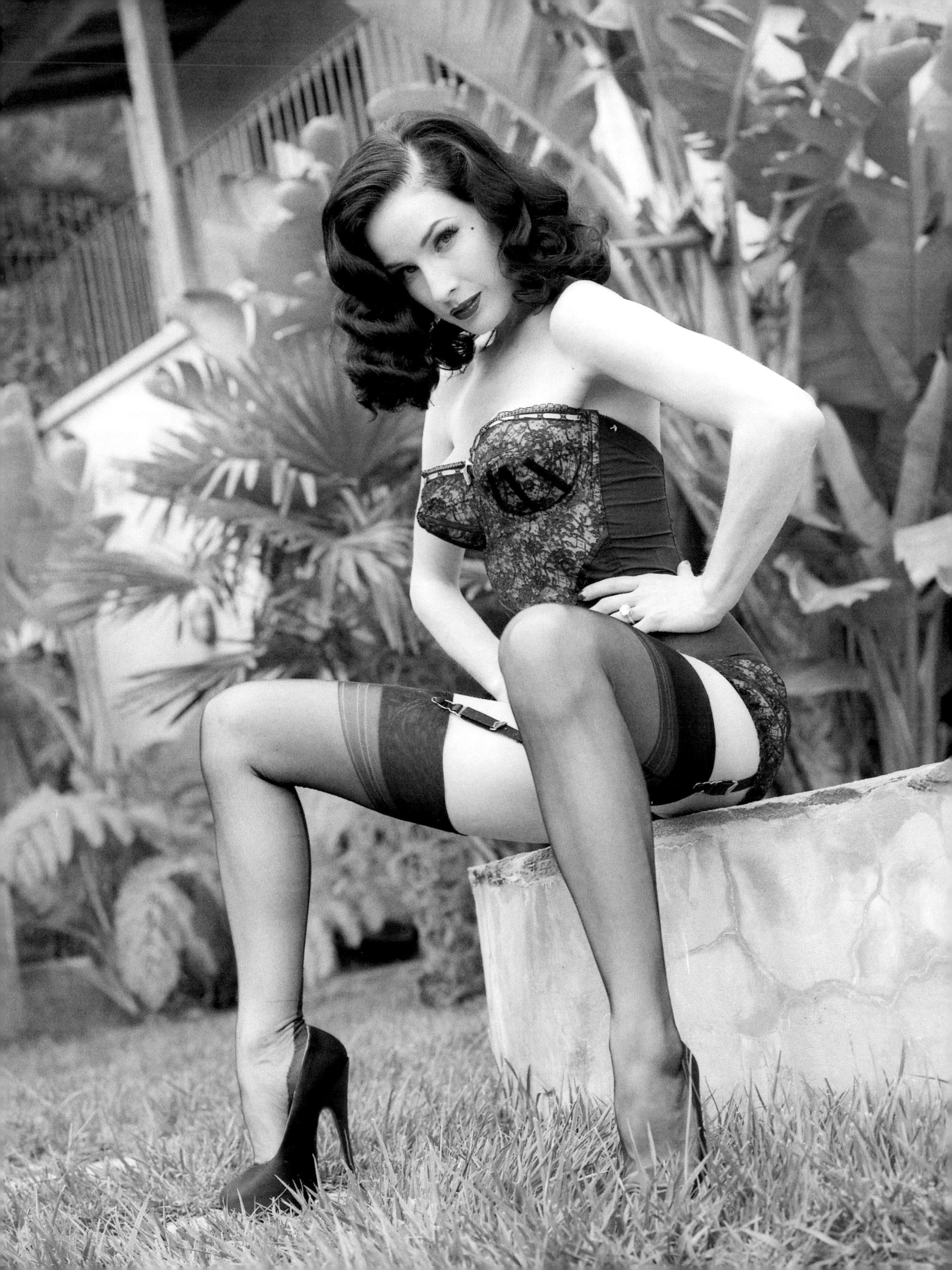

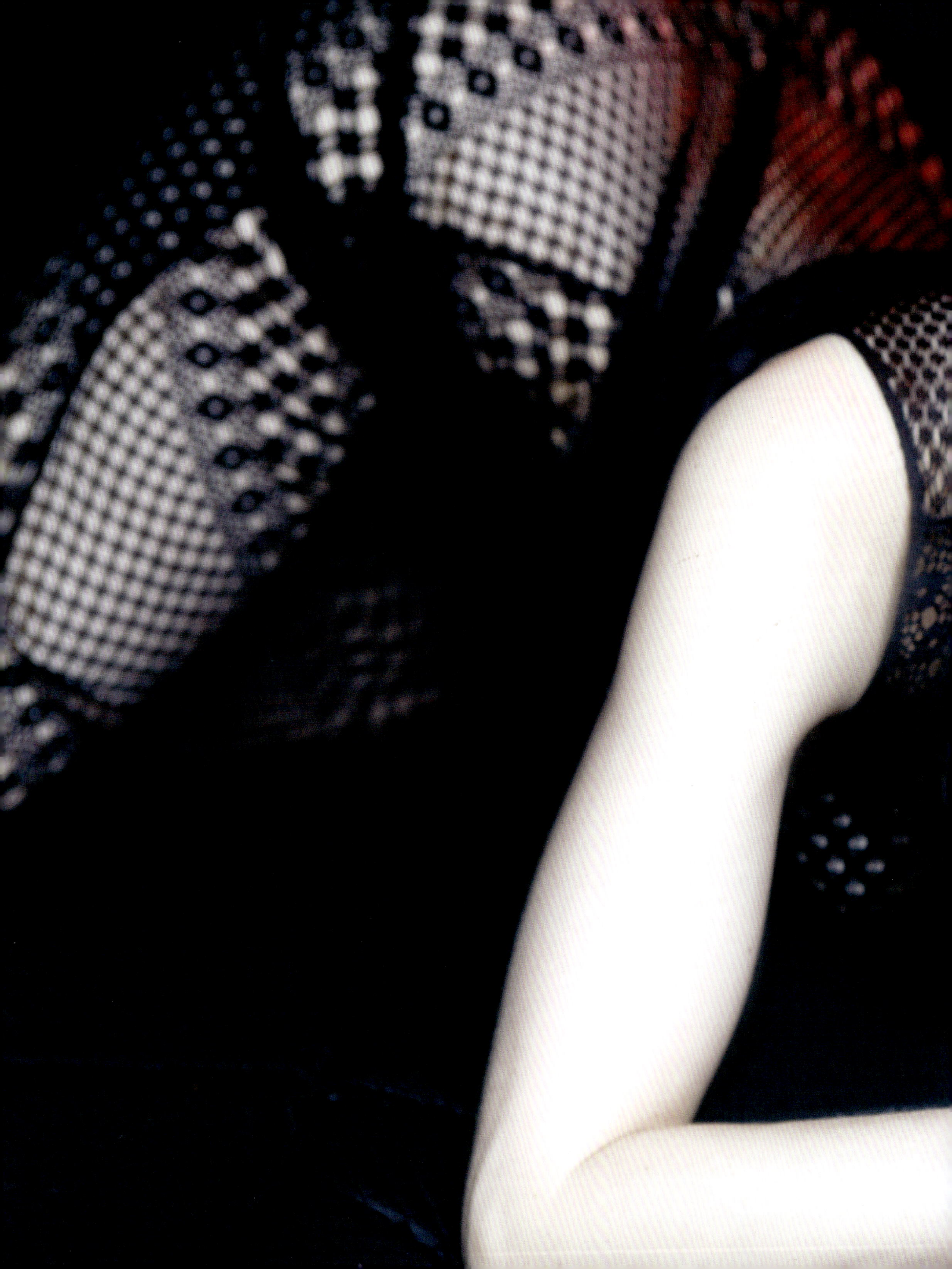

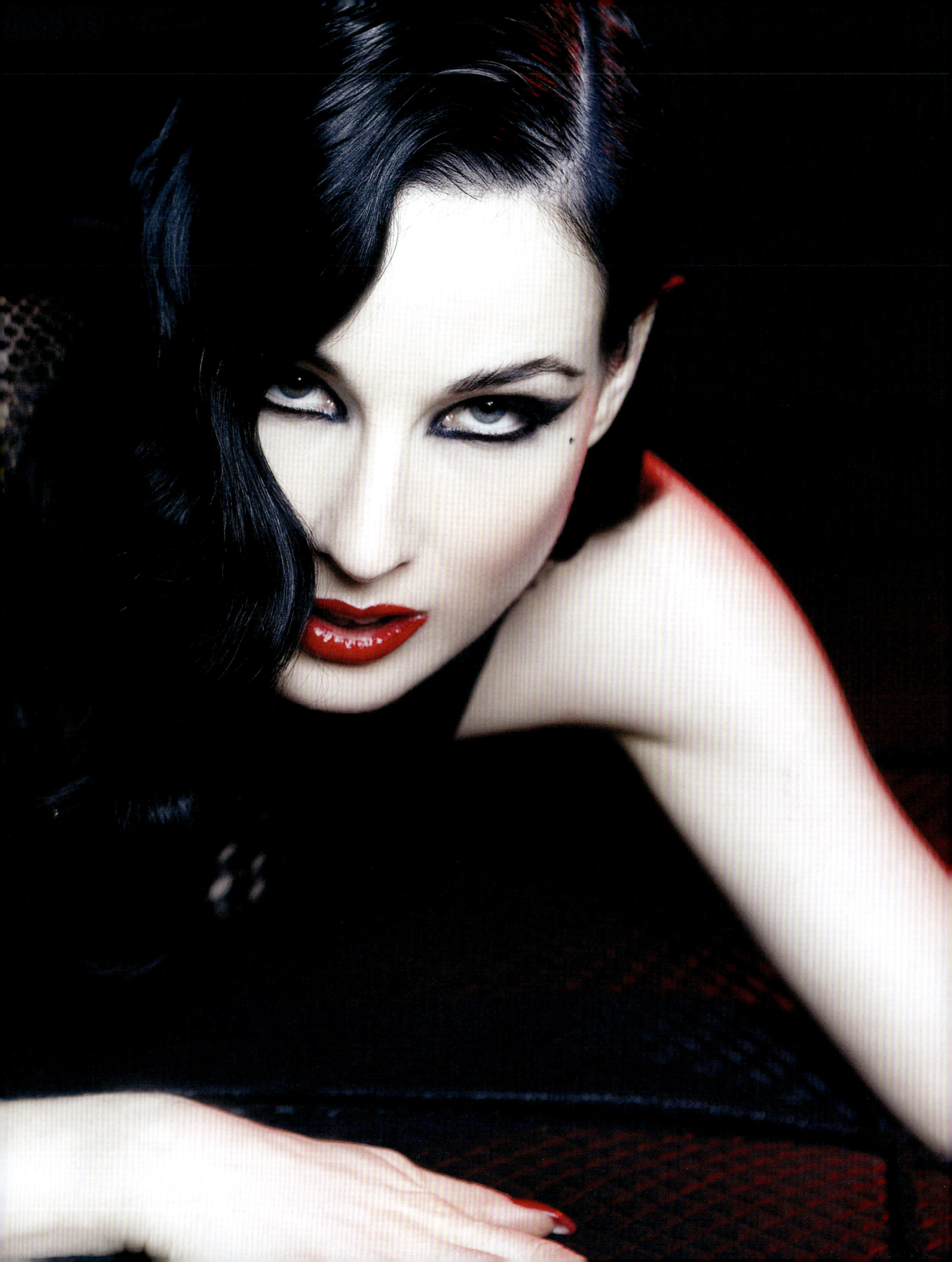

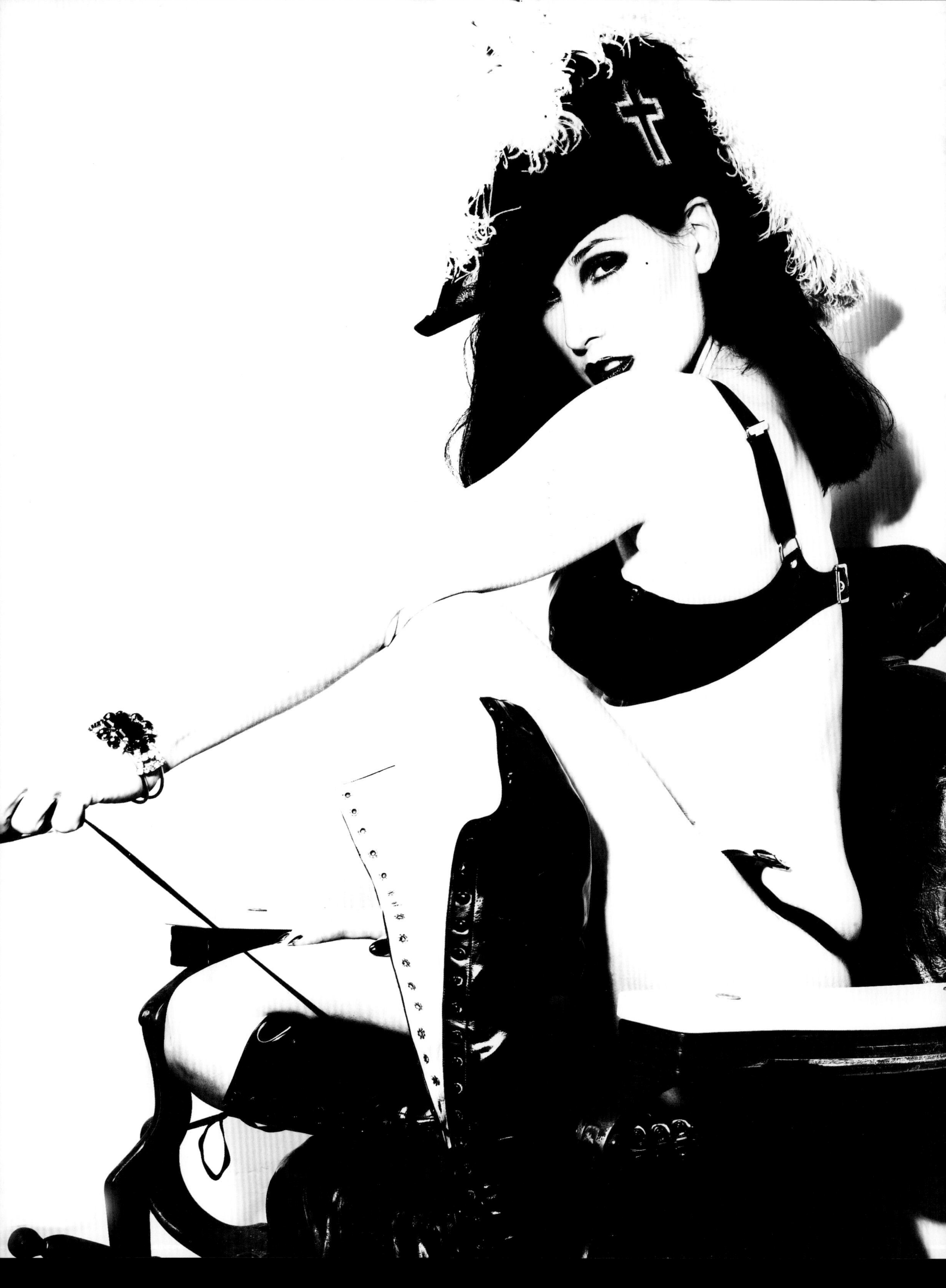

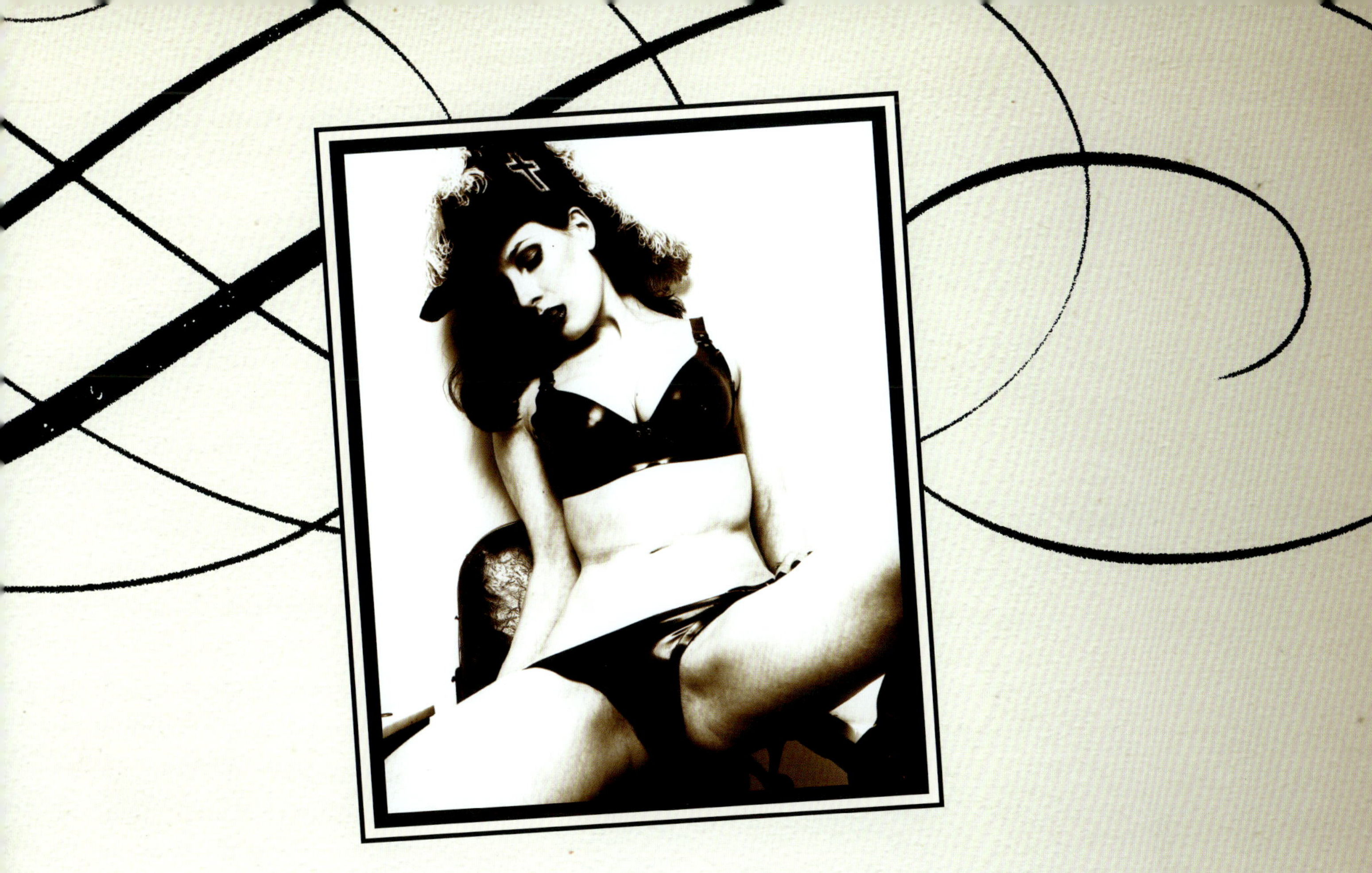

## Dita's Fetish Tips!

- Never trust a stranger to lace you up. I always lace my own corset, aside from allowing an expert like Mr. Pearl to do it.
- Never polish your latex on a tile or marble floor, or you'll regret it after the first of many bad falls you'll take for the next month!
- Don't haul off and whack someone with a whip just to make yourself look like a pro domina. There is an art to it, and it is not about who can hit the hardest! Be reserved. Be selective! And do your research!! There is, after all, such a thing as fetish etiquette!

*"Style can only be created at a risk,*
*it is a form of courage,*
*it is an exposed and often indefensible position."*
*—Edwin Denby*

# FETISH GODDESS

## *Make Fetish a Part of Your Everyday!*

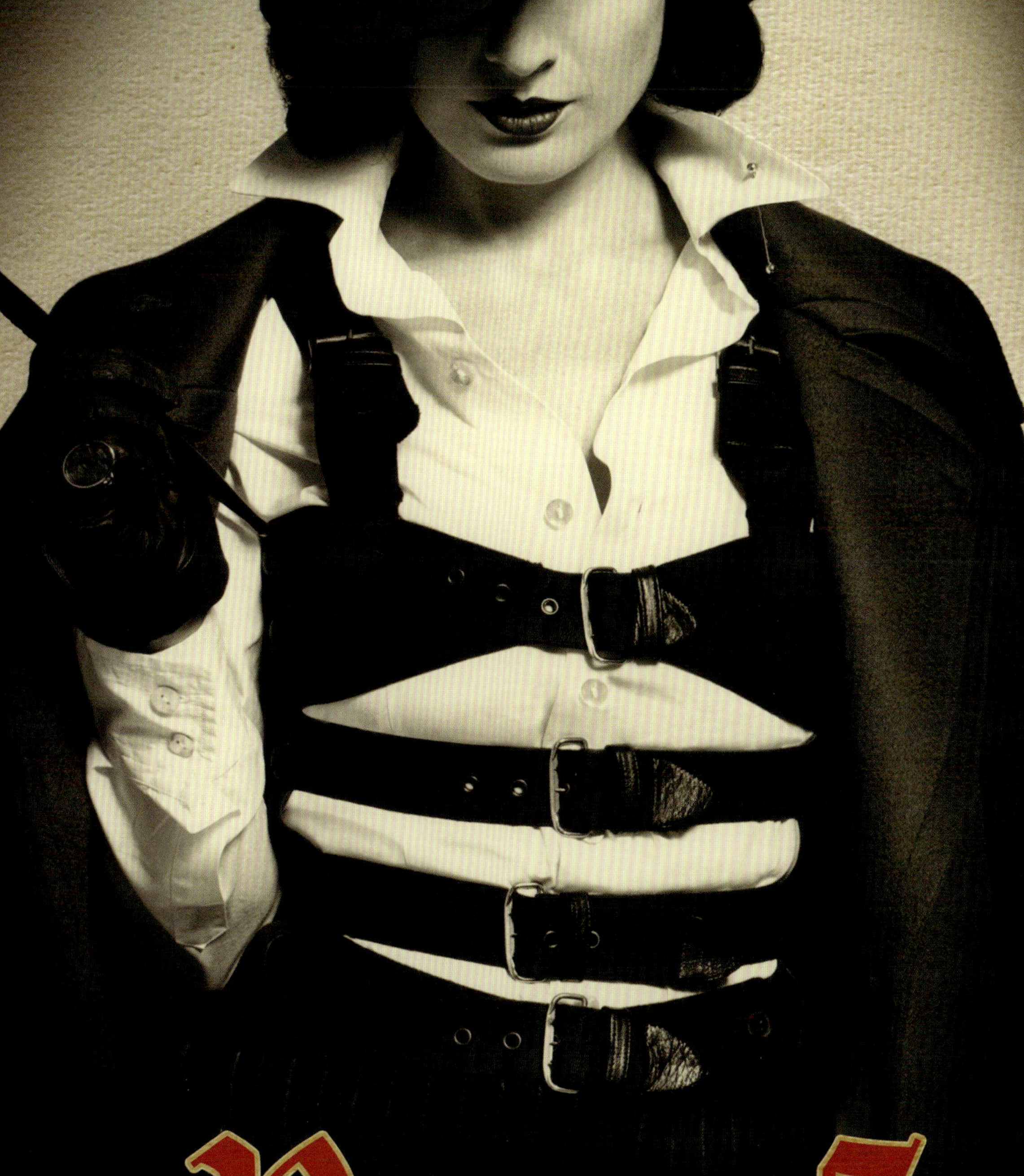

# Rule #5

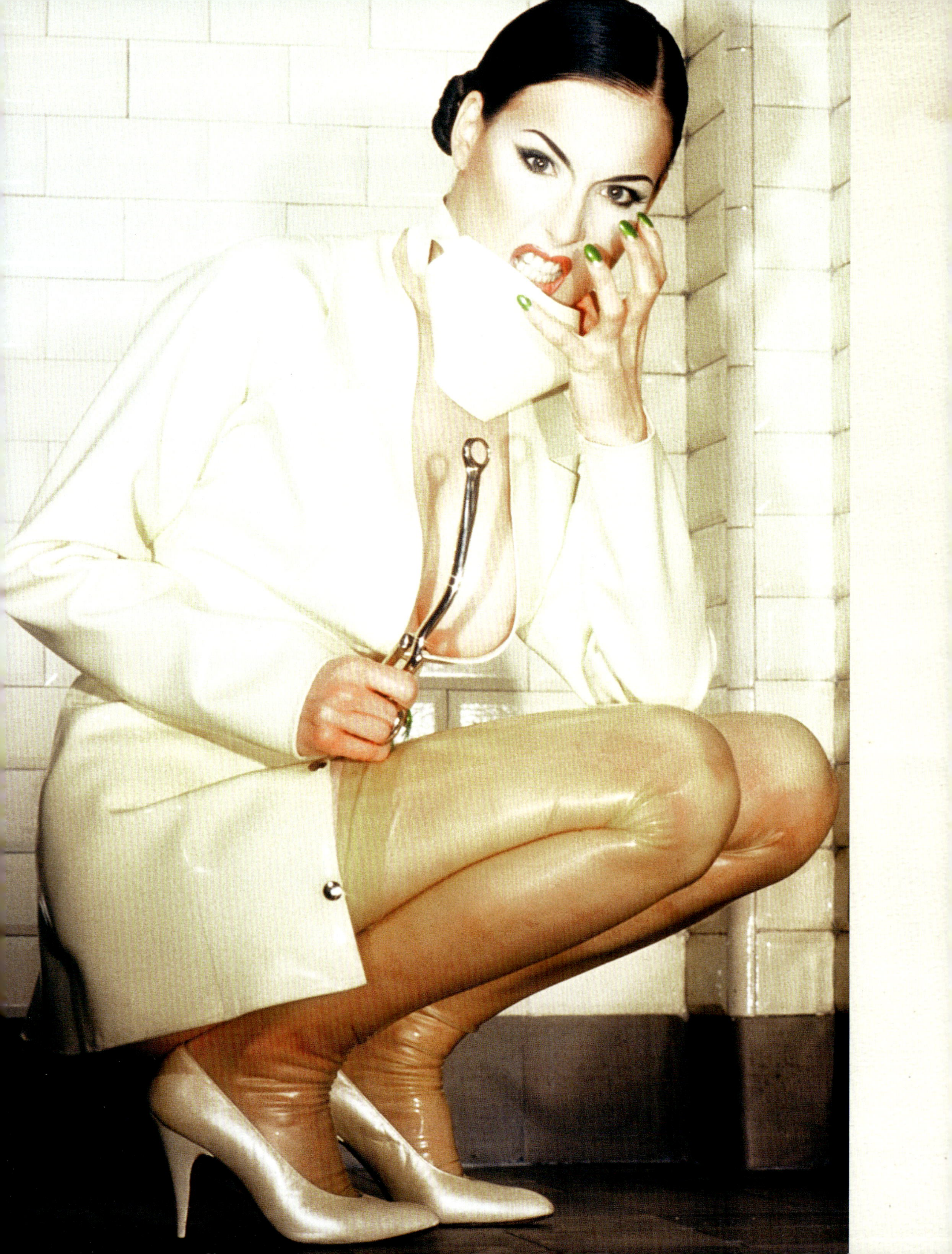

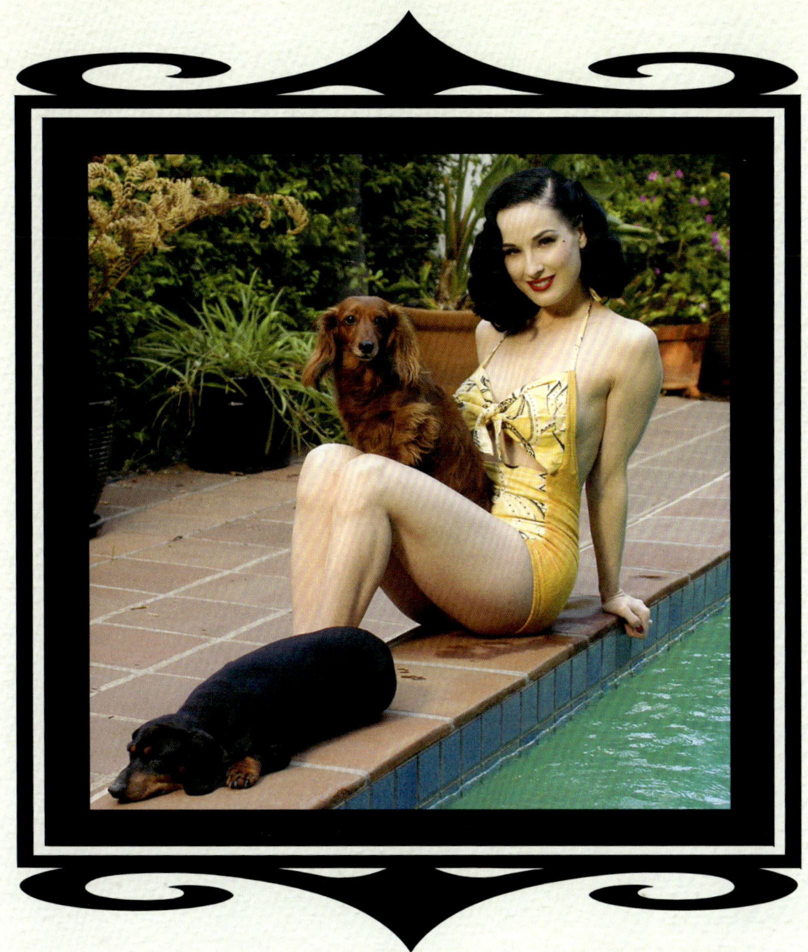

## The Fetish Vet

I used to take my two dachshunds, Eva and Greta, to a veterinarian in southern California. He was a reputable and highly respectable vet. My dogs loved him. I would drop into his office if one of the pups had a cough or needed a shot, and he and I would chat about the usual things—the weather, the news, the dogs' silly antics—while he conducted his business. And then one night I spotted my vet out on the dance floor at a fetish ball, wearing a black leather G-string and harness. A fetish vet? Yes, even I was surprised. He waved me over as if we were standing in line at the grocery store and introduced me to his rubberized wife.

"Sometimes we do this for fun," he smiled.

"Me too," I replied.

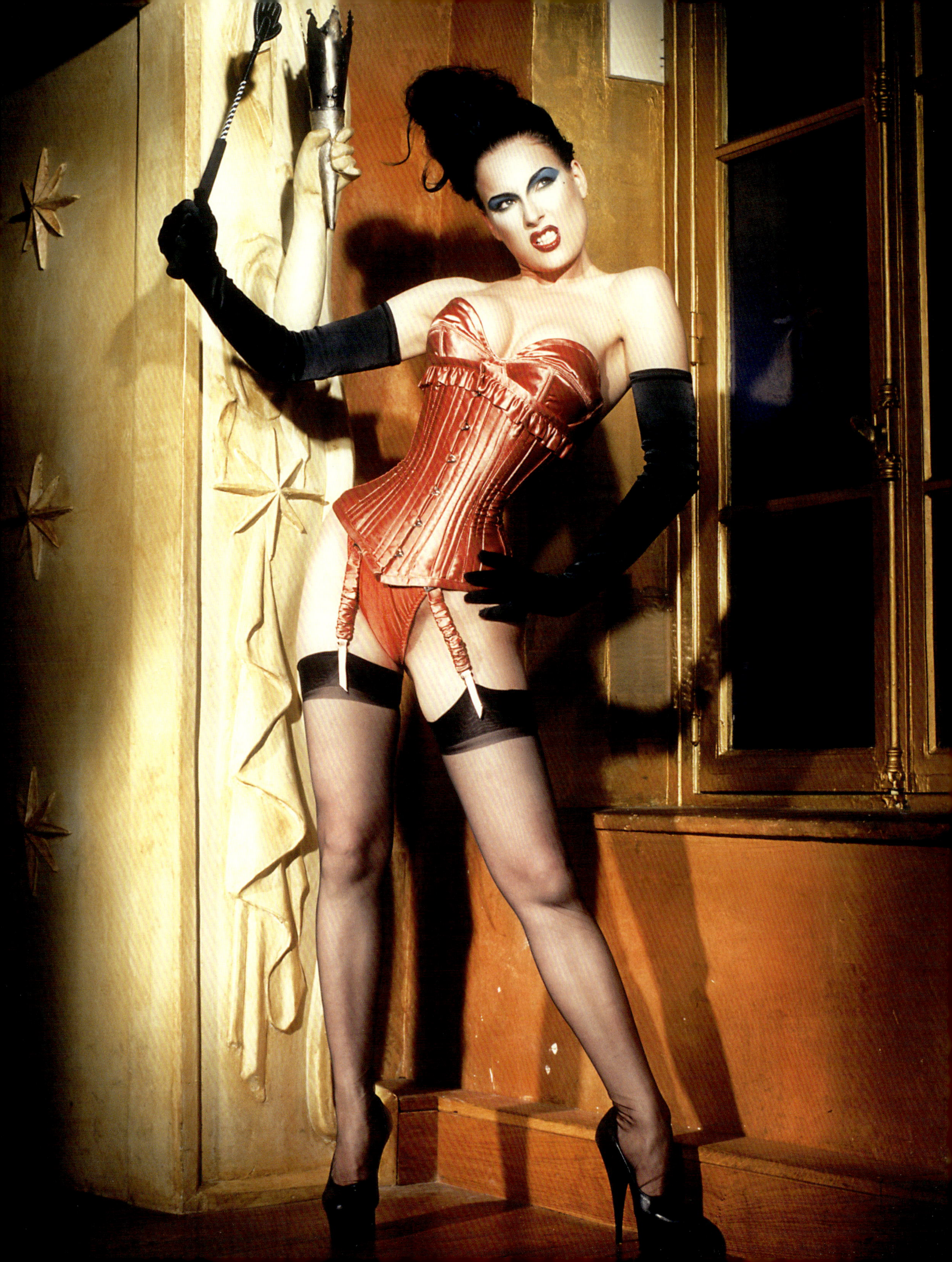

Fun is the best reason I can think of to enjoy fetish.

I learn of a new fetish every day.

What makes me sad is thinking about all the people who are ashamed of their desires, who keep their fetish for feet, cross-dressing, rubber, or bondage to themselves because they are afraid of what their wives, lovers, or friends will think. I want to send a memo to the world: *Don't worry, any fantasy you've had, someone else has had—and even more perverse!* To me, there just isn't anything creepy about most fetishes. It is a practice that has been around for hundreds of years, maybe, quite possibly, thousands, and it's here to stay. I think fetishism is something to be enjoyed, to be explored, to enrich our lives. On the other hand, without these taboos, I don't know what would happen to fetishism. It certainly wouldn't be as clever. Take one of my fetish heroes, John Willie. Now Mr. Willie published a little ol' fetish rag called *Bizarre* in the 1950s. He wrote, edited, and illustrated the magazines (some say he even penned the correspondence section). His drawings were gorgeous, just the sort of glamour I emulate: voluptuous women in slinky classics—stockings, high heels, beautiful makeup—bound and gagged and waiting for their hero.

Now, as this was the 1950s, such imagery was distinctly unacceptable where the censors were concerned. Willie's solution? Humorously misleading words: "Don't Let This Happen to You" read the caption under an image of a hog-tied beauty. "Learn Jiu-Jitsu, the Art of Self Defense" went another. As is the purpose of bondage, Willie had fun.

## The World's Top Fetish Parties

- Torture Garden (United Kingdom)
- The Rubber Ball (United Kingdom)
- The Vault (New York City)
- The Los Angeles Fetish Ball (Los Angeles)
- The Dressed to Thrill Ball (Las Vegas/Los Angeles)
- Manray's Annual B&D Ball (Boston)
- The Black and Blue Ball (New York City)
- Fetish & Fantasy Halloween Ball (Las Vegas)
- Miss Kitty's (Los Angeles)
- Club Fuck (Los Angeles)
- Sinamatic (Los Angeles)

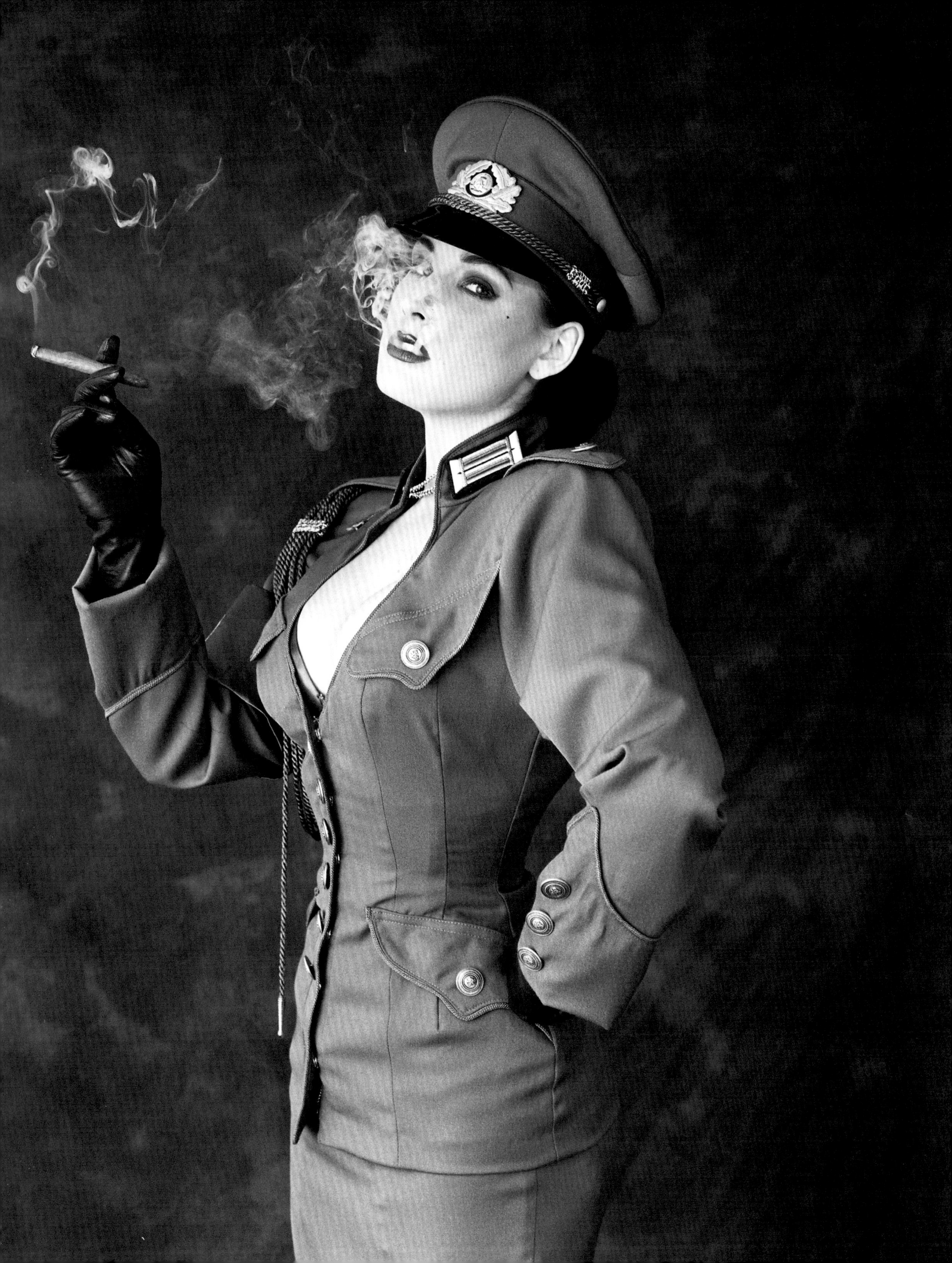

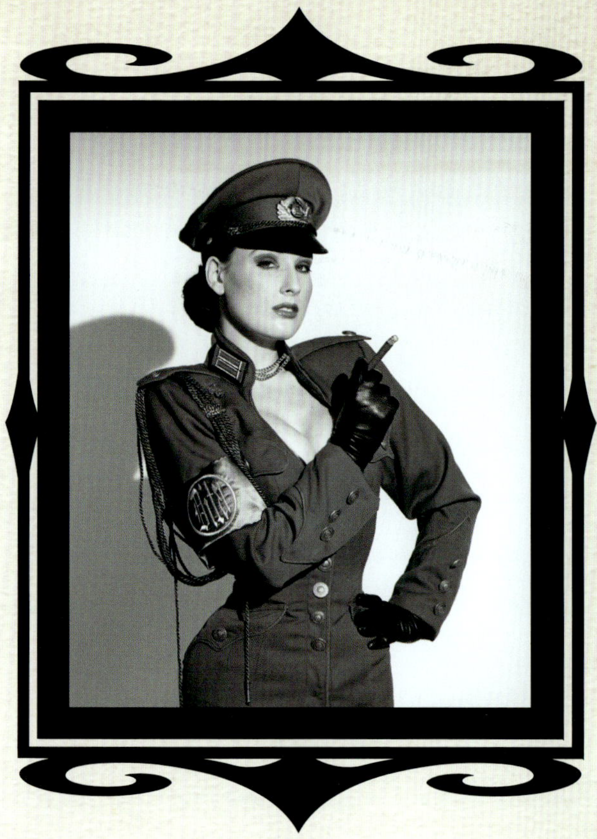

# Conclusion: The Afterglow

People often ask me if there is an element of feminism in my burlesque performances, or even in my boldly sexual fetish photographs. Yes, if you define *feminism* the way I do: *being as feminine as possible*. Now, I know a lot of people won't like that answer, and they won't find anything liberated in my representing myself as bound, weak, vulnerable—stereotypically female. John Willie called it "the realization of helplessness."

There is strength in submission. Why, I have to wonder, is it more acceptable to play a dominatrix than a damsel in distress? As my friend Ernest Greene says, "Feminine submission is the last stereotype to be liberated." So, perhaps I am interested in liberation.

Leopold von Sacher-Masoch put it this way: "Man is the one who desires, woman the one who is desired. This is woman's entire but decisive advantage." Perhaps things have changed—Sacher-Masoch wrote in the late 1800s, after all.

But once in a while, it's a devious lot of fun to pretend that they haven't.

# BURLESQUE

and the ART of the TEESE

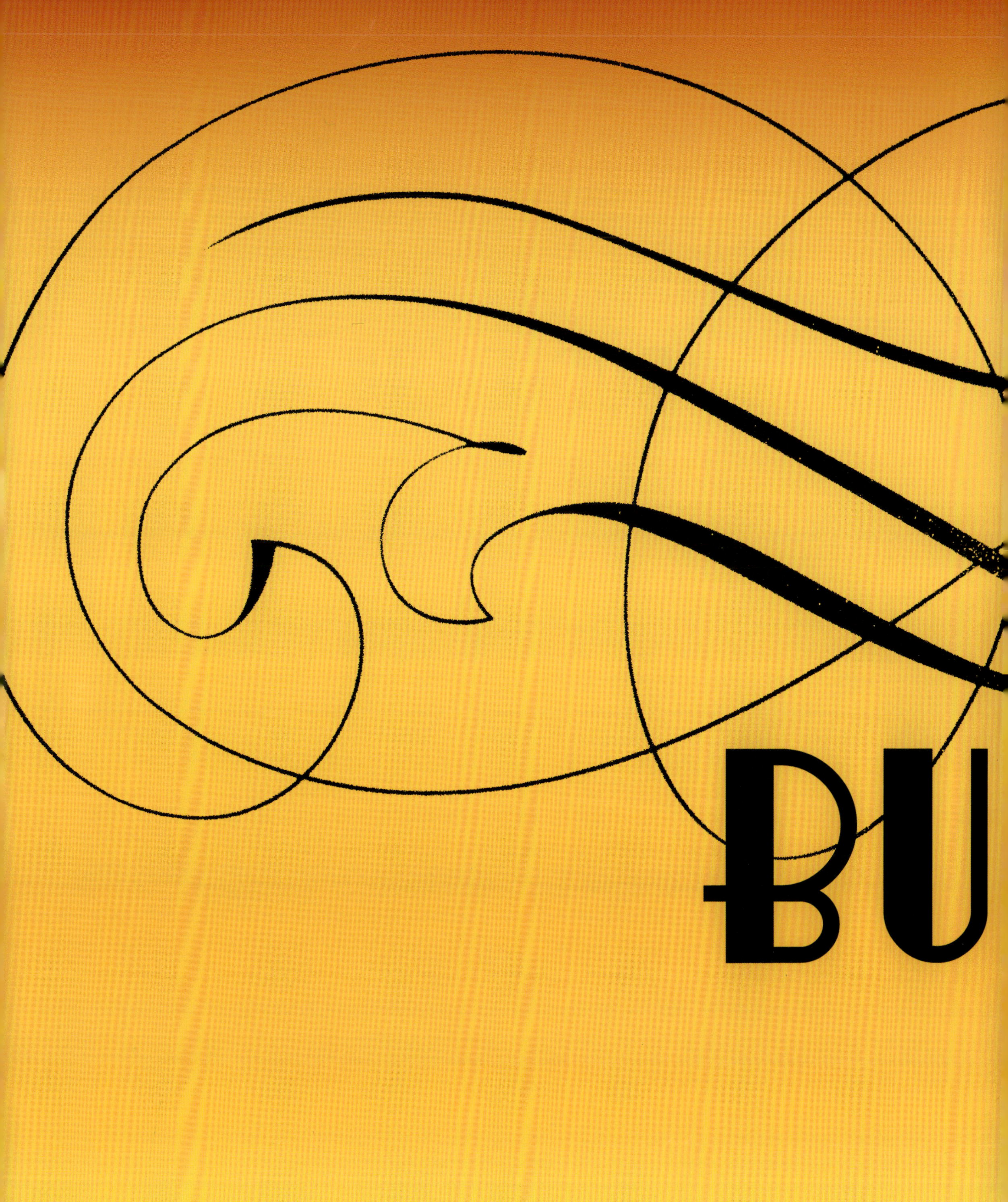
BU

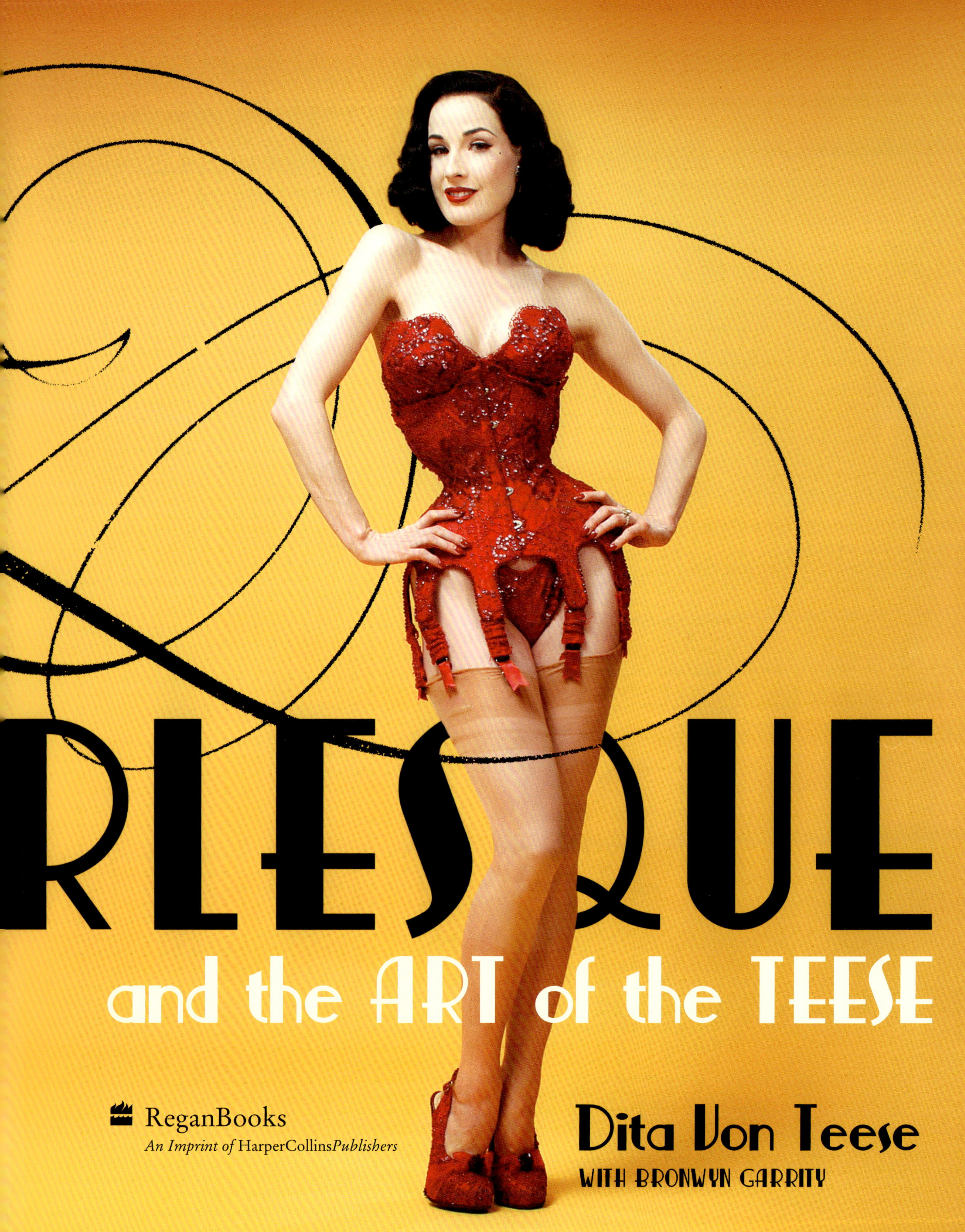
RLESQUE
and the ART of the TEESE
ReganBooks
An Imprint of HarperCollinsPublishers
Dita Von Teese
WITH BRONWYN GARRITY

WWW.DITA.NET



HarperCollins books may be purchased for educational, business, or sales promotional use. For information please write: Special Markets Department, HarperCollins Publishers Inc., 10 East 53rd Street, New York, NY 10022.

FIRST EDITION

*Designed by P.R. Brown @ Bau-da Design Lab*

Printed on acid-free paper

Library of Congress Cataloging-in-Publication Data

Von Teese, Dita, 1972–
Burlesque and the art of the Teese ; Fetish and the art of the Teese / Dita von Teese.— 1st ed.
p. cm.
No collective t.p.; titles transcribed from individual title pages.
ISBN 0-06-059167-6
1. Von Teese, Dita, 1972– 2. Stripteasers—United States—Biography. 3. Striptease—United States. 4. Burlesque (Theater)—United States. 5. Fetishism. I. Title: Fetish and the art of the Teese. II. Title.

PN1949.S7V66 2006
792.7—dc22

2004050914

25 RTLO 20

FOR MY MOTHER

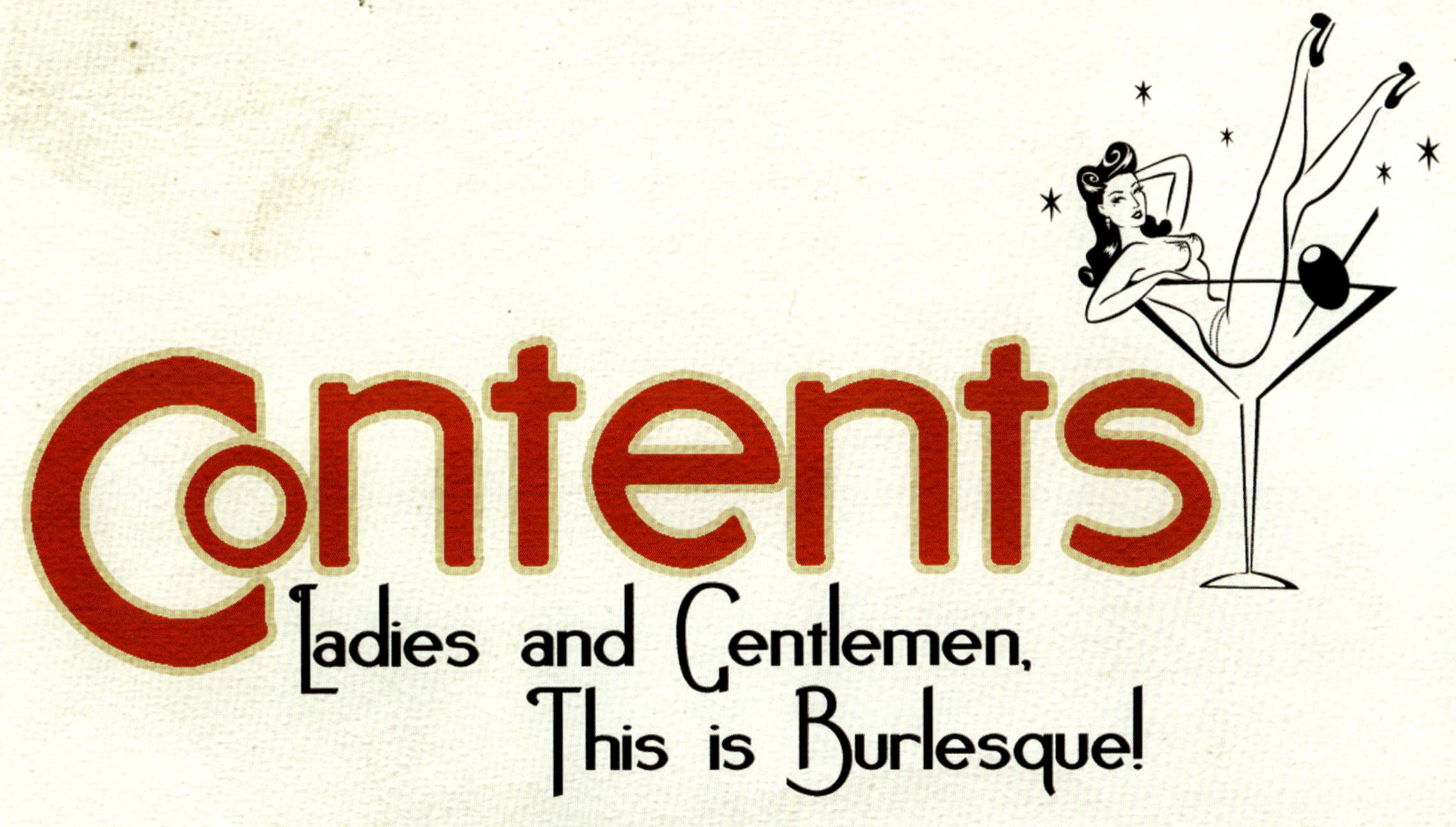
Contents
Ladies and Gentlemen,
This is Burlesque!

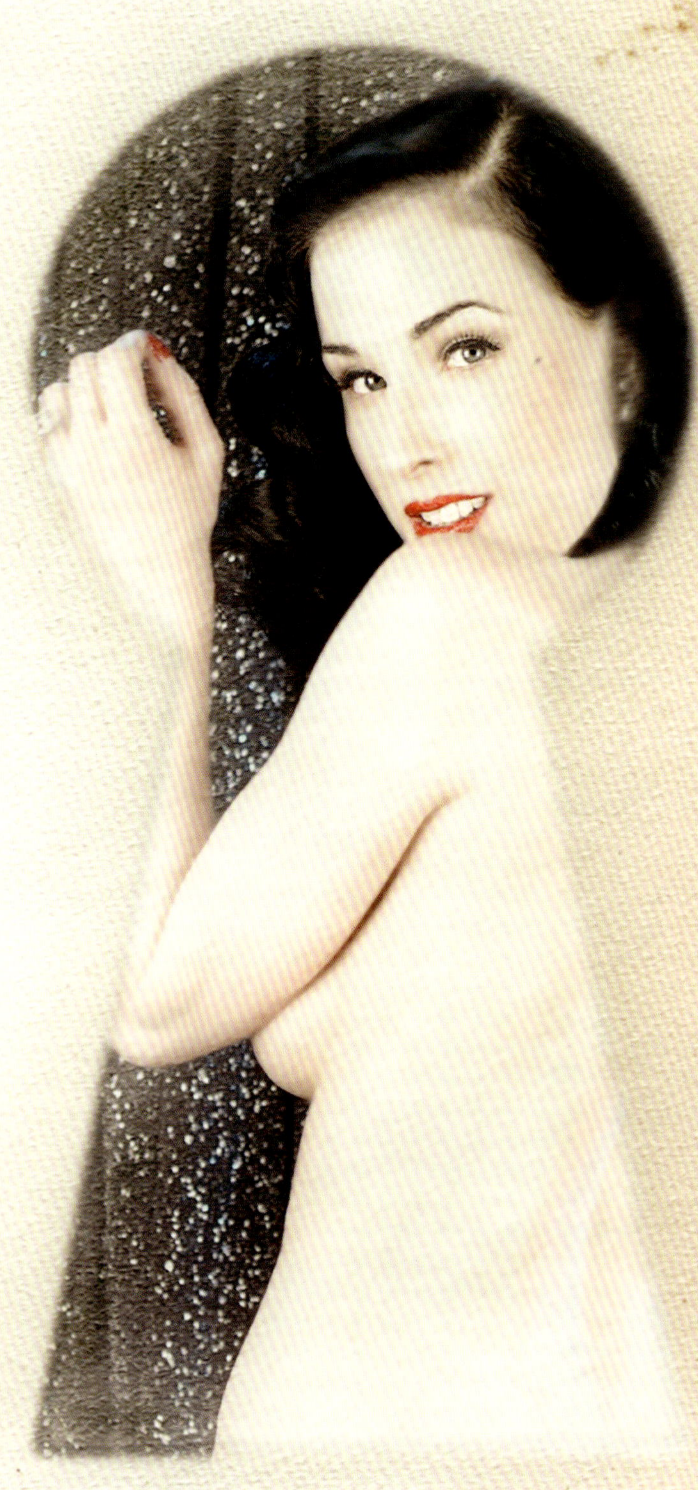

Introduction:
DITA VON TEESE, IF YOU PLEASE... xi

Part 1:
TITILLATION AND TIGHTS IN TIME 1

Part 2:
THE CURTAIN RISES, THE KNICKERS FALL, AND THE MEN WERE ROARING IN THE '20S! 31

Part 3:
GIVING THE BOYS THE BUSINESS: HEADLINE HONEYS AND THE 1930S 51

Part 4:
TECHNICOLOR TAKEOVERS, MAKEOVERS, AND MOVIES OF THE '40S 81

Part 5:
RETURN OF BURLEYCUE... BIGGER AND BETTER IN THE '50S! 101

Conclusion:
CURTAIN 125

Acknowledgments 130

Sources 131

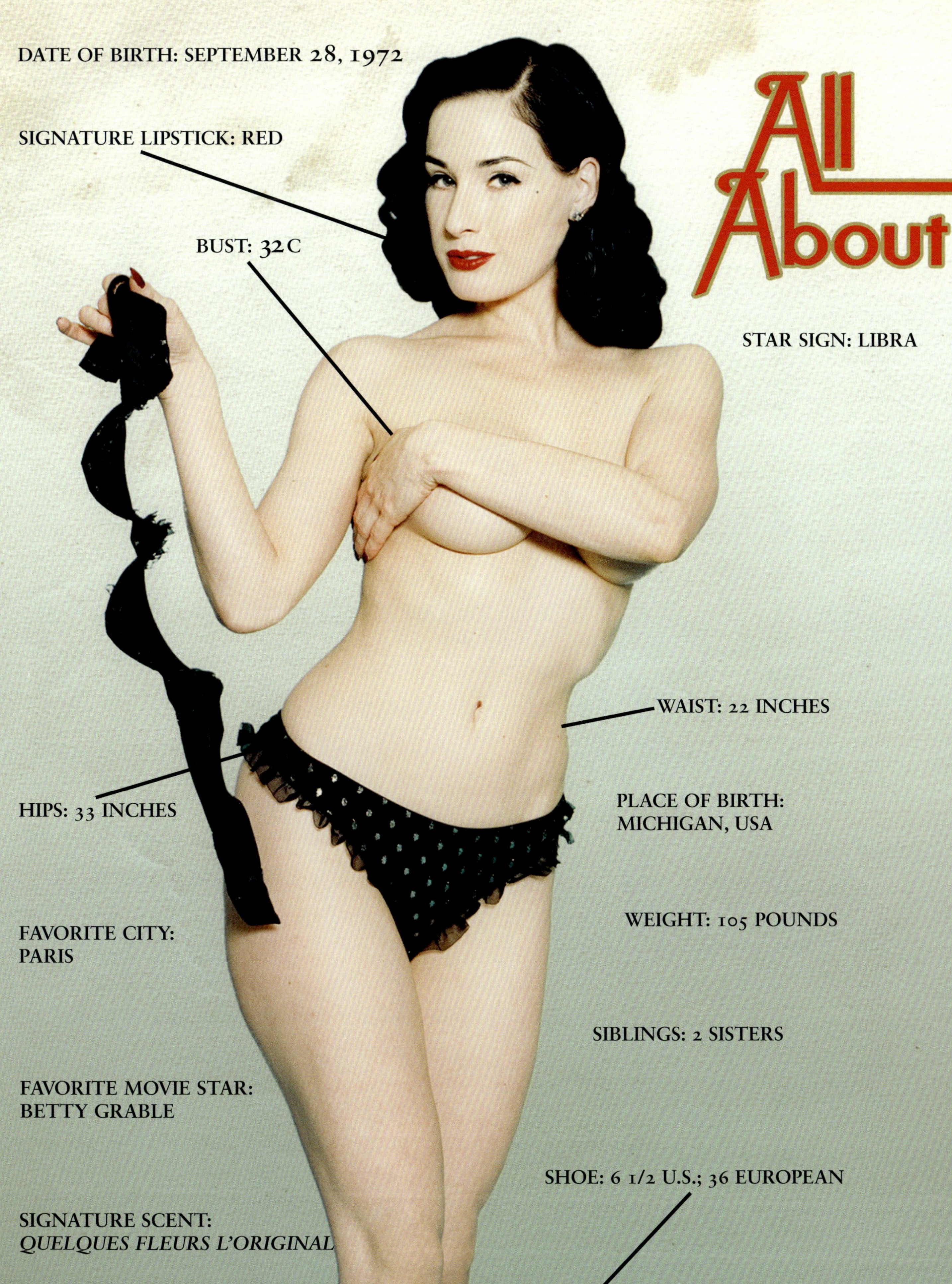

DATE OF BIRTH: SEPTEMBER 28, 1972
All About
SIGNATURE LIPSTICK: RED
BUST: 32C
STAR SIGN: LIBRA
WAIST: 22 INCHES
HIPS: 33 INCHES
PLACE OF BIRTH: MICHIGAN, USA
WEIGHT: 105 POUNDS
FAVORITE CITY: PARIS
SIBLINGS: 2 SISTERS
FAVORITE MOVIE STAR: BETTY GRABLE
SHOE: 6 1/2 U.S.; 36 EUROPEAN
SIGNATURE SCENT: *QUELQUES FLEURS L'ORIGINAL*

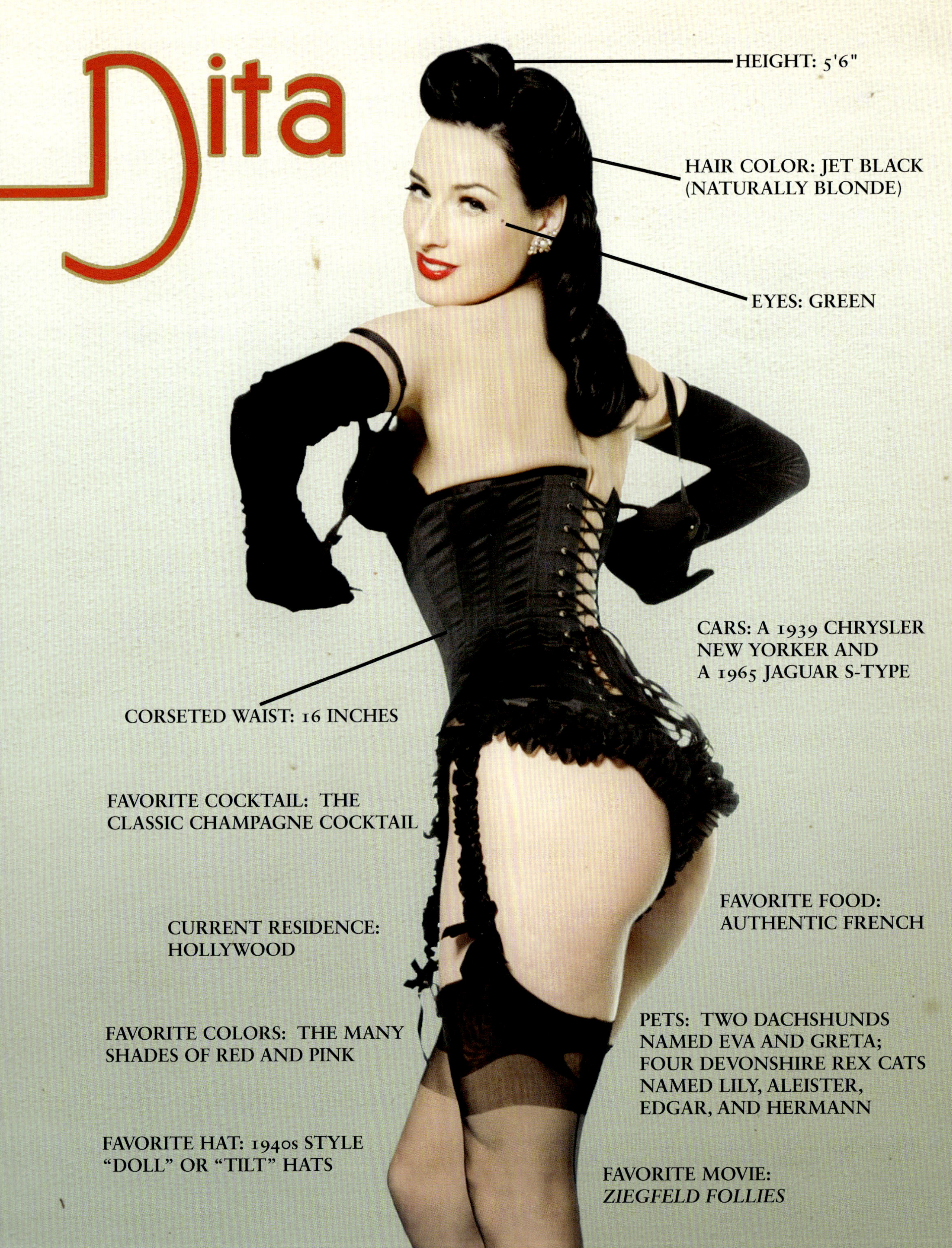
Dita
HEIGHT: 5'6"
HAIR COLOR: JET BLACK
(NATURALLY BLONDE)
EYES: GREEN
CARS: A 1939 CHRYSLER
NEW YORKER AND
A 1965 JAGUAR S-TYPE
CORSETED WAIST: 16 INCHES
FAVORITE COCKTAIL: THE
CLASSIC CHAMPAGNE COCKTAIL
FAVORITE FOOD:
AUTHENTIC FRENCH
CURRENT RESIDENCE:
HOLLYWOOD
PETS: TWO DACHSHUNDS
NAMED EVA AND GRETA;
FOUR DEVONSHIRE REX CATS
NAMED LILY, ALEISTER,
EDGAR, AND HERMANN
FAVORITE COLORS: THE MANY
SHADES OF RED AND PINK
FAVORITE HAT: 1940s STYLE
"DOLL" OR "TILT" HATS
FAVORITE MOVIE:
ZIEGFELD FOLLIES

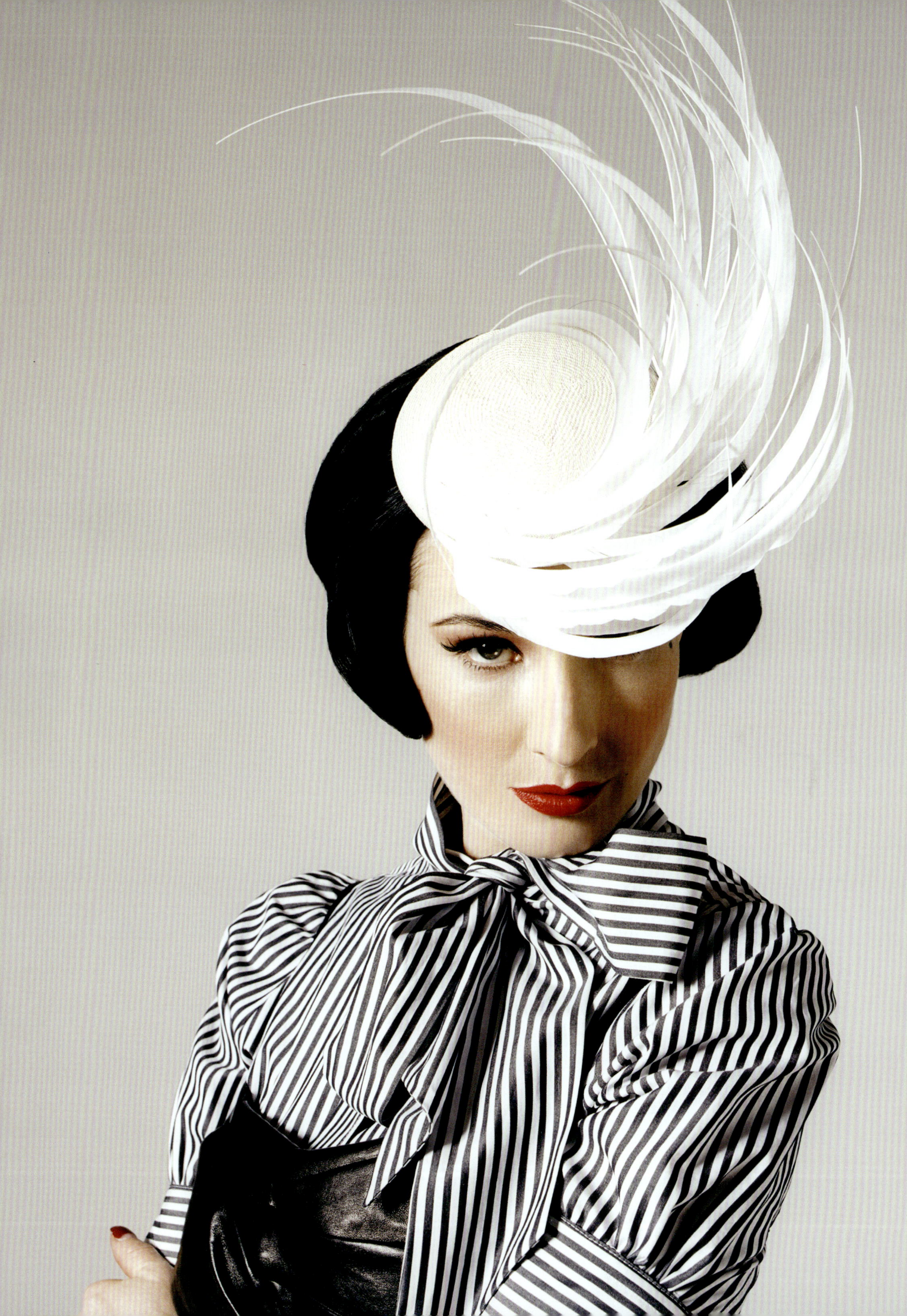

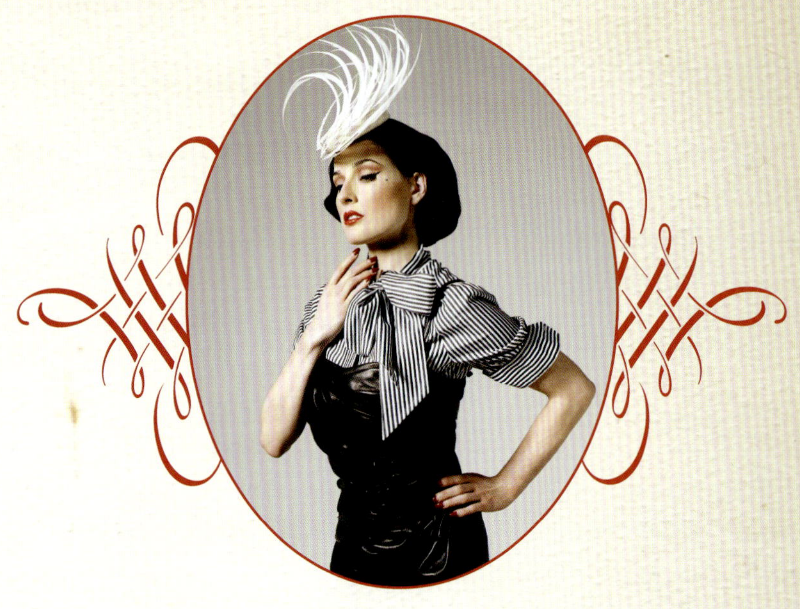

# Introduction
# Dita Von Teese, If You Please!

I advocate glamour. Every day. Every minute. Glamour. Sweatpants (at least spiritually) chafe me. If I am chilled, I nuzzle a fur stole. I pull seamed stockings over my gams. I may even wrap a cashmere robe around myself if I am staying at home on a winter night. Glamour above all things. This is what I say.

There was a time, after all—well, *before* all—when a lady dressed to the nines no matter what her destination. This great girl wore seamed stockings and garter belts *every single day.* She curled her eyelashes and she set her hair in luscious waves. She painted her lips a flushed, rich scarlet. Wherever the day took her, she wore high heels and satin gloves to her elbows, soaring cocque feathers and veils of the finest netting over her eyes.

And so do I.

You might say that I abide by the ancient advice of Billy Minsky, who owned and operated the National Winter Garden, the Prohibition-era New York theater where burlesque got its real start. Minsky believed that glamour reached beyond the stage—that it was an attitude, a way of life. Minsky saw to it that his footlight favorites wore hats and gloves, stockings, garters, and heels *offstage*. That they carefully applied their makeup before going to the post office. That they took the time to sweep their hair into sky-high jelly rolls if that's what their audiences loved. Glamour was a way of life.

Seventy years after Minsky and his brothers opened the National Winter Garden, I was coming of age in Orange County, California. To celebrate the occasion, my mother handed me a plastic egg with a desiccated pair of pantyhose huddled inside.

"Where is the garter belt?" I demanded, searching the egg. I was usually a soft-spoken, sweet girl, but this was too much.

"Oh, you don't need one of those, honey," said my mom. "See?" She throttled the waistband to reveal the idea. "Elastic."

This grotesque scene ended when she uttered six wonderful words: "Now, let's get you a bra."

I would forgive her the pantyhose, for I was about to achieve the holy grail of lingerie. My brain pulsed: bullet bras, silky satin, lace trim, ribbon detail, Chantilly lace! We drove to the shopping mall, my head filling with the big bright dreams of a girl who has sneaked peeks at a year's worth of *Playboy*s under her father's bed.

The white, snap-front cotton bra we left with bore an appalling resemblance to the bulky child's underpants I had been sentenced to wear.

I was pissed. Real ladies wore beige seamed stockings and garter belts. I knew they did.

"That was a long time ago," my mother said gently. "Women don't have to wear such cumbersome underpinnings. Not since the sixties."

Cumbersome? The only thing I found cumbersome was modernity. What a joke. My mother bent to kiss my cheek, and a black lace bra winked at me from beneath her blouse. The duplicity!

The very next day, I walked to Lady Ruby's Lingerie, the delightfully cluttered boutique next door to the pizza place where I worked. In contrast to the washed-out Italian décor at Rubino's, Lady Ruby's glowed in rosy pinks and bold, lacy blacks. I ducked inside and chose a ravishing pair of garters and stockings. I glided out, a blissfully unmodern woman. (I would have to save up for a bra.)

People ask me all the time if, *perhaps,* I was born to the wrong generation. They view my seamed stockings, my vintage dresses, and my grandly set, jet-black coiffure, and they say, "Dita, would you have been happier living in another time, when it was *normal* to look the way that you do?"

I pet my luxurious fox stole and laugh because this question tells me that I am living in *just* the right time; that these people—here, now—need me.

"Darling," I say, with the gentlest admonishment. "There should be nothing *normal* about glamour. Except that it should be, for you, the most normal thing in the world."

If you think about what I am saying, you will see that it makes sense.

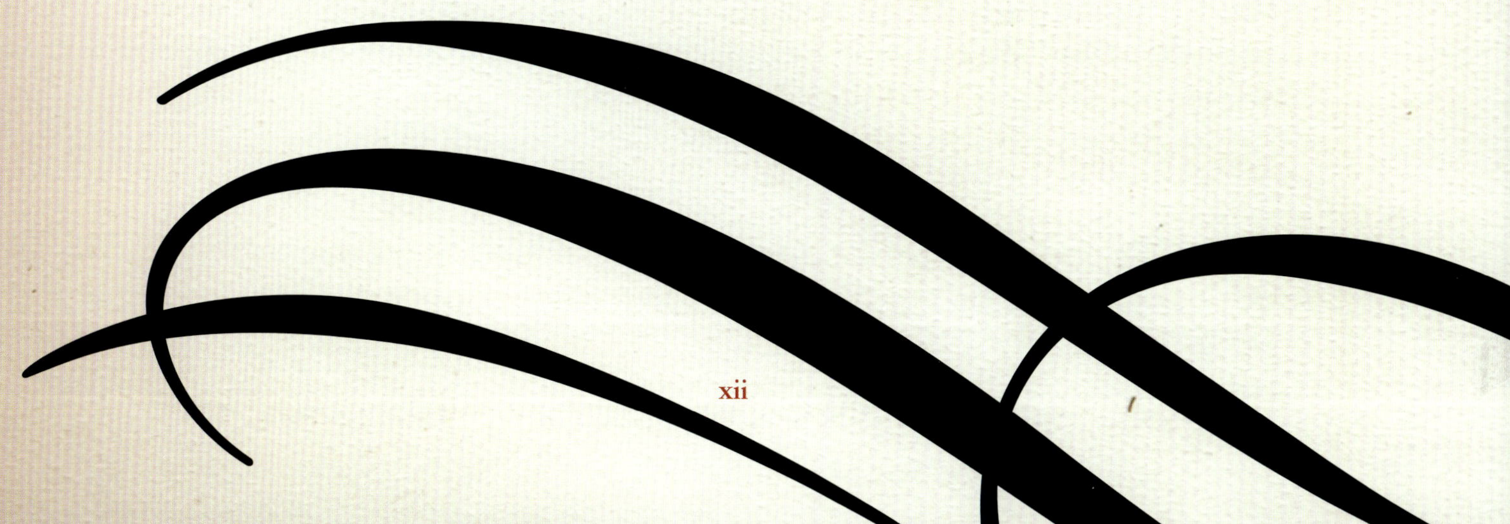

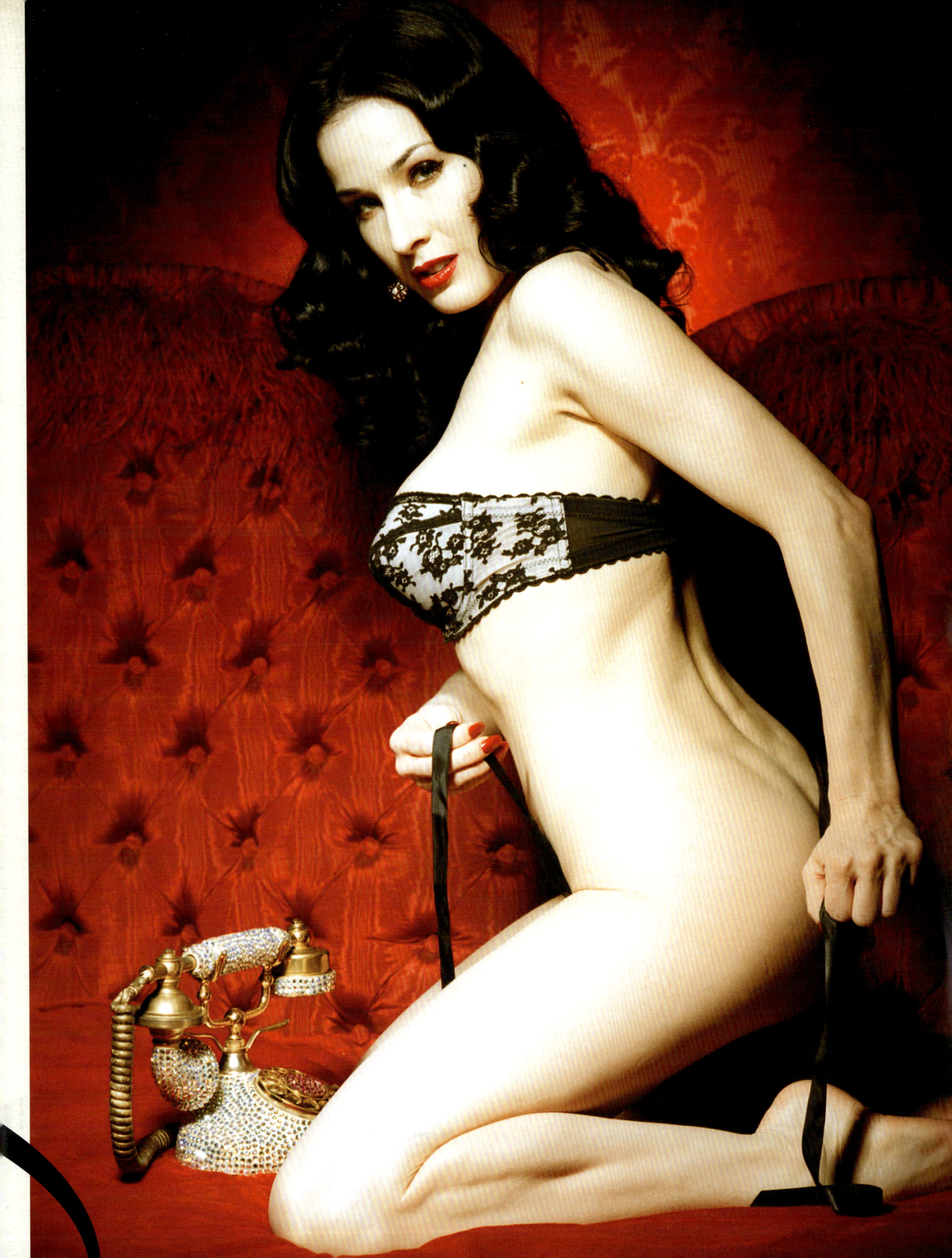

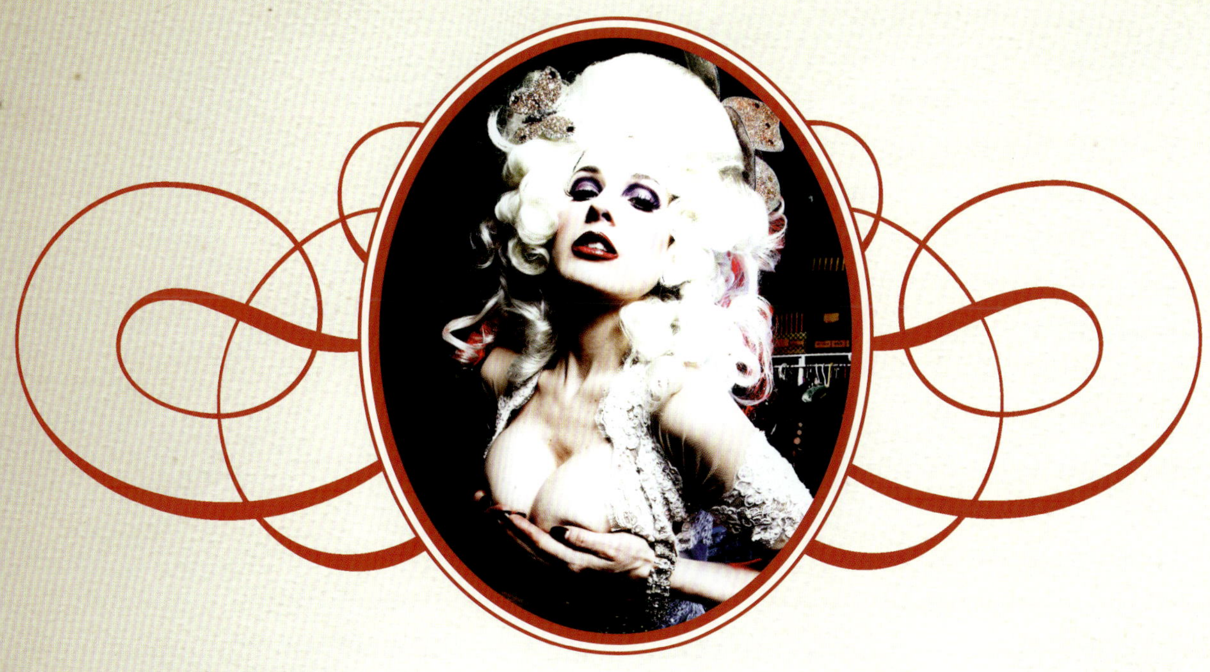

# The Opulence of Paris!

The other day, I was at the Ritz in Paris—my favorite hotel in my very favorite city. I had come for a photo shoot and to meet the legendary corset-maker, the charming Mr. Pearl, on the scene to measure for my very own Pearl corset. Mr. Pearl, you should know, is the picture of masculine refinement. Corseted (as always) under a finely tailored suit, he is a gorgeous reminder of the days when dandies were the height of fashion in Paris.

Well, the room was an editorial zoo, and I watched Mr. Pearl drift away to the window to look out over the historic Place Vendome. You can be certain I left the editors prattling at the sofa and walked to where Mr. Pearl stood. Not far below, people were strolling in and out of the couture boutiques, but I was not seeing *them*. No, no. I was seeing the starched, sky-blue magnificence of Napoleon's trumpeters marching in the sunshine. I was seeing the lustrous glinting diamonds of visiting royalty disembarking from their carriages. I could see every stitch of the silk brocades, the rustling petticoats, the embroidered, lace-encrusted finery of long-ago ladies swanning about the boulevard!

Mr. Pearl saw it, too. "Can you imagine?" he whispered, his voice delicate as crystal. "The centuries, the treasures passing forever along these busy streets?"

I had met my *soul mate de glamour.*

I should say that although I have something of an ongoing love affair with the past, I do not wear *only* vintage; there are many modern designers whose work I admire. But, as I discovered at twelve, modernity has removed breathtaking costumes from our closets to make room for sweatpants and "sensible" threads. History is so rich in style and story—in femininity—I cannot resist it. Indeed, I have many closets full of dazzling finds; I devote entire rooms

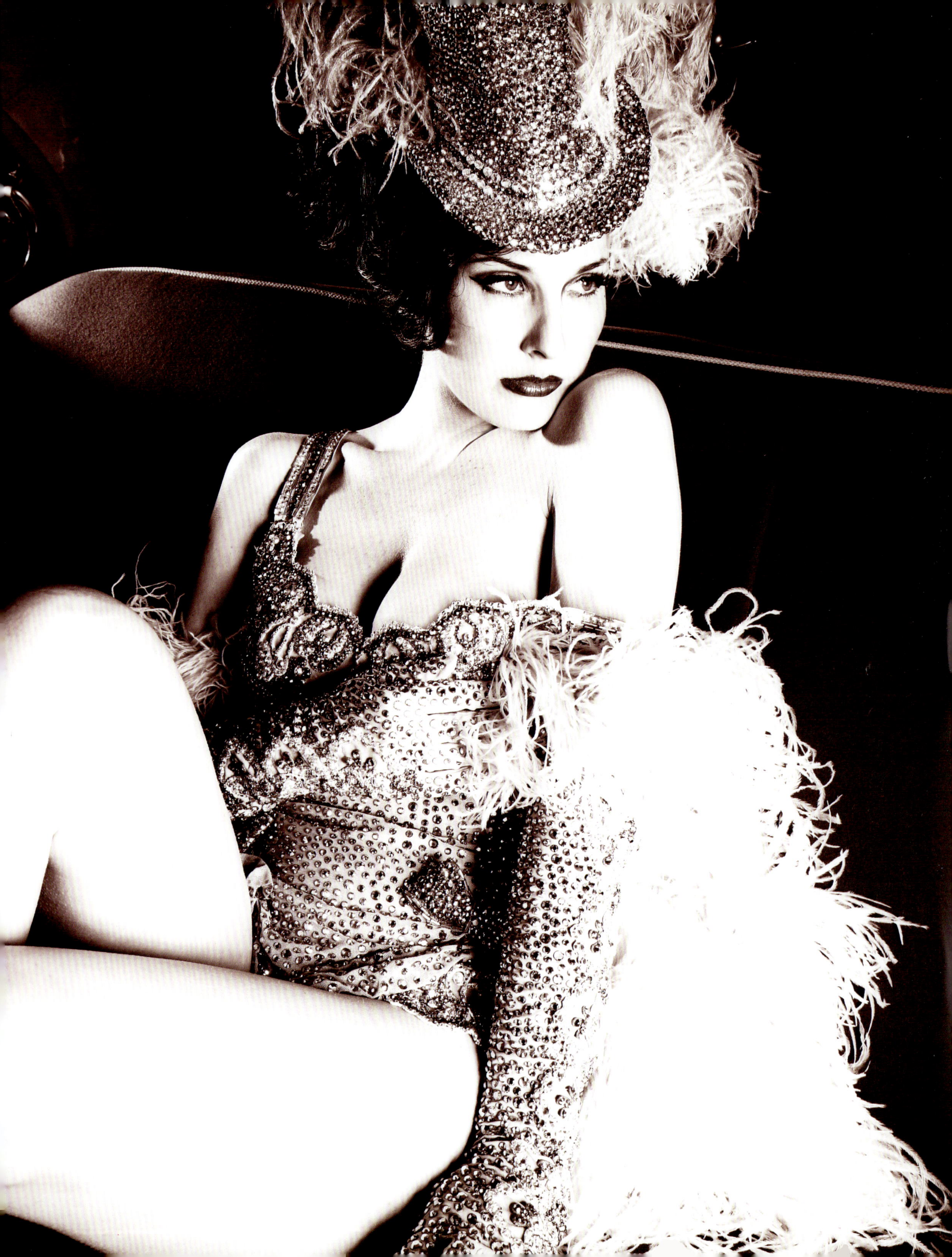

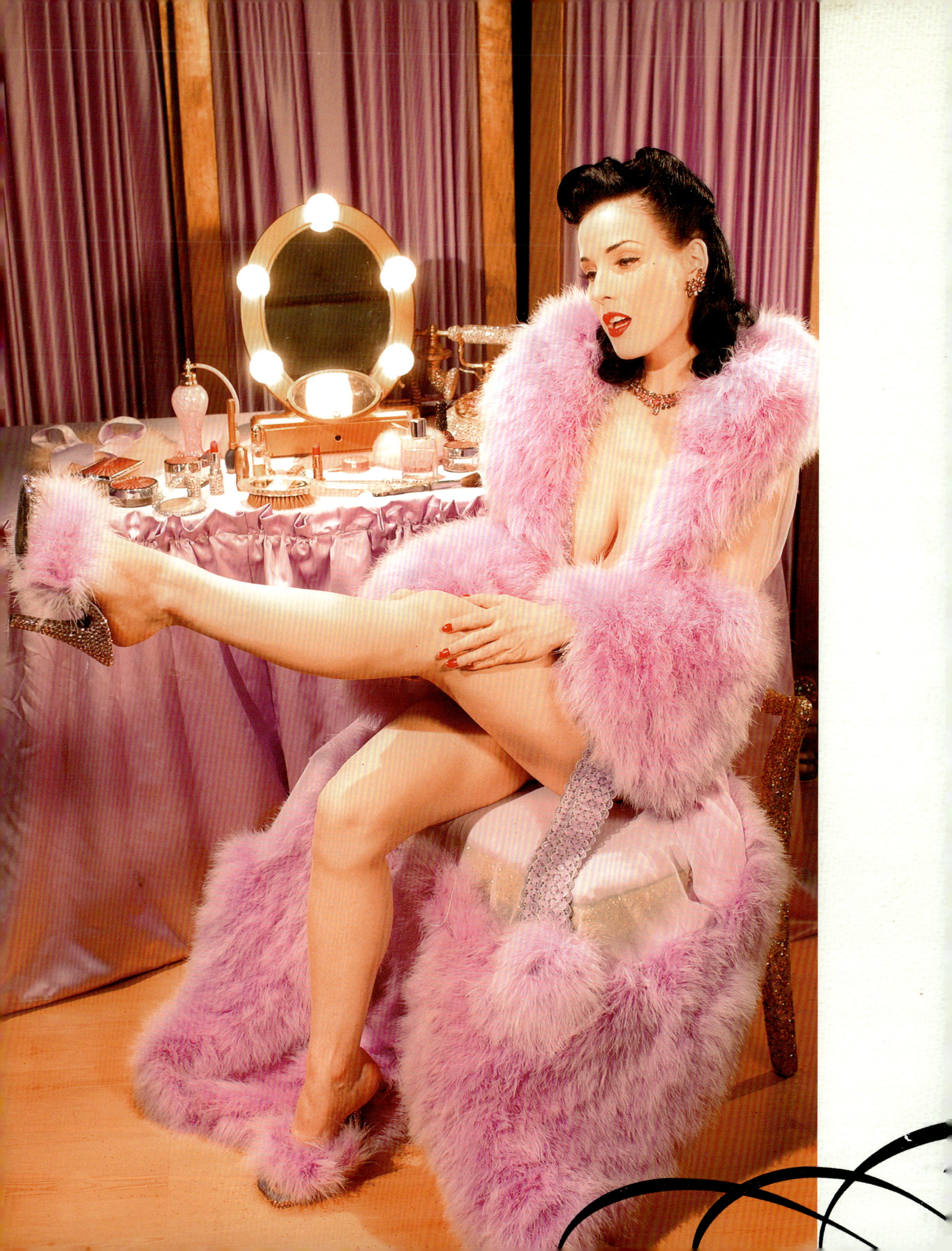

to my trove. I own a hand-sewn corset from la belle époque in Paris, detailed with creamy silk bows for a petite child of a girl. And, I am guardian to a 1940s shoe collection owned by the wife of a wealthy doctor. They are tiny things, and gorgeous still. Whoever she was, she took meticulous care, housing them in their original billiard green boxes, complete with receipts inside. This lady signed each ticket over to her husband—now, he kept her in style!

Of course, I must wear my things very carefully. Though I believe the world should see them—that wearing them keeps them alive—these pieces have survived more than sixty years, and I cannot be the person to extinguish them. If I take extra care with my doll hats, my fancy dresses, my slips, and marabou robes, they will live as long as I, stories intact.

## DON'T CALL ME A STRIPPER!

### OTHER CREATIVE WAYS TO REFER TO YOUR HEADLINE HONEY!

**Ecdysiast**
**(a term coined for Gypsy Rose Lee, who actually preferred the word *stripper*)**
**Peeler**
**Stripteuse**
**Bump-and-Grinder**
**Stripteaser**
**Showgirl**
**Exotic Dancer**
**Erotic Dancer**
**Burly-Q Queen**
**Slinger**
**Burlesquer**
**Effeuilleuse**
**Strip-Woman**
**Burlesque Queen, Star, Dancer, or Artist**
**Stripper!**
**(and you can call me that anytime; it was a term that was good enough for Gypsy, and it's good enough for me!)**

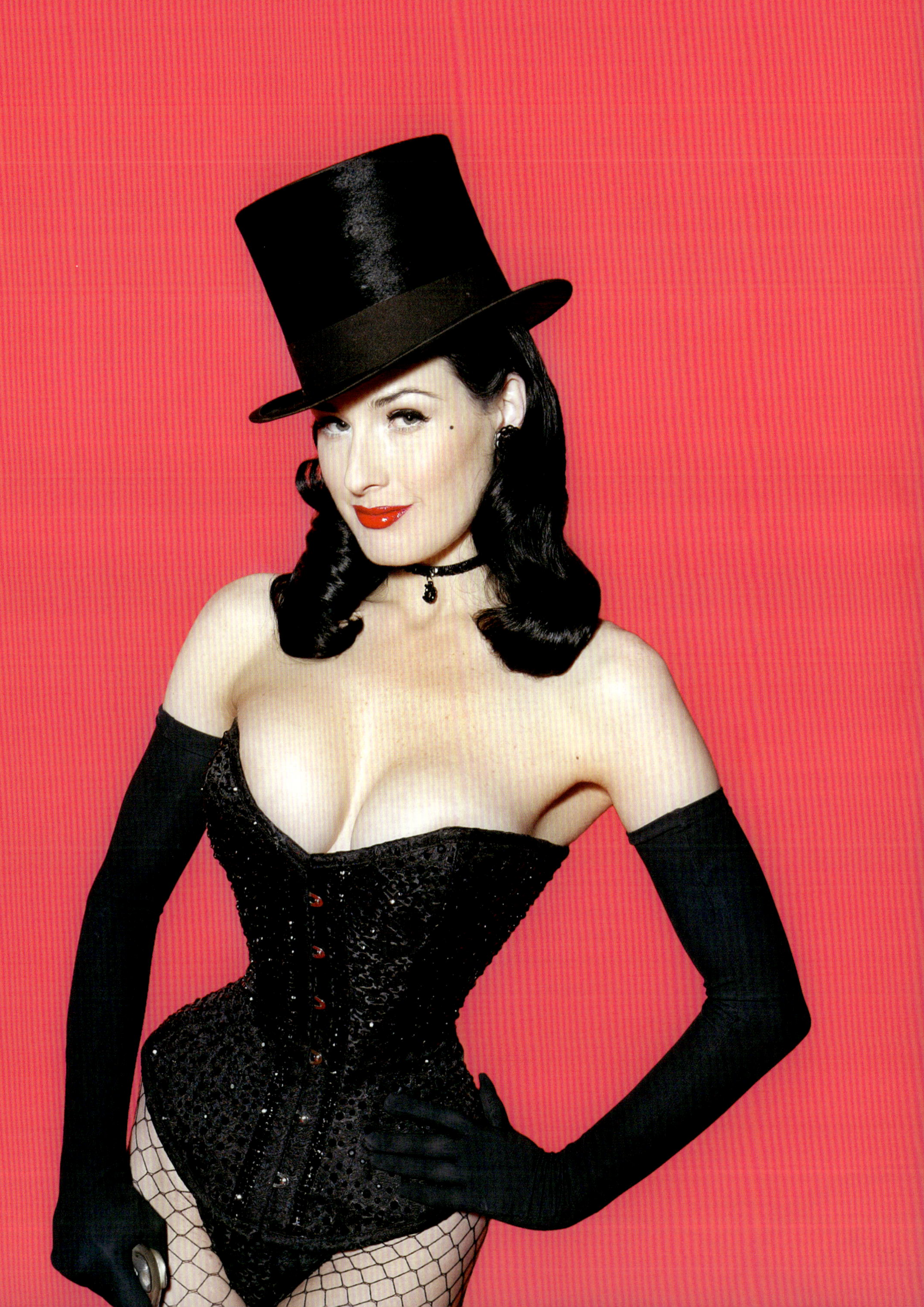

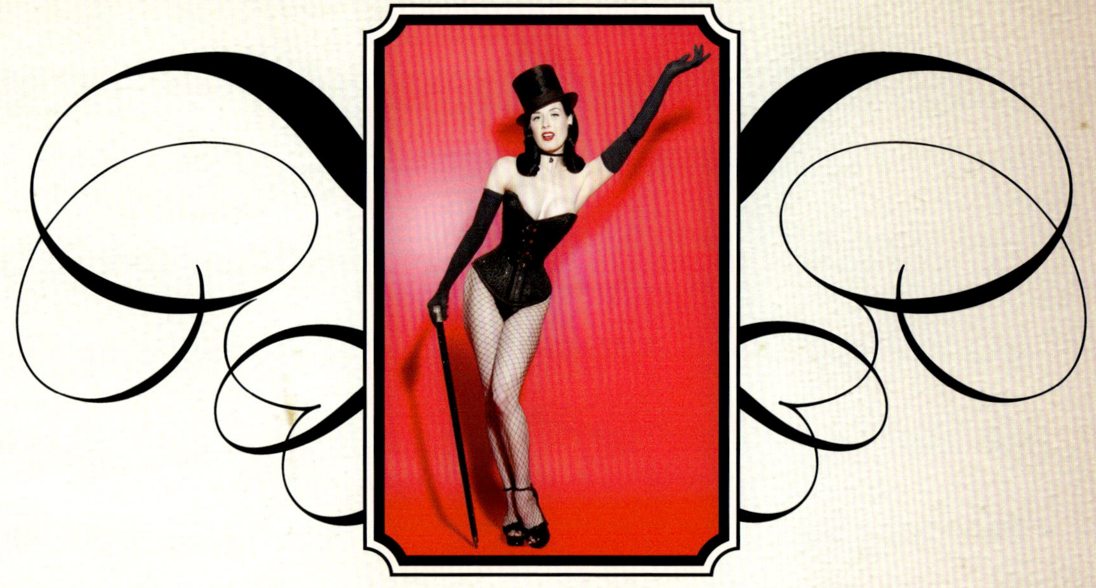

# When I Take the Stage . . .

I have a few rules for my shows. Number one: if something dazzles me, I may use it. This includes cocktail glasses, ballet slippers, rhinestones, bathtubs, friends. Number two: though I will describe to you the famous burlesque shows of the last century, I *do not* perform replicas. One of the consequences of time, you see, is that some elements may not translate at eighty years' distance. (Besides, I have ideas of my own!) My influences include so many things in addition to historic burlesque: Technicolor musicals, old movie stars, cheesecake pinups, fetish objects, the ballet. But this should not lead you to believe that my work is any less authentic—burlesque has always been a medley of the best kind. The great Mr. Minsky himself was influenced by everything from Shakespeare to stag reels. Number three: I strip. Always. Some people give me a lot of nonsense about stripping as being excessively modern and bad-mannered, insisting that the heavenly bodies of burlesque were proper goody-goodies in long white gloves and full dresses. Of course they were. This made the peeling off of it—piece by ever-slower piece—drive the jerks into a sweaty, roaring frenzy. You see, burlesque—in America—has *always* been about putting dirty thoughts into people's heads. It was for the biggest names in the business—Gypsy Rose Lee, Sally Rand, Lili St. Cyr—and it is for me.

Now, I do not mean to propose that *you* strip, or that everything I will tell you about burlesque and its history is correct. No, no. Burlesque is a world of illusion and dreams and fun. What you will see on these pages is just the way that I do it; the way I dance and dress and see the world. The history of burlesque is endlessly, wondrously fascinating, but my book can only be so long. I have dusted off only those characters that kindle my imagination. There may be many more that arouse yours.

I have been called so many things (if you know what I mean), but my very favorite moniker of all time is the *Queen of the New Burlesque*. Burlesque, as you will see, is an artifact of a departed culture, a gem of American invention, and now, my very own bread and butter.

Welcome, ladies and gentlemen, to burleycue.

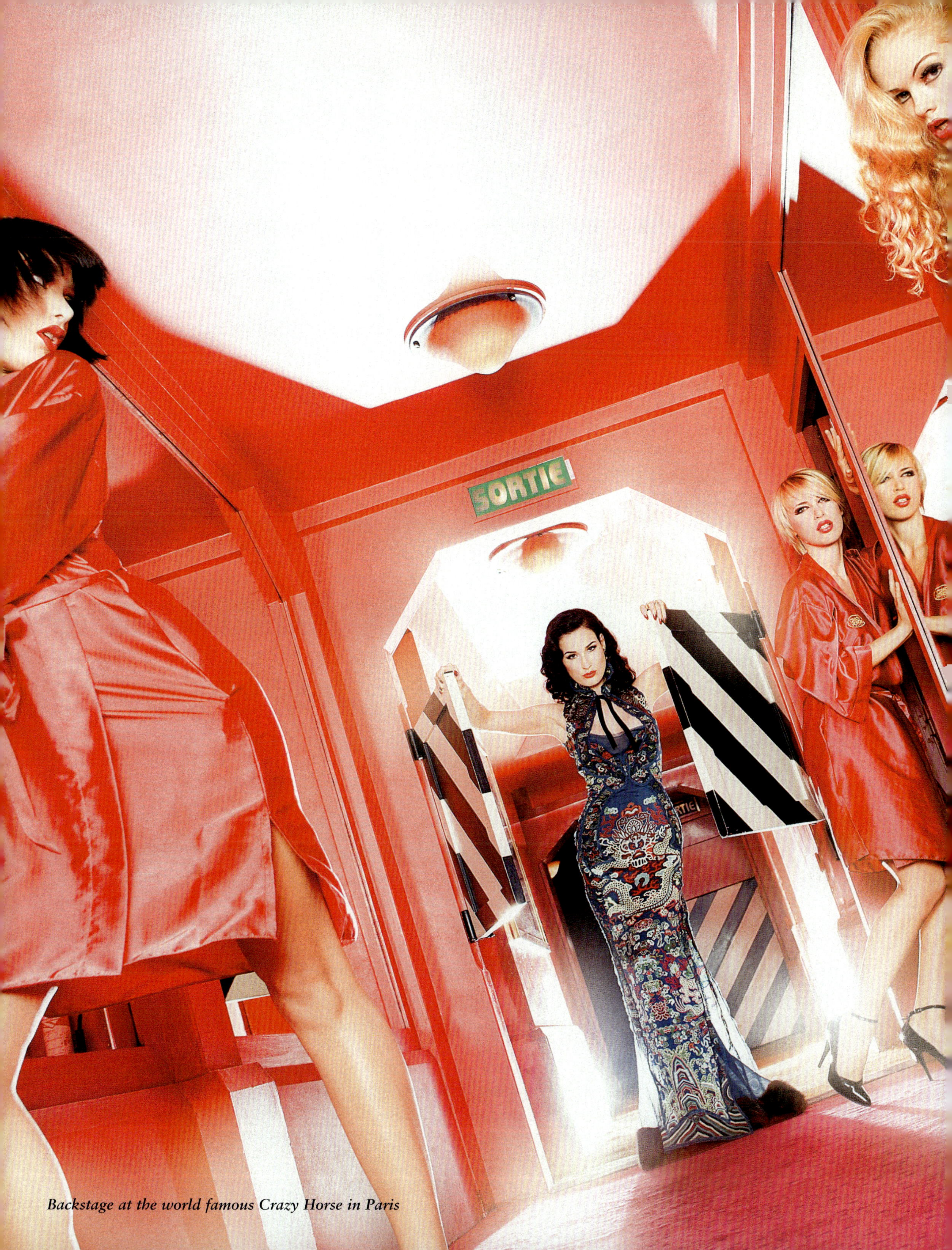


*Backstage at the world famous Crazy Horse in Paris*

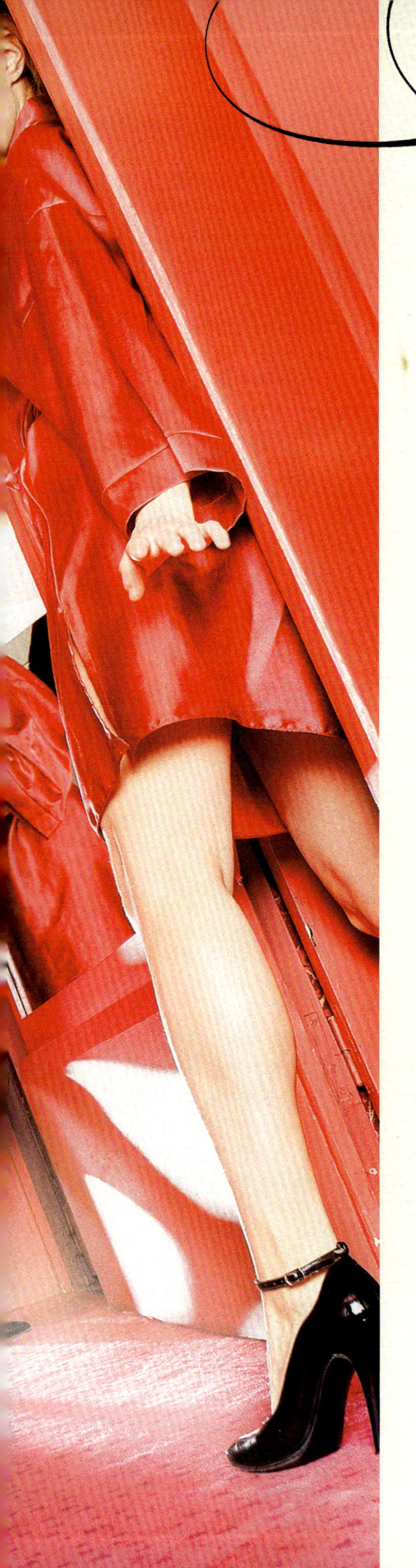

# BURLESQUE GLOSSARY

## VINTAGE STRIPTEASE SLANG YOU SHOULD KNOW

**Bit = skit between burlesque acts**
**Bluenose = police**
**Boston version = cleaned up version of a show**
**Bump = to spring the hips forward**
**Bust developer = offstage crooner on a strip number**
**Cacky = smutty**
**Five percenter = artist's representative**
**Flash = to expose part of the body**
**Gadget = G-string**
**Grind = to circle the hips forward to back**
**Honey = a greeting to anyone**
**Jerks = the audience**
**Knock herself out = to work hard**
**Milk the audience = beg for applause**
**Money guy = the owner**
**Nets = bras or panties**
**Quiver = the shake of the bosom**
**Shimmy = to shake the entire body**
**Slingers = the dancers**
**Snake type = provocative teaser**
**Snappers = buttons**
**Sunday school version = the cops are in the house!**
**Swell set up = a good figure**
**Trailer = the strut before the strip**

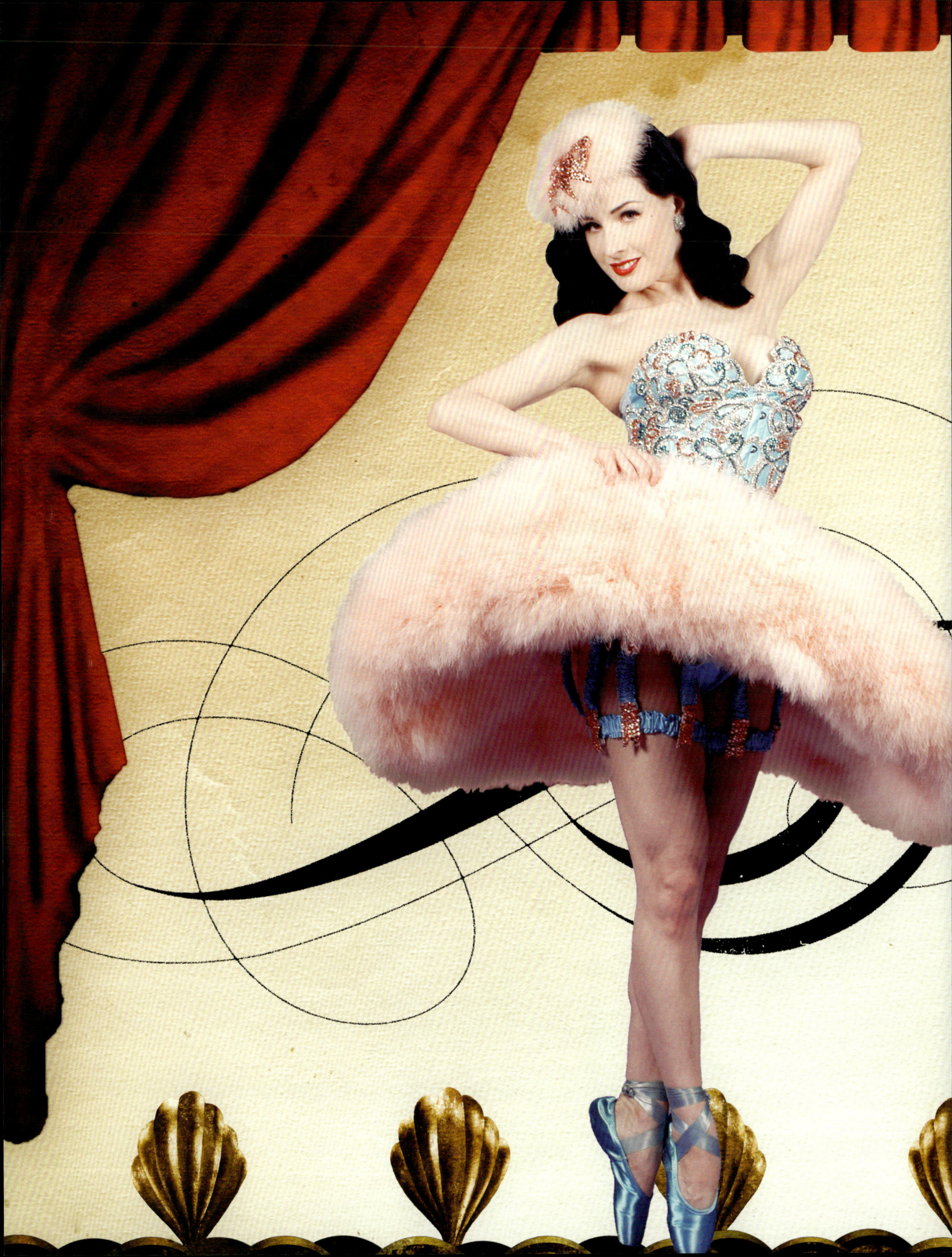

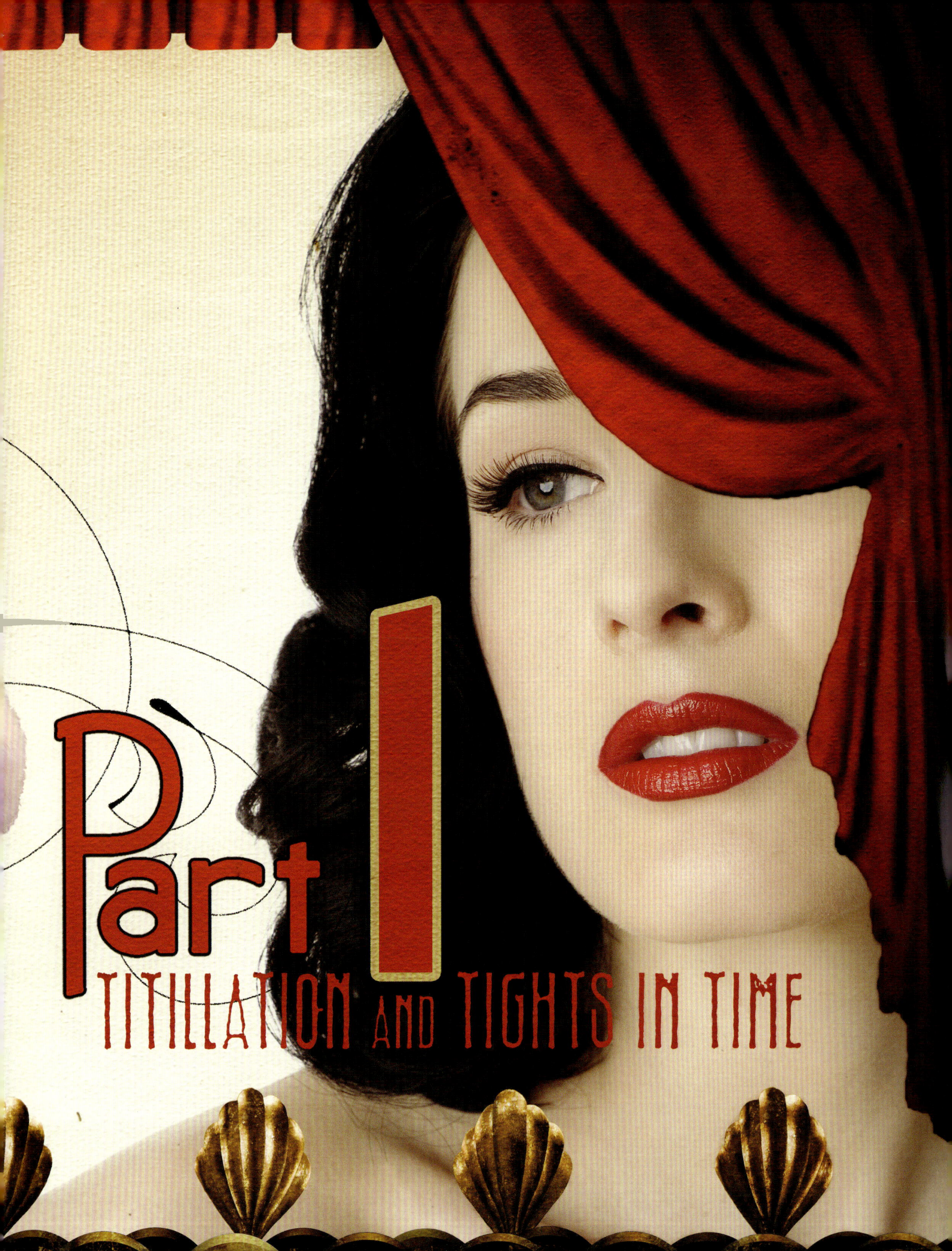

Part I
TITILLATION AND TIGHTS IN TIME

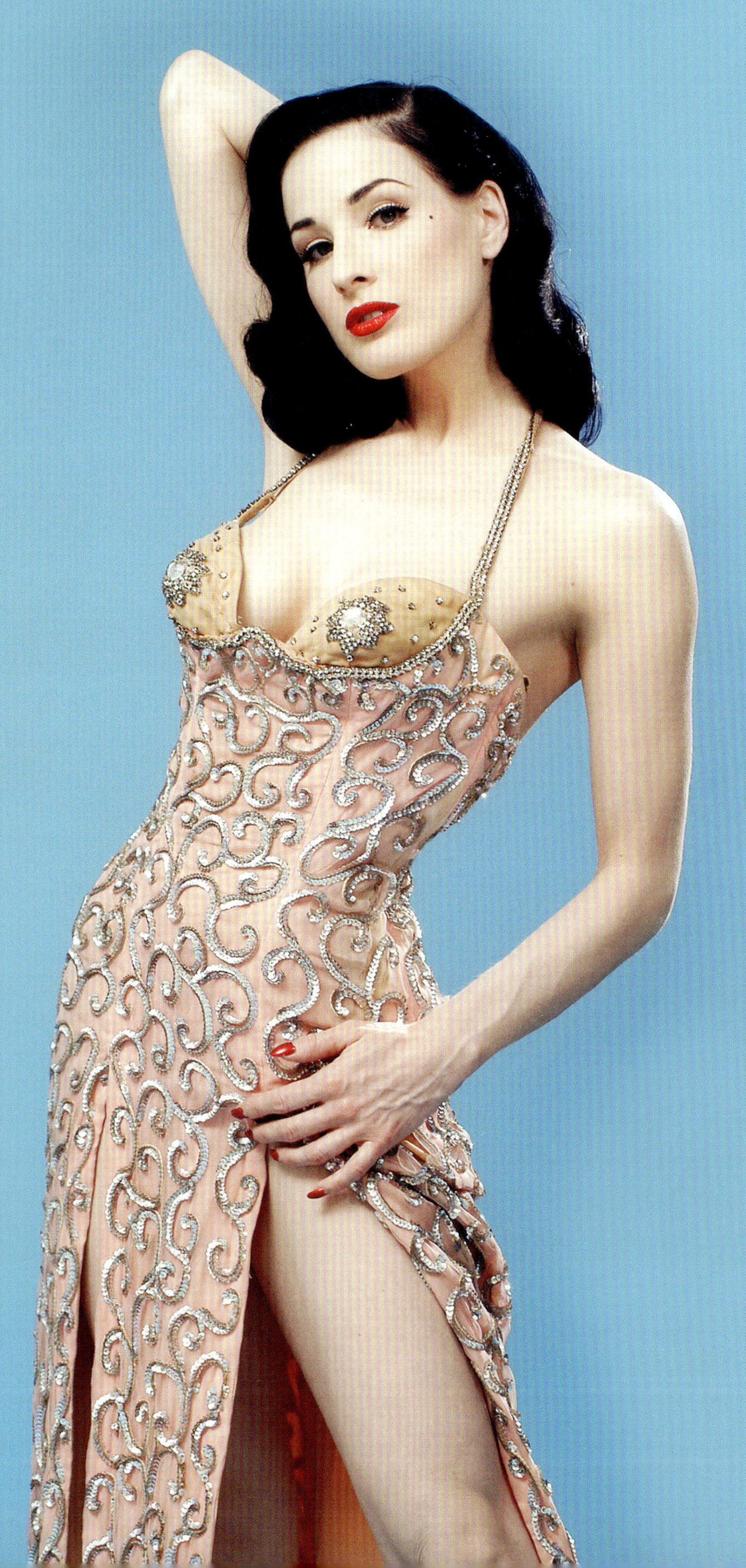

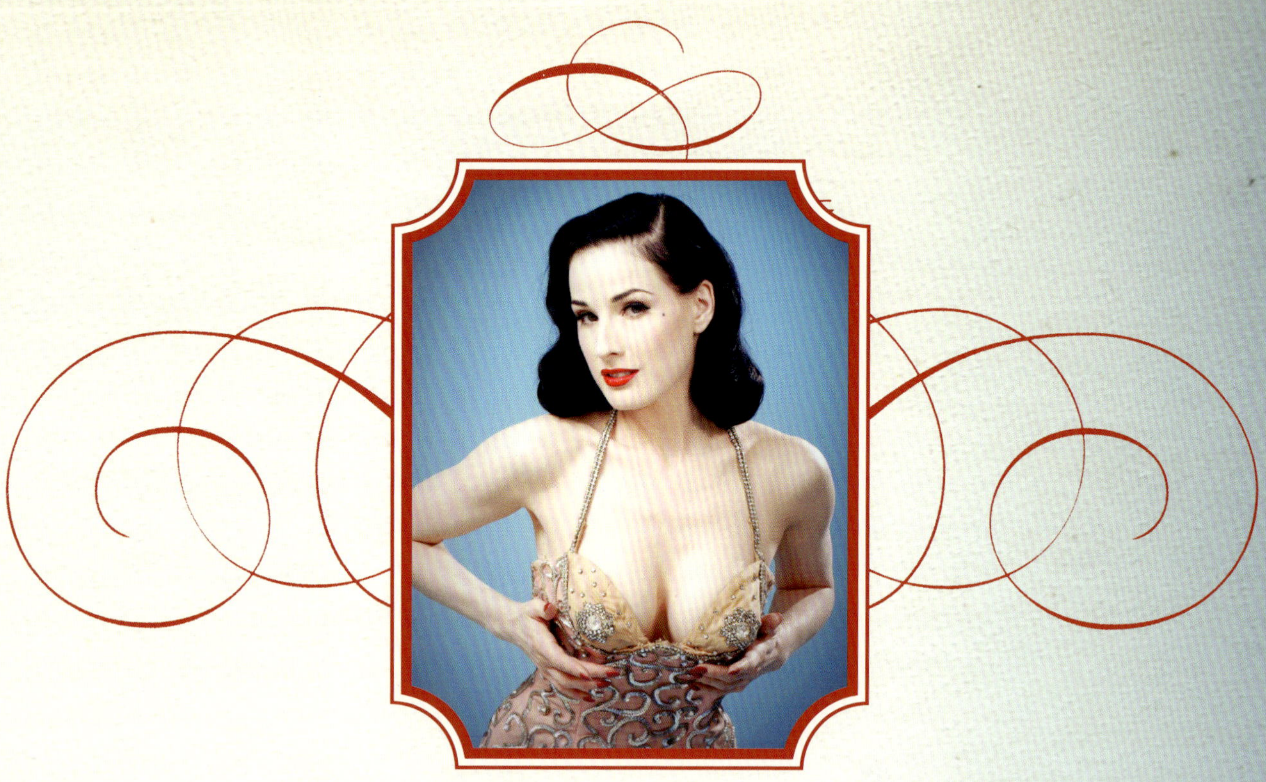

# Father Tease, Aristophanes

The things people tell me!

I like to chat with my fans after a show, so I put on my hat and gloves and walk out there, shaking hands and listening to my new—and returning—friends. Here is one story I have heard at least once.

"Dita," they will say, "did you know that burlesque has been around for hundreds of years as political satire?"

I cannot help but do a little shimmy in response. "What do you mean? No striptease?" I tease.

He's right, this fan, and a little bit wrong. The thing about burlesque is that it has led two lives. One in ancient Greece and all over Europe, where it was a theatrical form of satire—though still bawdy for the times. The other burlesque grew up right here in America, and is otherwise known as the *striptease*. Of course, nothing is so simple, as you know.

Some people like to tell me that America guttered burlesque, that it was a well-intentioned visitor to New York City promptly debased by horny blue-collar workers with drinking problems. An amusing interpretation, and a little bit true. But if you look more closely, you will find that the revered father of burlesque, a playwright of fifth century BC Athens, had his head in the proverbial gutter long before there was anything but forests and teepees in America.

Anyway, chances are you learned something about him in school (though I'll wager your teacher kept his dirty side to herself!). Aristophanes was the playwright, poet, and reformer who

penned the sexy masterpiece called *Lysistrata* in which the wives of the Athenian soldiers hole up in the Acropolis, depriving their husbands of sex until the termination of the Peloponnesian War. This play set the stage for centuries of ribald, faux Greek drama. A good credit for old Daddy A, but I like to give him even more.

The way I read it, these women are *teasing* their husbands, guiding their minds toward sex and then locking it away. Of course, like good *teuses,* they take their acts to the next level. "We will just be up here, *together,*" I can hear them whispering into their husbands ears before they climb the steps, swinging their hips ever so carelessly. Think of what this simple *notion*—women locked inside the castle, waiting for *sex*—does to the male psyche. Wonderful, isn't it? Mind you, since men acted in the roles of women back then, the story was sexy in idea alone. But, *idea,* dolls, *is* the art of the tease.

Now, I should not give you the impression that sexy was *all* Aristophanes had going for him—though I do imagine him as an enterprising romantic. The man is remembered predominantly for his humor, his use of wisecracks, puns, satire, and what have you—contributions that held burlesque firmly in the "parody" category until it reached America near the turn of the century. So my fan is right, you see, quite right.

Even when burlesque began its career in America, comics were staples of its stage—they still are in many of the revivals. People such as Eddie Cantor, Bert Lahr, Jackie Gleason, Fanny Brice, and Al Jolson all came out of these theaters. The word itself has Italian roots in the word *burlare,* which means "to laugh at."

But me, I am more interested in "to tease." So, ultimately, was the audience. For, as the good virus spread across America—worrying a self-appointed "Society for the Suppression of Vice"—the comedian was relegated to second banana.

As my hero Billy Minsky used to say, "if that's what they want, we'll give it to 'em."

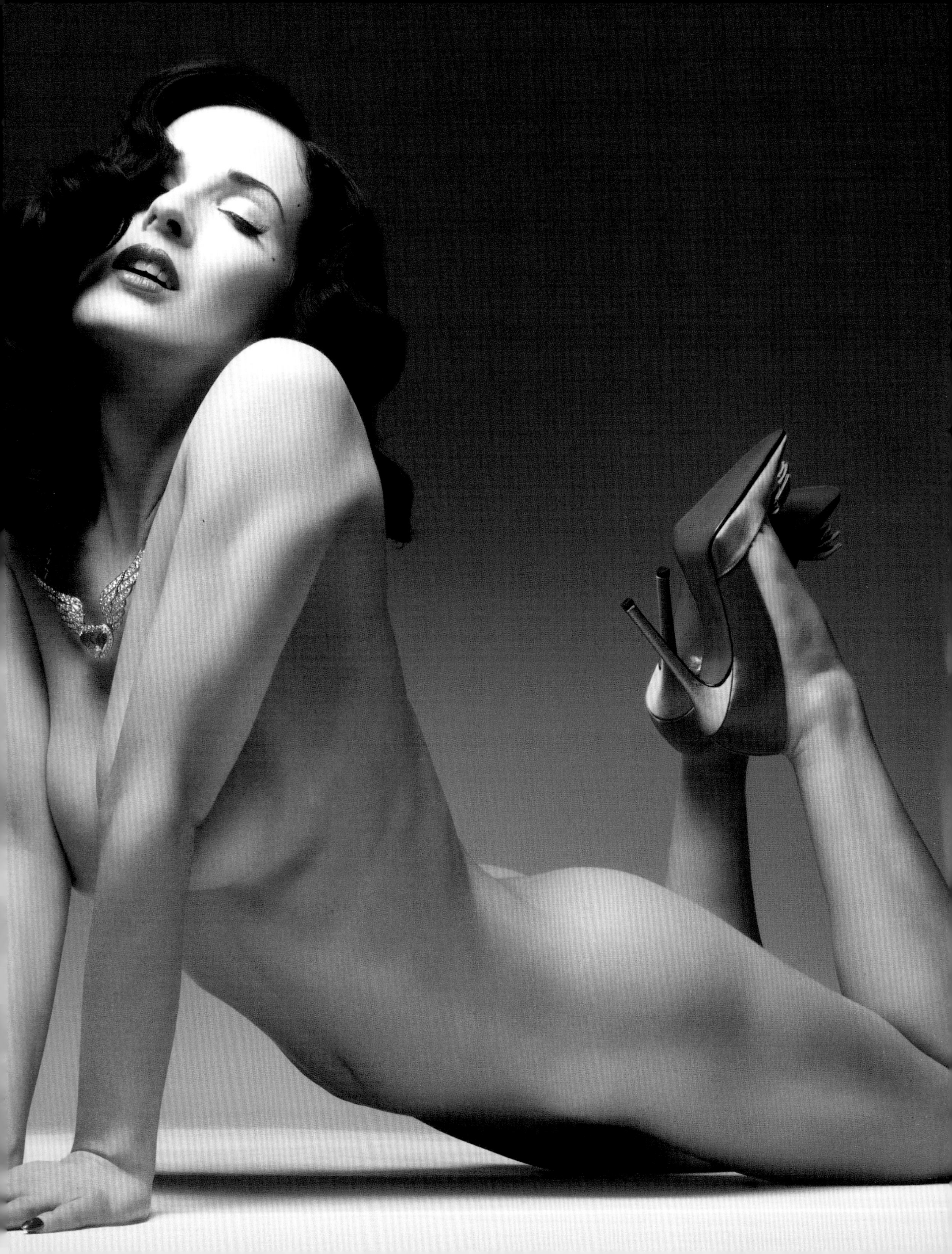

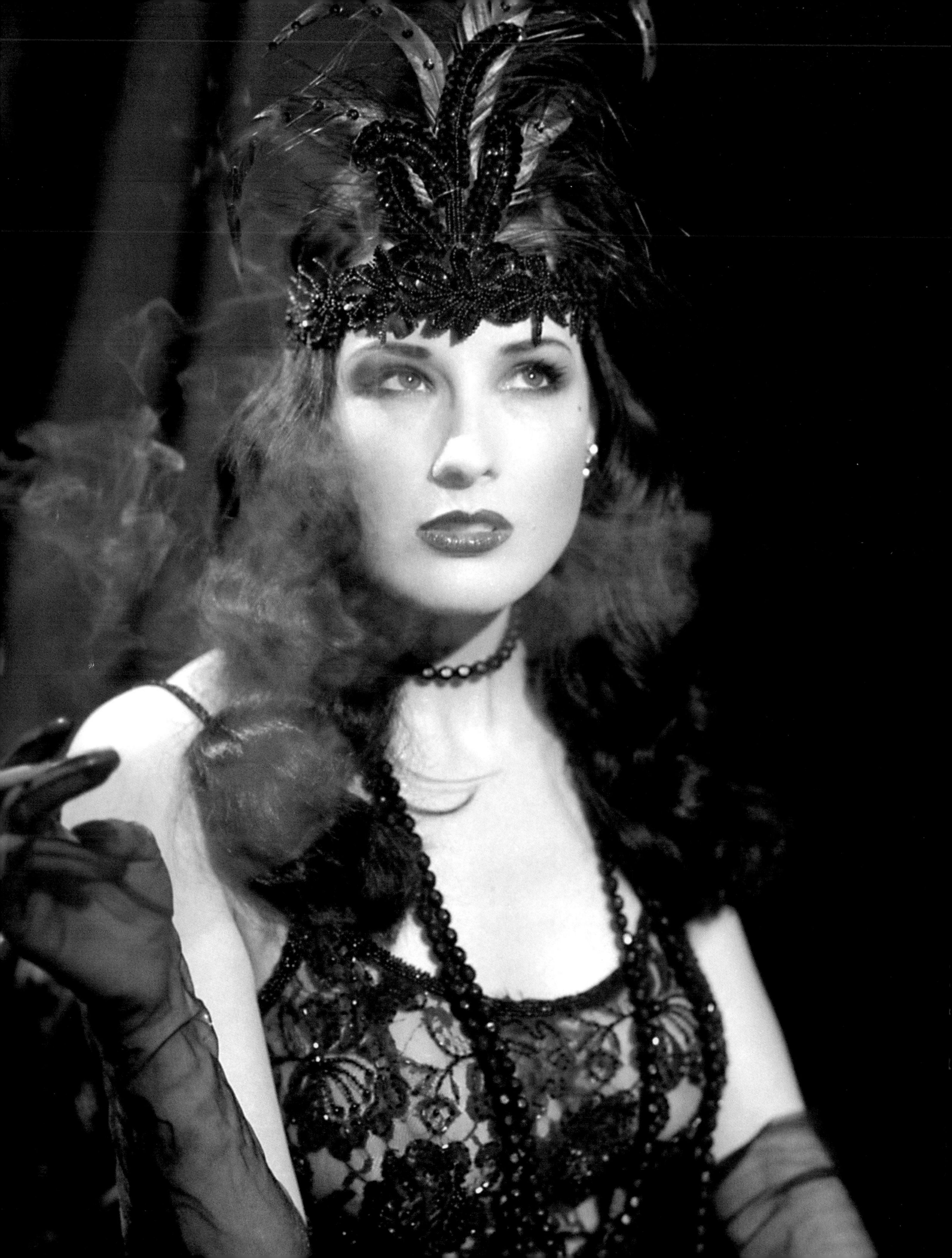

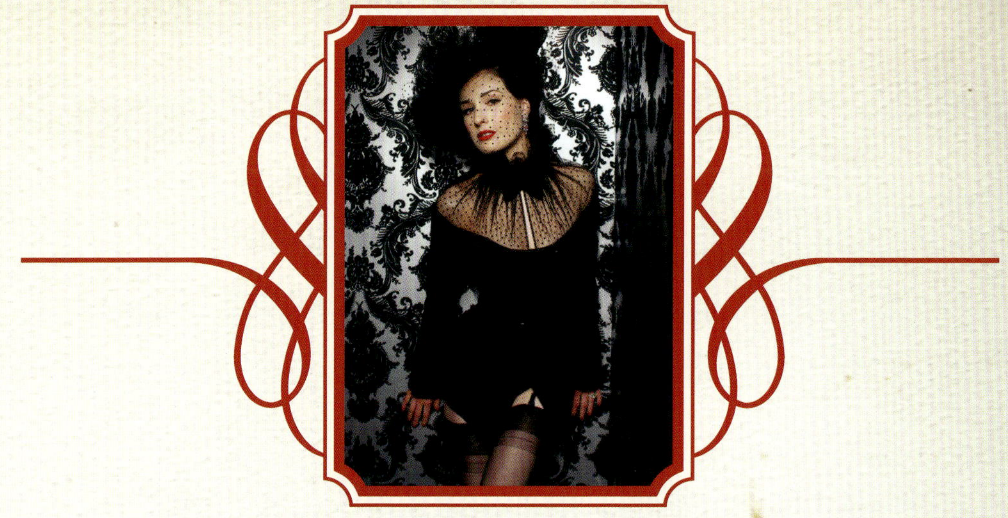

# The Scandal of the Tights

The Victorian era was not kind to flesh; the softer and lovelier the skin, the more fabric they dumped on top of it. Thus, when a group of young Englishwomen bleached their hair and donned flesh-colored tights for the stage, they scandalized—and thrilled—Britain. It was an ingenious coup, those tights: they gave the impression of naked flesh even though they covered it. What was the Queen to say? Who cared? Aristophanes was hooting from his grave.

The credit for the first onstage *tease* generally goes to Lydia Thompson, an ambitious darling of English music hall theater who assembled a peroxided burlesque dance troupe she called the British Blondes. The public was outraged—and bought tickets galore.

When Lydia and her Blondes took to New York on September 28, 1868, the city was waiting, pleading to be ravaged . . . by tights. Isn't it astonishing what a hundred years will do? Anyway, the anticipation may have had something to do with an early mastery of publicity and the art of the fabricated story. Here's one of the many tales that preceded Lydia's New York debut:

> Captain Ludoc Baumbarten of the Russian dragoons took some flowers and a glove belonging to Miss Thompson, placed them on his breast; then shot himself through the heart, leaving on his table a note stating that his love for her brought on the fatal act.

I have no idea whether the tale is true—after all, illusion is the nature of burlesque. However, stories like these so inflamed (wink, wink) the men in America that they all seemed willing to die for Lydia—if only *she* would be kind enough to dash their hearts out herself. Lydia was a tease. Absolutely. Yet, she should be credited with something else just as American: creating the enduring sex symbol of the "long-legged blonde."

Back in America, men were behaving as if they had never seen ladies' lower limbs in their lives, which was a curious thing, because opera houses had been serving up "leg shows" since the Civil War. Was it Lydia herself, I must then wonder, who inspired such fervor? Now, I don't like to be cruel, but my suspicion—since Lydia wasn't considered to be a great beauty, even for the times—is that the full hour's devotion to sex and the cheapie ticket were as hot as the show itself. Whatever the reason, for the rest of the century, burlesque flourished, developing into a full-night's entertainment that included chorus girls, comedy routines, and song and dance.

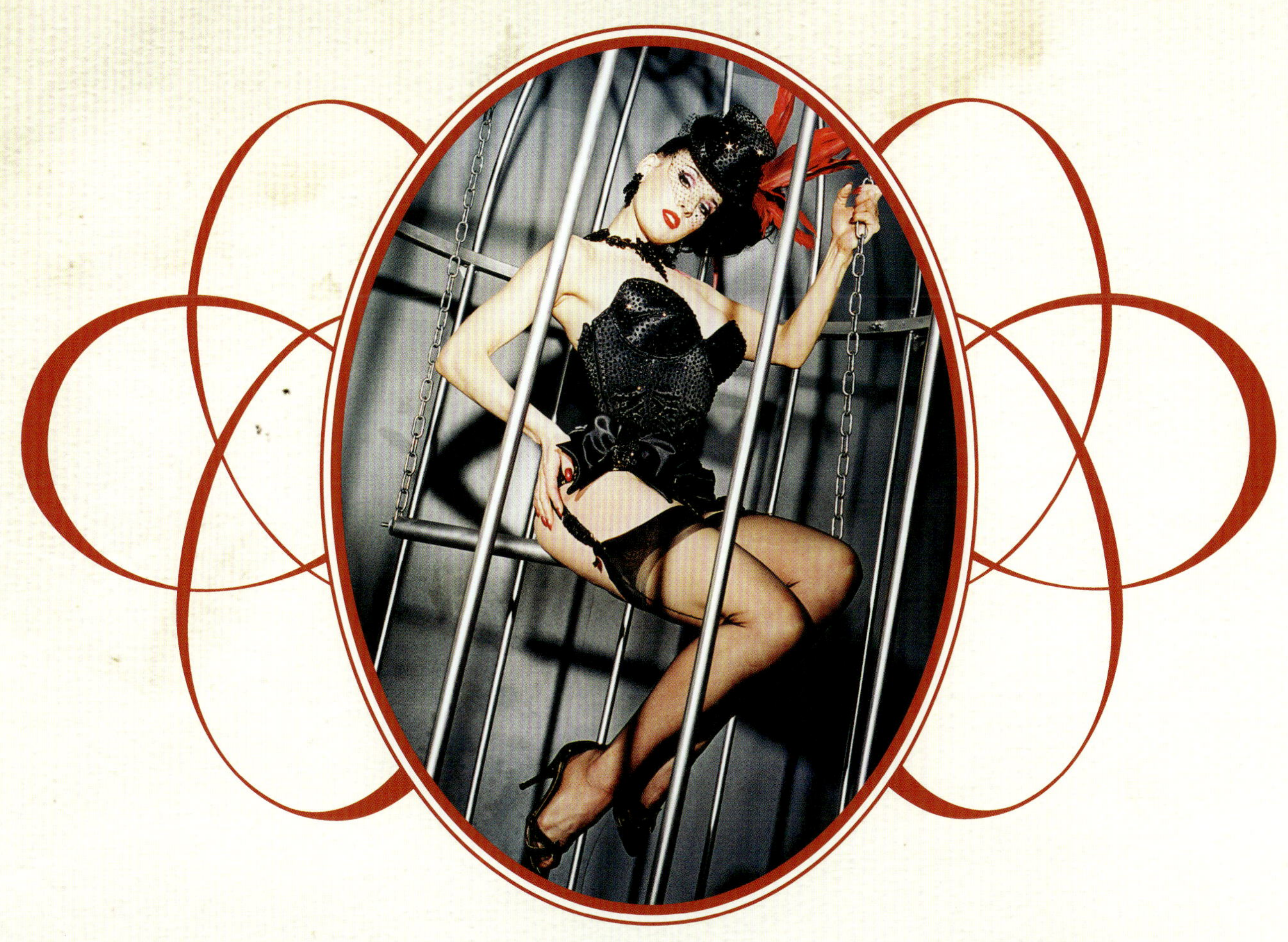

# Moonbeams, Gelatin, and Showgirls!

Miss Thompson was a smart businesswoman, and I do recognize her contributions toward breaking down the prudish morals of Anglos in America. However, my personal brand of burlesque owes more to the fabulous showgirls of la belle époque in Paris and mid-century American burlesque queens. Henry James once called the Paris of the end of the nineteenth century "a massive flower of national decadence, the biggest temple ever built to material joys and the lust of the eyes . . ." (Wonderful, wasn't he?) You see, while England and America were scandalized by tights, it was the age of the cancan, the Folies Bergère, and the Moulin Rouge in Paris. Oh, what an age! This was a time when any girl—no matter her background—transcended class by lighting up the stage. The very best "dancers"—mostly they just swanned about in luxurious fabrics and gems—consorted with kings, artists, and legendary writers. Take my very favorite showgirl of the day, Mistinguett, who was linked romantically with Alphonso XIII, the King of Spain, and the Russian Prince Orloff, while merely socializing with Jean Cocteau and Oscar Wilde (the writers never got the girl!).

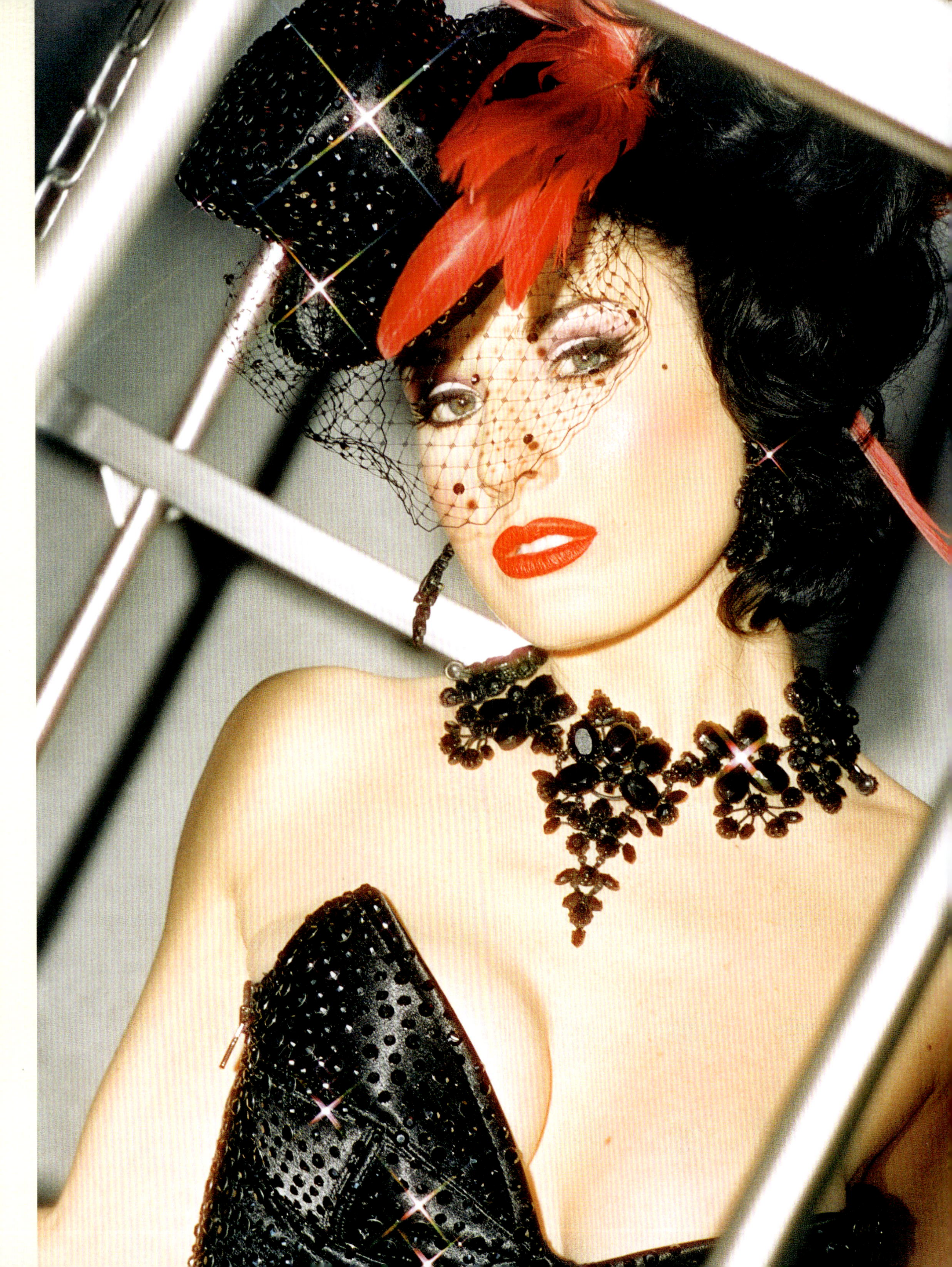

Miss, as she was known, was born Jeanne Marie Florentine Bourgeois (yes, this was her last name!), a member of the new petit bourgeoisie. But, her transformation occurred in more than her name. The girl was *not* a beauty and so, as she herself said, "the rest had to be created. I had to invent something . . . my legs [were called] 'the loveliest legs in the world', [an idea that] came out of my head." The girl was convincing. Mistinguett, with her playful onstage personality (once, when she was singing an audience member yelled "higher!"—to which she lifted her skirt!), transcended looks and bourgeois life to become one of the greatest showgirls of all time.

Of course, the term *courtesan* did not then reverberate with the bells of indecency it does today. Though not everyone approved of her lifestyle, the young woman was generally esteemed as a model of impeccable beauty, captivating style, and mysterious feminine power. She was a careerist, a society girl, an emulated celebrity. It may be true that she indulged in high-end affairs and accepted gifts, but who wouldn't? Returning a gift to a prince is not equal to returning a sweater to Bloomingdale's—one simply doesn't do it. But, the truth is that this courtesan was not dependent on any man. She made her living onstage. Yes, she was decadent, but this is the art of showmanship!

Consider Liberace, dripping in diamonds and furs, sitting under his glimmering candelabra. Was any American showman *more* fabulous? Some say he didn't have the greatest talent in the world, but he was lavish in costume and lifestyle. Liberace made people talk about him, journalists write about him, all of us want to *see* him. *That* is the draw of the showman. His art is creating spectacle and inspiring dreams.

As Mistinguett said, "We sell [the audience] a trip to nowhere, canvas landscapes, moonbeams made out of gelatin." The showgirl sells, in a word, magic.

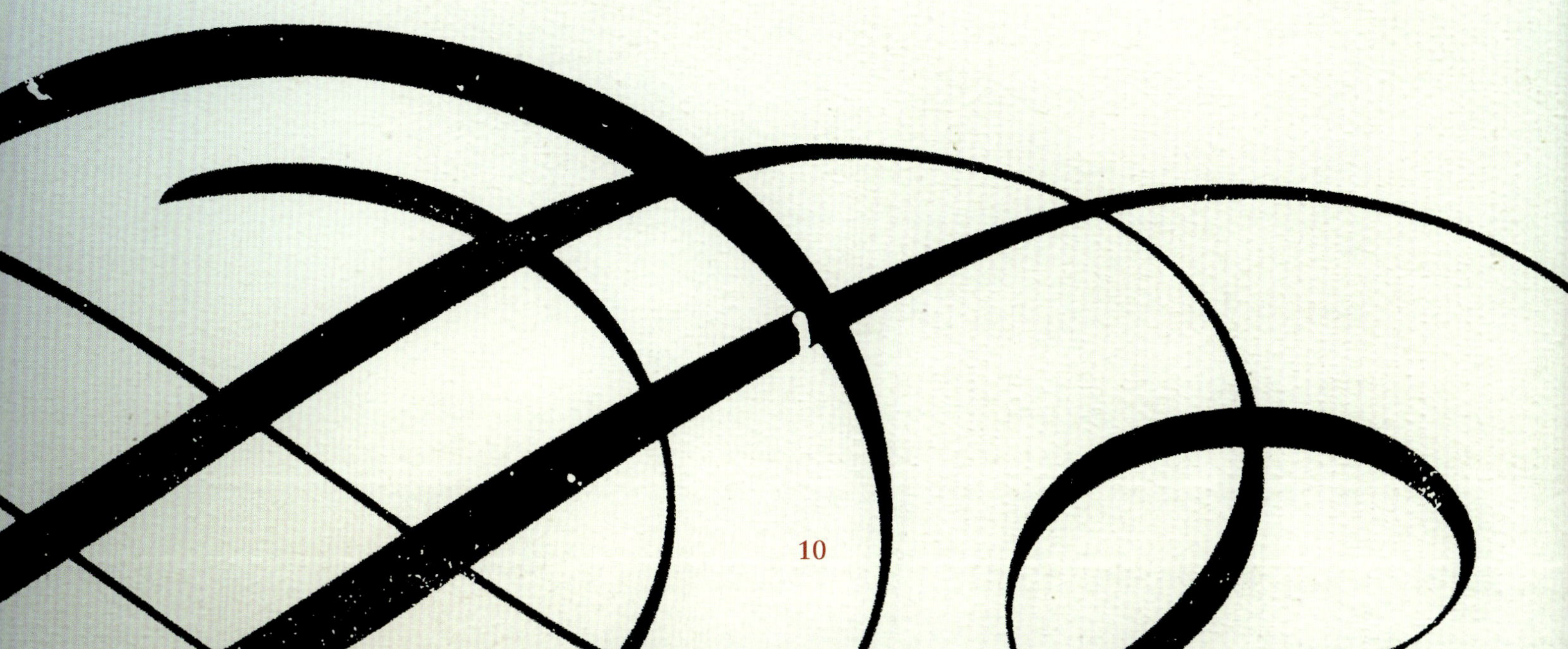

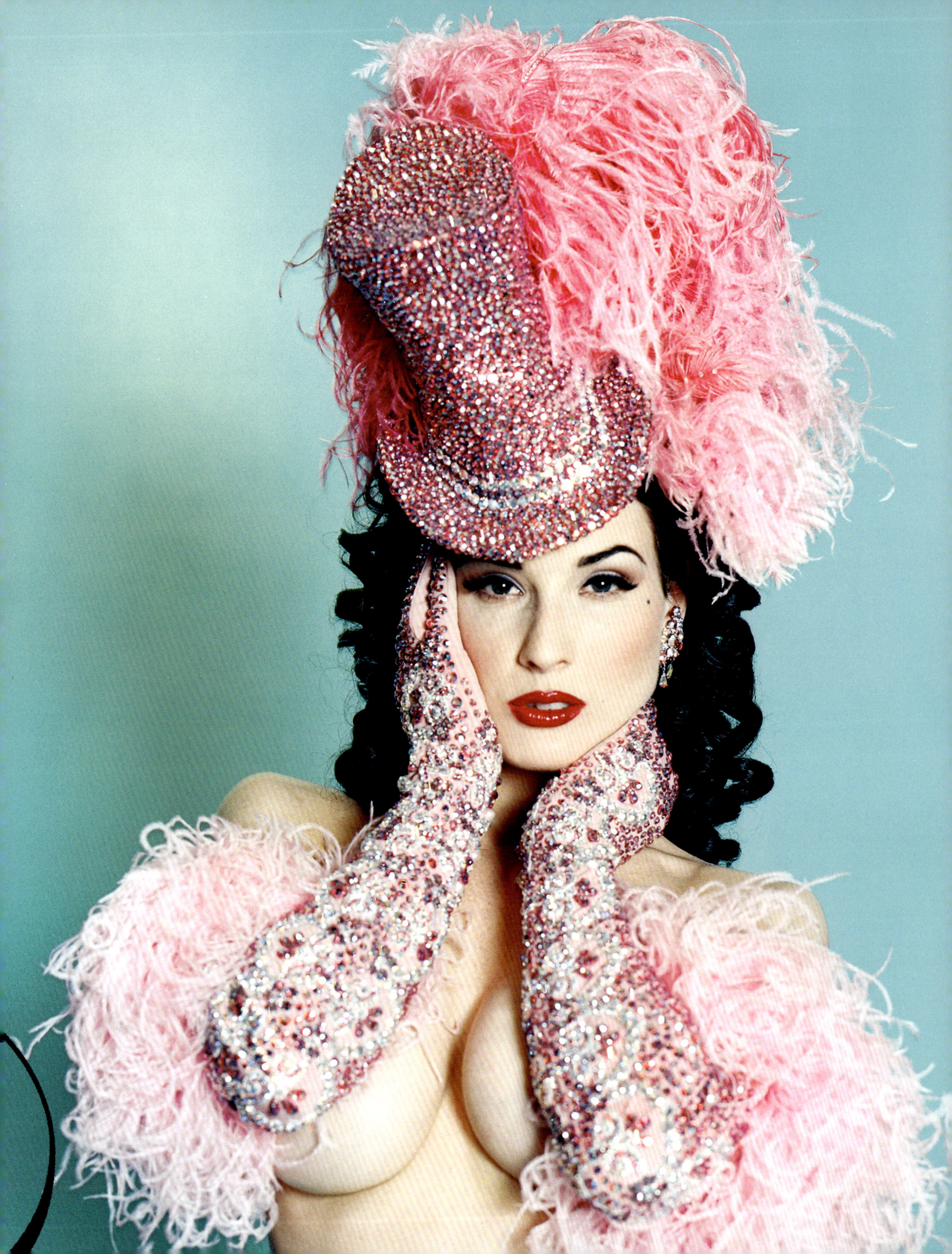

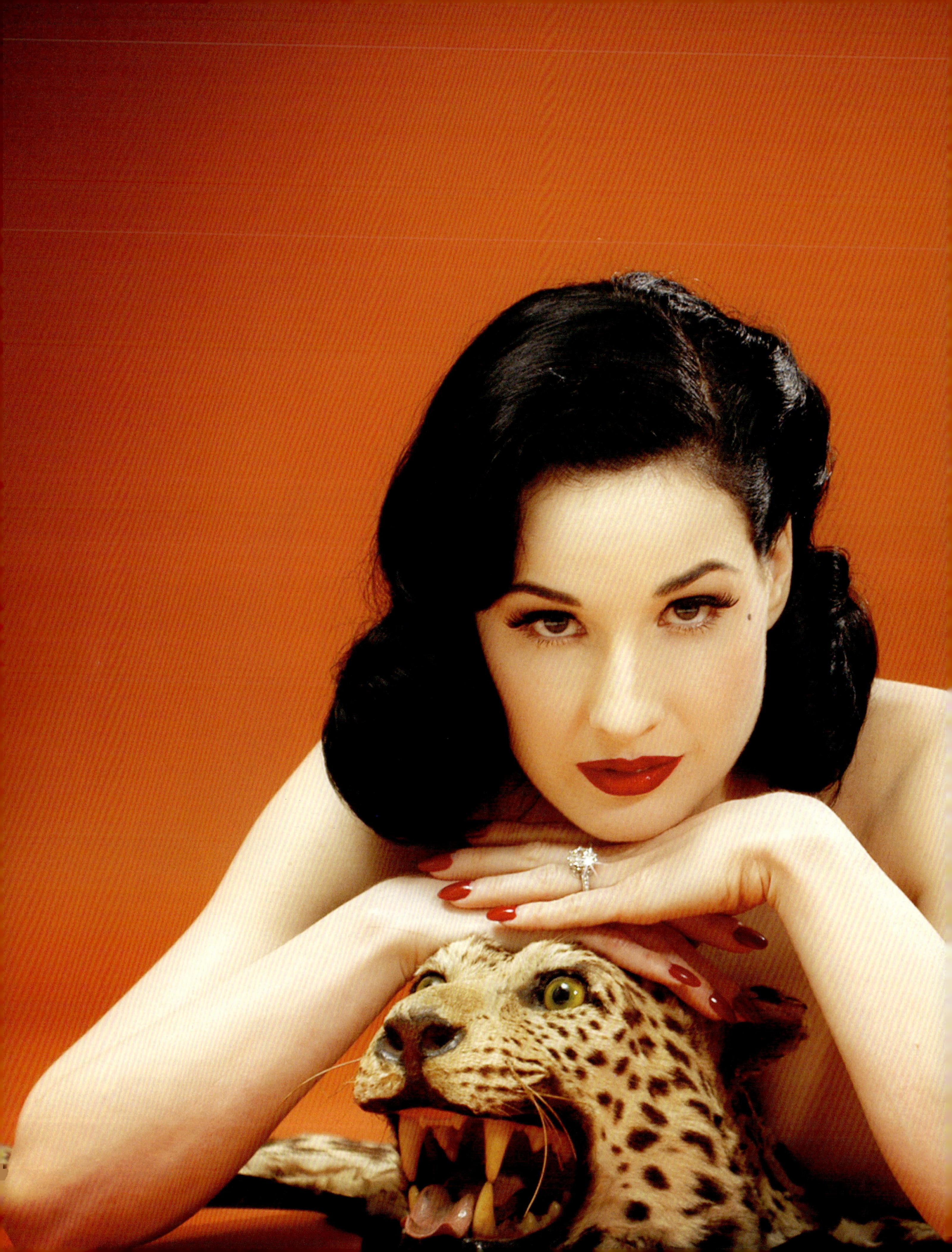

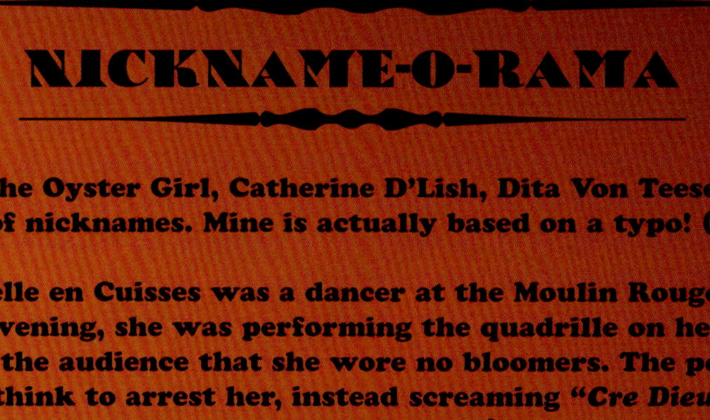

# NICKNAME-O-RAMA

**Evangeline the Oyster Girl, Catherine D'Lish, Dita Von Teese—burlesque is a reservoir of nicknames. Mine is actually based on a typo! (see *Fetish*, page 43)**

**Nini la Belle en Cuisses was a dancer at the Moulin Rouge in the late 1800s. One evening, she was performing the quadrille on her hands, thus revealing to the audience that she wore no bloomers. The policeman on duty didn't think to arrest her, instead screaming "*Cre Dieu! Les belles cuisses!*" ("Holy God, what beautiful thighs!") The name stuck. Here are a few other good showgirl monikers:**

**FROM LA BELLE ÉPOQUE:**

***La Mome Fromage* (the cheese kid)**
***La Sauterelle* (Grasshopper)**
***Cigarette***

**FROM MINSKY'S:**

***Hazel Nutt* from Brazil**
***Bettie Blushes* from Peking**
***Lita Butt* from Havana**
***Etta Herring* from Bismark**
***Mademoiselle Sprouts* from Brussels**

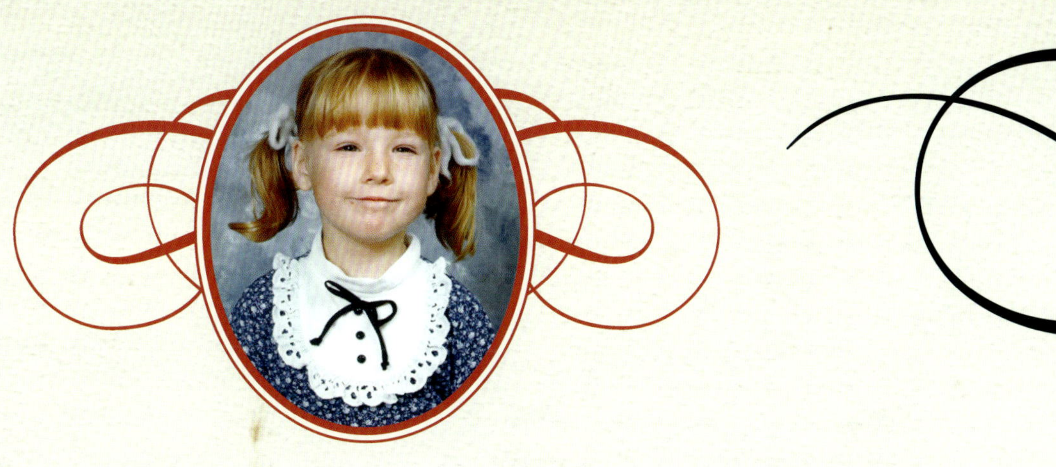

# Little Girl, Time Traveler

Even as a little girl, I understood that beauty was a luxury ticket to the world. One summer when I was eleven, my parents took my two sisters and me for a cruise. It was a marvelous English boat with glistening pools and grand buffets. In preparation for my trip—I have always believed in meticulous planning—I checked out library books about legendary sunken ships. Because I was a light sleeper as I child, I rose before my sisters each morning and wandered the wet wooden decks sipping orange juice, listening to the waves splash the steel hull, and imagining that I was really a girl from the twenties aboard the doomed luxury liner *Lusitania*. I dressed the part, of course—long black gloves, hat, and veil. I was a connoisseur of dress-up in those days, and my mother picked up vintage things in resale shops just for my games. I thought I looked glamorous and mysterious, and besides, it gave me a little thrill to pretend I was someone long gone . . . not to mention the only one on board who knew a torpedo was coming!

One afternoon, my parents gathered us together in the ship's photography studio for a family portrait. A tall, handsome man was snapping pictures this way and that, and I was surprised to find myself smiling easily, enjoying the session. When we returned to pick up our photos, a woman stood before our portrait, pointing. "Those girls are so lovely." I basked in the wonderful news.

"The two on the ends."

But I was in the middle. What did she mean by . . . ? Oh. My heart broke. In my eleven long years, I had never considered, not for a moment, that I might not be pretty. Perhaps this was the problem—I had given beauty no special thought. I looked into the delicate features of my mother and sisters for a sign of exertion. They were smiling vacantly—as lovely women do. But, I knew my mother was beautiful. Men's faces turned toward her when she passed on the street. And my sisters? People always commented on the pink loveliness of them.

No one ever talked about me. It was true. Recognition ached my brain. I am that girl. You know that girl, the milquetoast whose name you never learned. She sits in the back of the schoolroom and is barked at by the teacher. "Speak up!" If you had asked me before the cruise to identify "That Girl," I might have given you any list of overlooked fifth-grade names. Now I would give you one.

I am not suggesting that an average-looking girl cannot succeed. On the contrary. I mean to say she can, with a little practice, be as memorable as the "natural beauty" who, heaven

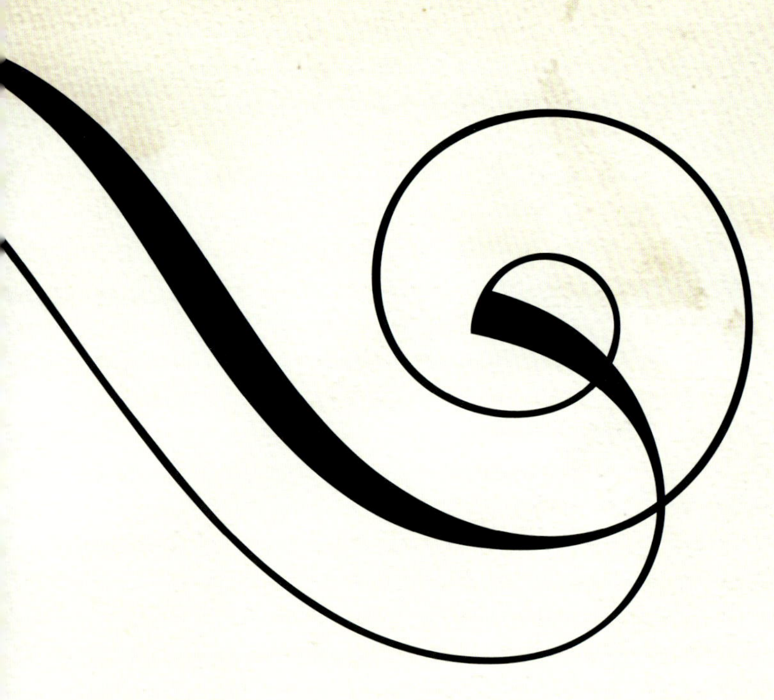

knows, enjoys life under a warmer sun. Besides, we burlesquers tend to be beauties of the created kind. Take Billy Minsky's first star stripper, Gypsy Rose Lee. She was skinny and flat-chested, quite plain indeed. But she worked her assets off, mastering makeup, costume, and timing. The result? She was the greatest headline honey in the history of the business.

I decided, then and there, to master makeup application and curling irons and skillfully, artfully enrapture the world. Then, because I had flunked social studies, I imagined that I would be crowned Queen of America.

You might try to add dumb to the day's list of epiphanies, but I was a damn smart kid. Even at eleven I understood the power of illusion. If Billy Minsky could have seen me then—and if I were really that girl from the 1920s and my ship was not going down—he would have hired me on the spot. After all, he hired Georgia Sothern when she was only twelve. But then, that was Minsky, the mischievous visionary running New York's naughtiest cartel. And anyway, Georgia lied about her age. I never lie . . . about my age.

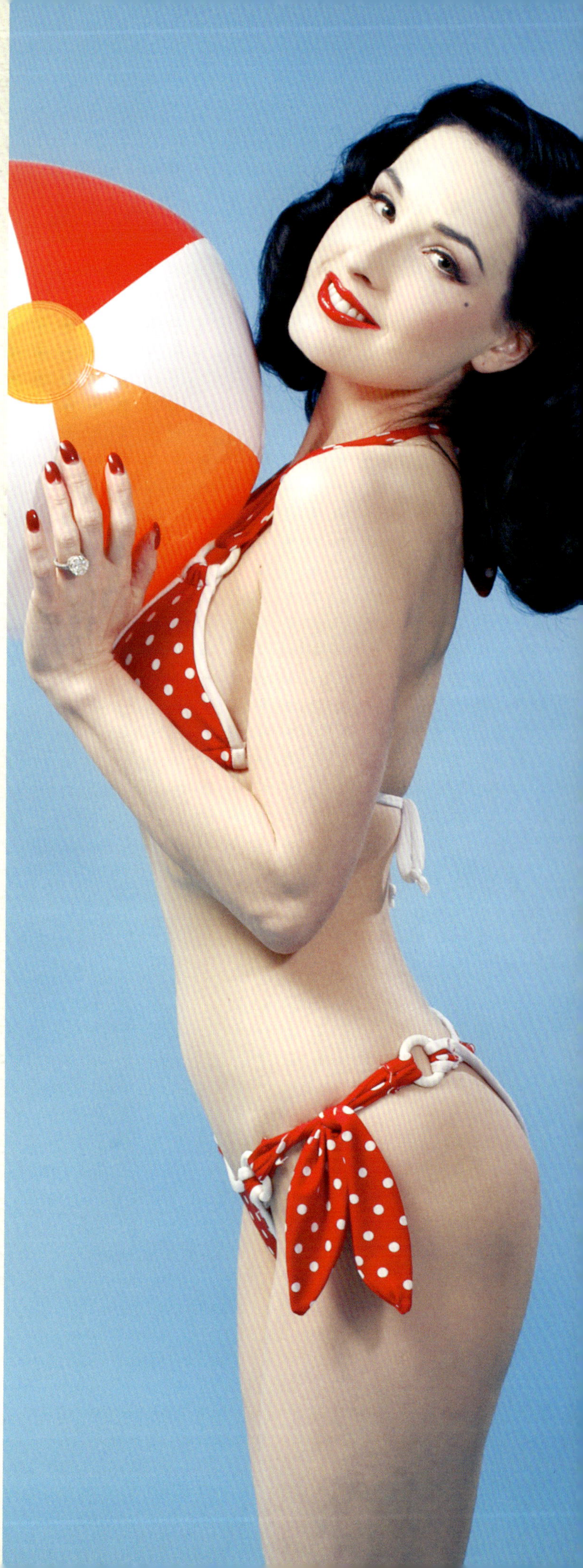

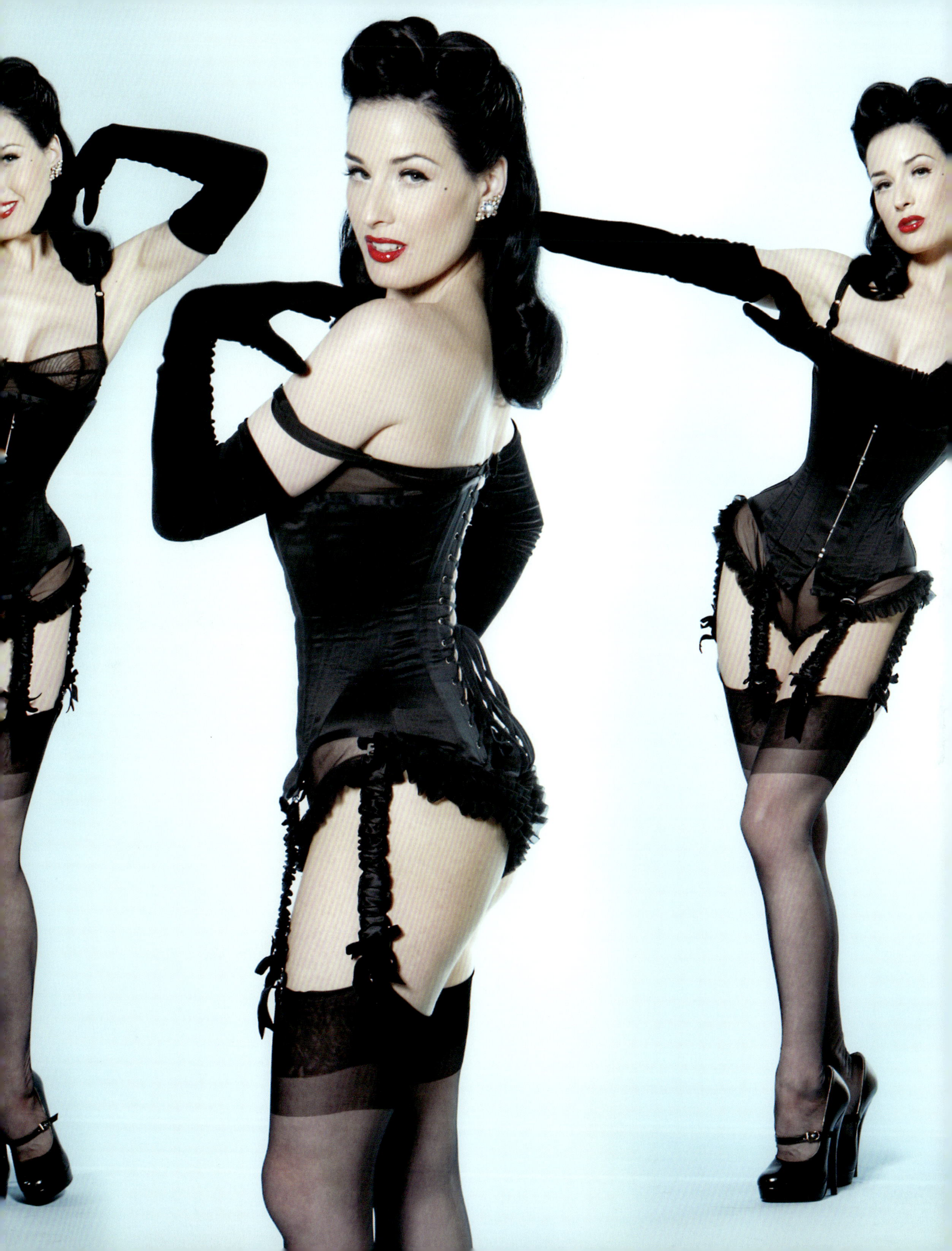

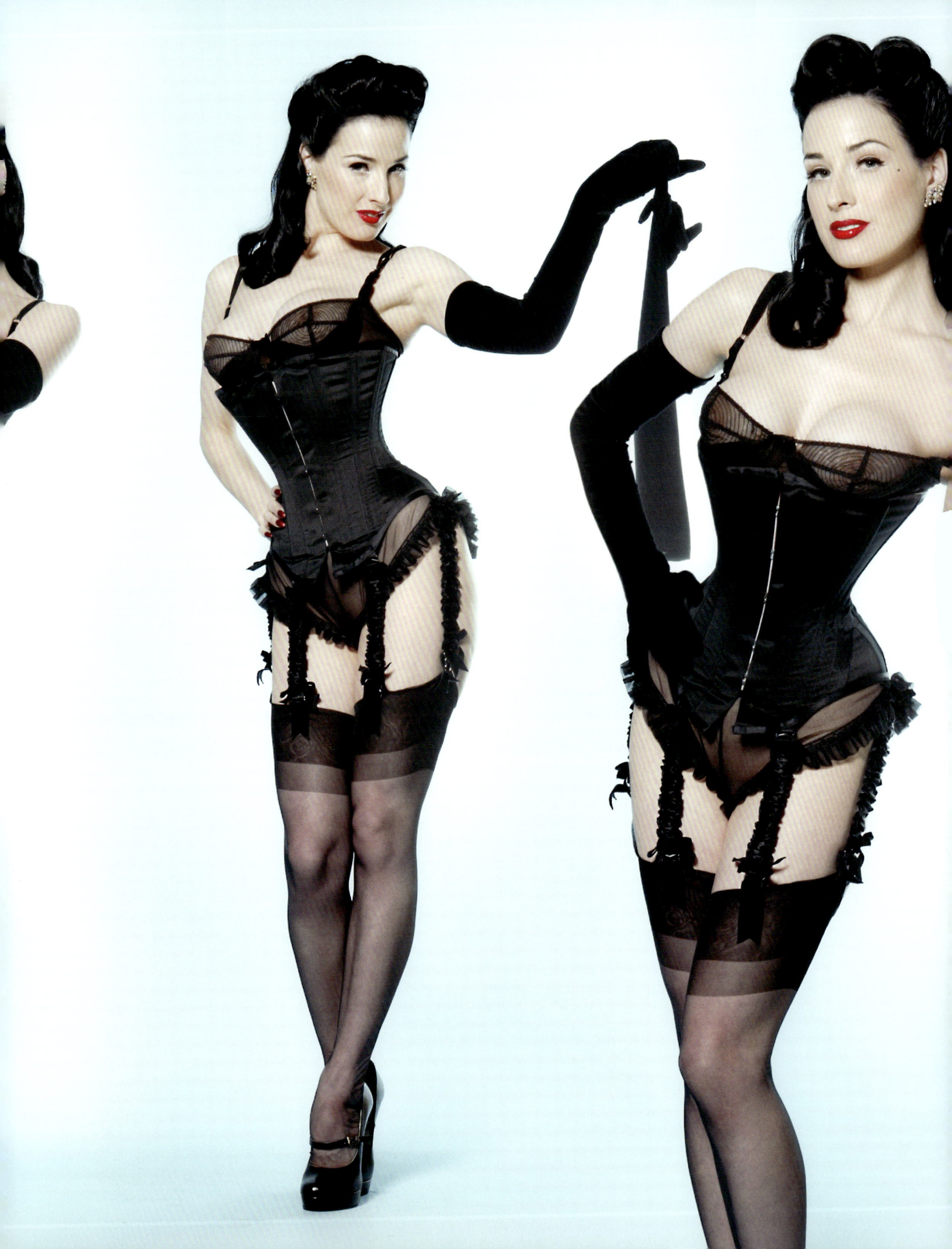

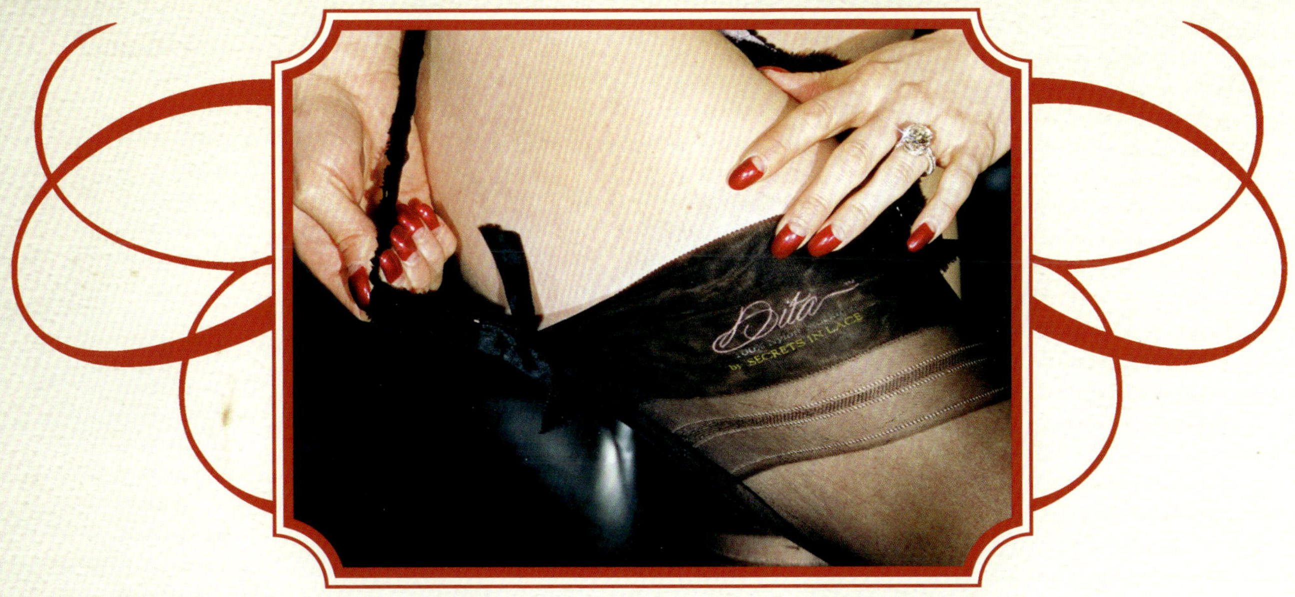

# The Snap Heard 'Round New York

Before Minsky ever met the speed-stripping Georgia or the witty Gypsy Rose Lee, a chorus girl snapped a strap during one of her numbers at a jammed little nightclub called Gotham's. The jerks caught on before the girl thought to refasten herself, screaming so boisterously they brought on the cops. Though the local bluenoses threatened and eventually performed an arrest, this girl refused to replace her top, even in the paddy wagon. I like to think she is resisting still, her strap—and her name—lost to burlesquean history.

The story goes that by the next morning, hundreds of girls had taken credit for the crime, and by evening "accidents" were happening all over town. Mind you, this is legend, not low-down, though it raises a good point. Burlesquers are notoriously competitive. Thieves even. If you're in this business, girls, it's wise to take some precautions, because times haven't changed. If you have a unique act that becomes your bread and butter, copyright your choreography and your props. Sally Rand did it after copycat fan dancers popped up all over the place, and so do I. Anyway, since Gotham or any of the other stories of the First, every stripper has upped the ante, aiming to titillate the audience a wee bit more. It is precisely this up-the-ante factor that gave rise to the modern strip club in which bronzed girls emerge in neon bikinis, tear them off, spin round a pole, and exit. It is also for this reason that there is, once again, room for someone like me. Nudity is fine. But, if everyone is naked, it's the costumes that rule the stage.

I was nineteen when I learned this lesson, visiting a strip club for the first time. Some friends and I were drinking Champagne in the smoky, wood-paneled room, watching girls spin

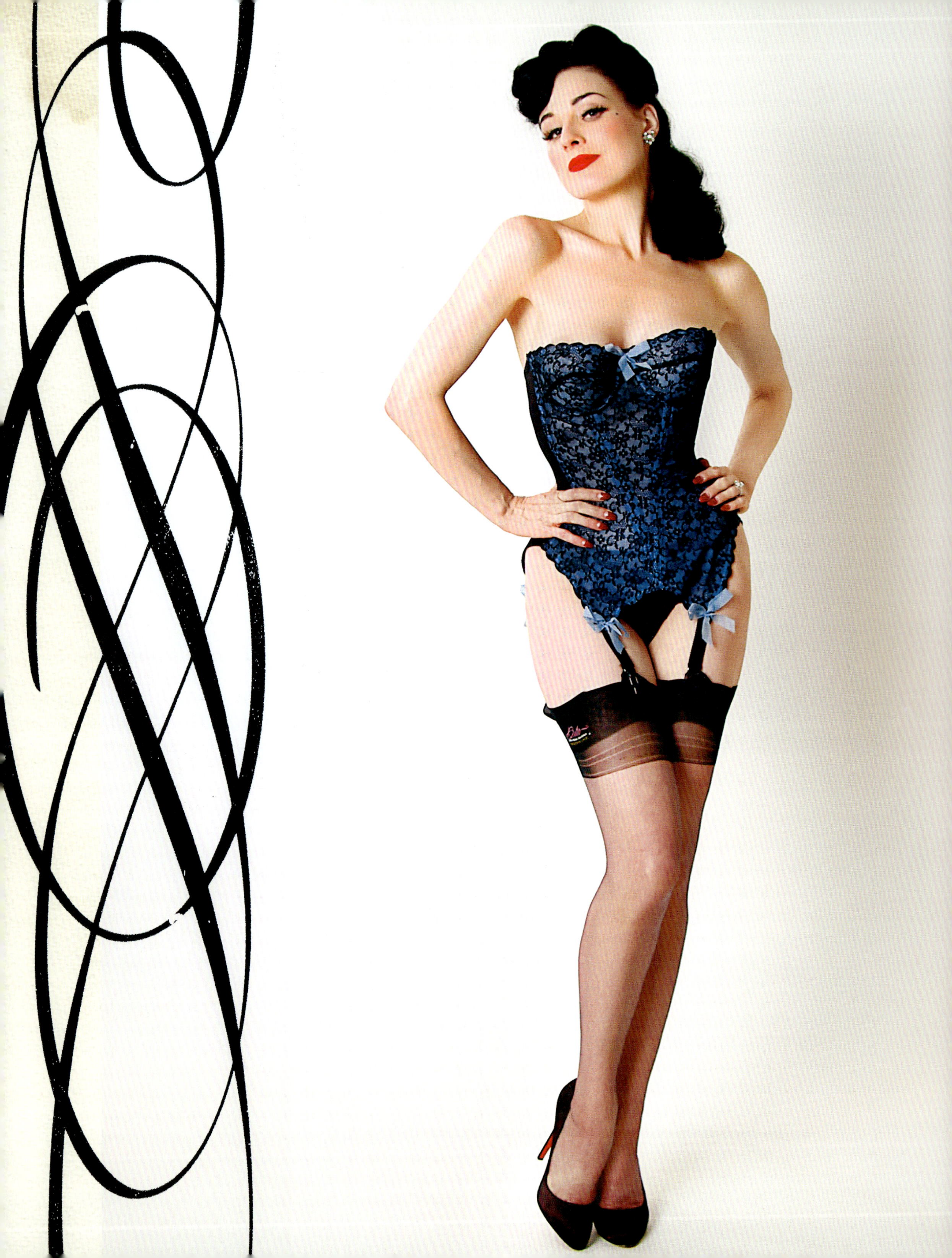

round and round those poles. The man next to me shook his head and grumbled, "Five minutes to do their thing, and every damn act is the same."

I, too, was stunned at the lack of originality. The things I could do, I whispered, if I had five minutes to construct my fantasy. Well, this chap owned the nightclub. I had a new job.

My first night onstage was a shock for the crowd, but one I like to think they needed. I was not yet studying burlesque per se, but I possessed enough of its artifacts to confound the room. I wore a proper crinoline dress over a tightlaced corset with seamed stockings, garters, and long black opera gloves. (Keep in mind that these punters were used to tan, big-bosomed blondes in bikinis.) I was a femme fatale—maybe the first in the club's history—and I slowly, but surely, took it off.

When I left the club, I left a lady—in hat, gloves, and cockroach stompers.

Back in the real world, where I worked as a makeup artist, people gasped when I told them about my new night job. "But Dita," they would stammer (because it always made them stammer), "you . . . you don't look like a stripper."

I did a spin in my big circle skirt, the wholesome rose print flaring, reaching for my inquirer. "What does a stripper look like?"

"A . . . an . . . a . . ."

I winked. "Not the good ones."

During burlesque's heyday, strippers did not look like strippers. One could argue that their makeup was a bit ravishing for daytime, and that they cursed more than the average girl, but they dressed like ladies. (Whether they were in fact ladies is another question.)

I love the challenge of making something beautiful for which people don't always have such high regard. Maybe it is the ballerina in me, the girl who has been doing pliés since she could walk, who believes everything can be as lovely as a pirouette. When I was little I cleaned the dance studio bathroom in exchange for my lessons. I owned a pair of toe shoes before I was allowed to wear them. I used to hang them up on my bunk bed and caress the peach-colored satin until I fell asleep, dreaming about becoming a big girl and dancing onstage. I incorporate ballet into many of my shows because there simply is not a single ugly move in ballet. Not one ugly move. I like to hold burlesque to the very same standards.

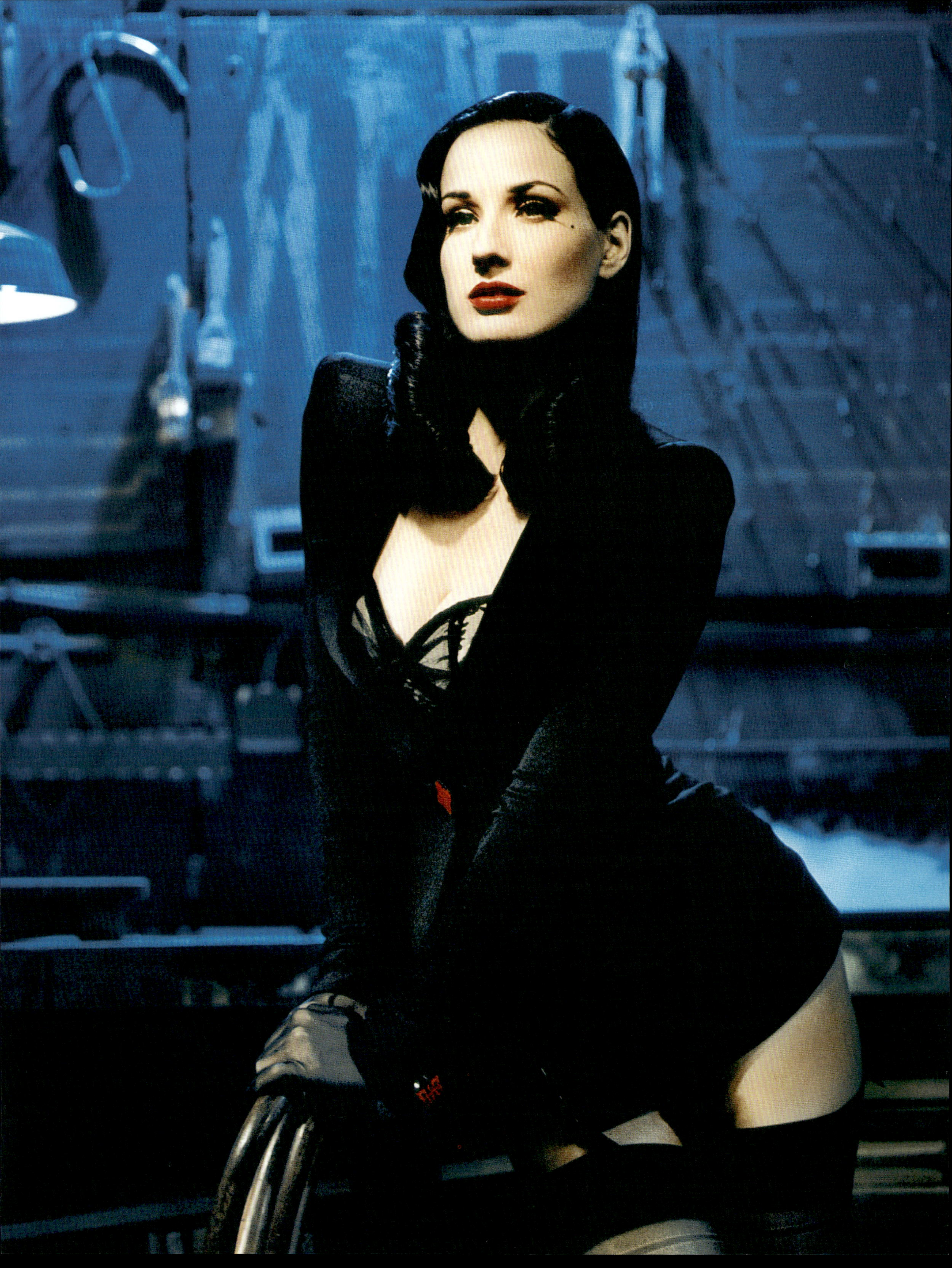

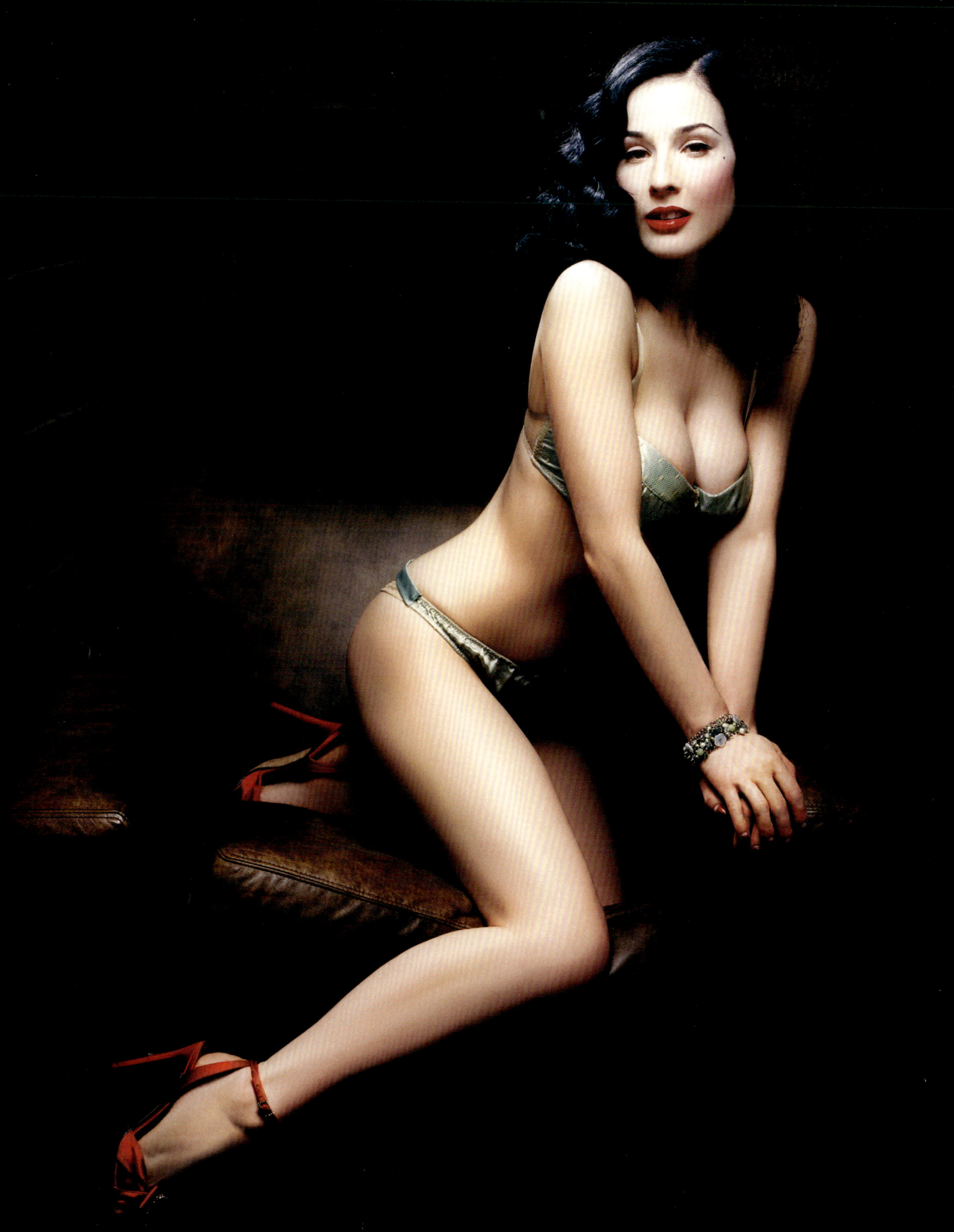

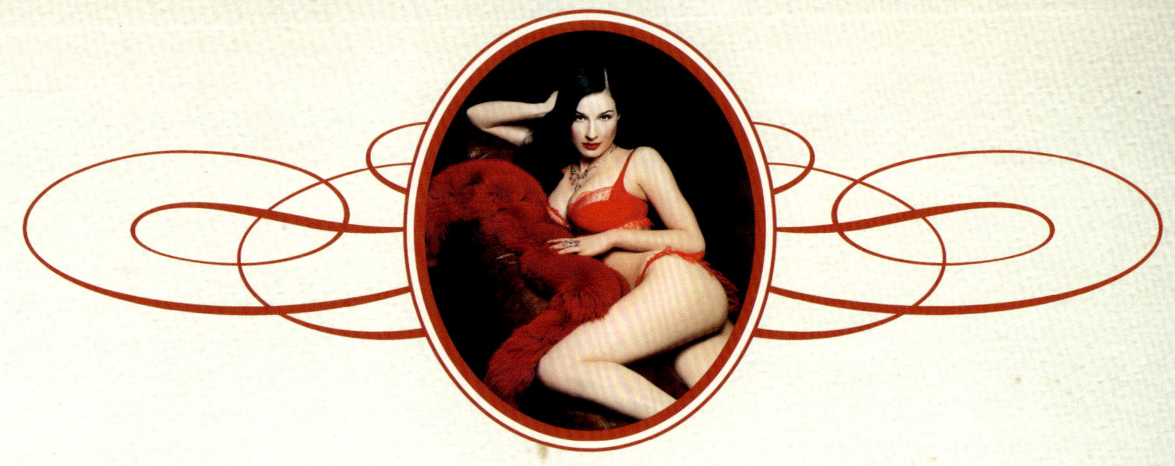

# Femme Fatale, Come Hither

Where does the ballerina meet the femme fatale, you wonder? In her confidence, her elegance, her steps. Above all, in her history. You may not believe this, but long before the *Nutcracker* and all the fearfully pristine ballet companies, the ballet dancer was a *showgirl.* That's right. In the eighteenth century, opera always included ballet—an art form bearing little resemblance to what we think of now. Yes, the girls wore tights and they pranced around the stage, but the ballet girl, or the *danseuse a' l'opera,* as she was once called, was more akin to a chorus girl dancing in a revue. Kick, spin, kick—you get it. More important, this was a *naughty* girl—at least her reputation was. Besides cavorting with powerful men, she was said to be a teasing exhibitionist. In fact, even in Napoleon's time, the most coveted ticket was one that would gain its holder access to the *foyer de la danse,* the backstage room where the girls—in various stages of undress, including complete nudity—warmed up at the barre. (Napoleon himself maintained a private room in one of these foyers!)

It makes perfect sense to me, then, that a ballerina should have a sense of her own role as a temptress—as Cyd Charisse surely did in *Singin' in the Rain*!

Hoping to make my new burlesque shows more authentic, I checked out books and old magazines from the library, studying, practicing the femme fatale's incarnations through the ages. I cut my hair shorter and dyed it red, and then magenta, and then black. I curled it, straightened it, and sprayed the bells out of it. I drew dramatic ebony cat eyes with heavy liquid liner. I read up on her attitude, her history.

The way I understand it, America first discovered the femme fatale in a petite, dark-skinned dancer they called "Little Egypt" at the 1893 Chicago World's Fair. She performed the *danse du ventre,* or what we imaginatively renamed "the belly dance." Fahreda Spyropolos captivated us, pulling up ticket sales and, say historians, single-handedly reviving the struggling World's Fair—while tantalizing America with a new fantasy. As for her dance, burlesquers saw it, mastered it, and gave it a new name: the *hootchie coochie.* (Originality was not their strong suit!)

But the femme fatale is, as you know, much more than a dark look or a saucy step. This woman is a study in shock psychology. She is the lady who turns up for meetings to remove her coat and "discovers" she is nude, and then asks her scandalized companion, "Do you have a cigarette? I don't seem to have my case on me." Sound like a James Bond girl? Not just yet.

This growing appetite for a dark enchantress led America to import a Western European stage production of *Salome,* giving America a real look into the femme fatale's *psyche* (it was the

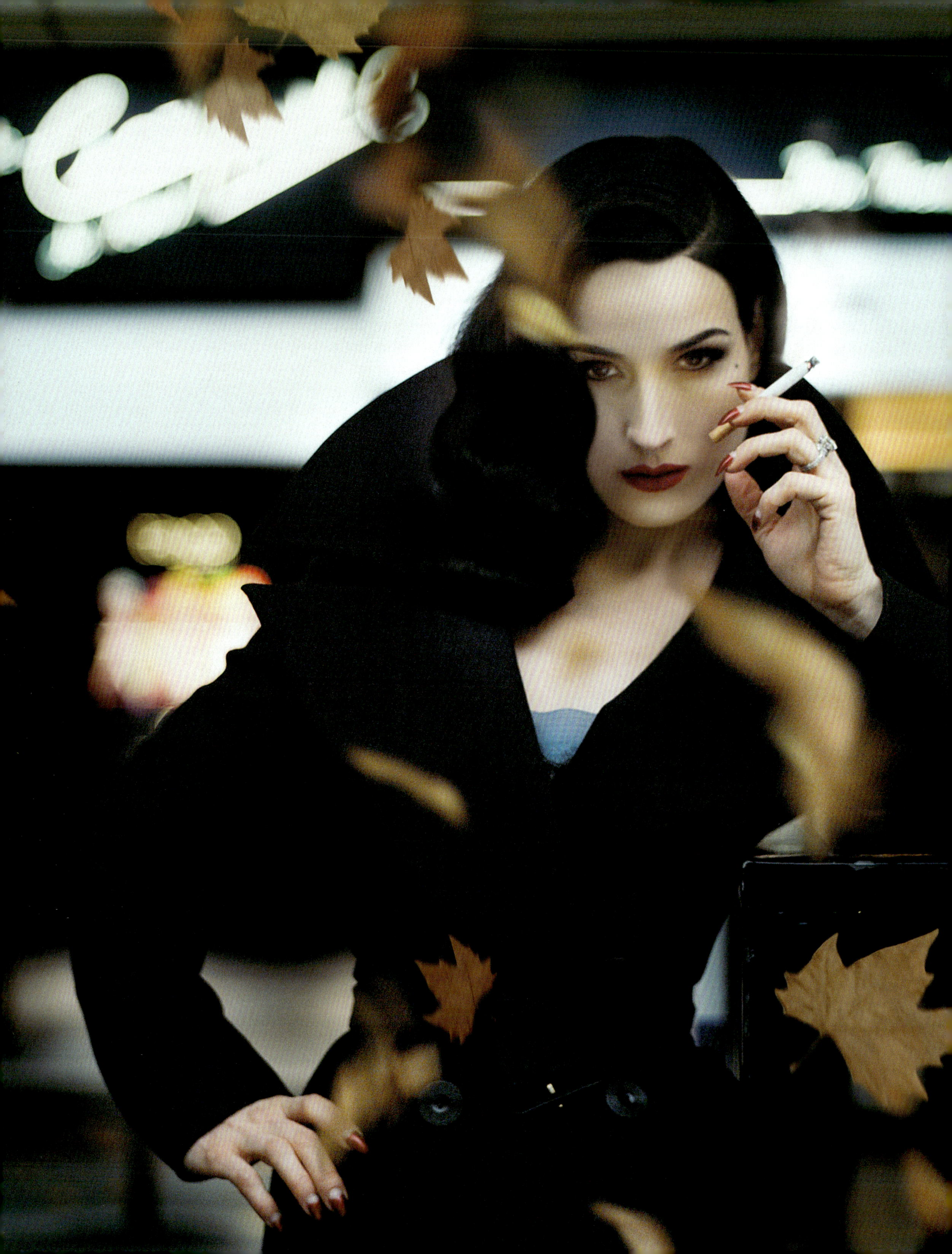

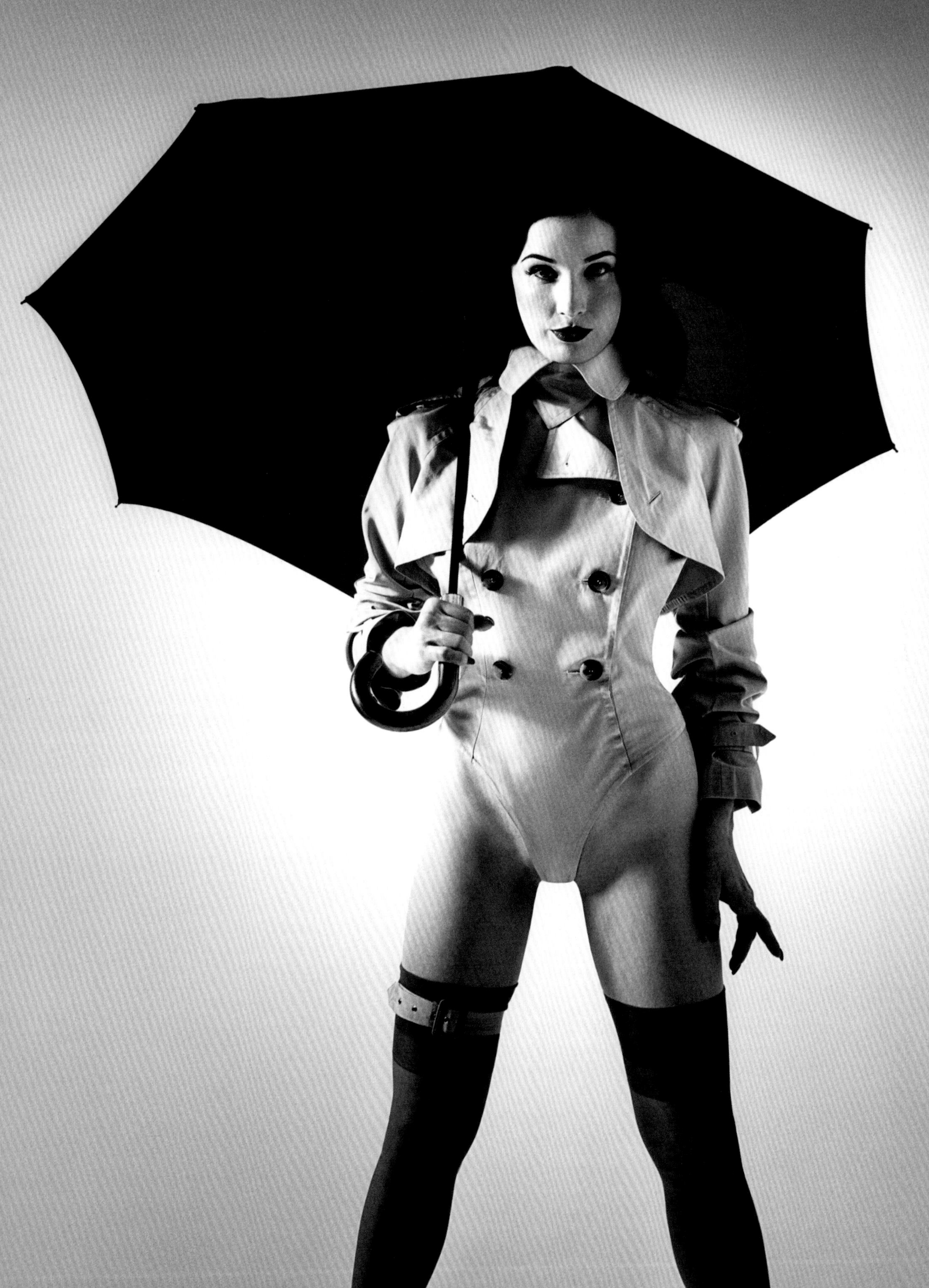

era of Sigmund Freud, remember). With *Salome,* the experience audiences were used to having in theaters reversed itself. Where they once concentrated upon *their own* sensations in watching a woman dance, they now considered *her pleasure* at being watched. Salome's was a strong, assertive, and destructive psyche—both tantalizing and terrifying. More to the point, the lady was a stripper. At the Metropolitan Opera, soprano Mary Garden shimmied away her coverings during the Dance of the Seven Veils, inciting passion and fervor in her audience that would last forever.

The femme fatale was who I wanted to be.

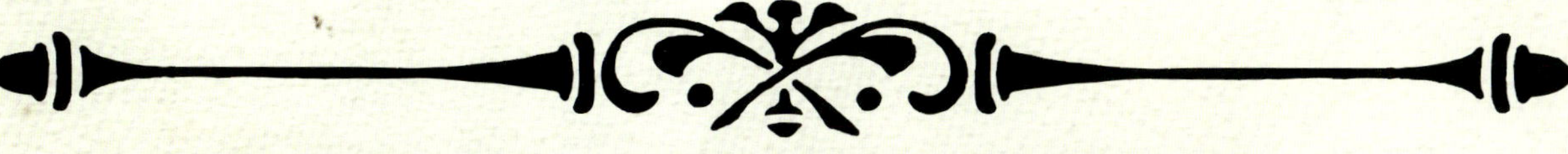

## ONE FIRST STRIP, SO MANY STRIPPERS . . .

**ALTHOUGH NO ONE WILL EVER KNOW WHO PERFORMED THE FIRST STRIP, SINCE SO MANY PEELERS TOOK CREDIT FOR IT, HERE ARE A FEW OF THE GEMS HISTORY REMEMBERS**

- **Salome, first century BC: Salome disrobed so gracefully that King Herod offered her anything she desired, which happened to be the head of John the Baptist on a platter. A little decadent, but she'd earned it.**
- **Adah Isaac Menken, 1861: Riding across the stage in pink tights and a short tunic, strapped to the back of a horse, English Adah climbed down and removed her cloak, partially shielded by actors.**
- **Anna Held, 1906: Flo Ziegfeld's wife, Anna, changed in and out of costumes onstage behind the chorus line in a performance of *The Parisian Model* in New York.**
- **Mae Dix, about 1917: This Minsky's girl was looking to save money on her laundering bill, so she pulled off the collar as soon as her number was over—and the audience nearly rioted. Mae reemerged and unbuttoned her bodice. When the crowd screamed for more, she teased and shimmied. The house manager fined her ten dollars for breaking the rules. Minsky repaid her the ten and gave her a raise to keep it up.**
- **Hinda Wassau, 1920: Hinda layered her costumes for quick changing. Yet one fateful evening she was unable to remove one for another. Hinda went out onstage and began a violent shimmying dance, hoping the first costume would come off. *Everything* came off.**

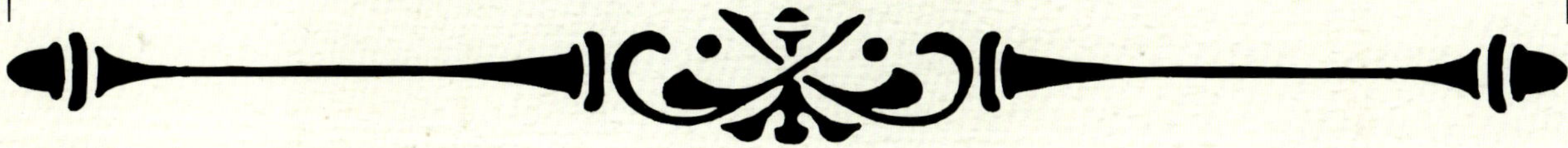

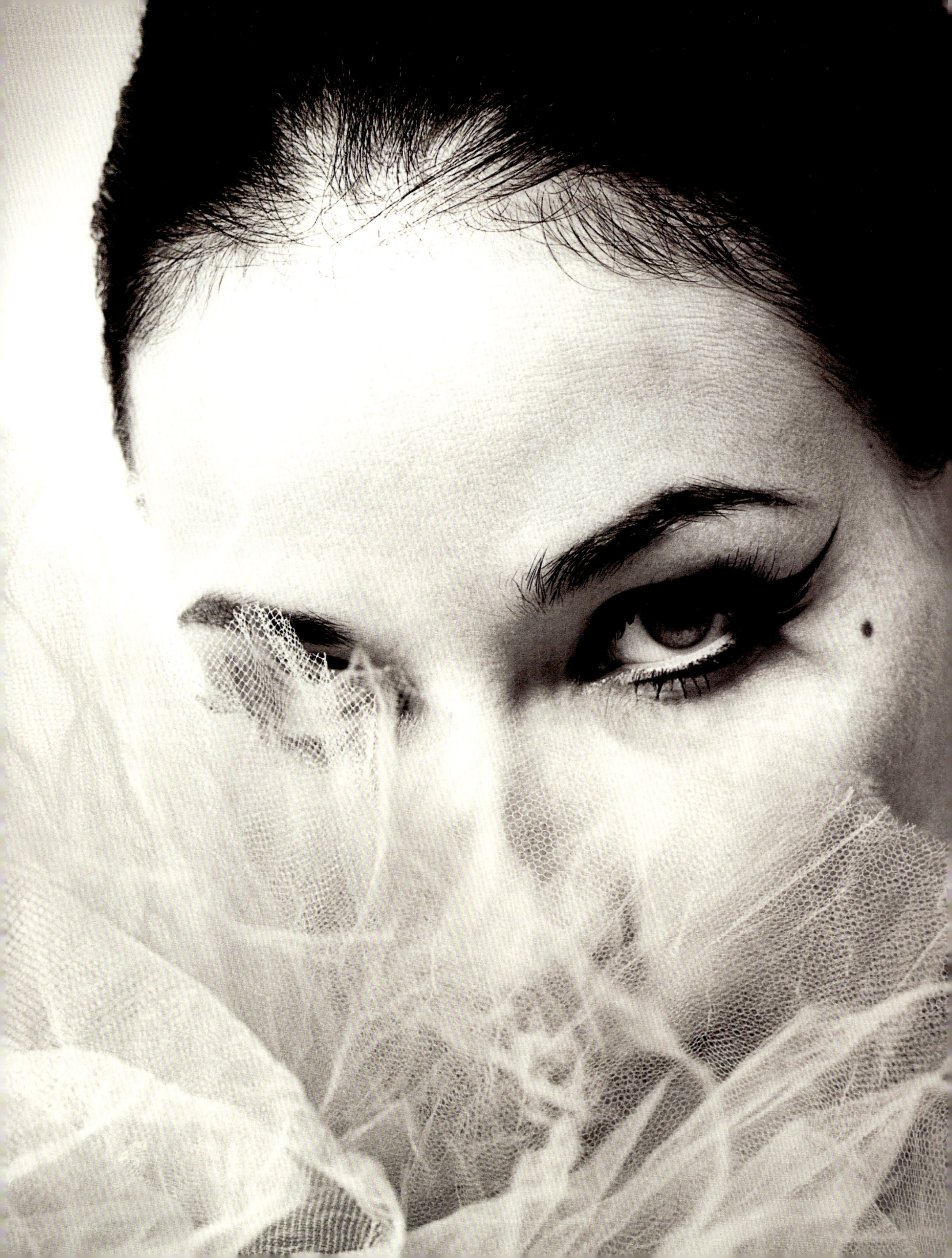

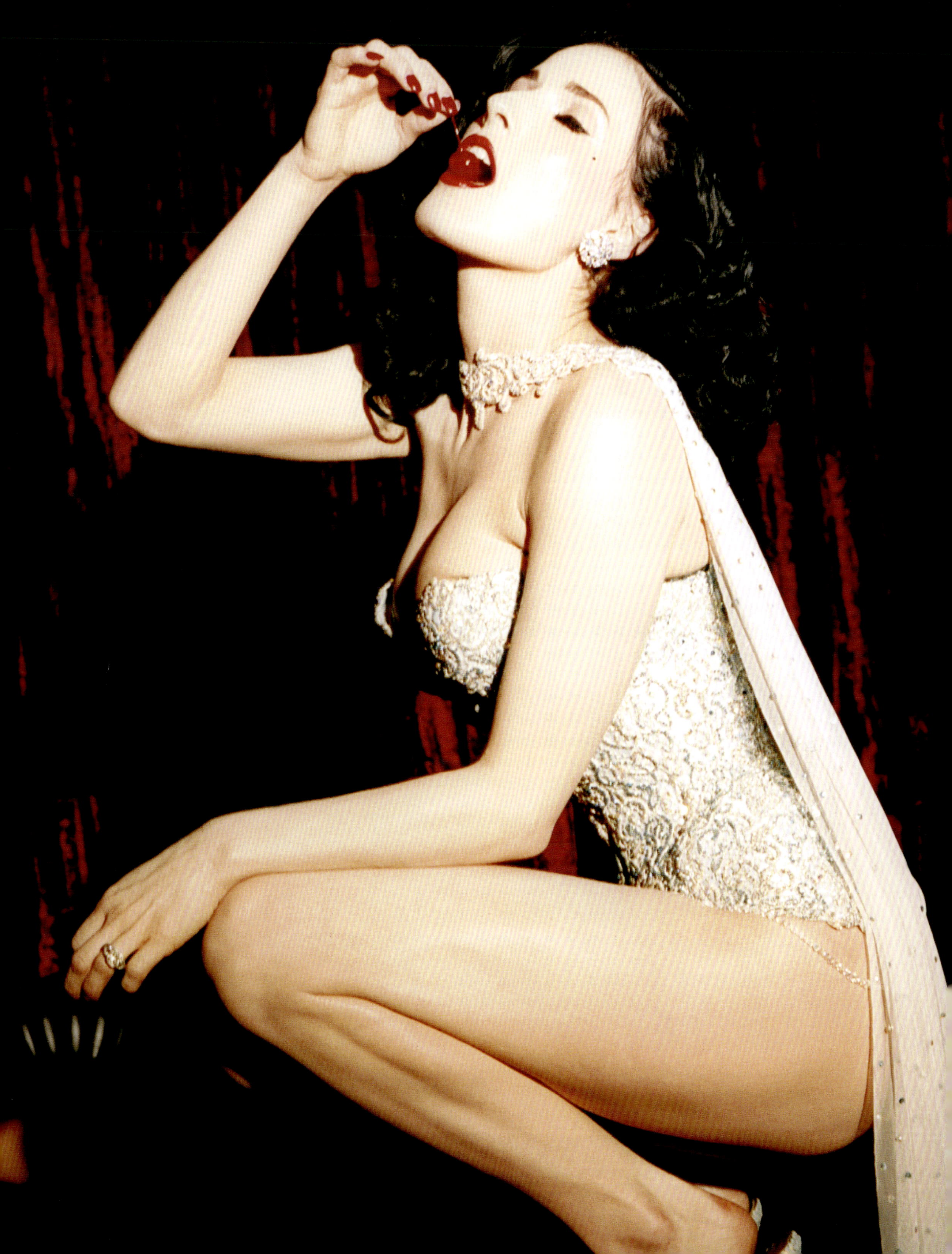

# OFFSTAGE SEDUCTION SECRETS

## USE YOUR WOMANLY WILES ONSTAGE AND OFF . . .

1. Apply lipstick in full view of your victim. This is particularly effective when done slowly and with a pretty compact.

2. Adjust your garter or stockings as though you were attempting to do it discreetly.

3. Allow your stiletto heel to dangle from one foot.

4. Touch yourself lightly in places you would want him to touch (not there!)—your neck, décolletage, hair, face. Do this subtly as he talks to you, and remember to be fascinated by every word he says!

5. Go to the powder room—alone! Captivate every man in the room by gliding confidently and effortlessly across the room in your stilettos.

6. Wear something that feels nice to the touch . . . velvet, silk, cashmere.

7. Wear your signature scent lightly. Make him lean in close to smell it.

8. Eat sexy foods . . . strawberries, cherries. This isn't about tying a cherry stem with your tongue to show off, it's about effortless and natural seduction, and this principle should be applied to all of the above tips.

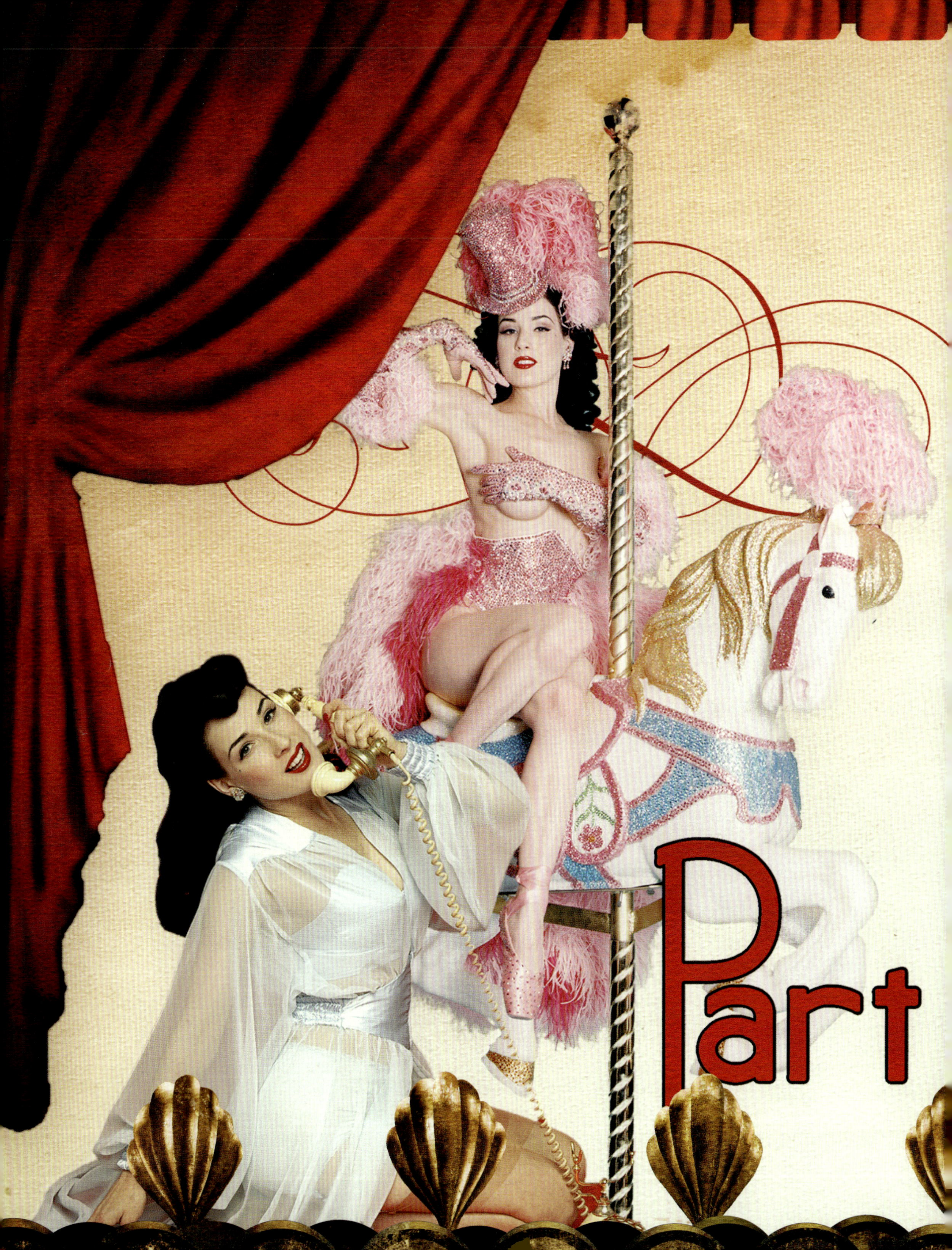
Part

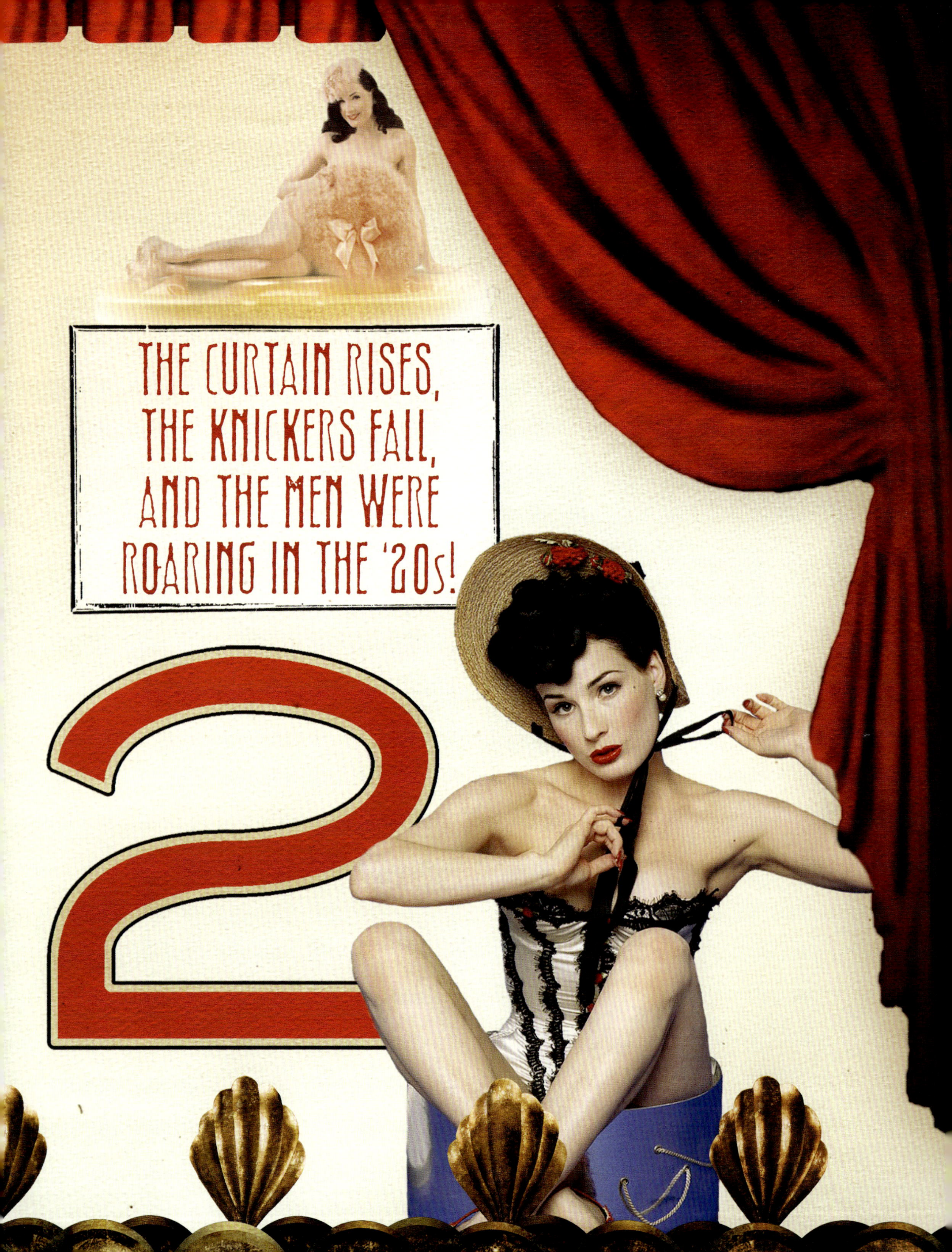
THE CURTAIN RISES,
THE KNICKERS FALL,
AND THE MEN WERE
ROARING IN THE '20s!
2

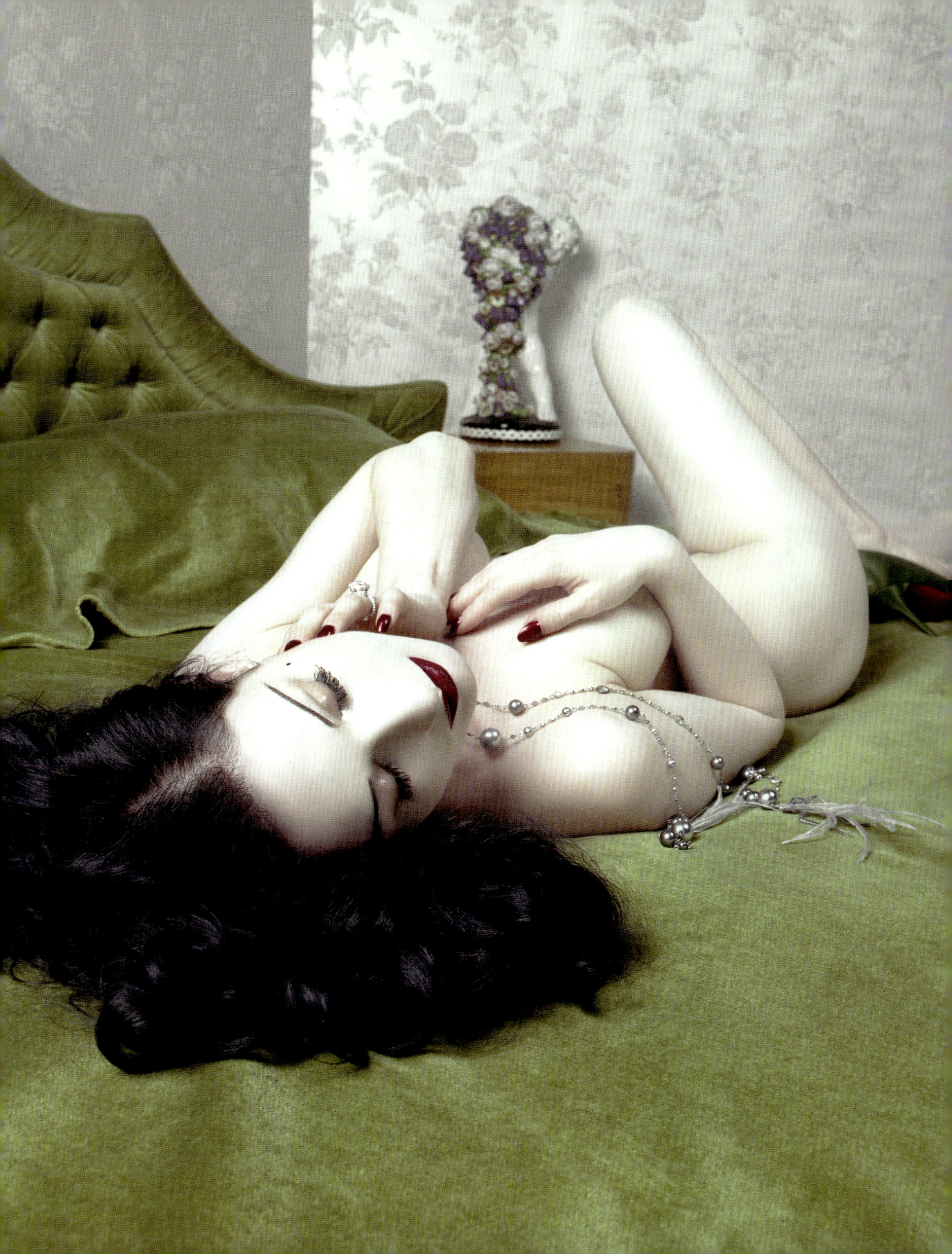

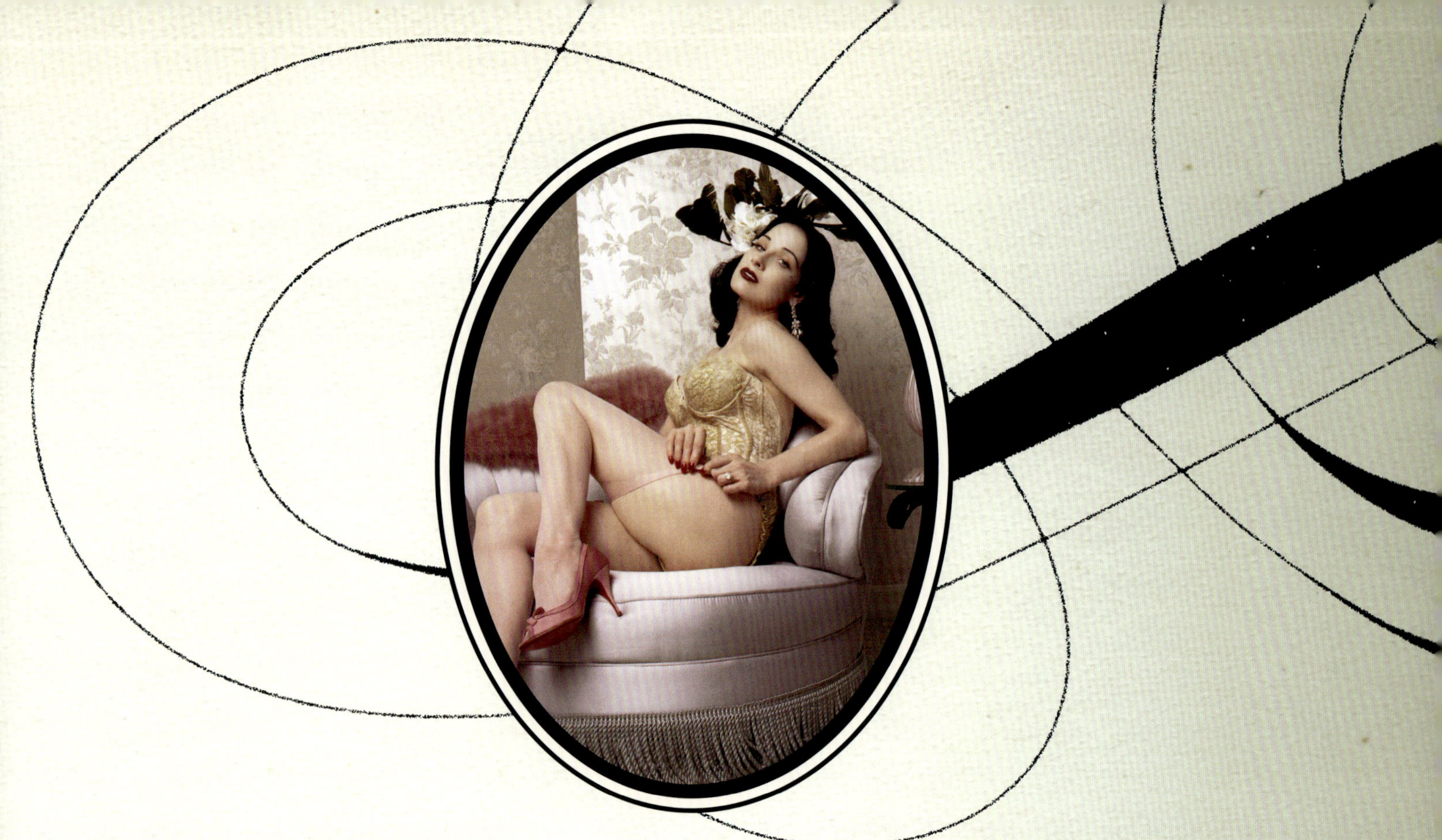

# A Time of National Undress

The 1920s were—as I like to think of it—a time of national undress, and *not* just for the showgirl. Out on the street, hemlines were rising, baring first the ankle, then the calf, and nearly the knee by decade's end. Alarm consumed the nation, with citizens storming city councils demanding dresses, dresses, dresses! Imagine it! Laws passed making it illegal to wear skirts more than seven-and-a-half inches off the floor in Philadelphia, for instance, and in Utah, skirts could be no more than three inches above the ankle. Similar regulations concerned the ever-naughty throat: in Ohio a lady could expose no more than two inches of neck!

In Europe and much of the rest of the world, people were allowed to drink to their heart's content, and women kept their clothes on. In America, where alcohol and too much leg were both deemed illegal, we developed the art of the striptease. Call me crazy, but the connection is obvious. One: weary men drain into the speakeasies (one of the most popular was Manny Wolf's, a few hundred yards from the Minsky's door). Two: drunk and looking for fun, the guys cross the street to where the girls were twirling their tassels on the National Winter Garden's newly built runways—the first in America!

I'm not talking merely about blue-collar clientele. In an exchange that became known as the silk hat trade, uptowners haunted downtown speakeasies, following the pack into Minsky's den. In fact, "slumming" became so much the thing to do that Minsky's saw an assortment of uptown regulars, including magazine publisher Condé Nast; writers John Erskine, John Dos

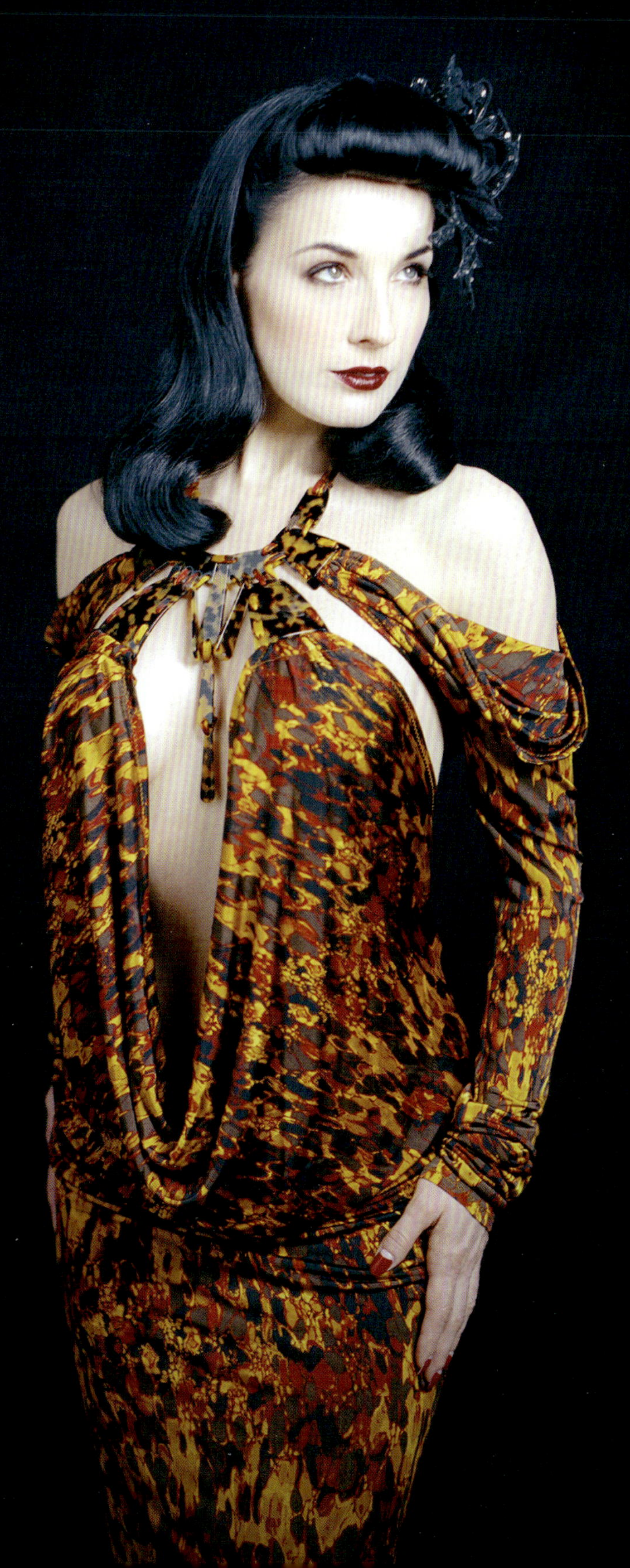

Passos, and Walter Winchell; and the poet Hart Crane, who wrote this charming ditty about the Minsky's productions:

*National Winter Garden*
Outspoken buttocks in pink beads
Invite the necessary cloudy clinch
The world's one flagrant sweaty cinch.
And while legs waken salads in the brain
You pick your blonde out neatly through the smoke,
Always you wait for someone else though, always—
(Then rush the nearest exit through the smoke).

Business was so good at Minsky's that old Billy opened two more theaters uptown, including the now legendary Little Apollo on 125th Street. But with the Minsky brothers' immense popularity came trouble with the law. My favorite Minsky raid has a horse-drawn paddy wagon pulling up in front of the Winter Garden, with the officers handcuffing the brother on duty. Once the bluenoses berated him for soiling neighborhood morals, Herbert Minsky walked them out, innocently inviting them to "drop in any time," with the assurance that they would "never see anything off-color at Minsky's." To make good on this promise, the brothers rigged footlights from the ticket booth through the theater so that when an officer entered, whoever was in the booth would hit a button flashing red through the rooms and to the stage, alerting the cast to promptly switch to what they called their "Boston" or "Sunday school" versions. Theaters all over town adopted the light rigging.

You might think things have changed. A few years ago, before burlesque had truly hit the mainstream media, my best friend, costume designer and co-burlesquer Catherine D'Lish, and I were "invited to leave" an establishment where we had earlier been "invited to perform." As we left the building, the venue manager explained, "We can't have entertainment like this here. This is a family place." Eighty full years after Minsky! It amazes me that if I do my show the way I like to do it—as it was done in burlesque's heyday so long ago—some people still find it too racy (after all, they are adults!). Of course, once word got out about our expulsion, Catherine and I found ourselves with a dozen new engagements on our wayward hands.

Anyway, back in Minskyville, what I think of as the Lonely Guy Club of Censors, officially known as the New York Society for the Suppression of Vice, finally hauled old Billy into court on obscenity charges.

You may as well know that just about every big star in the history of burlesque has been hauled in on obscenity charges. And with Minsky as a defendant, the spectacle was as good as anything he ever put onstage. The state's attorney and leader of the SSV (I'll call him State's A) complained to the judge that the "lascivious pelvic contortions . . . during the dance programmed as 'The Shame of La Boheme' were . . . indecent and immoral." You can still hear the judge snicker as he demanded a demonstration.

Surprised and morally appalled, State's A protested that he could not dance sans musical accompaniment. It was an insincere objection, and the judge nailed him. The judge (I'll call

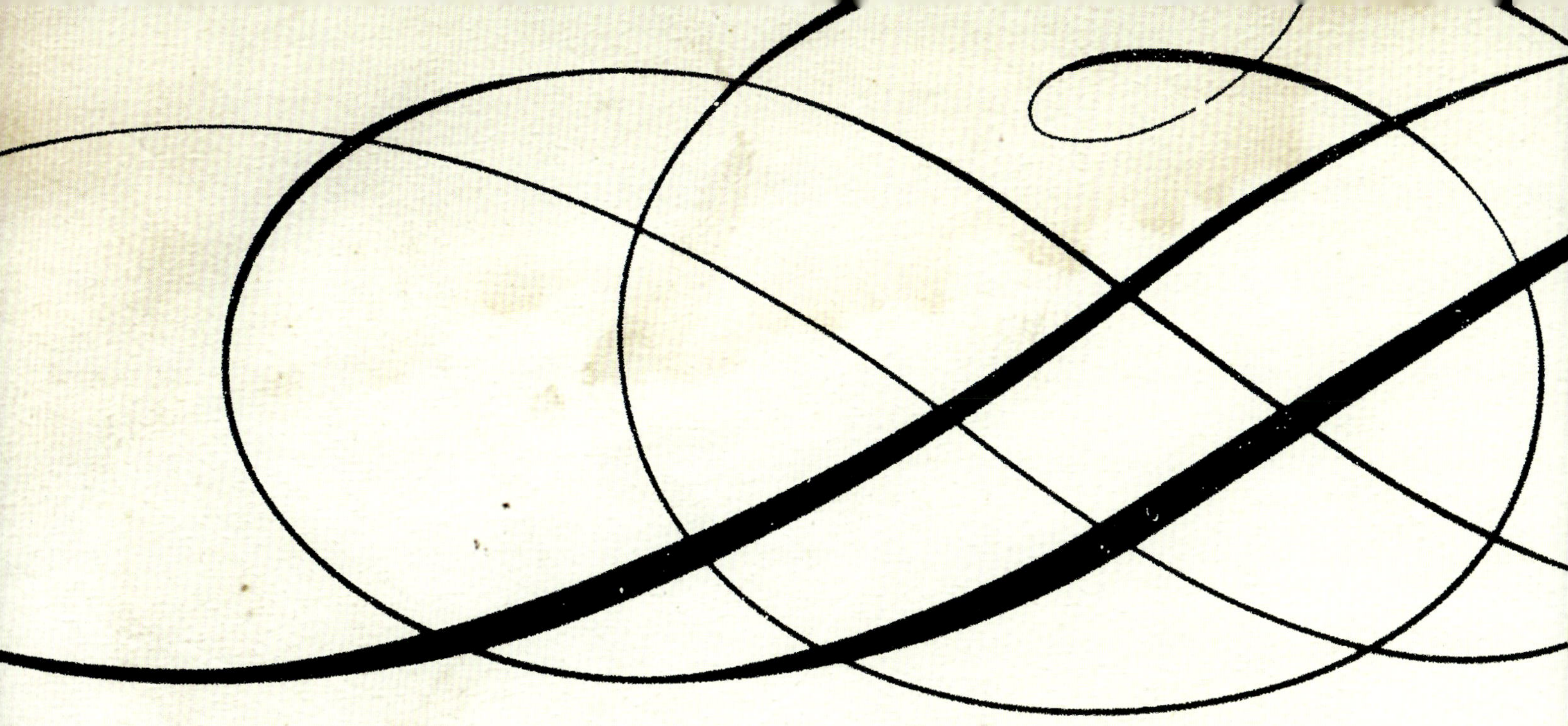

him Cheeky) asked for volunteers among the cast (who were in court on their own charges), ordering the shaken State's A to dance while the cast sang. State's A opened with a bump-and-grind number, his ineptitude demonstrating that there was in fact art involved in the striptease. Cheeky stopped the performer mid–hootchie cootchie and turned to the defendant. "Mr. Minsky, would you as proprietor of the National Winter Garden hire this dancer for your show?"

"Your honor," Billy Minsky replied, "I wouldn't wish this dancer to waltz on the grave of my worst enemy."

Did I mention that New York was *fun* in the twenties?

State's A blushed hard and raised his most important point so far: the Minsky dancer "did bare her breasts and move indecently." Now Cheeky was not going to sit through a shimmy, too. He asked the defense for their rebuttal.

Oddly, Minsky's lawyer questioned State's A as if *he* were a witness! "Have you visited any shows *uptown* by Shubert, Carroll, or Ziegfeld?"

"Yes," went the response.

"Are the women there 'nude from the waist up?'" queried Minsky's lawyer.

"Yes," was the answer, cheeks flushing.

"Why did you not stop *them*?"

State's A explained that the uptown performances were not "immoral" but works of beauty, art.

Minsky's lawyer continued his line of questioning—of the prosecuting attorney. "Could you explain why exposed breasts are decent *north* of Fourteenth Street, but indecent south of it?"

The prosecutor uttered the party line that would distinguish *revue* from *burlesque* for the next thirty years. "The difference is movement. On Broadway, unadorned female figures are used to artistic advantage in tableaux. They do not move."

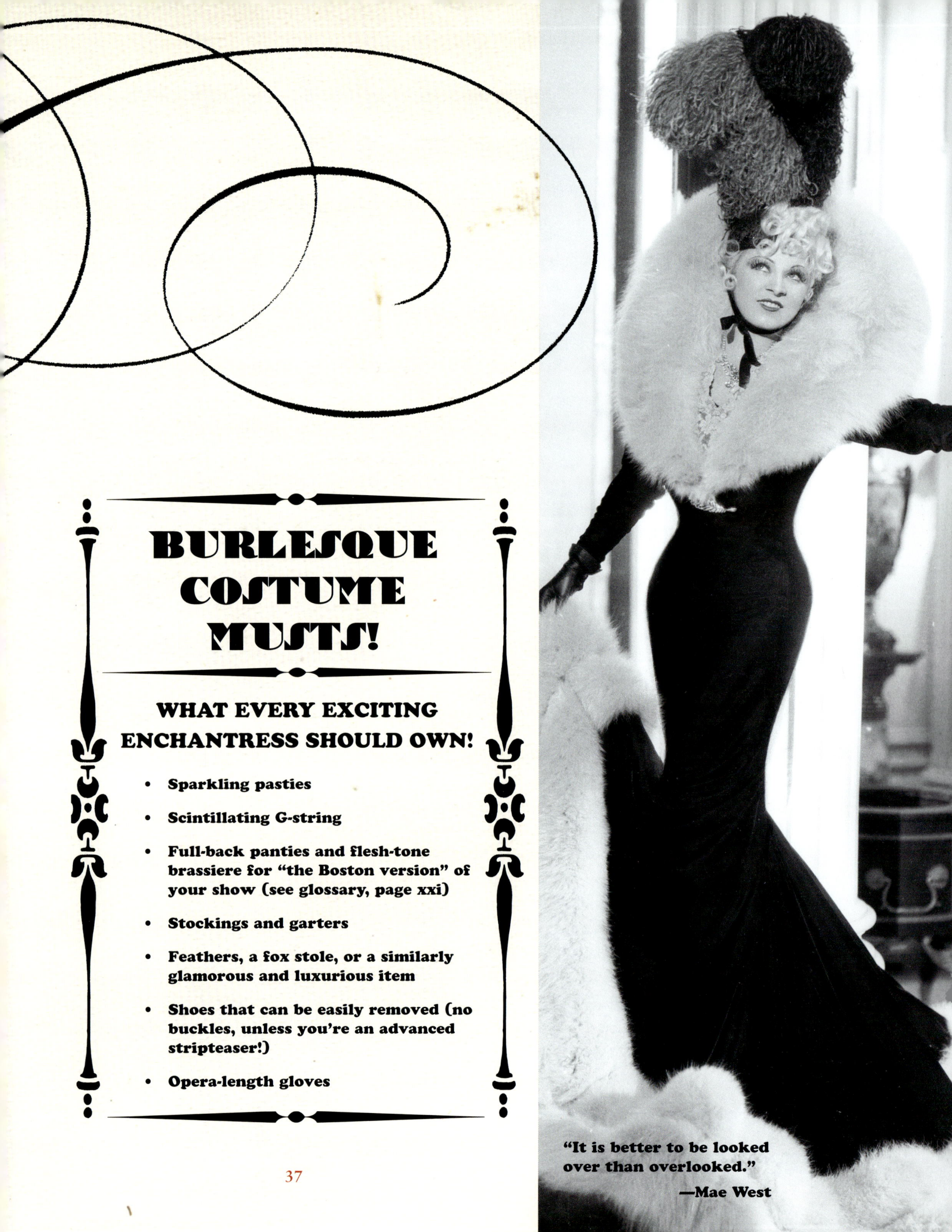

# BURLESQUE COSTUME MUSTS!

## WHAT EVERY EXCITING ENCHANTRESS SHOULD OWN!

- Sparkling pasties
- Scintillating G-string
- Full-back panties and flesh-tone brassiere for "the Boston version" of your show (see glossary, page xxi)
- Stockings and garters
- Feathers, a fox stole, or a similarly glamorous and luxurious item
- Shoes that can be easily removed (no buckles, unless you're an advanced stripteaser!)
- Opera-length gloves

"It is better to be looked over than overlooked."

—Mae West

The difference—at least morally—is nil. Minsky and Ziegfeld both knew their seats would sell if they showed fair flesh. Plain and simple. But Ziegfeld was sneakier: he reasoned that a naked woman posing as a classical painting or sculpture was immune to police intervention. The *tableaux vivants* had been, after all, used for hundreds of years in the theater. Their revival on Broadway was welcome to the audience (which included many more women than downtown), and the courts bought it, too. But don't you buy it. Though the audiences and the courts called the shows uptown *revues*, you may consider all of it burlesque.

Minsky's case was dismissed, and in the short term, the courtroom drama paid off. What, after all, is better for business than publicly calling a program "lascivious"? The words those brothers painted on the marquee out front said it all: BURLESQUE AS YOU LIKE IT—THE POOR MAN'S FOLLIES! *NOT* A FAMILY SHOW! The National Winter Garden was standing room only for months after.

Now, Flo Ziegfeld is one of my heroes. The man "celebrated the American girl" as I would like to be celebrated myself—in couture and feathers and diamonds. Ziggy was a study in decadence. Take his revue in 1910, for example, when his star, Lillian Lorraine, rode a pony onto the stage and was lifted, horse and all, by an elevator onto a festooned swing fastened to a track in the ceiling. Now, girl and horse flew out high over the audience, swinging back and forth, back and . . . you realize this was the era of the Model T? This man was innovative in his extravagance! Ziggy's final revue, scored entirely by Irving Berlin, cost a stunning $300,000. In 1927!

Ziegfeld believed in opulence, and so do I. Flo taught me that performance is not *all* about the performer: spectacle and skill are a winning mix, but if you hide talent beneath a pile of rags, it cannot shine. Not the way I like it to shine anyway, with unimaginably ornate sets, props that exist mostly in dreams, and gowns that glisten with the intensity of one hundred thousand hand-cut Swarovski crystals.

Would you believe I devise my entire show based upon a single one of these jewels? It's true. I choose a color from my collection (I keep a three-tiered glass box full of samples at all times), and with it I can imagine a whole world. It may take hours or days, this thinking process. Catherine and I will sit, sipping Dom Perignon and dreaming up ridiculous, over-the-top fantasies . . . and suddenly one of them works! And then we set to work, creating the dress, the prop, and the corset—the setting, if you will, for this crystal.

Of course, locating one hundred thousand crystals of a single color can be daunting. Recently, for example, Catherine was set to construct a dress founded upon a subtle lavender rhinestone. I possessed a few thousand of the gems and ordered the others while Catherine made the dress, then the shoes, the corset, and the jeweled, flowered headdress. We affixed the "few" crystals I had in my cache, and we waited. And waited. Could ninety thousand rhinestones be lost in the mail? I called the importer. The crystal, it seemed, was no longer available. I had been looking at an outdated color chart. There were others in the same color range, but did I want those? No! This crystal was the foundation of my performance—it was my muse, my inspiration.

Besides, we had already fastened a few thousand of them onto the exquisite French lace—one by one by one.

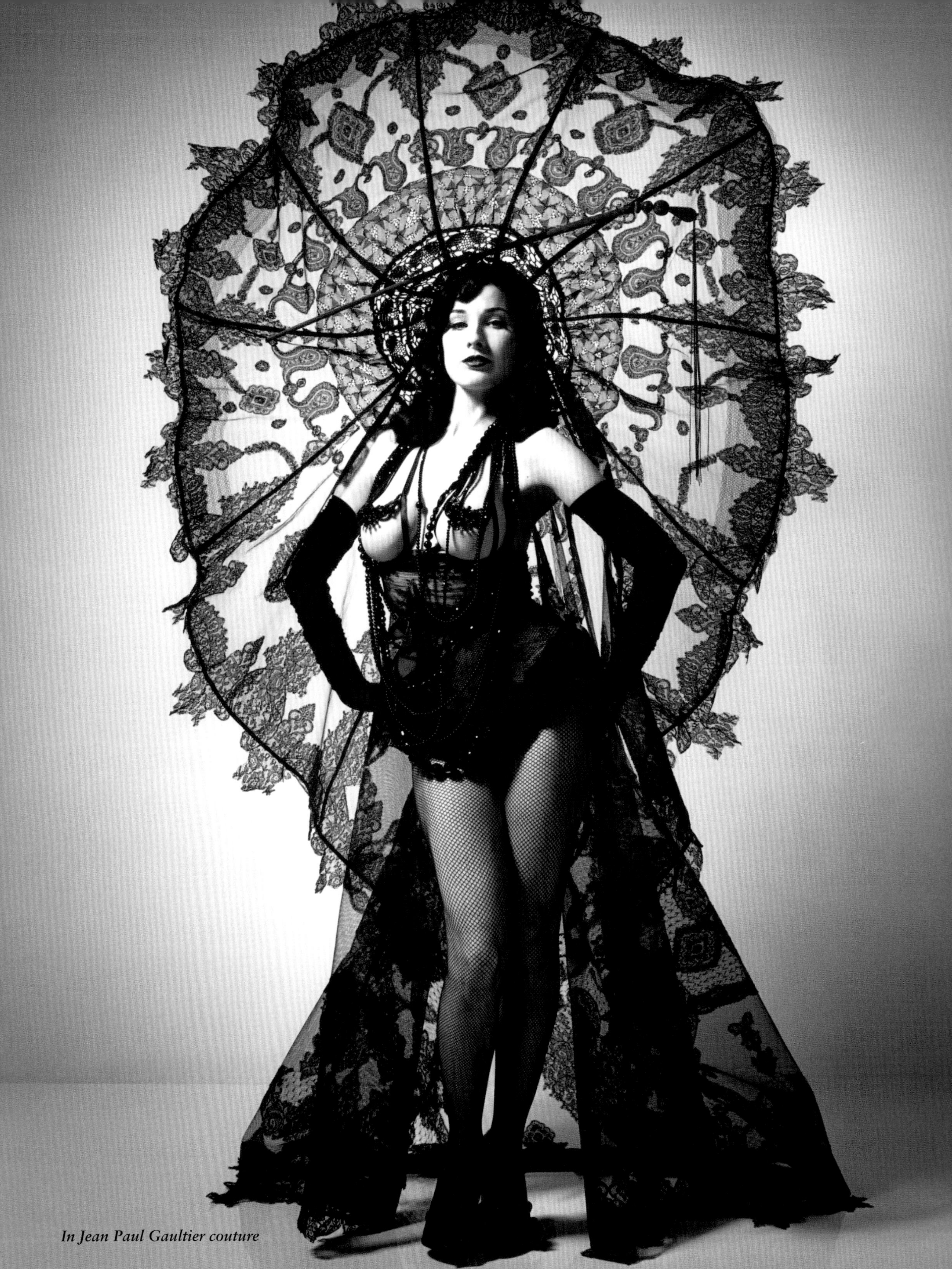

*In Jean Paul Gaultier couture*

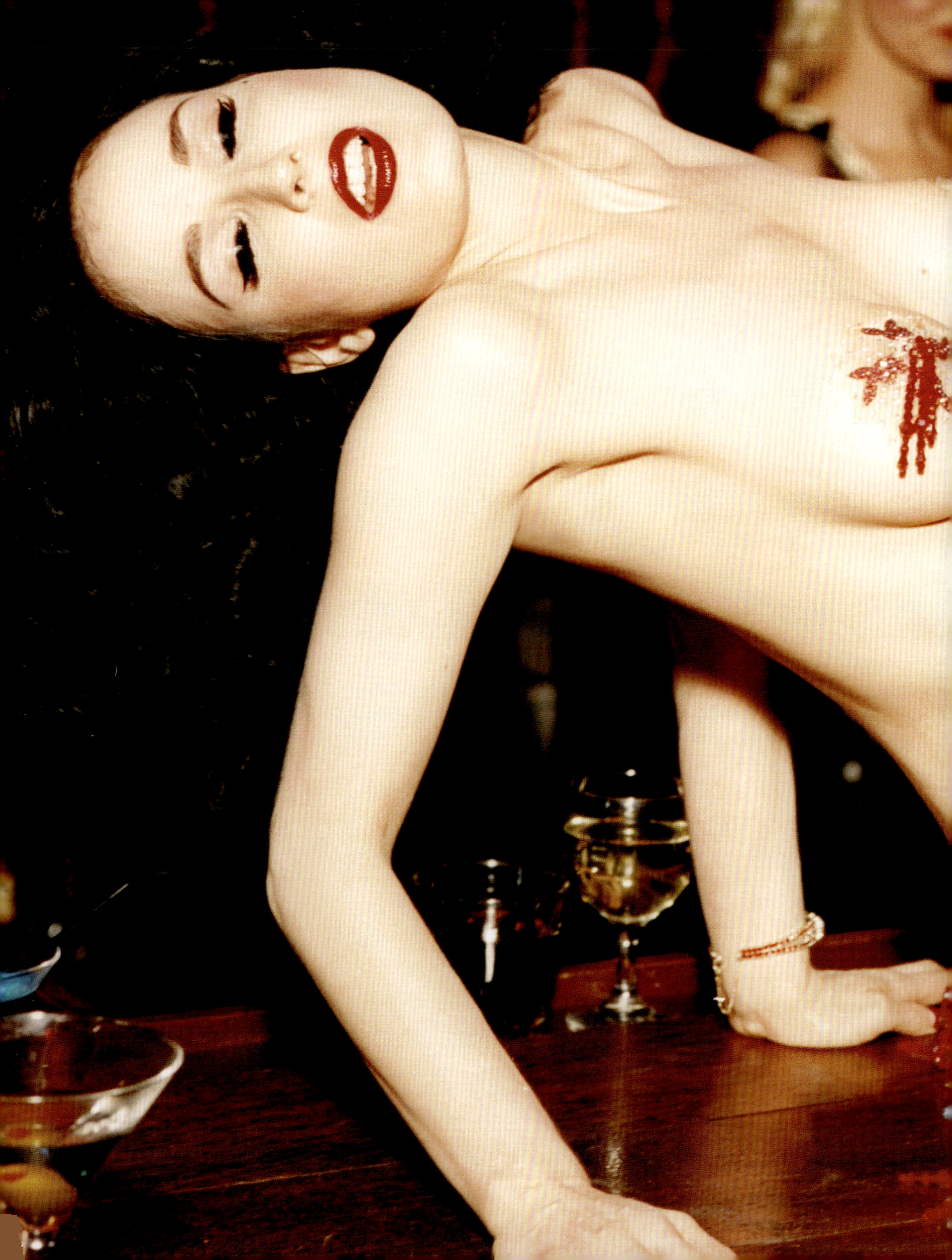

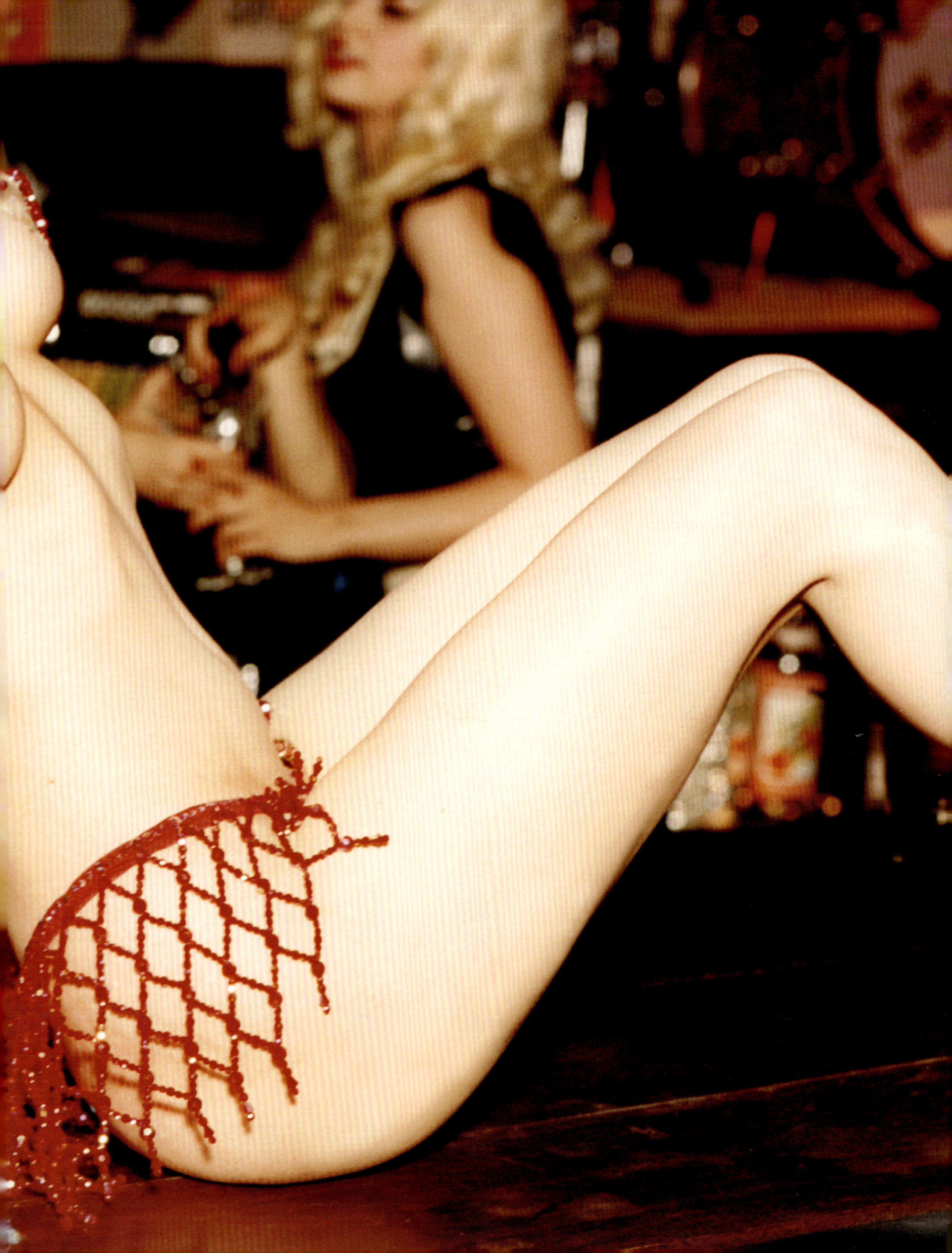

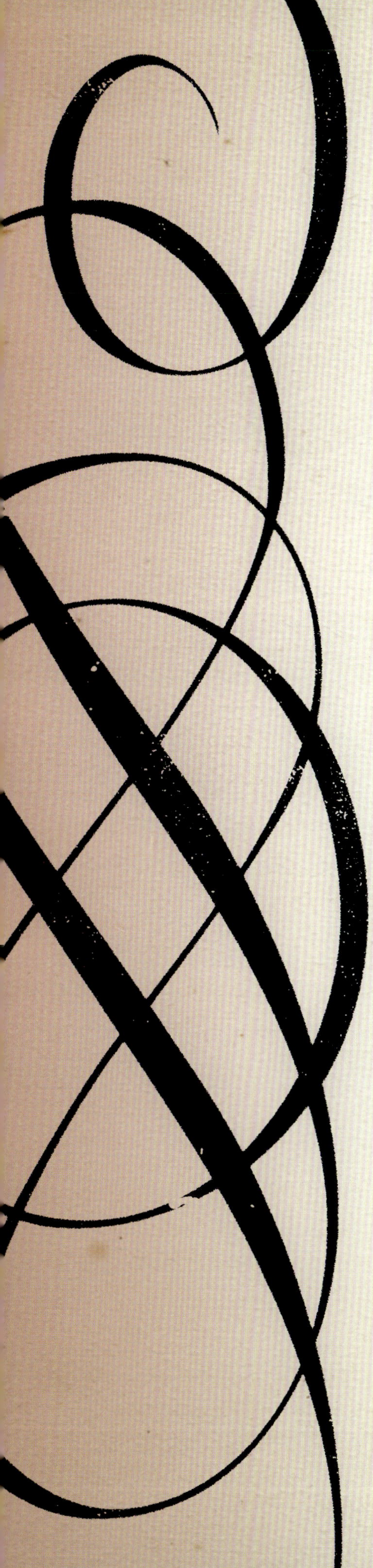

Anyway, I hung up the phone with the supplier, and set about frantically placing calls all over the world. After what seemed like thousands of dead ends, I located a woman working out of a minivan in my own city! This lady owned *all the stones left in the world*. What a coup! She held me rhinestone hostage, charging me double! What could I do but submit? Still, the dress is stunning.

Catherine has made me one dozen (and counting!) such jewel-encrusted costumes, using only the finest fabrics and drawing me perilously toward bankruptcy with every stitch. When I feel desperate about it, I remind myself that I am investing in my art, that opulence is my signature. Some people will suggest that I rely too heavily on showmanship. These people are absolutely right. I'm a good dancer and a nice girl, but I'm a *great* showgirl.

Gypsy Rose Lee, burlesque's first superstar, was every bit for the showmanship I'm talking about. In her heyday in the 1930s and 1940s, she had her clothes and costumes made to order by the pricey couture designer Charles James—who also constructed the wardrobes for royalty and movie stars. Gypsy spent obscene amounts of money on her costumes, tags that would amount to five figures today. She insisted on Louis Vuitton trunks for her costumes and a custom-designed Rolls Royce in which to arrive at her bookings. Why? Because for Gypsy it was about creating a fantasy, being untouchable, *not* being the girl next door.

Besides, if I ask Catherine to make anything but the very best, she will refuse.

She's right to. Once you have worn the finest materials on Earth, you can hardly return to the snap-front bra. Hold up an ordinary rhinestone to the light and you will see what I mean. That rhinestone, it may glitter some. You might even think it is pretty. Now, hold up a Swarovski crystal. That's right. It shines with an intensity you prefer to the sun's. Perhaps I exaggerate a little, but it is the nature of my business. What is costume and makeup—what is burlesque—but a delicious parade of hyperbole?

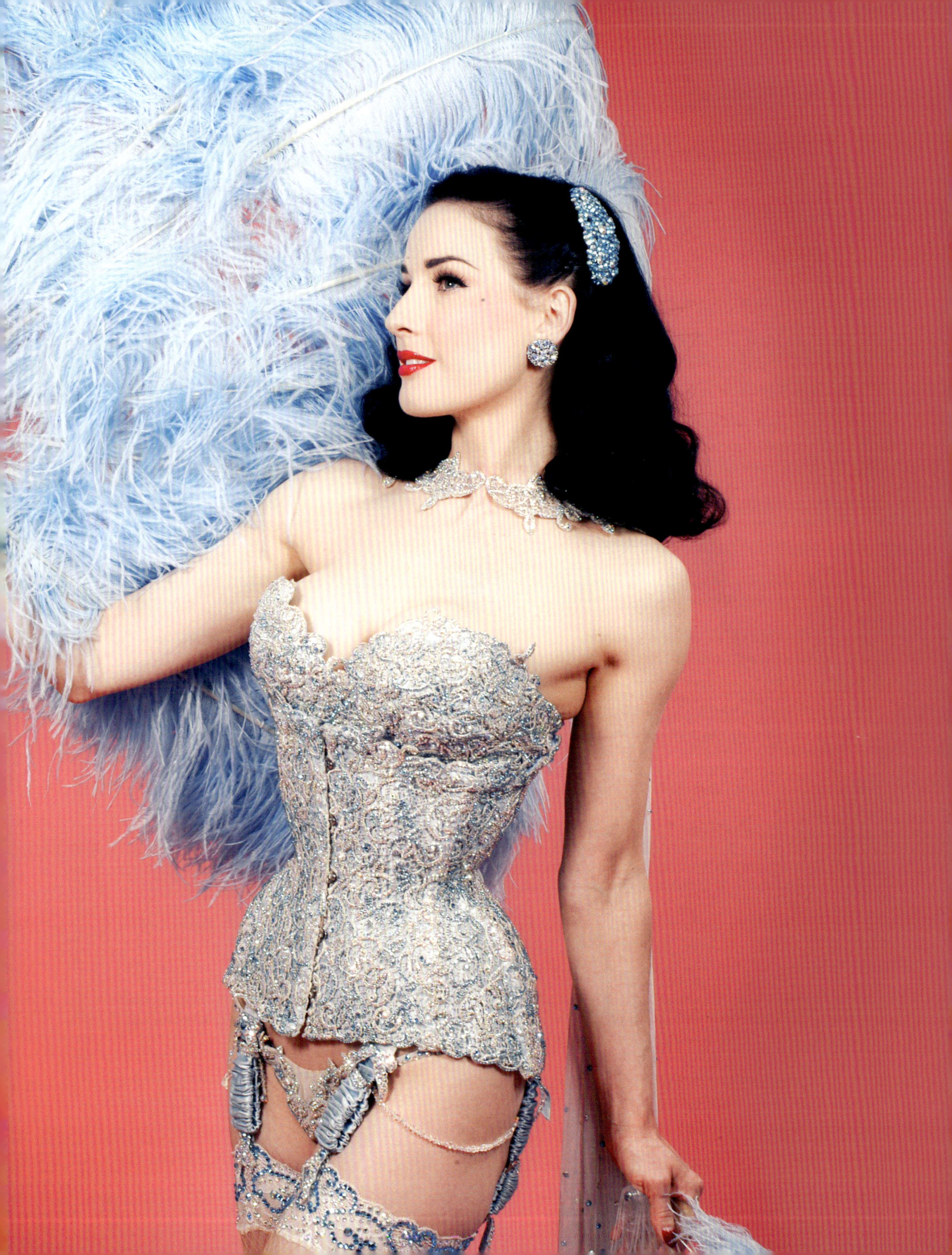

# SO YOU WANT TO BE A STRIPTEUSE?

**BILLY MINSKY WROTE THE BOOK ON HOW TO TRANSFORM FROM SWEETIE PIE TO SEX GODDESS. HERE ARE HIS GOLDEN RULES, WITH SOME OF MY OWN SAGE ADVICE FOR THE MODERN TEMPTRESS . . .**

**COSTUME: It should be luxurious, have lots of layers, and be easy to take off. A quick path to a bad performance is having to wrestle with your costume. Practice so that you can do it all with one hand, blindfolded (see *Fetish*).**

**HAIR: Back in Minsky's day, the girls had to dye it a definite color—red or yellow or black—because only certain colors worked with the spotlights. I find this is still good advice. However, in these days of independent burlesque you can choose your spot according to your hair. If your hair is flaming red, try the magenta. If it's black like mine, a pale blue or lavender spot works wonders for beauty and mood. Or, if you're blonde, go with an amber spot.**

**MAKEUP: Create a powdered and flawless foundation for face *and* body. I use an all-over pale shimmering white powder à la Sally Rand.**

**HANDS: I recommend you study ballet dancers—their hands are always lovely. Ballet is about grace and elegance, two things that have been proven time and time again to be attractive.**

**WALK: Be consistent and make it fit the music—whether it is graceful tiptoeing or a grand old strut. Videotape yourself, analyze yourself.**

**SIGNATURE: You've got to have one. Mine is the martini glass. What's yours?**

**PEELING PACE: Again, consistency is everything, ladies. If you're fast, keep it up-tempo. If you're a slow seductress, resist the temptation to turn it up.**

**TIMING: If you're up first or your audience looks bored, you'd better take it off early. If they are two sheets to the wind, take your time and tease, tease, tease.**

**PERFORMANCE LINE-UP: Minsky's feature peelers used to arrive onstage at the evening's middle and before the finale. If you can't have this slot, follow a comic routine—the audience will already be in a great mood, or they will just be happy to see someone stripping again!**

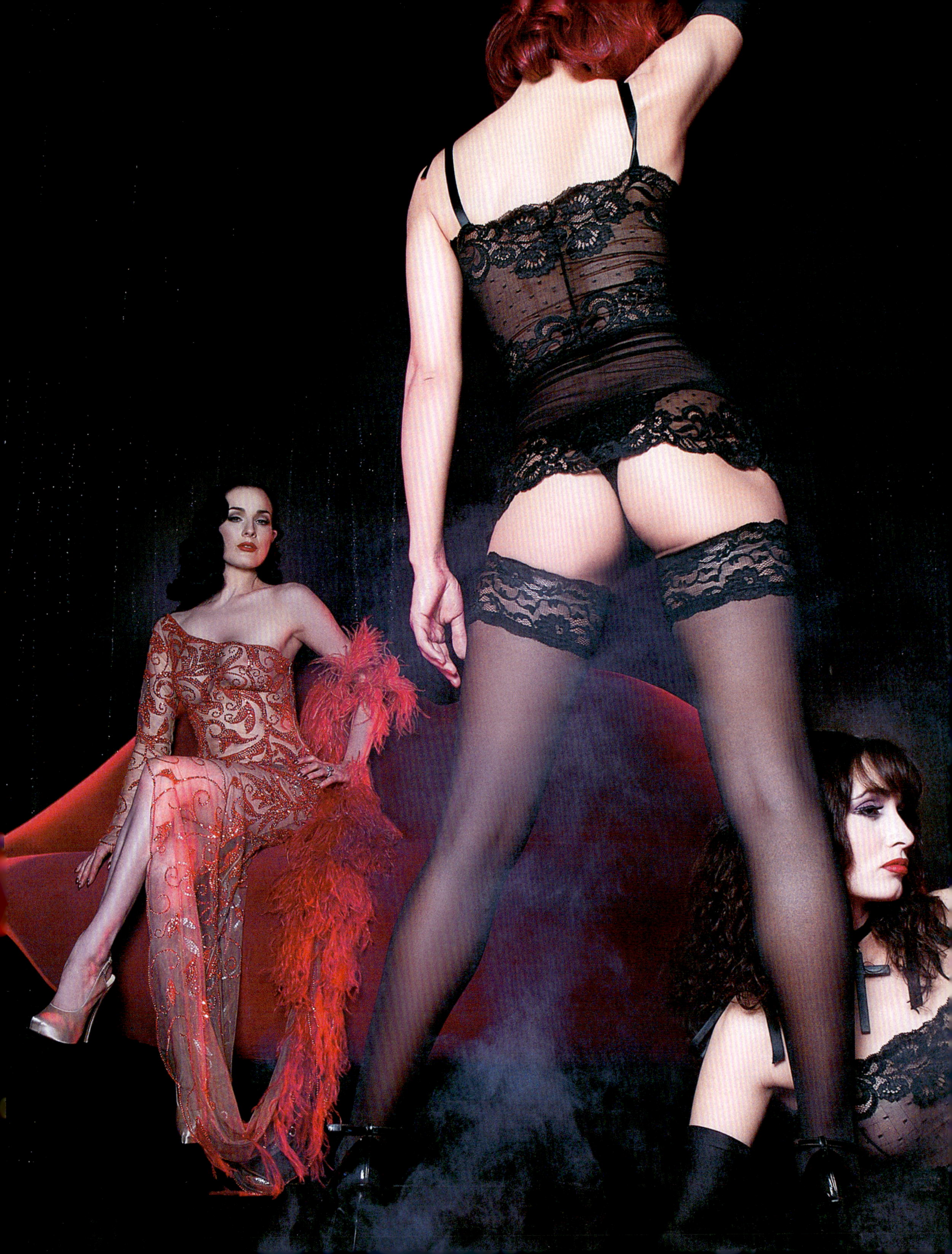

# PERFORMANCE PROBLEMS STRIPTEASERS MAY FACE . . . AND HOW TO THWART THEM!

## BEFORE YOU GET FOOTLOOSE AND FANCY FREE, TAKE NOTE!

**HANDS-ON AUDIENCES:** Steer clear and adjust your costume . . . keep just barely out of reach!

**A STUCK ZIPPER:** I always try to get an audience member to assist, and although they rarely succeed in fixing the problem, it buys you a little time to get it undone on your own.

**CANNED MUSIC PROBLEMS:** When using prerecorded music, whether it skips or stops playing altogether . . . just keep dancing!

**LOSING A PASTIE:** This sometimes happens, particularly if the show involves water: Hold it in place lustily with one finger, or live dangerously and lose it altogether! (Lili St. Cyr did it in the fifties, and I did it just this year!)

**TAKING A SPILL, OR STUMBLING:** What can you do but either laugh at yourself and look on the floor to see what tripped you, or just act like you meant to do it?

**GETTING VON FLEECED!:** I can't tell you how many jeweled stockings, velvet corsets, and lacy panties have been swiped from my stage over the years. I have since learned that no one is to be trusted. Keep an eye on each garment, and toss them out of reach, or better yet, employ a lovely assistant to retrieve them and keep a watchful eye.

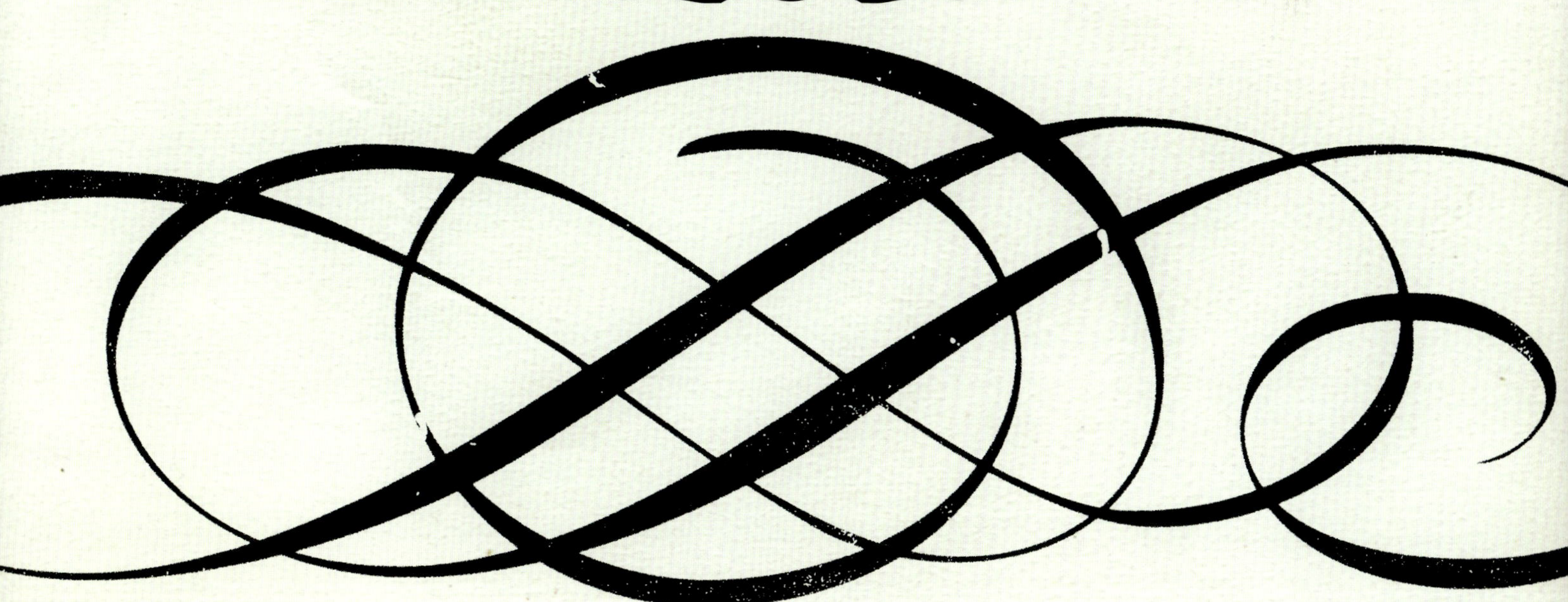

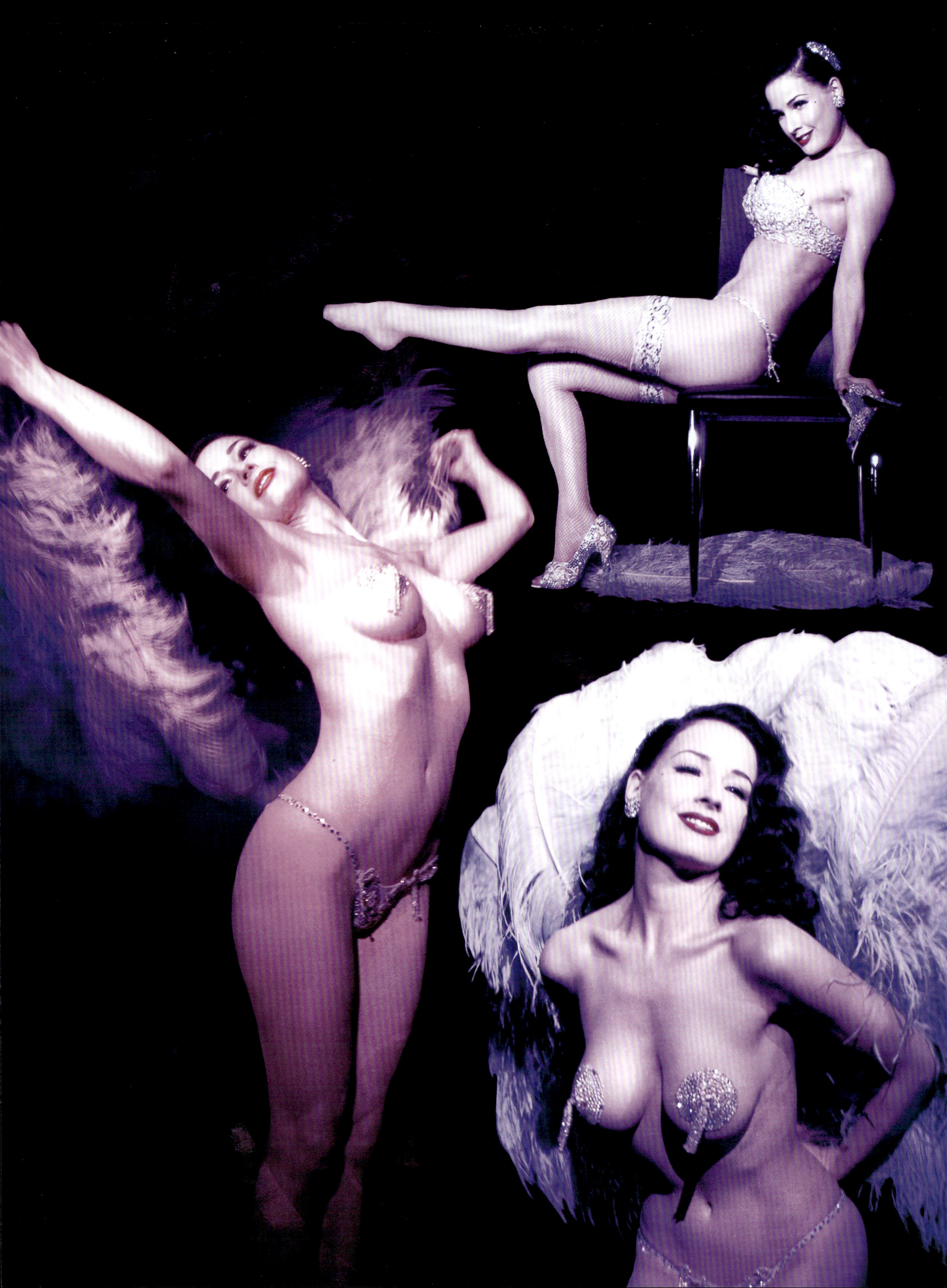

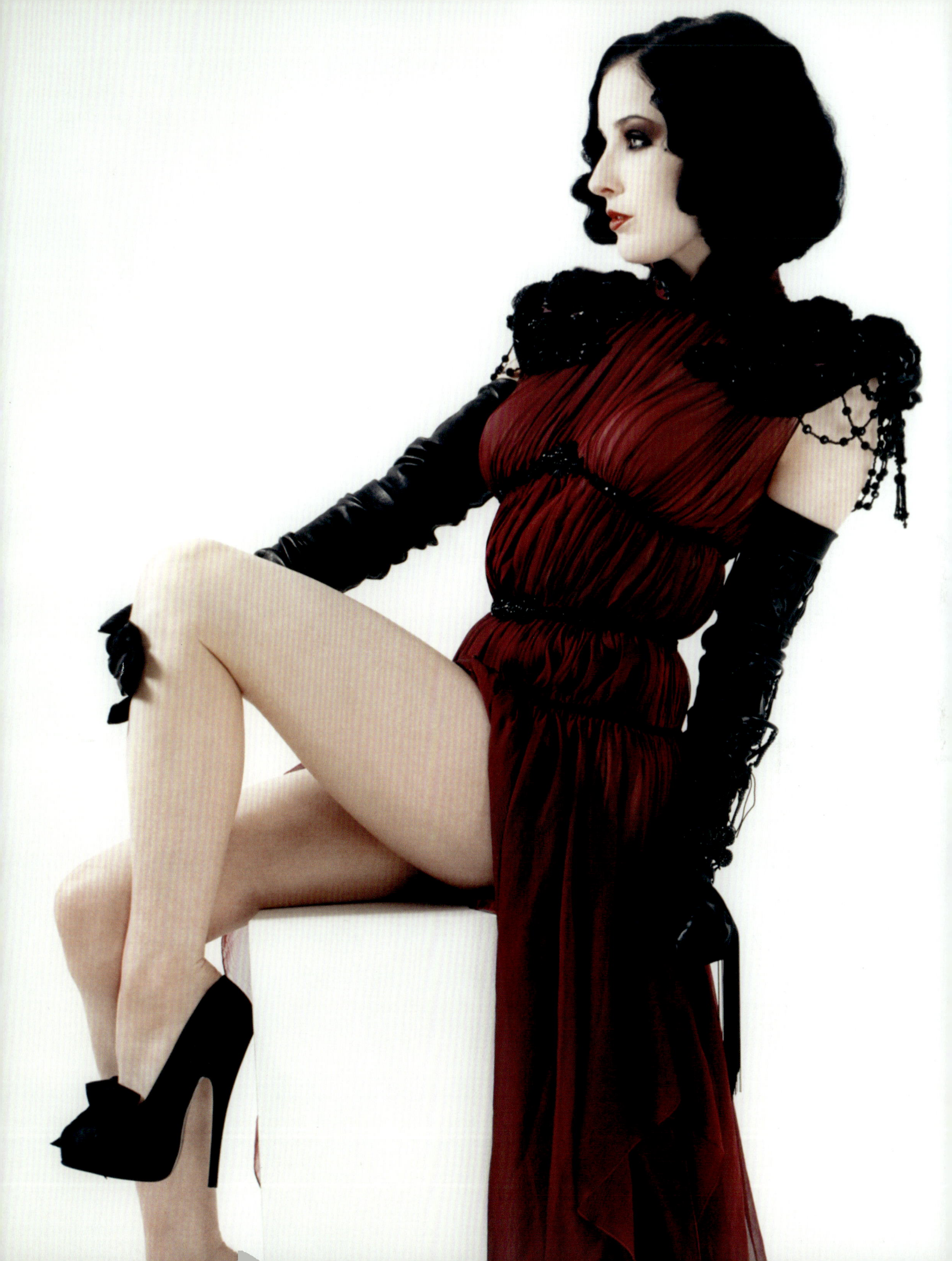

# FIRST-CLASS FACE: HOW TO GET THE LOOK OF THE '20S VAMP

**THE 1920s WAS THE ERA OF THE FEMME FATALE. HER HAIR WAS BOBBED, HER LIPS BEE-STUNG, AND HER EYES SMOKY. AS ONE OBSERVER PUT IT: "THE VANITY-CASE AND THE CIGARETTE-HOLDER ARE THE SYMBOLS OF THIS DECADE . . . THE WEAPONS OF A FANTASTIC COQUETRY." HERE'S WHAT I DO WHEN I'M LOOKING TO BE A LITTLE BIT WICKED . . .**

**'20s SHOW GIRLS**
Mistinguett
Josephine Baker
Mae Dix
Hinda Wassau

**FILM STAR FLAPPERS**
Theda Bara
Louise Brooks
Clara Bow

**SKIN:** Very pale ivory without rouge and a matte flawless finish.

**BROWS:** Penciled dark, thin, and dramatically arched.

**EYES:** Dark and exaggerated with the deepest jet black pencil liner smudged all around the eye. Apply a deep smoky gray or black shadow over the crease and blend well.

**LIPS:** Penciled into a small rosebud shape and rouged with a matte wine or plum shade.

**NAILS:** Worn either very short and painted entirely in a deep vamp crimson or burgundy. Or for a true vampy look, wear nails long with pointed tips and color applied only in the center with the tips and moons near the cuticle left natural or painted white.

**HAIR:** In this era of the jazz baby, it was all about sleek, glossy pixie bobs and tight marcel waves! If your hair is long, try a short bob style wig, or pin back the length of your own hair to create a classic flapper 'do.

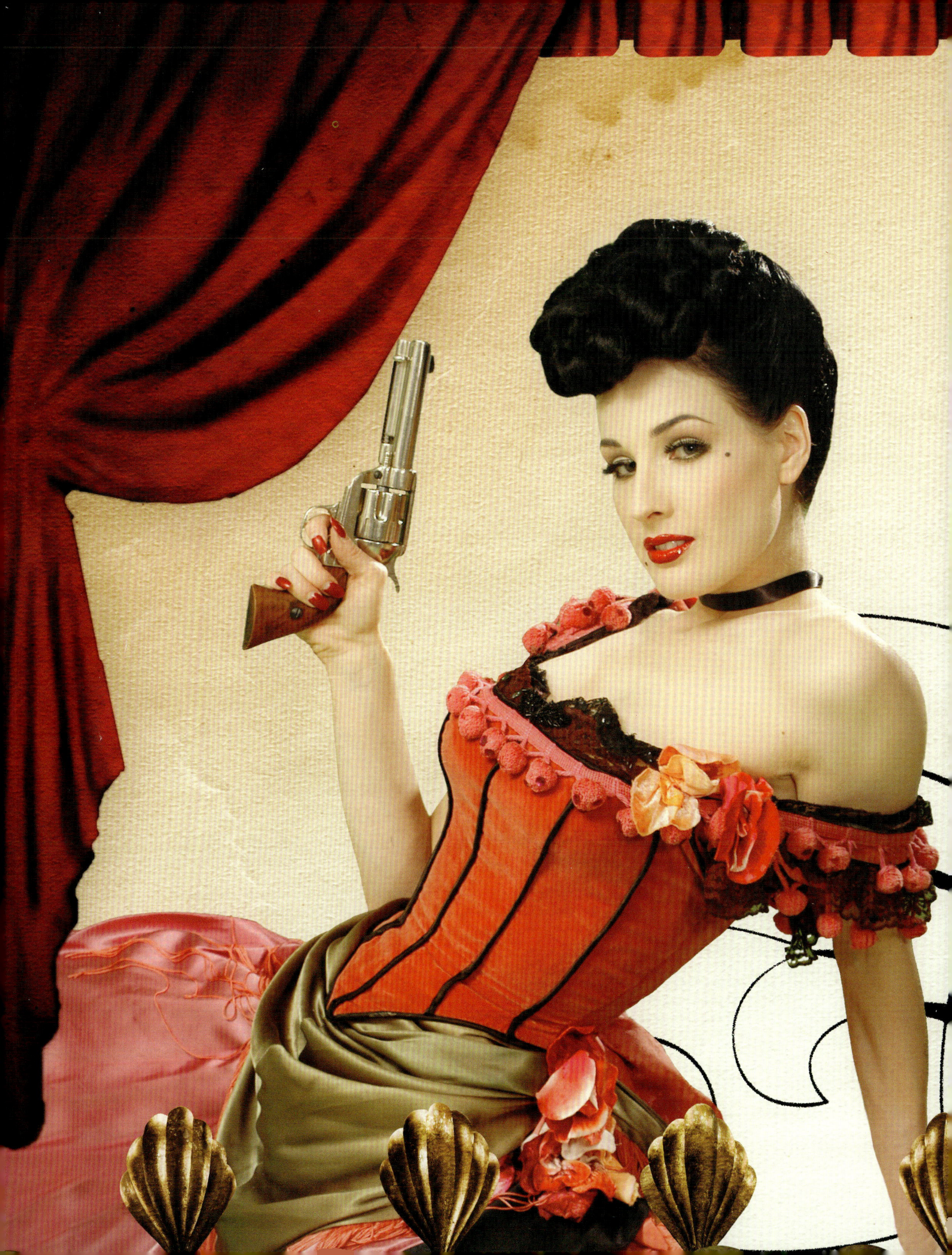

# Part 3

## GIVING THE BOYS THE BUSINESS: HEADLINE HONEYS AND THE 1930s

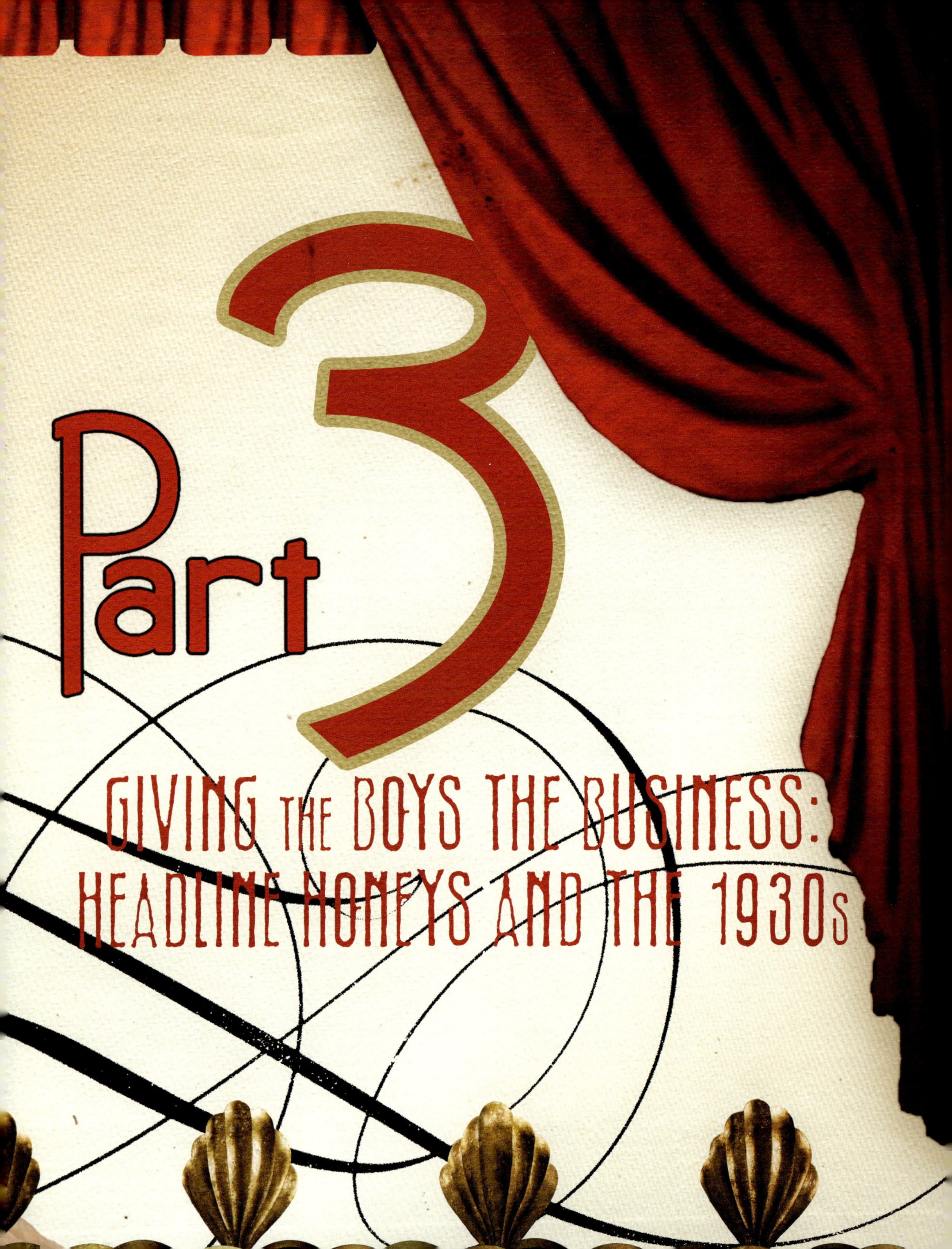

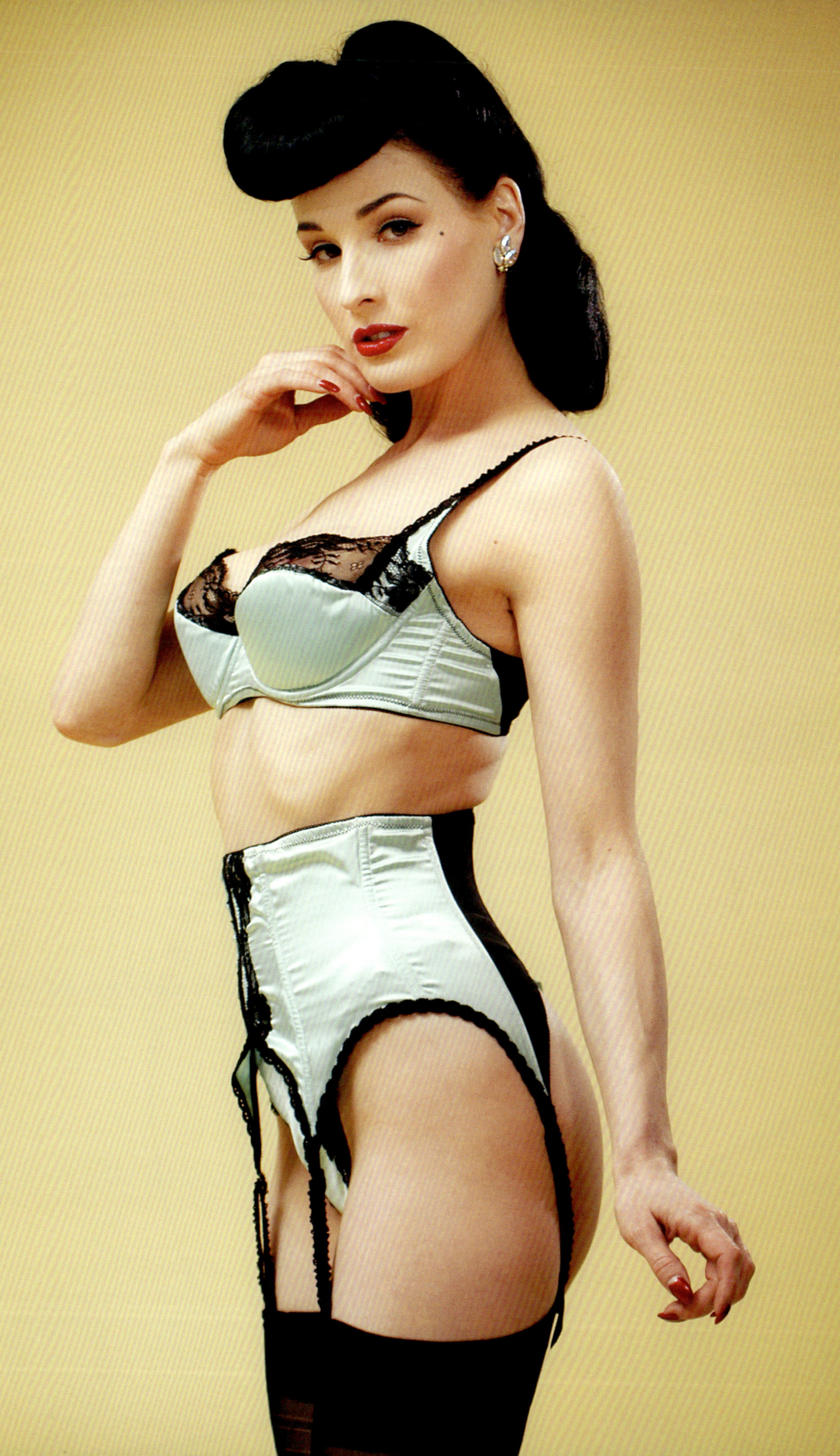

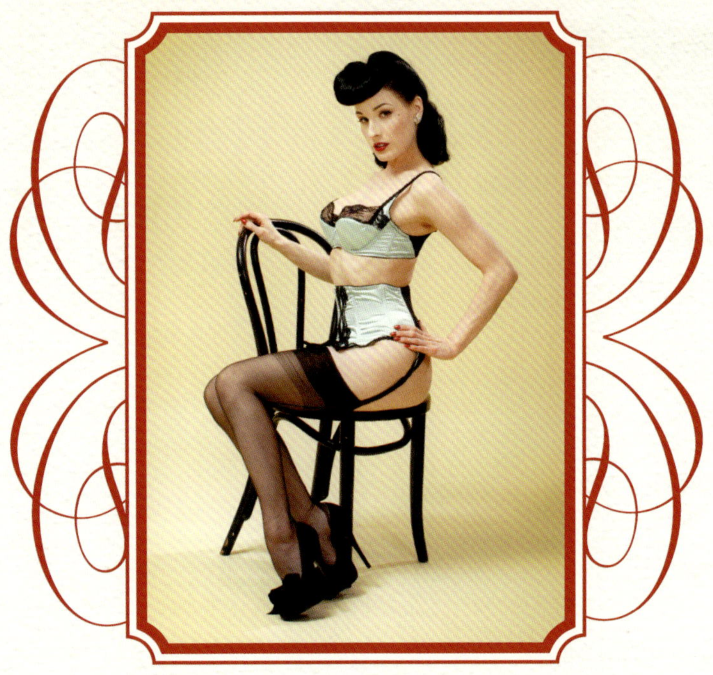

# Little Girl Lingerie

By the time I turned thirteen, it was pretty clear to me that pizza was not my calling. My future, I sensed, was waiting somewhere on the racks of Lady Ruby's Lingerie. Of course, I would need to convince the boutique owners of our mutual destiny. Every day during my break, I browsed the French lace garters, regaling the salespeople with descriptions of Betty Grable's costume lingerie, planting what I considered the seed of my employment. Then one day it happened. I still don't know why they hired me, but one must never question her *deus ex machina* (especially when mine was probably my mother, who worked as a manicurist in the same shopping center and had terrific powers of persuasion). From that fateful moment on, *all* my paychecks went to *all* those underpinnings.

It made me feel feminine to wear lingerie—I loved its history and its persistence in fashion. I devoured books about current and past styles, picked through vintage clothing and costume shops, and studied ancient issues of *Vogue* with an ardor I never bestowed upon calculus. I was the picture of D.I.Y. glamour.

Prom, as you may have feared, would be my heyday. My junior year, I was determined to wear a couture-style gown, and so I spent weeks flipping through my *Vogue* trove, scanning the images for something extraordinary. And then I saw perfection in a silver sequined sweetheart bodice dress. I tore out the page and ran with it into my mother's studio. She was lacquering a client's nails, but a better sport there never was. She smiled big, gulped, and said, "We can try."

I mined the stores for a similar pattern and splurged on what I still stand by as the brightest silver sequins in the world (I hadn't yet discovered the power of the rhinestone). Mom

made that dress for me, and it's likely that University High School has still not seen a flashier costume to this day. But I was in heaven. I had found the hundred-and-fifty-dollar solution to the five-thousand-dollar dress, and it was fabulous. You know, sometimes I think about the boyfriend who took me to that prom. He may have thought the dress was a little wild—everyone else was donning those 1980s Gunny Sax dresses by Jessica McClintock—but the poor guy probably thought all girls wore black merry widows and stockings.

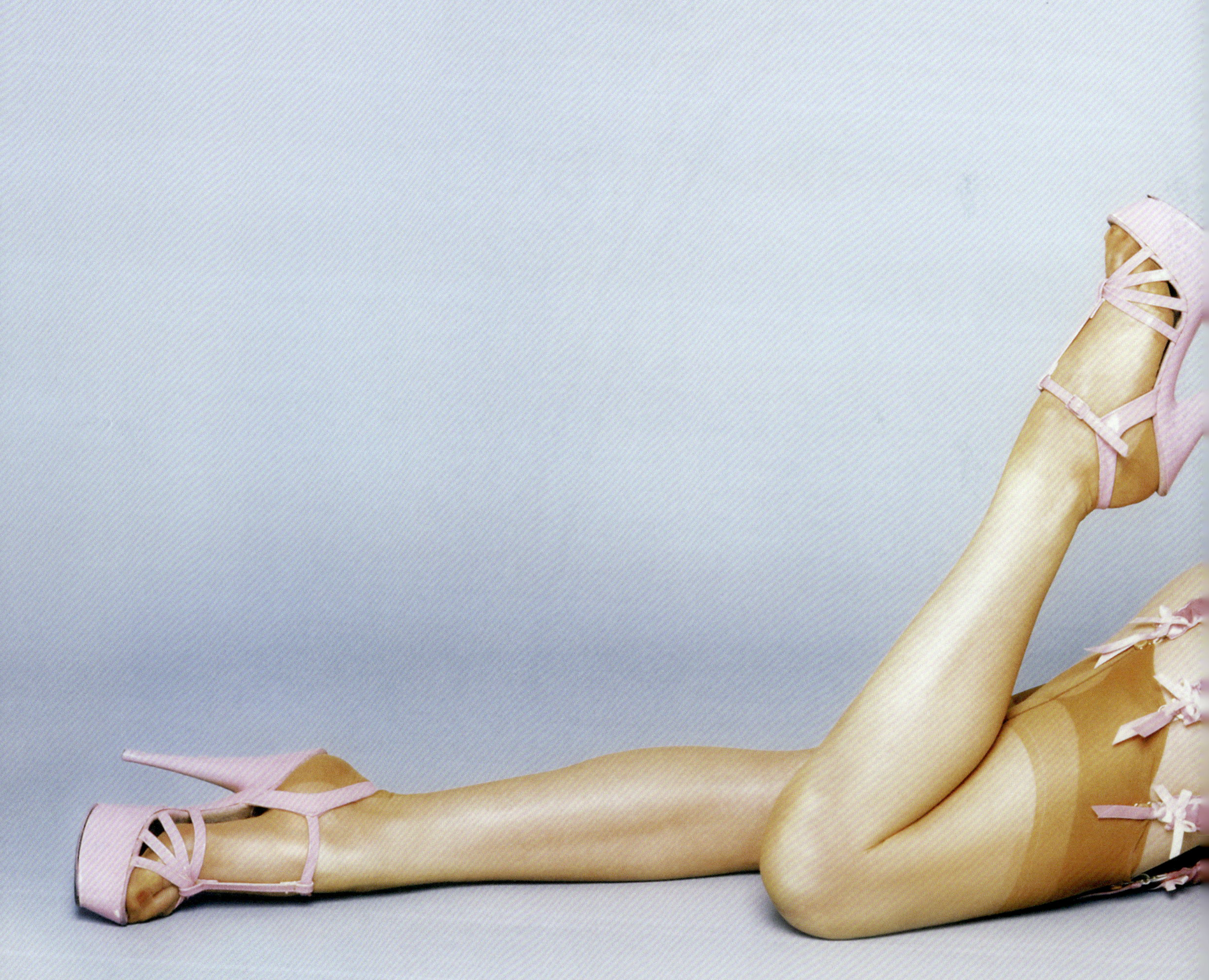

At the time, I hoped one day to work in historic costuming (I imagined that Hollywood had a department by this name), and I gave myself a pretty well-rounded education. You may as well know that I was not a glowing student of traditional academia—although I did pride myself on my resourcefulness. In horticulture class, for example, I was told to "grow something." Imagine it. I ran right over to the supermarket and chose a lovely cabbage. One cannot expect to be a star in every show. But resourcefulness, this is the pride of burlesque.

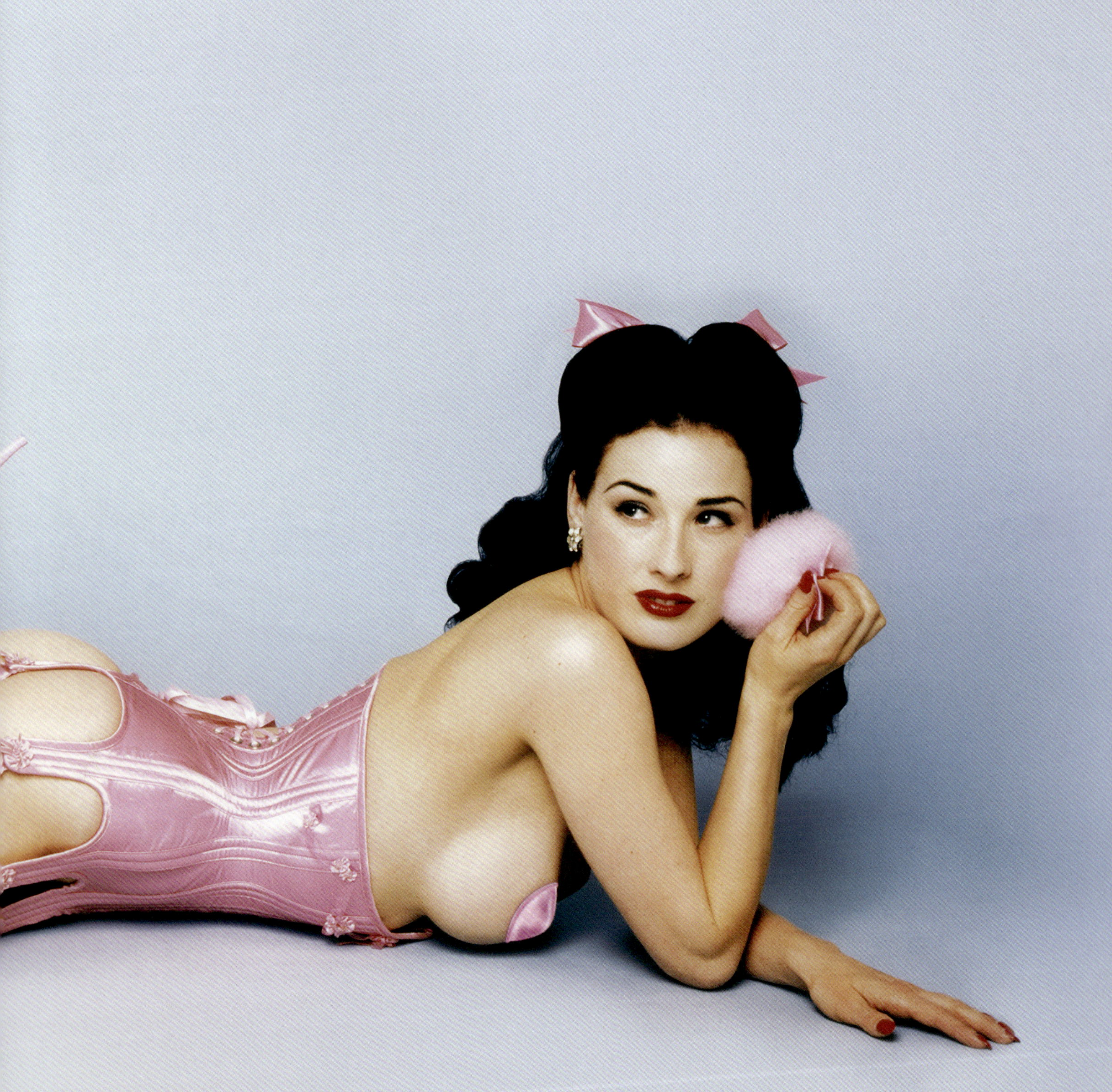

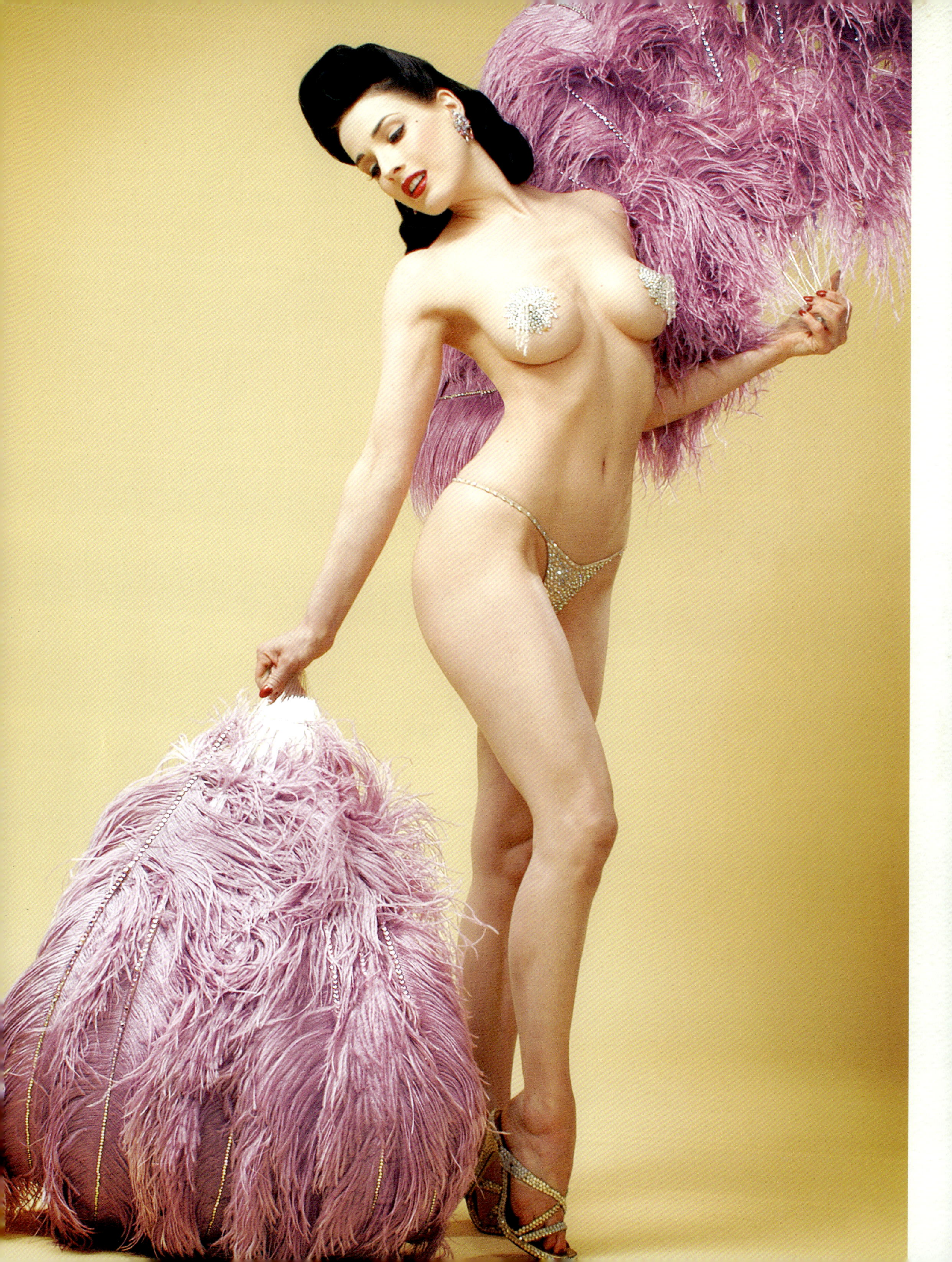

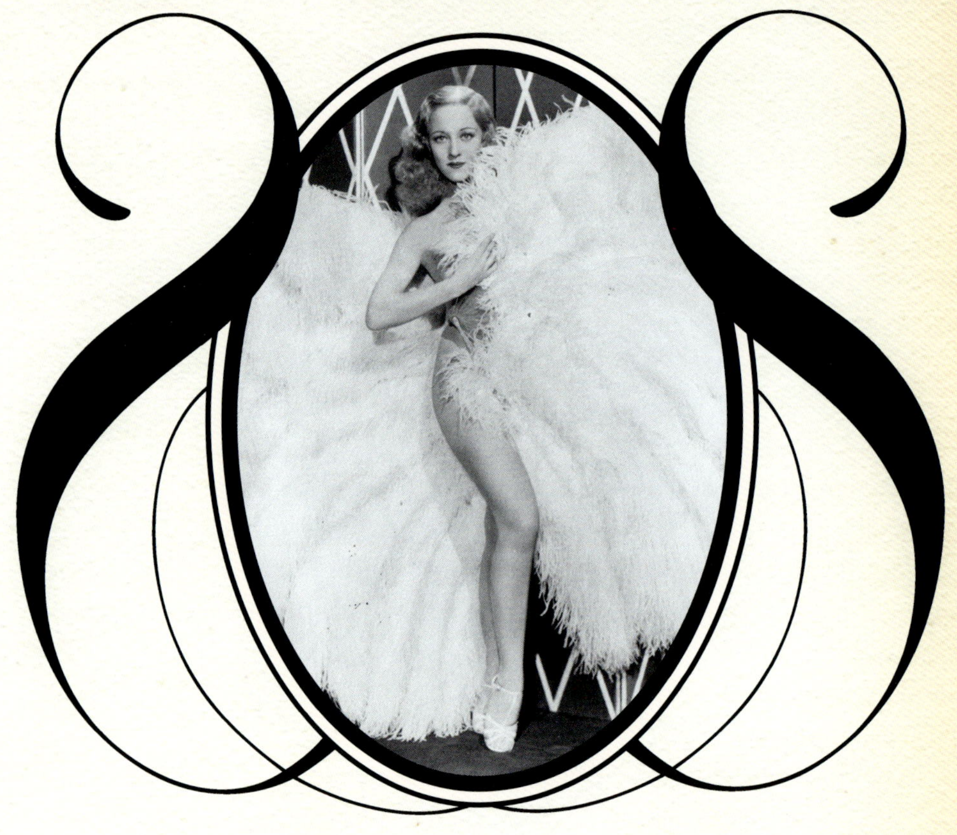

# The Rand Is Quicker Than the Eye

Take Sally Rand. Sally was a silent film star on contract with Cecil B. DeMille's stock company, early in the "star system." Poor Sally had a slight lisp, and when films became "talkies" she was out of a job. Just like that, finished. Sally turned to "exotic dancing" (a term in use since, you guessed it, Little Egypt danced Chicago) because she had to.

A club on the loop called The Paramount promptly hired her (she was a dashing little blonde, after all), provided she get a costume together and appear onstage that same evening. Walking home, Sally stepped into a resale shop and saw two huge pink ostrich feather fans restrained by spiderwebs begging to be freed. When the clerk wrapped them up in an old silk chemise, Sally even imagined she would cut and sew and style it into a Grecian gown to wear under the fans. And then Sally ran out of time.

Sally did what all good burlesquers do: she improvised. She asked the drunk at the piano to play "Clare de Lune" and she stepped out onto the stage *au naturel*—dancing carefully and gracefully behind the feathers. Her ballet training came in very handy this evening, very handy. The audience loved the ethereal performance, and even the classical music, which was not then in vogue at exotic clubs. Oh, and they rather enjoyed the nudity—though as she liked to say, "the Rand is quicker than the eye." She was a star again, even if she was not entirely clear on *why*: You see, after the show, she assured the club's owner that her act would be even better *with* the Grecian gown. This new boss looked at her funny, you can be sure. The show, he said, would stay *exactly* as it was. Silly Sally.

Anyway, pretty soon Sally had established herself as something of a celebrity on the loop, and was determined to gain entrance to the 1933 Chicago World's Fair, where she imagined she could reach superstardom. The fair was not exactly thriving, but Sally was nonetheless denied admission several times due to her conspicuous state of undress. When she sneaked through a side entrance and rode gloriously through the fair on a white horse, donning only a long blond wig and her signature head-to-toe thick white body makeup, the listless audience cheered for the first time in hours. Resourceful Sally (a.k.a. Lady Godiva) got her show time and was arrested that very evening on obscenity charges. Lucky for her, the judge's response was nearly as sane as Judge Cheeky's:

> If you ask me, these [people] are just a lot of boobs to come to see a woman wiggle with a fan with or without fig leaves. But we have the boobs and we have the right to cater to them. Case dismissed.

So, Sally and her fans saved the Chicago fair from financial ruin, just the way Little Egypt had done at the turn of the century—with boobs!

Now, Sally's shows weren't as rowdy as the ones that played at Minsky's, but they still enraptured the audience. Some people do not consider her performances burlesque for the very reason that she was a one-woman act engaged in something so simple, so unusual. The way I see it, Sally brought ethereal beauty onto burlesque's stage. But if that doesn't convince you, maybe this will: Billy Minsky signed Sally on the spot when he saw her at the Chicago World's Fair.

What modern day burlesquer hasn't been influenced by Sally Rand? My own pink ostrich fans—designed by Catherine, naturally—were the largest fans on any stage in the world (even I must up the ante). They are absolutely stunning! Made with four graduated shades of pink and hundreds of rose-colored crystals, they measure seven feet across and weigh 2.3 pounds each. (They are now on display in a museum because I have given up lifting them!) I know, I know, 2.3 pounds sounds like nothing. But keep in mind, the weight is spread out over seven feet. My moon show is another Sally-inspired act. Equal parts Sally ethereal and 1930s Erte-style art deco flair, I dance to a slow Harry James classic, and then I undress while standing on tiptoe inside a shimmering, twelve-foot-tall art deco crescent moon, held up by two enormous clouds. I even toss about a six-foot diaphanous bubble—much like the one with which Sally herself performed in lieu of the fans. The moon show captivates my audience . . . like a strong cognac.

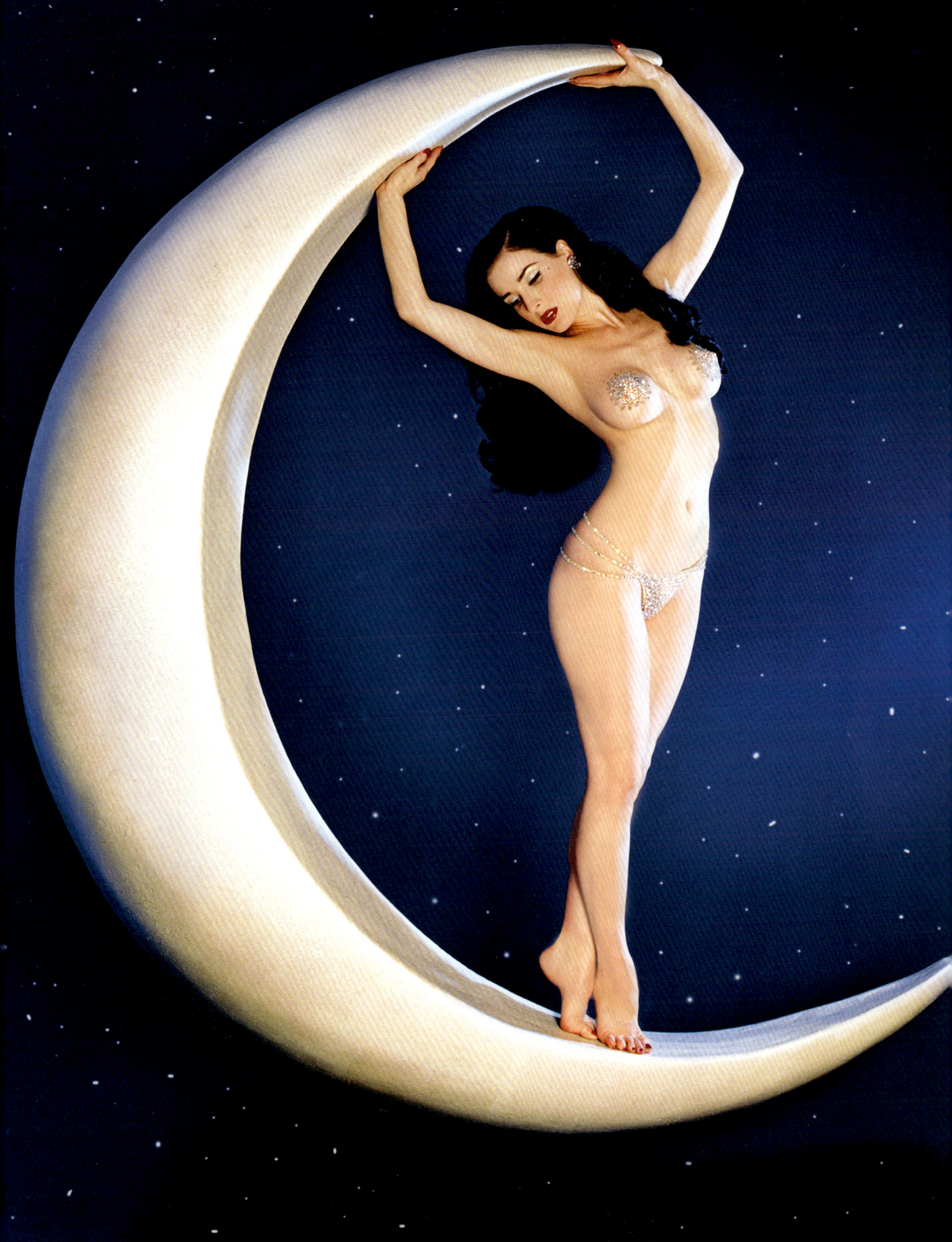

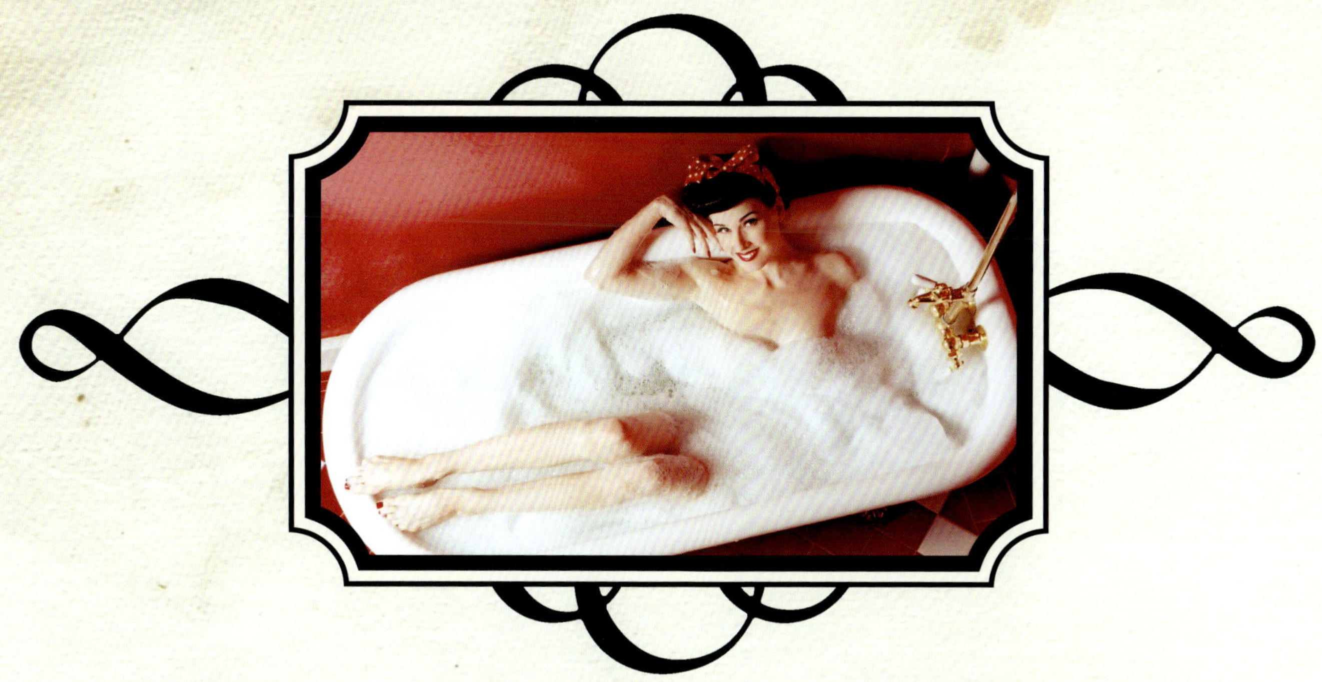

# Billy Minsky Cleans Up

When Wall Street crashed in 1929, Billy Minsky must have seemed like the only guy in town making any money. Minsky's brand of burlesque thrived in his family-run theaters all over New York and Brooklyn, at least in part because people needed cheap escapes. Sure, Ziegfeld's girls wore fancier dresses and danced amidst more elaborate stage sets for $6.60 a night, but Minsky's Poor Man's Follies was cheap. $1.50 cheap.

With business thriving, Billy realized his dream and opened two theaters on Broadway, the Central Theater on 47th Street and the Republic on 42nd. *The New Yorker* magazine quickly dubbed the area "Minskyville." Of course, "legitimate" producers were resentful from the get-go. How could they compete with their cheap and naughty new neighbor? They may have thought him vulgar, but Billy rose to the Broadway occasion, constructing a lush theater that the most famous tease of the decade, Gypsy Rose Lee, remembered as

> the most elegant burlesque theatre I had played. The doorman was garbed as a French gendarme, complete with mustache and red-lined cape. The girl ushers, wearing Frenchy-type maids' costumes with frilly skirts and long, black silk stockings, squirted perfume on the customers as they came in. For the ladies there were gardenia corsages. . . . The name of the show was in lights on the marquee . . .

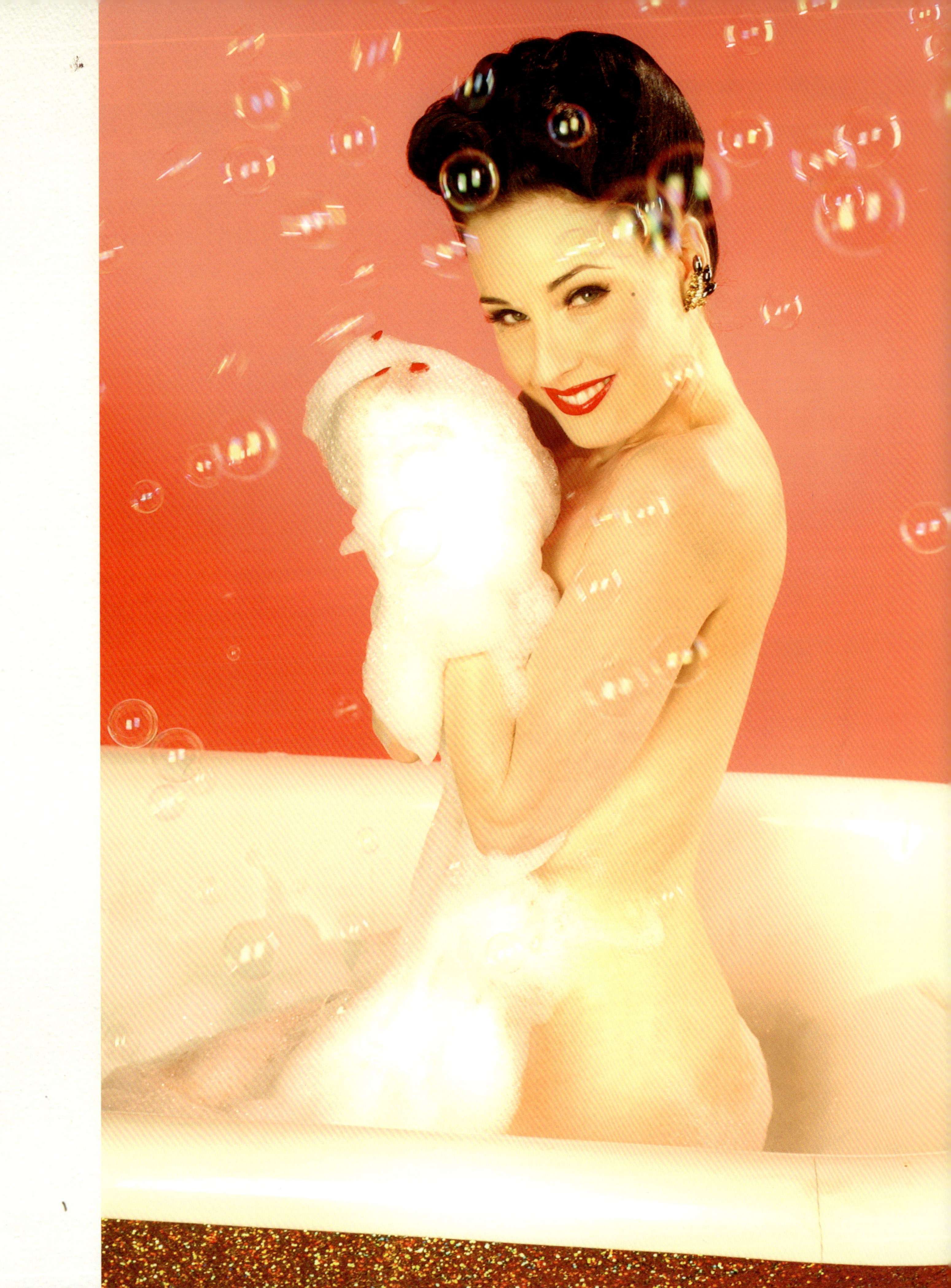

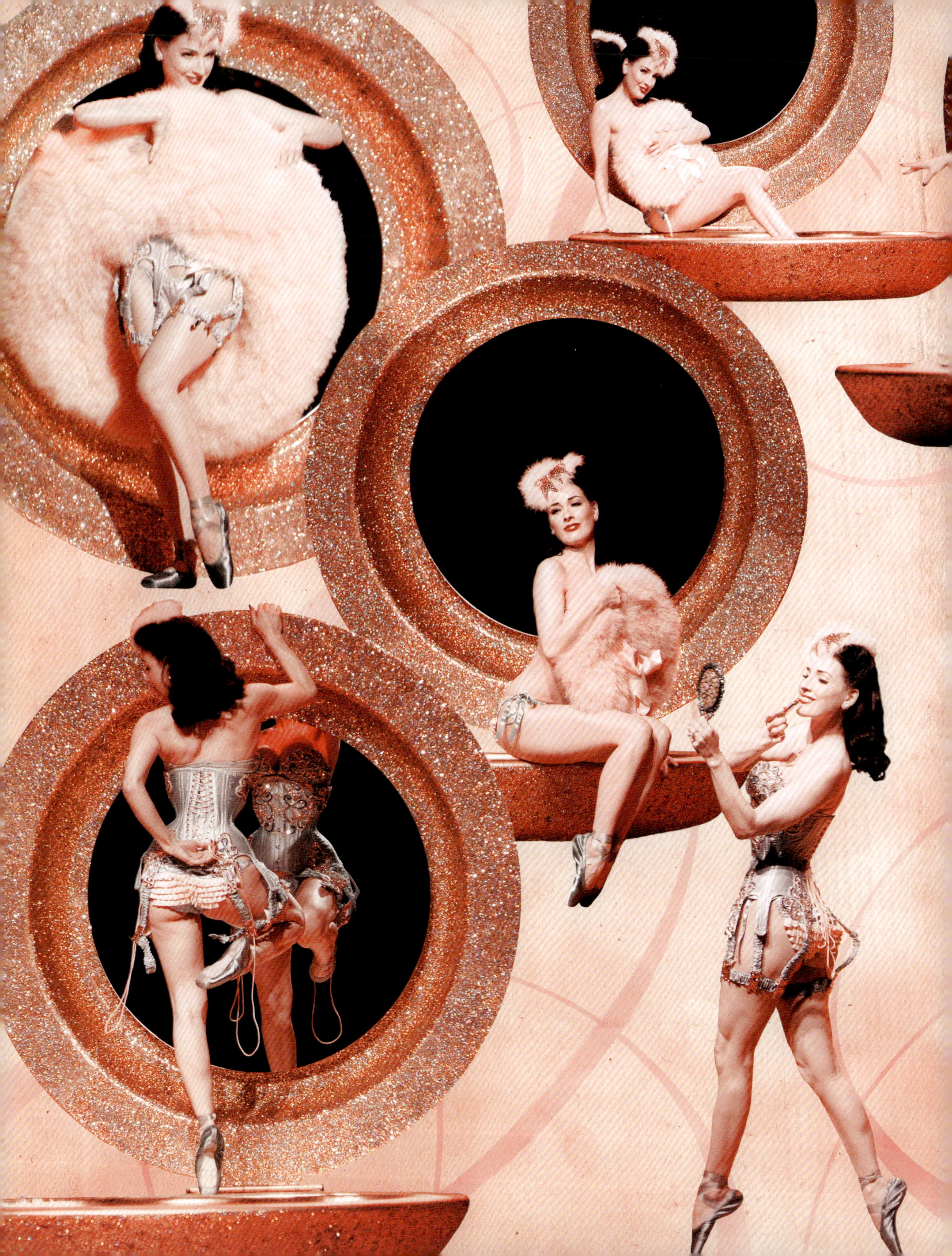

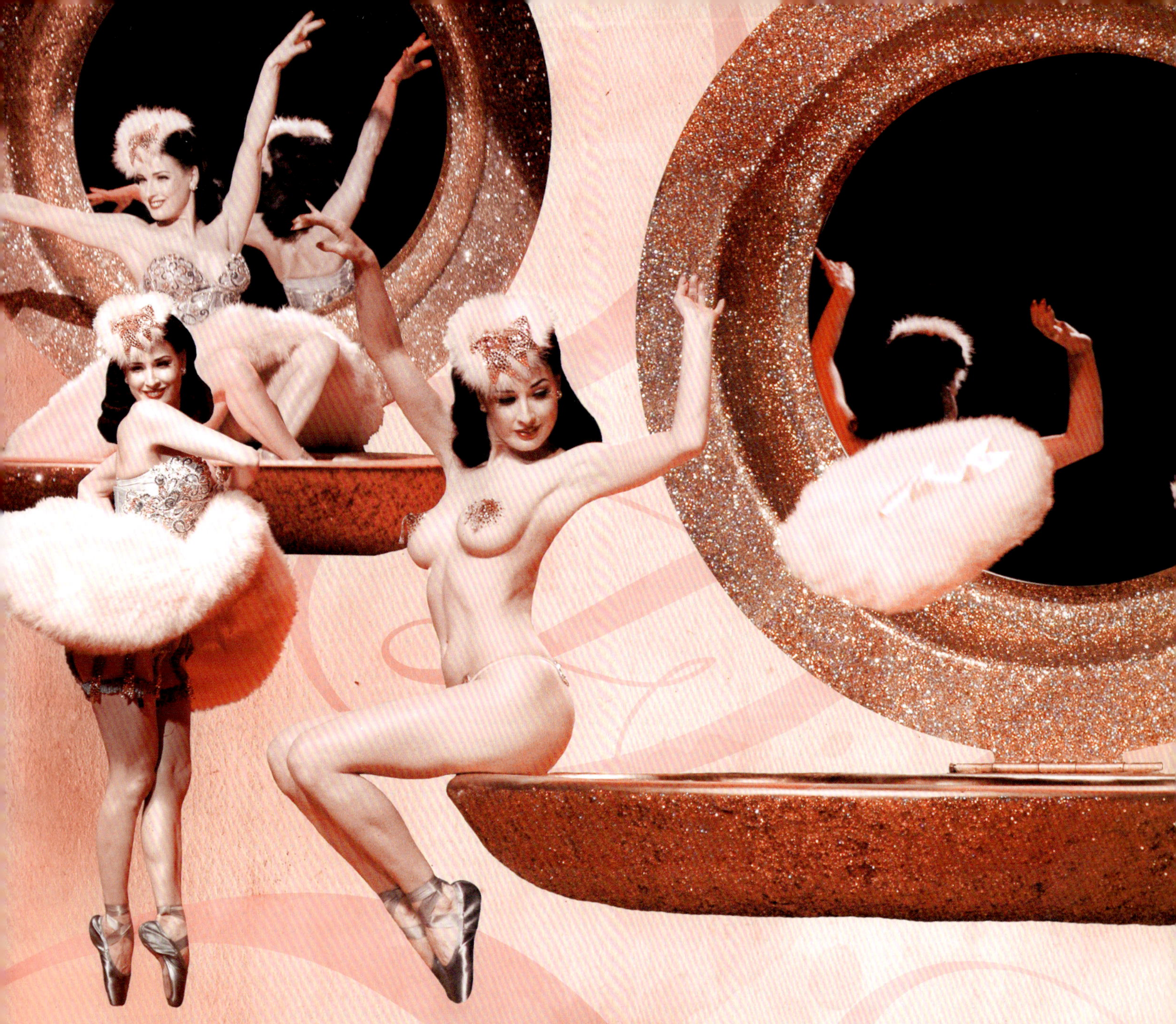

## THE MAKING OF A GREAT SHOWGIRL

Most of burlesque's great performers were not trained dancers; they were just women who had charisma, that "je ne sais quoi" that makes someone a star! Dance training certainly helps if you incorporate the right elements, but traditionally, burlesque wasn't about a choreographer mapping out a dancer's moves. It was about a woman wanting to make a name and a place for herself on the burlesque circuit. She didn't have a team of people instructing her. Not a single name in burlesque was "made" strictly by another person's styling and vision. This is perhaps the single most important element missing in the high-profile burlesque troupes and nightclubs you see today.

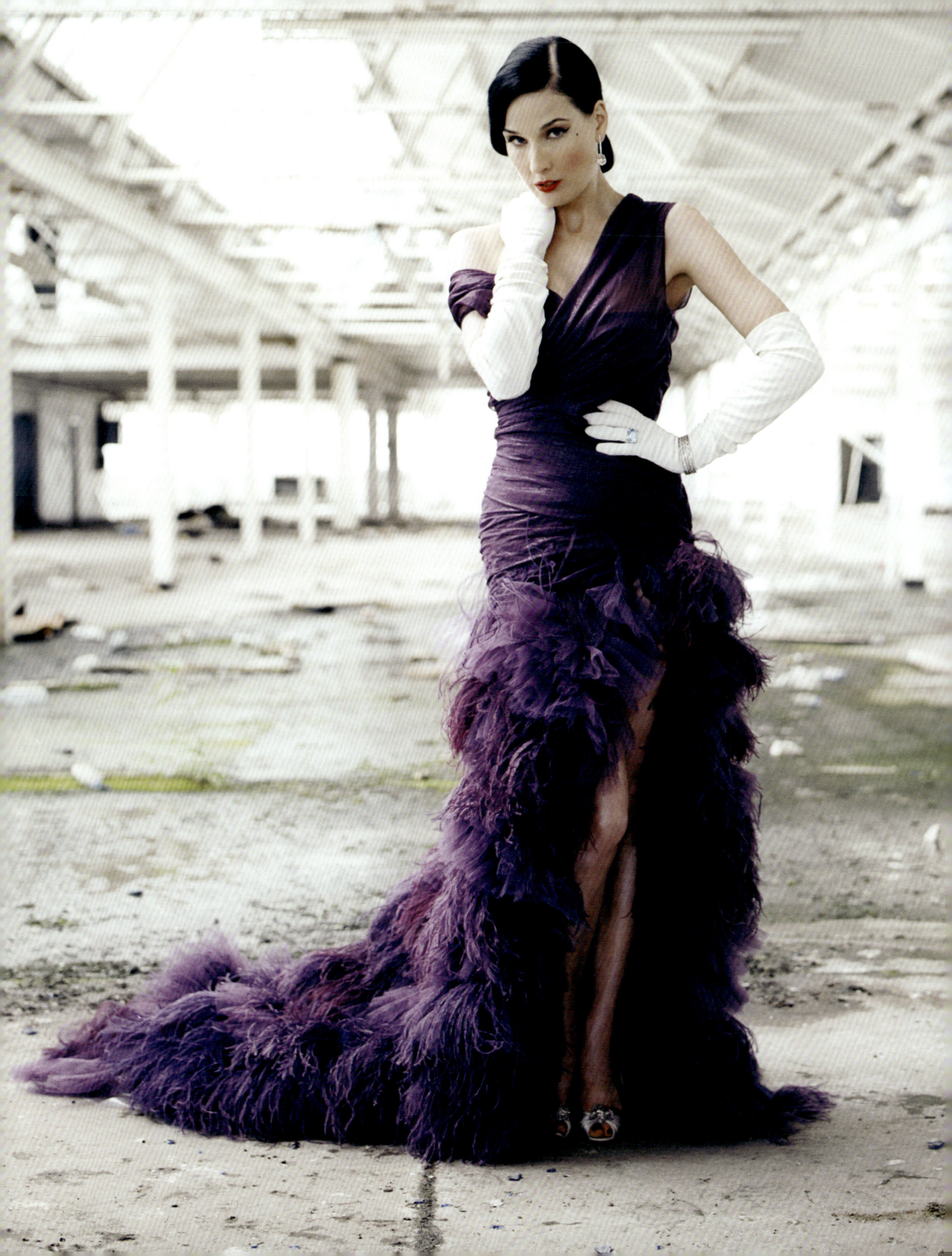

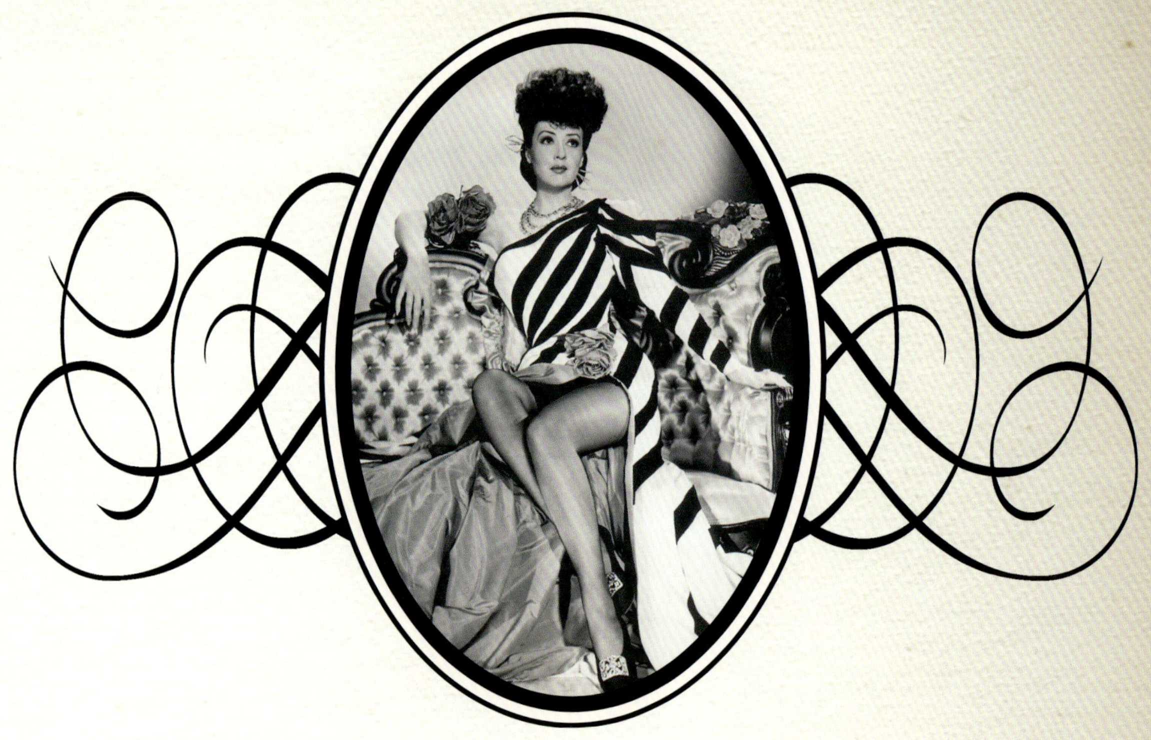

# The Reign of the Headline Honey

Broadway was big billing for a spanking new headline honey, but that was Billy. If he was going to bet on someone, he was going to bet everything. To ensure that the world embraced his latest star, Minsky planted articles (he had begun his career as a newspaperman and still had plenty of contacts), ignited controversy, and even made her debut a black tie affair on February 12, 1931. He bet and he won. Gypsy was the biggest sensation burlesque had ever seen. And, as far as I'm concerned, at least half of it was her own business acumen.

When Minsky got wind of her, Gypsy Rose Lee (born Rose Louise Hovick) was traveling the burlesque circuits with a mother who had already taught her daughter a thing or two about the hoodwink. The story goes that wherever young Gypsy performed, she received a reliable thunder of applause and a basket of flowers over the stage lights from "Anonymous," while everyone else—particularly the best talents—suffered booing and poison-pen letters. Gypsy found the abuse of the other performers puzzling, but assumed it was as her mother said: she was more talented, and the audience appreciated it.

One day, Gypsy opened her dressing room door to discover her mother preparing the basket of flowers. The girl was devastated—to think she had been blushing with every "Anonymous" card that arrived. But Momma Rose just looked up with relief. "Good," she said,

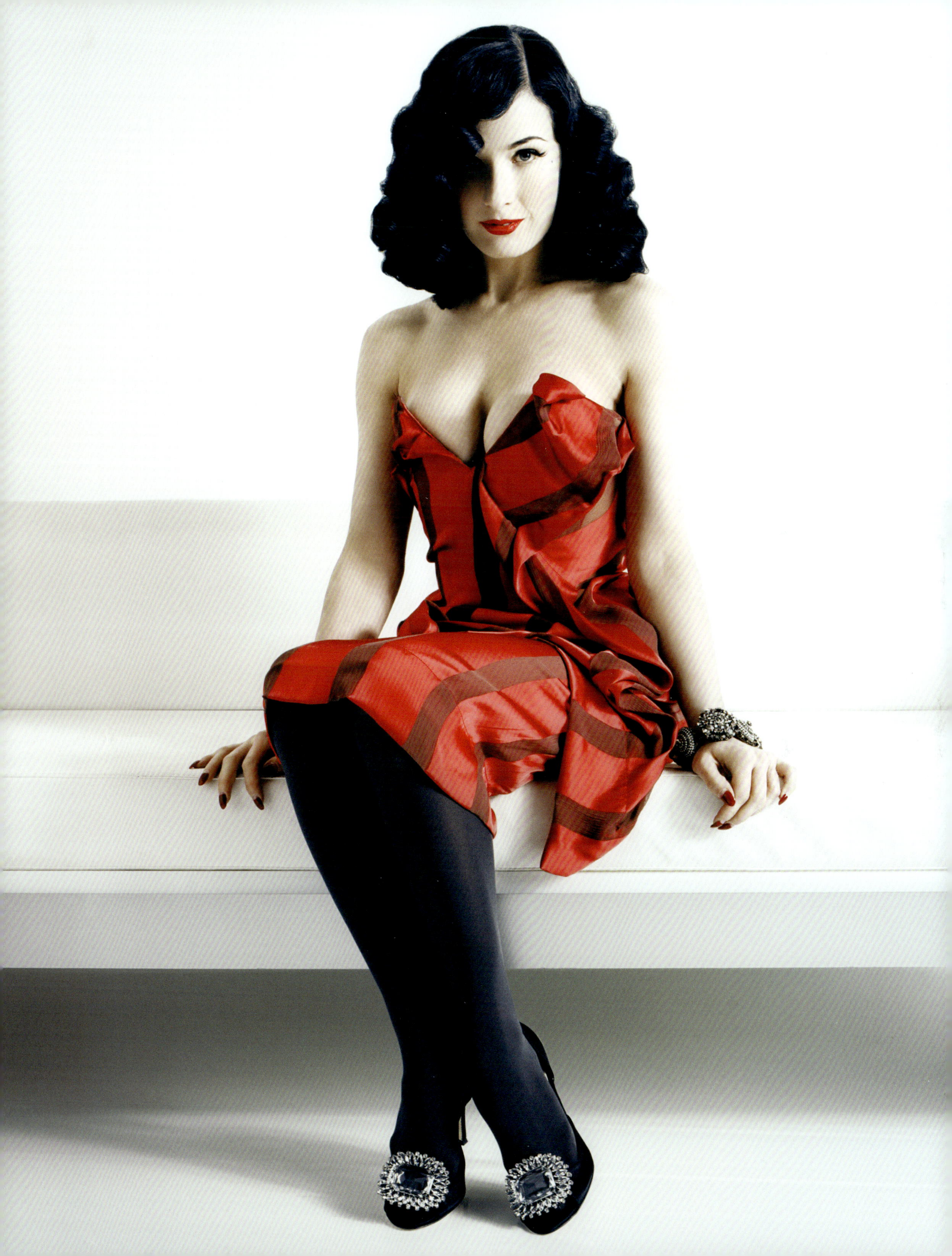

"Now I won't have to go on preparing these myself." Gypsy had—quite literally—discovered the "art" of publicity. Working for Minsky would give her occasion to master it.

Seeing her act in Philadelphia—and perhaps succumbing himself to her mother's guiles—Billy invited Gypsy to join his theater in New York. She was only sixteen, but she was studious as a schoolgirl . . . in black stockings and red garters. When she discovered that the Minskys paid a publicist, she hired one for herself, drumming up the most fabulous gossip in town. Opening night at the Met? Gypsy emerged from her limo in a floor-length cape made of real orchids. Worried that her extraordinary jewelry collection would be stolen, Gypsy confided to every newspaper in town that she wore it into the bath and even to bed. Readers loved the decadence of their star, and Gypsy became burlesque's first household name.

But lest you think Gypsy was all hoodwink and no wink wink, I can promise you the woman knew a thing or two about titillating an audience. Gypsy was famous for chatting up her punters directly with an enchanting combination of sweetness and mockery. They say she got the audience so riled up that she didn't have to strip. The youngest Minsky brother, Morton, remembered that: "After all this hocus-pocus, mumbo-jumbo of suggestiveness and promise, there would be the quick flash of a breast and a bare hip bone as [Gypsy] slid off chuckling into the wings." Billy himself was heard to call her show "seven minutes of sheer art."

Gypsy's signature on- and offstage was the head on her shoulders—and she wasn't going to lose control of her best asset. For that reason, she stayed away from opium (popular in those days), famously saying, "[it] makes me too agreeable. I'm not giving anything away, I'm selling it. . . . Nope, it dims my luster, makes me resemble the others—that's the worst thing that could happen."

I'm with Gypsy. I enjoy one glass of Champagne before going onstage. Just one! Though some dancers I know think they are better boozy, the truth is that they just look drunk. And if there are cameras, forget it! Two glasses and the camera will pick up the wooze in anyone's eye. Bubbly is a gift from the wine gods, but one must be professional in her profession, if you know what I mean. "Dimming your luster" is the thing to avoid at all costs.

With the ascent of Gypsy into the society pages, the audiences came to adore the ecdysiast, as H. L. Mencken, a Minsky regular, described Gypsy (though she despised the term). Girls now dreamed of climbing the ranks at Minsky's instead of being swept up into the dreamlike world of Ziegfeld's Follies. Why? Stripping's stigma had vanished with Gypsy's famous pins (she tossed straight pins that pieced her costume together out to the audience; they could be redeemed for a free show) and besides, feature strippers of the early 1930s could command salaries of $250 to $1,000 or more each week (up to eight times as much as at Ziegfeld's). Even though the girls worked much harder in the burlesque houses—fourteen-hour days with four performances were typical—Broadway producers couldn't lure the dolls uptown, even with drastically lighter schedules.

It may be true that I don't take much from Gypsy's raucous performance style, but I very much admire her business acumen, the seriousness with which she approached her work, and, above all, her love of all things opulent. Gypsy Rose Lee was an original American showgirl!

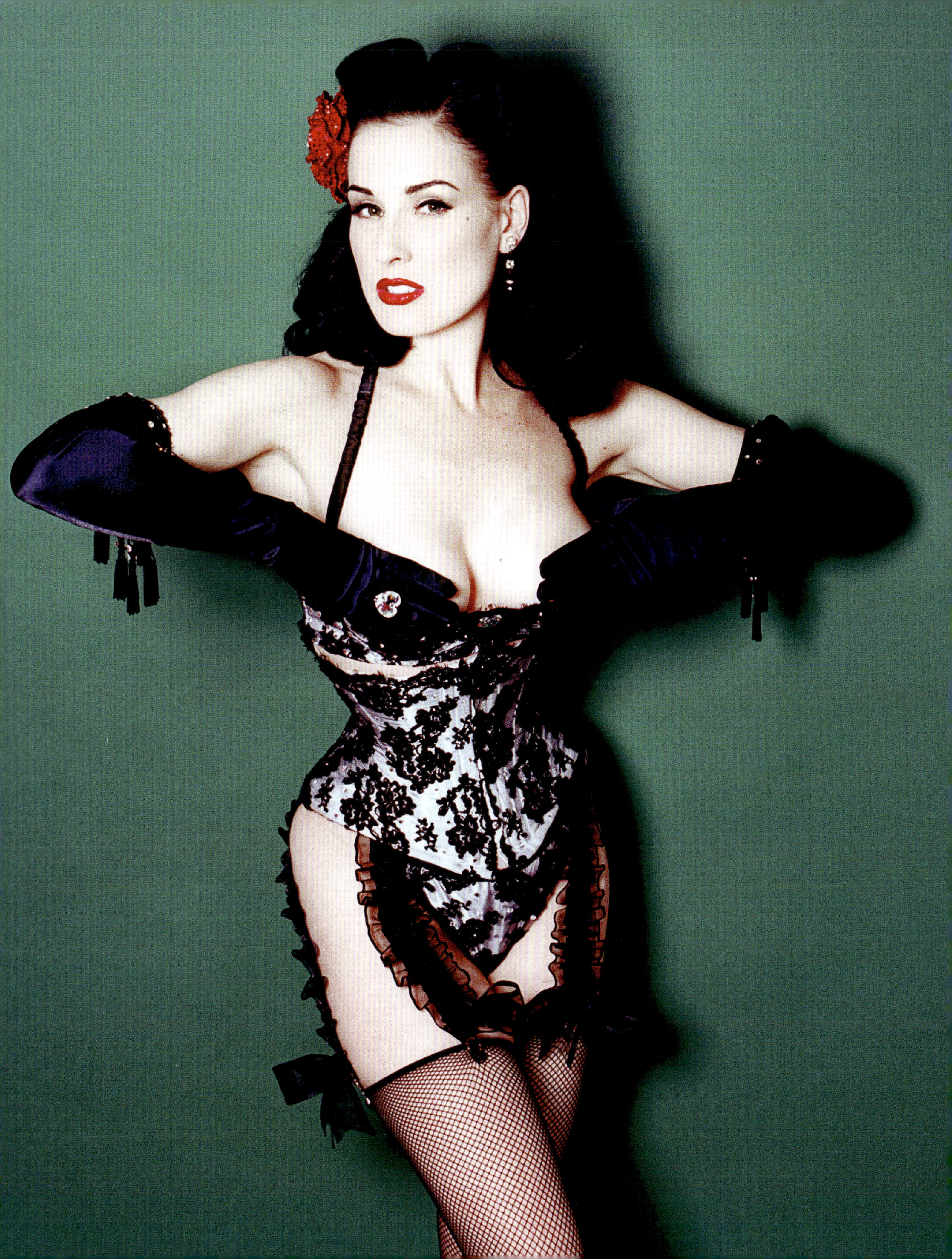

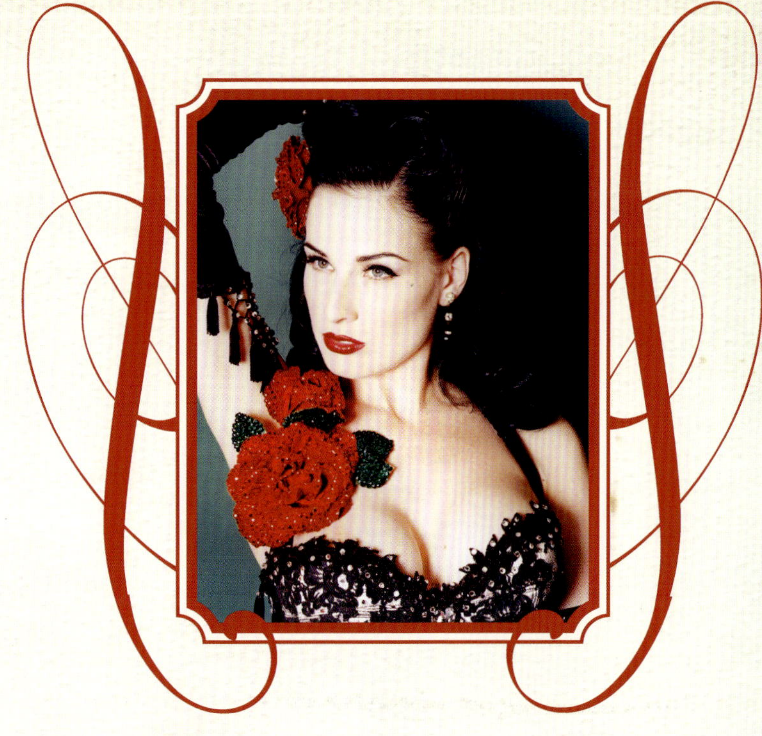

# The Fall of the House of Minsky

Even as Gypsy's adored stripteases lit up the stages of Minskyville, the lights were quietly going down. In 1932, Billy Minsky died suddenly at forty-one from Paget's disease. Burlesque had lost its king, and without him, the gelatin castle would show a new crack every day. Burlesque had survived Aristophanes, and it would likewise outlive Billy Minsky. But it would suffer.

Resentful Broadway producers, local real estate owners, the Catholic Church, and the disgraced Tammany Hall government (who hoped this crusade would restore its soiled public image) united to fight burlesque. Even more bizarre, a new mayor, Fiorello La Guardia, installed a failed Broadway producer named Paul Moss to the office of License Commissioner. This guy was wolf bait who harbored real resentment for the whole Minsky family. As the *The New Yorker* reported it: "There is a conspiracy of rival interests to clean up Minskyville."

Indeed, between 1932 and 1936 the Minskys' licenses were revoked and renewed endlessly, causing Billy's beloved Republic Theater to be shut down again and again. Then, unbelievably, on April 30, 1937, Mayor La Guardia signed a law killing the entire industry in the city of New York. At Moss's urging, La Guardia went a step further, banning the words *burlesque* and, most stunningly, *Minsky* from use in connection with any theatrical production in New York, effectively putting an entire family out of business.

On the tail of the depression, La Guardia was putting nearly one thousand actors out of work in New York, not to mention the huge number of stagehands and musicians who were dependent on the business. When it was all over, the *Herald Tribune* sadly noted, "The last vestiges of the once flourishing art of burlesque disappeared yesterday afternoon."

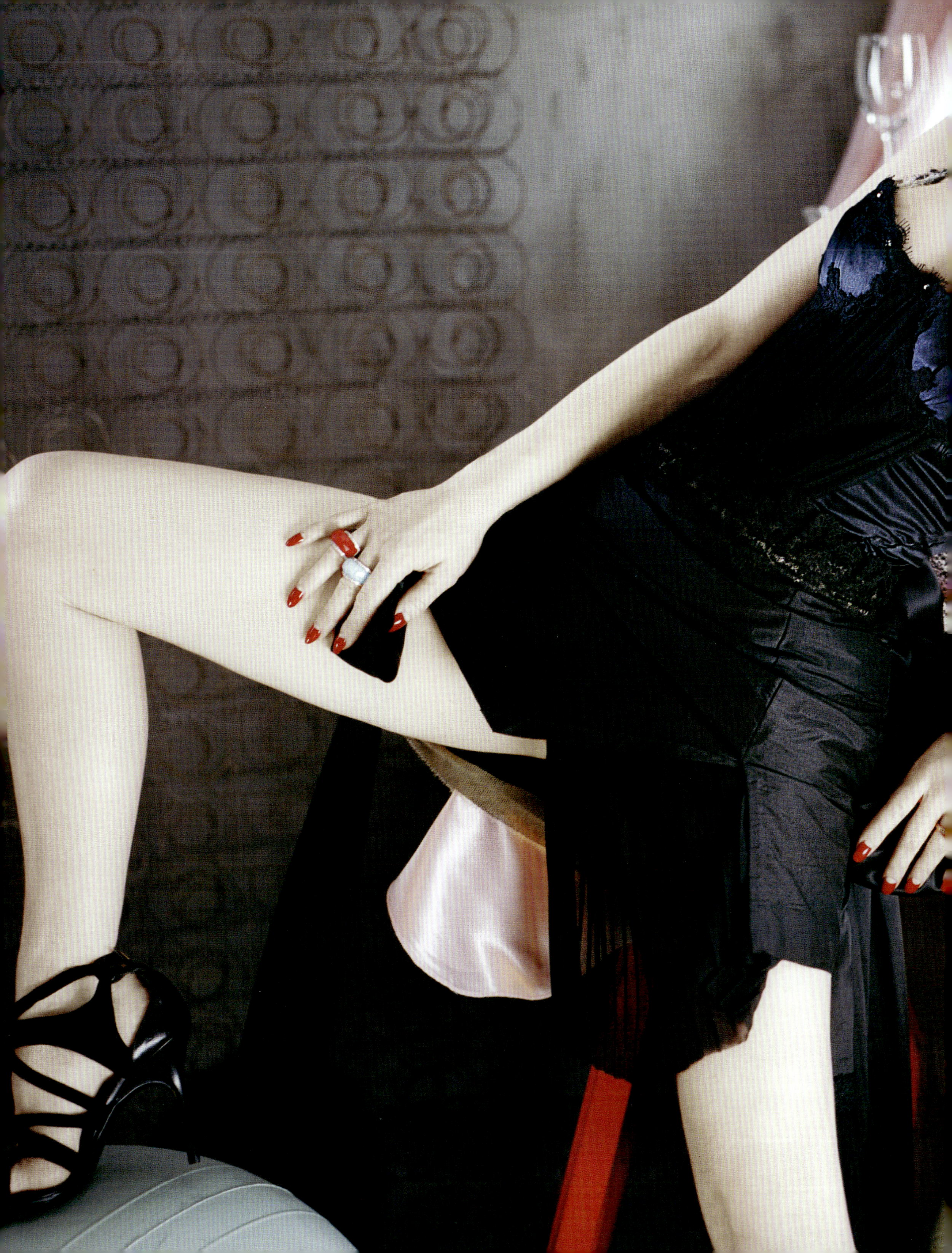

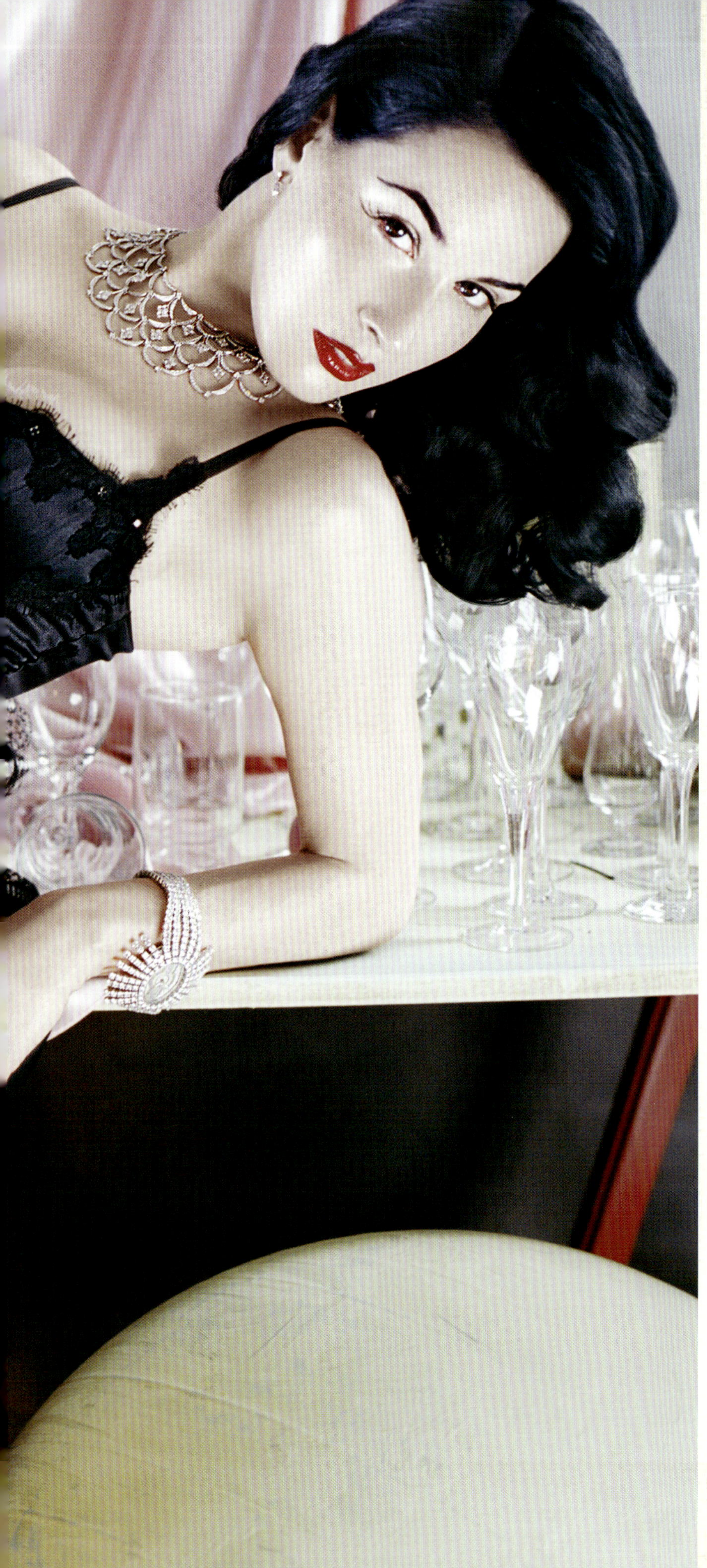

All that fluffy warmth had been a sort of soothing confectionary that quieted the ache of poverty. For the "silk-hat" regulars it may have been just a diversion, but for many others it was an antidote to despair. New York's Bowery was a squalid home to a large population of unemployed, unwed male immigrants. Billy Minsky must have seen it as a lovely accolade that his patrons fought to hold onto their seats all day, but he must have also felt the tragedy in the men who carried bedroom slippers and brown bag lunches into his theaters, hiding out alongside the magenta spots until the lights came up.

To me, that's the darkest part of La Guardia's attack on burlesque. Sure, burlesque would survive—revues were still legal, so Broadway producers such as Michael Todd and Billy Rose took stock burlesque material and presented it as *revues* in such popular shows as the *Star and Garter*. Ploys like this saved the material from obscurity—but what of its audience? The so-called "Poor Man's Follies" were now available only to those wealthy enough to afford a Broadway ticket.

What of the rest of the country? With New York as burlesque's epicenter, the reverberations of the new prohibition were felt far and wide. *Billboard* reported that even "Chicago, once the home of a robust burlesque theater, was now devoid of a single standard burlesque house."

It was time to go to the movies.

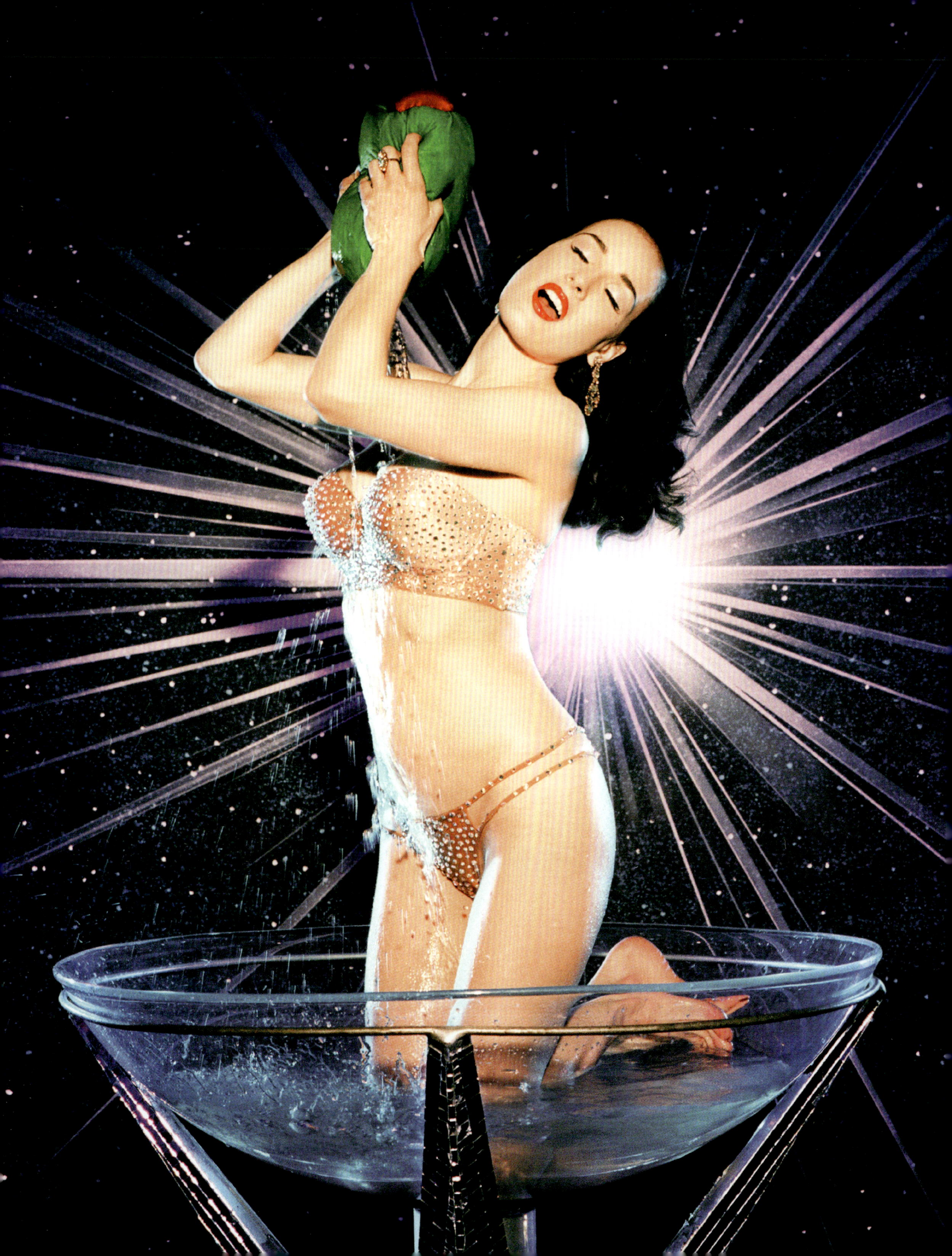

# The Birth of a Signature

People know me best for my martini glass act. How did I think of it? Over a bottle of Dom, of course! My friend Catherine D'Lish had already performed a show with a giant champagne glass, so we figured that I needed a drink with a different flavor and style and a different clientele, and most important, it had to be completely new and unique to the burlesque stage. A margarita? Unique indeed, but I wasn't so sure about that topless Mexican hat dance. A shot glass? Nope, too small. A highball? I may have drowned! A martini? Yes. I would be hip and swingin' while Catherine the champagne girl would remain classic and refined. We'd duke it out in style—onstage—and then take a bath in our drinks of choice.

We edited the music to cut back and forth between classic big band and '50s swing music (each girl could peel only to her own), and then we had a strip-off. At the end, we toasted each other and climbed into our glasses for a wet and wild finale! Since then, my martini glass show has become my "signature," and it has taken me all over the world . . . London, Paris, Vienna, Lisbon, Hong Kong, Moscow, Ibiza, Belgrade, Frankfurt, Berlin, and just about every major city in the United States. I've performed everywhere from the seediest strip clubs to the most prestigious events, and it's been a terrific time.

After all of these years, my glass show is still the most in-demand of all of my performances. But I love to perform each and every one of my shows that I have dreamed up, and I can't wait for the day when I can perform all of them as a full-length show, with another signature of mine, the elegant striptease, leading the way.

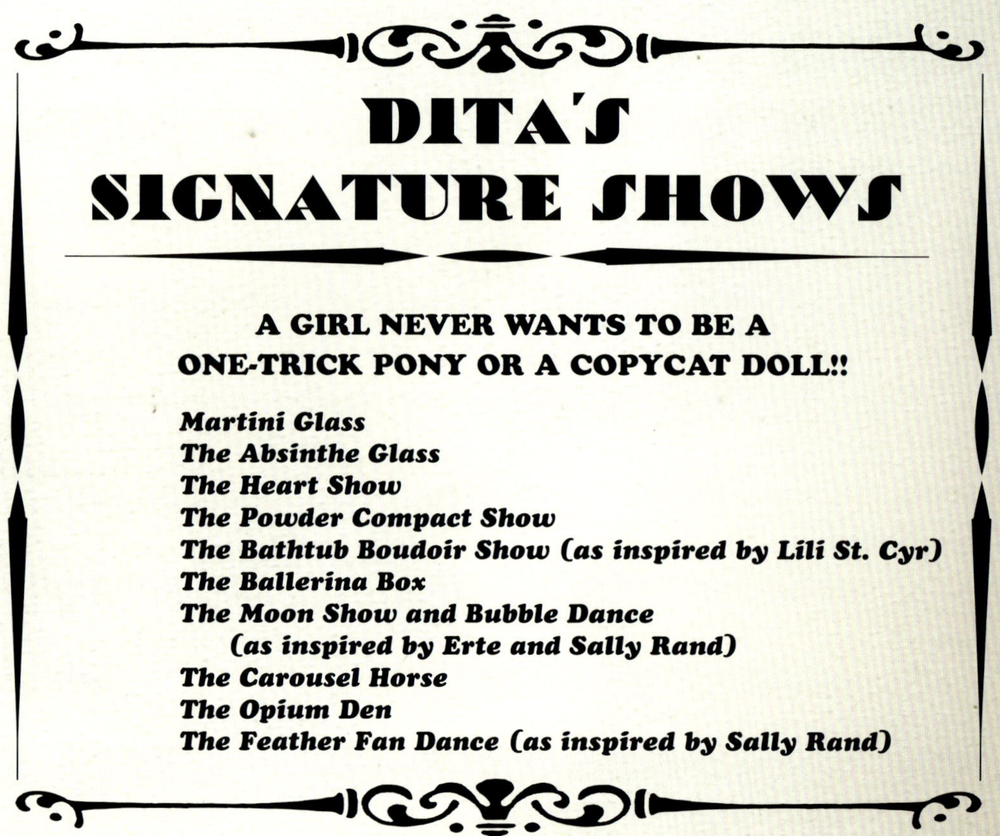

## DITA'S SIGNATURE SHOWS

**A GIRL NEVER WANTS TO BE A ONE-TRICK PONY OR A COPYCAT DOLL!!**

***Martini Glass***
***The Absinthe Glass***
***The Heart Show***
***The Powder Compact Show***
***The Bathtub Boudoir Show (as inspired by Lili St. Cyr)***
***The Ballerina Box***
***The Moon Show and Bubble Dance (as inspired by Erte and Sally Rand)***
***The Carousel Horse***
***The Opium Den***
***The Feather Fan Dance (as inspired by Sally Rand)***

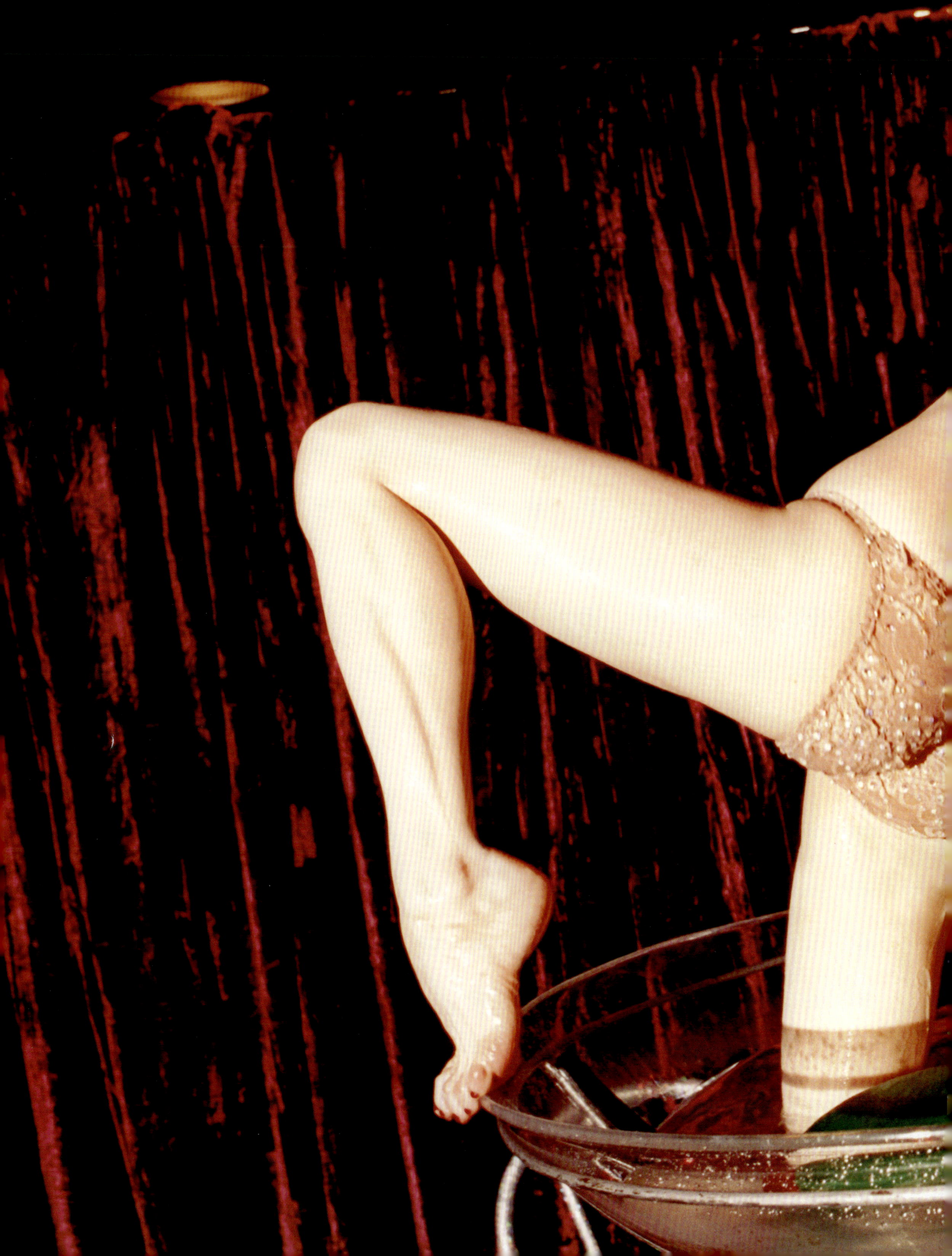

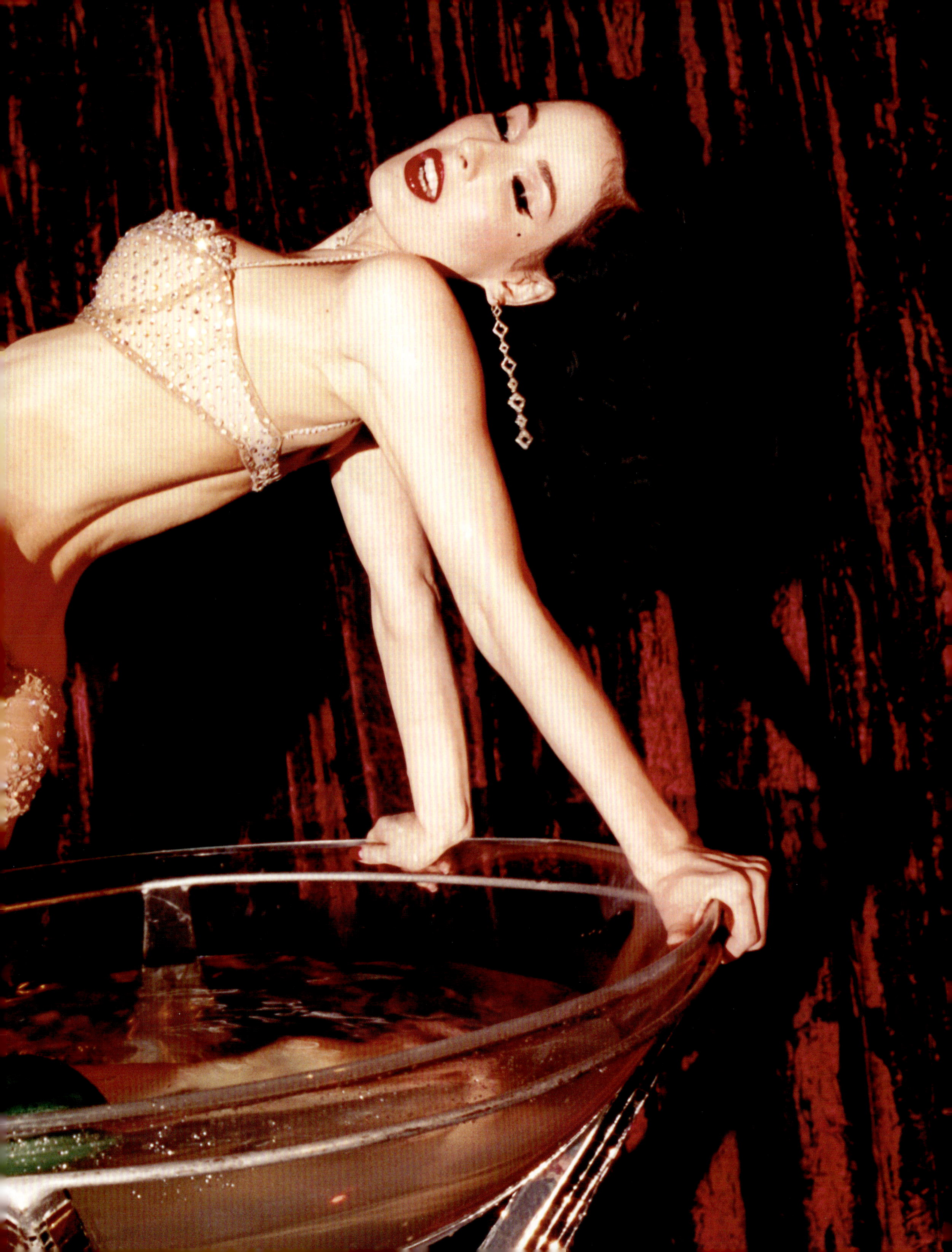

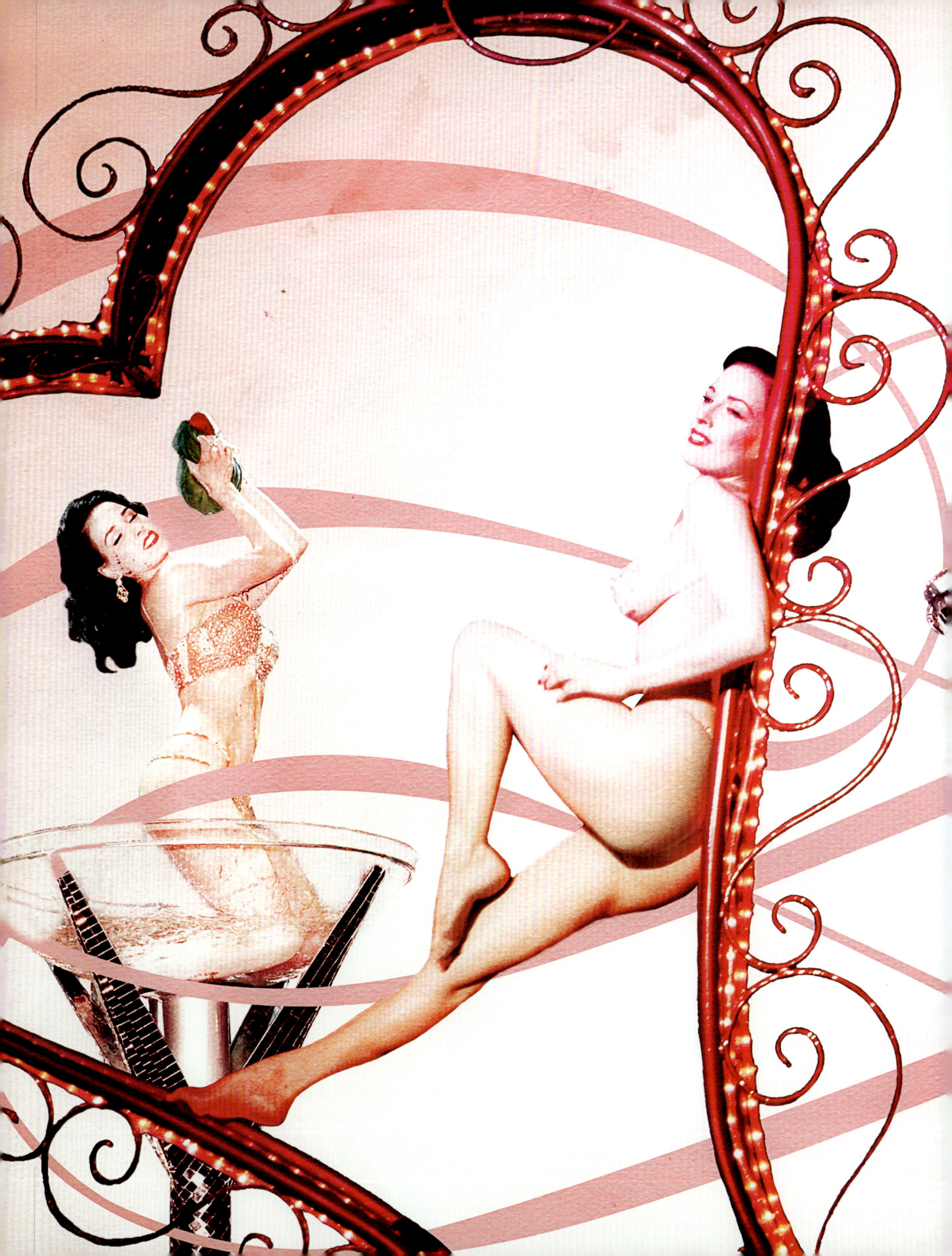

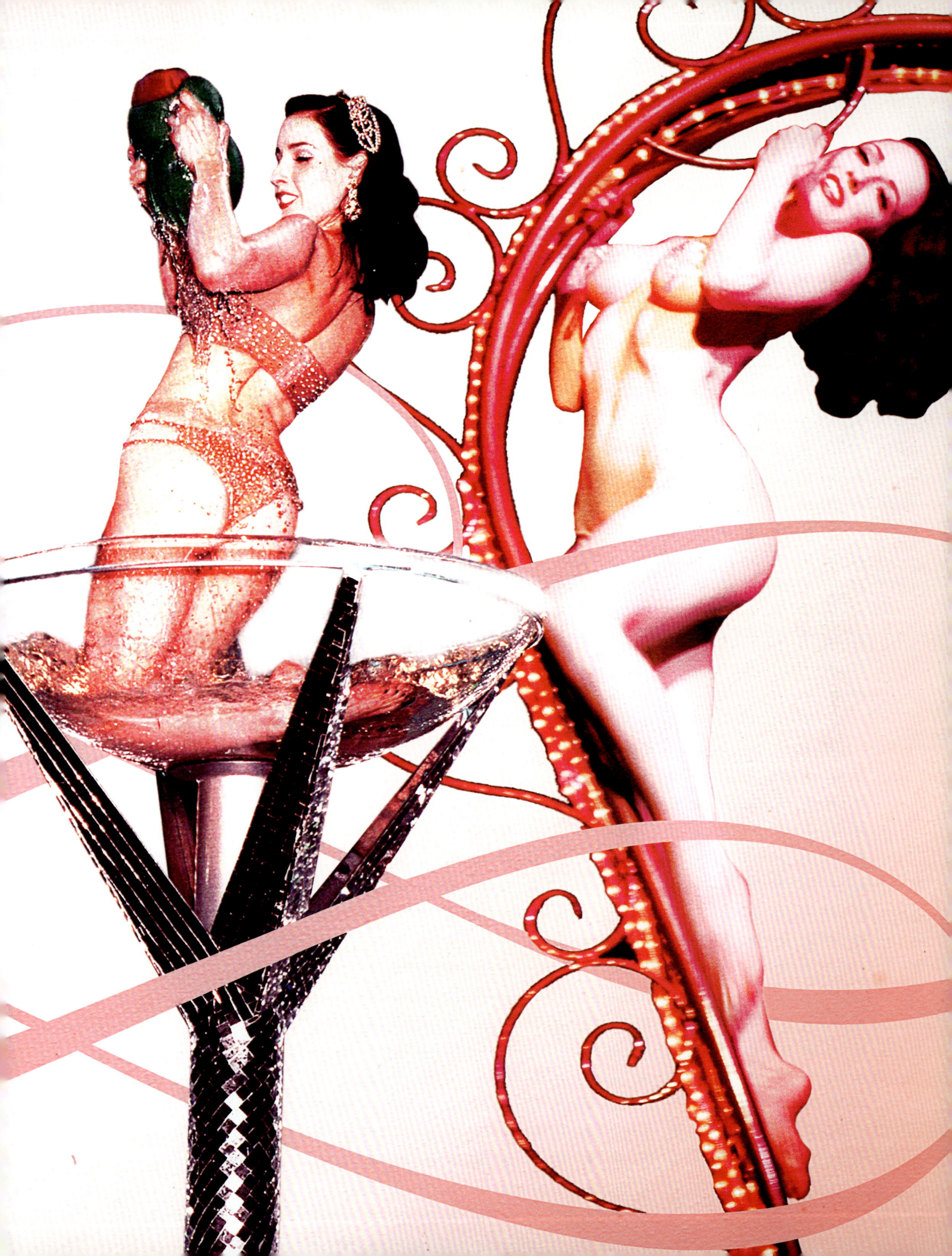

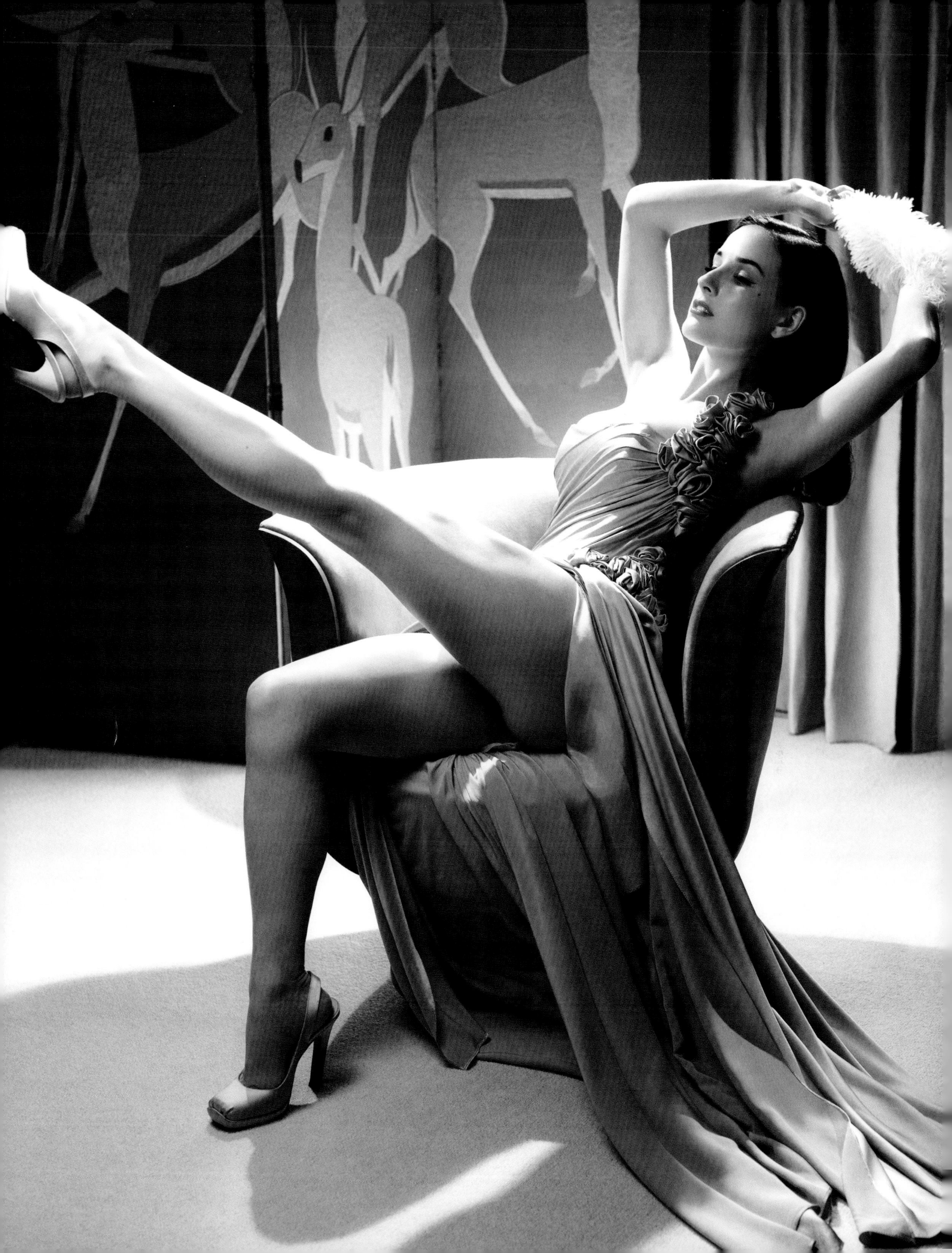

# FIRST-CLASS FACE: LOOKING LIKE A 1930S SILVER SCREEN SIREN

**THE 1930s WAS THE ERA OF THE SILVER SCREEN STAR! THE '30s OWNED A LOOK THAT WAS SEXY, BUT SOULFUL, WITH CURVE-SKIMMING SILKY GOWNS, MARCEL WAVES, AND BOBBED HAIR.**

**BURLESQUE QUEENS**

**Gypsy Rose Lee**
**Sally Rand**
**Georgia Sothern**

**MOVIE STARS**

**Marlene Dietrich**
**Jean Harlow** →
**Mae West**
**Hedy Lamarr**
**Greta Garbo**
**Ginger Rogers**

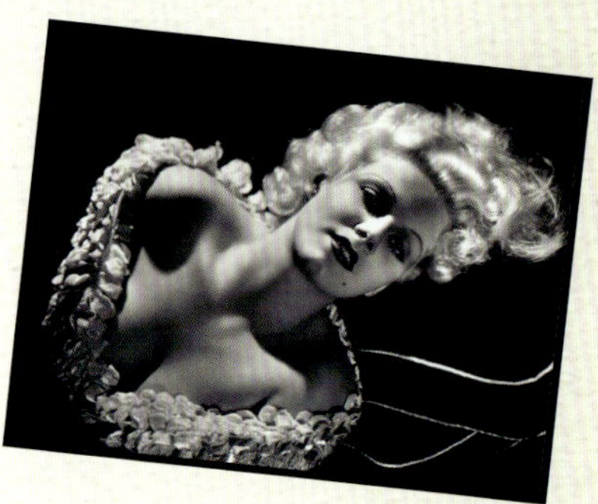

**SKIN:** Creamy pale ivory with rose-toned cream blush applied to the apples of the cheeks with a dusting of powder.

**BROWS:** Sleek and elongated with high arches. Some '30s stars like Jean Harlow wore shaved brows that were penciled in thinly with very high arches, but you can also achieve a lovely '30s brow simply by enhancing your own natural brows with a pencil.

**EYES:** Either light with long, thin false lashes and just a touch of soft liner at the lash line, or smoldering with glossy heavy lidded eyes like Greta Garbo.

**LIPS:** Lined fuller and painted a satiny raspberry or ruby tone.

**NAILS:** Oval-shaped and painted a pale pink with the moons and tips left natural or painted silver.

**HAIR:** Marcel waves were all the rage! I like to set my hair in very tight rollers and then use a comb to form the waves. You can also buy small metal clips to create the "ridges" of the waves. (Or make an appointment at a beauty school . . . students must master finger waves to graduate!)

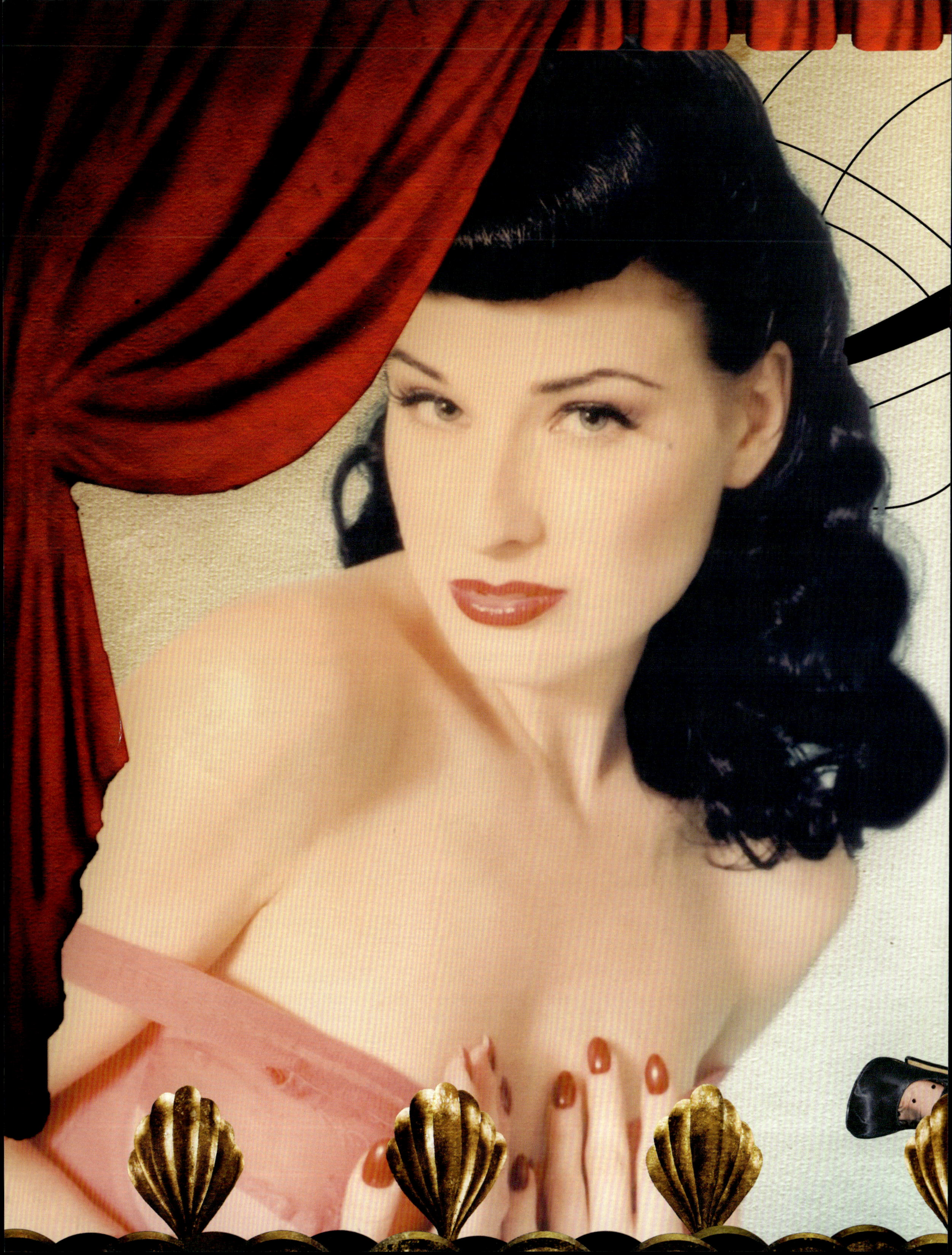

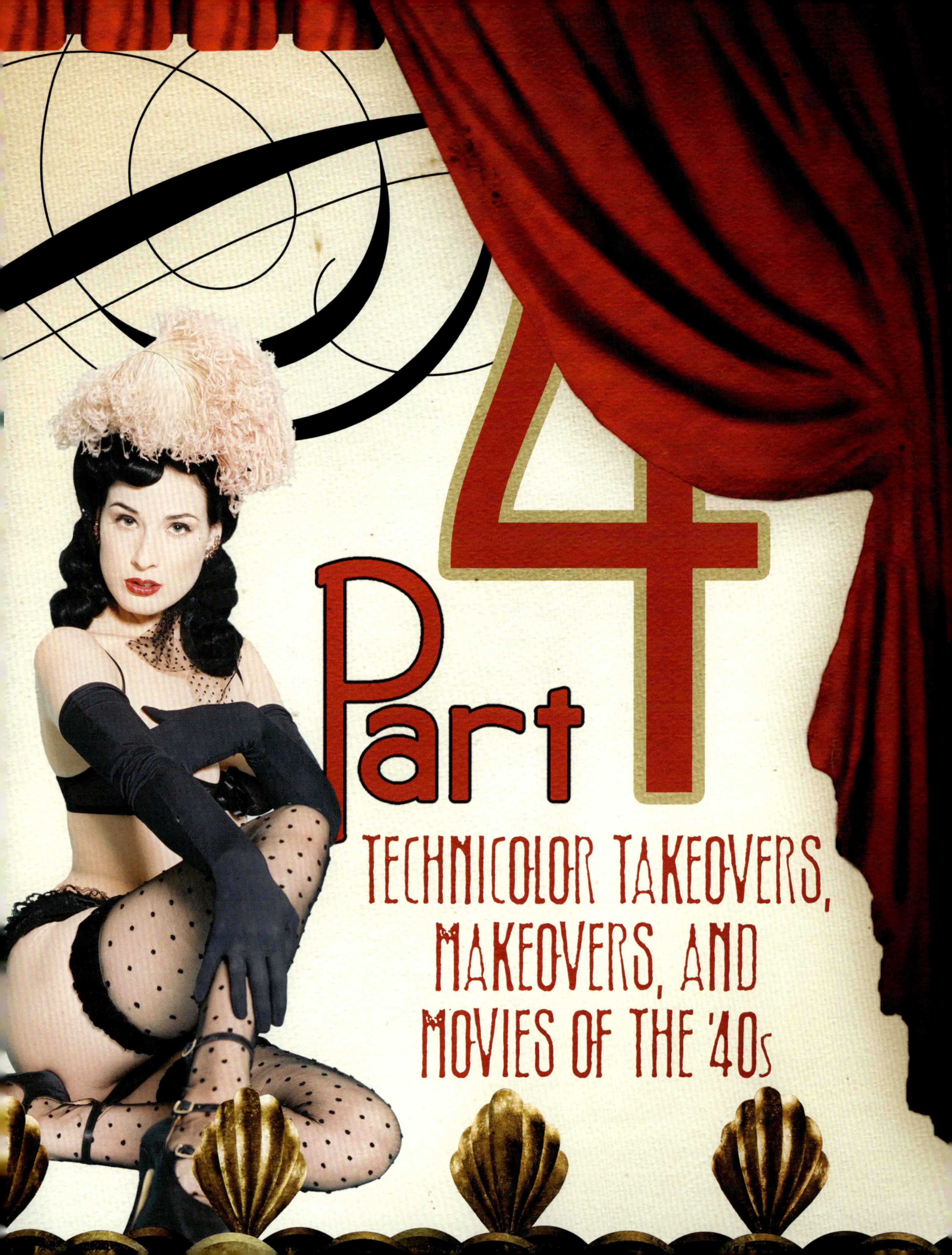
Part 4
TECHNICOLOR TAKEOVERS,
MAKEOVERS, AND
MOVIES OF THE '40s

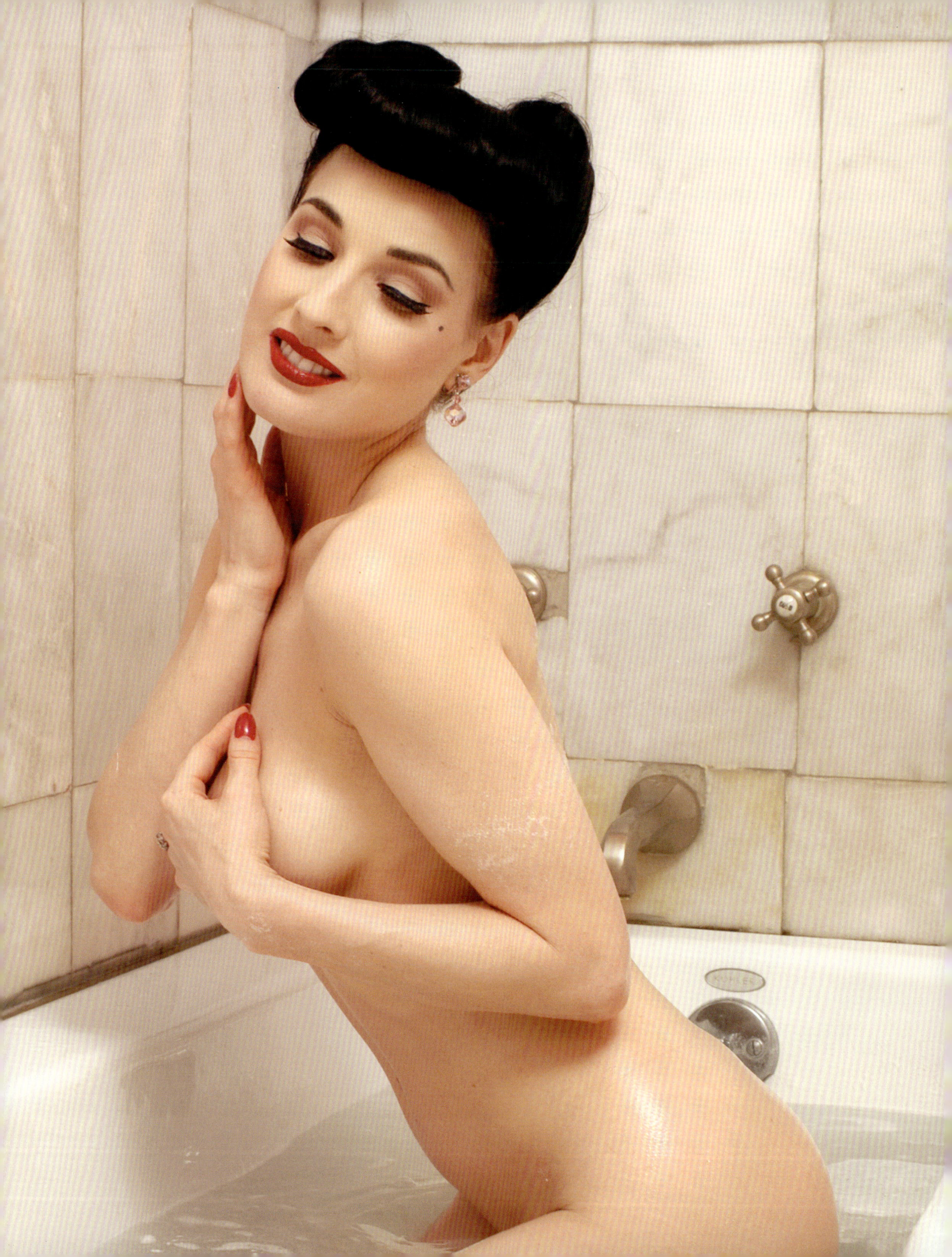

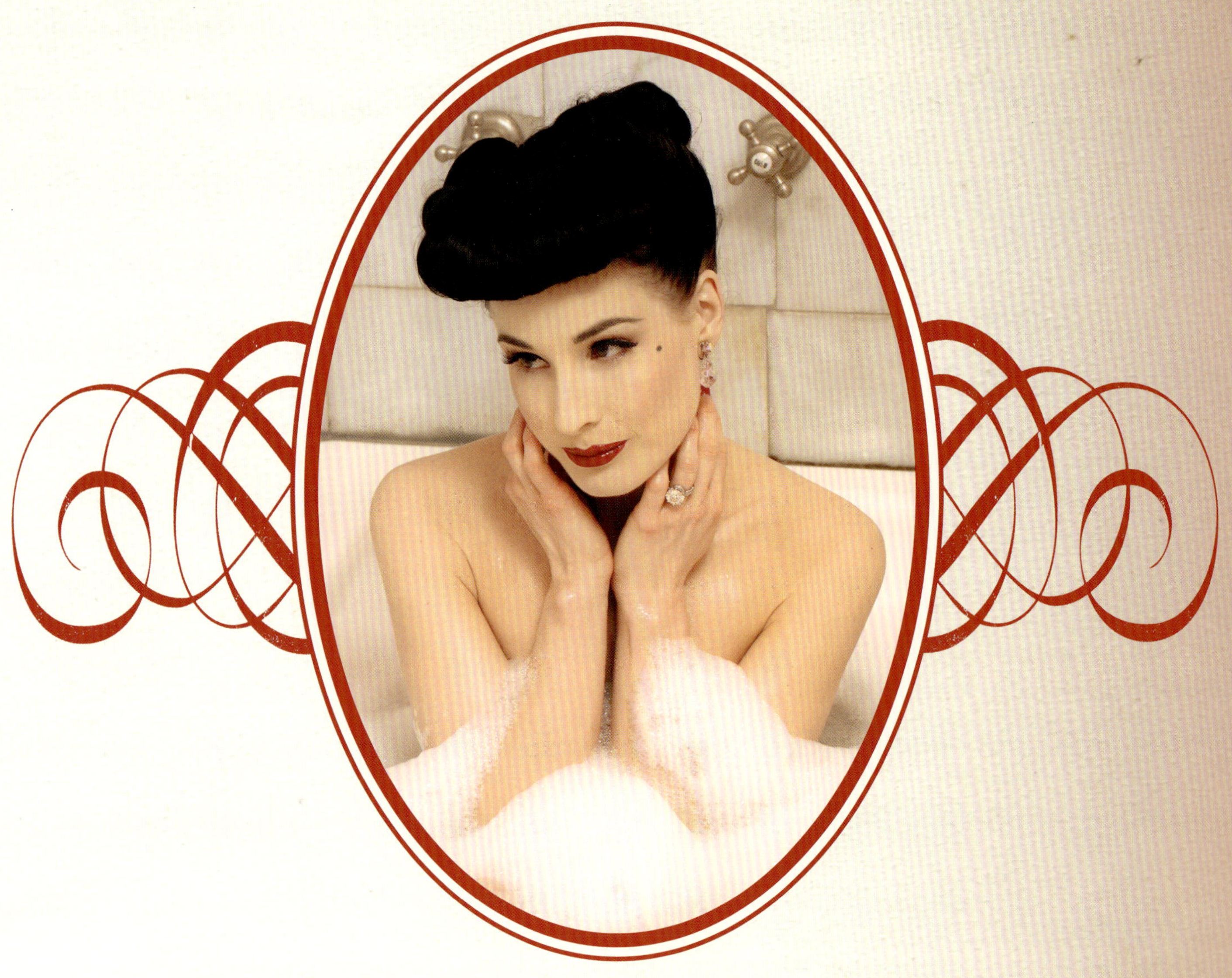

# Pink Room Daydreams

There were times when I was little—rainy Saturdays or days I was sick and home from school—that my mom would brew a pot of chamomile tea and we would stay in our pajamas and watch old movies in the Pink Room. Mom would eventually go off to work, but I was delighted to stay there all day watching old MGM Technicolors.

In my mind, the Pink Room was like the first scene in any movie. The walls were painted with 1950s-style poodles, the ceiling was sparkly, and best of all, the floor was carpeted in cotton candy pink shag. The styling was solidly outside my mother's sense of decency, but she left it alone, never quite "getting to it" as she renovated our house, and for this I was grateful.

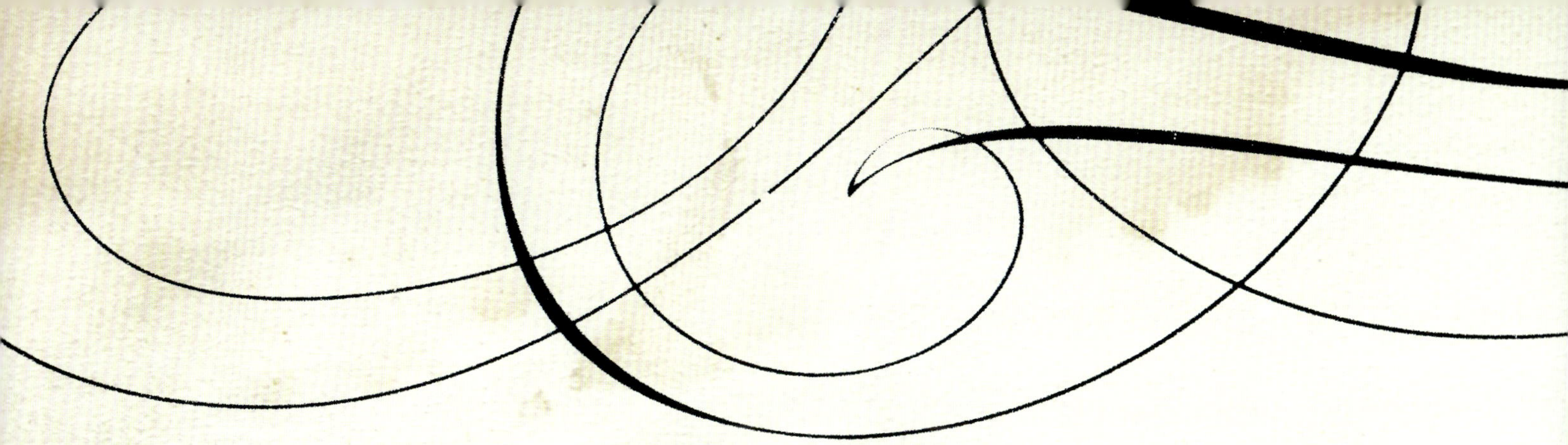

I was sitting on that rug when I first saw *Ziegfeld Follies,* the most enchanting film on earth. Have you seen it? My dreams are set on the same twinkling stage! The first scene is drenched in glittering pink and white, with a pinup pretty ballerina twirling amid dozens of beautiful girls riding around a carousel on live horses. Talk about decadence! Then Lucille Ball emerges, a splendid red-headed siren with a serious face. Who knew she was ever *not* cracking jokes? My goodness, whenever I watch the film, I expect *I Love Lucy* to bubble up through the flawlessly young features. I cannot tell you how this scene has influenced my shows. Of course, I do not use live horses. Not yet. But I do ride a full-size free-standing carousel pony wearing pounds of aurora borealis–colored rhinestones and luxurious, curled, cotton-candy-pink ostrich feathers. Call me loopy, but I find it appalling that Hollywood can spend zillions of dollars on movies that never amount to half of one serving of *Ziegfeld Follies!*

It was in this room, sitting in the shag, with my too-large toe shoes in my lap, that I had my first encounter with my favorite actress of all time, Betty Grable. I loved Betty Grable because she was a nice girl and she would sing and dance, and above all, she had the ultimate 1940s hair. You know, she's one of the first images I remember from the Pink Room. Even today, when I can't think of anything to wear or I am tired of my hairstyle or confused about my next show, I turn on a Betty Grable musical. For added inspiration, I slip into the ivory corset she wore in *The Farmer Takes a Wife.* (I acquired it at an auction.)

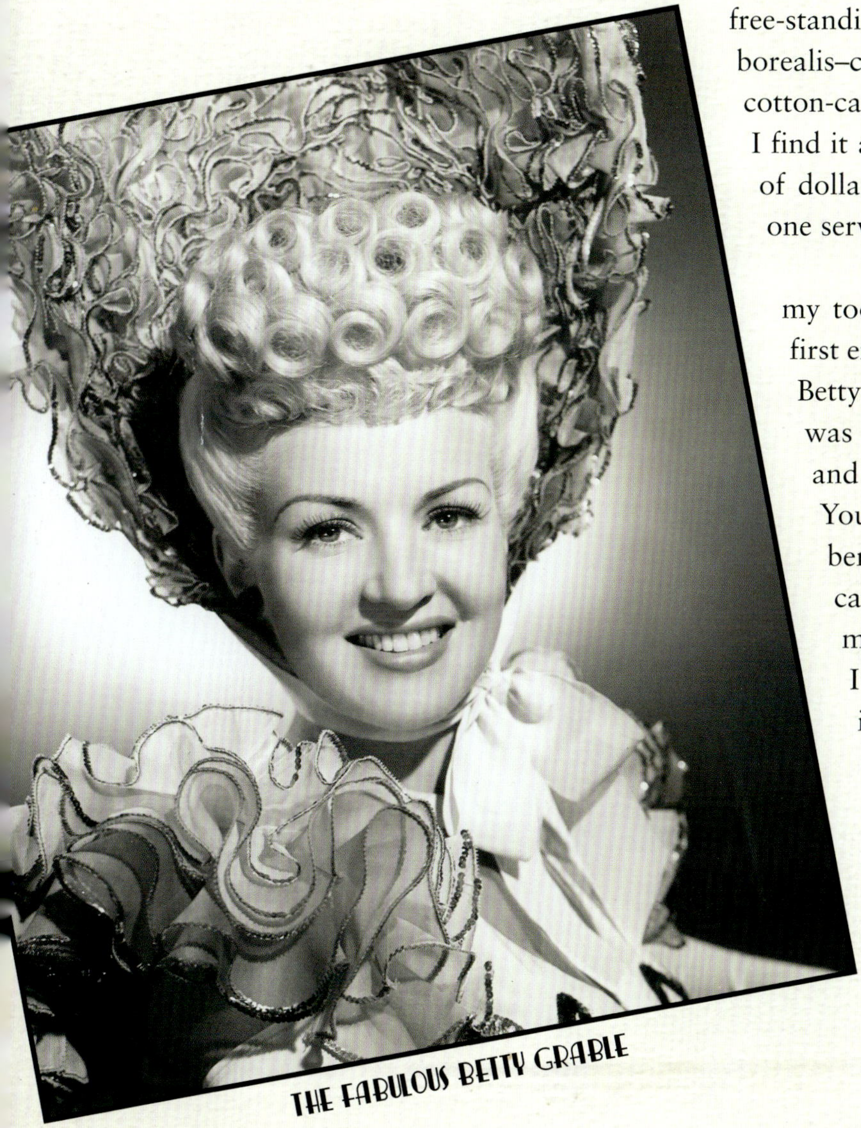

THE FABULOUS BETTY GRABLE

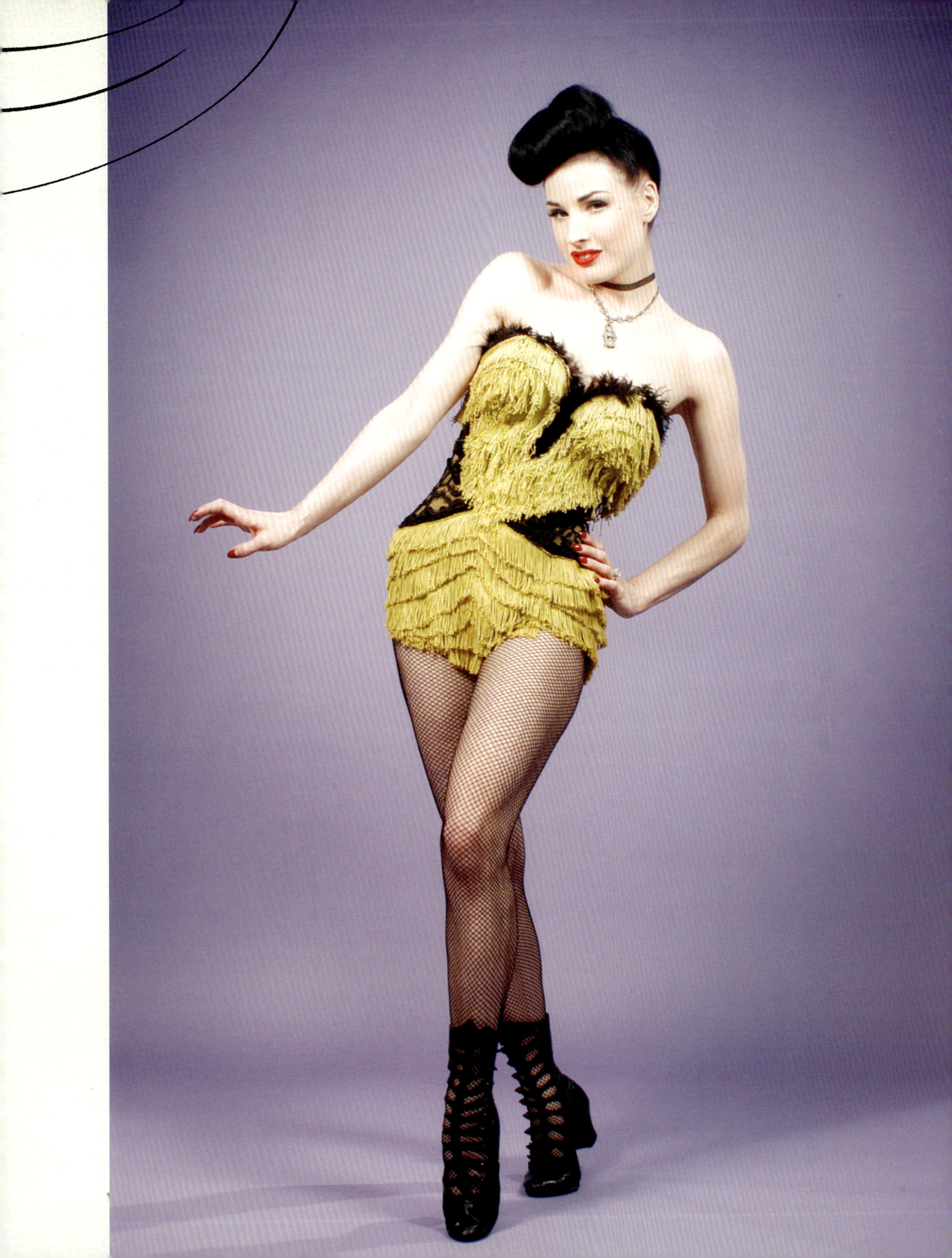

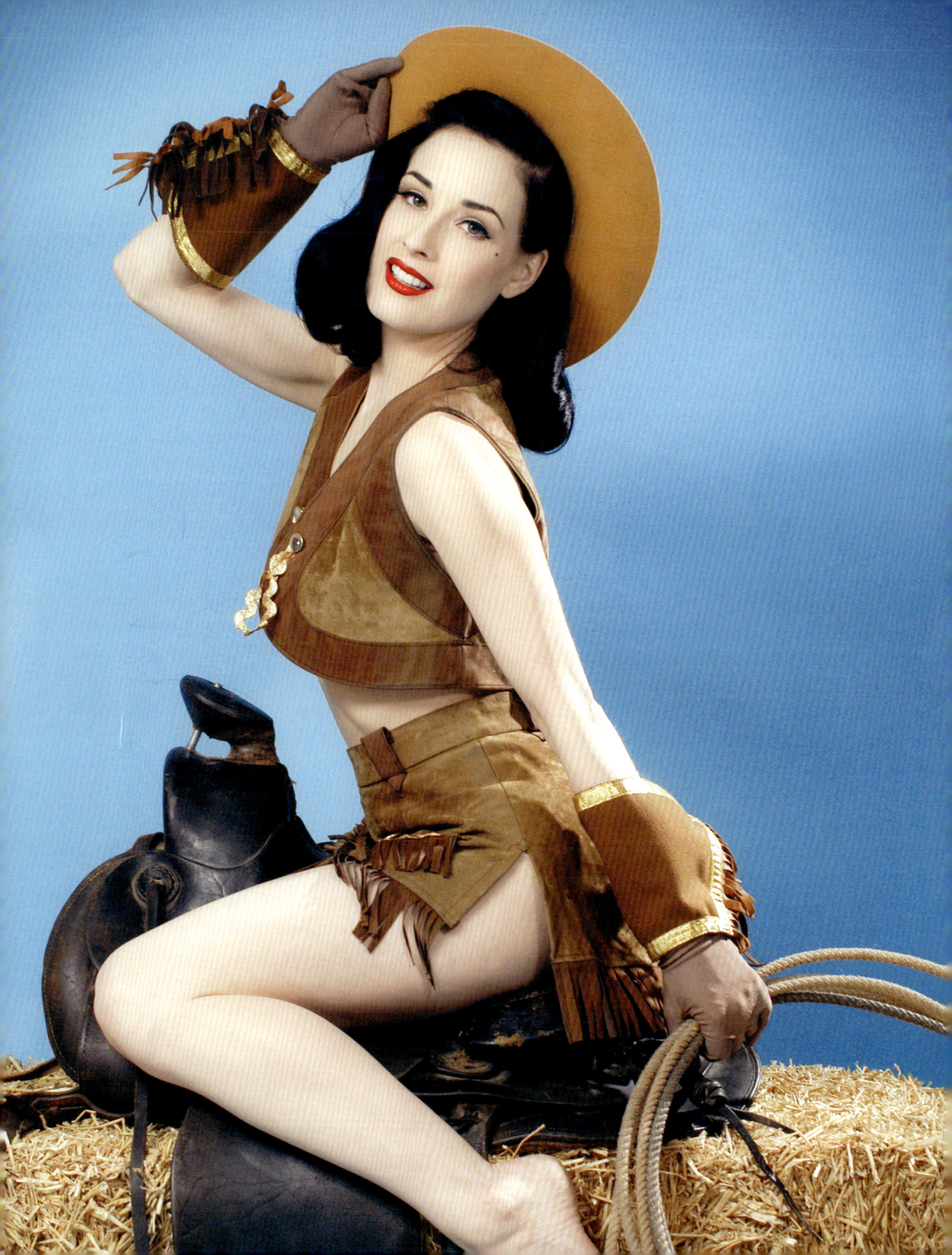

# MUST-SEE MOVIES OF TECHNICOLOR

FOR A REAL TREAT—AND A STUDY IN '40s AND '50s GLAMOUR—SEE THESE STUNNING TECHNICOLORS! THESE ARE THE MOVIES THAT MAKE ME SCOOT UP UNTIL I'M FIVE INCHES FROM THE TELEVISION SET!

1. **ZIEGFELD FOLLIES**

   Nothing is more inspiring to me than the opening scene with the women on a grand carousel. I have this scene along with other favorite clips playing as a loop on the television above my clawfoot bathtub at home, for constant inspiration.

2. **ZIEGFELD GIRL**

   This film was my introduction to Hedy Lamarr and the young Lana Turner—and the darker side of being a showgirl!

3. **COVER GIRL**

   This film, starring Rita Hayworth, has influenced my street dressing style more than any other. The fashion is to die for, especially the miniature doll hats (the kind I am most often seen wearing).

4. **PINUP GIRL**

   Betty Grable is the very epitome of World War II pinups in this movie! She has the best '40s bouffant hair you'll see in any film.

5. **GENTLEMEN PREFER BLONDES**

   I can't leave out a Marilyn film or two. This flick is full of great dance numbers with fantastic costumes and curves for days. Take a close look at the "Diamonds Are a Girl's Best Friend" scene. It opens with women hanging from chandeliers!

6. **THE DOLLY SISTERS**

   Starring Betty Grable and another '40s beauty, June Haver, this movie is based on the true story of twin showgirl sisters. In one fantastic scene the stars emerge from a giant evening bag, and girls, dressed as cosmetics, sing and dance with them. It's deliciously absurd!

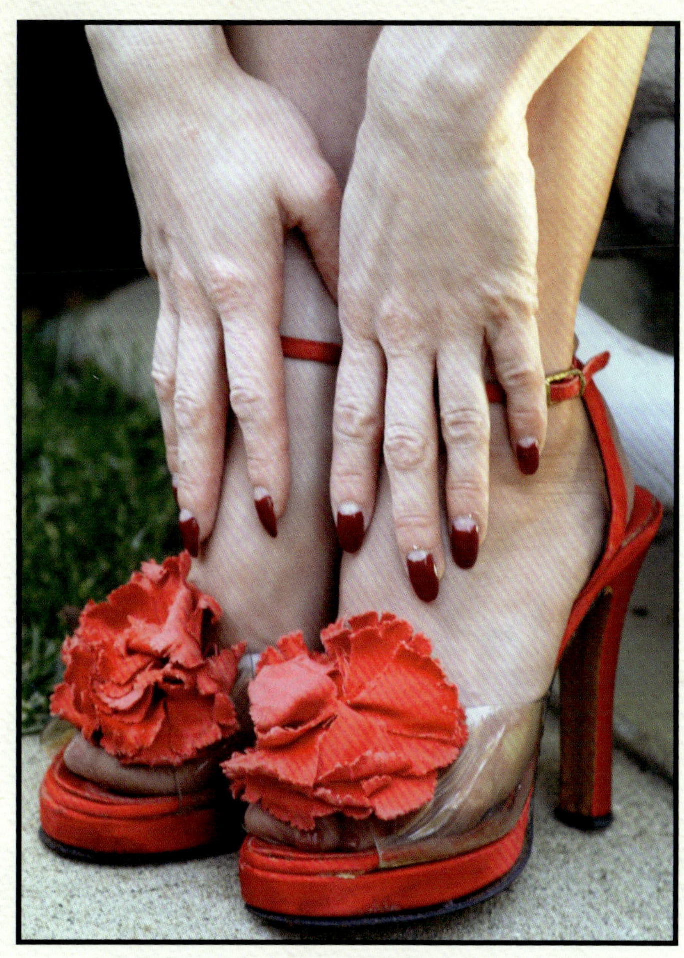

## DITA'S VINTAGE MANICURE TIP

I have always loved the look of the classic bare moons you will notice in the most glamorous movie star portraits and also on the nails of Vargas and Petty pinups, so I taught myself how to do this look. It is a stunning detail that shows you know your stuff when it comes to vintage beauty! My secret? Either take a photo to your manicurist, or learn to do it yourself! Look for those little curved stickers used for creating French manicures, but place them just over your natural "moons," and then paint the length of your nails. Remove the sticker, touch up mistakes with a Q-tip and polish remover, and follow with a coat of clear varnish! Voila!

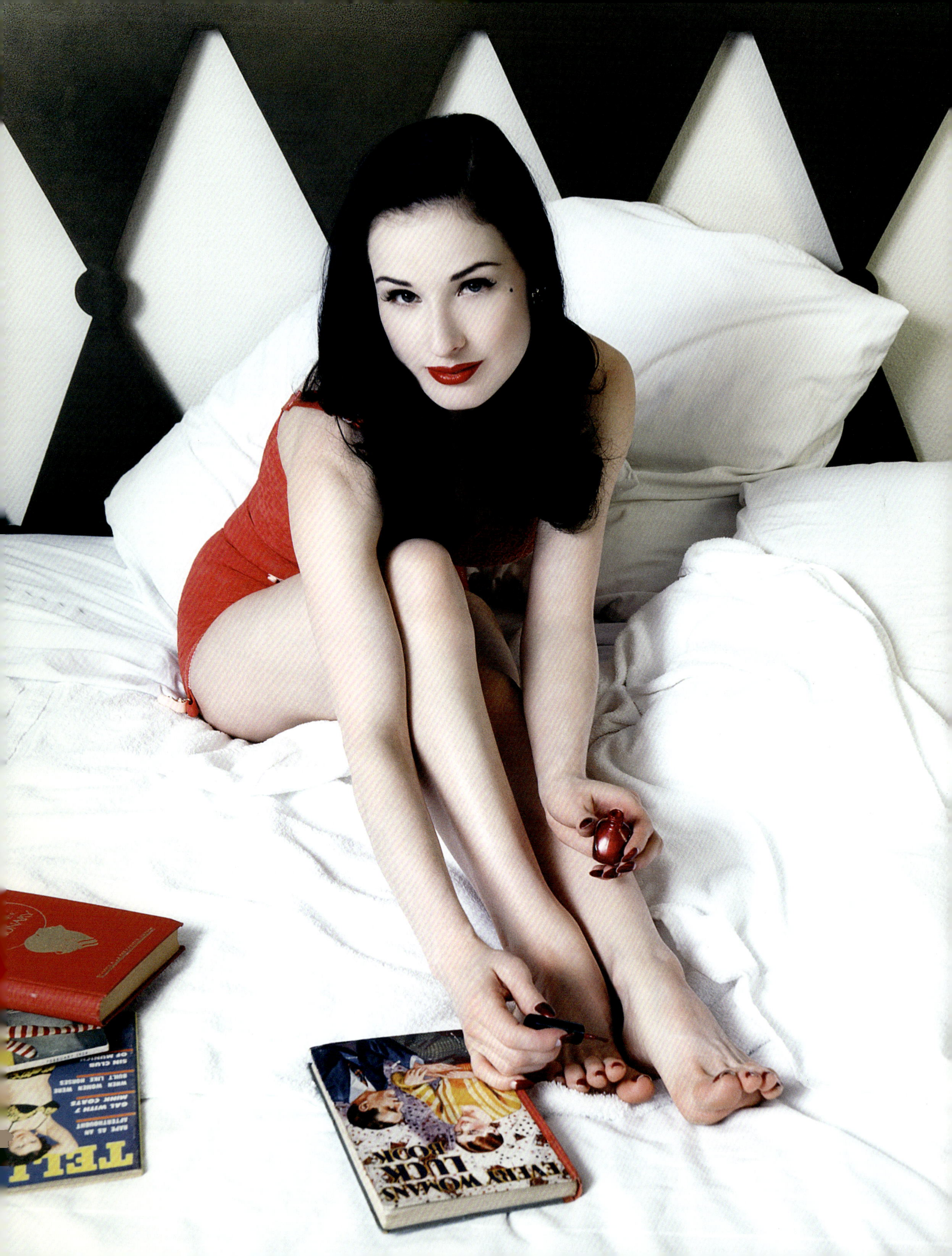
TELL
RAPE AS AN AFTERTHOUGHT
GAL WITH 7 MINK COATS
WHEN WOMEN WERE BUILT LIKE HORSES
SIN CLUB OF MUNICH
EVERY WOMAN'S LUCK BOOK

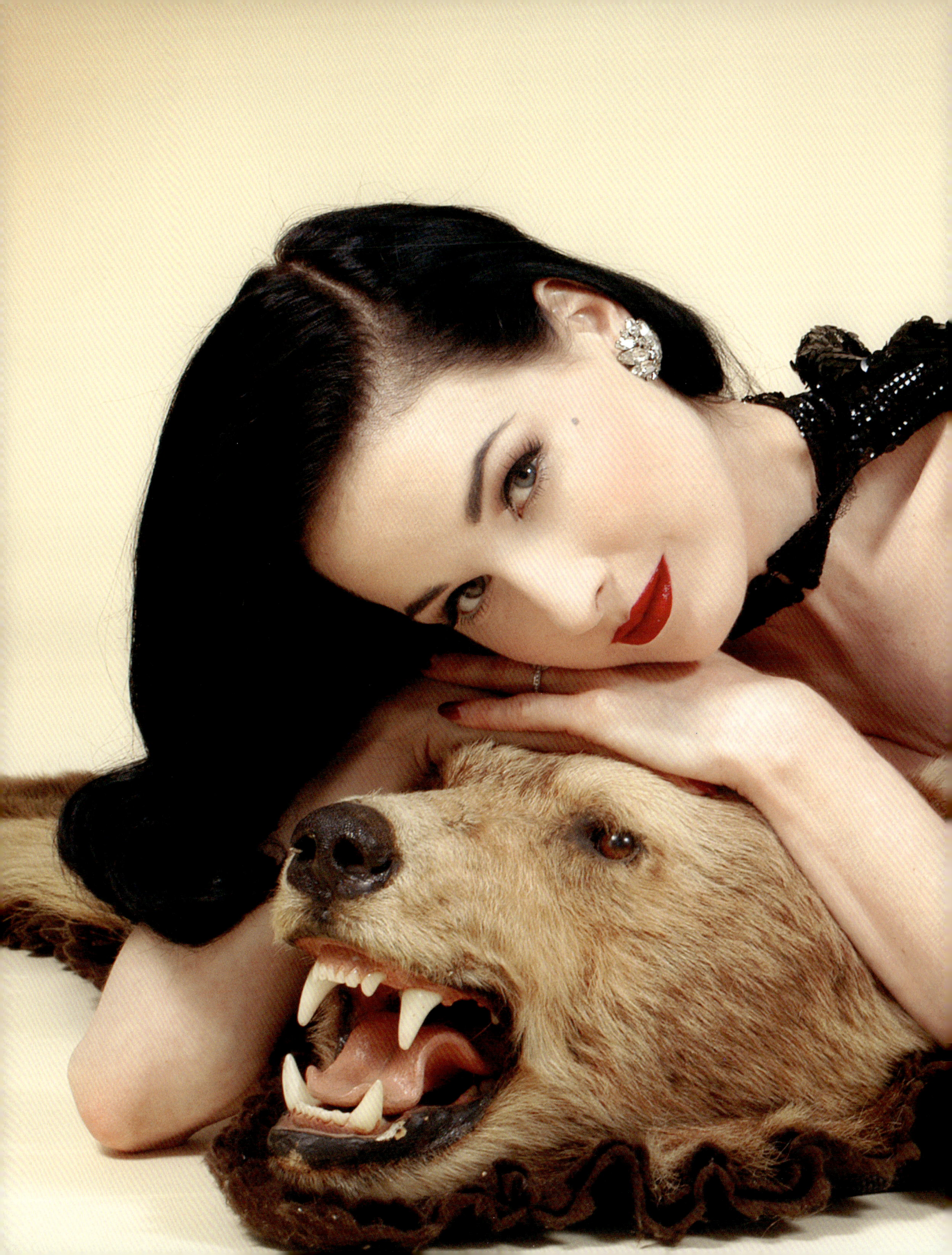

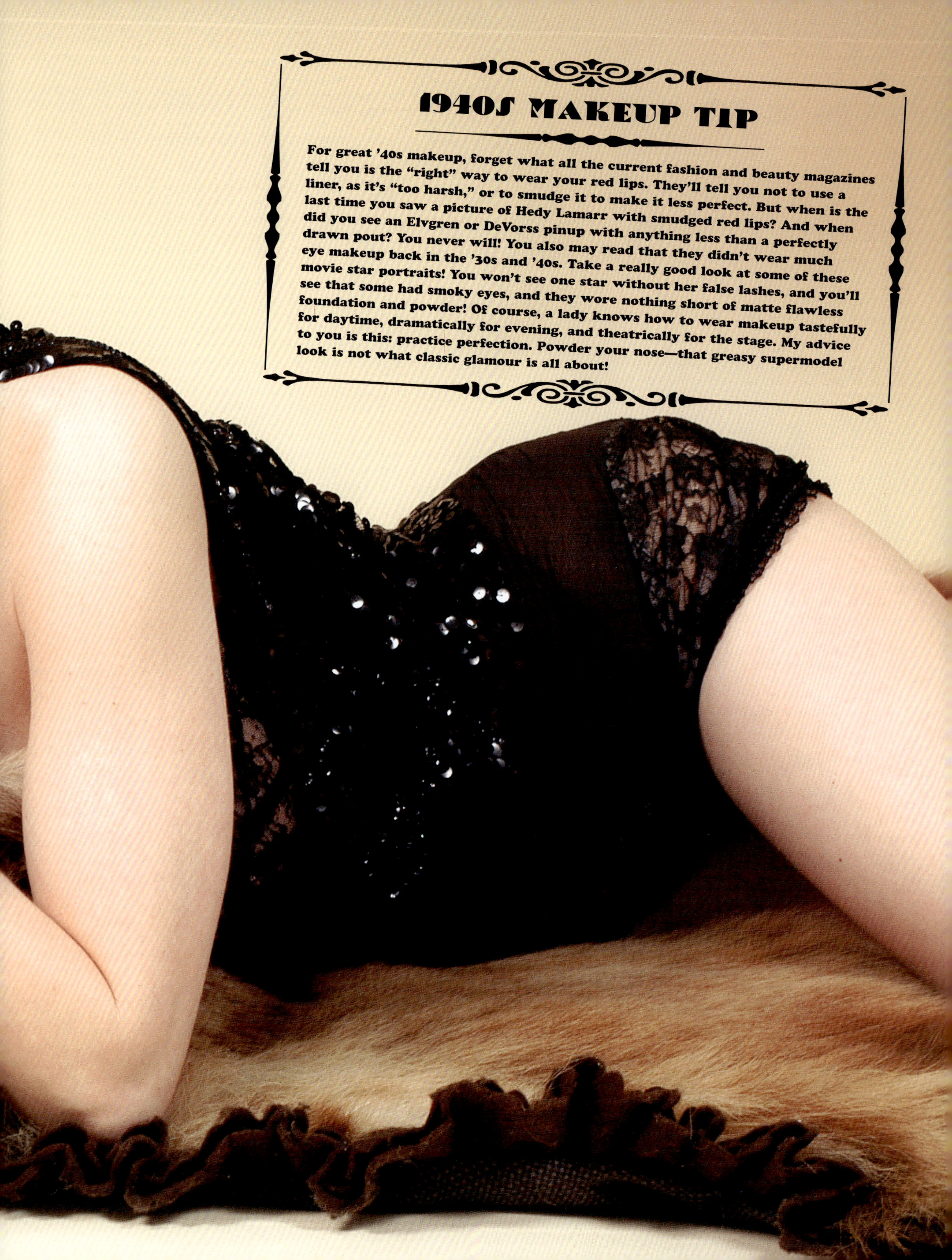

## 1940S MAKEUP TIP

For great '40s makeup, forget what all the current fashion and beauty magazines tell you is the "right" way to wear your red lips. They'll tell you not to use a liner, as it's "too harsh," or to smudge it to make it less perfect. But when is the last time you saw a picture of Hedy Lamarr with smudged red lips? And when did you see an Elvgren or DeVorss pinup with anything less than a perfectly drawn pout? You never will! You also may read that they didn't wear much eye makeup back in the '30s and '40s. Take a really good look at some of these movie star portraits! You won't see one star without her false lashes, and you'll see that some had smoky eyes, and they wore nothing short of matte flawless foundation and powder! Of course, a lady knows how to wear makeup tastefully for daytime, dramatically for evening, and theatrically for the stage. My advice to you is this: practice perfection. Powder your nose—that greasy supermodel look is not what classic glamour is all about!

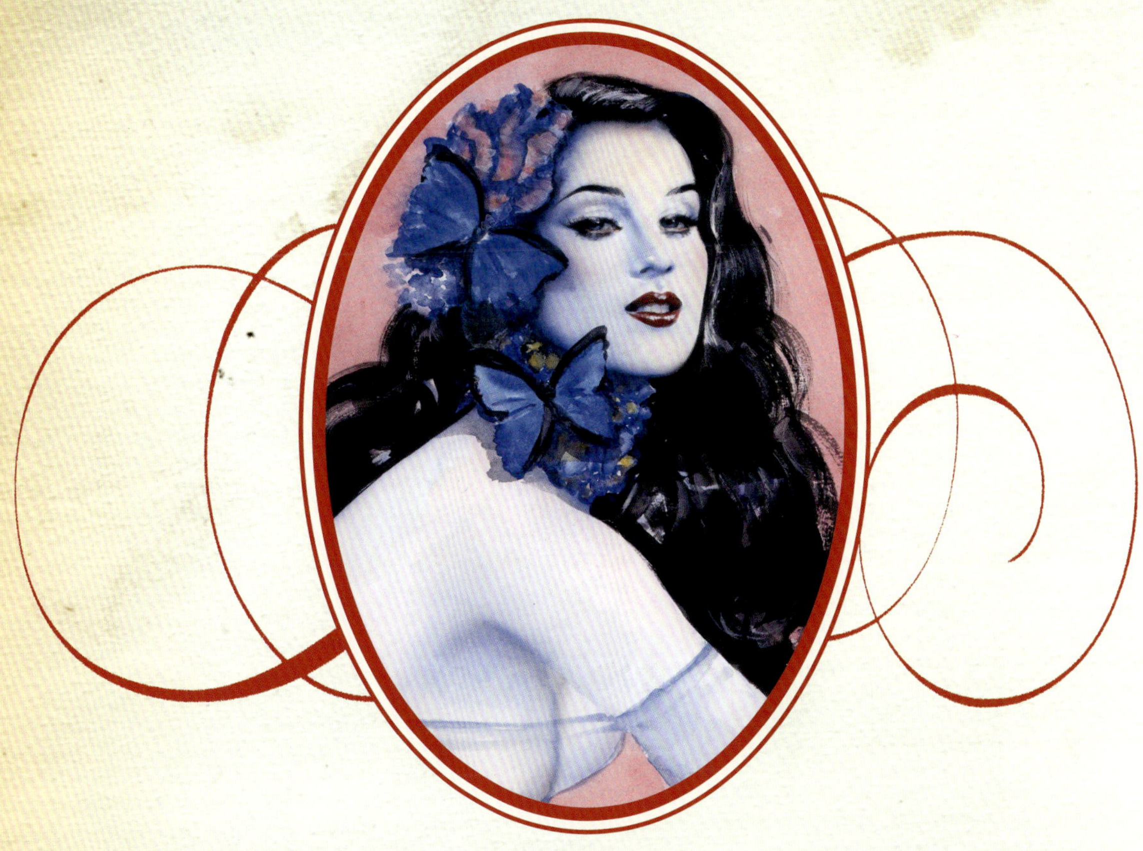

# Pinup Pretty, Can I Be You?

Betty Grable is everyone's favorite pinup. Just ask your grandfather or great-grandfather. I'll bet he loved that classic shot of her, looking over her shoulder, wearing a one-piece bathing suit, her shiny golden hair in the perfect '40s bouffant. I adore every photo ever taken of Betty. Those pictures make me deliriously happy; they inspire me. But, then that was the point.

Let me tell you about the first cheesecake pinup. The year was 1915, and a lusty newspaper photographer caught sight of a red-hot Russian opera singer disembarking from a ship in New York's harbor. He begged her to lift her skirt *for the sake of the photo* (I've heard that one!), and the curvy cookie obliged, tugging at her ruffles ever so slightly, smiling deliciously into the camera. When the photographer's editor saw the image, he cried out, "Why, this is better than cheesecake!" And wasn't he right.

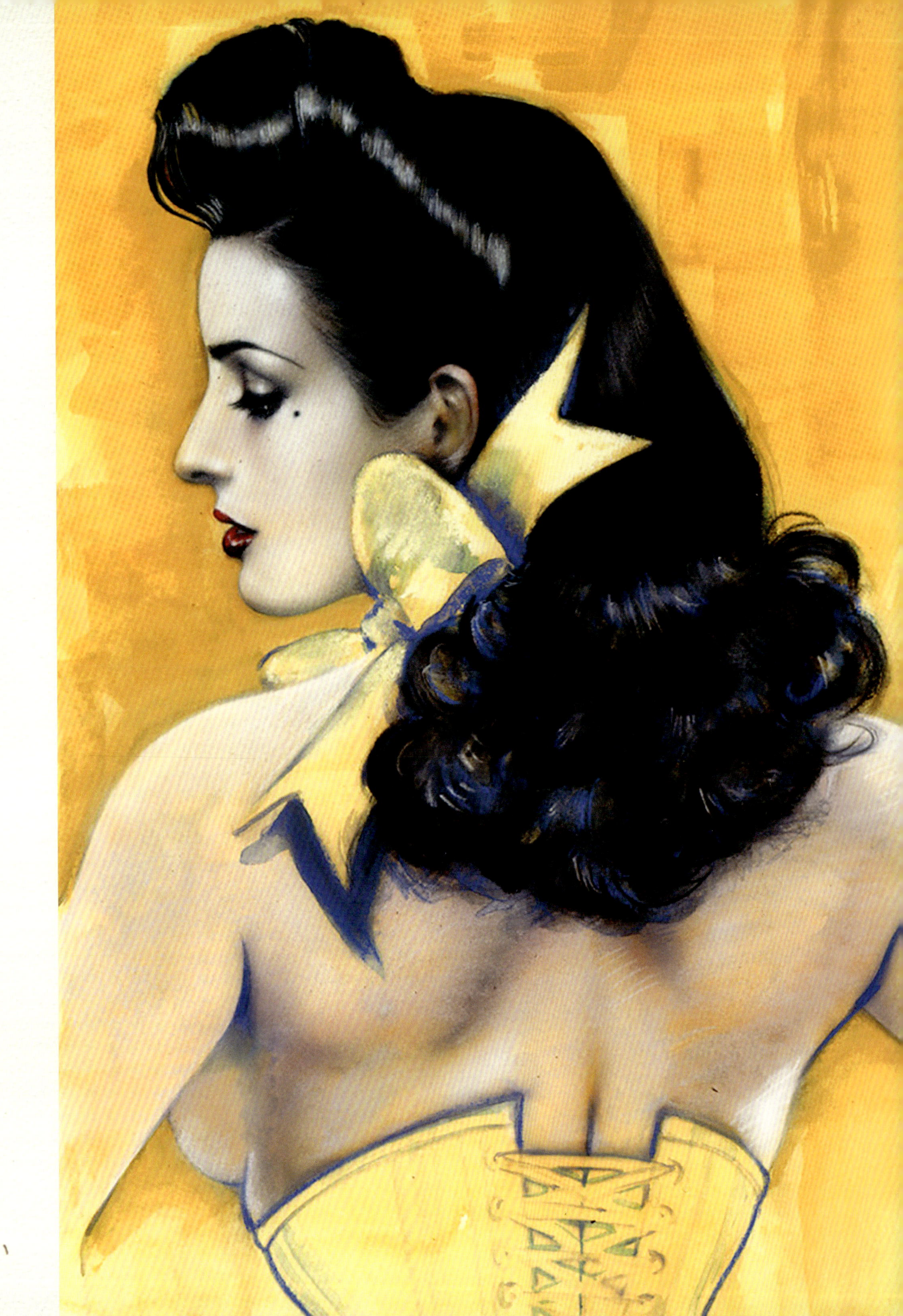

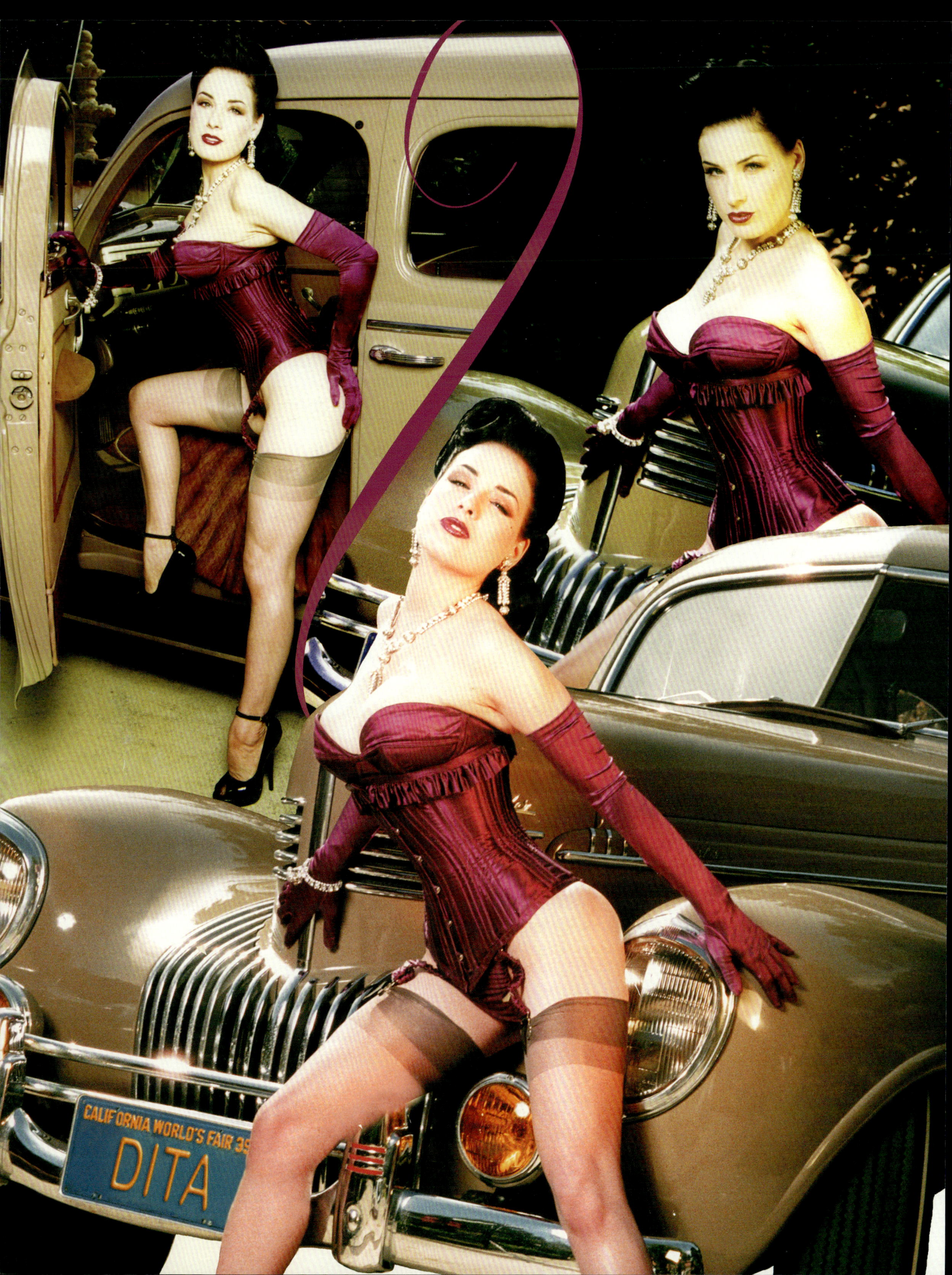
CALIFORNIA WORLD'S FAIR 39
DITA

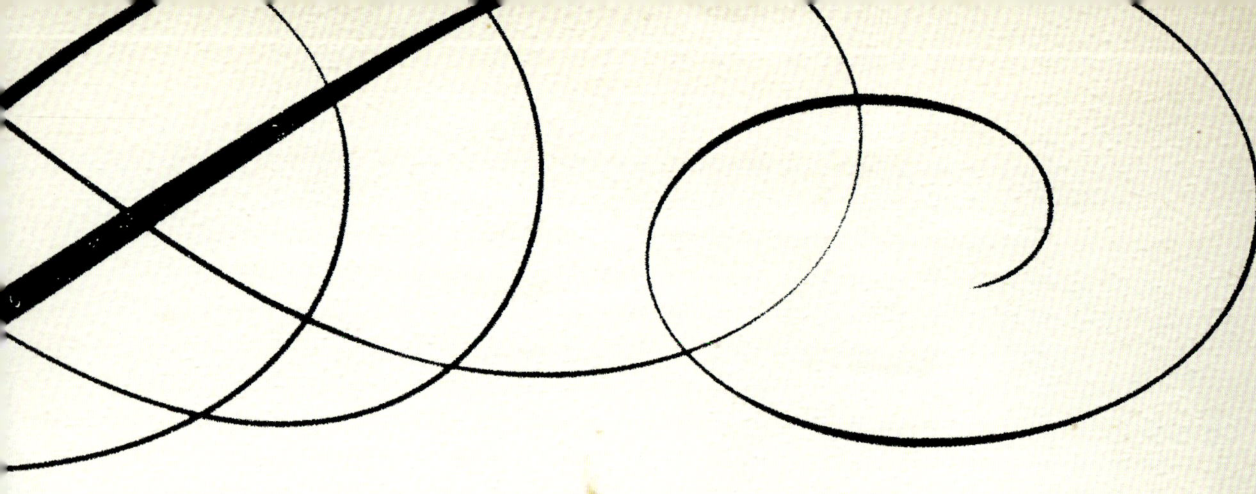

Who doesn't love the cheesecake pinup? The long-limbed all-American temptress with the wholesome hourglass figure—sometimes illustrated, sometimes photographed—always wearing something revealing. As Betty Grable does in that World War II classic, the cheesecake invites you in to join her on the beach or for a picnic—to do whatever she's doing right along with her. Every man wants to *be with* the American pinup. I want to *be* her. Why, she's an illustrated Ziegfeld Girl!

It seems too perfect, then, that my hero Flo played a hand in the pinup's evolution. But then again, if there was a pretty girl under the lights, you could bet Flo was behind the curtain. When he opened the Follies in 1907, he realized pretty quickly that what the audience wanted were the girls. Sensing that he could enhance their allure by making audiences more "familiar" with them offstage, Flo hired a young Peruvian-born painter named Alberto Vargas to paint the girls in repose, in their dressing rooms, on smoke breaks—inviting viewers into these intimate settings. Vargas moved on to *Esquire* in 1940, where he took over for another famous pinup artist named George Petty, and went on to paint so many of the dazzlingly sweet girls America associates with cheesecake pinup: the Varga Girl.

Old Flo, as you know, believed in the power of imagery. But, would you believe he hired most of the girls for his Follies without ever meeting them? He presumed that pictures could more accurately gage whether they enjoyed being looked at. As usual, I'm with Flo. Modeling and performing feel like two parts of a whole to me, too—I've always attempted to blend the mediums. Some people may not consider modeled photos a form of entertainment, but I like to think that each of my pictures tells a story, and that all of my performances are also pinups. It's for this reason that I do my own makeup and hair for shows, and that I conceive of all my own props and costumes. For me, it's important to be the model *and* the artist.

Of course, it's a ton of work, living D.I.Y. Perfecting a look and a style takes a lot of practice—which I got during my obsession with swing dancing in my early twenties. I used to go out every single night—meaning that every evening I sat down at my little vanity with my books and magazines, fingered waves into my hair, applied fake lashes, and drew my lips into a full Hedy Lamarr pout. I even bought a car to match my new style—a gorgeous 1939 Chrysler New Yorker in desert beige! Best of all, the roof on that car—high and rounded—is a testament to the fabulous hats of those days. One can't very well drive a modern compact to go swing dancing when one is trying to live the dream!

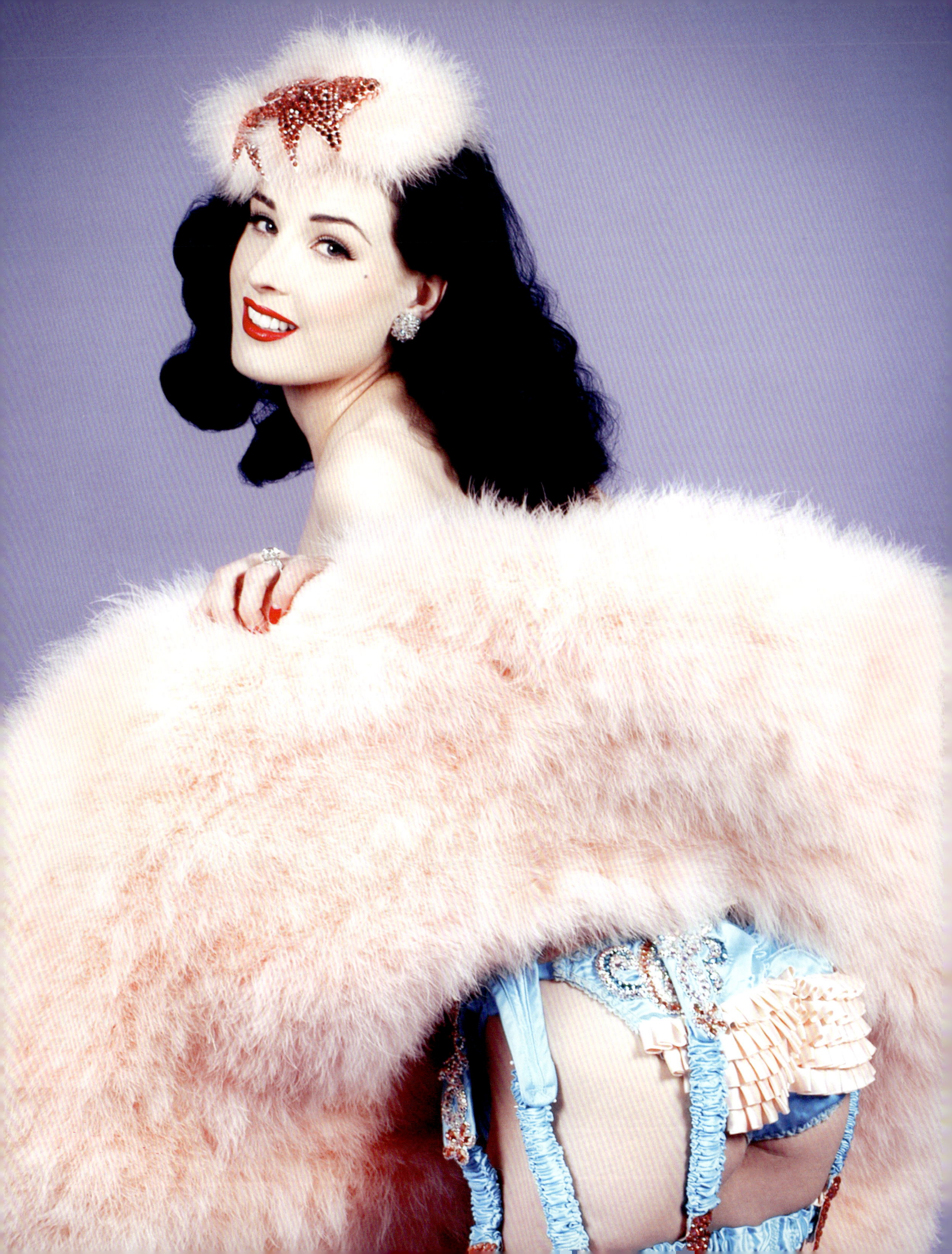

# FIRST-CLASS FACE: HOW TO LOOK LIKE A CHEESECAKE PINUP DOLL!

**THE WORLD WAR II PINUP IS MY PERSONAL FAVORITE FOR BEAUTY. WELCOME TO THE PRETTY ERA OF THE PINUP DOLL!**

**BURLESQUE QUEENS**

**Ann Corio**
**Gypsy Rose Lee**
**Margie Hart**
**Sherry Britton**

**MOVIE STARS**

**Betty Grable**
**Rita Hayworth** →
**Gene Tierney**
**Lana Turner**
**Vivien Leigh**

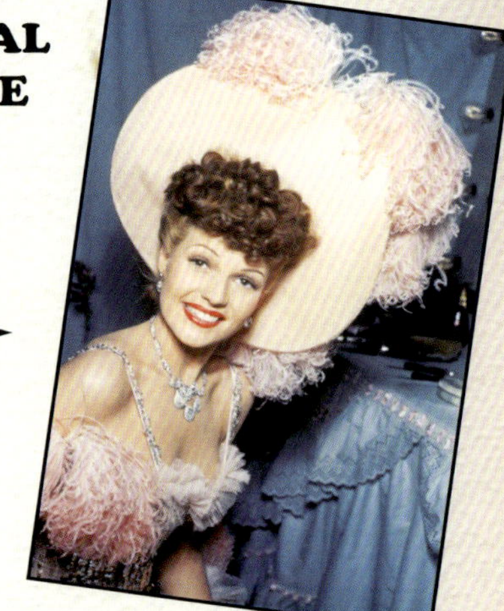

**SKIN:** Natural-toned with rosy or peach rouge blended onto cheeks with a powdery matte finish.

**BROWS:** Neatly tweezed, but kept naturally full and defined with pencil to create nice arches.

**EYES:** Long, curled lashes with muted shadow near the lashline or a touch of liner. Eye shadow may be a creamy ivory, soft lavender, or pale powder blue, blended well.

**LIPS:** Drawn with red pencil into a rounded full bow. All shades of red satin or glossy lipstick make the perfect pinup pout!

**NAILS:** Long oval shape painted to match the lips, with the moons left natural.

**HAIR:** Bouffants and Victory rolls! Pay no mind to books that tell you to do a pincurl set . . . hot rollers are a much better and simpler option for creating the volume you need to get 1940s bouffant styles. I prefer very small barrel hot rollers to create tight curls. Be sure to take special care to learn to roll the ends perfectly, and use a setting lotion or spray gel.

To create big Victory rolls, section the front of your hair and do a little bit of back combing before smoothing out the sides and rolling it from the ends and pinning it. Practice makes perfect!

I also like to use the classic "rat" foundations to make big "bumper bangs" or an enormous chignon! Look for the kind made from woven nylon, and don't bother with the ones made out of spongy material. The best tip I have is to practice, practice, practice! That's my secret!

You can create that classic Betty Grable curly bangs 'do by sweeping your hair into a very tight ponytail at the front of your head and then pinning each section into big pincurls.

You can also pin fresh gardenias in your hair, as I did for the cover of *Playboy* (see *Fetish*, "Playboy Fetish Forum," page 43), or buy silk roses, lilies, or cherry blossoms and pin them in with small bobby pins. Try pinning on vintage rhinestone earrings or brooches and wearing a hairnet or a snood for a really classic World War II–era style.

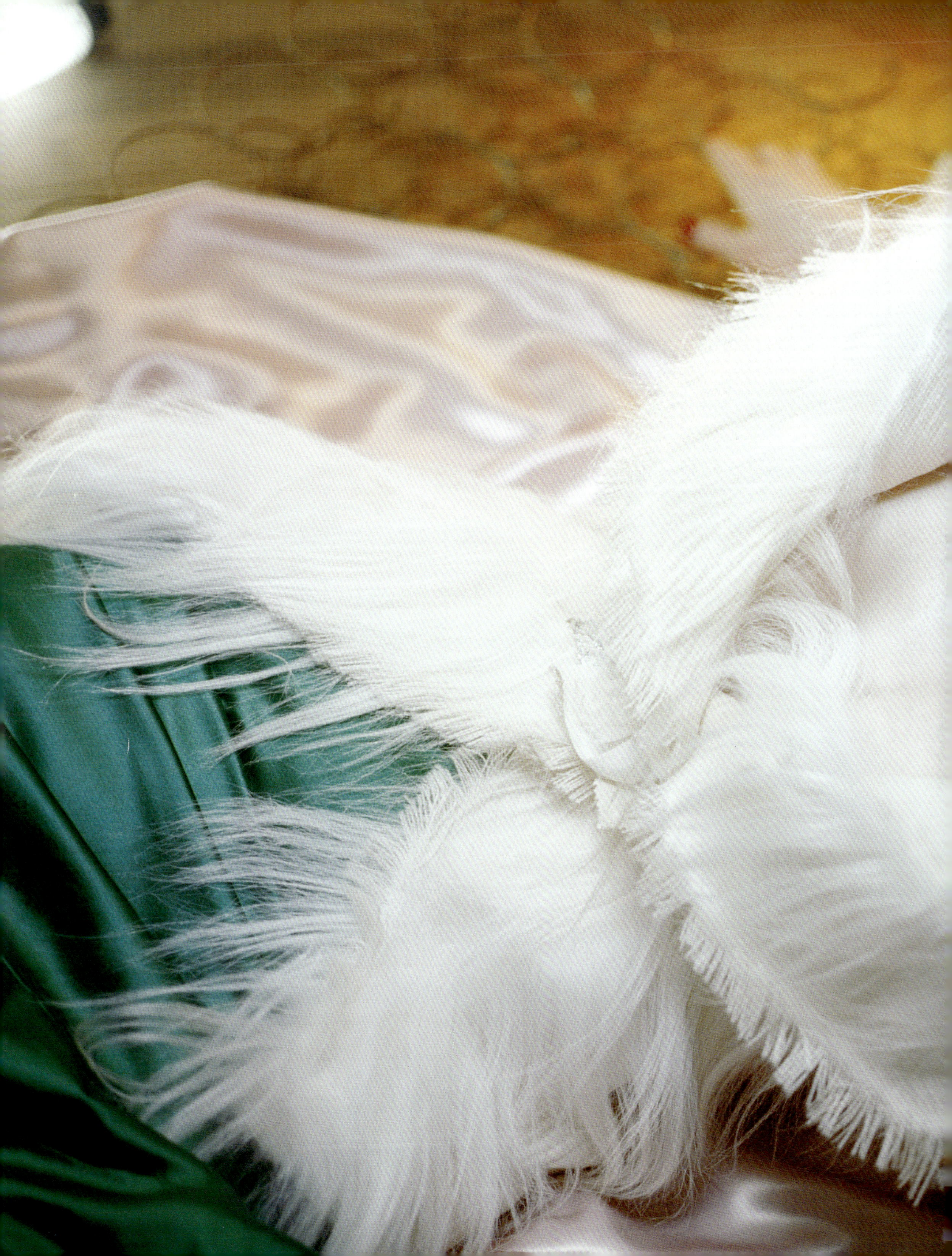

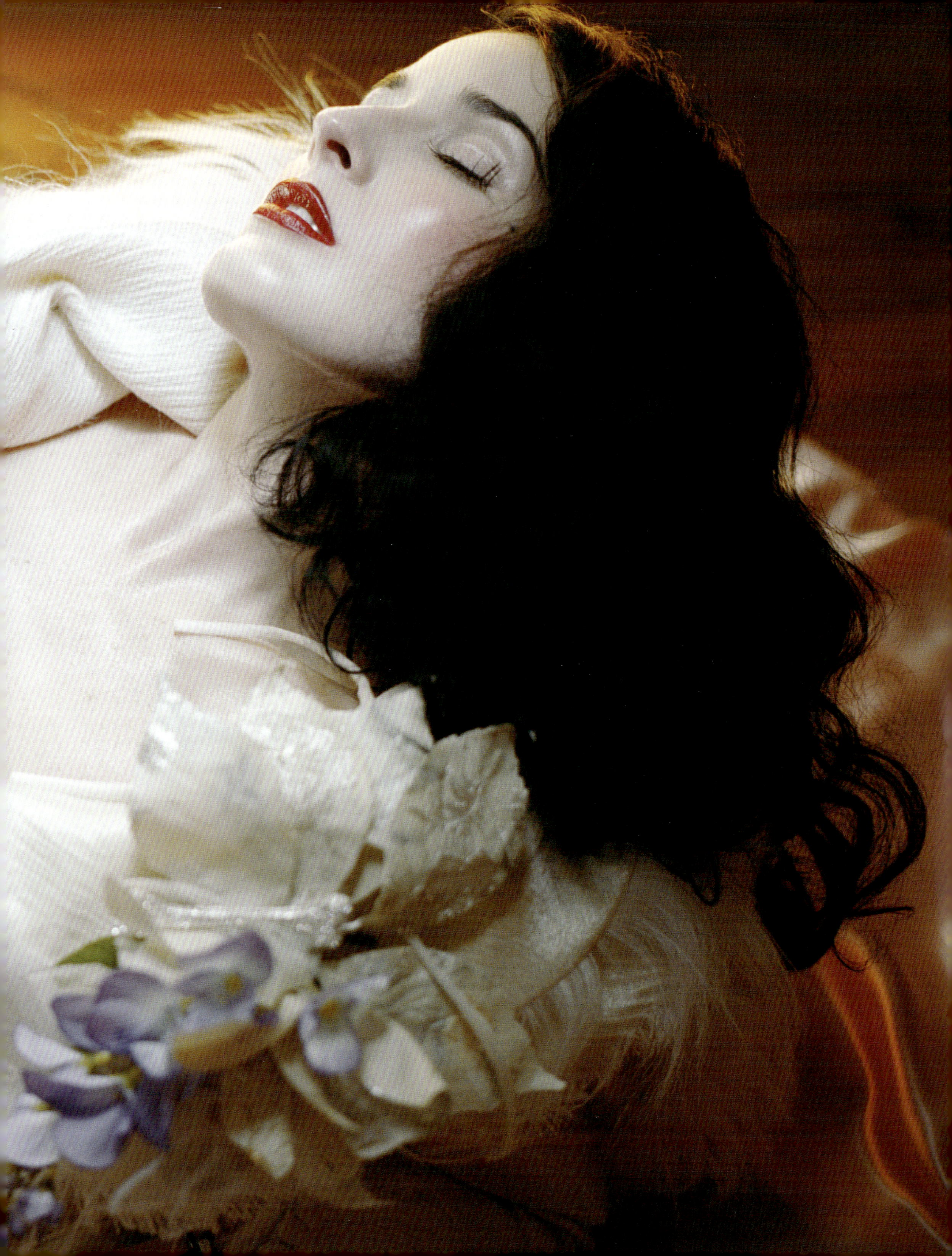

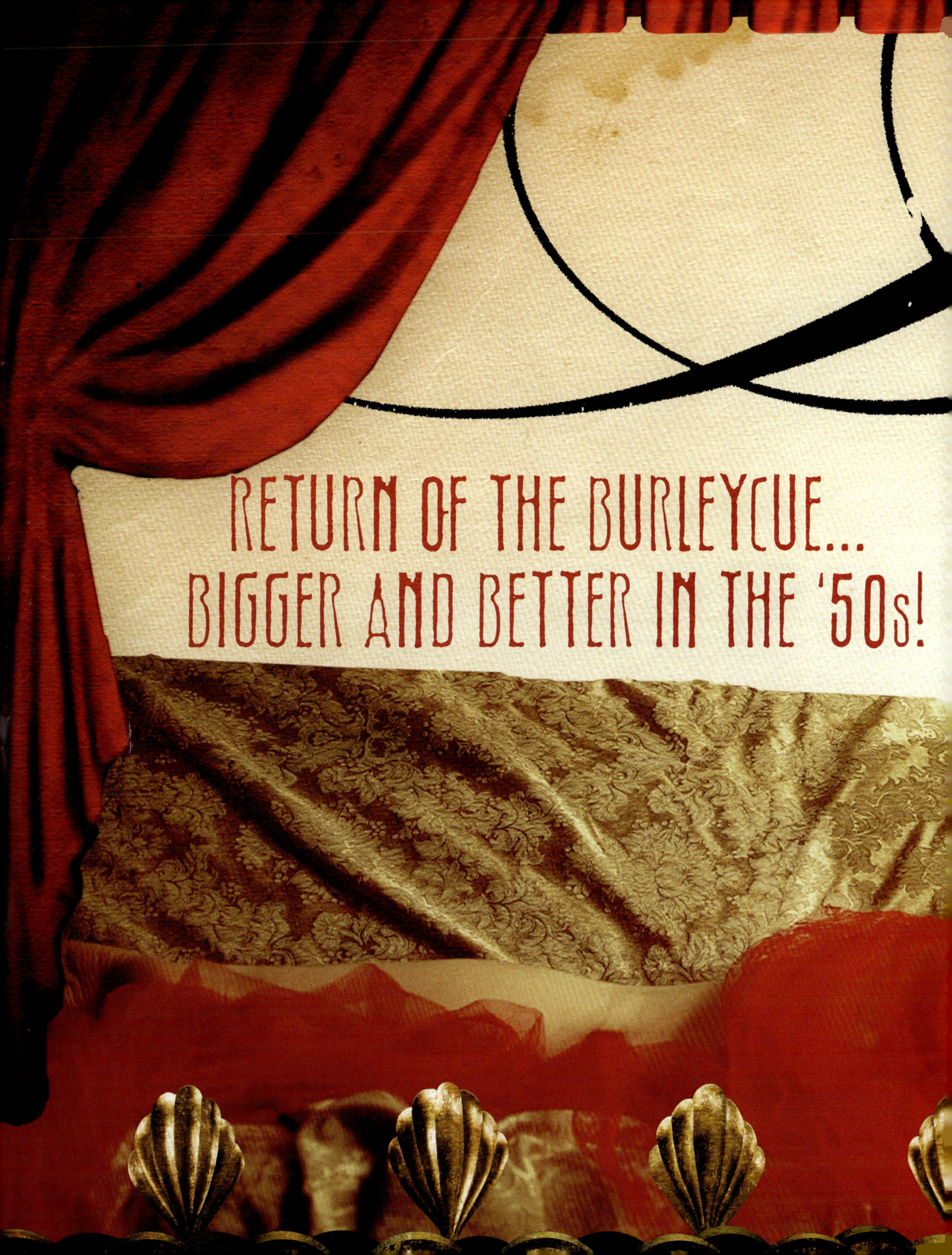
RETURN OF THE BURLEYCUE...
BIGGER AND BETTER IN THE '50s!

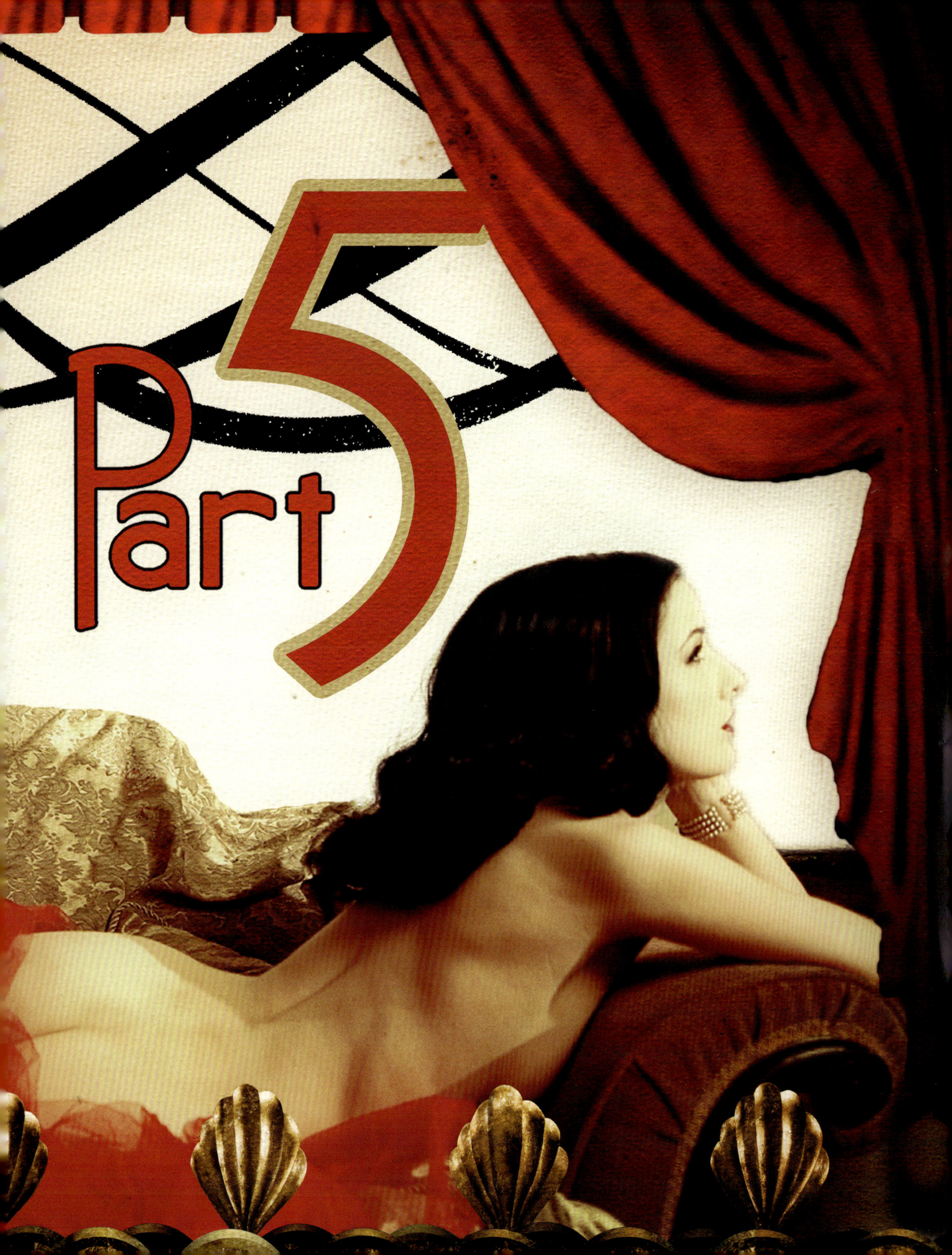
Part 5

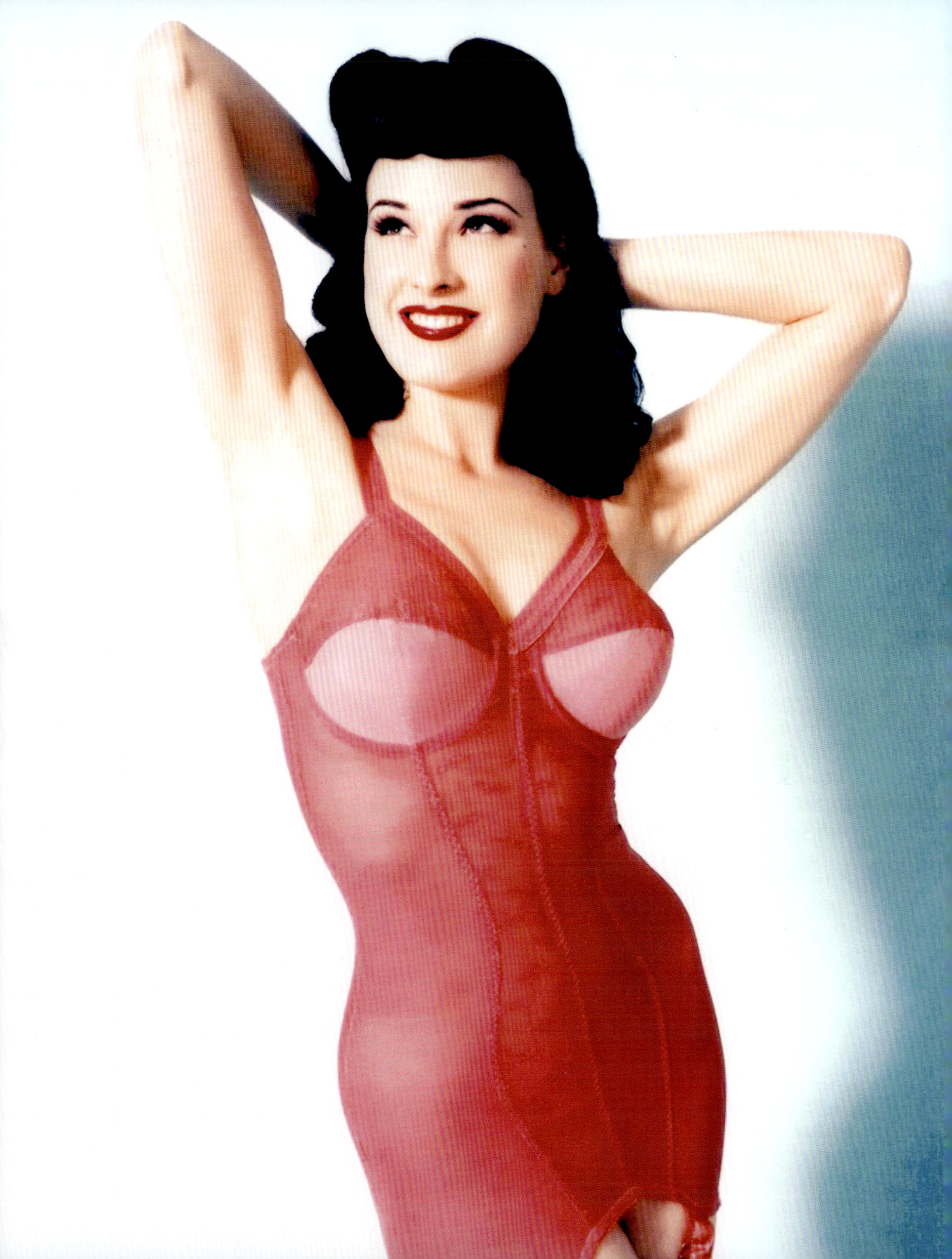

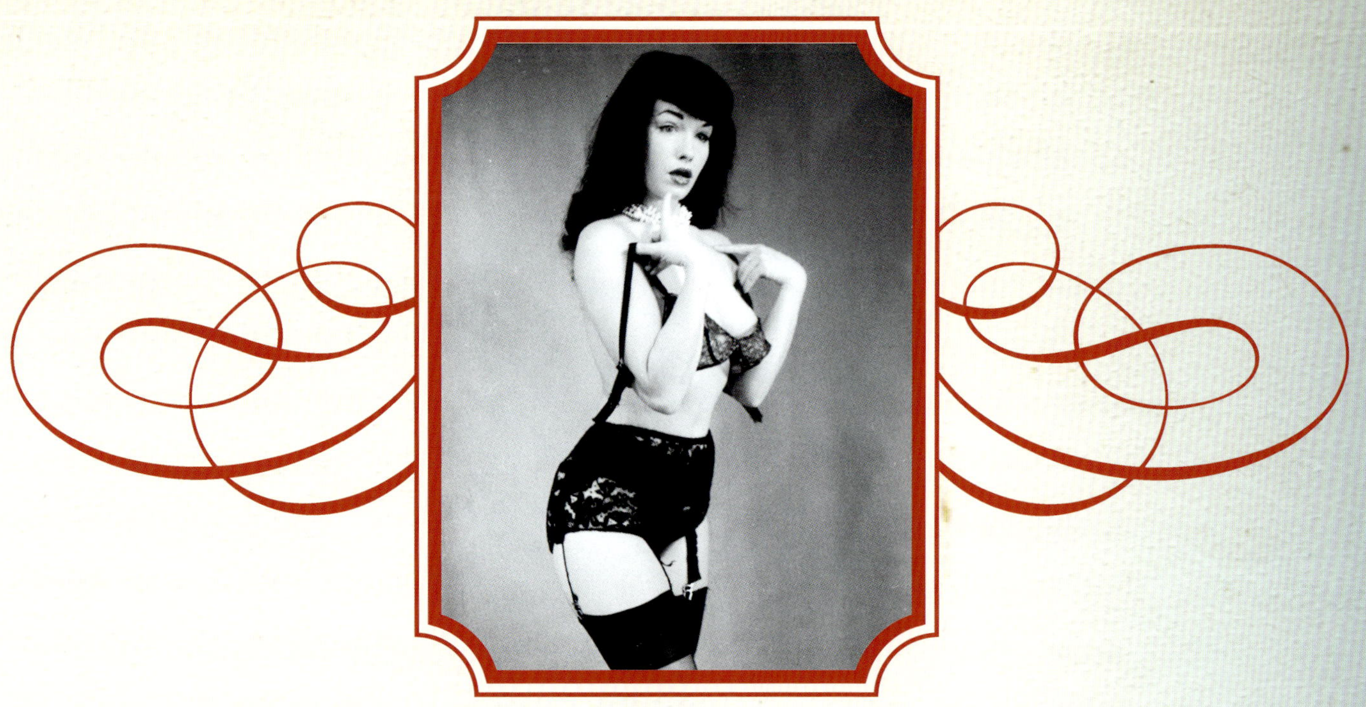

# Finding Bettie Page

When I was seventeen and had been working at Lady Ruby's for four years, I found myself hunting a new white whale: the corset (coincidentally structured with whalebone when it was first introduced). I discovered in my increasingly fraught search for it that the corset was the ultimate, unattainable piece of lingerie. I must have placed one hundred calls and talked to as many people in my quest for it. I finally found an advertisement in a magazine, which led me to a bland little door tucked into an Orange County minimall. Behind it, I found a whole world of what I might have described in high school as "totally perverted"—rubber capes and hoods, whips and chains, cruel shoes. I didn't know anything about this stuff, but I wasn't going to lose my nerve now. I asked the clerk where I could find a corset, and I picked out a luscious three-hundred-dollar steel-boned pink satin number, with black velvet trim and black lacing down the back. I was only in high school, so this was big money, but oh, was it beautiful! When the salesman laced me into it, I knew I had discovered a lost world. More to the point, I loved the way it exaggerated my body shape, pushing everything up, up, up. My curves were in all the right places. I still remember the feeling of being laced up that first time: it was bizarre and erotic and wonderful.

Per my request, the salesman guided me through a reserve of what I later understood were fetish magazines. (The corset itself is a bona fide fetish icon, see *Fetish*, "A Corset in History," page 51.) I was surprised to see that the photos were so, well, amateurish, and the models seemed like ordinary people posing in unexciting rooms and unfortunate positions. And then I came across a beautiful brunette with shiny black bangs and pale skin. The woman seemed to be smiling straight out of another era, reminding me somehow of the World War II pinups I had seen . . . but naughtier. I pulled the glossy closer.

"That's Bettie Page," said the clerk, holding onto the image as if it were more than a photocopy. "My favorite."

I had found another grail.

The clerk, Jim Thompson, with whom I am still friends, loaned me one of his Bettie videos, and I went home and watched this dark temptress shimmy and pose. But I discovered something else in those videos: the beautiful girls encircling her, wearing sequined dresses and feathers, teasing, taunting. I began collecting more and more men's magazines from Bettie's heyday and even earlier with such names as *Wink* and *Eyeful*. In these, too, I saw the enigmatic young models in various positions of undress and dance. I studied the photos and then I noticed it. These models weren't models—they were burlesque dancers. The captions underneath their images spelled it out: *"So and so dances at Minsky's."*

And that is how Billy Minsky introduced me—sixty-eight years after his death—to burlesque.

Having "discovered" these Bettie Page photos and artists' renditions, particularly those by modern pinup artist Olivia DeBerardinis, and becoming familiar with her passionate following, I decided to re-create her look, with aspirations of becoming the greatest fetish pinup since she reigned. Of course, I didn't just want to look like Bettie Page. I wanted to look the way she looked in Olivia's paintings—classic, but lush and sexy in satin and silks, seamed stockings, corsets. Olivia's Bettie was sophisticated and ultrafeminine, irrepressibly, decadently alluring. What did I do? I sat right down at my vanity and set about perfecting Bettie's gorgeously clean-skinned, black-banged visage.

I would say I had her down pretty well by the time I got to meet Olivia. I was twenty-one and attending the Glamourcon convention for showgirls, artists, and models. I had already

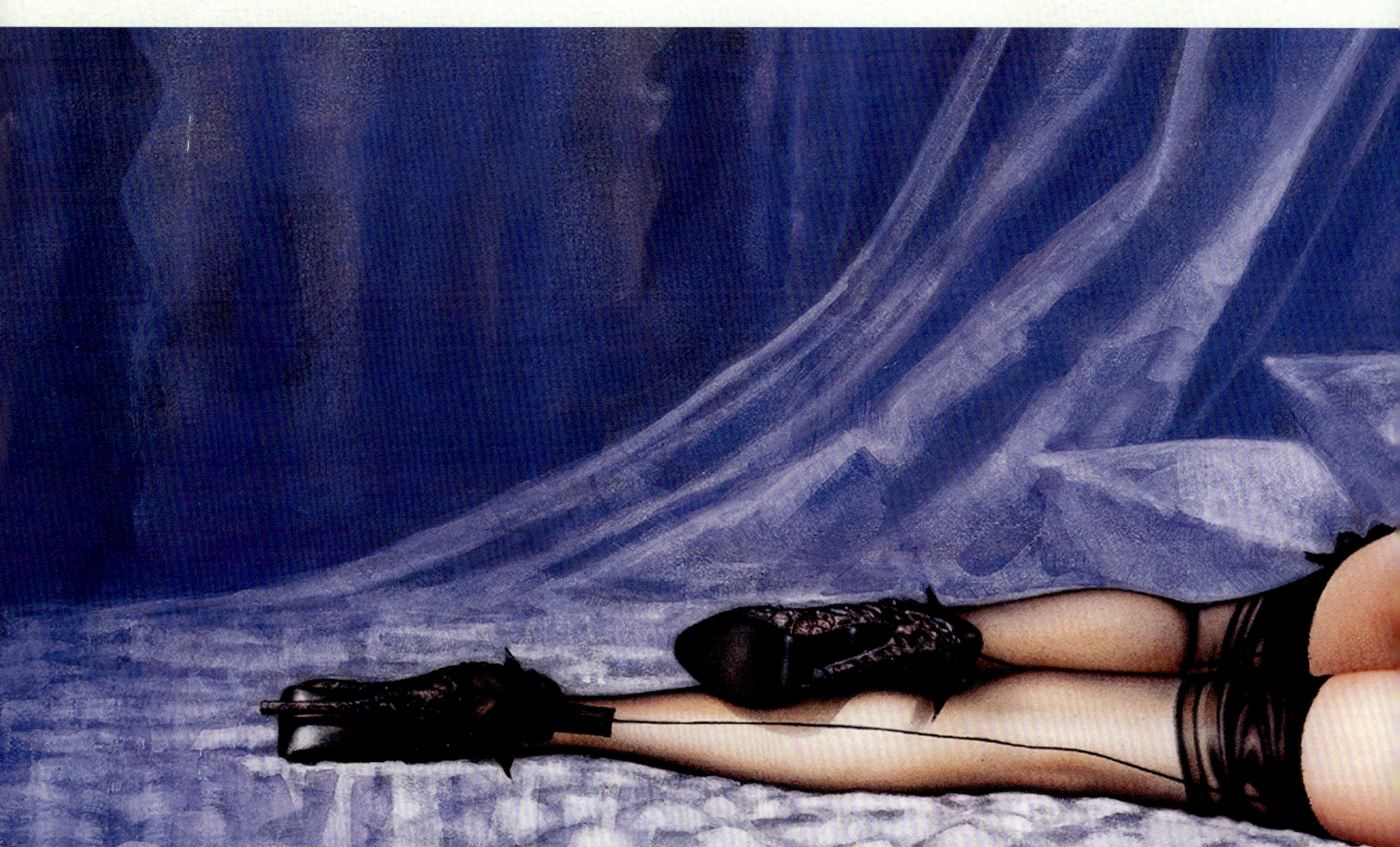

begun to make a name for myself in fetish modeling, and one of my fans remarked that I looked like an Olivia pinup. I was thrilled! And, there was more good news: Olivia was at Glamourcon. I remember approaching her booth to find the artist herself standing, chatting with an evident admirer, in front of those splendid paintings. When it was my turn, I introduced myself and we had quite a chat. Before I left, I seized one more opportunity. "I'm a big fan of yours," I said. "If you ever need a model, I would be honored and forever grateful." Yes, I was begging!

Olivia looked at me and said very seriously, "But I already painted you." I shook my head, and again she stopped me. "I already painted you when I painted Bettie." Now, I might have taken this as a compliment since I was attempting to master Bettie's look. But, at that moment, a bell sounded in my brain and I realized that I don't want to be a lookalike. Winning imitation is not what makes somebody great.

After Glamourcon, I gave serious thought to what it means to be a star. I studied my books and my pictures of Bettie Page, and I realized that her looks weren't the thing that made her popular (or any of my other heroes, for that matter). It was her chameleon-like persona: she was sweet and innocent on the one hand, and then she could turn around and be a bad girl. I love that. A '50s femme fatale, the contradiction every man adores. What's more, she looked like a girl I would have liked to have known. These were the qualities—not her hair and not her makeup—that I resolved to emulate. That bit of Bettie combined with elements I discovered in my travels through burlesque history, film, fashion, and beauty have helped me compose my signature style.

I heard that Vargas himself confessed his best pinups were actually amalgamations of women he knew and models he drew. A composite of American girls!

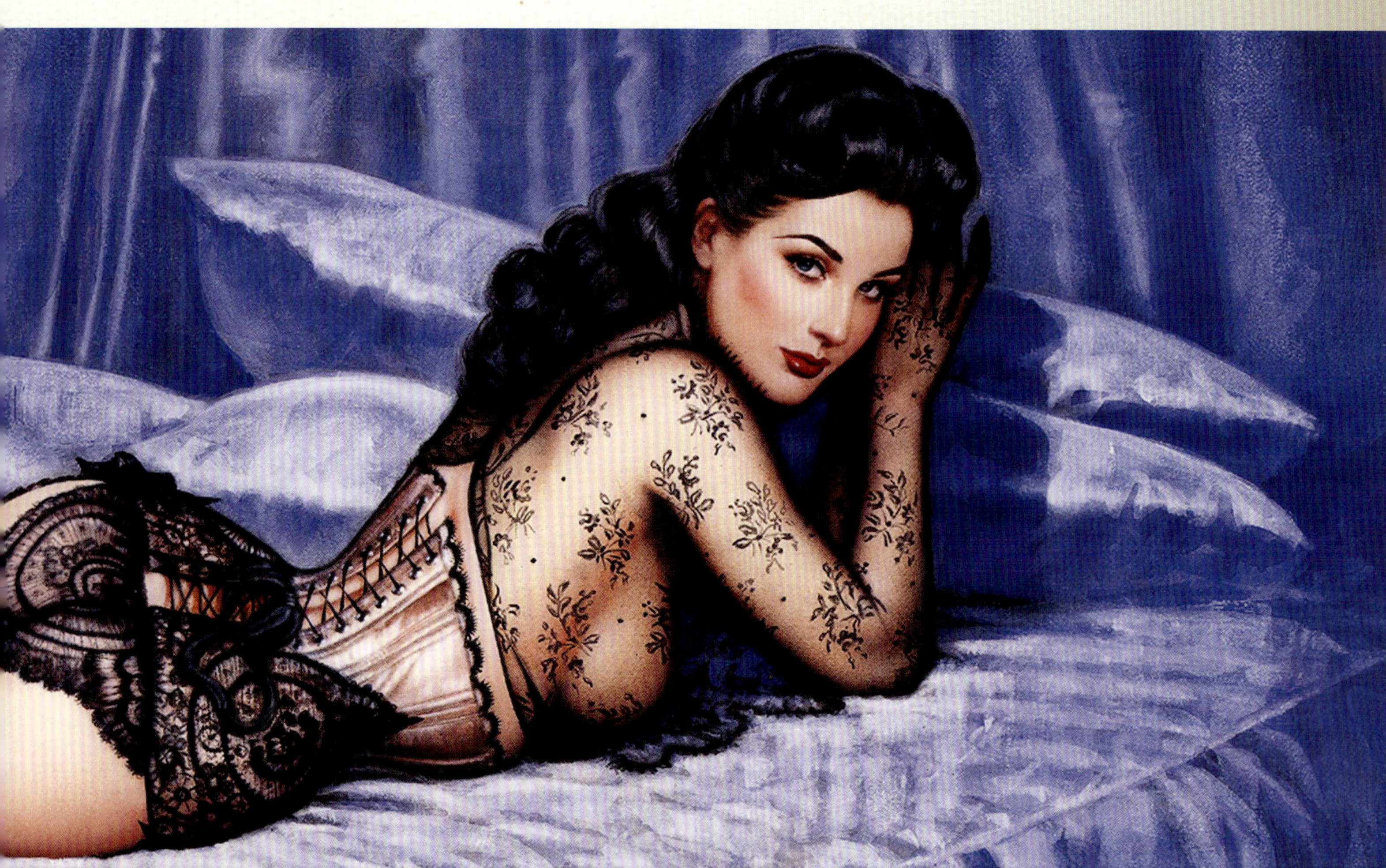

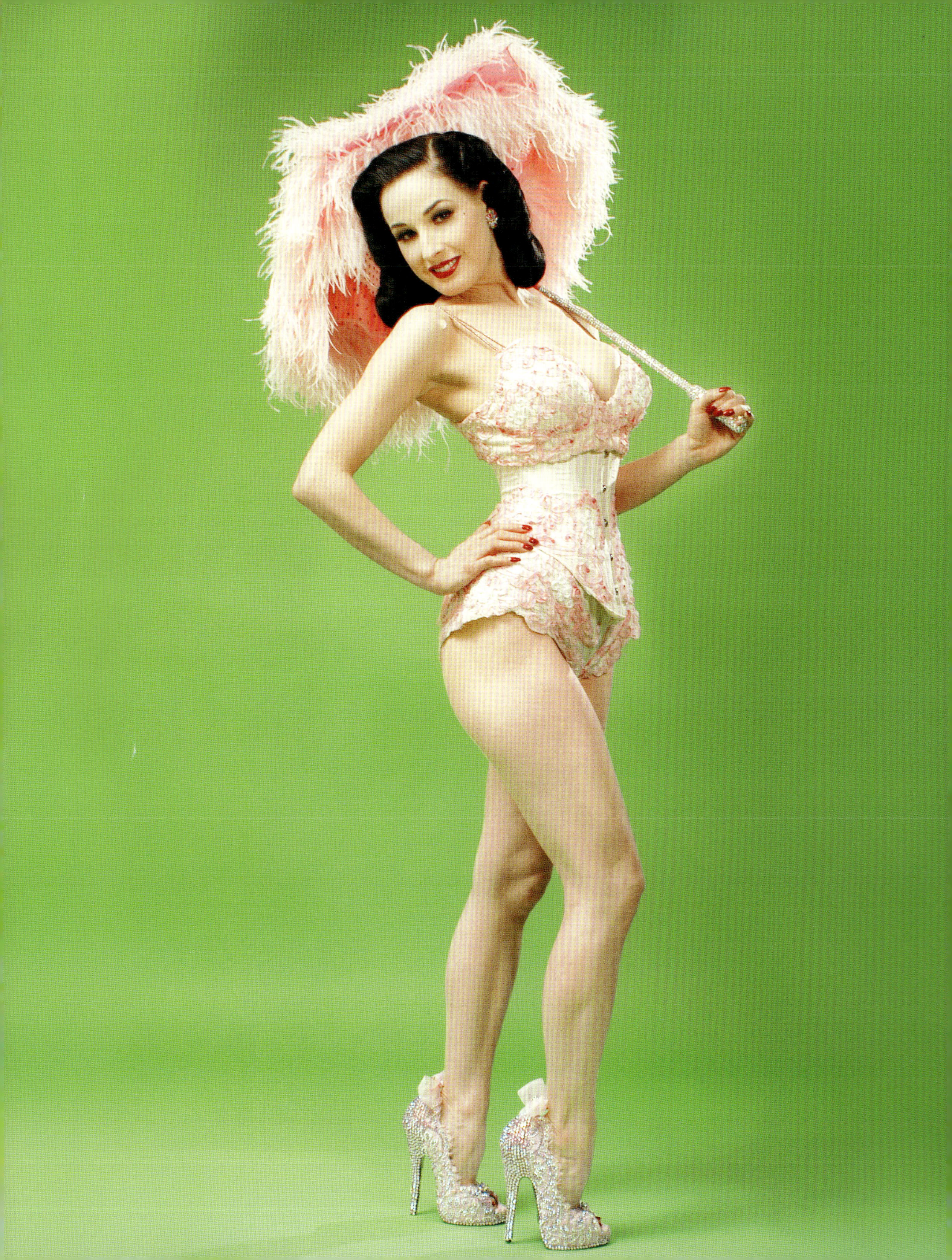

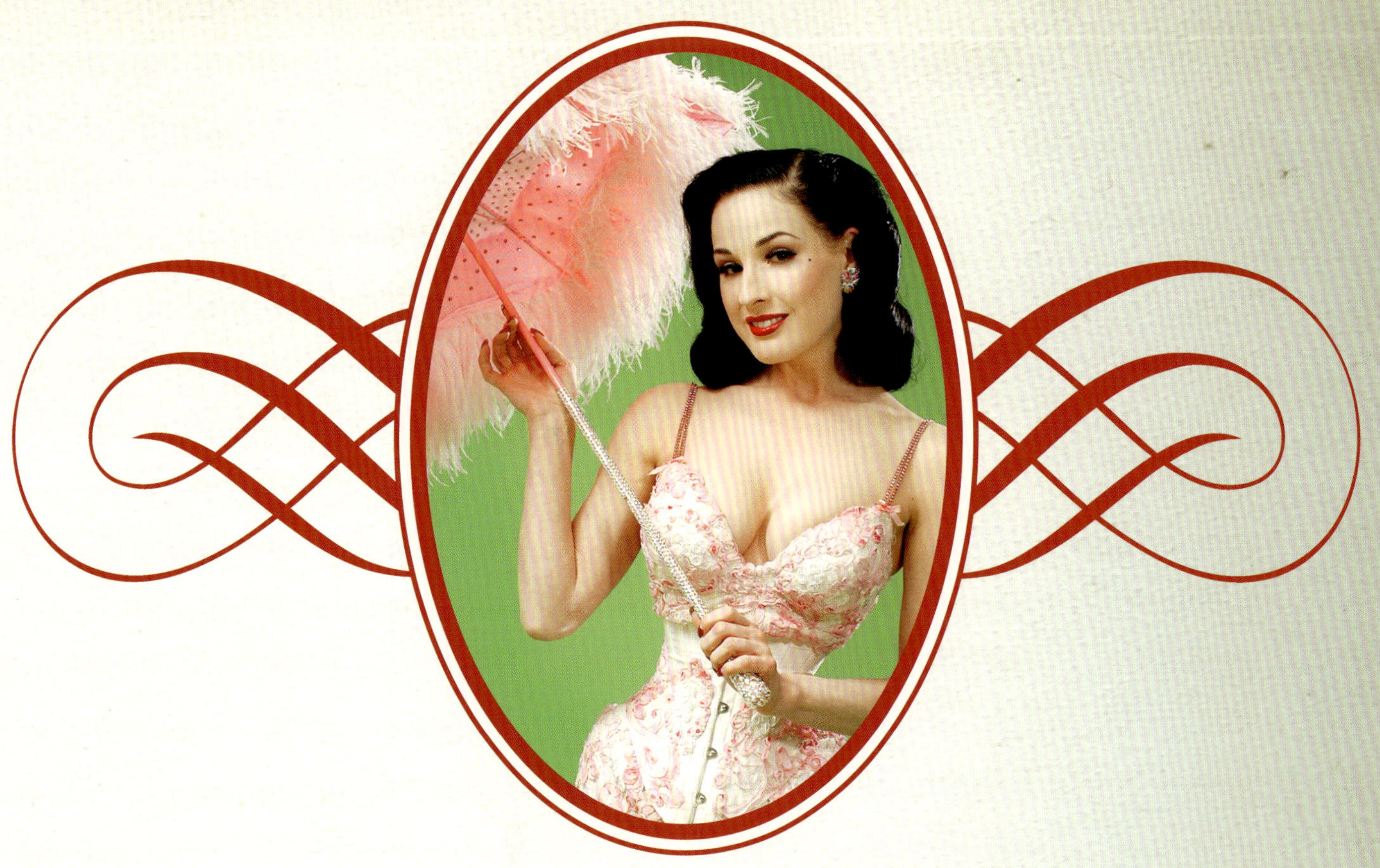

# Curvy Corset Cuties

It's no coincidence that Bettie Page's heyday coincided with the end of World War II, the era that brought burlesque back. Our grandparents were celebrating Americana of all kinds, and burlesque was as American as baseball. Though censors lingered, by 1951 burlesque was again flourishing in thirty theaters across America, incorporating new and old into a tantalizing contemporary stew.

The new acts' major influences were movies and their curvy queens Brigitte Bardot and Marilyn Monroe. With their big blonde hair, ample breasts, and highly fertile hips, these bombshells inspired women everywhere to exaggerate their own voluptuousness. The best part? Flouncy, bouncy underpinnings were back! *The bigger the chests and hips and the smaller the waists, the better* was the decade's mantra. Yes! It was a rebirth for the corset, the girdle, and crinoline. You have to see the Jayne Mansfield movie *The Girl Can't Help It* for a sneak peek into this era. Every time I think of it, I am astonished they didn't call it *The Sex Bomb Can't Help It!* She is *so* not a girl in this movie! Oh no, she is every inch a woman. She simply walks down the street and I promise you, her hourglass curves blow your mind. Her breasts are absolutely giant, and her waist is flawlessly tiny. The reason? Ms. Mansfield is corseted under all those clothes. Welcome the return of artifice and the created beauty!

Of course, I am not a blonde bombshell—but I still adore this era's voluptuous, overemphasized femininity. When I feel a little bombshelly (who doesn't have a day like this?), I slip into a wiggle dress, a bullet bra, or a full, crinoline skirt.

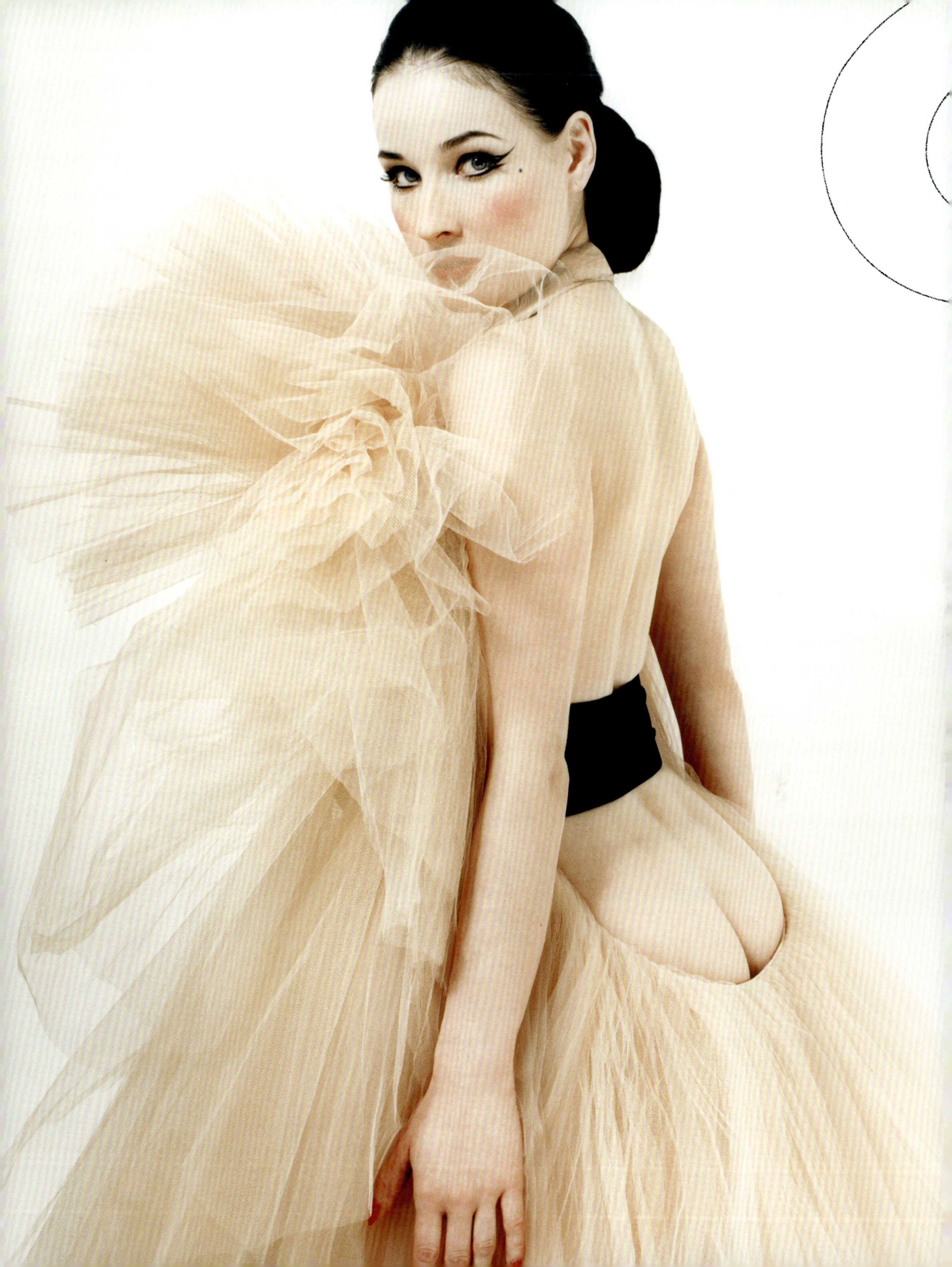

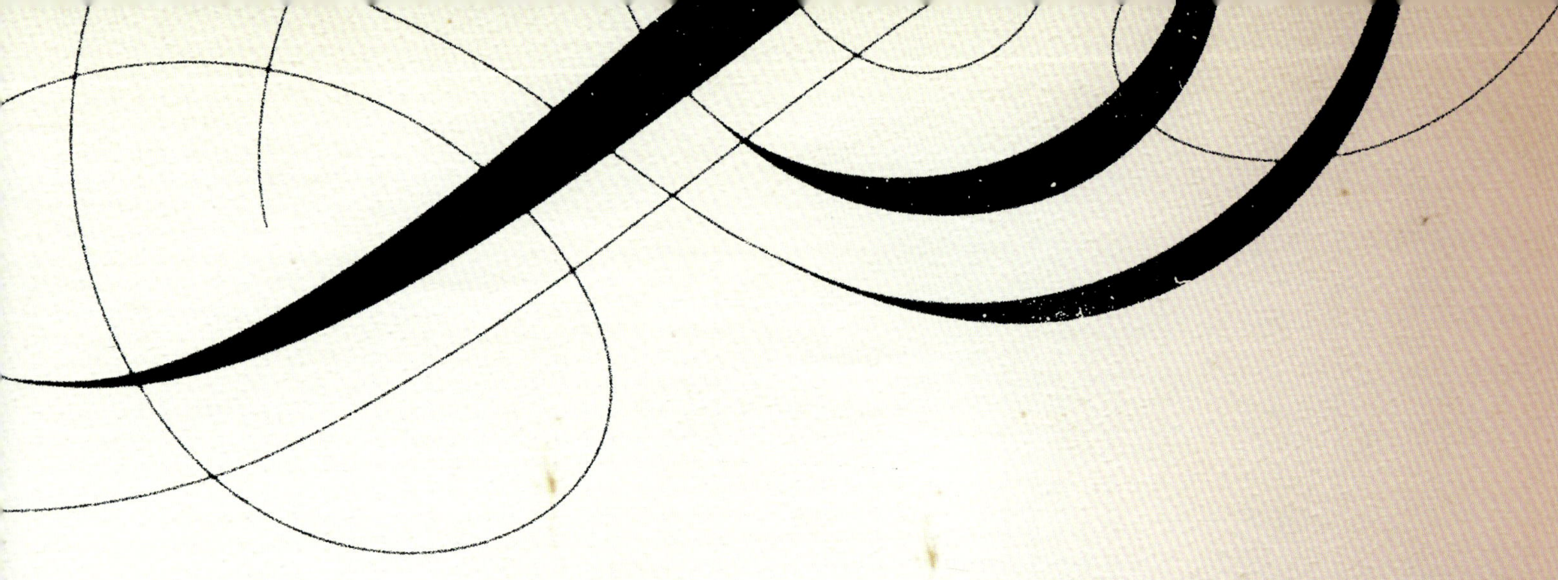

The 1950s marked the glorious pinnacle of Hollywood movie glamour. Marilyn Monroe was undeniably the most beautiful woman ever to grace the screen. But like me and Gypsy and the others, Marilyn may have been a "created" beauty. Many experts insist that adorable Marilyn had her nose slightly altered. Well, she didn't deny it. Of course, people back then didn't think to ask such things. I want to point out though, that this prevailing belief that plastic surgery is a modern phenomenon is tacitly false. Books I own from the thirties and even earlier discuss surgical options for facial rejuvenation and remodeling. Of course, my favorite, *Beauty's Question and Answer Dictionary,* published in 1931, also calls plastic surgery "not dangerous." But, the point is, these women were doing it, even though it was not reported in the press, and certainly not acknowledged by the stars!

I confess, I don't understand the taboo. If you want to change something about yourself, whether it is your hair color, your makeup, or your nose, I support you. If you do not, then I support you in that. I urge you to do exactly what you want to do to make yourself feel beautiful. And I'm not talking about beauty according to magazine standards or Hollywood standards, but *your* standards. Cosmetic surgery is a form—albeit a dramatic one—of makeup.

The 1950s burlesquers were similarly bent on exaggeration. Their personalities, like their chests and hips, were *big*. Competition was fierce, and every girl had a signature. Not just a look or an attitude, mind you—this was the age of the big-time *prop*. There was Rosita Royce with her fly-away bikini of trained pigeons; Evangeline the Oyster Girl emerging, slow and swampy, from a giant shell; or my favorite of the era, Lili St. Cyr, splashing about in her trademark transparent bathtub.

These girls took more off than ever before. The reason? They were strippers *first*. If the fifties were more flagrantly sexy than previous decades, we can thank the Society for the Suppression of Vice. Banishing burlesque to the nightclubs and bars for a decade drove the dancers to emphasize less art and more flesh. In fact, voyeurism reached a new level in the fifties, with "sneaking a peek" of a woman "unawares" developing as one of burlesque's new themes. Lili St. Cyr performed the voyeur's show best, with her bathtub and boudoir acts in which she dressed and undressed, bathed, and otherwise luxuriated in being a woman. The performances were decadent in their indulgence of the girl and the audience—a quality that has inspired a few of my own acts.

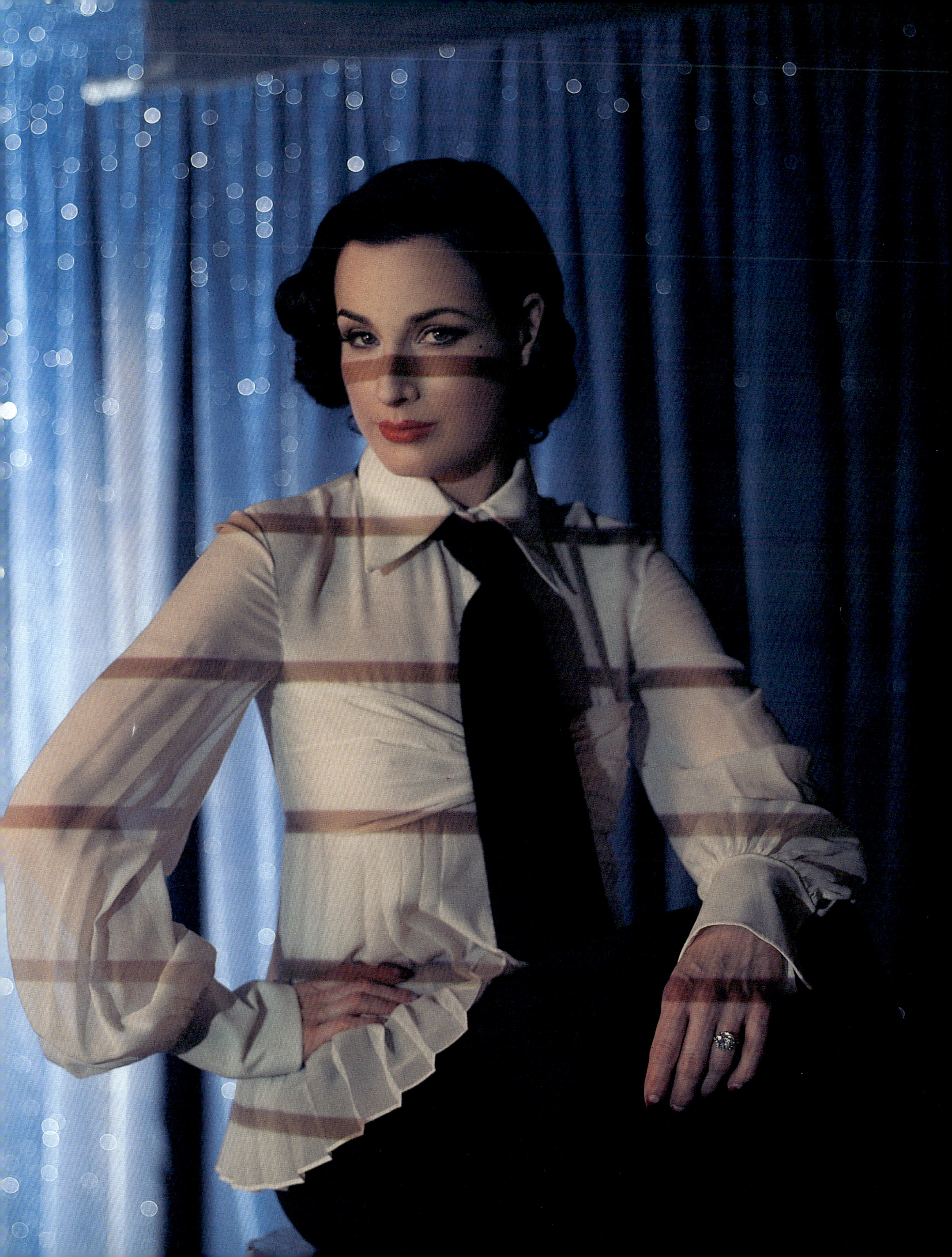

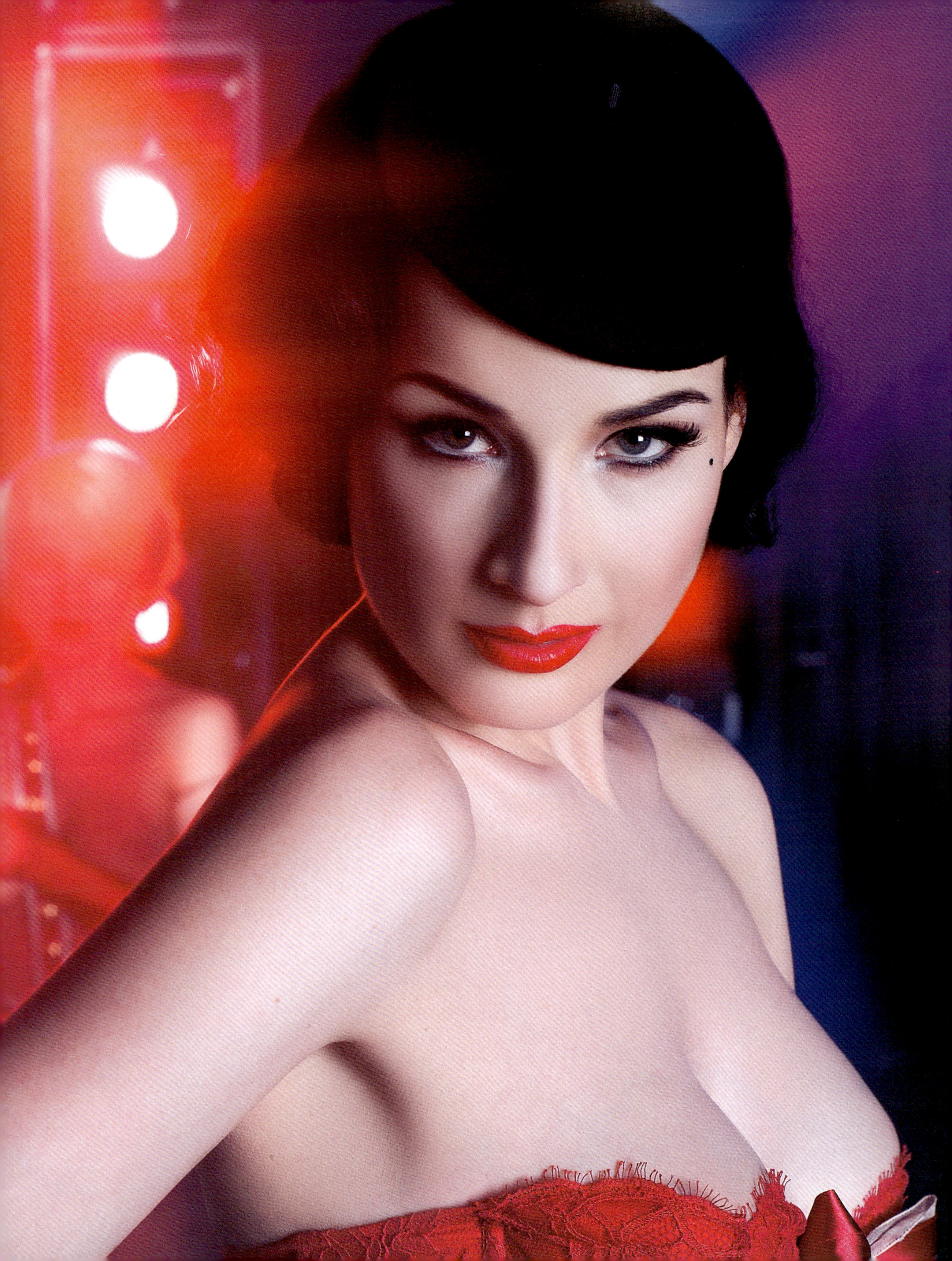

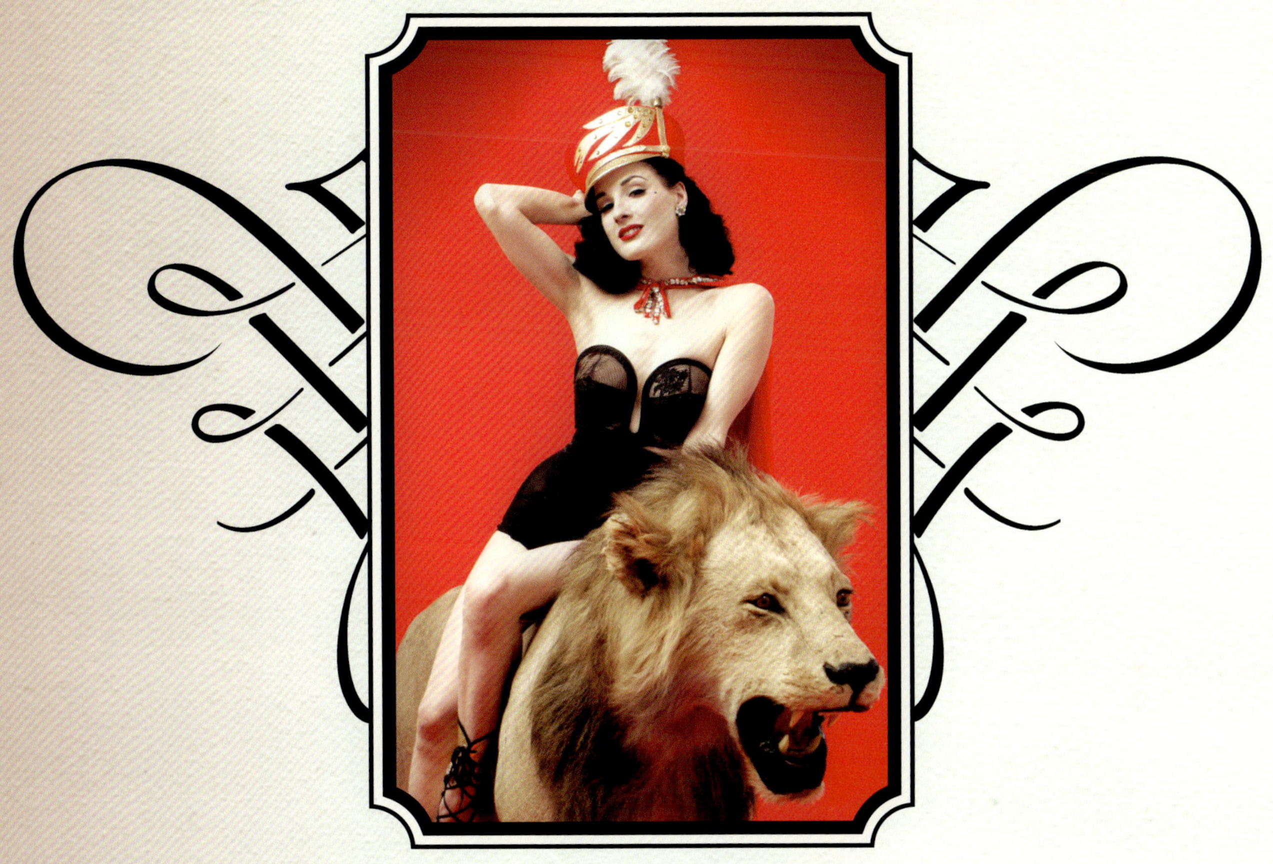

## Publicity Stuntwomen

*Everything* about this generation was big—and I mean the stories, too. Gypsy Rose Lee may have introduced the art of the publicity stunt, but the ladies of the 1950s mastered it. Take Evangeline the Oyster Girl, whose rivalry with an underwater peeler—the girl held her breath and disrobed in a tank of water onstage—led her to storm the performance and hack at the glass with a hammer until it shattered. The stripper inside sunk to the floor and the audience nearly drowned. Wily Evangeline was shown off the stage and onto the pages of *Time*.

Well, the times sure have changed! If you ask me, publicity stunts are one of the things regrettably lacking from today's burlesque scene. When I sit down and read the histories, I cannot imagine that the world was ever so silly, so colorful, so *fun*. It seems to me that every great burlesquer was at one point arrested on obscenity charges. I think it's time burlesque renewed the art of the stunt.

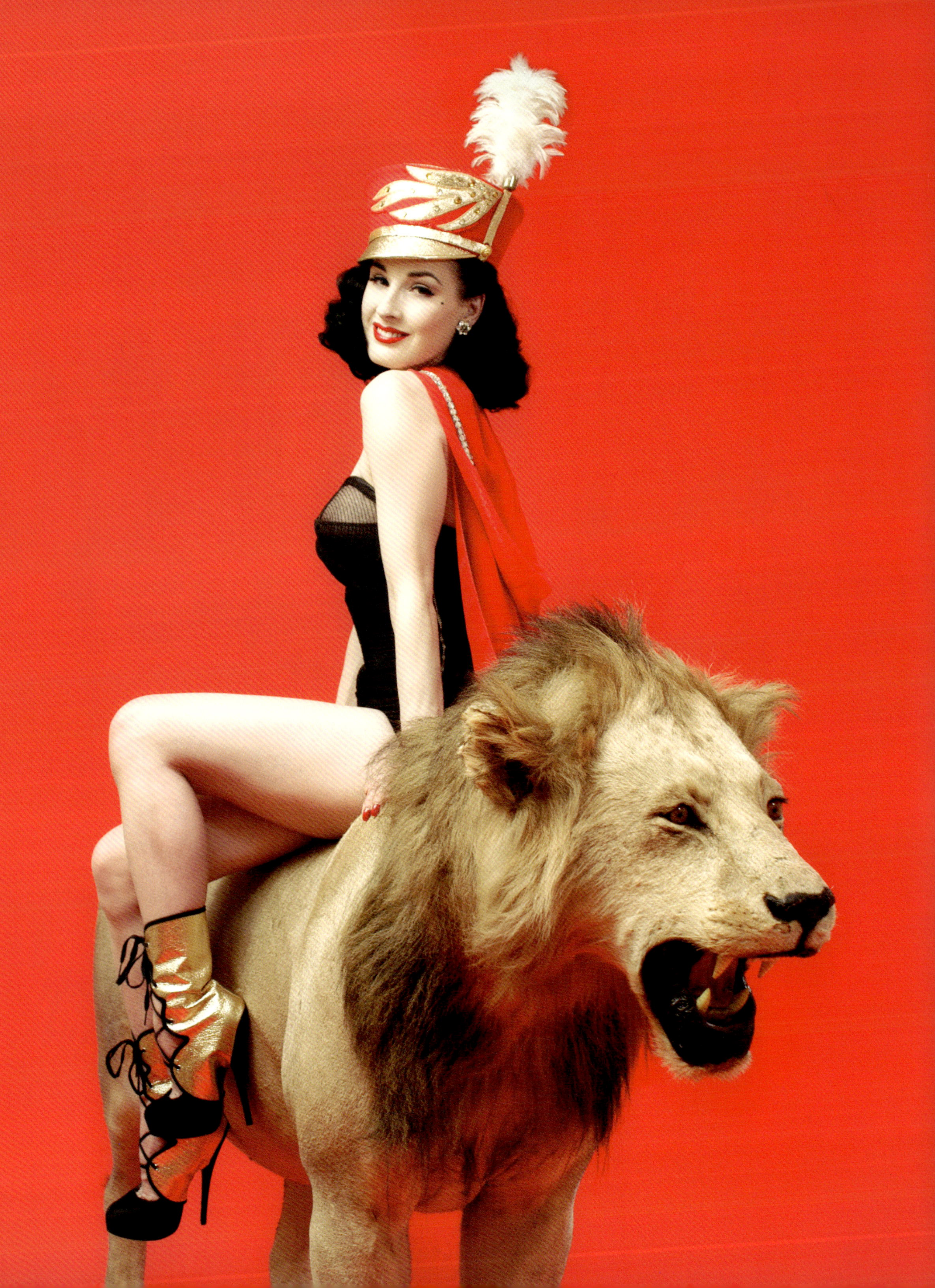

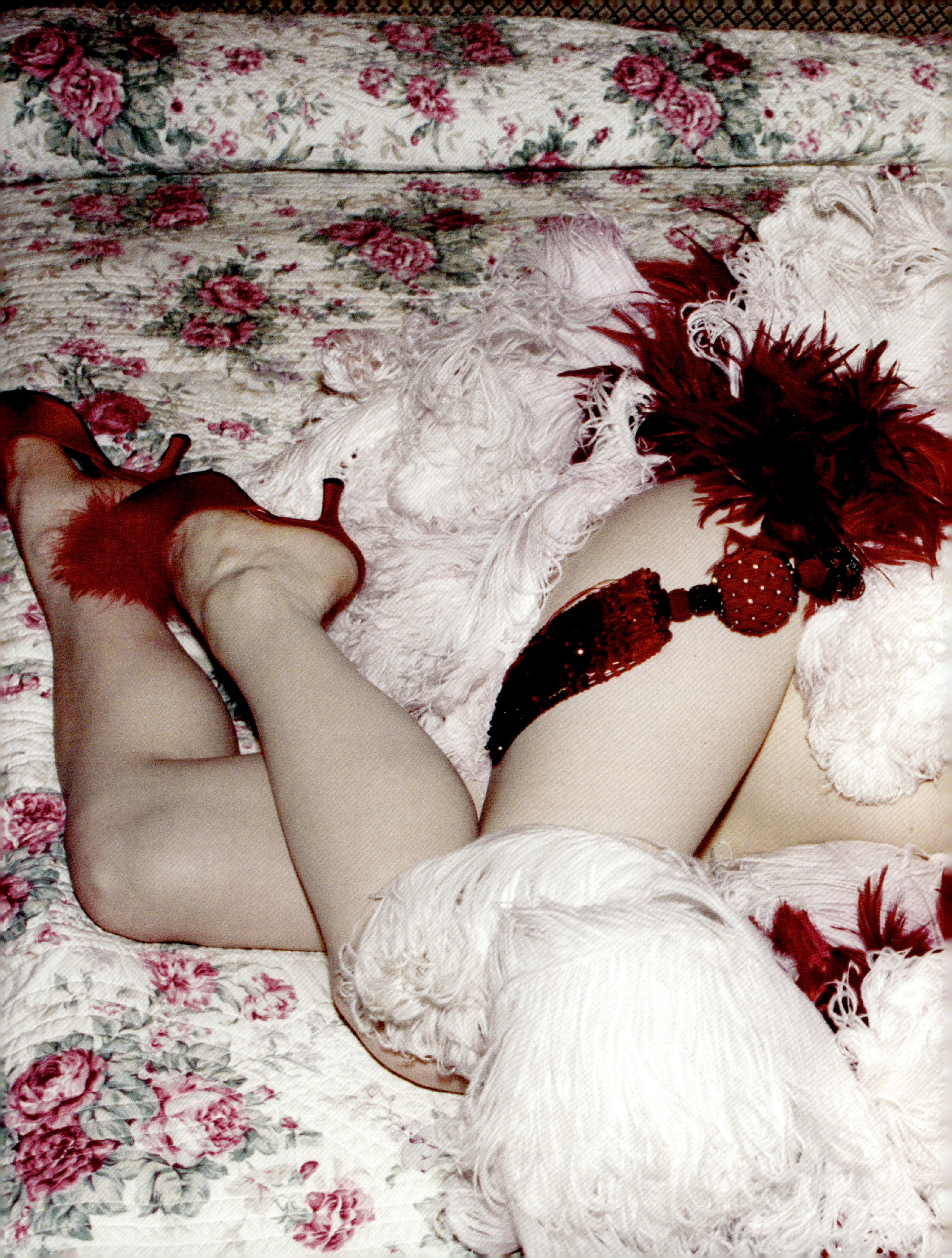

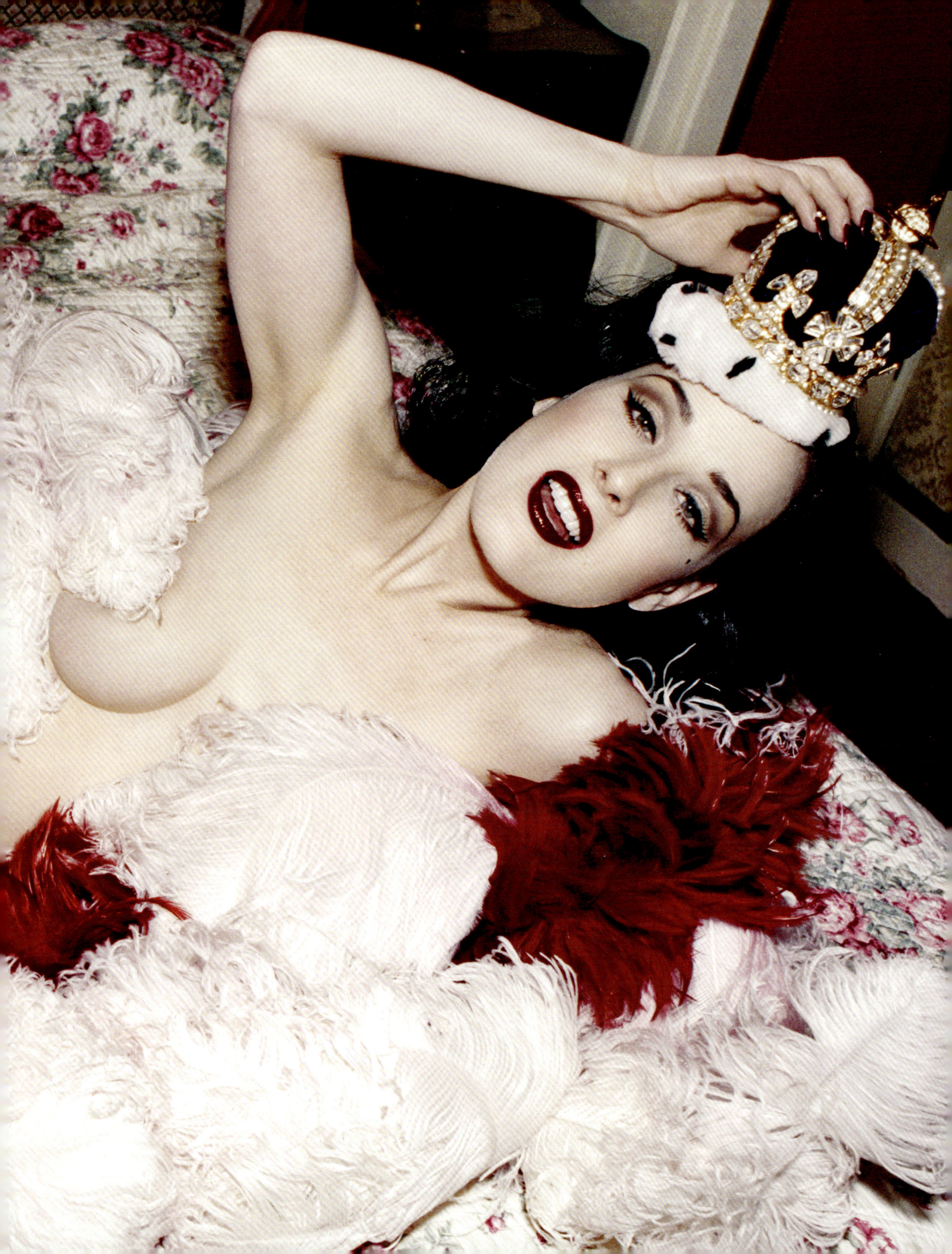

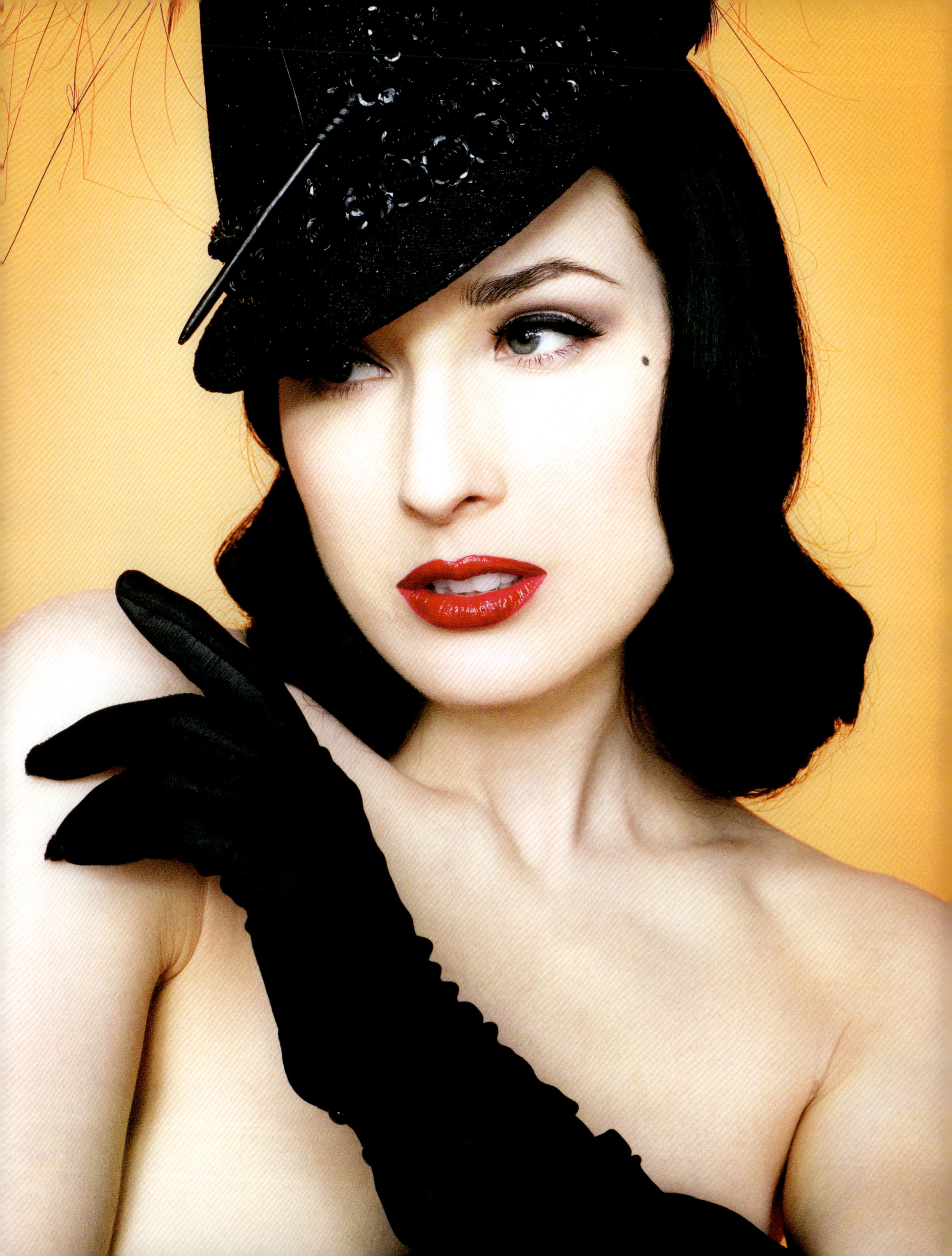

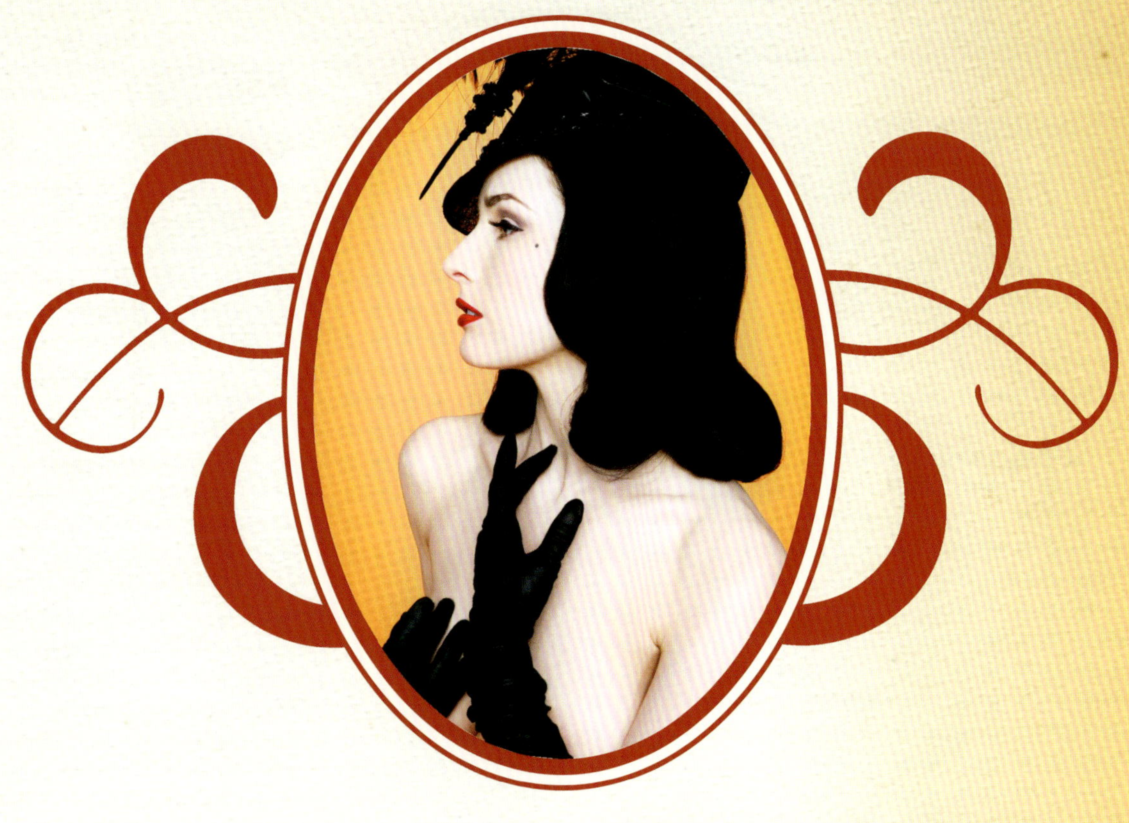

# Music Matters . . . A Pretty Girl Is Like a Melody

The way I think about it, every dress has its own mood, and every mood has its own sound. To that end, I mine vintage archives and modern recordings for music to fit my shows.

For instance, in my carousel show, my fabulous costume—a massive bustle of pink ostrich and a rhinestone top hat with even more ostrich plumes—calls for a big showy traditional strip anthem, such as "The Stripper." When wearing the lavender tulle dress I peel off in my boudoir show, I use traditional striptease tunes, such as "A Pretty Girl Is Like a Melody." The moon show is very ethereal, so I choose music that is less va-va-voom and allows ballet over the traditional striptease moves. On that note, you should use two or three songs. That's it! A lady knows when to leave. . . .

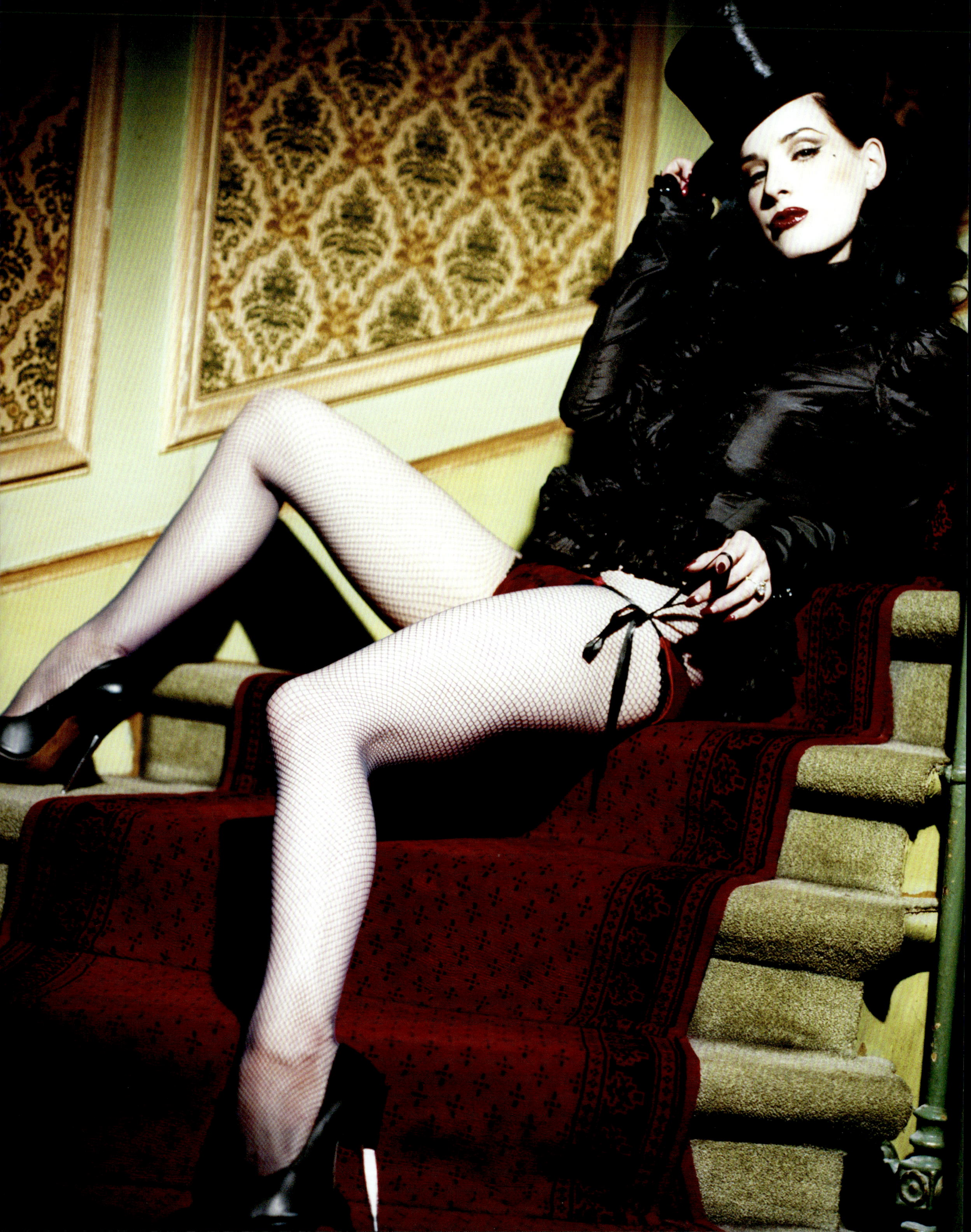

# HERE ARE SOME OF MY FAVORITE STRIP TUNES!

**THESE SONGS SHOULD HAVE YOU PEELING IN NO TIME!**

- **"A Pretty Girl Is Like a Melody"**
- **"The Stripper"**
- **"The Big Strip"**
- **"Bumps and Grinds"**
- **"More Bumps and Grinds"**
- **"Melancholy Serenade"**
- **"Hubcaps and Taillights"**
- **"Boulevard of Broken Dreams"**
- **"Night Train"**
- **"The Mooche"**
- **"Strangers in the Night"**

# DITA'S BEAUTY TIPS

- Remember that well-manicured hands and feet are beauty essentials!
- There is no such thing as a plain woman. Every woman has attractive points, so accentuate your best assets!
- Perfume is the magic touch that transforms a charming woman into an enchanting one! When properly used, it creates an aura of mystery and romance!

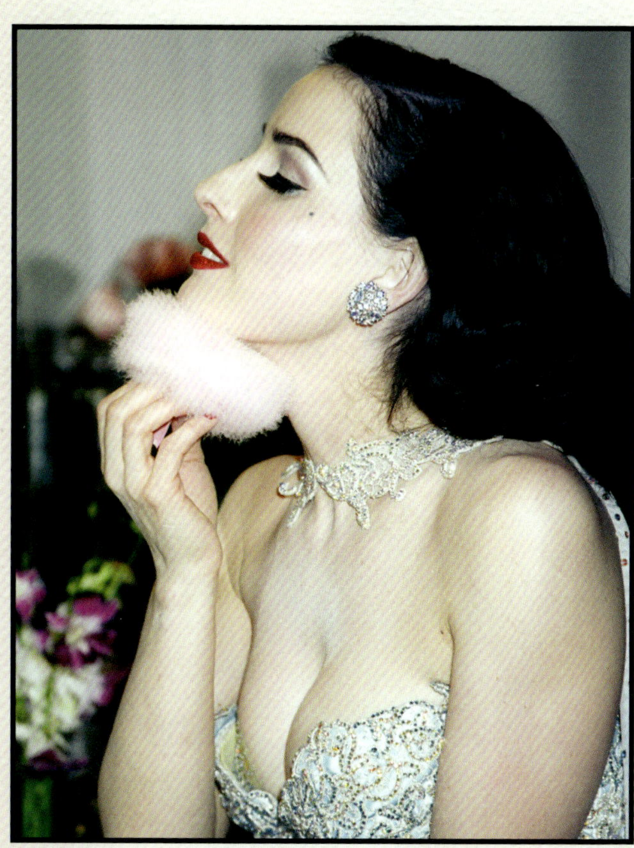

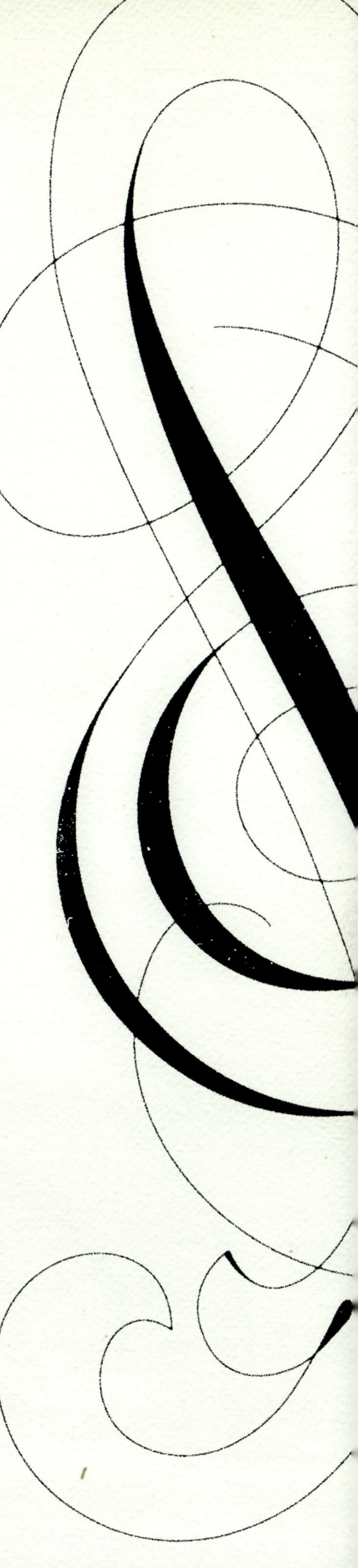

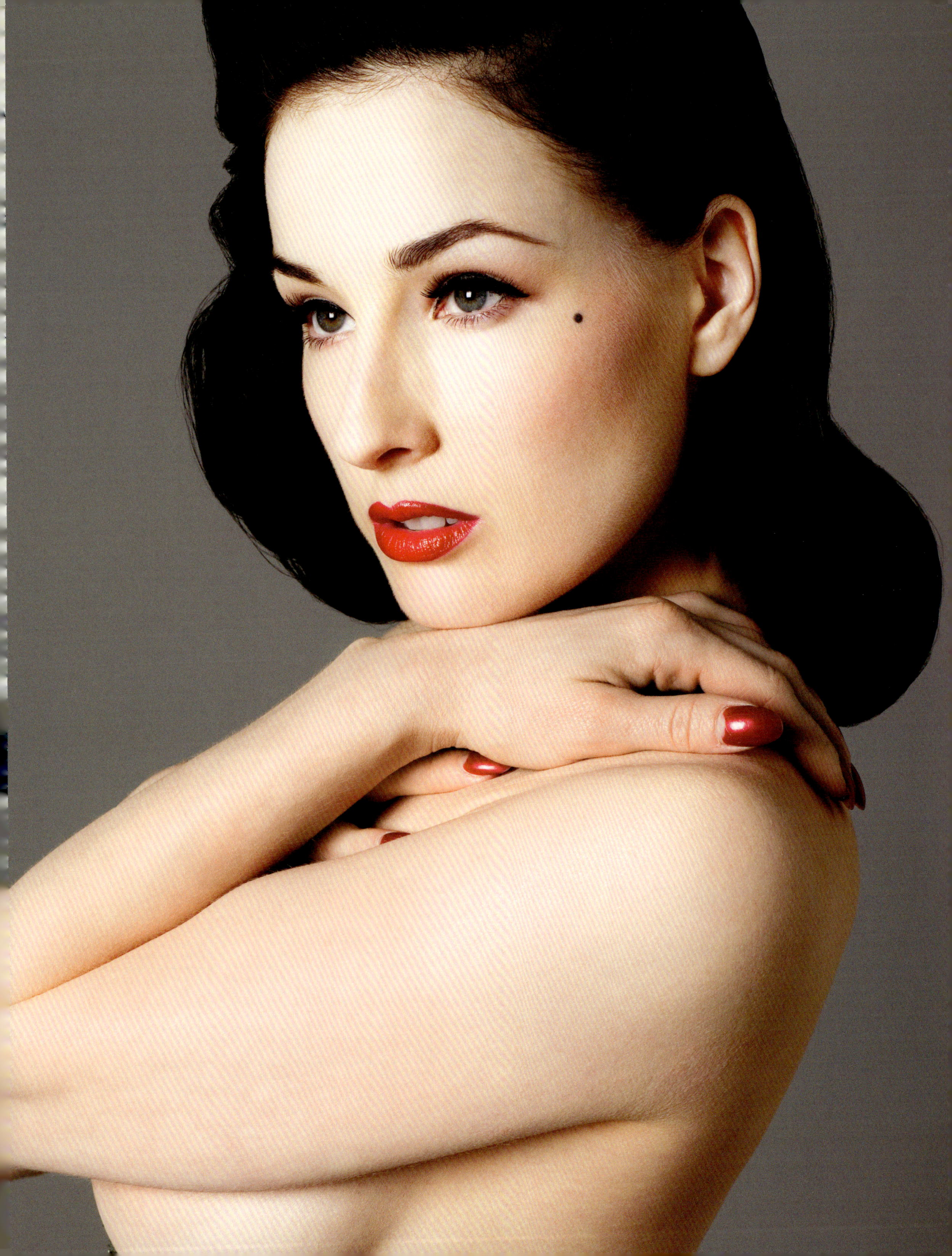

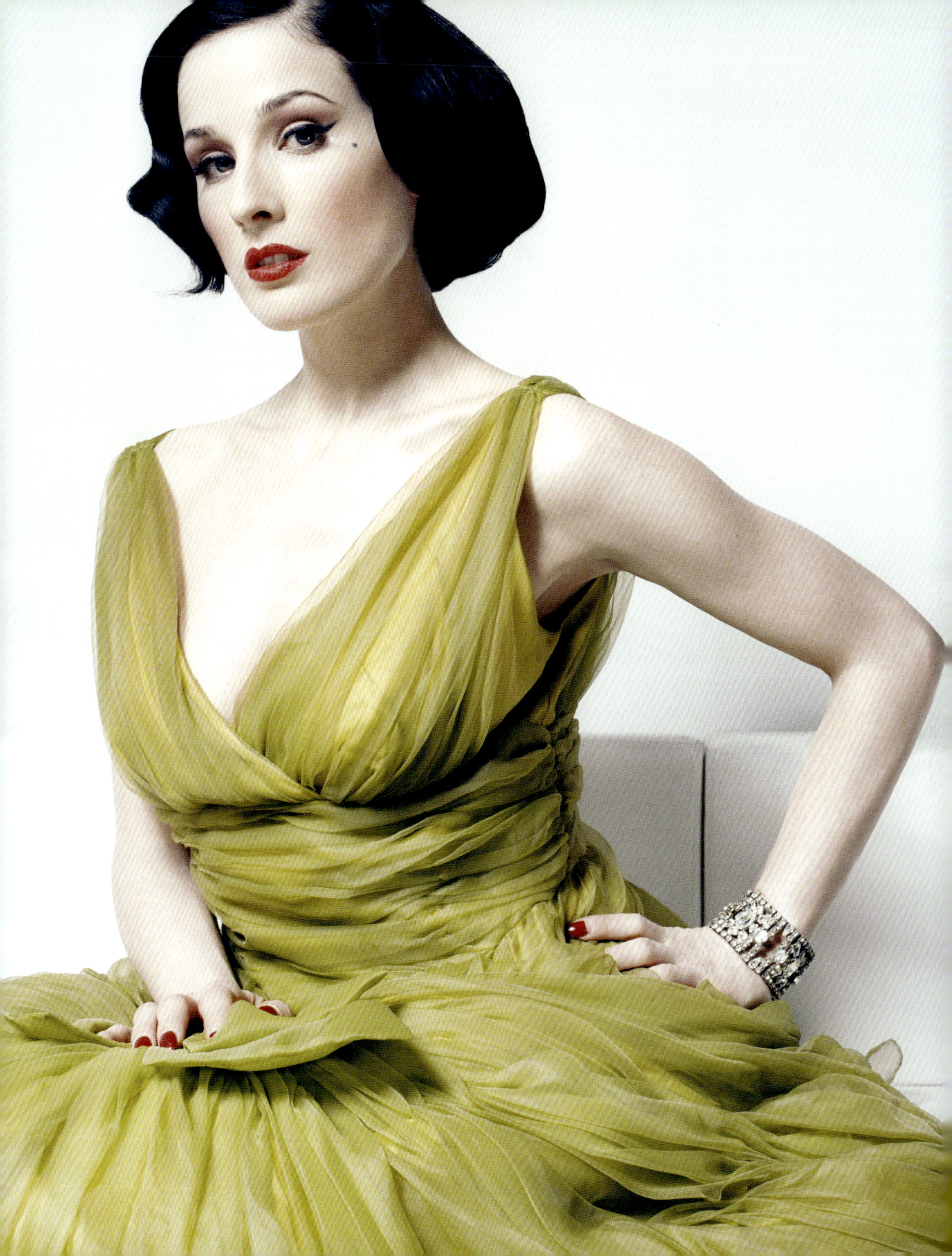

# FIRST-CLASS FACE: HOW TO GET THE LOOK OF A BOMBSHELL

## THE 1950s WAS THE ERA OF THE BOMBSHELL, THE AGE OF MARILYN! NEED I SAY MORE?

| BURLESQUE QUEENS | MOVIE STARS |
|---|---|
| Lili St. Cyr | Marilyn Monroe |
| Tempest Storm | Brigitte Bardot |
| Dixie Evans | Elizabeth Taylor |
| Jennie Lee | Jayne Mansfield |
| Blaze Starr | Mamie Van Doren |

**SKIN:** Natural in color with a matte and smooth powdered base. Powder blush is applied along cheekbones in a peach, coral, or rose tone.

**BROWS:** Thick, dark, and highly arched.

**EYES:** Lined on top with winged liner and thick, dark, long lashes. You can apply lashes to the entire eye or just to the corners for an extra sexy cat gaze.

**LIPS:** Full with pointed peaks in various shades of bright red, ruby, fuchsia, or coral glossy lip color.

**NAILS:** Should match your lipstick, of course.

**HAIR:** Think Elizabeth Taylor and Marilyn Monroe . . . This era is about BIG styles. Shorter hair was quite chic, and considered to be very sexy. Use combs to pin one side up leaving a sexy wave over your eye on the other. Use medium-size hot rollers rather than small ones.

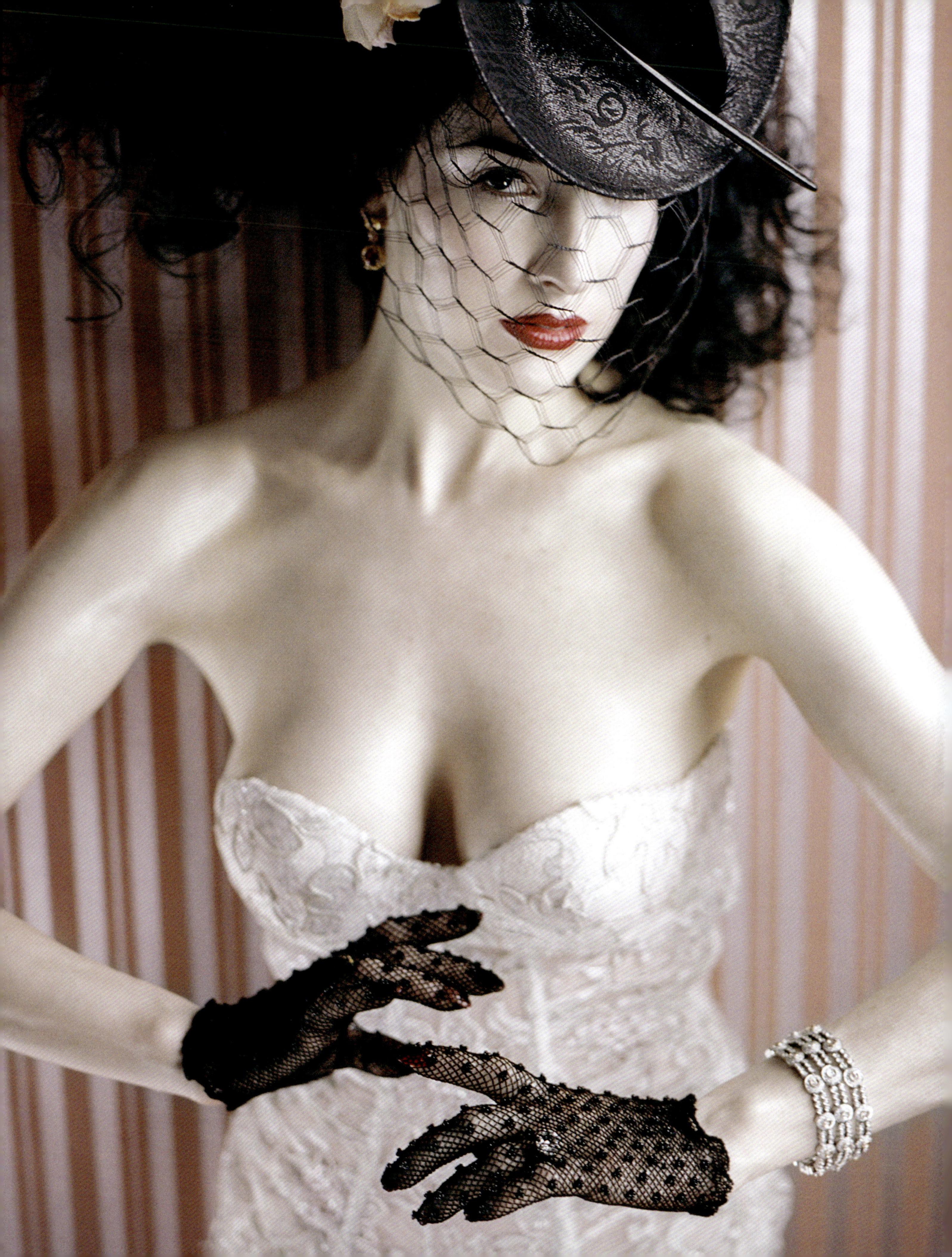

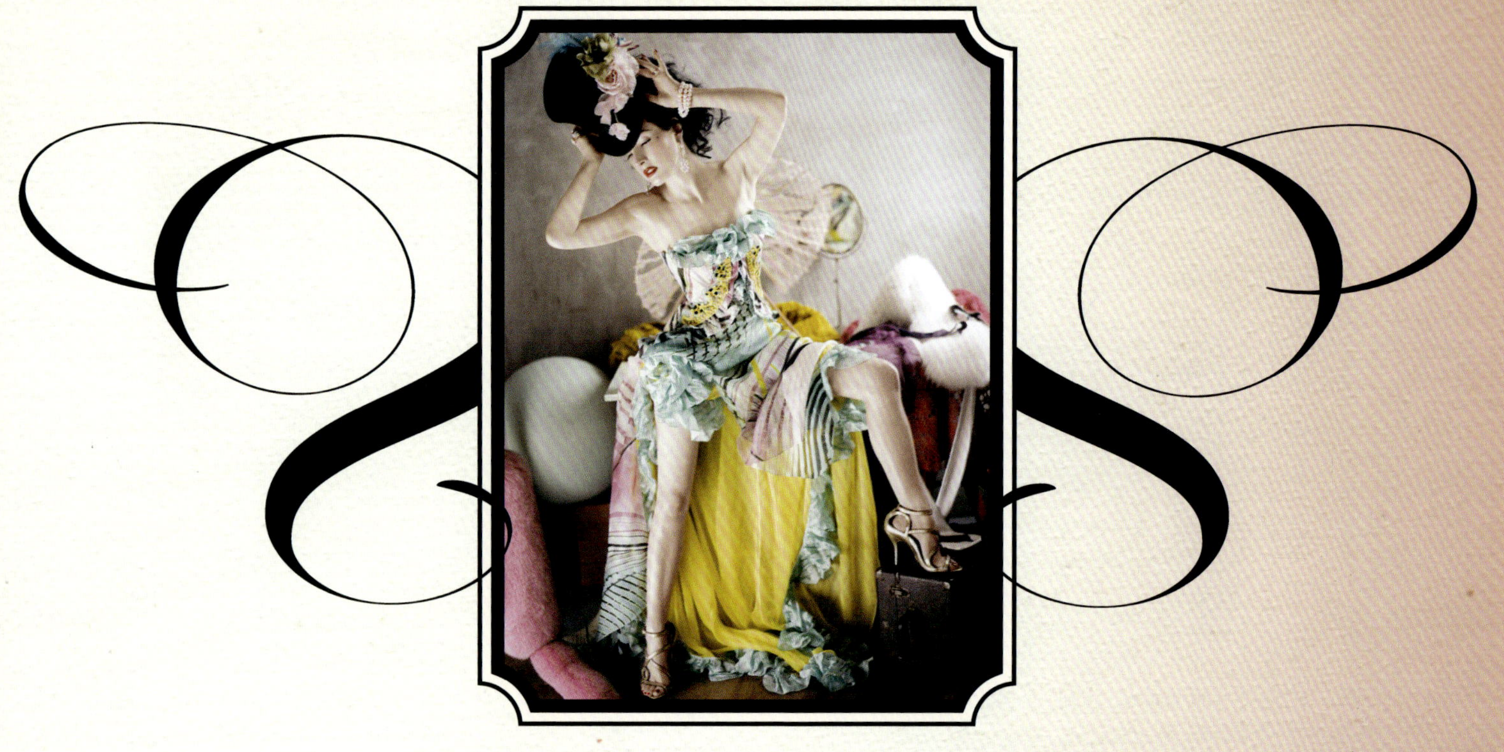

# Conclusion: Curtain

I house all of my costumes and vintage treasures in their very own room, complete with pink velvet wallpaper and pink chandeliers. This is the sort of room I visited in my sleep as a little girl.

As I look around, I see a garment from every era I love, from a vast number of cities, a thousand women. Hundreds of hats—picture hats, tilt hats, veiled hats, cloches, top hats, doll hats—decorate the room. My finest dresses—of lush silk and satin and velvet—are here, as are my lace-trimmed slips; my rainbow-colored collection of fur stoles; and pointe shoes of pink, ruby red, and tiffany blue satin. The whalebone corsets from la belle époque are here, and so are the shoes from the '40s—that long-ago lady's feet are up, I like to think, in front of the fireplace.

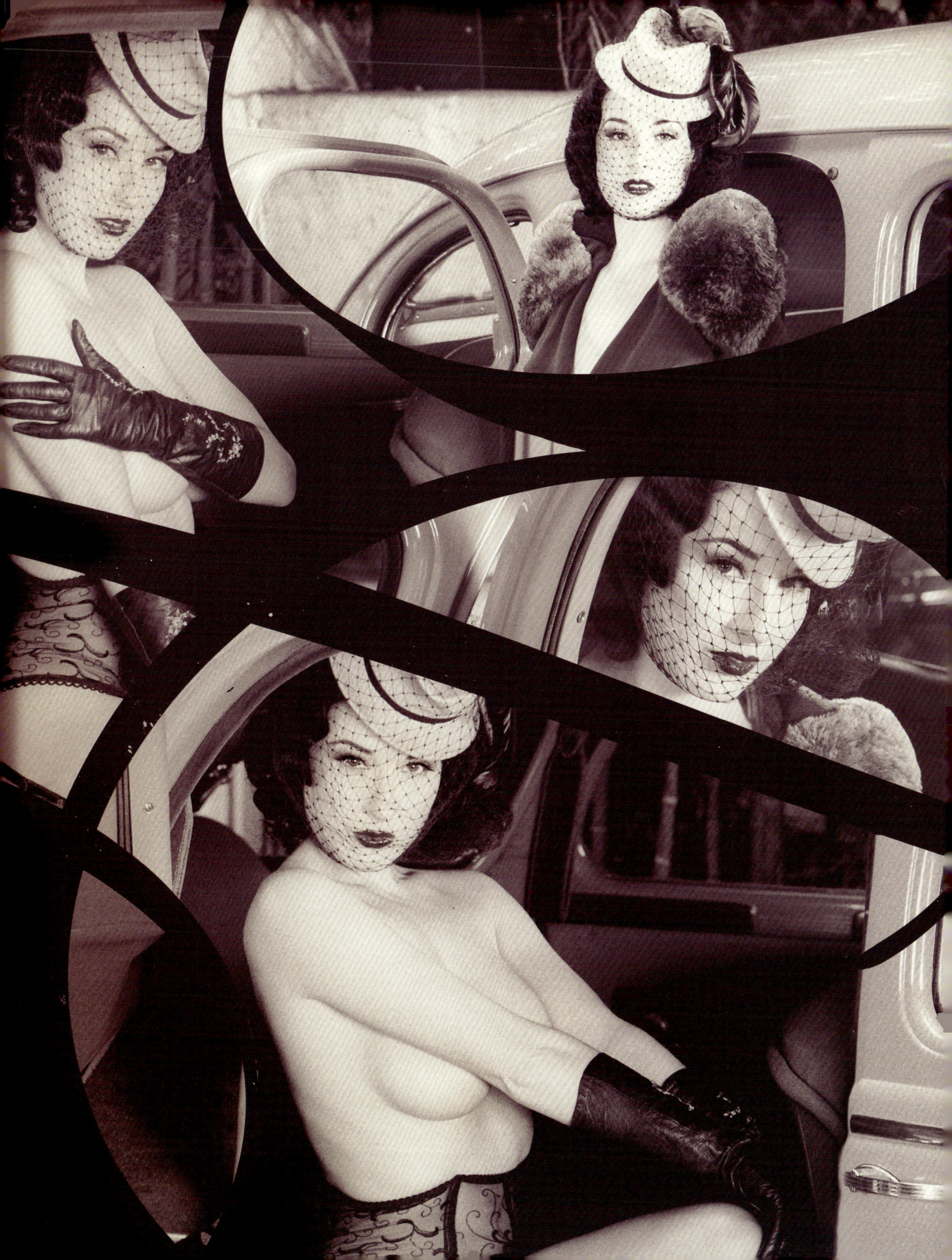

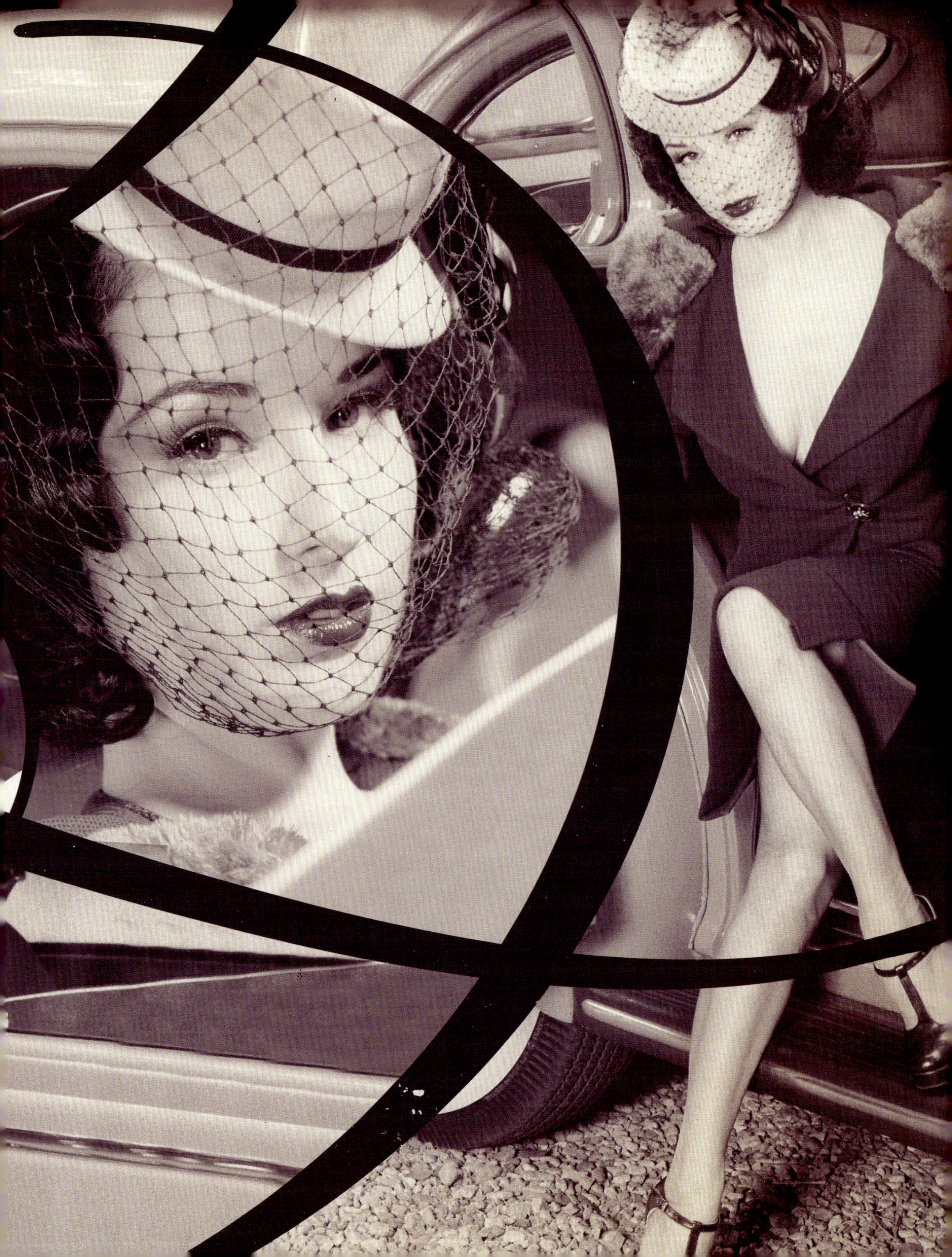

Each and every piece, whether it's vintage or new, has its own story to tell. When I look at each item I recall the time I acquired it and where I was, and the places and important moments in my life where I wore it. To me, each hat, bracelet, and coat is more than just a "vanity item". . . it is a memento of sorts, a souvenir from my travels and a reminder of the places I have been.

In my childhood dreams I would explore the world, dressed in a pretty, sparkling gown that I always wanted to take back to real life with me.

In a way, I guess I did.

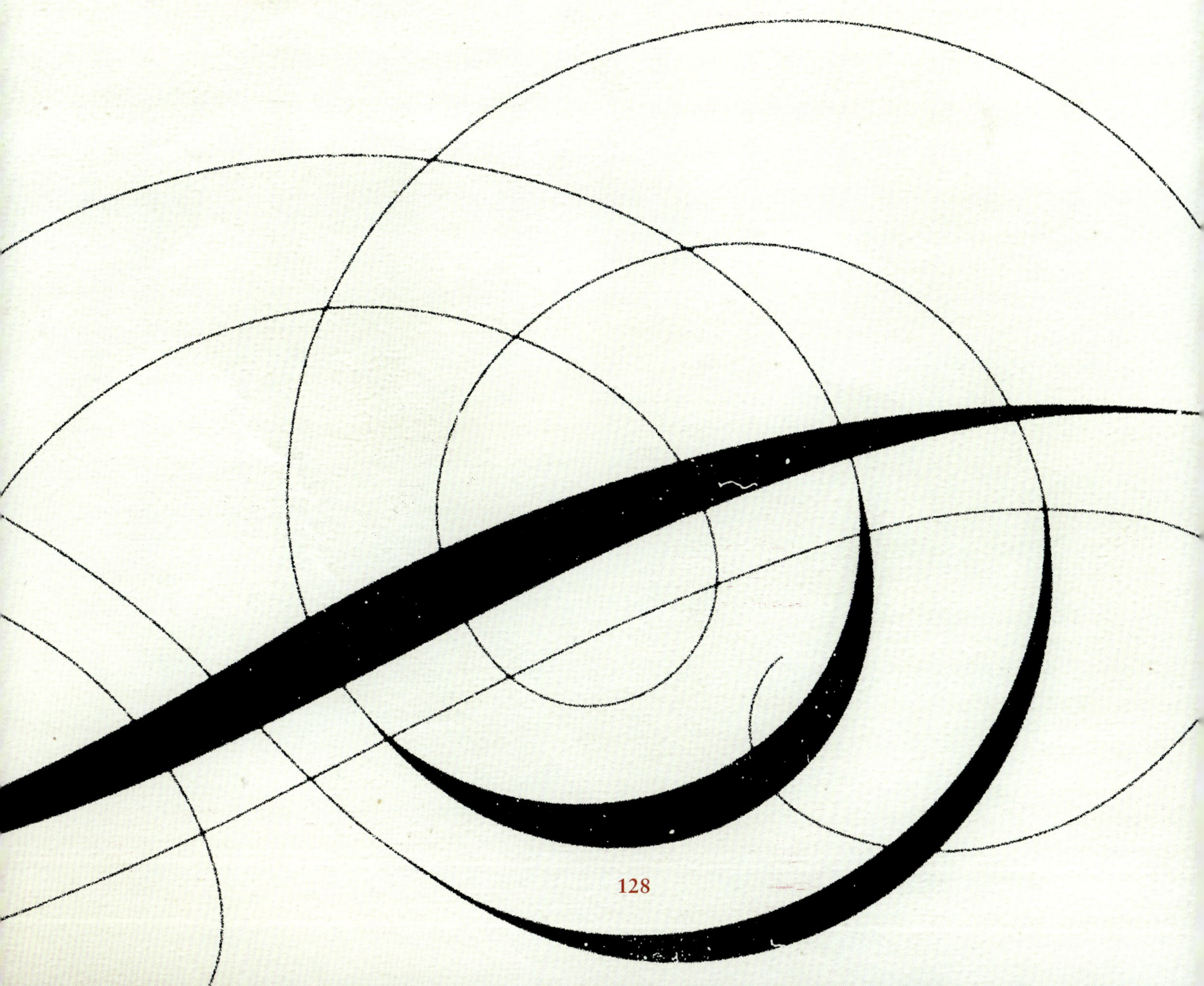

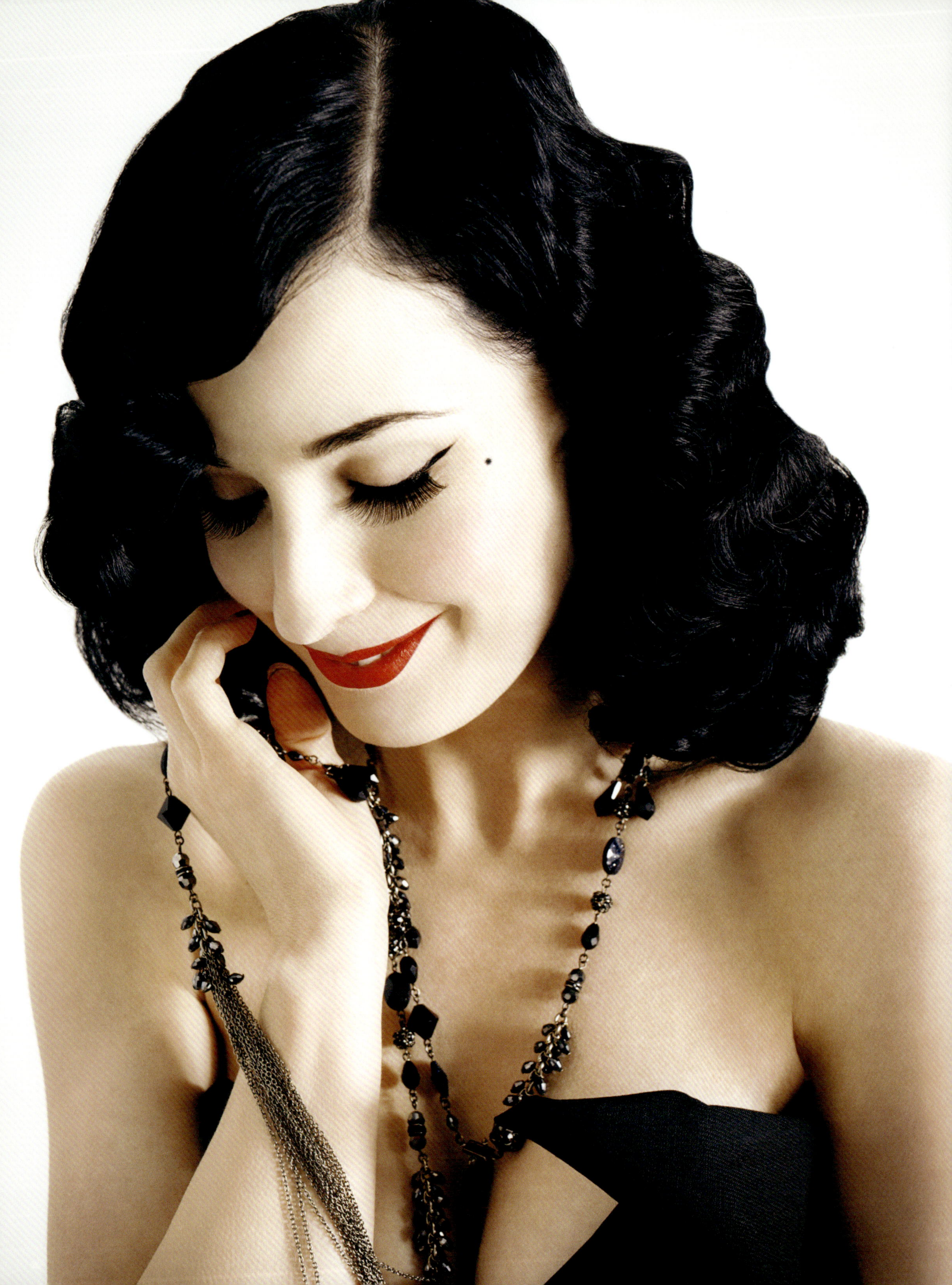

# Acknowledgments

I would like to thank my fans and members of Dita.net, Hugh Hefner and everyone at *Playboy*, Mary O'Conner and Captain Bob, Steve Martinez, Marilyn Grabowski, Lawrence Lanoff, Bill Farley, Moshe Brakha, Arny Freytag, Joel and Olivia, Dixie Evans and The Exotic World Museum, The Crazy Horse and La Femme, Tempest Storm, Eddie DeBarr, Andrea Sikie, Yvonne Baxter, Dr. Lee, Charles Koutris, "Wolfie," Eric Szmanda, Stacia Dunnam, Erica Elliott and Heather Minges, Mr. Pearl, Ali Mahdavi, Suzanne von Aichinger, Betony Vernon, Jean Paul Gaultier, Christophe Mourthe, Yves Riquet, the Osbourne Family, Bettie Page and Mark Roesler, Ellen Von Unwerth, Sascha Lilic, George Bone, Mack Prevatte, Steven Klein, David Friedlander, Tony Glassman, Gottfried Helnwein and the Helnwein Family, Christian Louboutin, Anne Muhiethaler, Fiona Leahy, Levi Pharoah Gonzalez, Sara Forage, Perou, Pierre et Gilles, Anna Wintour, Sally Singer, Hamish Bowles, and everyone at *Vogue*, Marc Jacobs, Robert Duffy, Kate Waters, everyone at Louis Vuitton, Dark Garden Corsetry, Secrets In Lace, ReVamp, Trashy Lingerie, Versatile, Jim Thompson, everyone at Roland Mouret, Lionel Deluy, Sean McCall, Christina Radish, Mimi Legg, Julie Strain, Matthew Burda, John Juniper, Ronnie Magri, Rick Delaup, Morgan Higby, Erica Ludwig, Ira Levine and Nina Hartley, Danilo, Julia Grimm, Danielle at White Rabbit Studio, Vivienne Westwood, Andreas Kronthatler, Brigitte Stepputis, Jason Lane, Bob Schultz and everyone at Glamourcon, Hamilton Stansfield, James O'Reilly, John Galliano, Alexis Roche and everyone at Galliano, Stephen Jones, everyone at *Harpers & Queen*, *Vanity Fair*, everyone at Moschino, Stella McCartney, Rose Apodaca, *Elle* UK, Lars and everyone at Nina Ricci, Zac Posen, Agent Provocateur, Jade Jagger and Garrard, Giuseppe Zanotti, Lulu Guinness, Diane von Furstenberg, Victoire de Castellane, M.A.C., Victoria's Secret, Club Lux, Luis and *Flaunt* magazine, Peter Czernich and everyone at *Marquis*, Teaseorama and all of my fellow neo-burlesquers.

Special thanks to Bronwyn Garrity, Melissa Dishell, Andrea Martin, Albert Murcia, Paul Brown, and all the contributing photographers for making this book possible.

I am forever indebted to all the showgirls and the legends of burlesque who inspired the neo-burlesque movement.

All my love to my family for supporting and believing in me since the beginning: Bonnie and Dan Lindsey, Ken Sweet and the Sweet Family, Jennifer Fears and the Fears Family, Sarah Sweet, and Hugh and Barbara Warner.

Much gratitude to Catherine D'Lish for dreaming big with me and for making the most beautiful burlesque costumes a girl could ever wish for. We always knew we were meant to be either the greatest rivals or the greatest friends and it is my privilege to call you both! (www.cdlish.com)

*Thank you to my Grand Amour, Marilyn Manson,*
*for being the best reason I can think of to take my clothes off.*

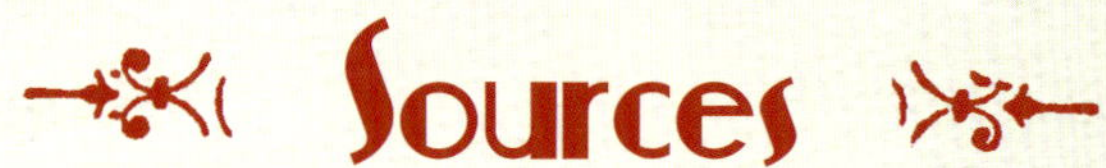

# Sources


Bardey, Catherine. *Lingerie: A History and Celebration of Silks, Satins, Laces, Linens and other Bare Essentials.* New York: Black Dog & Leventhal Publishers, Inc., 2001.

Bressler, Karen W. *A Century of Lingerie: Revealing the Secrets and Allure of 20th Century Lingerie.* Edison, New Jersey: Chartwell Books, 1997.

Cary, David, Ph.D. *A Bit of Burlesque.* San Diego: Tecolote Publications, 1997.

Castle, Charles. *The Folies Bergere.* New York: Franklin Watts, Inc., 1985.

Corio, Ann with Joseph Dimona. *This Was Burlesque.* New York: Madison Square Press/Grosset & Dunlap, 1968.

Dache, Lily. *Lily Dache's Glamour Book.* New York: J.B. Lippincott Company, 1956.

Davis, Lee. *Scandals and Follies: The Rise and Fall of the Great Broadway Revue.* New York: Proscenium Publishers Inc., 2000.

Essex, Karen and James L. Swanson. *Bettie Page: The Life of a Pin-up Legend.* Santa Monica: General Publishing Group, Inc., 1996.

Higham, Charles. *Ziegfeld.* Chicago: Henry Regnery Company, 1972.

Jarret, Lucinda. *Stripping in Time: A History of Erotic Dancing.* London: Pandora-Harper, 1977.

Knox, Holly. *Sally Rand: From Films to Fans.* Bend, Oregon: Maverick Publications, 1988.

Kroll, Eric, ed. *John Willie's Best of Bizarre.* New York: Taschen, 2001.

Lee, Gypsy Rose. *Gypsy.* New York: Dell Publishing Co., 1957.

Leeds, Lois and Hilda M. Kaji. *Beauty and Health: A Practical Handbook.* New York: P.F. Collier & Son, Co., 1929.

Minsky, Morton and Milt Machlin. *Minsky's Burlesque.* New York: Arbor House, 1986.

Rice, Ann. *Beauty's Punishment.* New York: Penguin Books, 1984.

Rothe, Len. *The Bare Truth: Stars of Burlesque From the 40s & 50s.* Atglen, PA: Schiffer Publishing Ltd., 1998.

Ryersson, Scot D. and Michael Orlando Yaccarino. *Infinite Variety: The Life and Legend of the Marchesa Casati*, 1st ed. Viridian Books, 1999.

Sacher-Masoch, Leopold von. *Venus in Furs and Selected Letters.* New York: Blast Books, 1989.

Sobel, Bernard. *Burleycue: An Underground History of Burlesque Days.* New York: Farrar & Rinehart, Inc., 1931.

Steele, Valerie. *The Corset: A Cultural History.* New Haven: Yale University Press, 2001.

Steele, Valerie. *Fetish: Fashion, Sex and Power.* New York: Oxford University Press, 1996.

Stuart, Andrea. *Showgirls.* London: Random House, 1996.

Swan, Viola and Alexander. *Beauty's Question & Answer Dictionary.* Hollywood: Beauty Arts Institute, 1931.

Wortley, Richard. *A Pictorial History of Striptease: 100 Years of Undressing to Music.* London: Octopus Books Ltd., 1976.


*Burlesque and the Art of the Teese* Photograph Credits: **Danielle Bedics/whiterabbitstudio.com:** pages iii, xxii, 2, 3, 7, 12–13, 15, 31 (top), 43, 50, 52, 53, 56, 82, 83, 85, 86, 90–91, 96, 106, 107, 112, 113; **Claudette Barjoud:** page vi; **Sean McCall:** pages vii, xvi, 6, 61, 126–127; **courtesy of www.dita.net/photographer Matt Naylor:** pages viii, 11, 30 (top), 59, 81; **Estradaphoto.com:** pages ix, xviii, xix, 16–17, 30 (bottom), 31 (lower right), 54, 55, 60, 68, 69; **www.perou.co.uk:** pages x, xi, 25, 27, 39, 48, 64, 66, 108, 122, 129; **Scott Macaulay/J.M.E.:** page xiii; **Lionel Deluy:** pages xiv, xv; **Amedeo M. Turello:** pages xx–xxi, 24, 45, 110, 111; **Chris Cuffaro:** pages 1, 116, 117, 121; **© Rankin:** pages 4–5; **Christophe Mourthé:** pages 8, 9; **courtesy of Dita:** page 14; **Silvercanvas Photography:** pages 18, 19; **ali mahdavi & Suzanne von Aichinger:** pages 20–21; **Gavin O'Neill:** pages 22, 23; **Ellen Von Unwerth:** pages 28, 40–41, 74–75; **Ellen Von Unwerth/Above Magazine:** pages 114–115, 118; **Gitte & Delaney/Gdphoto.net:** pages 32, 33; **David Raccuglia:** page 34; **John Kobal Foundation/Getty Images:** page 37; **Frank Mullen/www.matteblack.com:** page 47; **Library of Congress:** page 57; **Aaron D. Settipane:** pages 62–63, 76 (right), 77 (right); **courtesy of Photofest:** pages 65, 84; **Sheryl Nields:** pages 70–71, 98–99, 124, 125; **Greg Endries:** page 72; **Christina Radish:** pages 76 (left), 77 (left), 120; **Wayne Maser/Vanity Fair/451 Imaging Ltd.:** page 78; **The Kobal Collection, Photographer George Hurrell:** page 79; **courtesy www.dita.net/Photographer Danielle Emerick:** pages 80, 102; **Keith Williams, KEW Productions for Glamourcon:** page 88; **James and James:** page 89; **copyright © 2005 Olivia De Berardinis:** pages 92, 93, 104–105; **Pierre & Gary Silva Photography:** page 94; **Everett Collection:** page 97; **Marilyn Manson:** pages 100–101; **© Bettie Page, www.BettiePage.com:** page 103; *Fetish and the Art of the Teese* Photograph Credits: **www.perou.co.uk:** pages iii, viii, xiii, 14-15, 60, 61, 70, 71, 76, 95; **Lionel Deluy:** pages vi-vii, 8, 9, 74–75, 90–91, 92, 93; **John Dietrich:** page xi; **Jim Weathers:** pages xiv, 38, 40–41; **Christophe Mourthé:** pages xvi–xvii, 6, 7, 12, 13, 16, 77, 87, 96, 98; **Peter W. Czernich/www.marquis.de:** pages 1, 32, 66, 67; **Gitte & Delaney/Gdphoto.net:** pages 2, 62, 80–81; **Reb Stout:** page 3; **Gavin O'Neill:** page 5; **Chas Ray Krider:** pages 10–11, 50, 58, 59, 84, 85, 86; **www.dita.net:** page 17; **Amedeo M. Turello:** pages 18–19, 20, 21; **Chris Cuffaro:** pages 23, 25; **Silvercanvas Photography:** pages 24, 27, 51, 69; **Sean McCall:** pages 26, 36, 37, 100, 101; **courtesy www.dita.net/Photographer Danielle Emerick:** pages 28, 31; **© Bettie Page, www.BettiePage.com:** page 29; **Wayne Maser/Vanity Fair/451 Imaging Ltd.:** page 33; **Ellen Von Unwerth:** pages 34–35; **Copyright © Olivia De Berardinis 2005:** pages 45, 72; **David Slijper:** pages 46, 53; **© Steven Klein:** pages 48, 49; **courtesy www.dita.net/Photographer Matt Naylor:** page 54; **ali mahdavi & Suzanne von Aichinger:** pages 56–57; **Marilyn Manson:** page 78; **Steve Diet Goedde:** pages 88, 89; **Pierre & Gary Silva Photography:** pages 66, 82, 83; **Danielle Bedics/whiterabbitstudio.com:** page 97